ALGORITHMS
from P to NP

Volume 1
Design & Efficiency

B.M.E. Moret   H. D. Shapiro

P

Executive Editor: Alan Apt

Acquisitions Editor: John Thompson

Production Coordinator: Catherine E. Lewis

Copy Editor: Robert Klingensmith

Cover Designer: Irene Imfield

Composition: ETP Services

Library of Congress Cataloging-in Publication Data

Moret, Bernard M. E.
     Algorithms from P to NP / Bernard M.E. Moret, Henry D. Shapiro
          p.   cm.
     Includes bibliographical references and index.
     Contents: v. 1. Design and efficiency.
     ISBN 0-8053-8008-6
     1. Electronic digital computers—Programming. 2. Algorithms.
  I. Shapiro, Henry D.   II. Title
QA76.6.M667   1990
005. 1—dc20   90-1015
                                                 CIP

ISBN 0-8053-8008-6
ABCDEFGHIJ-MA-9543210

The Benjamin/Cummings Publishing Company, Inc.
390 Bridge Parkway
Redwood City, CA 94065

PREFACE

This book is the first volume of a two-volume work on algorithms intended for use by seniors and graduate students, as well as computing professionals. This volume, *Design and Efficiency*, emphasizes algorithmic techniques for tractable problems, while the second, *Heuristics and Complexity*, presents search and approximation techniques for hard problems and also addresses computational complexity theory. Together, the two volumes cover the full range of algorithmic techniques of practical interest, with the exception of mathematical programming techniques, such as linear programming. Each technique is illustrated by a number of important applications. We discuss applications in depth, starting with a high-level design, then providing a proof of correctness and an analysis, and continuing with details of implementation, often including an empirical study of competing designs. This preference for depth over breadth prevents us from covering all applications of importance; whenever choices must be made, we give preference to combinatorial problems that arise in practice.

Our purpose in this volume is to expose the reader to a range of problems, to teach methods of algorithmic analysis and to justify their need, to introduce specific paradigms for algorithm design, to emphasize the importance of coding choices, and to provide a basic set of useful algorithms. We have mixed a problem-specific approach with a paradigmatic one; the latter is obvious in the organization of the chapters, while the former is embodied as a set of problems, which are introduced in the first chapter and then taken up again with each paradigm, thus acting as a bundle of threads tying together the chapters of the two volumes. Much of the text is intended to support a discovery process and thus be useful for self-study. For each algorithmic technique, we begin by building up intuition through simple or general examples, then discuss important applications in great detail.

Because the problems that we mention arise in real applications, and because the algorithms that we present are both efficient and concise, we take particular care to discuss the implementation and coding of each algorithm. We do not simply present programs in pseudocode, but give actual running programs (in PASCAL—translation into C, FORTRAN, ADA, or other procedural languages is straightforward). We chose this unusual style of presentation for three reasons. First, the distance from the pseudocode description of an algorithm to its actual implementation is often considerable; bridging this gap often involves nontrivial decisions about the implementation and bad decisions can make the resulting code too time- or space-consuming for real applications. Secondly, it is often the case that many high-level algorithms with similar asymptotic behaviors have been proposed for the same problem, algorithms; in such cases, an informed choice can be made only after implementing the algorithms and experimenting with them. Finally, all of our programs work as written and can be used immediately by the reader, so that this text can also serve as a library of useful routines for combinatorial optimization. In the few cases where we present an algorithm of major theoretical, but little practical interest (such as the linear-time algorithm for Jordan sorting), we follow the standard convention of theoreticians and give only a high-level description of the algorithm.

To the Student

This volume contains a lot of material and exercises ranging from simple to very challenging. In order to read this book, you should be comfortable with elementary data structures, such as linked lists and search trees, including some type of balanced search tree. Chapters 2 and 3 review some of the required mathematics and data structures, but mostly they elaborate on the expected background.

Exercises, as mentioned, vary in difficulty. We have limited our selection to those that test your understanding of the material by asking you to take things further; with the exception of Chapter 2, no chapter includes "finger exercises" of a purely mechanical nature. In order to guide you through the exercises, we have classified them in four broad categories: (i) unmarked exercises (e.g., Exercise 1.1) are easier—we expect that you can solve most of them in ten to twenty minutes each; (ii) exercises with one star (e.g., Exercise 1.1*) are of medium difficulty—we expect that, with a good grasp of the material, you can solve most of these, spending less than an hour on each; (iii) exercises with two stars (e.g., Exercise 1.1**) are difficult, with somewhat varied levels of difficulty—we expect that, given sufficient time, you can solve a fair number of them, but we consider each such exercise to be a challenging problem; and (iv) exercises with a [P] following their numbers (e.g., Exercise 1.1[P]) are project exercises and typically require you to program algorithms and compare them empirically—the time needed and the level of difficulty will depend almost entirely on your and your instructor's expectations.

To the Instructor

This text includes more material than can be covered in a semester, even at the graduate level. As we mentioned in the introduction, it can be used with seniors as well as with graduate students; in either case, it can form the basis for a one- or two-semester class in algorithms. Over the several years of its development, we used it in our undergraduate class on algorithms, which is also a prerequisite to our graduate program. Our undergraduates come to this class having taken one year of calculus, one year of discrete mathematics, one and a half years of programming, and a course in intermediate data structures covering storage management, balanced tree structures, hashing, and basic priority queues, with an introduction to algorithmic analysis. Thus much of Chapters 2 and 3 is already familiar to them, albeit not at the level of our presentation. With these students, we cover parts of Chapter 1 and all of Chapters 2, 3, 4 (except Section 4.2.3), 5 (except Section 5.6), 7 (except Section 7.3 and skipping the material on sorting networks in Section 7.1), and 8 (quickly, because our students are already familiar with the standard sorting methods); even with a somewhat light touch, this schedule makes for a busy semester.

We see two main patterns of use for this text:

- A one-semester class at the senior or graduate level. Such a course can follow the outline we have just given. Chapter 1 is meant for assigned reading rather than for classroom use. Section 2.2.2 should and Section 2.4 can be skipped. If the students have not learned about recurrence relations, then Section 2.2.1 can be skimmed and Section 2.3.1 can be covered more slowly, since the text can be used by students who know how to set up a recurrence to describe the behavior of an algorithm, but not how to solve it. Chapter 8 and the material on sorting in Sections 3.1 and 7.1 should be covered early in the class. Time can be saved by skipping one or both of the connectivity algorithms of Section 4.1.2, the analyses of UNION-FIND and Fibonacci heaps, or some sections in later chapters. On the other hand, should there be additional time, we suggest covering Sections 6.3 and 6.5.

- A two-semester class at the senior or graduate level. The additional time allows a thorough coverage of all the material in this book and the exploration of many topics through term projects. The entire text can be covered, even with students whose preparation does not include much combinatorics. With graduate students, experimental and research projects can be assigned to take them beyond the material in the text—the project exercises and the double-starred exercises provide good starting points for these explorations.

For a description of the notation used to mark exercises, please refer to our comments to the student. Note that we deliberately abstained from lengthening this text with mechanical exercises ("show the effect of algorithm X on this input"); should any be required, we trust that you can provide them as fast as, and in greater variety than, we. Solutions to the double-starred exercises are generally mentioned in the bibliography section; these exercises should be used with caution. Some of the exercises are starred, not because of their intrinsic difficulty, but because they require specific background (matrix algebra, graph theory, number theory, etc.); for many students with the required background, they will be easy.

To the Professional

We hope that the inclusion of well-tested, working code will result in more professionals availing themselves of the fruits of 30 years of progress in the design of data structures and algorithms. Unfortunately, classes in data structures and algorithms are often taught "by theoreticians, for theoreticians," with the consequence that intricate (and often beautiful) algorithms of no practical use are discussed at length, to the exclusion of algorithms that may be less efficient in asymptotic terms, but are more effective in practice. While we always analyze carefully the asymptotic behavior of each algorithm, we also always discuss implementation issues and present only those algorithms that do well in practice because of their low overhead and the relative simplicity of their coding. Thus, not only does every routine printed in this text work correctly, but it also works efficiently.

Acknowledgments

Among the many researchers whose results are found throughout this volume, two must be given specific mention. Donald E. Knuth has been a source of inspiration to generations of computer scientists; his monumental work, *The Art of Computer Programming*, remains the standard by which all texts on algorithms are judged. He also developed the TEX system for typesetting, which we used to typeset this volume. Robert E. Tarjan has, more than anyone else, contributed to the development of data structures and algorithms for graph and other problems, as a quick look at our list of references and our bibliographic sections will show (almost 30 articles authored or coauthored by him appear in our list of references); as much as a third of the material in this text is due, directly or indirectly, to him.

It is our pleasure to acknowledge the help that we received from many sources during the five years of development of this text. Our friends and family gave us moral support. The first author particularly wants to thank his wife,

Carol P. Fryer, for her help; she it was who gave us a title that we both liked and who proposed the cover design. Our colleagues in the Department of Computer Science at the University of New Mexico were most supportive through the years; in particular, since we typeset the text ourselves, they suffered through long output queues on the laser printers. Similarly, our systems staff helped us with many unusual requests, from compiling a very large TeX processor to running some machines in stand-alone mode for our experiments.

We had the help of a number of reviewers, all of whom we wish to thank: Mustafa Akgul from North Carolina State University; Stephen T. Hedetniemi from Clemson University; William R. Nico from California State University at Hayward; Michael Ian Shamos from Carnegie-Mellon University; Jeremy Spinrad from Vanderbilt University; Matthias Stallman from North Carolina State University; and Ivan Hal Sudborough from the University of Texas at Dallas. Stephen Hedetniemi, in particular, gave us a very thorough critique, together with many suggestions for coverage; it was due to him that we included the section on matroids (Section 5.6). Other colleagues gave us advice and encouragement; we should like to thank particularly Gary Bloom from the City University of New York, Herbert Edelsbrunner from the University of Illinois, and Michael Fellows from the University of Victoria. Since we have used parts of this text in our classes, we have a large number of students to thank for putting up with sets of notes that changed somewhat during the course of the semester. An instructor learns the art of teaching from his or her students; in writing this text, we used lessons learned in ten years of teaching.

Finally, in producing this volume, we had the support of many people at Benjamin-Cummings. Our editor, Alan Apt, and his associate, Mary Ann Telatnik, were very patient with our constant delays and let us work our way to the best book we could write; our typesetting liaison, Sharon Weldy, gave us the book design and helped us novices to understand the production process; our copyeditor, Robert Klingensmith, was very thorough; and our production editor, Cathy Lewis, was unfailingly cheerful, always available, and very prompt.

Albuquerque, July 1990

Bernard M.E. Moret
    moret@cmell.cs.unm.edu

Henry D. Shapiro
    shapiro@vishnu.cs.unm.edu

NOTATION

Σ^*	the set of all strings on the alphabet Σ
$\exists$	"there exists," the existential quantifier
$\forall$	"for all," the universal quantifier
$\mathcal{Z}, \mathcal{Z}^+$	the (positive) integers
$\mathcal{R}, \mathcal{R}^+$	the (positive) reals
$[x,y], (x,y)$	the closed (open) interval from x to y
$f \circ g$	the functional composition of f and g; $f(g(n))$
$f^{(n)}(x)$	the nth derivative of $f(x)$; also, $f \circ f \circ \cdots \circ f$, n times
$\sum, \prod$	sum, product
$\lfloor x \rfloor$	the "floor" of x: the largest integer not greater than x
$\lceil x \rceil$	the "ceiling" of x: the smallest integer not less than x
$\log x, \lg x, \ln x$	the logarithm of x in any base, in base two, in base e
$\lg^* n$	the "log star" function
lub	least upper bound
$\alpha(m,n)$	the inverse Ackermann function
H_n	the nth harmonic number
F_n	the nth Fibonacci number
$n!$	the nth factorial number
$\binom{n}{k}$	"n choose k," the number of ways to choose k objects from n objects
$\mathbf{v}, \|\mathbf{v}\|$	a vector, its (Euclidean) norm
$\mathbf{A}, \mathbf{A}^{-1}, \mathbf{A}^{\#}$	a matrix, its inverse, its pseudoinverse
$O(\ ), o(\ )$	"big Oh," "little oh"
$\Omega(\ )$	"big Omega"
$\Theta(\ )$	"big Theta"
$\asymp$	asymptotically equal to
$\approx$	approximately equal to
$\ll, \gg$	much less (greater) than
$\prec$	lexicographically less than
$\oplus$	addition modulo n; also, symmetric difference of sets
$\circledast$	the convolution operator
$G = (V, E)$	the undirected graph G with vertex set V and edge set E
$G = (V, A)$	the directed graph G with vertex set V and arc set A
$\|$	concatenation of paths

CONTENTS

PROGRAMS

CHAPTER 1

A Sampling of Problems

The study of algorithms cannot be dissociated from the study of problems. The first step in the solution of any problem is the specification, in terms as clear as possible, of the problem's parameters and objectives. In spite of appearances, this step may prove quite challenging: the range of problems that algorithm designers have to face can be quite broad, and each problem may be initially presented in an extremely complex manner, encumbered by a myriad of details. In order to analyze the problem and develop algorithms for its solution, it is crucial that the problem be reduced to an abstract formulation, devoid of any details—however important in practice—that have no bearing on algorithmic development. Since optimization problems often spring from real situations—many tracing their sources to the planning of production and delivery schedules and the reduction of manufacturing costs—developing a suitable abstract formulation requires some thought and some experience. In this first chapter we propose to take the reader through a guided tour of typical combinatorial optimization problems, with three goals in mind: (i) to illustrate the development of formal problem specifications from informal English descriptions; (ii) to provide an overview of the type of problems that we shall examine (and thus demonstrate, albeit indirectly, the wide range of applicability of the methods that we shall study); and (iii) to instill in the reader a sense of adventure, a spirit of exploration, and a mood for play, all attitudes which we think are both elicited by and conducive to the study of algorithms.

We propose a tour of *combinatorial optimization* problems, not of all possible types of optimization problems. The common feature of all combinatorial problems is their discrete and finite nature: their parameters can only take on discrete values, and their solutions can only be drawn from a finite set of possibilities. The finiteness of these problems generally ensures the existence of some brute-force method of solution: simply generate all possible solution structures, always keeping the best one. Such methods, however, can only succeed with fairly small solutions sets. Thus the subject of these two volumes is the design of efficient algorithms for the solution of combinatorial optimization problems characterized by the enormous size of their set of potential solutions. All of the problems introduced in this chapter share this feature; for convenience of presentation, they have been further grouped into categories based on their fields of application.

1.1 Integer Programming Problems

Many situations of economic interest can be modelled as a set of linear equations in which the variables represent continuously varying quantities which are required to remain within certain limits. The objective in studying such systems is to maximize or minimize some aspect of the system—for example, profit, cost, or equitability of distribution of goods—without violating any of the constraints imposed on the variables by the linear equations. Problems of this nature are formalized as *linear programs*, and the study of their solution is called *linear programming*. However, the problems that we shall consider differ from the linear programming formalism in a significant way: the variables will be restricted to a finite set of values. We begin with an example known as the *knapsack* problem.

A hiker planning a backpacking trip feels that he can comfortably carry at most 20 kilograms. After laying out all the items that he wants to take and discovering that their total weight exceeds 20 kilograms, he assigns to each item a "value" rating, as shown in Table 1.1. Which items should he take to maximize the value of what he can carry without exceeding 20 kilograms?

Table 1.1: An Instance of the Knapsack Problem

Item	Tent	Canteen (filled)	Change of clothes	Camp stove	Sleeping bag	Dried food
Weight	11	7	5	4	3	3
Value	20	10	11	5	25	50

Item	First-aid kit	Mosquito repellent	Flashlight	Novel	Rain gear	Water purifier
Weight	3	2	2	2	2	1
Value	15	12	6	4	5	30

Although we do not yet know how to obtain the solution, the way to fill the knapsack to carry the most value is to take the sleeping bag, food, mosquito repellent, first-aid kit, flashlight, water purifier, and change of clothes, for a total value of 149 with a total weight of 19 kilograms. An interesting aspect of the solution is that it is not directly limited by the weight restriction. There are ways of filling the knapsack with exactly 20 kilograms, such as substituting for the change of clothes the camp stove and rain gear, but this decreases the total value.

Formally, the knapsack problem can be stated as follows.

Problem 1 [Knapsack] Given M, the capacity of the knapsack, $\{\, w_i \mid w_i > 0,\ i = 1, 2, \ldots, n \,\}$, the weights of the n objects, and $\{\, v_i \mid v_i > 0,\ i = 1, 2, \ldots, n \,\}$, their corresponding values,

$$
\begin{aligned}
\text{maximize} \quad & \sum_{i=1}^{n} v_i x_i \\
\text{subject to} \quad & \sum_{i=1}^{n} w_i x_i \leq M \\
\text{where} \quad & x_i \in \{0, 1\}.
\end{aligned}
\tag{1.1}
$$

($x_i = 0$ means that item i should not be included in the knapsack, and $x_i = 1$ means that it should be included.) □

If x_i equals zero, then $v_i x_i$ and $w_i x_i$ will be zero, so that the value of the ith item will not be included in the sum that represents the total value and its weight will not be included in the sum of the weights. If, on the other hand, x_i equals one, then the value of the ith item contributes to the combined value of all things selected for inclusion and its weight similarly contributes to the combined weight. In consequence, the solution space has size 2^n, since there are two choices for each of n independent variables. This method of encoding is used over and over again for problems where something is being included or excluded, made true or false, etc.

A more realistic version of the knapsack problem would add volume restrictions to the weight restrictions, thereby obtaining a multidimensional version of the knapsack problem. However, modelling the volume constraints by a simple inequality ignores the fact that objects are three-dimensional solids; it models a soft knapsack to be filled with plastic objects (e.g., objects that come in instant, powdered form). An accurate model of the real-world knapsack problem requires large numbers of constraints to express the various restrictions placed on three-dimensional arrangements; moreover, a solution to such a problem should include not only a list of the chosen objects, but also packing instructions.

Problems of this type are called *optimization* problems, because there is some function, called the *objective function*, which is to be maximized or minimized. The restrictions placed on the variables, x_i, $i = 1, 2, \ldots, n$, in words or in formulae, are called *constraints*. When formalized in this way, the knapsack problem has an extremely simple form. The single "subject to" constraint in 1.1 is a linear inequality, and the objective function is also linear. A problem that can be formalized as

$$
\text{optimize} \quad \sum_{i=1}^{n} c_i x_i
$$

$$
\text{subject to} \quad
\begin{cases}
a_{11}x_1 + a_{12}x_2 + \cdots + a_{1n}x_n \le b_1 \\
a_{21}x_1 + a_{22}x_2 + \cdots + a_{2n}x_n \le b_2 \\
\quad \vdots \qquad\quad \vdots \qquad \ddots \qquad \vdots \qquad \vdots \\
a_{m1}x_1 + a_{m2}x_2 + \cdots + a_{mn}x_n \le b_m
\end{cases}
$$

$$
\text{where} \quad x_i \ge 0, \quad i = 1, 2, \ldots, n
$$

is called a *linear programming* problem (LP). When specific numerical values are assigned to the constants in the above formulae (for c_i, a_{ij}, and b_i; or for v_i, w_i, and M), we say that we have an *instance* of the problem, so that names like "knapsack problem" actually refer to a family of similar problems. Unlike the x_i, the c_i, a_{ij}, and b_i may be negative. The point—or more precisely a point, since there can be more than one—that satisfies the constraints and makes the objective function achieve its maximum or minimum is called an *optimal solution*; we denote it by $(\hat{x}_1, \hat{x}_2, \ldots, \hat{x}_n)$. The direction of each inequality in the "subject to" constraints depends on the problem; strict equalities can also be used, since an equality can be replaced by two inequalities.

The formulation of the knapsack problem does differ from this prototype in an important way, however. In a linear programming problem, the x_i are not restricted to discrete values, but are continuous variables. Certainly the presence of a constraint of the form "x_i integral" can affect the optimal solution, since a formerly optimal solution, such as $(12^1/_4, 2^2/_3)$, no longer satisfies all the constraints. It is intuitively reasonable to expect that the introduction of integrality constraints will force the optimal solution to an all-integer point that is near the optimal solution that would otherwise be obtained. Unfortunately, as the following example shows, this intuition is incorrect.

A brewery makes two types of beer: lite and light. The key ingredients used, malt, hops, and yeast, are in limited supply, while other ingredients, like water, can be considered in infinite supply. It takes 2 units of malt, 4 of hops, and 2 of yeast to make 100 liters of lite and 3 units of malt, 1 of hops, and 9 of yeast to make 100 liters of light. (The unit of measurement is not the same for the three ingredients.) The brewery can sell all its output at a profit of $21 per 100 liters of lite and $31 per 100 liters of light. They are able to obtain 25 units of malt, 32 of hops, and 54 of yeast. How should they schedule their production to maximize profit?

This problem is embodied in the linear program

$$\text{maximize} \quad 21x + 31y$$

$$\text{subject to} \quad \left\{ \begin{array}{rcl} 2x + 3y & \leq & 25 \\ 4x + y & \leq & 32 \\ 2x + 9y & \leq & 54 \end{array} \right.$$

$$\text{where} \quad x, y \geq 0.$$

In this linear program, the variables x and y represent the amount, in 100-liter units, of lite and light to make, respectively, and each of the constraints given by the linear inequalities says that the amount of one of the critical ingredients used cannot exceed the supply. "$x, y \geq 0$" is the obvious condition that a negative quantity cannot be produced. Constraints such as "$x, y \geq 0$" or "$x_i = 0$ or 1," which do not appear in the problem statement, which are generic to all of the problems that we shall be considering, and which can be imposed by a computer program without significant computation, are called *implicit constraints*. The constraints that define the essence of the problem are called *explicit constraints*, or often simply "the constraints," as if to say that the implicit constraints are so obvious as to make their statement redundant. The methods used today to solve linear programs are variations on the *simplex method*, developed by George Dantzig and a number of colleagues in the late 1940s. For our simple problem, however, it is possible to proceed graphically. Figure 1.1 indicates the regions of the first quadrant ($x, y \geq 0$) for which each inequality holds. The points in the shaded region satisfy all of the constraints, both implicit and explicit, and are termed *feasible solutions*. The shaded region itself is called the *feasible region*. Points that satisfy the implicit constraints, especially if they are of the form "$x_i = 0$ or 1," define what is often called the *solution space*; the individual points are then referred to as *solutions*. This use of the term *solution* is an abuse of language, since a solution as just defined need not satisfy all explicit constraints and thus is not a solution at all in the normal sense of the word. What would normally be called a solution is what we have defined as a feasible solution.[1]

We can picture the line $21x + 31y = C$, which describes the set of solutions which have the same objective function value, being slowly moved toward the origin. As the value of C decreases, the line moves closer to the feasible region.

---

[1]One reason for the terminology is that enumeration of only those solutions which are feasible is often not practical, since the distinction between a feasible and an infeasible solution requires a significant amount of computation and is best done after the solution has been generated.

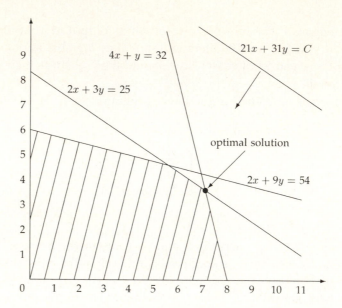

Figure 1.1: A Graphical Solution to the Problem of Planning Brewery Production

At $(x, y) = (7^1/_{10}, 3^3/_5)$, where the objective function first crosses the feasible region, the objective function is maximized. The brewery achieves a maximum profit of \$260.70 on 710 liters of lite and 360 liters of light. Notice that all of the malt and hops available will be used but that there is an excess of yeast.

We now consider a problem that appears extremely similar. Instead of a brewery producing two types of beer, imagine a seamstress who plans to produce a limited number of copies of two suit styles. The suits require three fabrics, 2 meters of the first, 4 of the second, and 2 of the third being required for one style and 3 meters of the first, 1 of the second, and 9 of the third being required for the other style. If the seamstress has available the same amounts of material—her ingredients—that the brewery had available to it and if the slope of her objective function is also $-^{21}/_{31}$, how many suits of each type should she make? The explicit constraints are identical to what we had before, but the answer of $(x, y) = (7^1/_{10}, 3^3/_5)$ is unacceptable: a fraction of a suit cannot be sold. The two problems are not quite the same. The implicit constraint is now

$$x, y \geq 0, \quad x, y \text{ integer}.$$

Of the four points closest to $(7^1/_{10}, 3^3/_5)$ with integer components, three of them, $(7, 4)$, $(8, 3)$, and $(8, 4)$, violate at least one of the explicit constraints. The truncated solution of $(7, 3)$ is feasible, with an objective function value of \$2400, if we assume \$210 and \$310 profit per suit, respectively. It is not optimal, however,

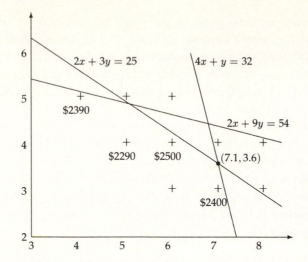

Figure 1.2: The Effect of Integrality Constraints on the Solution to a Linear Programming Problem

since $(6, 4)$ provides a profit of \$2500; $(4, 5)$, with a profit of \$2390, is not far behind. The situation is illustrated in Figure 1.2. A linear programming problem, that includes the additional constraint that all variables be integer valued, is called an *integer linear programming* problem (ILP). If the variables are further restricted to 0 or 1, the problem is called a *0-1 integer linear programming* problem, or just a *0-1 programming* problem for short. The feasible region of an ILP is a set of discrete points in n-dimensional space, those points with all integer components that satisfy the explicit and nonnegativity constraints.

Definition 1.1 Let P_1 and P_2 be two LPs or ILPs over n variables with the same objective function. If the feasible region of P_1, $F(P_1)$, is a subset of the feasible region of P_2, $F(P_2)$, then P_2 is called a *relaxation* of P_1.   □

An obvious result which will be very useful is the following:

Theorem 1.1 If P_2 is a relaxation of P_1, then the value of the objective function at the optimal feasible solution for problem P_2 is greater than or equal to (less than or equal to for minimization problems) the value of the objective function at the optimal feasible solution to P_1.   □

The proof consists merely of noting that, in maximizing the objective function for P_2, the arguments to the objective function range over $F(P_2) \supseteq F(P_1)$. An immediate corollary is the following:

Corollary 1.1 Let P_2 be a relaxation of P_1; if the optimal feasible solution to P_2 is also contained in $F(P_1)$, then it optimizes P_1 as well.   □

We have overlooked a subtle point in the proof of Theorem 1.1. If the feasible region is *bounded* (i.e., every variable satisfies $x_i \leq u_i$, the u_i constants) and the problem is an ILP, then the objective function will achieve its maximum, since then there are only finitely many feasible solutions. For the case of continuous variables, the existence of a definite point that is the optimal feasible solution (in certain circumstances there can be infinitely many optimal solutions) may not be apparent. The proof that such a point exists, while not complex, depends on some elementary real analysis, and we shall not present it. The u_i can be explicit in the problem or implied by the other constraints; for example, $2x + 3y \leq 25$ and $y \geq 0$ implies $x \leq 12.5$. If the feasible region is unbounded, the objective function may also be unbounded. It is also possible for an LP or ILP to have conflicting constraints that reduce the feasible region to the empty set; such a problem is called *infeasible*.

Exercise 1.1 Show that if an LP has two or more distinct optimal solutions, then it has infinitely many optimal solutions. *Hint*: Construct, pictorially, a two-dimensional LP problem with two distinct optimal solutions in order to see how the infinitely many solutions arise.   □

A case of special interest arises from an ILP and the corresponding LP with the integrality constraints removed. The resulting LP is a relaxation of the ILP, since its feasible region is defined by the same explicit and nonnegativity constraints. The corollary becomes:

Corollary 1.2 Let an LP be formed from an ILP by dropping the integrality constraints; if the optimal solution to the LP is all integer, then it also optimizes the ILP.   □

As we saw in the preceding example, merely truncating the fractional solution may lead to a feasible but nonoptimal solution. If the point formed by truncating the solution to the LP is feasible, then it does provide a useful bound for the potential error. If we let $\mathbf{x}_0$ be the optimal solution to the LP, $\lfloor \mathbf{x}_0 \rfloor$ be the truncated feasible solution to the ILP, and $\hat{\mathbf{x}}$ be the optimal solution to the ILP, then

$$f(\lfloor \mathbf{x}_0 \rfloor) \leq f(\hat{\mathbf{x}}) \leq f(\mathbf{x}_0),$$

where f is the objective function and we have assumed a maximization problem.

In many applications, where the solutions are fractional but have a large integral component, truncation may provide an acceptable solution. Consider an automobile manufacturer planning the production levels of several models of cars with the goal of maximizing its profit. Since the production figures are very large, the truncated solution, while not necessarily optimal, will show only a small percentage decrease in the value of the objective function. The values of some of the coefficients in the constraints will have enough uncertainty— some are likely to be based on economic forecasts or consumer surveys—that the true optimal solution is no more meaningful than any nearly optimal feasible solution. On the other hand, when the discretization is relatively coarse, as in a 0-1 programming problem, the use of the truncated solution in place of the true optimal is often unacceptable.

Other problems can also be formulated as 0-1 programming problems.

Problem 2 [Set Cover]   Given S, a set containing m elements, and n subsets of S, $\{ S_i \mid i = 1, 2, \ldots, n \}$, with $\bigcup_{i=1}^{n} S_i = S$, what is the smallest collection of the S_i, the union of which is S? (A collection of sets, the union of which is S, is called a *cover*. The problem is to find the cover consisting of the fewest subsets.) $\square$

As an example, consider the following subsets of a set of 16 elements:

$$
\begin{aligned}
S_1 &= \{1,\, 5,\, 13\} & S_2 &= \{4,\, 8,\, 12\} \\
S_3 &= \{1,\, 2,\, 3,\, 4\} & S_4 &= \{5,\, 6,\, 7,\, 9,\, 12\} \\
S_5 &= \{9,\, 10,\, 12,\, 14\} & S_6 &= \{8,\, 10,\, 11,\, 13,\, 14\} \\
S_7 &= \{11,\, 12,\, 15,\, 16\} & S_8 &= \{13,\, 14,\, 15,\, 16\} \\
S_9 &= \{2,\, 3,\, 6,\, 7,\, 10,\, 11,\, 14,\, 15\} &&
\end{aligned}
$$

The collection $\{S_3, S_4, S_6, S_8\}$ forms a minimum cover, since their union is S and there is no cover consisting of three subsets. (In this problem, the optimal cover is not unique.) The set cover problem can be formulated as a 0-1 programming problem in much the same manner as the knapsack problem. Again, $x_i = 0$ (or 1) is taken to mean that S_i is not (is) included in the cover. In addition, define a_{ij}, for $i = 1, 2, \ldots, m$ and $j = 1, 2, \ldots, n$, by

$$
a_{ij} = \begin{cases} 1, & \text{if element } i \in S_j \\ 0, & \text{otherwise.} \end{cases}
$$

The a_{ij} vary from instance to instance, but are constants once the instance is specified. The x_i, however, are truly variables. With these definitions, the set covering problem becomes

$$
\text{minimize} \quad \sum_{i=1}^{n} x_i
$$

$$
\text{subject to} \quad \begin{cases} a_{11}x_1 + a_{12}x_2 + \cdots + a_{1n}x_n \geq 1 \\ a_{21}x_1 + a_{22}x_2 + \cdots + a_{2n}x_n \geq 1 \\ \quad \vdots \qquad \quad \vdots \qquad \ddots \qquad \vdots \qquad \vdots \\ a_{m1}x_1 + a_{m2}x_2 + \cdots + a_{mn}x_n \geq 1 \end{cases}
$$

$$
\text{where} \quad x_i = 0 \text{ or } 1, \quad i = 1, 2, \ldots, n.
$$

The value of the objective function at the optimal solution is the number of sets in the minimum cover. Each linear inequality in the constraints guarantees that an element is in the union of the selected subsets. S_j contains element i and S_j is included in the cover if and only if $a_{ij}x_j$ equals 1. The value of the left-hand side of the ith inequality is the number of times the ith element is covered by the subcollection comprising the cover, and this number must be one or more.

Of all the problems considered, set covering appears to be the most theoretical, with no possible application. In fact, this problem does model important practical problems, however imperfectly, and has received considerable attention in the professional literature. The *airline crew scheduling problem* is an example. An airline has m flights scheduled every day; management wants to know the minimum number of crews needed to service all flights. In the terminology of the set covering problem, a flight is an element of the set S. A subset corresponds to a set of different flights that can be serviced by the same crew. The S_j are determined in advance by consulting the schedule—a crew can serve on flight k after serving on flight i only if flight k departs from the same airport that serves as the destination for flight i and the departure time for flight k is suitably later than the arrival time for flight i—and by heeding various regulations. To say that S must be covered is to say that every flight must have a crew assigned to it. The value of the objective function is the number of required crews.

In this problem, the number of subsets will greatly exceed the number of flights, since the number of flight-to-flight transfers possible at some destinations may be quite large, creating many options for any one crew. The number of crews actually required can be expected to be smaller than the number of flights by a factor of three or more, since one crew normally services several domestic flights in a day. The set covering problem only models the airline crew scheduling problem inexactly, since a number of realistic secondary constraints are not correctly handled. For example, if two or more crews are scheduled for the same flight, i.e., an element is contained in more than one subset that composes the cover, presumably all but one of the crews rest. The airline may consider this to be a penalty situation, since seats that could be sold to passengers must now be reserved to move crews to their next destination. The objective function can be modified to take this situation into account. Another difficulty that is easily handled is that wide-body aircraft may require staffing by more than one crew. Yet another aspect of the real problem not captured in the set covering formulation is that management presumably prefers schedules in which the crew does not change aircraft, since this prevents delays from propagating through the entire schedule and alleviates the need to call up reserve crews on short notice to handle flights for which the correct crew has not arrived. This can be handled partially by imposing additional rules on the formation of the S_j, effectively eliminating certain combinations of flights that fulfill all legal requirements, but are deemed to be too risky. An additional advantage of this formulation is that it decreases n, the number of subsets, and thus reduces the size of the instance.

1.2　Path Problems in Graphs

Many problems reduce to finding paths in a graph that are optimal under some measure. Probably the most widely known optimization problem, the travelling salesperson problem, falls into this category.

A salesman has customers in each of n cities, including that in which he lives. He is planning a round trip in order to visit each of his customers. In what order should he visit them to minimize the distance travelled? There are many abstract formulations of this problem, each version incorporating various constraints designed to model the problem with greater realism. In its most general form, the problem can be expressed as follows.

Problem 3 [Travelling Salesperson] Given a directed graph, $G = (V, A)$, of n vertices and a distance function, $d: V \times V \to \mathcal{R}^+ \cup \{\infty\}$, such that[2]

$$d(v_i, v_j) = \begin{cases} D_{ij} \in \mathcal{R}^+, & \text{if } (v_i, v_j) \in A \\ \infty, & \text{if } (v_i, v_j) \notin A, \end{cases} \qquad (1.2)$$

find a simple cycle, $v_{i_0} \to v_{i_1} \to \cdots \to v_{i_n} = v_{i_0}$, which minimizes

$$\sum_{k=0}^{n-1} d(v_{i_k}, v_{i_{k+1}}). \qquad \square$$

A *simple cycle* is a path that passes through no vertex twice, except for the starting and ending vertices, which are the same. That the number of edges of the path is specified to be n, the same as the number of vertices, implies that each vertex is visited exactly once in the cycle. The size of the solution space can reach $(n-1)!$; that is, there can be up to $(n-1)!$ possible cycles from which the cycle of minimum length must be found. The worst case occurs in complete graphs where $(n-1)!$ is derived as follows. The starting and ending vertex can be considered to be v_0, since any vertex in a cycle is just as good a starting and ending point as any other; also, the first vertex on the path after v_0 can be chosen arbitrarily from the remaining $n-1$ vertices. There are then $n-2$ choices for the next vertex, given that v_0 and the vertex chosen already have been eliminated,

---

[2]Directed graphs are composed of vertices and arcs and will be denoted by (V, A), while undirected graphs are composed of vertices and edges and will be denoted by (V, E). $\mathcal{R}^+$ will generally be taken to include zero as well as the positive reals; whether zero is included can usually be told from context, and no special mention of zero will normally be made.

etc. The size of the solution space to this problem is even larger than the 2^n size for the knapsack and set covering problems.

The distance function can be viewed in greatest generality by considering it as an $n \times n$ matrix, D, the entries of which are the values returned by the function. The values do not necessarily have to represent distances in a geometric sense: they can be travel time or travel cost (gasoline $+$ tolls $+ \cdots$). If the minimum-cost tour yields an objective function value of infinity, then no tour is possible, i.e., the problem is infeasible. The distance function and the corresponding distance matrix do not have to be symmetric, that is, $D_{ij} = D_{ji}$ need not hold for all i and j. When symmetry does hold, the graph can be thought of as undirected and the problem is known as the *symmetric travelling salesperson problem*. A more important additional constraint for modelling the original, informal statement of the problem is to insist that the *triangle inequality* hold:

$$d(v_i, v_k) \leq d(v_i, v_j) + d(v_j, v_k), \quad \forall\, i, j, k.$$

In other words, while it may be preferable, in the context of the entire problem, to visit v_j on the way from v_i to v_k, the direct route, when considered in isolation, cannot be bettered. The importance of this property derives from the fact that any distance matrix can be transformed into one that obeys the triangle inequality: it is enough to allow multiple visits to a vertex, thereby letting the new distance from v_i to v_k equal the length of the shortest path from v_i to v_k (instead of the length of the arc from v_i to v_k). In terms of a real salesperson travelling between cities, a multiple visit can be regarded as "passing through on the way to someplace without stopping," a liberty that one would not be denied in practice. Thus the optimal tour obtained from the new matrix, although it is a simple cycle in terms of the new "arcs," may in fact pass through the same vertex more than once, since each new arc corresponds to a path in the original graph. Indeed, this path will have to be stored for each new arc in order to print out the optimal tour in terms of the original graph, G. Figure 1.3 shows an instance of the symmetric travelling salesperson problem with triangle inequality. The graph at the top shows only the direct connections, with the matrix below formed from the shortest paths from each vertex to every other vertex. The optimal tour, starting at Washington, D.C., goes successively to Baltimore, Philadelphia, New York, Buffalo, Detroit, Cincinnati, Cleveland, Pittsburgh, and finally back to Washington, D.C., for a total distance of 1790 miles.

There is a related graph traversal problem, which those of us who always seem to be late to engagements and appointments are continually called upon to solve—the shortest-path problem.

Problem 4 [Shortest Path] Given a directed graph, $G = (V, A)$, of n vertices, a distance function, $d : V \times V \to \mathcal{R}^+ \cup \{\infty\}$, and two vertices, $v_a, v_b \in V$, find a path,

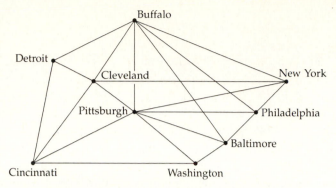

(a) The graph, showing only direct connections

Baltimore	0	345	514	355	522	189	97	230	39
Buffalo	345	0	430	186	252	445	365	217	384
Cincinnati	514	430	0	244	265	670	589	284	492
Cleveland	355	186	244	0	167	507	430	125	356
Detroit	522	252	265	167	0	674	597	292	523
New York	189	445	670	507	674	0	92	386	228
Philadelphia	97	365	589	430	597	92	0	305	136
Pittsburgh	230	217	284	125	292	386	305	0	231
Washington	39	384	492	356	523	228	136	231	0

(b) The distance matrix

Figure 1.3: An Instance of the Symmetric Travelling Salesperson Problem with Triangle Inequality

$v_a = v_{i_1} \to v_{i_2} \to \cdots \to v_{i_m} = v_b$, which minimizes

$$\sum_{j=1}^{m-1} d(v_{i_j}, v_{i_{j-1}}),$$

i.e., find a path of minimum length from v_a to v_b.   □

Note that a path of minimum length need not be a path with the fewest arcs.

A variant on this problem is the *all-points shortest-paths problem*, which is simply the problem above applied to all pairs of vertices. We have already encountered this problem in converting the general travelling salesperson problem to one in which the triangle inequality holds.

Problem 5 [All-Points Shortest Paths] Given a directed graph, $G = (V, A)$, of n vertices and a distance function, $d: V \times V \to \mathcal{R}^+ \cup \{\infty\}$, find the shortest path from each vertex in V to every other vertex in V.   □

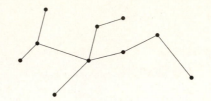

Figure 1.4: An Example of a Free Tree

Another problem of the same general type, but with a somewhat different twist, is the minimum spanning tree problem.

Problem 6 [Minimum Spanning Tree] Let $G = (V, E)$ be an undirected, connected graph of n vertices and let $d: E \to \mathcal{R}^+$ be a distance function defined on the edges. Find $E' \subseteq E$ such that $G' = (V, E')$ is still connected and $\sum_{e \in E'} d(e)$ is minimized. □

We claim that the edges composing the optimal E' form a tree.

The word *tree* is used here in a sense familiar to graph theorists and mathematicians, and not in the sense typically associated with computer science, where it is often equated with a binary tree, which has a designated root and directed edges.

Definition 1.2 A *free tree* (or just a *tree*) is an undirected, connected graph with no cycles. □

Figure 1.4 highlights several aspects of this definition. Notice that there really is neither a root nor a parent-child relationship and that the number of edges incident upon a vertex is variable. The definition does not even require the number of vertices in the graph to be finite, although we shall always assume finiteness. With this assumption, we have the following result:

Theorem 1.2 The following are equivalent:

1. G is a free tree (with n vertices).

2. G is connected, but if any edge is deleted, G becomes disconnected.

3. G is connected and has $n - 1$ edges.

4. G has no cycles, but the addition of an edge between any two vertices of G creates a cycle.

5. G has no cycles and has $n - 1$ edges.

6. There is a unique simple path connecting any two vertices of G. □

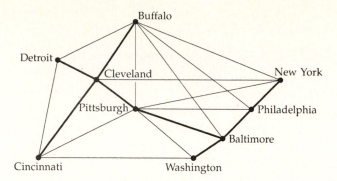

Figure 1.5: The Graph of Figure 1.3 with Its Minimum Spanning Tree

Proving this result would be too much of a digression at this point, but the reader is encouraged to do so, if only in an informal manner.

The optimal set of edges, E', must leave the vertices connected, as required by the problem statement, and cannot contain a cycle, since removing any edge from a cycle will produce a set of lower cost that nonetheless connects all vertices. Thus $G' = (V, E')$ is a tree by Definition 1.2. Any set of edges that connects all of the vertices of a graph is termed spanning. Taken together, these two observations explain the name given to the problem.

Figure 1.5 shows the graph of Figure 1.3 with the minimum spanning tree superimposed. While it is possible to go from any vertex to any other, the route can be quite circuitous, such as the path from Cincinnati to Washington, D.C., which has a length of 638 miles, compared with the direct route of 492 miles. Minimum spanning trees are effective models for certain applications—although road building is not one of them. Consider, for example, a chain of department stores located in the Mid-Atlantic region and the Ohio valley. The management has decided to implement a distributed database system with computing facilities located in the cities shown in Figure 1.5. They intend to lease telephone lines to connect the computing facilities, where the charge for the leased line is a linear function of the distance. By selecting the edges that compose the minimum spanning tree, they will connect all facilities at minimum cost.

Let us now change our viewpoint slightly. Consider the problem of conveying material or data from one point to another in a labelled graph. Each edge corresponds to a section of pipe or transmission line of limited carrying capacity; the labels, which are positive real numbers, represent these capacities. In its full generality, the problem statement allows for two different capacities to be associated with the same edge, one for each direction of flow. In most applications, these two capacities are the same (the graph is effectively undirected) or one of the capacities is zero (the graph is effectively directed). Each vertex is a *source*

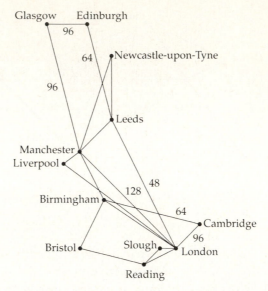

(Capacities are 56 kbps unless otherwise indicated.)

Figure 1.6: The British Public Data Transmission Network (PSS) *circa* 1981

(generating materials or data), a *sink* (consuming material or data), or a simple interconnection point. Our problem is to determine how to maximize the flow of material or data from one given point to another. This problem is an appropriate model for gas, oil, and water distribution networks, as well as for many data transmission applications.

Most data transmission networks use a transmission technique known as packet switching, in which a message is broken into packets and the individual packets are sent independently. Each packet contains a sequence number (to merge it correctly with the other packets when reconstituting the message at the destination) and a destination code; routing is done by each node in the network, so that different packets may be sent concurrently along different paths. The question then arises: What is the maximum amount of data that can be transferred from one network node to another, making the best possible use of concurrency? To illustrate the problem, consider the British public data transmission network, PSS, in its early stages (*circa* 1981), as illustrated in Figure 1.6.[3] Assuming perfect routing, the maximum rate of data transmission from Cambridge to Glasgow is 160 kbps (kilobits per second), using several links in parallel, as shown in Figure 1.7. This problem can be formalized as follows.

---

[3]The line transmission capacities have been altered somewhat to make the problem more interesting: as a rule, data networks use the same type of line throughout.

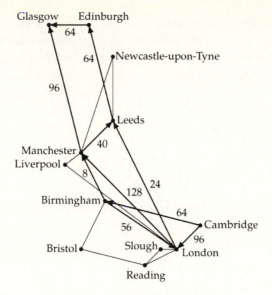

Figure 1.7: The Graph of Figure 1.6 with a Maximum Flow from Cambridge to Glasgow

Problem 7 [Network Flow] Let $G = (V, E)$ be an undirected, connected graph of n vertices and let $c: V \times V \rightarrow \mathcal{R}^+$ be a capacity function. (This formalism allows for different capacities for the two directions of flow through an edge; by convention we let $c(v, w) = 0$ when there is no edge connecting v and w.) Let $s, t \in V$ be distinguished vertices (the source and the sink). A flow from s to t is a real-valued function on pairs of vertices which obeys five conditions, for all vertices v and w:

1. The flow assigned to an arc does not exceed its capacity: $-c(w, v) \le f(v, w) \le c(v, w)$.

2. The flow through an edge is positive when seen from one end and negative when seen from the other: $f(v, w) = -f(w, v)$; in other words, f is skew-symmetric.

3. Material is conserved at all vertices except s and t: $\sum_w f(v, w) = 0$ for all vertices v other than s and t.

4. There is no flow into the source: $f(s, w) \ge 0$.

5. There is no flow out of the sink: $f(w, t) \ge 0$.

The *value* of a flow from s to t is simply the value of the net flow out of s, $\sum_w f(s, w)$. We want to find a flow from s to t of maximum value.   □

In thinking about these conditions, it is best to think of $f(v, w)$ as the amount of flow from v to w. A negative value for $f(v, w)$ means that the actual, physical flow of material is really from w to v. This is why $f(v, w)$ can be as negative as $-c(w, v)$ (the flow is at its maximum, but the direction of flow is from w to v); why $f(v, w) = -f(w, v)$ (it is just a change of perspective); and why $\sum_w f(v, w) = 0$ represents conservation of material. The fourth and fifth conditions can be enforced by the convention that $c(v, s) = c(t, w) = 0$ for all v and w.

Exercise 1.2 Prove that the net flow out of the source, $\sum_w f(s, w)$, is equal to the net flow into the sink, $\sum_v f(v, t)$. □

The path problem underlying the network flow problem is apparently complicated by the infinite number of possible flow assignments: this is the first problem we have encountered where the solution space is infinite.

1.3 The Efficiency of Elementary Calculations

How efficiently a certain task can be performed is a central theme of computer science. Here we consider problems, the origins of which are not rooted in classical computer science, but rather stem from elementary mathematics.

Problem 8 [Exponentiation of Integers] Let x and n be natural integers. How should x^n be computed in order to minimize the number of multiplications performed? □

The problem statement just given is sufficiently open-ended that it permits a number of solutions that are not really intended. First, since x is an integer, it is reasonable to presume that x^n is to be computed exactly. Methods for computing x^n approximately, appropriate when x is real, and possibly already represented inexactly inside the computer, such as executing the FORTRAN code

```
Y=EXP(N*LOG(X))
```

corresponding to $e^{n \ln x} = \left(e^{\ln x}\right)^n = x^n$, are not being considered here. More in the spirit of integer arithmetic, but still not intended, is to compute x^{2047} as x^{2048}/x. This method is effective because x^{2048} can be computed using only 11 multiplications when constructed by the sequence

$$x, \quad x \cdot x = x^2, \quad x^2 \cdot x^2 = x^4, \quad x^4 \cdot x^4 = x^8, \quad x^8 \cdot x^8 = x^{16}, \dots$$

How to judge the "cost" of computing x^{2047} in this manner is not clear; divisions are normally considered to be more time-consuming than multiplications. In general, for an exponent of the form $n = 2^m - 1$, this method takes m multiplications and one division. If methods like this, which are strictly integer (the division leaving no remainder), are to be considered invalid, a precise set of rules must be given. We shall permit only multiplications under the following rules:

1. A fixed pool of memory locations is available; initially, all memory locations have undefined values, with the exception of one location, which contains the value x.

2. Multiplication must be performed by taking the values from two defined memory locations, multiplying them, and putting the result into a memory location. The operands may come from the same defined memory location, and either a defined or an undefined memory location can receive the result of the multiplication.

If only two storage locations are allowed, one in which x itself is held and one in which the answer is being accumulated, then the optimal way to compute x^{15} is to form the sequence

$$x, \quad x \cdot x = x^2, \quad x^2 \cdot x = x^3, \quad x^3 \cdot x^3 = x^6,$$
$$x^6 \cdot x = x^7, \quad x^7 \cdot x^7 = x^{14}, \quad x^{14} \cdot x = x^{15}.$$

There really is very little choice in the matter. Each computation must correspond to

```
answer := answer*answer;    or
answer := answer*x;         or
answer := x*x;
```

where answer holds the result as it is being accumulated. This sequence requires six multiplications. The ability to store an indefinite number of intermediate results and to use them later with no cost penalty reduces the number of multiplications to five, since x^{15} can then be computed as

$$x, \quad x \cdot x = x^2, \quad x^2 \cdot x = x^3, \quad x^3 \cdot x^2 = x^5,$$
$$x^5 \cdot x^5 = x^{10}, \quad x^{10} \cdot x^5 = x^{15},$$

which requires that two intermediate values, x^2 for the computation of x^5 and x^5 for the computation of x^{15}, be retained. If x need not be preserved, then this method of computing x^{15} still requires only two memory locations. If x must be preserved for some other purpose, then three memory locations are required. This analysis raises the possibility of optimizing a secondary objective function:

Among all ways to compute x^n that use the fewest number of multiplications, which uses the least additional storage?

Since multiplying x^p by x^q is equivalent to adding p and q, and since the value of x does not affect our evaluation of the cost, the original problem, after clarifying the legal operations, can be rephrased as shown in Problem 9.

Problem 9 [Shortest Sum Decomposition] Given n, find the shortest sequence of integers, $1 = p_1, p_2, \ldots, p_{k-1}, p_k = n$, such that each integer in the sequence, other than 1, is the sum of two integers already included in the sequence.

□

x^{2047} can be computed in 15 multiplications, corresponding to the following sequence:

Value	1	2	3	5	7	14	21	42	47
from		$1+1$	$2+1$	$3+2$	$5+2$	$7+7$	$14+7$	$21+21$	$42+5$

Value	89	178	267	445	890	1780	2047
from	$47+42$	$89+89$	$178+89$	$267+178$	$445+445$	$890+890$	$1780+267$

If only x and one other storage location to accumulate the answer are permitted, then computing x^{2047} requires 20 multiplications. Notice that 15 multiplications would appear more expensive than the computation of x^{2048}/x, but that approach violates our ground rules.

Exercise 1.3 What is the optimal way to compute x^{77}? (The minimum length sequence requires eight multiplications, and it is not unique.)   □

Why the ground rules, and where did this problem come from in the first place? In recent years, considerable attention has been paid to *public key encryption*, systems for sending coded messages that have several advantages over earlier cryptographic methods. These advantages include the following:

1. An encrypted communication between two people can be established without a clandestine meeting to exchange secret coding and decoding keys; in fact, the exchange of keys can be done over an insecure communications channel using plain language.

2. Bogus messages from third parties can be detected and disregarded; that is, the authenticity of the sender can be determined. (Not all public key encryption systems incorporate this feature.)

3. Since these systems are based on problems assumed to be intractable, it may be possible to prove that the code cannot be deciphered in any reasonable length of time.

The basic computation required to use the public key encryption system due to Rivest, Shamir, and Adelman is the rapid calculation of $x^e \bmod N$ for x, e, and N positive integers of up to 1000 digits in length. In this system, x is the message (or a portion of it) to be encoded; it can simply be the ASCII representation of the message viewed as one large binary number. Note that x changes with each transmission but that e and N are calculated once and for all. The large size of the numbers implies that an unbounded precision arithmetic package, that stores numbers in multiple words, will be needed, so that a multiplication will take considerable time. Division by x is disallowed for the following reason: if the arithmetic is done modulo N at every stage, performing a division by x is really multiplying by x^{-1}, a value which must be determined at a fairly large cost and which might not even exist (because N is composite). On the other hand, performing the entire computation in $\mathcal{Z}^+$, which permits the division, and taking the result modulo N requires multiplying far larger numbers at each stage, which slows down the overall computation. Since e does not change, but $x^e \bmod N$ is being constantly computed, it pays to spend some time finding the optimal way to compute x^e.

Problem 10 [Matrix Chain Product] Given the matrix computation, $A_1 \times A_2 \times \cdots \times A_n$, where the matrices have compatible dimensions, but need not be square, in what order should the matrices be multiplied to minimize the computation time?   □

To avoid some cumbersome details, we shall assume that the matrix multiplications are carried out in the "standard" manner, where if $C = A \times B$, c_{ij} is computed as $\sum_{k=1}^{s} a_{ik} \cdot b_{kj}$, where A is $r \times s$ and B is $s \times t$. This results in $r \cdot s \cdot t$ scalar multiplications for the matrix multiplication, which will be used as the measure of computation time, since the number of additions performed is essentially the same. If the matrices are all square, say $s \times s$, then the order of multiplication is irrelevant and $(n-1) \cdot s^3$ scalar multiplications are required. If the matrices are rectangular, on the other hand, the order of multiplication can make a significant difference. Consider, for example, four matrices with dimensions 100×4, 4×50, 50×20, and 20×100. Table 1.2 shows the five different orders of computation possible and their respective computation times. The worst order requires almost 12 times more work than the best.

   If the order of multiplication is thought of as a list of instructions that states the order in which the multiplications are to be carried out, there are six orders of multiplication, but

$$
\begin{array}{lll}
T_1 \leftarrow A_1 \times A_2 & & T_1 \leftarrow A_3 \times A_4 \\
T_2 \leftarrow A_3 \times A_4 & \text{and} & T_2 \leftarrow A_1 \times A_2 \\
T_3 \leftarrow T_1 \times T_2 & & T_3 \leftarrow T_2 \times T_1
\end{array}
$$

Table 1.2: The Effect of the Order of Evaluation on the Number of Scalar Multiplications

Order of multiplication	Number of scalar multiplications
$\big((A_1 \times A_2) \times A_3\big) \times A_4$	320,000
$(A_1 \times A_2) \times (A_3 \times A_4)$	620,000
$A_1 \times \big(A_2 \times (A_3 \times A_4)\big)$	160,000
$\big(A_1 \times (A_2 \times A_3)\big) \times A_4$	212,000
$A_1 \times \big((A_2 \times A_3) \times A_4\big)$	52,000

require the same number of computations, for both are linearizations of the order specified by

$$(A_1 \times A_2) \times (A_3 \times A_4).$$

In order to keep the solution space, each member of which is an order of multiplication, as small as possible, it makes sense to find a representation for an order of multiplication that treats these equivalent sequences as indistinguishable. The fully parenthesized form used in Table 1.2 is one way of representing the computation that ignores the ordering of logically independent subcomputations. Another way of achieving the same effect is to specify a computation as an *expression tree*. Each internal node of the tree is an operator, the only operator here being "matrix multiplication," and each leaf represents an operand, one of the matrices. The five orders of multiplication corresponding to the five parenthesizations are shown in Figure 1.8. Notice that the n leaves are always labelled in the same order, $A_1, A_2, \ldots, A_n$, when viewed from left to right, or more precisely when listed in the order in which they are encountered in a pre-, in-, or postorder traversal of the tree.

It should be apparent that there is a one-to-one correspondence among the fully parenthesized form for the specification of the order of multiplication, the use of expression trees to convey the order, and what we intuitively would call distinct orders of multiplication. Therefore the size of the solution space is equal to the number of binary trees with $n-1$ internal nodes (or n leaves).[4] Table 1.3 shows the number of binary trees with n leaves, b_n, for the first few values of n. Note that, while the values increase only slowly at first, they seem to grow

---

[4]Different authors define *binary tree* differently. Some insist that every node have either zero or two children, as is the case for expression trees, while others allow zero, one, or two children, with the case of a single left child distinguished from that of a single right child. We use the term *binary tree* to designate either kind, with context or a brief comment specifying which definition obtains.

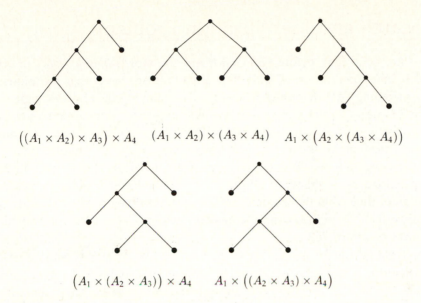

$((A_1 \times A_2) \times A_3) \times A_4$ $(A_1 \times A_2) \times (A_3 \times A_4)$ $A_1 \times (A_2 \times (A_3 \times A_4))$

$(A_1 \times (A_2 \times A_3)) \times A_4$ $A_1 \times ((A_2 \times A_3) \times A_4)$

Figure 1.8: Tree Representations of Fully Parenthesized Matrix Products

exponentially after that, tripling or more at each step for $n \geq 6$.

While for some problems, such as the knapsack and travelling salesperson problems, only the most elementary principles of counting were needed to determine the size of the solution space, finding a closed form formula for b_n is considerably more difficult. The required mathematics, as well as the derivation itself, will be presented in the next chapter; we content ourselves here with quoting the result,

$$b_n = \frac{1}{n}\binom{2n-2}{n-1}.$$

Table 1.3: The Number of Binary Trees with n Leaves

n	b_n	n	b_n
1	1	7	132
2	1	8	429
3	2	9	1,430
4	5	10	4,862
5	14	11	16,796
6	42	12	58,786

1.4 Search and Identification Problems

Chances are good that, before you first heard the words *binary search* or wrote your first computer program, you had already discovered this technique for rapidly searching an ordered list, probably while playing the children's guessing game of 20 questions. In one version of this two-person game, one player picks a number between 1 and 1000 and the second player tries to guess the number by asking questions of the form, "Is it bigger than ...?" or "smaller than ...?" or "equal to ...?" If the second player manages to guess the number in 20 or fewer questions, he or she wins; otherwise, he or she loses. Children quickly tire of this game: they soon realize that the first question they ought to ask is, "Is it bigger than 500?" and, based on the answer, next ask about the relationship of the number to 250 or 750.

The code for binary search, given in Program 1.1,[5] is effective for searching large ordered lists since the length of the interval of search, $r - l + 1$, is reduced by a factor of two with every pass through the while loop. Thus, for a list of length n, the search time is proportional to $\lg n$. To see just how effective this algorithm really is, imagine a stack of punch cards with the name of every man, woman, and child in the United States, in alphabetical order, on a separate card. The stack would stretch for a distance of 25 miles, yet the card associated with any individual could be retrieved in just 28 fetches.

By placing the binary search technique in a more abstract and general setting, we can see more clearly what it does and perhaps how to improve on its performance. Let us first generalize the problem setting, using as a specific example a program to detect spelling errors in large documents. We begin with a key space, K, which is quite enormous or even infinite. K must have the property, however, that any two keys in K can be compared with the "<" relation. In the application we are considering, K would consist of all possible strings of letters, that is, wordlike objects, where $k_1 < k_2$ means that k_1 precedes k_2 in alphabetical order. From K we select a distinguished finite subset, $\hat{K}$, which defines the dictionary of correctly spelled words. The use to which we intend to put $\hat{K}$ is as follows: for every wordlike object in a document, determine whether or not the object is also in $\hat{K}$. If it is, ignore it, but if it is not, then print it out as a potential misspelling. Thus we anticipate searching $\hat{K}$ for different keys time and time again. (Of course, this scheme is not perfect: foreign or technical words and proper names may be absent from $\hat{K}$ and will be printed, and some misspellings will produce legitimate words and not be caught.)

---

[5]Note that we pass the array A as a var parameter, in spite of the fact that it is not modified by the procedure; otherwise, the whole point of the algorithm would be lost, because the array would be copied on entry to the procedure, a linear-time operation. On the other hand, we choose to pass the objects to be compared by value, as we assume them to be small.

```
const MaxN = ...;
type datum = ...; (* anything comparable by (generalized) '<' *)
     data = array [1..MaxN] of datum;
function BinarySearch(var (* for speed *) A: data; n: integer;
                         k: datum): integer;
  (* Return location in A of k, if present, or 0 if absent.
     n is the location of the last valid datum in A. *)
  label 1;
  type order = (less, equal, greater);
  var l, m, r: integer; (* left, middle and right *)
       (* The value k, if present, is always located in A[l..r]. *)
  function Compare(first, second: datum): order;
    begin
      (* Determine relationship between first and second. *)
      ... not shown ...
    end; (* Compare *)
  begin (* BinarySearch *)
    l := 1; (* If present, surely in A[l..r] at this point. *)
    r := n;
    while l <= r do (* There still is a potential range. *)
      begin
        (* Find the middle element of A[l..r], more or less. *)
        m := (l+r) div 2;
        case Compare(k,A[m]) of
          less:    r := m - 1; (* If present, then to the left of m. *)
          equal:   begin (* found it *)
                     BinarySearch := m;
                     goto 1 (* return *)
                   end;
          greater: l := m + 1 (* If present, then to the right of m. *)
        end
      end;
    (* Not present in the list. *)
    BinarySearch := 0;
  1:
  end; (* BinarySearch *)
```

Program 1.1: Binary Search

We can apply binary search to the alphabetized $\hat{K}$, but this approach is not entirely satisfactory. With a bit of bad luck, the most common word in English, *the*, will fall into a position on the list that requires the maximum number of passes through the `while` loop of Program 1.1. Indeed, if the dictionary is 250,000 words long, a total of 118,929 words take the maximum number of passes; even if *the* is not among them, other common English words, such as *of*, *and*, and *if*, are sure to be. Conversely, a rare word like *numismatist* is likely to fall exactly at the halfway point, requiring only one pass. Unlike in the 20 questions game, where each integer had the same probability of being selected for the secret number, the elements of $\hat{K}$ in this example are looked up with unequal probabilities. We shall therefore assume that each key, $k_i \in \hat{K}$, for $1 \le i \le n$, where $|\hat{K}| = n$, has an associated probability, p_i, that it will be the object of the search. Another feature that distinguishes this search from the game of 20 questions is the possibility of requesting a key that is absent from $\hat{K}$. We define q_i as the probability of a search for a key, absent from $\hat{K}$, that falls between the adjacent keys k_i and k_{i+1}. The two boundary cases, q_0 and q_n, are the probability of searching for a key preceding k_1 or following k_n. In some problems, the p_i and q_i can be determined *a priori*; for the example at hand, these values would have to be determined empirically by gathering frequency statistics from a number of large documents. (We shall ignore the fact that many of the p_i will be so small as to be meaningless and that the q_i probably cannot be determined with any accuracy.) Since the p_i and q_i represent probabilities of successful and unsuccessful search, respectively, and between themselves account for all keys in K, we must have

$$\sum_{i=1}^{n} p_i + \sum_{i=0}^{n} q_i = 1.$$

Given that we have K, $\hat{K}$, the p_i, and the q_i, the question is: How do we organize the search to minimize the average search time? As with the problem of rapid exponentiation of integers, this question is also too open-ended. For instance, if hashing is permitted, we might achieve constant average search time. On the other hand, if we restrict ourselves to the binary search procedure, there is no problem at all because, given $\hat{K}$, there is only one way to apply this procedure. We need an appropriate generalization.

Definition 1.3 A *binary search tree* is a binary tree (of the zero, one, or two children variety) in which there is a one-to-one correspondence between the keys of $\hat{K}$ and the nodes of the tree and in which every node has the following property: if k is the key associated with the node, k_1 is any key associated with a node in its left subtree, and k_2 is any key associated with a node in its right subtree, then $k_1 < k < k_2$.   □

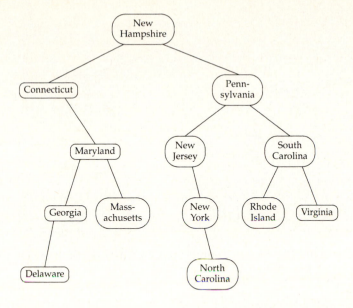

Figure 1.9: A Binary Search Tree for the Original 13 States

A binary search tree containing the names of the original 13 states is shown in Figure 1.9. Notice that, if a binary search tree is traversed in inorder, the nodes are visited in increasing order with respect to the "<" relation.

The process of searching a binary search tree for a specified value is essentially the same as searching an array of ordered values with binary search, as illustrated in Program 1.2. In searching for Massachusetts, we first try the root; since Massachusetts precedes New Hampshire, we go down the left branch; then, since Massachusetts follows Connecticut, we go to the right, where we compare

```
p := root;
while p <> nil do
  case Compare(k,p^.data) of
    less:    p := p^.left;  (* equivalent to r := m - 1 *)
    equal:   goto 1;
    greater: p := p^.right  (* equivalent to l := m + 1 *)
  end;
  (* p = nil; no node with key equal to k *)
1: ...
```

Program 1.2: Searching a Binary Tree

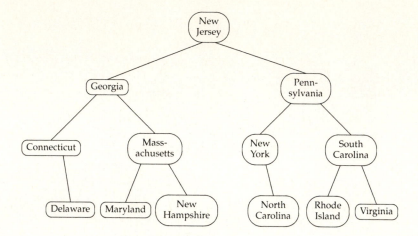

Figure 1.10: The Binary Search Tree Dictated by Binary Search

it with Maryland and go right again; finally, we find Massachusetts on the fourth probe of the data structure. While the process is the same, there is an important difference: in binary search we reduce the search space by half with each test. For an arbitrary binary search tree, the gain may be much smaller—in Figure 1.9, New Hampshire creates a 5 *vs.* 7 split, while Connecticut splits its two subtrees 0 *vs.* 4.

Not only is the search algorithm of Program 1.2 analogous to the search procedure of Program 1.1, but also the behavior of binary search is emulated exactly if the tree is constructed according to the following rule:

> Select as the root of the tree and every subtree the key which divides the remaining search interval most nearly into two equal pieces, giving the extra key to the right subtree in case the original search interval had an even number of keys.

Whenever a move is made down the right subtree in Program 1.2, binary search adjusts 1 in Program 1.1, etc. For the original 13 states, the tree that is equivalent to binary search is shown in Figure 1.10.

Binary search never performs poorly, because the associated binary search tree is balanced fairly evenly and the height of the tree is $\lfloor \lg n \rfloor + 1$. On the other hand, as the spelling error detection program suggests, binary search is completely insensitive to the probability distribution of search requests inherent in the data—the rule just given for constructing the binary search tree equivalent to binary search concerns itself with only the number of data items. Therefore, it might be possible to find a somewhat skewed binary search tree that exhibits better performance characteristics by placing items that are frequently requested closer to the root.

So that we can be precise about what we mean by one binary search tree being better than another, we need to define an objective function. Intuitively, we want to minimize the average execution time of the search described in Program 1.2 under the probability distribution specified by the p_i and q_i. Exact analysis is difficult, because the time through the while loop depends on whether one or two tests (the one in the while and the one in the case) are performed. In order to simplify our work, we assign unit cost to the test of the case, but ignore the work done in the test of the while. This charging policy can be viewed as a crude model of the situation where the binary search tree is kept on disk. Checking whether a pointer is nil is done in main memory and so is very fast; similarly, once the data at p^ have been retrieved, performing the case test is irrelevant. The disk access time dominates all other computations.

Let the root be at depth 1; if a node at depth j is the object of the search, we incur a cost of j. Since node k_i is the object of the search p_i percent of the time, it contributes an average cost of $p_i \cdot \mathrm{depth}(k_i)$. An unsuccessful search presents a slight difficulty, because it does not correspond to nodes of the tree; to remedy this situation, we imagine that the nil pointers are replaced by a special type of node, the key of which matches anything in the range $k_i < k < k_{i+1}$ (or $k < k_1$ for q_0 and similarly for q_n). Calling such a node k_i', the cost of an unsuccessful search is now $q_i \cdot (\mathrm{depth}(k_i') - 1)$, where the -1 is due to the fact that determining that we are at node k_i' is really the test p <> nil, for which we agreed not to incur any cost. Thus, for any binary search tree, the cost of the tree equals the average search length:

$$\sum_{i=1}^{n} p_i \cdot \mathrm{depth}(k_i) + \sum_{i=0}^{n} q_i \cdot (\mathrm{depth}(k_i') - 1).$$

The binary search trees of Figures 1.9 and 1.10 have costs of 3.62 and 3.45, where we have used for p_i the population of the state relative to the population of all 50 states according to the 1980 census. The q_i are the percentages of people who lived in the states alphabetically between k_i and k_{i+1}. Since no state falls alphabetically between Maryland and Massachusetts, $q_4 = 0$. On the other hand, q_9 is 0.0757, since North Dakota, Ohio, Oklahoma, and Oregon fall between North Carolina and Pennsylvania.

We can now pose the following problem.

Problem 11 [Optimal Binary Search Tree] Given K, $\hat{K}$, $\{ p_i \mid 0 \le p_i \le 1, i = 1, 2,$ ..., $|\hat{K}| \}$, and $\{ q_i \mid 0 \le q_i \le 1, i = 0, 1, \ldots, |\hat{K}| \}$, with $\sum_{i=1}^{n} p_i + \sum_{i=0}^{n} q_i = 1$,

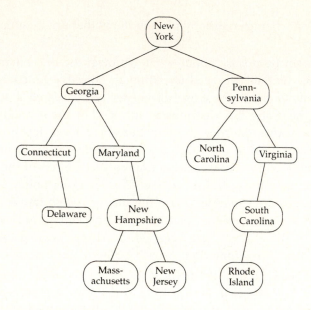

Figure 1.11: The Optimal Binary Search Tree with Probabilities Based on 1980 Populations

what is the binary search tree that minimizes

$$\sum_{i=1}^{n} p_i \cdot \operatorname{depth}(k_i) + \sum_{i=0}^{n} q_i \cdot (\operatorname{depth}(k_i') - 1)\,?$$ □

The tree of Figure 1.11 is optimal for the data described, with a cost of 3.27.

The use of trees to guide searches is not limited to searching lists, the elements of which come from a totally ordered domain. Consider the problem of a microbiologist attempting to determine which one of eight species from genus *Pasteurella* is present in a specimen brought into the laboratory for identification. He has at his disposal a collection of tests that he can apply to samples of the specimen, such as the motility of the bacteria at 22°C or the ability of a colony to grow on an agar medium in the presence of various chemical compounds. The results of applying these tests to control strains are published in the microbiological literature and can be summarized as in Table 1.4, where "+" indicates a positive response and "−" a negative response. Unless every row of such a table is distinct from every other row, there will be species that are inseparable, because these species behave identically under any and all tests applied to them. For the time being, we shall assume that any two species can always be separated.

Table 1.4: Test Results on Eight Species of *Pasteurella*

Organism	Name of test									
	Motility at 22°C	Haemo-lysis	Indole	Methyl red	Urease	Oxidase	Litmus	Orni-thine	Arab-inose	Cello-biose
P. pneumo-tropica	−	−	+	−	+	+	−	−	−	−
P. hemolytica var. ureae	−	+	+	+	+	+	+	−	−	−
Pasteurella multocida	−	−	+	−	−	+	−	+	−	−
P. hemolytica type A	−	+	−	−	−	+	−	−	+	−
P. hemolytica type T	−	+	−	−	−	+	−	−	−	+
Pasteurella X	+	−	−	+	+	−	−	+	+	+
Pasteurella pestis	−	−	−	+	−	−	+	−	+	−
P. pseudo-tuberculosis	+	−	−	+	+	−	+	−	+	−

The microbiologist could proceed by applying all of the tests and then matching the observed results against each row of the table until an exact match is found. However, this procedure is inefficient. Notice that applying any one test will divide the species into two disjoint subsets, based on the reaction of each species to the test. The result of performing the test on the unknown species will narrow the possibilities to those species in one subset or the other. The microbiologist can then select another test to apply, further restricting the possibilities for the unknown, and continue in this manner until the species is identified. There are two subtle points to notice about this procedure:

1. The tests are to be applied sequentially, with the knowledge gained on previous tests guiding the selection of subsequent tests. The test that the microbiologist chooses to apply as the $(i + 1)$st test generally depends on the outcome of the first i tests.

2. Unlike when binary search is applied to an ordered list, the two subsets produced cannot always be forced to be of (approximately) equal size. The size of the subsets created by applying a test depends on the data in the published table, and nature does not always conveniently divide things along a 50–50 split.

A testing procedure can be specified by an *identification tree*, such as that shown in Figure 1.12. An identification tree differs from a binary search tree in a

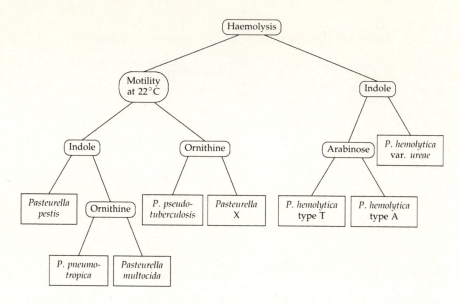

Figure 1.12: An Identification Tree for Eight Species of *Pasteurella*

few relatively inconsequential ways. The interior nodes now correspond to tests and no longer contain a key value, so that the search cannot terminate before reaching a leaf. The `nil` pointers have been replaced by nodes that involve no testing but that specify the name of the identified object, here a species of *Pasteurella*.

While technically an interior node can have only one child, applying such a test would provide no useful information, since having only one child corresponds to not splitting a subcollection further. Just as in the case of binary search trees, we may associate a probability, p_i, with each species: the probability that this species will be brought into the laboratory for identification. These probabilities are presumably determined by gathering statistics over a period of time. There is no analogue to the q_i, as every identification will terminate at a leaf. As an unfortunate consequence, if the unknown species is not any of those listed in the table, a misdiagnosis will result. The code of Program 1.2 must undergo minor modifications to accommodate our new problem.

Problem 12 [Optimal Identification Tree] Given that objects drawn from m categories, $O_1, O_2, \ldots, O_m$, with relative frequencies $p_1, p_2, \ldots, p_m$ (with $\sum_{i=1}^{m} p_i = 1$) must be identified with the help of n dichotomous tests, each of which is applicable to any object and is specified by an $m \times 1$ vector of outcomes, find the identification tree that minimizes the average path length

$$\sum_{i=1}^{m} p_i \cdot (\text{depth}(O_i) - 1),$$

where $\text{depth}(O_i) - 1$ is the number of tests that must performed to identify an object in category O_i. ☐

If the eight species of *Pasteurella* are equiprobable, the identification tree of Figure 1.12 is not optimal.

1.5 Puzzles and Decision Problems

Every so often combinatorial games and puzzles appear in toy stores and for a short period of time become the rage, only to be relegated to attics and garages when their owners become sufficiently frustrated with them. The number of puzzles of this type is truly staggering. We present here four such puzzles, which hold some theoretical interest and have the advantage that they can be expressed easily in the two-dimensional format of a book.

Problem 13 [n-queens] The queen in the game of chess attacks in the horizontal, vertical, and diagonal directions, as shown in Figure 1.13. How, if at all, can n queens be placed on an $n \times n$ chessboard so that no two queens are mutually attacking? ☐

A few minutes of thought should convince the reader that there are no solutions to the two-queens and three-queens problems. A solution to the four-queens problem is shown in Figure 1.14.

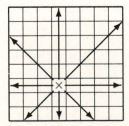

Figure 1.13: The Lines of Attack of a Queen on an 8×8 Chessboard

Figure 1.14: A Solution to the Four-Queens Problem

Problem 14 [Tiling a Square] A tile is a square with a side of unit length divided into four independently colored quarters, as shown below:

(The back of the tile is blank.) There are m different tile types, i.e., color arrangements, and t_i tiles of type i available, with

$$\sum_{i=1}^{m} t_i = n^2.$$

How, if at all, can the tiles be placed in an $n \times n$ square so that, whenever two tiles have a border in common, they have the same color along that border? The tiles may be rotated, they need not agree in any sense if they share only a point in common, and any colors can be on the boundary of the $n \times n$ square.   □

Problem 15 [Pentominoes] Five unit squares can be connected into rigid shapes in exactly the following 12 ways:

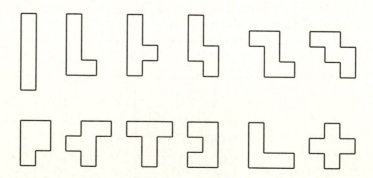

Since $12 \times 5 = 60$, how, if at all, can the 12 shapes be placed into a 6×10 rectangle so that it is completely covered?   □

Problem 16 [Peek] This is a two-person game played with a stack of perforated plates placed in a fixed order in a rack. Each plate has one or more holes centered at integer coordinates. All plates have the same dimensions, with their length exceeding the length of the rack, and all holes have the same diameter. A plate can be in one of two positions in its slot: flush on one side or flush on the other. The top of the rack is itself a plate, but it is shorter and fixed in place. (Figure 1.15 shows a sample configuration for the game.) Each player knows the perforation pattern of all plates and can observe the other player's moves. Each plate is marked "first" or "second," and players can move only their own plates. Players take turns sliding their plates back and forth until one player succeeds in aligning holes so that one can "peek" clear through the stack. The problem is to determine, given an initial configuration, whether the first player can force a win. □

These problems, unlike the earlier ones in this chapter, are not usually viewed as optimization problems. What is desired here is to exhibit one or more solutions or, perhaps, to decide whether or not a solution exists. In general, we can formulate the same problem in several ways by slight rephrasings; we distinguish the following forms:

1. A *decision* problem has a yes or no answer. Typical questions are, "Does a solution exist?" or "Is there a sufficiently good solution?"

2. In a *search* problem, one must exhibit a solution. Puzzles are search problems. Optimization problems are search problems, too: it does not do the travelling salesperson much good to know the length of the optimal tour while remaining ignorant of which tour has this length.

3. In an *enumeration* problem, one must exhibit all solutions. Many enumeration problems may require long running times simply because the number of solutions is very large; to avoid this constraint, an enumeration problem is often defined as requiring that all distinct solutions only be counted. The latter requirement might be met implicitly—which could prove much faster than counting solutions one by one.

The initial reaction to decision problems is often to dismiss them as hidden search problems (and thus just as difficult). How, in general, are we to solve a decision problem, except to solve the corresponding search problem, then emit yes or no? While it is true that, for most decision problems, solving the corresponding search problem is the only technique that suggests itself, this need not always be the case: mathematics does allow nonconstructive existence proofs.

As an example of this distinction, consider the following two-person game, which is a generalization of the game of *hex*. (The reasoning to follow applies to

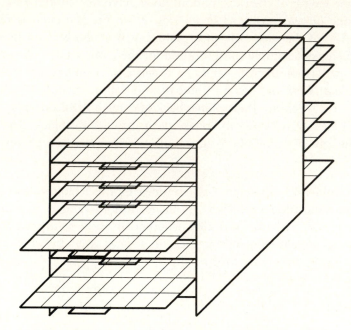

(a) A box with eight movable plates, six slid in and two slid out

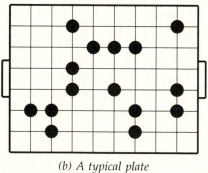

(b) A typical plate

Figure 1.15: A Sample Configuration of the Peek Game

any two-person game where an extra piece or an extra move can only help the player who has it available.) The game board consists of a connected, undirected graph, $G = (V, E)$, with two distinguished vertices, s and t. The players alternate turns, coloring a vertex from $V - \{s, t\}$ that has not already been colored, until all vertices are colored. Let the first player color vertices green and the second color them red. If the first player can form a path from s to t passing through only green vertices and the second player cannot form a path from s to t passing through only red vertices, then the first player wins. A win for the second player is similarly defined. If neither or both players can form paths from s to t passing through only vertices of the proper color, then the game is a draw. Consider the decision problem: given G, s, and t, and assuming perfect play by the first player, can he or she force a win or a draw? We can prove that the answer to this question is always yes—although the proof is a little hard to accept on first reading. The argument, a proof by contradiction, establishes that the second player cannot win. *Ad absurdum*,[6] suppose that there exists an instance of the game in which the second player can win according to some strategy. The first player can effectively adopt the second player's strategy as follows. For the first move, he or she chooses a vertex randomly and "forgets" that he or she has it. The second player then moves. The first player then chooses his or her next vertex using the second player's strategy, treating the second player's first move as if it were the opening move of the game. This style of play continues until the first player, according to the second player's strategy, must pick the vertex that he or she originally chose and forgot. If this occurs, and there are any vertices left, he or she chooses his or her next vertex randomly, making it the new forgotten vertex. Play continues in this manner. At the end of the game, the first player holds all of the vertices that the second player would hold according to the latter's strategy, plus possibly one more. Having an extra vertex cannot harm a winning position, so the first player wins, contradicting our hypothesis. Thus the decision problem is solved, yet we do not have the slightest inkling as to what is the perfect strategy! Note that the fact that the answer to the decision problem is yes for all instances of the game plays no role in the proof; other games exist for which the decision problem is also solvable without search and where the answer does vary with the instance.

One of the most important decision problems concerns Boolean expressions; it has applications in automated theorem proving, logic circuit verification (since each circuit implements a Boolean function), and system testing (in which we are interested in only Boolean values: Does the system work or does it not?). It is also fundamental in the study of problem complexity (see Volume II).

---

[6]Literally, "towards absurdity," i.e., in order to obtain a contradiction.

Problem 17 [Satisfiability]   Given a Boolean expression in *conjunctive normal form*—that is, as a conjunction (logical "and") of clauses, each of which is a disjunction (logical "or") of literals (variables or their complements)—can the variables be assigned truth values that make the expression evaluate to true?

□

For instance, the expression

$$(x \vee z) \wedge (\bar{x} \vee \bar{y} \vee \bar{z}) \wedge (\bar{x} \vee y) \wedge (\bar{z}),$$

where $\bar{x}$ denotes the complement of x, is satisfiable (the truth assignment $x = true$, $y = true$, $z = false$ makes the expression evaluate to *true*), but the expression

$$(\bar{x} \vee y) \wedge (x \vee \bar{y}) \wedge (\bar{x} \vee \bar{y}) \wedge (x \vee y)$$

is not. Like generalized hex, it is conceivable that the satisfiability of an expression can be determined nonconstructively, i.e., without producing a satisfying truth assignment; however, once again, most of us would approach this problem as a search problem.

We also note that this problem, like many other decision problems, is easily rephrased as an optimization problem: find the truth assignment that maximizes the number of clauses that evaluate to *true*. In fact, this slight transformation is only one of several among the problem forms. Clearly, a search problem can be turned into an enumeration problem. An optimization problem is easily converted into a decision problem by adding one parameter, a bound assigned to the objective function, and asking whether there exists a solution for which the objective function exceeds the bound. A search problem can also be converted into an equivalent decision problem by means other than changing the question from "show a solution" to "does a solution exist?" For instance, one can convert the search version of satisfiability (find a truth assignment, if any, that makes the expression evaluate to *true*) into the pure decision problem of *tautology* (is a Boolean expression true under all possible truth assignments?) by transforming the original expression, (E), into the new Boolean expression $(E \rightarrow false)$. The new expression is a tautology if and only if E can never be satisfied; in particular, a solution to the tautology problem would provide a (presumably) nonconstructive solution to the satisfiability problem.

1.6   Geometric Problems

With the increasingly widespread use of graphics and the advent of computer-aided design and manufacturing (better known as CAD/CAM), geometric prob-

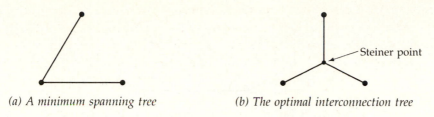

(a) A minimum spanning tree   (b) The optimal interconnection tree

Figure 1.16: Interconnection Trees for Three Cities

lems are receiving more and more attention. Most geometric problems consist of an underlying set or graph problem, where the set or graph is *embedded* in Euclidean space. An embedding of a set or graph in n-dimensional space is a function that assigns an n-tuple of coordinates to each element or vertex. The embedding automatically induces a distance measure between the set elements or the graph vertices. Thus most set or graph problems can give rise to geometric problems; however, we shall reserve the term for those problems that depend on geometry for their existence, such as the problems introduced in this section.

Let us consider once again the problem of a communication network, which we discussed in Section 1.2, but let us shift our focus from the use of such a network to its design. Given a collection of cities, we are to construct the least expensive network that will allow communication between any two cities. Let us define the cost of any such network as the sum of the lengths of its communication links. From our discussion in Section 1.2, the reader may be tempted to propose using a minimum spanning tree. That the least expensive network is indeed a tree is easily proved: if it were not, then a cycle would exist; removing any edge of the cycle would produce a less expensive, and still connected, network. However, the minimum spanning tree only rarely provides an optimal solution. In most cases, it is advantageous to add extra nodes (relay stations) to the network. Figure 1.16 presents a simple example with three cities, where the length of the minimum spanning tree is $2/\sqrt{3}$ times that of a tree using an additional node. A tree that spans all the given vertices and possibly includes additional vertices is called a *Steiner tree* and the additional vertices are called *Steiner points*. We can now formulate our first geometric problem.

Problem 18 [Geometric Steiner Tree] Given a set of points, S, in the plane, find a Steiner tree of minimum total length for S. □

The search space for this problem appears infinite, because we can locate the Steiner points at any real coordinates. However, Steiner points must satisfy a number of strong conditions; as a result, the choice of locations remain finite (see Exercise 1.14).

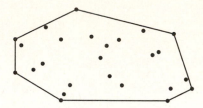

Figure 1.17: The Convex Hull of a Set of Points

Of particular importance in both linear programming and computational geometry is the notion of a convex domain or region.

Definition 1.4 A set of points in space is said to be *convex* if and only if, given any two points, p_1 and p_2, in the set, all points on the line segment $\overline{p_1 p_2}$ are in the set as well. □

Examples of convex domains include half-spaces, (hyper)planes, the interiors of (hyper)spheres, and the interiors of regular polygons. Since convex domains are closed under intersection, the feasible region of a linear programming problem is itself convex, since it is the intersection of half-spaces, each defined by one of the linear constraints. For the same reason, the concept of the smallest convex domain containing a set of points is well defined, because it is just the intersection of all convex domains that contain the given set. This minimal convex domain is called the *convex hull* of the set. Due to the finiteness constraints of computing, we are particularly interested in convex domains that can be specified finitely.

Definition 1.5 Given a collection of points, $P = \{p_1, p_2, \ldots, p_k\}$, in n-dimensional space, a point, $p = \sum_{i=1}^{k} \alpha_i p_i$, where each $\alpha_i \geq 0$ and $\sum_{i=1}^{k} \alpha_i = 1$, is called a *convex combination* of the points in P. □

In two dimensions, the set of convex combinations is just the line segment connecting the two points; in general, the set of convex combinations is a convex domain, as a little algebra shows. Furthermore, any convex domain containing the points must contain all of their convex combinations, so that the points describe their own convex hull. The p_i are referred to as the *generators* of the convex set. Note that some of the points of P may themselves be convex combinations of other points in P; such points serve no useful purpose, since their contributions to a convex combination can always be absorbed into the α_i of the other points. Thus there is a minimal subset of generators, no element of which can be generated from any subset of the others. As suggested by Figure 1.17, the generators are the vertices of a polygon which forms the convex hull of the set of points. Although this picture offers only a two-dimensional illustration,

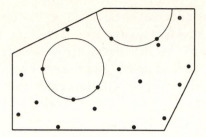

Figure 1.18: An Instance of the Largest Empty Circle Problem, Showing Two Large Empty Circles

we can see that, if the points lie in n-dimensional space, then the minimal set of generators form the vertices of a polytope (the n-dimensional version of a polygon), which is also the convex hull of the set of points. Thus, even though the convex hull of a finite set of points is infinite, it has a finite representation, so that the problem of finding the convex hull is basically a subset search problem.

Problem 19 [Convex Hull] Given a finite set of points in n-dimensional Euclidean space, find the summits of its convex hull. □

While we have discussed several problems concerned with connecting things as tightly as possible, we have not considered the reverse, that is, how to keep things as far apart as possible. One application of this problem derives from environmental considerations: if some pollution-producing plant is to be located within some political jurisdiction, it would be well to place it as far as possible from all human habitation, water sources, and other environmental resources. If each habitation and environmental resource is represented by a point on a map, then the problem becomes one of placing within specified boundaries a vertex that will maximize the distance to its closest neighbor. We formalize this problem as follows.

Problem 20 [Largest Empty Circle] Given a collection of points in the plane and a boundary enclosing these points, find the largest circle containing none of the points, the center of which lies within the boundary. .□

A sample instance is shown in Figure 1.18.

Although the search space may at first appear infinite, a basic result of Euclidean geometry serves to restrict it to a subset search: each circle is fully characterized by three points on its perimeter. Thus we can simply examine each subset of three points, find the center of the circle that they describe, and then determine whether or not that circle is empty. The state space reduces to $\binom{n}{3}$, and the obvious algorithm takes quartic time. However, the algorithm sketched above does not really work, because the center of the circle determined by three points might lie outside the boundary, and thus not be feasible. In particular, it follows that the largest empty circle with its center within the boundary might not touch three obstructions, so that our state space might not be limited after all. In fact, a little more geometric analysis indicates how to handle the cases where the largest empty circle touches only two, or even one, obstruction. Similar work takes care of more possible problems, such as nonconvex regions or even regions with holes (nature preserves, for example, where no development is allowed); the state space remains cubic in size, where n now counts both points and boundary edges. The challenge is to come up with a faster algorithm, that is, an algorithm that uses the geometric nature of the problem in order to consider only a small subset of the $\binom{n}{3}$ circles.

Given the presence of walls (segments) or more general obstructions (solid figures) in the plane, an astoundingly large array of interesting questions may be formulated. Of particular interest are problems of visibility. Consider the design of a prison or fortress; we can assimilate it to a simple polygon (roughly speaking, a polygon with no crossing edges). Both require guards: in the case of a fortress, in order to survey the outside of the polygon; in the case of a prison, in order to watch over both the inside and outside. Towers are commonly built at vertices of the polygonal perimeter, for structural reasons as well as for convenient placement of guards. For a given polygonal enclosure, what is the minimum number of guards, placed at vertices of the polygon, required to keep the entire area (inside or outside) under watch? We formalize these problems as follows. A point, p, is *visible* from a vertex, v, of a simple polygon, P, whenever the line segment, $\overline{vp}$, does not cross the perimeter of P. The internal (external) *visibility area* associated with v is the set of all points inside (outside) of P visible from v.

Problem 21 [Art Gallery] Given a simple polygon, P, find a minimal set of vertices of P such that the union of their internal visibility areas covers the inside of the polygon. □

Problem 22 [Fortress] Given a simple polygon, P, find a minimal set of vertices of P such that the union of their external visibility areas covers the outside of the polygon. □

Problem 23 [Prison Yard] Given a simple polygon, P, find a minimal set of vertices of P such that the union of their internal and external visibility areas covers the plane. □

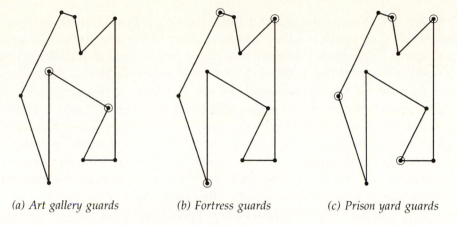

(a) *Art gallery guards*   (b) *Fortress guards*   (c) *Prison yard guards*

Figure 1.19: A Simple Polygon with Optimal Guard Emplacements

An immediate consequence of our definition of convexity is that a single guard is needed to watch over a convex art gallery; similarly, $\lceil n/2 \rceil$ guards are needed to take care of a convex fortress with n vertices. Thus the problem is of interest for only nonconvex enclosures. Figure 1.19 shows a simple polygon with optimal guard emplacements for all three problems.

1.7 Comments and Additional Problems

By now, the reader will have developed some intuition about the formulation of problems, as well as about the nature of what we have chosen to call combinatorial optimization problems. It may still be difficult to gauge accurately the importance of an abstract formulation; yet the value of a precise formulation should at least be clear. Although we have made an effort to present each problem in a natural manner, as it arises from its real-world constraints, we must acknowledge that we have described very few problems in a complete, realistic manner. The point of the model is the expression of the fundamental combinatorial question present within the problem: there can be no solution to the problem without consideration of this question, although solving this question alone may not be sufficient. The additional constraints and parameters typically complicate the problem (although they may so much constrain it that very few potential solutions are left, so that the design of a solution algorithm becomes easy); consequently, they are often best handled in an *ad hoc* manner through modifications to the algorithm designed to solve the basic underlying question.

In fact, not only do our abstract formulations deliberately omit many parameters and constraints, but they also omit many of the objectives. It is a rare situation in a company or government where a single, quantifiable objective is to be pursued. An airline is not only interested in scheduling its flight crews efficiently, but must also pursue a wide variety of other objectives: customer satisfaction, growth, shareholders' profits, and more. A time-dependent travelling salesperson tour problem may be used to model the flight path of a space shuttle on a satellite maintenance and repair mission; but, even with the inclusion of such parameters as payload, fuel consumption, human reliability, and insurance costs, the tour problem remains a small part of the goals pursued by the astronautic agency in charge of the mission. Other objectives include production of more craft, testing and development of new parts, training of personnel, image building, and advertising with potential contributors and customers. The clear impossibility of modelling all of these constraints and objectives together justifies our insistence on the extraction, from each real-world problem, of the combinatorial core, i.e., of a greatly streamlined version which retains the essential flavor of the original, captures as well as possible the difficulties involved in its solution, and yet lends itself to a concise and precise mathematical formulation.

Providing abstract formulations of problems has been a major concern of mathematicians and scientists throughout the ages; even in its few years of existence, the field of computer science has accumulated a large collection of such abstract problems. In order to round out the reader's impression of the field of combinatorial optimization, we present a few more problems, but this time only in their formalized, purified versions. We encourage the reader to relate each of these problems to possible real-world applications.

Problem 24 [Vertex Cover] Given an undirected graph, $G = (V, E)$, a *vertex cover* is a subset of the vertices, $V' \subseteq V$, such that, for each edge, $(u, v) \in E$, at least one of u and v is contained in V'. Find a vertex cover of minimum cardinality.

□

Problem 25 [Chromatic Number] A *vertex coloring* of an undirected graph is an assignment of colors to the vertices of the graph such that no edge of the graph connects vertices of the same color. The *chromatic number* of a graph is the minimum number of colors needed for a legal vertex coloring.   □

Problem 26 [Chromatic Index]   An *edge coloring* of an undirected graph is an assignment of colors to the edges of the graph such that no two edges of the same color share an endpoint. The *chromatic index* of a graph is the minimum number of colors needed for a legal edge coloring.   □

Problem 27 [Monochromatic Triangle] Given an undirected graph, $G = (V, E)$, is it possible to partition E into two subsets, E_1 and E_2, such that neither $G_1 = (V, E_1)$ nor $G_2 = (V, E_2)$ contains a "triangle," i.e., a complete subgraph of three vertices?

The problem is called *monochromatic triangle*, because the edges in E_1 can be thought of as being blue and the edges in E_2 can be thought of as being red. The question is then: Can the edges of the graph be colored in such a way that the resulting graph contains neither a blue nor a red triangle?   □

Problem 28 [Minimum Testing Collection]   Let us take another look at our microbiologist. While the optimal identification tree affords, on the average, the minimum number of tests, it may prove very costly in terms of time. Because many of the tests require a day to perform (the specimen has to incubate), the sequential nature of the identification procedure induces unacceptable delay when a medical diagnosis must be made as rapidly as possible. Even in this situation, it is possible to improve on the procedure of applying all of the tests and then looking for a match between the results and a row of a table similar to Table 1.4. As already pointed out, what is required is that no two rows be identical. Certain columns, i.e., tests, can be eliminated from such a table, and the resulting collection of tests can still separate all bacteria. For example, in Table 1.4, the tests labelled haemolysis, urease, litmus, and arabinose suffice to separate the eight species of *Pasteurella*. Given a table of test results, the minimum testing collection problem is to find the smallest subset of tests that still separates all object categories.   □

Problem 29 [Bipartite Matching or Marriage]   Recall that an undirected graph is *bipartite* if and only if its vertex set can be partitioned into two subsets, U and V, such that each edge of the graph has one endpoint in U and the other in V. A *matching* in an undirected graph, $G = (V, E)$, is a subset of the edges, $M \subseteq E$, with the property that no two edges in M share an endpoint (one endpoint of each edge in M is "matched" with the other endpoint). A bipartite graph can be considered as giving a list of possible matches between elements of U and elements of V. The maximum bipartite matching problem is to find a matching of maximum cardinality. The alternate name of marriage derives from another interpretation: the vertices of one subset are women, those of the other subset are men, the edges denote marriageable (compatible) pairs, and the problem is to produce as many married couples as possible.

When the two subsets U and V have equal size, we can formulate the decision problem variant known as *perfect matching* by asking whether or not all of the vertices can be matched.   □

Problem 30 [Bin Packing] Given a set of elements, S, a size function, $s\colon S \to \mathcal{R}^+$, and given a bin capacity, $B \in \mathcal{R}^+$, determine the minimum number of bins necessary to pack all the elements of S, where the bin capacity cannot be exceeded and elements are indivisible. This problem can be generalized to a finite inventory of bin capacities by asking that the total amount of wasted space be minimized. $\qquad\square$

Problem 31 [Clustering]   Given a set of elements, S, with a "dissimilitude" function, $d\colon S \times S \to \mathcal{R}^+$ (which we can regard as a distance measure, as an incompatibility measure, as a cost measure, etc.—this diversity helps explain why clustering problems are a frequent occurrence in many diverse fields), and given a positive integer, $k < |S|$, partition S into k nonempty subsets—which we shall call *clusters*—such that a suitable objective function is optimized. Two optimization criteria suggest themselves:

1. Minimize the total *intracluster* dissimilitude, that is,

$$\text{minimize} \sum_{i=1}^{k} \sum_{x.y \in C_i} d(x,y),$$

   where C_i is the ith cluster. This criterion gives rise to the problem known as *k-min clustering*.

2. Maximize the total *intercluster* dissimilitude, that is,

$$\text{maximize} \sum_{i=1}^{k} \sum_{\substack{j=1 \\ j \neq i}}^{k} \sum_{\substack{x \in C_i \\ y \in C_j}} d(x,y).$$

   This criterion gives rise to the problem known as *k-max cut*.

$\qquad\square$

1.8   Exercises

Exercise 1.4 Rank all problems presented in this chapter (including the additional problems) in order from most difficult to solve to least difficult to solve. (You will want to form groups of approximately equally difficult problems.) We shall refer back to this list on occasion as new techniques are covered—it will be interesting to see how your initial intuition corresponds to your intuition after reading this book! $\qquad\square$

Exercise 1.5 Recast the vertex cover, monochromatic triangle, and minimum testing collection problems as 0-1 programming problems. How many constraints do your formulations produce in terms of the original problem size? (Note that the monochromatic triangle problem provides an example of formulating a decision problem as an integer linear programming problem. In such a case, there is no natural objective function; what matters is whether there are any feasible solutions at all.)   □

Exercise 1.6 Show that, if all inequalities are of the "≤" variety and $a_{ij} \geq 0$ for all i, then truncation of the optimal solution of the LP obtained by dropping the integrality constraints from the ILP yields a feasible solution to the ILP.   □

Exercise 1.7 Show that, if the conditions of Exercise 1.6 do not hold, then it is possible that an optimal all-integer solution exists, but that neither truncating nor rounding up the variables yields a feasible solution to the ILP.   □

Exercise 1.8 Explain why the following 0-1 programming formulation for the travelling salesperson problem is incorrect.

$$\text{minimize} \quad \sum_{\substack{1 \leq i,j \leq n \\ i \neq j}} d_{ij} x_{ij}$$

$$\text{subject to} \quad \begin{cases} \sum_{\substack{j=1 \\ i \neq j}}^{n} x_{ij} = 1, & \text{for } i = 1, 2, \ldots, n \\ \sum_{\substack{i=1 \\ i \neq j}}^{n} x_{ij} = 1, & \text{for } j = 1, 2, \ldots, n \end{cases}$$

$$\text{where} \quad x_{ij} = 0 \text{ or } 1$$

There is an x_{ij} for each ordered pair (i,j) with $i \neq j$. In the optimal solution, x_{ij} equals one whenever the edge from i to j is included in the minimum-cost tour of the graph; x_{ij} equals zero otherwise. The first set of n constraints states that each vertex will be left exactly once, since i is fixed and j varies over all potential next vertices. The second set of n constraints states that every vertex will be entered once.   □

Exercise 1.9 If $G = (V, E)$ is a free tree, then $\sum_{i=1}^{|V|} d_i = 2(|V| - 1)$, where d_i is the degree of vertex i. Show that the converse is true, namely: given n positive integers with $\sum_{i=1}^{n} d_i = 2(n - 1)$, there is a free tree of n vertices such that the d_i describe the degrees of its vertices.   □

Exercise 1.10[*] Present an informal argument to show that, if all capacities in a network flow problem are integral, then there is an integral flow that is also a maximum flow. (Thus the search space for integral problems is at least finite.)

□

Exercise 1.11 Construct an example to show that the collection of tests composing the minimum testing collection can be of lower cardinality than the collection of those tests that occur (somewhere) in the optimal identification tree. This highlights the difference between the sequential searching process embodied in identification trees and the parallel nature of the testing procedure described here—the identification based on the optimal identification tree performs, on average, fewer tests, but requires more capability in the arsenal of tests that may potentially be applied.

□

Exercise 1.12 Prove that the following recursive procedure calculates the cost of an identification tree when called externally with a pointer to the root of the tree.

```
const NumObjects = ...;
      NumTests = ...;
type class = (object, test);
     ptr = ^node;
     node = record
                case kind: class of
                    object: (who: 1..NumObjects);
                    test:   (what: 1..NumTests; left, right: ptr)
             end;
var prob: array [1..NumObjects] of real;
        (* probabilities of request for identification for individual
           object categories *)
procedure CalcCost(p: ptr; var cost, weight: real);
  (* On exit, weight equals sum of the probabilities of request for
     identification of all objects in the subtree rooted at p. *)
  var lcost, rcost, lweight, rweight: real;
  begin
    if p^.kind = object
      then begin
              weight := prob[p^.who];
              cost := 0.0
           end
      else begin
              CalcCost(p^.left,lcost,lweight);
              CalcCost(p^.right,rcost,rweight);
              weight := lweight + rweight;
              cost := lcost + rcost + weight
           end
  end; (* CalcCost *)
```

□

Exercise 1.13 [P] Study and compare Steiner trees and minimal spanning trees; in particular, attempt to estimate how much can be gained by using a Steiner tree rather than a minimal spanning tree.   □

Exercise 1.14* Prove that any additional vertices present in the Steiner tree have degree three and that the three edges incident upon such vertices form a regular star (i.e., the angle between two consecutive edges is exactly 120°). *Hints*: Consider splitting Steiner points of degree higher than 3 into two or more closely spaced vertices and compute the length of the resulting trees. Consider small motions of the Steiner points and compute the lengths of the resulting trees.

□

Exercise 1.15 Prove that a partition is an optimal solution to k-min clustering whenever it is an optimal solution to k-max cut. Thus the two clustering problems are very closely related.   □

Exercise 1.16* Each of the combinatorial optimization problems that follow is presented in a deliberately vague manner and sometimes also obscured by algorithmically irrelevant details. For each problem, devise one (or more, as a problem may contain more than one combinatorial core) abstract formulation in the spirit of those presented in this chapter.

1. (Database optimization) An airline reservation system must be distributed across many computer systems for purposes of efficiency and reliability. The information to be stored is fairly well known: the list of flights changes neither much nor often. However, updates and queries are frequent: schedule queries, seat reservations, rate requests, and similar operations emanate from all nodes with predictable frequencies. How should the airline pick its computing nodes, connect them, distribute the data between them (including duplications, of course), and organize the flow of queries and updates in order to maximize the efficiency and reliability of the system and minimize its cost?

2. (The MX missile shuffle) Missiles loaded on railroad cars must be moved on a network of tracks in such a manner as to: (i) make it difficult to predict their next location; and (ii) make it impossible to destroy more than one missile with the same shot.

3. (City planning) The city of Albuquerque has spent many years gathering statistics about commercial and residential fires in terms of time and place of occurrence, severity, demands placed on the city's emergency services, and additional damage resulting from the time taken by the emergency crews to get to the scene. Now that it is about to renovate much of its

vehicle inventory, it also wants to relocate its emergency facilities so as to make the entire system as effective as possible.

4. (The copy editor) You are writing a book, a software manual, or a very large, well-documented program. You have several versions stored on disk and are working on the latest version, which is to be amended according to a collection of notes. You would very much appreciate a program which would take as inputs the current and the new versions and produce as output as succinct and organized a list of the changes as possible. This program might recognize not only simple word alterations, but also data movement at any structure level (such as moving words within a sentence, sentences within a paragraph or section, paragraphs within a section or chapter), addition and deletion of data (words, sentences, paragraphs), and substitution of words within a pattern (such as use of synonyms).

□

1.9 Bibliography

Linear and integer programming have long been the main object of study of operations research and thus predate computer science; most of the texts discussing these methods have a markedly different flavor from that encountered in texts on algorithms, with the exception of the graduate text of Papadimitriou and Steiglitz [1982], which takes its inspiration from both fields. The simplex method for linear programming was invented by Dantzig in 1947, and his text [1965] remains one of the best sources for linear programming problems and methods; for a more modern exposition, the reader should consult the text of Chvátal [1983]. Readers who want to learn more about integer programming techniques should consult the aforementioned text of Papadimitriou and Steiglitz [1982] and the text of Nemhauser and Wolsey [1988]. Formalized problems appear in all writings dealing with algorithmic design; particularly interesting sources include the monographs on graph algorithms of Christofides [1975] and of Even [1979]; the three volumes of Knuth [1968, 1969, 1973] on general combinatorial problems as well as on seminumerical problems and on search problems; the two-volume work of Berlekamp, Conway, and Guy [1982] on games; the three-volume monograph of Mehlhorn [1984] on search problems, graph problems, geometric problems, and general combinatorial optimization problems; and the text of Pearl [1985] on difficult combinatorial problems. In addition, the text of Garey and Johnson [1979] contains a list, organized by areas of application, of over 300 combinatorial problems (all hard to solve) stated in a very succinct, clear, and precise manner. Whole books have been devoted to some particularly important problems: examples include the travelling salesperson problem (Lawler *et al.* [1985]), the job scheduling problem (Brucker [1981]), the network flow problem (Ford and Fulkerson [1962], the original study of the problem), and the guard problems (O'Rourke [1987]).

The airline crew scheduling problem is discussed in detail by Giannessi and Nicoletti [1979]; they model the problem as closely as possible to reality—in fact, Nicoletti actually worked for an airline (Alitalia). The game of hex was invented by Piet Hein; the argument demonstrating that the first player has a forced win is a special case of a class of arguments first formalized by Hales and Jewett [1963].

CHAPTER 2

Mathematical Techniques for the Analysis of Algorithms

A major concern throughout this book will be determining the running time of algorithms. Experimentally determined execution times are an important tool for judging program performance, especially when the problem instances are derived from real-world data and contain biases that cannot be characterized mathematically. On the other hand, mathematical analysis can provide important information on the running time of an algorithm as a function of the problem size. In this chapter we present mathematical techniques that are useful in such analyses. We begin with the language used in describing the efficiency of algorithms, the big Oh, big Omega, and big Theta notations. We then turn to methods used both for establishing the size of the solution space for certain problems and for determining the running time of many programs, presenting first the mathematical background and following with a discussion of the use of these methods in various types of analysis. We close the chapter with an illustration of the consequences for algorithm design of our mathematical development.

2.1 Big Oh, Big Omega, and Big Theta Notations

While it would be desirable to give a precise running time for an arbitrary algorithm as a function of the size of its input, it is generally impossible to do so. The difficulty is only partly due to the use of different compilers and target machines. More importantly, all but the simplest algorithms contain conditional statements, like if and while, so that the flow of control and resulting execution time depend on the actual data and not just on the number of data (the "size" of the input). Thus a reasonable description should ignore constants of proportionality and start-up costs and simplify the picture by choosing a common measure for all inputs of the same size. To say that heapsort can sort an arbitrary list of n numbers in time proportional to $n \log n$ and that bubblesort can sort the same list in time proportional to n^2 gets at the essential fact that heapsort is a far better choice than bubblesort if the lists to be sorted are reasonably long. The statement also hides two important, but secondary, details that must be kept in mind:

- If the lists to be sorted are short, the overhead associated with the internal workings of heapsort may actually cause it to be the slower algorithm.

- There are some lists of length n, even for large n, on which bubblesort makes very few passes over the data and is the faster algorithm.

The notion of execution time "roughly proportional to ..." is formalized by the "big Oh," "big Omega," and "big Theta" notations.

Definition 2.1 Let $f, g \colon \mathcal{Z}^+ \to \mathcal{R}^+$. $f(n)$ is said to be $O(g(n))$, read "$f(n)$ is 'big Oh' of $g(n)$"—or just "$f(n)$ is 'Oh' of $g(n)$"—if and only if there exists $n_0 \in \mathcal{Z}^+$ and $c \in \mathcal{R}^+$ such that we have

$$f(n) \leq c \cdot g(n), \quad \forall n \geq n_0. \qquad \square$$

(Actually, the letter O used here is a capital omicron—all letters used in asymptotic algorithmic notation are Greek letters; however, since the Greek omicron and the English 'o' are indistinguishable in most fonts, it has become customary to read $O(\ )$ as "Big Oh" rather than as "Big Omicron.") In terms of the graphs of the two functions, $f(n)$ is $O(g(n))$ if and only if there exists a c such that the graph of f is at or beneath that of $c \cdot g$ after a certain point, n_0, is reached on the abscissa. The $O(\ )$ notation formally captures two ideas that are important to us: (i) the exact function, g, is not critically important, since the function can be multiplied by any arbitrary positive constant, c; and (ii) the relative behavior of the two functions is compared only for large n (asymptotically) and not near the origin, where overhead may cloud the issues. Of course, if the constants involved are very large, then the asymptotic behavior is of no practical interest; in most cases, however, the constants remain fairly small. In terms of the running time of algorithms, we shall (after some necessary modifications to be discussed shortly) use this definition with $f(n)$ equal to the "exact" running time on inputs of size n and $g(n)$ equal to the rough approximation to the running time.

For the moment, let us explore the consequences of this definition through examples and theorems.

Example 2.1 $2n^3 + 5n^2 + 3$ is $O(n^3/100)$. To prove this, we must exhibit a c and an n_0 which satisfy the definition. Suppose we take $c = 201$ and $n_0 = 501$. We must then show that

$$2n^3 + 5n^2 + 3 \leq 201(n^3/100)$$

holds for all $n \geq 501$. This is equivalent to showing that

$$5n^2 + 3 \leq 0.01n^3$$

holds for $n \geq 501$, which reduces to showing that

$$n^3 - 500n^2 - 300 \geq 0$$

holds for $n \geq 501$. This follows from elementary algebra, and the result is established.   □

There are several things to notice about this choice of c and n_0:

1. For $c = 201$, the smallest choice for n_0 is 501, but any value larger than 500 could have been chosen. While $f(n) \leq c \cdot g(n)$ must hold for all $n \geq n_0$, the definition places no requirements on the relationship between f and g for values less than n_0. In particular, n_0 need not be the smallest possible choice given the value selected for c.

2. Other choices of c and n_0 are possible. For example, $c = 300$ and $n_0 = 100$ also cause f to satisfy the conditions of the definition. Actually, for this choice of c, n_0 could be selected as small as 6. It is not hard to see that any $c > 200$ will do, but, as c gets closer to 200, the corresponding minimum n_0 increases.

3. $2n^3 + 5n^2 + 3$ is also $O(n^3)$. To see this, take $c = 3$ and $n_0 = 6$ (or $c = 4$ and $n_0 = 3$ or $c = 5$ and $n_0 = 2$). While saying that $2n^3 + 5n^2 + 3$ is $O(n^3/100)$ is correct, it is more natural to say that it is $O(n^3)$. The idea behind the use of $O(\ )$ notation is to ignore coefficients that hide the growth in the running time of algorithms as the size of the input increases.

Even stranger than saying that $2n^3 + 5n^2 + 3$ is both $O(n^3/100)$ and $O(n^3)$ is to say that it is $O(n^4)$. Taking $c = 1$ and $n_0 = 4$ shows this to be true. Stating that $2n^3 + 5n^2 + 3$ is $O(n^4)$ is weaker than stating that it is $O(n^3)$, since any function that is $O(n^3)$ is also $O(n^4)$, but not conversely. When saying that $f(n)$ is $O(g(n))$, we usually require $g(n)$ to be a "simple" function, such as n^2, $\log n$, 3^n, etc.,[1] since such functions illustrate the growth rate better than functions with more terms.

---

[1] We do not state the base of the logarithm when dealing with $O(\ )$, since $\log_a n = \log_a b \cdot \log_b n$, and part (2) of the theorem which follows applies.

It is also understood that the $g(n)$ chosen is the "best" (i.e., tightest) for which we can find an appropriate combination of c and n_0.

The $O(\ )$ notation describes an upper bound on the growth rate of a function; even if this bound is as tight as possible, it may not characterize the behavior of the function very well. Consider

$$f(n) = \begin{cases} 2^n/3, & \text{if } n \text{ is a perfect square} \\ n^2/2, & \text{if } n \text{ is even, but not a perfect square} \\ 4n, & \text{if } n \text{ is odd, but not a perfect square.} \end{cases}$$

Here $f(n)$ is $O(2^n)$—take $c = 1$ and $n_0 = 4$—but not $O(n^2)$ nor $O(n)$. For any values of c and n_0, it is always possible to find an $n \geq n_0$ with $f(n) > c \cdot n^2$; just let n be a sufficiently large perfect square. Notice that, for $c \geq \frac{1}{2}$, the inequality $f(n) \leq c \cdot n^2$ holds for infinitely many values of n, and, in fact, the values for which $f(n) > c \cdot n^2$ holds become increasingly rare as n gets larger—but they are always present. This type of situation is not totally artificial. Consider a procedure that determines if an integer, n, is prime by first checking for divisibility by 2 and then successively dividing n by the odd integers up to the square root of n. The number of divisions performed by the procedure as a function of n is $O(\sqrt{n})$, but, for randomly selected n, the procedure does three or fewer divisions almost three-fourths (73.33%) of the time.

The arithmetic of $O(\ )$ is governed by the following theorem.

Theorem 2.1

1. [Transitivity] If $f(n)$ is $O(g(n))$ and $g(n)$ is $O(h(n))$, then $f(n)$ is $O(h(n))$.

2. [Scaling] If $f(n)$ is $O(g(n))$, then, for any $k > 0$, $f(n)$ is $O(k \cdot g(n))$.

3. [Rule of sums] If $f_1(n)$ is $O(g_1(n))$ and $f_2(n)$ is $O(g_2(n))$, then $(f_1 + f_2)(n)$ is $O(\max(g_1(n), g_2(n)))$.

4. [Rule of products] If $f_1(n)$ is $O(g_1(n))$ and $f_2(n)$ is $O(g_2(n))$, then $(f_1 \cdot f_2)(n)$ is $O((g_1 \cdot g_2)(n))$. Note that $(f_1 \cdot f_2)(n)$ refers to the product of the values of the two functions at n and not to the value at n of the composition of the two functions.

□

Proof:

1. $f(n)$ is $O(g(n))$ says that there exist $\tilde{c}$ and $\tilde{n}_0$ such that $f(n) \leq \tilde{c} \cdot g(n)$ holds for all $n \geq \tilde{n}_0$; similarly, $g(n)$ is $O(h(n))$ says that there exist $\hat{c}$ and $\hat{n}_0$ such that $g(n) \leq \hat{c} \cdot h(n)$ holds for all $n \geq \hat{n}_0$. Take $c = \tilde{c} \cdot \hat{c}$ and $n_0 = \max(\tilde{n}_0, \hat{n}_0)$. Now for any $n \geq n_0$, we have

$$f(n) \leq \tilde{c} \cdot g(n) \leq \tilde{c} \cdot (\hat{c} \cdot h(n)) = c \cdot h(n),$$

where the first inequality follows from $n \geq \tilde{n}_0$ and the second from $n \geq \hat{n}_0$. Thus, for any $n \geq n_0$, we have $f(n) \leq c \cdot h(n)$, so that $f(n)$ is $O(h(n))$.

2. Again, $f(n)$ is $O(g(n))$ means that there exist $\tilde{c}$ and $\tilde{n}_0$ such that $f(n) \leq \tilde{c} \cdot g(n)$ holds for all $n \geq \tilde{n}_0$. Take $c = \tilde{c}/k$ and $n_0 = \tilde{n}_0$. Then, for $n \geq n_0$, we have $f(n) \leq \tilde{c} \cdot g(n) = (ck)g(n) = c(k \cdot g(n))$, so that $f(n)$ is $O(k \cdot g(n))$.

3. Before proving this result, note that $\max(g_1(n), g_2(n))$ is a function defined *pointwise*, i.e., independently for each n; for some n it takes on the value of g_1, and for others it takes on the value of g_2. Take $c = 2 \cdot \max(\tilde{c}, \hat{c})$ and $n_0 = \max(\tilde{n}_0, \hat{n}_0)$. The remaining details are left to the reader.

4. The proof is left as an exercise.

$$Q.E.D.$$

Computations with $O(\ )$ are rarely done directly from the definition; instead, the theorem just proved is used. For example, to verify that $2n^3 + 5n^2 + 3$ is $O(n^3)$, we can use the rule of sums to eliminate the $5n^2 + 3$, i.e., $2n^3 + 5n^2 + 3$ is $O(2n^3)$, and then scaling, with $k = 1/2$, to eliminate the factor of 2.

Thus far, our formal discussion of $O(\ )$ has addressed functions from $\mathcal{Z}^+$ to $\mathcal{R}^+$, not the running time of algorithms. It is natural to let $f(n)$ be "the running time of the algorithm on an input of size n" and $g(n)$ be a function that roughly approximates the running time, and to say, "the algorithm is $O(g(n))$," dropping the words *running time*, which are understood. As hinted at earlier, this usage is a little too simplistic. The problem is that $f(n)$ thus defined is not really a well-defined function—the running time not only depends on the size of the input, but also on the input data themselves. A more precise definition of $f(n)$ is required. There are two natural choices:

1. [Worst-case analysis] $f(n)$ is the longest running time exhibited by the algorithm on any legal input of size n.

2. [Average-case analysis] $f(n)$ is the average running time exhibited by the algorithm over all legal inputs of size n, using a probability distribution representing the expected frequency of occurrence of the various possible inputs.

Which is the more appropriate definition for $f(n)$ depends on the circumstances; in general we would like to know the performance of an algorithm with respect to both measures. Worst-case analysis is more common: it is easier to carry out and depends only on the algorithm, whereas the average-case analysis also requires knowledge of the probability distribution. Unless stated otherwise, the phrase "running time of an algorithm" will mean worst-case running time.

Regardless of which method of analysis is employed, $O(\ )$ notation does not suffice to characterize the performance of the algorithm. As mentioned earlier, if $f(n)$ is $O(n^3)$, it is also $O(n^4)$. It may be the case that the running time of an algorithm is reported to be $O(g(n))$, not because this is the true worst-case performance, but because the mathematics needed to derive a tighter upper bound is just too difficult. What is desired is a proof that not only is the algorithm $O(g(n))$, but also that no better $g(n)$ can be found, i.e., a proof that $g(n)$ is a lower bound. In order to express lower bounds, we introduce the big Omega and big Theta notations.

Definition 2.2 Let $f, g: \mathcal{Z}^+ \to \mathcal{R}^+$. $f(n)$ is said to be $\Omega(g(n))$, read "$f(n)$ is 'big Omega' of $g(n)$," if and only if there exists a constant $c \in \mathcal{R}^+$ such that, for any N, there exists an $n \geq N$ with $f(n) \geq c \cdot g(n)$. $\qquad \square$

This definition is not symmetrical with the $O(\ )$ definition. Notice that c is chosen first and then, for any N, which is chosen subsequently, there must exist an $n \geq N$ with $f(n) \geq c \cdot g(n)$. With $O(\ )$ notation, we must have $f(n) \leq c \cdot g(n)$ for all n beyond a certain point; whereas, with $\Omega(\ )$ notation, we require the existence of only one sufficiently large n with $f(n) \geq c \cdot g(n)$ for each choice of N. Since N is arbitrary, just one n will not do—an infinite number will be required. The definition is sometimes phrased in the following equivalent manner:

> ... there exists a constant $c \in \mathcal{R}^+$ such that $f(n) \geq c \cdot g(n)$ holds infinitely often.

Note the wording: "infinitely often," not necessarily "always." In rough terms, to say that an algorithm is $O(g(n))$ is to say that it cannot require more than time proportional to $g(n)$. To say that it is also $\Omega(g(n))$ is to say that sometimes it performs that badly. Since most algorithms are rather well behaved, the $\Omega(\ )$ notation is often unnecessarily general; when applicable, a better way to express a lower bound for the function $f(n)$ is to state that some bounding function, $g(n)$, is $O(f(n))$. Since this means $1/_c \cdot g(n) \leq f(n)$ for all sufficiently large n, such a statement implies that $f(n)$ is $\Omega(g(n))$, although the converse is not necessarily true.

Why then did we define $\Omega(\ )$ asymmetrically? The main reason derives from the uses of $O(\ )$ and $\Omega(\ )$ notations in algorithmic analysis. We use an upper bound to provide a limit on the worst-case behavior of an algorithm; we want such a bound to be valid for all but a small number of instance sizes. Such a guarantee is precisely what $O(\ )$ notation offers: for all instances sizes larger than some constant, the bound holds. On the other hand, we use a lower bound to indicate that the algorithm may exhibit such behavior; that such behavior only shows itself for certain instance sizes does not decrease its importance as long as the sizes on which the algorithm behaves poorly do not constitute just a finite set of anomalies. Again, this characterization is precisely that given by $\Omega(\ )$: the set of values for which it holds is infinite, but need not include all possible values. Another reason for using an asymmetric definition is that, since $\Omega(\ )$ as defined is weaker than a symmetric version would be, it often holds where the symmetric version would not, as we illustrate shortly with our primality testing example. A final reason is that, in the most interesting case of symmetry, that is, whenever f is $O(g)$ and g is $O(f)$, we shall make use of a special notation. A new notation is well justified in this case, since the behavior of an algorithm has then been characterized very precisely—the characterization is exact within a constant factor.

Definition 2.3 Let $f, g: \mathcal{Z}^+ \to \mathcal{R}^+$. $f(n)$ is said to be $\Theta(g(n))$, read "$f(n)$ is 'big Theta' of $g(n)$," if and only if $f(n)$ is $O(g(n))$ and $g(n)$ is $O(f(n))$. $\square$

For instance, any nonzero constant is $\Theta(1)$ and any polynomial of degree k is $\Theta(n^k)$. The Θ notation is reflexive, symmetric, and transitive, and thus is an equivalence relation defined on functions from $\mathcal{Z}^+$ into $\mathcal{R}^+$. Since it is defined in terms of $O(\ )$, the rules governing its arithmetic may be readily derived from those governing the arithmetic of $O(\ )$.

Our primality testing example demonstrates that not every algorithm can be described with $\Theta(\ )$ notation. The number of divisions performed is $O(\sqrt{n})$ because the upper bound on the loop that controls the choice of divisors is $\sqrt{n}$. While the number of divisions performed is also $\Omega(\sqrt{n})$, since this is roughly the number of divisions performed if n is prime, $\sqrt{n}$ is not O of the number of divisions performed. In this case we must settle for saying that the algorithm is both $O(\sqrt{n})$ and $\Omega(\sqrt{n})$, even though this may not be a very apt characterization of its performance. When an algorithm is both $O(g(n))$ and $\Omega(g(n))$ we do know, however, that the $O(\ )$ bound cannot be improved.

Even when it is applicable, $\Theta(\ )$ notation does not completely characterize the behavior of an algorithm, because it effectively reduces the input to a single number. While many algorithms, such as mergesort, radix sort, and others that we shall discuss in Chapter 4, are essentially insensitive to the input data, and thus well characterized by reducing their input to a single parameter, many more, such as the flow algorithms of Chapter 6 and the geometric divide-and-conquer algorithms of Chapter 7, are not. Unfortunately, $\Theta(\ )$ notation does not discriminate between these two types of algorithms. Hence the reader should keep in mind that an algorithm said to be running in $\Theta(f(n))$ time may well run much faster on most inputs.

Intractability

When an algorithm is reported to be $O(n \log n)$, we feel that the algorithm is "good," because fairly large problem instances can be solved—assuming that the

Table 2.1: The Largest Problem That Can Be Solved by an Algorithm with Running Time $\Theta(f(n))$ for Various $f(n)$

Efficiency of algorithm	Length of time algorithm is run							
	1 second	1 minute	1 hour	1 day	1 week	1 year	1 decade	1 century
$\Theta(n)$	0	10	600	14,400	100,800	5,256,000	52,588,800	525,945,600
$\Theta(n \log n)$	1	10	250	3,997	23,100	883,895	7,640,268	67,193,510
$\Theta(n^{1.5})$	0	10	153	1,275	4,666	65,128	302,409	1,403,763
$\Theta(n^2)$	1	10	77	379	1,003	7,249	22,932	72,522
$\Theta(n^3)$	2	10	39	112	216	807	1,738	3,746
$\Theta(2^n)$	4	10	15	20	23	29	32	35
$\Theta(n!)$	8	10	11	12	13	15	15	16
$\Theta(n^n)$	9	10	11	12	13	14	15	15

constants involved are reasonable. Conversely, if an algorithm has *exponential* performance, which technically means that its running time is not $O(n^m)$ for any m, but in practice generally means a running time of $\Omega(2^n)$ or worse, we can conclude that an adequate solution has yet to be found.[2]

Table 2.1 is designed to give a concrete feel for the effect of the order of an algorithm on the size of problems that can be solved effectively. These data have been normalized so that all algorithms can solve a problem of size 10 in exactly one minute. Another way to view these data is to realize that, if technology were to improve to the point where we had computers 10,000 times as fast as current machines (10,000 is approximately the ratio of a week to a minute), then, for the same amount of computing time, we could solve a problem 100 times larger than before if our algorithm were $\Theta(n^2)$, 21.6 times larger than before if our algorithm were $\Theta(n^3)$, but a problem with only 13 additional input values if the algorithm were $\Theta(2^n)$.

We define a problem as *intractable* if the most efficient known algorithm for solving it requires exponential time. What we propose appears to be a rather fuzzy boundary: a polynomial-time algorithm that requires $10^3 \cdot n^{20}$ time is not

---

[2]There are functions that are not $O(n^m)$ for any m, but have growth rates far slower than 2^n. The function $n^{\lg n}$ is an example. The function $n^{\lg \lg \lg n}$ has an exponent which grows so slowly that, for values of n less than $2^{16} = 65,536$, it is less than n^2 and, for values of n less than $2^{256} \approx 10^{77}$, it is less than n^3; yet it is not $O(n^m)$ for any m and so is exponential according to our definition. The reader may encounter a definition of *subexponential* functions as those nonpolynomial functions $f(n)$ which are $O\left(2^{n^\epsilon}\right)$ for any $\epsilon > 0$, yet such that 2^{n^ϵ} is not $O(f(n))$ for any $\epsilon > 0$. This definition attempts to capture the difference between *bona fide* exponential functions and those "intermediate" functions, neither polynomial nor truly exponential. For instance, $n^{\lg n}$ is subexponential, as $n^{\lg n} < 2^{n^\epsilon}$ is equivalent (by taking logarithms of both sides, followed by square roots) to $\lg n < n^{\epsilon/2}$, which is easily verified for large n.

likely to make the problem which it solves tractable, while an exponential-time algorithm that runs in $10^{-1} \cdot 1.1^{\sqrt[4]{n}/50}$ time will provide an efficient solution method for all but the largest instances. The distinction is justified in practice by the fact that known polynomial-time algorithms for standard problems usually run in $O(n^3)$ time or better, while most exponential-time algorithms tend to run in $\Omega(2^n)$ time or worse. Thus the difference between actual polynomial- and exponential-time algorithms is indeed one between practical and impractical solution methods. (In fact, even a quadratic- or cubic-time algorithm can be quite useless in practice if the size of the problems on which it is to be run begins to get large.)

Our definition of intractability suffers from a more troubling defect: it is a "moving definition," since today's best performing algorithm can be supplanted by a better one tomorrow. It would be preferable to prove that a problem is intractable—that no algorithm can ever be devised that solves the problem and has polynomial-time complexity. However, such proofs appear, at least initially, to be forever beyond reach: how can one show that some task is impossible when one cannot know all of the methods that can be devised for that task? As surprising as it may seem at first, it is possible to show that certain tasks cannot be accomplished. The most famous example is one of the problems left unsolved by the Greek geometers: how to trisect an arbitrary angle with a compass and straight edge. For centuries, mathematicians tried in vain to solve this problem; building upon the work of Karl Friedrich Gauss (1777–1855) and Évariste Galois (1811–1832), P. L. Wantzel (1814–1848) proved that such a construction is impossible.

Until recently, it had been possible to prove inherent intractability results only for "artificial" problems; similar results have now been proved for several problems from logic and automata theory, as well as for some combinatorial games. Indeed, determining the winner in the game of peek, introduced in Section 1.5, is one such problem. There are also a large number of important problems (i) for which no polynomial-time algorithm has been found; (ii) which are not known to be provably intractable; (iii) the solution of which is easy to verify (if not to find); and (iv) which are of roughly equivalent complexity, in the sense that either they are all provably intractable or they all can be solved in polynomial time. This class of problems is referred to as the class of $\mathcal{NP}$-complete problems. The fact that no one has been able to devise a polynomial-time algorithm to solve any of these problems is taken as strong evidence of intractability; indeed, such conjectural results are often the best that we can achieve when analyzing the inherent complexity of problems. We shall study the issue of problem complexity in Volume II.

2.2 Recurrence Relations and Their Solution

It is said that in a Buddhist monastery in Hanoi stand three diamond spikes, on which rest 64 gold disks of progressively larger outside diameter. The disks were initially placed on one of the spikes, with the largest on the bottom and the smallest on the top, as pictured (with fewer disks) in Figure 2.1. The monks must maneuver the disks so that they are arranged largest on the bottom to smallest on the top on another of the spikes. Divine decree imposes the following two strictures on the constantly laboring monks:

1. Only one disk may be off a spike at any one time. Thus only the top disk on a spike may be transferred to another spike.

2. A larger disk may never be placed atop a smaller one.

When the monks finish their task, the world will end.... Assuming that they perform the task optimally, i.e., with the fewest transfers possible, how much longer do we have?

The recursive procedure in Program 2.1 prints out the optimal sequence of moves when initially called with `Tower(64,1,2)`. To see that the sequence is indeed optimal, note that just to move n legally arranged disks from spike a to spike b requires that the $n-1$ disks above the largest of the n disks be transferred (retaining the same order) to the third spike. Then the largest of the n disks can be moved from spike a to spike b. Moving the $n-1$ disks from the third spike to spike b completes the transfer. This sequence of moves will therefore be optimal if the two nonprimitive movements of the $n-1$ smaller disks are done optimally. Since these moves are done by recursive calls to `Tower` and since a direct transfer occurs on calls made with a first parameter equal to 1, it follows by induction that the entire procedure yields the optimal sequence of moves.

The number of motions that the monks must make equals the number of times that `writeln` is executed. Let us define T_n to be the number of `writeln`

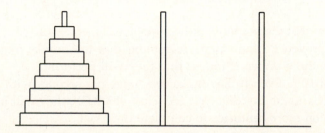

Figure 2.1: The Initial Configuration for the Towers of Hanoi Problem

```
procedure Tower(n, a, b: integer);
  (* Recursive procedure to print the optimal way to move
     n legally arranged disks from spike a to spike b. *)
  var third: integer;
  begin
    if n > 1
      then begin
             (* The indices of the three spikes sum to the constant 6. *)
             third := 6 - a - b;
             Tower(n-1,a,third);   (* Move the top n-1 disks out of the way. *)
             writeln('Move a disk from spike ',a:1,' to spike ',b:1);
             Tower(n-1,third,b)    (* Move the n-1 disks back. *)
           end
      else writeln('Move a disk from spike ',a:1,' to spike ',b:1)
  end; (* Tower *)
```

Program 2.1: A Procedure to Generate the Optimal Sequence of Transfers

statements executed when Tower is called with a first parameter of n. We can write

$$\begin{cases} T_n = T_{n-1} + 1 + T_{n-1} = 2T_{n-1} + 1 \\ T_1 = 1, \end{cases} \tag{2.1}$$

since, if $n > 1$, Tower initially calls itself with a first parameter of $n - 1$, incurring a charge of T_{n-1}, then does one writeln, and finally calls itself again with a first parameter of $n - 1$, incurring another charge of T_{n-1}.

By successively substituting already known values we see that

$$T_1 = 1$$
$$T_2 = 2T_1 + 1 = 3$$
$$T_3 = 2T_2 + 1 = 7$$
$$T_4 = 2T_3 + 1 = 15$$
$$T_5 = 2T_4 + 1 = 31$$

and might guess that the nth term of the sequence, T_n, equals $2^n - 1$. This formula can easily be proved by induction. Assuming that the monks make no errors along the way, the number of moves that they will perform is $2^{64} - 1$, which is on the order of 10^{20}. Even if they make one move per second, with a head start of 2500 years (Gautama Buddha *circa* 563–*circa* 483 B.C.), they will have to labor for several billion more centuries to complete their task.

An equation with the form of (2.1), which defines T_n "in terms of itself," is called a *recurrence relation*—at least by computer scientists; engineers call it a *difference equation*. The equation $T_1 = 1$ is called a *basis* or an *initial condition* for the recurrence. When a function can be formulated as a recurrence, finding the value of any particular term of the function is simply a matter of substituting known values to generate successive terms until the desired term is produced. Of greater interest, partially because computation may be made easier, but primarily because the growth of T_n as a function of n is more apparent, is to develop a *closed form* expression for T_n, that is, what we would traditionally call a "formula." Solving recurrence relations in this manner plays a fundamental role in the analysis of algorithms because the running time of many algorithms is best described by a recurrence relation—either because the algorithm makes direct use of recursion, as for the Towers of Hanoi, or because it involves iteration, which can be considered as tail recursion for the purposes of analysis.

In the case of the Towers of Hanoi, the closed form expression was guessed by inspecting the first few terms of the sequence. Now consider the sequence of numbers 1, 7, 29, 103, 341, ... defined by the recurrence relation

$$\begin{cases} a_n = 5a_{n-1} - 6a_{n-2} \\ a_1 = 7 \\ a_0 = 1. \end{cases} \qquad (2.2)$$

This recurrence relation appears more complex than that of (2.1): a_n depends on two previously defined values, a_{n-1} and a_{n-2}, and, accordingly, two initial conditions are specified. It is unlikely that the reader will guess the closed form expression for a_n, namely $a_n = 5 \cdot 3^n - 4 \cdot 2^n$. A more systematic approach is clearly needed; we now discuss two such approaches, restricting ourselves to simple cases only. The first and simpler, but also less powerful, method uses the *characteristic roots* of an equation derived from the recurrence to determine the general form of the solution; constants within the general form are then determined by using the initial conditions. The second method embeds the problem in the more general problem of finding a closed form for the power series

$$G(z) = a_0 + a_1 z + a_2 z^2 + \cdots + a_n z^n + \cdots, \qquad (2.3)$$

called a *generating function*, where the coefficients of the terms are the successive values defined by the recurrence relation.

2.2.1 The Method of Characteristic Roots

The method of *characteristic roots* parallels an approach developed in the 18th century for solving linear differential equations with constant coefficients. The method involves assuming a certain form for the solution and using the initial conditions to resolve coefficients and determine the actual solution to the problem at hand. Of course, the choice of a form for the solution is informed by a body of mathematical theory; in fact, various important classes of problems can be solved mechanically. If the idea of assuming a solution (somehow putting the cart before the horse) disturbs the reader, he or she can take comfort in the knowledge that any proposed answer, no matter how obtained, can be verified with a proof by mathematical induction.

Equation 2.2 is an example of a *homogeneous linear recurrence with constant coefficients*. The general form is given by

$$\begin{cases} a_n + c_1 a_{n-1} + \cdots + c_k a_{n-k} = 0 \\ a_{k-1} = \ldots \\ \quad \vdots \\ a_0 = \ldots, \end{cases} \tag{2.4}$$

where k is a fixed value (that depends on the problem) and $c_1, \ldots, c_k$ are constants (the constant coefficients). The word *homogeneous* refers to the fact that the right-hand side of the recurrence is zero. (Note that, despite its simplicity, the recurrence of (2.1) is not of this form because its right-hand side, after rearranging the terms, is 1.) The equation is called *linear* because its left-hand side is a linear combination of the a_{n-i} terms; that is, the left-hand side is a first-degree polynomial in the unknowns a_{n-i}. In particular, there are no terms of the form $c_i a_{n-i}^p$ ($p \neq 1$) nor any cross products, such as $a_{n-i} a_j$. The linearity of the recurrence has an extremely important consequence: if $a_n = f(n)$ and $a_n = g(n)$ are two solutions to (2.4), then another solution is $a_n = \alpha f(n) + \beta g(n)$ for arbitrary constants α and β. This follows immediately from distributivity and from the form of (2.4):

$$(\alpha f(n) + \beta g(n)) + c_1 (\alpha f(n-1) + \beta g(n-1)) + \cdots$$
$$+ c_k (\alpha f(n-k) + \beta g(n-k)) =$$
$$\alpha (f(n) + c_1 f(n-1) + \cdots + c_k f(n-k))$$
$$+ \beta (g(n) + c_1 g(n-1) + \cdots + c_k g(n-k)) =$$
$$\alpha \cdot 0 + \beta \cdot 0 = 0.$$

Combining multiple solutions in this manner yields a more general solution. Such combination is known as *superposition*, taking its name from the superposition of waveforms in classical physics.

Let us pick the form of a solution to a homogeneous recurrence with constant coefficients to be the function $a_n = r^n$. Using this "guess" in recurrence (2.2), we substitute for a_n, a_{n-1}, and a_{n-2} to obtain

$$r^n - 5r^{n-1} + 6r^{n-2} = 0.$$

Ignoring the trivial solution of $a_n \equiv 0$ $(r = 0)$, we can divide through by r^{n-2}, which yields

$$r^2 - 5r + 6 = 0.$$

This is known as the *characteristic equation* of the recurrence; the roots of this equation, $r_1 = 2$ and $r_2 = 3$, are called the *characteristic roots* of the recurrence. Thus, if $a_n = r^n$ is to be a solution to (2.2), we must have either $a_n = 2^n$ or $a_n = 3^n$. Since both are solutions to the recurrence (as can be checked by substitution), our earlier discussion of superposition suggests that the general solution has the form $a_n = \alpha 2^n + \beta 3^n$.

At this point we have two degrees of freedom, α and β, and two initial conditions, $a_0 = 1$ and $a_1 = 7$. We can use the initial conditions to determine α and β:

$$a_1 = 7 = 2\alpha + 3\beta$$
$$a_0 = 1 = \ \alpha + \ \beta.$$

Solving this linear system gives $\alpha = -4$ and $\beta = 5$, so that the closed form solution to our problem is $a_n = 5 \cdot 3^n - 4 \cdot 2^n$.

To summarize, solving recurrence relations by the method of characteristic roots proceeds in three steps:

1. Write down the characteristic equation for the recurrence,

$$r^k + c_1 r^{k-1} + \cdots + c_k = 0.$$

2. Find the characteristic roots, $r_1, r_2, \ldots, r_k$, and form the general solution

$$a_n = \alpha_1 r_1^n + \alpha_2 r_2^n + \cdots + \alpha_k r_k^n.$$

3. Use the k initial conditions to form k linear equations in k unknowns and solve for the α_i.

Note that the solution produced by this method need not always be a sum of exponentials; if a characteristic root equals 1, then its corresponding term is just a constant.

There are a number of complications involving irrational, complex, and repeated roots. Irrational and complex roots pose no technical problems, but it is unsatisfying to see terms involving radicals or imaginary numbers when the original recurrence uses integer coefficients and each a_n is integral. Consider, for example, the recurrence

$$\begin{cases} a_n = 4a_{n-1} - 5a_{n-2} \\ a_1 = 6 \\ a_0 = 2. \end{cases}$$

The sequence of values is 2, 6, 14, 26, 34, 6, -146, -614, -1726, -3834, $\ldots$; the characteristic equation has complex conjugate roots $2 \pm i$. Solving for the coefficients yields complex values and the closed form solution of the recurrence is

$$a_n = (1 - i)(2 + i)^n + (1 + i)(2 - i)^n.$$

Note that, for any value of n, the imaginary parts cancel and a_n is indeed an integer. However, neither the sequence of values nor the closed form gives us a clear picture of the behavior of a_n as n gets large. Indeed, we might even conclude incorrectly that, after some curious initial values, the sequence decreases steadily and tends toward minus infinity as n grows large. Because the roots (and the coefficients) are complex conjugates, we gain more insight if we write a_n in polar form,

$$a_n = (\sqrt{2} \cdot \sqrt{5}^{\,n}, -\frac{\pi}{4} + n\theta) + (\sqrt{2} \cdot \sqrt{5}^{\,n}, \frac{\pi}{4} - n\theta),$$

where $\theta = \arctan \frac{1}{2}$. Thus we get

$$a_n = 2\sqrt{2} \cdot \sqrt{5}^{\,n} \cos(n \arctan \frac{1}{2} - \frac{\pi}{4})$$

and can see that a_n oscillates in sign, but has ever increasing magnitude. This oscillation is characteristic of complex roots.

Simple situations involving irrational roots are less confusing. Since one of the roots will have the largest magnitude, its corresponding term will dominate all others as n goes to infinity, regardless of the values of the coefficients.

Repeated roots are more of a problem. Having two terms αr_i^n and βr_i^n really gives no more flexibility than the one term γr_i^n (just let $\gamma = \alpha + \beta$) so that, upon using the initial conditions to determine the values of the coefficients, we would wind up with an overdetermined system—k equations in $k - 1$ unknowns. As it turns out, the problem is with our guess at the form of the solution, which only allows for simple exponentials or constants. If we modify our guess to allow for polynomials, then the problem is easily resolved. If r_i is a repeated root of the characteristic equation with multiplicity m_i, then the form of the solution is $P_{m_i-1}(n) \cdot r_i^n$, where $P_{m_i-1}(n)$ is a polynomial of degree $m_i - 1$ in n. For simple roots the multiplicity is one, the polynomial is of degree zero and thus a constant, and the general form reduces to our earlier one.

Solving the following recurrence involves most of the problems and techniques just discussed:

$$
\begin{cases}
a_n - 5a_{n-1} + 8a_{n-2} - 4a_{n-3} = 0 \\
a_2 = 35 \\
a_1 = 14 \\
a_0 = 0.
\end{cases}
\tag{2.5}
$$

The characteristic equation is

$$r^3 - 5r^2 + 8r - 4 = 0,$$

which has two roots, 1 and 2, the latter being a double root. Thus the general form of the solution is

$$\alpha_1 \cdot 1^n + (\alpha_2 n + \alpha_3) \cdot 2^n.$$

The initial conditions give us

$$
\begin{aligned}
\alpha_1 + 8\alpha_2 + 4\alpha_3 &= 35 \\
\alpha_1 + 2\alpha_2 + 2\alpha_3 &= 14 \\
\alpha_1 + 0\alpha_2 + \alpha_3 &= 0,
\end{aligned}
$$

whence $\alpha_1 = -21$, $\alpha_2 = -7/2$, and $\alpha_3 = 21$. Thus the closed form solution to the recurrence is $a_n = (-7/2 n + 21) \cdot 2^n - 21$.

While we now have a method for solving homogeneous linear recurrences with constant coefficients, we still cannot solve the simple recurrence of (2.1). The difficulty comes from the inhomogeneous right-hand side, known as the *driving function*, which prevents us from dividing through by a power of r. The principle of superposition tells us that, if $a_n = f(n)$ is a solution to the linear inhomogeneous equation with constant coefficients

$$a_n + c_1 a_{n-1} + \cdots + c_k a_{n-k} = F(n) \tag{2.6}$$

and $g(n)$ is a solution to the homogeneous part of the same equation, namely

$$a_n + c_1 a_{n-1} + \cdots + c_k a_{n-k} = 0,$$

then $a_n = f(n) + g(n)$ is also a solution to (2.6). Thus we can solve inhomogeneous equations in two steps: we first solve the homogeneous part of the equation by the method just described; we then obtain somehow a solution to the inhomogeneous recurrence. Finally we sum the two to derive the general solution. The solution to the inhomogeneous equation used in this process is known as the *particular* solution; note that it need satisfy only the recurrence in the definition of a_n, not the initial conditions, as those can be satisfied by using appropriate coefficients in the part of the solution derived from the homogeneous equation. We may obtain a particular solution by any method available; in practice, we consult tables of standard forms for typical driving functions in the hope that the driving function at hand will be found on the list. If the driving function is a sum of terms, linearity again allows us to use superposition; thus we break the recurrence into a collection of inhomogeneous recurrences, one for each driving term, find particular solutions to each, and sum them to derive a particular solution to the original recurrence.

A particular solution often has the same form as the driving function. This is due to the linearity of the recurrence: since the driving function is just a linear combination of various forms of the solution, the two must be very similar. No linear combination of fourth-degree polynomials will make a fifth-degree polynomial or an exponential; no linear combination of terms of the form 3^n will make a term of the form 2^n; etc. In Equation 2.1, the driving function is a constant, so we look for a particular solution of the form $T_n = d$, where d is a constant. Substituting in the recurrence $T_n - 2T_{n-1} = 1$, we get

$$d - 2d = 1,$$

which tells us that $d = -1$; hence $T_n = -1$ is a particular solution. Our proposed general solution to (2.1) is thus

$$T_n = \alpha 2^n - 1,$$

where $\alpha 2^n$ is the general solution to the homogeneous equation $T_n - 2T_{n-1} = 0$. We now use the initial condition to get

$$T_1 = 1 = 2\alpha - 1,$$

so that the closed form solution to (2.1) is indeed

$$T_n = 2^n - 1.$$

In general, if the driving function (or part of it) has the form $P_k(n) \cdot b^n$, where $P_k(n)$ is a polynomial of degree k in n, then there is a particular solution of the same form, namely $Q_k(n) \cdot b^n$. This result covers a number of important special cases: constants ($k = 0$ and $b = 1$), simple polynomials ($b = 1$), simple exponentials ($k = 0$ and $b \neq 1$), and combinations of polynomials and exponentials. Situations in which the driving function is not of the proper form can sometimes be handled by transformation; for instance, $2^{n/2}$ can be changed into $\sqrt{2}^n$. When b also happens to be a characteristic root, then the particular solution will be of the form $P_{k+m}(n) \cdot b^n$: the degree of the polynomial in the particular solution is increased by m, the multiplicity of b. As an example, consider modifying recurrence (2.5) to include a driving function of $2n + 1$, i.e., using the inhomogeneous recurrence

$$a_n - 5a_{n-1} + 8a_{n-2} - 4a_{n-3} = 2n + 1$$

with the same initial conditions. The general solution to the homogeneous equation remains $\alpha_1 + (\alpha_2 n + \alpha_3)2^n$. Since the driving function is a polynomial of degree 1 and since $b = 1$ is a characteristic root of multiplicity 1, a particular solution has the form of a polynomial of degree 2:

$$\beta_2 n^2 + \beta_1 n + \beta_0.$$

Since both the homogeneous and particular solutions have an arbitrary constant term, we can ignore it (β_0) in the particular solution and capture it later in the homogeneous portion. By substituting $a_n = \beta_2 n^2 + \beta_1 n$ in the recurrence, we get

$$(\beta_2 n^2 + \beta_1 n) - 5\big(\beta_2(n-1)^2 + \beta_1(n-1)\big)$$
$$+ 8\big(\beta_2(n-2)^2 + \beta_1(n-2)\big) - 4\big(\beta_2(n-3)^2 + \beta_1(n-3)\big) = 2n + 1,$$

which yields

$$\beta_2 n + \beta_1 - 9\beta_2 = 2n + 1.$$

Since this formula is true for all n, the coefficients of terms of the same degree must be equal, so that we get

$$2\beta_2 = 2$$
$$\beta_1 - 9\beta_2 = 1$$

and thus $\beta_1 = 10$ and $\beta_2 = 1$. Now our general solution is

$$a_n = \alpha_1 + (\alpha_2 n + \alpha_3)2^n + n^2 + 10n.$$

Using the initial conditions, we solve for the remaining constants. The final solution is $a_n = (n + 1) \cdot 2^n + n^2 + 10n - 1$. Note that we used the recurrence to resolve the coefficients in the particular solution first. Only then did we use the initial conditions to solve for the remaining constants in the general solution.

As described so far, the method of characteristic roots applies only to linear recurrences with constant coefficients. Fortunately, most recurrences that arise in the context of algorithmic analysis are of this type. Even when they are not, it is often possible to transform them into recurrences that are. Our average-case analysis of insertion into a binary search tree (Section 2.3.1) and of quicksort in Section 8.4 provides a fairly elaborate example of such transformations. Here we present a simple example. A common recurrence in algorithmic analysis arises from divide-and-conquer algorithms (Chapter 7):

$$T(n) = p \cdot T(n/q) + g(n), \text{ with } T(1) = \ldots, \tag{2.7}$$

where p and q are positive integers and $g(n)$ is some driving function. This recurrence does not lend itself directly to the method of characteristic roots: the characteristic equation would appear to be $r^n - p \cdot r^{n/q} = 0$, which has only the trivial solution $r = 0$ (unless p equals 1). However, note that the recurrence does not define $T(n)$ for all values of n, but only for those values of n that are powers of q. Thus, we can let $n = q^k$ and consider the new function $H(k) = T(q^k)$; note that $H(k)$ is defined for all values of k. This function obeys the recurrence

$$H(k) = p \cdot H(k - 1) + g(q^k), \text{ with } H(0) = T(1).$$

This new recurrence does lend itself to the method of characteristic roots; we have transformed an apparently intractable recurrence into a fairly simple one by a change of variables. For the sake of clarity, assume that $g(n)$ is a polynomial of degree 1 (an important case in actual divide-and-conquer algorithms, where the nonrecursive part often does constant work per element on top of some fixed overhead), so that $g(q^k)$, a function of k, is of the form $\gamma_1 q^k + \gamma_2$, the sum of an exponential and a constant. The homogeneous equation has a solution of the form αp^k, while a particular solution is $\beta_1 q^k + \beta_2$ (this time assuming $p \neq q$ and $p \neq 1$). Thus the general solution is of the form

$$H(k) = \alpha p^k + \beta_1 q^k + \beta_2.$$

To convert this back to a function of n, we substitute $k = \log_q n$ to get

$$T(n) = \alpha n^{\log_q p} + \beta_1 n + \beta_2.$$

Exercise 2.1 The two cases $p = q \neq 1$ and $p = 1$ account for the majority of recurrences derived from divide-and-conquer algorithms. Mergesort (Section 7.1) is an example of the first (with a linear driving function), and binary search is an example of the second (with a constant driving function).

Analyze each case separately, assuming first a constant and next a linear driving function. Compare your solutions against the table below.

	$g(n) = \Theta(n)$	$g(n) = \Theta(1)$
$p = q \neq 1$	$\Theta(n \log n)$	$\Theta(n)$
$p = 1$	$\Theta(n)$	$\Theta(\log n)$

Can you think of algorithms with running times described by each of these cases?

□

2.2.2 The Method of Generating Functions

When the method of characteristic roots fails, even after suitable transformations and changes of variables, the more powerful method of generating functions may be useful. We begin by considering a class of problems we already know how to solve: linear recurrences with constant coefficients. Referring back to Equation 2.3,

$$G(z) = a_0 + a_1 z + a_2 z^2 + \cdots + a_n z^n + \cdots,$$

notice that, by design, each term of the infinite power series $G(z)$ is of the form $a_i z^i$: the coefficient of z^i is the ith term in the sequence generated by the recurrence relation. Since a linear recurrence involves only a few of the a_i terms, some way must be found to relate the infinite series of the generating function to the finite collection of terms of the recurrence. Starting from the recurrence and working toward the generating function, we force $G(z)$ to appear by taking suitable infinite sums. We use the recurrence of (2.2) as an example:

$$a_n - 5a_{n-1} + 6a_{n-2} = 0, \quad n \ge 2.$$

The equality remains true if both sides are multiplied with the same power of z:

$$(a_n - 5a_{n-1} + 6a_{n-2}) \cdot z^n = 0 \cdot z^n, \quad n \ge 2.$$

We now have an $a_n z^n$ term, but to obtain $G(z)$ we need an infinite sum of such terms. Hence we sum an infinite number of these equalities, one for each power of z:

$$\sum_{i=2}^{\infty} (a_i - 5a_{i-1} + 6a_{i-2}) \cdot z^i = \sum_{i=2}^{\infty} a_i z^i - 5 \sum_{i=2}^{\infty} a_{i-1} z^i + 6 \sum_{i=2}^{\infty} a_{i-2} z^i = 0.$$

Notice that the lower bound on the infinite sums is the first value for which the recurrence applies. Now, the first of the three sums is $G(z)$, except that it lacks the first two terms of the infinite series, $a_0 + a_1 z$. The second and third sums also resemble $G(z)$, but the subscripts on the a_i do not match the exponents. This is easily remedied by factoring out z and z^2, respectively. Doing this and adjusting indices finally yields

$$\sum_{i=2}^{\infty} a_i z^i - 5z \sum_{i=1}^{\infty} a_i z^i + 6z^2 \sum_{i=0}^{\infty} a_i z^i = 0.$$

Now the second sum is seen to be $G(z)$ minus its first term, a_0, while the third sum is exactly $G(z)$. Substituting accordingly, we obtain

$$\big(G(z) - a_0 - a_1 z\big) - 5z\big(G(z) - a_0\big) + 6z^2 G(z) = 0.$$

A closed form for $G(z)$ can now be obtained by replacing a_0 and a_1 with their respective values and collecting terms:

$$G(z) = \frac{1 + 2z}{1 - 5z + 6z^2}.$$

A closed form for $G(z)$ is not exactly what we want: what we are looking for is a closed form for a_n in terms of n. In order to derive this, we shall expand $G(z)$ into an infinite series; as Equation 2.3 shows, the coefficient of z^n will be a_n. We start by rewriting $G(z)$ in a simpler form,

$$G(z) = \frac{1 + 2z}{(1 - 3z)(1 - 2z)} = \frac{A}{1 - 3z} + \frac{B}{1 - 2z},$$

where the coefficients A and B remain to be determined. This last step, known as *partial fraction decomposition*, is a technique taken from calculus, where it is used to reduce the difficulty of performing certain integrations. Such decomposition simplifies our task, inasmuch as it allows us to consider each simple fraction independently: we recover from each the corresponding coefficient of the nth term and sum the results. To make the last equality true, we must have

$$
\begin{array}{ccc}
A + B = 1 & & A + B = 1 \\
-2Az - 3Bz = 2z & \text{or} & 2A + 3B = -2.
\end{array}
$$

Solving for A and B gives $A = 5$ and $B = -4$, so that

$$G(z) = \frac{5}{1 - 3z} + \frac{-4}{1 - 2z}.$$

To proceed further it is necessary to know a "magical fact," namely

$$\frac{1}{1 - rx} = 1 + rx + r^2 x^2 + r^3 x^3 + \cdots. \tag{2.8}$$

The simplest way to verify this "magical fact" is to multiply both sides of the equation by $1 - rx$ and observe the cancellation of terms on the right-hand side. This equation can also be derived directly by showing that $1/(1 - rx)$ is the closed form for the generating function associated with the simplest of recurrences,

$$
\begin{cases}
a_n = r a_{n-1} \\
a_0 = 1,
\end{cases}
$$

the solution of which, by inspection, is $a_n = r^n$.

Exercise 2.2 Derive Equation 2.8 using the technique outlined for obtaining $G(z)$ from a homogeneous linear recurrence with constant coefficients.   □

Applying (2.8) first to $5/(1 - 3z)$ and then to $-4/(1 - 2z)$, we find that the coefficients of the nth terms are $5 \cdot 3^n$ and $-4 \cdot 2^n$, respectively. Thus the coefficient of the nth term of $G(z)$, i.e., the solution to the recurrence, is $a_n = 5 \cdot 3^n - 4 \cdot 2^n$.

   Had our recurrence been inhomogeneous, it would have been necessary to include the driving function in the derivation of the generating function. Let us return to the recurrence of (2.1) and solve it by the method of generating functions. Notice that the first term defined is T_1; this is a slight problem, inasmuch as generating functions assume the existence of a zeroth term. This is rectified by letting $a_n = T_{n+1}$, solving for a_n, and recovering the solution in terms of T_n. Proceeding as before, from the recurrence

$$\begin{cases} a_n - 2a_{n-1} = 1 \\ a_0 = 1, \end{cases} \tag{2.9}$$

we obtain the equation

$$\sum_{i=1}^{\infty} a_i z^i - 2 \sum_{i=1}^{\infty} a_{i-1} z^i = \sum_{i=1}^{\infty} 1 \cdot z^i.$$

The first two terms can be expressed in terms of $G(z)$ in the manner just used; the right-hand side is, but for the absence of the zeroth term, the generating function for the trivial recurrence $c_n = 1$. In order to derive a closed form for $G(z)$, we replace $\sum_{i=1}^{\infty} 1 \cdot z^i$ with its closed form and solve the resulting equation for $G(z)$. Finding the closed form for the generating function corresponding to the driving function has much in common with finding the particular solution in the method of characteristic roots: for the most part it is done from tables, but unusual cases require a great deal of ingenuity. For our simple case we have just Equation 2.8 with $r = 1$. Thus armed, we can now rewrite the infinite sums as

$$(G(z) - a_0) - 2zG(z) = \frac{1}{1 - z} - 1.$$

Substituting for a_0, we obtain

$$G(z) = \frac{1}{(1 - z)(1 - 2z)}$$

and partial fraction decomposition gives us

$$G(z) = \frac{-1}{1 - z} + \frac{2}{1 - 2z}.$$

Using (2.8) once again, we conclude that the solution of recurrence (2.1) is, in terms of a_n,

$$a_n = -1 + 2 \cdot 2^n = 2^{n+1} - 1,$$

from which the solution in terms of T_n follows.

In summary, converting a recurrence relation to a closed form expression for the nth term of the sequence by the method of generating functions involves four steps:

1. *Create the power series.* Write the equality, involving power series in the artificial variable z, obtained by taking infinite sums of the recurrence, with the homogeneous part on the left and the driving function on the right. Begin the infinite sums at the lowest index allowed by the recurrence.

2. *Convert the power series to closed form.* Replace the sums on the left-hand side with functions of $G(z)$ and the initial conditions. Replace the sums on the right-hand side with the appropriate closed forms of the generating functions.

3. *Manipulate the closed form.* Solve the resulting equation for $G(z)$ and decompose the closed form into partial fractions, so that $G(z)$ is written as the sum of simple functions with known infinite series expansions.

4. *Convert the closed form back to a power series and match terms.* Use the infinite series expansions to determine the nth coefficient of each and then collect terms and simplify.

In practice, conversions between generating functions and their infinite series are not derived from scratch every time; one consults tables of basic generating functions and relationships and uses the tables to obtain quickly the desired conversion.

As described, the method is also known as the method of *z-transforms*, with $G(z)$ viewed as the transform of the function described by $g(n) = a_n$.[3] Transform methods involve two domains: the original domain, in which the problem is given and in which the answer must be expressed, and the transform domain, in which the reformulated problem is more easily solved. A very similar method is used in solving differential equations; the transforms used in that field are known as Laplace transforms. Indeed, *z*-transforms can be thought of as the discrete equivalent of Laplace transforms.

---

[3]Many authors define *z*-transforms by using negative powers of z, rather than the positive powers used with generating functions. This difference alters only the domain of convergence of the series, not their manipulation.

Notice that we have been manipulating infinite series as if they were finite sums; but elementary calculus tells us that infinite series are not sums at all, but limits of sequences of finite sums—a fundamental difference which casts doubts on the validity of our manipulations. The discovery of the consequences of this difference came rather late in the development of calculus. Although generating functions were introduced by Abraham de Moivre (1667–1754) early in the eighteenth century, the rules for manipulating infinite series were first studied carefully by Niels Henrik Abel (1802–1829). Actually, all of the operations that we have performed are perfectly legal and can be made completely rigorous by resorting to the concept of a *formal power series*, where the powers of z are just symbols used to group certain coefficients.

As might be expected, each of our two methods for solving recurrences—characteristic roots and generating functions—has its advantages. Although transformations, such as substituting q^k for n in Equation 2.7, extend its range of applicability, the method of characteristic roots works best for the important, but restricted, class of linear recurrences with constant coefficients. The method of generating functions, as we shall see in some further examples, is more versatile, even if the methodology is often *ad hoc*. When both methods are applicable, the method of characteristic roots is generally preferred. Among other advantages, it allows an immediate estimate of the rate of growth of the solution, as no lengthy computations to determine exact coefficients are made until the form of the solution is known. In contrast, with generating functions the form of the solution is not known until after decomposition into partial fractions. The ability to estimate growth rate quickly is particularly important in view of our notation for algorithmic analysis, which essentially ignores the values of constants. The method of characteristic roots is also typically faster, although using tables of transformations, such as those of Exercise 2.28, allows generating functions with complicated coefficients to be expressed in terms of progressively simpler ones without resorting to intricate algebraic manipulations. We now illustrate the power of generating functions, and the use of tables in their derivation, with a few examples.

Consider the related problems of finding a closed form for $\sum_{i=0}^{n} g(i)$ as a function of n and that of determining the value of $\sum_{i=0}^{\infty} g(i)$, assuming that the infinite series converges. Although the problem of finding a closed form for $\sum_{i=0}^{n} g(i)$ may easily be transformed into a recurrence by letting

$$f(n) = \sum_{i=0}^{n} g(i), \tag{2.10}$$

yielding

$$f(n) = f(n-1) + g(n), \quad \text{with } f(0) = g(0),$$

this transformation appears to be of little use, as the recurrence has a trivial homogeneous part and packs all of its information into the driving function. In such problems, however, $g(n)$ is usually given explicitly (we shall use $g(n) = 6n/3^n$ as a concrete example), which will allow us to derive very easily a closed form for $G(z)$, the generating function for $g(n)$, in terms of which we can then formulate $F(z)$, the generating function for $f(n)$. The latter task is less formidable than it may at first appear. The second table of Exercise 2.28 establishes a correspondence between manipulations on generating functions and manipulations on their coefficients. The third entry of this table is a precise match, since the nth coefficient of $F(z)$ is, by definition (Equation 2.10), the sum of the zeroth through nth coefficients of $G(z)$; the corresponding relationship between their generating functions is thus

$$F(z) = \frac{1}{1-z} G(z).$$

Turning now to our concrete example, $g(i) = 6i/3^i$, we note that, according to the fourth entry of the table, the generating function for g is the generating function for $g_1(i) = i/3^i$, multiplied by 6. Again, the seventh entry of the same table allows us to express the generating function for $g_1(i)$ in terms of that for $g_2(i) = 1/3^i$, $G_1(z) = z\, dG_2(z)/dz$. Finally, $g_2(i)$ is just an instance of (2.8) with $r = 1/3$; we could also use the fifth entry of the table to conclude that $G_2(z)$ is equal to $G_3(z/3)$, where $G_3(z)$ is the generating function for $g_3(i) = 1$. $G_3(z)$ is our most basic relationship,

$$\frac{1}{1-z} = 1 + z + z^2 + \cdots,$$

a special case of the first entry of the first table. Putting this all together yields

$$G(z) = 6z \frac{d}{dz}\left\{ \frac{1}{1-z/3} \right\} = \frac{2z}{(1-z/3)^2},$$

so that the generating function for $f(n) = \sum_{i=0}^{n} 6i/3^i$ is

$$F(z) = \frac{2z}{(1-z)(1-z/3)^2}.$$

Recovering the closed form for $f(n)$ is now a straightforward, if computationally unpleasant, task.

   Having $G(z)$ in closed form allows us to answer our other question: what is $\sum_{i=0}^{\infty} 6i/3^i$? It is just $G(1)$, which is $9/2$. We must be careful when making this substitution: 1 must lie inside the radius of convergence of the power series. Since the radius of convergence of a power series is the absolute value of the smallest *pole* (i.e., a root of the denominator), the substitution is justified in our situation, where the two poles are both equal to 3.

The real field of application of generating functions is, however, in solving problems to which the method of characteristic roots is not applicable, even after suitable transformations. Consider the problem of determining the number of distinct ways of multiplying n matrices together (Problem 10) or, equivalently, of determining the number of binary trees with n leaves, b_n. In a binary tree representing a specific order of multiplication, one of the multiplications must be performed last, and it corresponds to the root of the tree. Once a multiplication has been selected for the root, it partitions the problem into two subproblems— the k matrices to the left of the root must be multiplied together somehow, and the $n - k$ matrices to the right of the root must also be combined. A nice feature of this partitioning into subproblems is that the k leaves to the left of the root can be formed into trees in b_k ways, each totally independent of how the $n - k$ leaves to the right of the root are formed into trees; that is, the two subproblems do not interact in any way, except that the total number of leaves always equals n. Therefore, once the last multiplication has been selected, with k matrices on the left and $n - k$ matrices on the right, there are

$$b_k \cdot b_{n-k}$$

possible trees with this root, since the number of ways in which two independent choices can be combined is the product of the number of ways in which each choice can be made. Of course, the split into left and right "halves" can be done in many ways: one matrix on the left and $n - 1$ matrices on the right, two on the left and $n - 2$ on the right, etc. No tree formed from a k_1 *vs.* $(n - k_1)$ split can be the same as any tree formed from a k_2 *vs.* $(n - k_2)$ split, so that the total number of binary trees with n leaves is given by

$$\begin{cases} b_n = b_1 b_{n-1} + b_2 b_{n-2} + b_3 b_{n-3} + \cdots + b_{n-2} b_2 + b_{n-1} b_1 \\ b_1 = 1. \end{cases} \tag{2.11}$$

This recurrence differs from all our preceding examples in that b_n does not depend on a fixed number of previously computed terms, but on all previous terms, a number that varies with n; moreover, the recurrence is nonlinear. The method of characteristic roots does not apply; no amount of manipulation appears to help in turning this recurrence into a linear recurrence with constant coefficients. What is even worse, the method of generating functions does not seem to apply either, because no equation with a fixed number of terms can be derived even after using infinite sums. However, notice that one entry in the table of Exercise 2.28 does apply: multiplying two generating functions, $G(z)$ and $H(z)$, corresponds to taking the *convolution* of the two original functions,

$$g \circledast h = \sum_{j=0}^{n} g_j h_{n-j},$$

and the recurrence defining b_n in (2.11) is a convolution of b_n with itself. Thus the generating function for b_n, $G(z)$, equals that for $b \circledast b$, which the table tells us is simply $G^2(z)$. We have

$$G(z) = b_1 z + b_2 z^2 + \cdots + b_n z^n + \cdots, \tag{2.12}$$

from which we get

$$G^2(z) = b_1 b_1 z^2 + (b_1 b_2 + b_2 b_1)z^3 + (b_1 b_3 + b_2 b_2 + b_3 b_1)z^4 + \cdots$$
$$+ (b_1 b_{n-1} + b_2 b_{n-2} + \cdots + b_{n-1} b_1)z^n + \cdots.$$

Note that the coefficient of the nth term of $G^2(z)$ is indeed the right-hand side of the recurrence in (2.11). Therefore,

$$G^2(z) = b_2 z^2 + b_3 z^3 + \cdots + b_n z^n + \cdots = G(z) - b_1 z.$$

Substituting 1 for b_1 gives

$$G^2(z) - G(z) + z = 0.$$

Replacing $G(z)$ with y and treating z as a constant yields the quadratic equation $y^2 - y + z = 0$, which gives us

$$y = \frac{1 \pm \sqrt{1 - 4z}}{2}.$$

Using (2.12), we get $G(0) = 0$, so that the negative sign is correct and we have

$$G(z) = \frac{1 - \sqrt{1 - 4z}}{2} = \frac{1}{2} - \frac{\sqrt{1 - 4z}}{2}. \tag{2.13}$$

Again we have a closed form formula for $G(z)$, where what we want is one for b_n. We need an infinite series formulation for $\sqrt{1 - 4z}$. Since our sole "magical fact" (Equation 2.8) does not cover this case, we derive the formulation from basic principles, using a technique through which the facts of the first table of Exercise 2.28 can be established. An infinite series for $\sqrt{1 - 4z}$ can be developed by expanding $\sqrt{1 - 4z}$ around zero using Taylor's theorem:

$$f(x) = f(0) + f'(0)x + \frac{f''(0)}{2!}x^2 + \cdots + \frac{f^{(n)}(0)}{n!}x^n + \cdots.$$

By letting $f(x) = (1 + x)^m$ (where m is not necessarily an integer), we obtain

$$(1 + x)^m = 1 + mx + \frac{m(m - 1)}{2!}x^2 + \frac{m(m - 1)(m - 2)}{3!}x^3 + \cdots$$
$$+ \frac{m(m - 1)\cdots(m - n + 1)}{n!}x^n + \cdots.$$

We now write $\sqrt{1 - 4z}$ as $(1 + (-4z))^{1/2}$ and substitute $-4z$ for x to derive the nth term:

$$\frac{(\frac{1}{2})(\frac{1}{2} - 1)(\frac{1}{2} - 2)(\frac{1}{2} - 3) \cdots (\frac{1}{2} - n + 2)(\frac{1}{2} - n + 1)}{n!}(-4z)^n$$

$$= \frac{1}{2^n} \cdot \frac{((1)(1 - 2)(1 - 4)(1 - 6) \cdots (1 - 2n + 4)(1 - 2n + 2))}{n!}(-4)^n z^n$$

$$= -\frac{2^n \cdot 1 \cdot 1 \cdot 3 \cdot 5 \cdots (2n - 5) \cdot (2n - 3)}{n!}z^n$$

$$= -\frac{2^n}{n!} \cdot 1 \cdot \frac{2}{2} \cdot 3 \cdot \frac{4}{4} \cdot 5 \cdots (2n - 3) \cdot \frac{2n - 2}{2n - 2}z^n$$

$$= -\frac{2(2n - 2)!}{n!} \cdot \frac{2^{n-1}}{2 \cdot 4 \cdots (2n - 2)}z^n$$

$$= -\frac{2(2n - 2)!}{n!\,(n - 1)!}z^n = -\frac{2}{n}\binom{2n - 2}{n - 1}z^n.$$

Thus, referring back to (2.13), the nth term of $G(z)$ is

$$b_n = \frac{1}{n}\binom{2n - 2}{n - 1}.$$

This formula is usually shifted over one term to yield

$$C_n = \frac{1}{n + 1}\binom{2n}{n}.$$

These numbers are called *Catalan numbers* after Eugène Charles Catalan (1814–1894), who studied their properties extensively—although they were known to Leonhard Euler (1707–1783).

As a last example of the use of generating functions, let us examine the difficult problem of deriving, if not a closed form, at least a closed form approximation for factorials. We shall have occasion to use functions such as $n!$ and $\log(n!)$ to describe the behavior of certain algorithms and shall then require an estimate of the growth rate of such functions. Factorials may be defined by the following linear recurrence with nonconstant coefficients:

$$\begin{cases} a_n = na_{n-1} \\ a_0 = 1. \end{cases}$$

Let us apply our summing technique:

$$\sum_{i=1}^{\infty} a_i z^i - \sum_{i=1}^{\infty} ia_{i-1}z^i = 0.$$

The first term is $F(z)$ minus its first element. The second term may be derived from the second table of Exercise 2.28: after rewriting the second term as

$$z\sum_{i=0}^{\infty} ia_i z^i + z\sum_{i=0}^{\infty} a_i z^i,$$

we can use the seventh entry to conclude that

$$F(z) - 1 - z^2\,dF(z)/dz - zF(z) = 0.$$

Gathering terms, we obtain the equation

$$(1-z)F(z) - z^2 F'(z) = 1, \text{ with } F(0) = 1.$$

This equation characterizes $F(z)$, but in a much more complex manner than any seen heretofore. It is a first order linear differential equation with nonconstant coefficients. Thus we have only managed to replace a difference equation with a differential equation. Fortunately, differential equations are often amenable to somewhat different methods of solution than difference equations. In this particular case, though, there is no closed form for $F(z)$ and, although a very close approximation can be derived (*Stirling's approximation*), its derivation involves both generating functions and integral equations and is very complex. We content ourselves with quoting the result:

$$n! = \sqrt{2\pi n}\left(\frac{n}{e}\right)^n\left(1 + \frac{1}{12n} + \frac{1}{288n^2} + O\!\left(\frac{1}{n^3}\right)\right).$$

2.2.3 Combining Recurrences and Asymptotic Notation

Since we have repeatedly stated that most algorithmic analysis is done in asymptotic terms and since we have defined a notation suitable for the expression of asymptotic relationships, it would seem only logical to combine this notation with recurrence relations, thereby enabling us to ignore small and presumably irrelevant details of coding. Specifically, there are two areas where the introduction of asymptotic notation would bring about welcome simplifications: the base cases, where we would like to write $\Theta(1)$, since the exact values of the constants ought not to matter; and the driving functions, where only the leading term appears relevant. However, recall that $O(\ )$ and $\Theta(\ )$ denote families of functions, so that their introduction in a recurrence yields a family of recurrences, one for each function in the family. The problem is that certain of these recurrences may yield solutions that differ considerably from what we would expect. Consider, for instance, the family of recurrences given by

$$\begin{cases} a_n - 5a_{n-1} + 6a_{n-2} = \Theta(n) \\ a_0 = \Theta(1) \\ a_1 = \Theta(1). \end{cases}$$

First note that, although we presumably expect the driving function to be a first-degree polynomial, the family of driving functions described by $\Theta(n)$ also includes functions such as $n + \sqrt{n}\log n$, the second term of which will yield additional terms in the general solution. Even considering only the leading term of the driving function, we come across significant problems. The general solution is then of the form $\alpha 3^n + \beta 2^n + \gamma n + \delta$, so that we might be tempted to conclude that all members of the family of solutions are $\Theta(3^n)$. However, some members of the family are $\Theta(2^n)$ (just choose $a_1 - 2a_0 = \gamma - \delta$) and some even are $\Theta(n)$ (additionally require $a_0 = \delta$ and $a_1 = \gamma + \delta$). Note that, for each specific choice of first-degree polynomial for the driving function, there exist choices for the initial conditions which change the behavior of the solution from the expected $\Theta(3^n)$ to $\Theta(2^n)$ or even $\Theta(n)$. Generalizing to arbitrary recurrences, for each specific driving function, one can always choose initial conditions which make the homogeneous solution disappear.

This behavior is perfectly reasonable in mathematical terms, but makes no sense whatsoever in programming terms: it would imply that an apparently exponential-time algorithm, normally requiring $\Theta(3^n)$ time, could be made to run in linear time by the simple device of tuning the code for the two base cases! This anomaly serves as a timely reminder, just as we are about to use our recurrence tools to analyze real algorithms: recurrences and asymptotic notation are just mathematical tools used to model certain aspects of the behavior of algorithms and, like all models, they are not universally valid. As the simple example just discussed makes abundantly clear, the mathematical model and the real program may exhibit wildly divergent behavior.

2.3 Worst-Case, Average-Case, and Amortized Analysis

Now that we are equipped with the necessary tools, we can tackle the real problem, *viz.*, the analysis of algorithms. We must first note that such analysis is likely to prove both simpler and harder than our mathematical exercises of the previous sections: simpler because we need only determine the asymptotic behavior of an algorithm and thus need not solve recurrences to the last constant; harder because we face the additional problem of deriving some type of recurrence to characterize the algorithm before we can solve it. Secondly, we must decide on the type of analysis that is to be performed: any algorithm uses many different resources, each of which can be measured in a number of ways. Since we restrict our study to sequential (as opposed to parallel or distributed) algorithms, the two resources of most interest to us are running time and running space (where the latter is understood to include only additional space, not the space needed to store the input and the output). Of the two, time is the more traditional and, at least for those algorithms that run reasonably fast, the more important. On the other hand, many exhaustive search algorithms run out of space while remaining within reasonable time limits: after all, space is bounded by a fixed constant on any system, while time is essentially unbounded. (Even with the large address space of current machines, one can easily write a program that will run out of space in just a few minutes of CPU time.) In most cases, however, the analysis of the space requirements of an algorithm is a very simple task. Thus we shall concentrate on the traditional measure of running time. How to measure it, though, is not immediately clear: do we wish to characterize the worst possible behavior, the average one, or the one most likely to arise in practice? The first is at least fairly well defined; moreover, it becomes of paramount importance in real-time applications (such as process control), where an answer must be produced within fixed delays. The last two are much harder to define: computing an average over all instances presupposes a knowledge of the probability distribution of the instances, and doing the same for a specific application requires even more *a priori* knowledge. Finally, we must acknowledge that algorithms rarely work in isolation, but instead within a rich context and in cooperation with other algorithms; thus a realistic analysis ought to take into account the influence of one algorithm's behavior on another's. This last consideration has led in recent years to the development of amortized analysis, which has quickly become an important tool for the analysis of algorithms that manipulate data structures.

In the following, we provide examples of worst-case, average-case, and amortized analysis—this last at somewhat more length than the first two, due to its relatively recent introduction. We assume that the reader is familiar with the basic premises and techniques of algorithm analysis; our examples are intended to illustrate more sophisticated applications of analysis techniques.

2.3.1 Worst and Average Case: Asymptotic Analysis

While solving recurrences arising from algorithmic analysis is often a difficult job and sometimes not possible with the techniques discussed in the previous section, the real challenge lies in the development of the recurrence itself. Of course, the analysis of an algorithm need not be approached solely through recurrences: many iterative algorithms with fixed loops are easily analyzed directly. Minor difficulties arise with algorithms that use a mixture of recursive and iterative control structures; they are easily disposed of by simply noting that each iterative construction can be viewed as a tail recursion. Much more difficult are the problems posed by algorithms which control the flow through variables that bear no direct relationship to the input size; a number of the iterative algorithms of Chapter 6 fall in this category. Generally speaking, it is best to develop the analysis in terms of the control variables first; when necessary, additional work can then be done to relate these variables to the input size. In the following, we present examples of increasingly complex analyses and attempt to illustrate a variety of sources for the difficulties. However, deriving recurrences that characterize the behavior of an algorithm remains an art: few rules apply, and only long practice will increase competence and confidence.

Worst-Case Analysis: AVL Trees

As a first example, consider the data structure known as a height-balanced binary search tree—also known as an AVL tree when the balance factor cannot exceed 1.

Definition 2.4 A binary search tree is an AVL tree if and only if the two subtrees of each node differ in height by at most 1.   □

How can we determine the worst-case behavior of the various operations on this data structure? Note that there are two types of analysis to consider: what is the worst possible tree that can be constructed, and what is the worst possible behavior for a single operation? Since the time required by a search, insertion, or deletion is directly proportional to the length of the search path, the worst-case behavior varies in direct proportion to the height of the tree. (Details of AVL tree operations are irrelevant to our development; they can be found in standard textbooks on data structures, for which the reader should see the bibliography.) Thus both types of analysis reduce to the same question: for a given number of nodes, what is the height of the tallest possible AVL tree? More formally, can

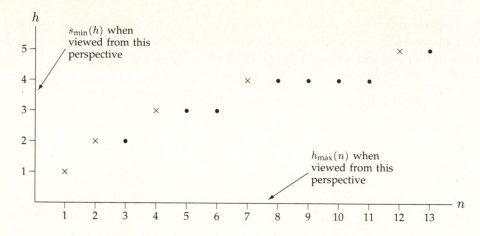

Figure 2.2: The Relationship Between $h_{max}(n)$ and $s_{min}(h)$

we characterize $h_{max}(n)$, where n is the size of the tree? Writing a recurrence to describe $h_{max}(n)$, say

$$h_{max}(n) = 1 + \max\{h_{max}(k), h_{max}(n - 1 - k)\},$$

presents a major problem, however, because we have no way of knowing how many nodes to allocate to each of the two subtrees of the root. First, several different allocations may all result in the maximal value; secondly, several others may not be permissible, since they prevent any possibility of meeting the height-balance requirement. In fact, h_{max} is a step function, remaining constant for a range of values. In this case, the problem can be solved by turning the question upside down and asking for the smallest possible AVL tree of a given height (see Figure 2.2). Denote the size of the smallest such tree of height h by $s_{min}(h)$; since this function increases monotonically with increasing h, we can write the recurrence

$$s_{min}(h) = 1 + s_{min}(h - 1) + s_{min}(h - 2),$$

with bases $s_{min}(0) = 0$ and $s_{min}(1) = 1$. The recurrence accounts for the root of the tree of height h and for its two subtrees, one of height $h - 1$ (obviously, since otherwise the larger tree would not have height h) and one of height $h - 2$, the smallest allowed by the height balance. This is a familiar recurrence: in homogeneous form, it defines the Fibonacci numbers (see Exercise 2.15). (Indeed, the trees built from the nonhomogeneous recurrence are called Fibonacci trees.) The nonhomogeneous constant term makes very little difference, and the reader can verify that the solution is simply $s_{min}(h) = F_{h+2} - 1$. From the results of

```
procedure SillySort(var A: arraytype; i, j: integer);
  (* sorts subarray A[i..j] *)
  var temp: integer;
  begin
    if i < j  (* If i = j there is nothing to do. *)
      then begin
              m := (i+j) div 2;
              SillySort(A,i,m);
              SillySort(A,m+1,j);
              (* Largest element in the entire array is the larger
                 of A[m] and A[j]. *)
              if A[m] > A[j]
                then begin (* swap *)
                        temp := A[m]; A[m] := A[j]; A[j] := temp
                     end;
              (* Largest element in place--sort the rest. *)
              SillySort(A,i,j-1)
           end
  end; (* SillySort *)
```

Program 2.2: A Subexponential Sorting Procedure

Exercise 2.15, we conclude that the asymptotic behavior of s_{min} is given by

$$s_{min}(h) \asymp \frac{\phi^{h+2}}{\sqrt{5}},$$

where $\phi = (1 + \sqrt{5})/2 \approx 1.618034$ is the *golden ratio*. Now we can recover the asymptotic behavior of h_{max}, the height of the tallest AVL tree on n nodes, by letting $n = s_{min}(h)$ and solving for h, yielding

$$h_{max}(n) \asymp \log_\phi(\frac{\sqrt{5}}{\phi^2}n)$$

or $h_{max}(n) = \Theta(\log n)$. Our analysis confirms that the worst-case behavior of AVL trees is logarithmic.

Worst-Case Analysis: Bounding

As a second example, consider the sorting algorithm implemented by Program 2.2 (maliciously designed to waste a lot of time in somewhat inconspicuous ways). Due to the recursive nature of the algorithm, setting up a recurrence to characterize its running time is fairly easy:

$$t(n) = t(\lfloor n/2 \rfloor) + t(\lceil n/2 \rceil) + t(n-1) + c_1, \qquad \text{with } t(1) = c_2.$$

Solving it, however, turns out to be much harder: none of the methods in our bag of tricks works—generating functions and characteristic roots, with or without transformations, all fail. This failure suggests bounding $t(n)$ rather than deriving an exact expression for it. We shall proceed in several stages, first deriving rough upper and lower bounds for $t(n)$, then refining our bounds, and finally deriving an accurate characterization of the function, all through a mix of recurrence work and inductive reasoning. First note that $t(n)$ grows no faster than 3^n, since 3^n characterizes the function, $t'(n)$, obtained from $t(n)$ by replacing each $t(n/2)$ term with the larger term, $t(n-1)$. Then note that $t(n)$ grows faster than any polynomial: if we had $t(n) = \sum_{i=0}^{k} a_i n^i$, then, substituting into the recurrence, looking only at the terms of highest degree, and ignoring the floors and ceilings, we should get

$$a_k n^k + \cdots = a_k (n-1)^k + \cdots + 2a_k \left(\frac{n}{2}\right)^k + \cdots,$$

which simplifies to

$$a_k n^k + \cdots = a_k n^k + \frac{a_k}{2^{k-1}} n^k + \cdots,$$

which is impossible for large n. Trying to show that $t(n)$ is exponential, i.e., $\Omega(2^{n^\epsilon})$ for some ϵ, we get a similar contradiction: $t(n)$ does not grow that fast, because we have $\lim_{n \to \infty} 2^{(n-1)^\epsilon}/2^{n^\epsilon} = 0$. Thus we must conclude that $t(n)$ is a subexponential function. In fact, another approximation gives us an explicit subexponential bound for the function: since the tail recursion results in n iterations on a steadily decreasing range, an upper bound can be derived by treating each tail recursive call as if it were working on the entire original array, giving us (for n a power of 2):

$$t(n) \leq n \cdot \big(2t(n/2) + c\big).$$

Substituting $n = 2^k$, we get the new recurrence

$$g(k) \leq 2^{k+1} g(k-1) + c \cdot 2^k.$$

If we ignore the driving function and use repeated substitution, we see that $g(k)$ grows roughly as 2^{k^2}. In fact, if we assume that $g(k)$ is of the form $2^{\alpha k^2 + \beta k + \gamma}$, we can derive the bound

$$g(k) = O(2^{\frac{k}{2}(k+4)}),$$

so that $t(n)$ is $O(n^{a \log n})$ for some suitable constant, a. Thus $t(n)$ grows no faster than a subexponential. In fact, $t(n)$ is $\Omega(n^{b \log n})$, as can be shown by further arguments in the same style.[4]

Average-Case Analysis: Binary Search Trees

We now turn to average-case analysis. As noted earlier, such analysis presupposes knowledge of the probability distribution of the instances of the problem; as we also noted, such knowledge is, in fact, rarely available, so that a uniform distribution (all instances are equally likely) is typically assumed. The difficulties associated with worst-case analysis all appear in average-case analysis, but they are compounded by the need to compute averages, i.e., expressions of the form $\sum_i p_i f(i)$, where p_i is the instance probability of object i. Such sums may not always lend themselves to reduction to a closed form and thus encumber the analysis throughout. As even uniform distributions often give rise to binomial coefficients, average-case analysis often requires familiarity with the manipulation of such coefficients.

Consider the problem of characterizing the average behavior of standard binary search trees. Although the worst-case behavior for all three operations (search, insertion, and deletion) is linear, as is easily shown on a tree constructed from a sorted list, it is well known that these trees behave much better in practice and usually exhibit logarithmic behavior. How can we prove that such is indeed the correct average behavior, say for insertion? We begin by postulating the usual assumption of uniformity: for a given input size n, all $n!$ distinct input sequences (of n insertions) are equally likely. Now let us build the binary search tree from the "average" input sequence, which we denote $k_1, k_2, \ldots, k_n$. The first key in the sequence becomes the root of the tree, thereby splitting our task into two subtasks: building the left subtree and building the right subtree, respectively. The left subtree contains all keys smaller than k_1; assume that there are n_l such keys and let $n_r = n - 1 - n_l$. Note that the $(n-1)!$ possible input sequences beginning with key k_1 consist of all possible mergings of the $n_l!$ possible sequences of keys smaller than k_1 and the $n_r!$ possible sequences of keys larger than k_1. This property allows us to proceed recursively.

---

[4]Program 2.2 is a good example of a "reluctant" algorithm; in fact, this could be termed a "multiply-and-surrender" algorithm (as opposed to the divide-and-conquer algorithms of Chapter 7). In the words of the inventors of this algorithm: "The basic multiply and surrender strategy consists in replacing the problem at hand with two or more subproblems, each slightly simpler than the original, and continue multiplying subproblems and subsubproblems recursively in this fashion as long as possible. At some point the subproblems will all become so simple that their solution can no longer be postponed, and we will have to surrender. Experience shows that, in most cases, by the time this point is reached the total work will be substantially higher than what could have been wasted by a more direct approach."

Since each node, once inserted, remains in place, a suitable measure need only account for the distance from the root to every node in the final tree. One such measure is the internal path length, $I(T)$, which is simply the sum of these distances and which equals the total number of comparisons made by all the insertions while building the tree. The internal path length obeys the recurrence

$$I(T) = |T| - 1 + I(T_l) + I(T_r),$$

where T denotes a binary tree, $|T|$ its number of nodes, and T_l and T_r its left and right subtrees. Now we can write a recurrence for $I_{av}(n)$, the average internal path length of binary search trees over n keys:

$$I_{av}(n) = n - 1 + \frac{1}{n} \cdot \sum_{i=0}^{n-1} \big(I_{av}(i) + I_{av}(n - 1 - i)\big). \qquad (2.14)$$

While the real base case is $I_{av}(1) = 0$, we use $I_{av}(0) = 0$, because we need a value to substitute into the recurrence. The sum includes all n possible choices for the root of the tree (i.e., all possible choices for k_1, the first key in the sequence); since each choice determines a unique partition of the keys into the left and the right subtrees, we simply use the defining recurrence for the internal path length to obtain (2.14).

Now, this recurrence is not in a form which we can handle, because it involves all terms of lower order. Such recurrences, called *full-history recurrences*, occur commonly in the analysis of algorithms and can almost always be reduced to a form with a fixed number of terms by the simple expedient of subtracting the value at $n - 1$ from the value at n, with coefficients chosen so as to cancel lower-order terms. In the present case, we choose the subtraction

$$n \cdot I_{av}(n) - (n - 1) \cdot I_{av}(n - 1),$$

so that, upon substituting from Equation 2.14 and simplifying (the two sums cancel except for the highest term), we get

$$n \cdot I_{av}(n) - (n - 1) \cdot I_{av}(n - 1) = 2n - 2 + 2 I_{av}(n - 1)$$

or

$$n \cdot I_{av}(n) - (n + 1) \cdot I_{av}(n - 1) = 2n - 2.$$

Only two function terms appear; however, they do not have constant coefficients. This difficulty can be overcome by dividing throughout by $n(n + 1)$ to yield

$$\frac{1}{n + 1} \cdot I_{av}(n) - \frac{1}{n} \cdot I_{av}(n - 1) = 2 \cdot \frac{n - 1}{n(n + 1)},$$

and by substituting $g(n) = I_{av}(n)/(n+1)$, to get the linear recurrence with constant coefficients

$$g(n) - g(n-1) = 2 \cdot \frac{n-1}{n(n+1)}, \text{ with } g(0) = 0.$$

Repeated substitution gives

$$g(n) = 2 \sum_{i=1}^{n} \frac{i-1}{i(i+1)}.$$

But note that, for $i > 3$, we have

$$\frac{1}{i+3} < \frac{i-1}{i(i+1)} < \frac{1}{i+2},$$

so that we may write

$$g(n) = \Theta\left(\sum_{i=1}^{n} \frac{1}{i}\right).$$

The sum term appearing in this equation is known as a *harmonic number*, more precisely in this case, the nth harmonic number, H_n. Recalling from calculus that $\sum_{i=1}^{n} 1/i$ is bounded below by $\int_1^{n+1} (1/x)\, dx$ and bounded above by $1 + \int_1^{n} (1/x)\, dx$, we get

$$\ln(n+1) \le H_n \le \ln n + 1,$$

and thus $H_n = \Theta(\log n)$. Hence we have $g(n) = \Theta(\log n)$ and thus $I_{av}(n) = \Theta(n \log n)$. At great expense of time and patience, we could obtain a more precise characterization by keeping the driving term intact, but we have argued that algorithmic analysis should be in asymptotic terms and thus have no need for additional precision. The result confirms our expectations: the average internal path length of binary search trees is optimal in $\Theta(\ )$ terms.

Since a successful search stops at a node in the tree, its average behavior can be characterized in terms of the internal path length of the tree, namely, by $I(T)/|T|$. Since insertion takes place at external nodes, it corresponds to an unsuccessful search, and thus its behavior can be characterized in terms of the external path length of the tree, namely, by $E(T)/(|T|+1)$. A simple induction argument shows that $E(T) = I(T) + 2|T|$. Therefore, our results also imply that, on average, both successful and unsuccessful searches run in logarithmic time; however, the same reasoning cannot be extended to the average height of the trees—although it is, in fact, logarithmic as well.

Average-Case Analysis: Hash Tables

Of all data structures, that which relies most heavily on average behavior is the hash table. (The mechanics of hashing are discussed in standard textbooks on data structures, for which the reader should see the bibliography.) Although a complete analysis of most hashing schemes is extremely complex, let us take a look at *uniform hashing*, an abstraction of hashing with open addressing (i.e., collision resolution within the table), which requires that all possible table configurations produced by the insertion of m keys be equally likely. Nonrepeating uniform hashing may be implemented, for a table of size n, with a family of n hash functions, $\{ f_i \mid i = 1, \ldots, n \}$, which must obey two conditions. First, for $i \neq j$, we must have $f_i(k) \neq f_j(k)$ for any key k—the nonrepeating aspect. Locating an item within the table is then simply a matter of using the hashing functions in order until either the item is located or an empty location is found; in some sense, of course, this search is the basis of all well-known schemes for collision resolution (even linear probing, which uses $f_{i+1}(k) = f_i(k) \ominus 1$). What makes our hashing scheme unique is the second condition: each function in the family must provide, within the constraints placed on it by the functions with lower indices, a uniform distribution of the keys over the table. In other words, given a key k that has gone through i collisions, function f_{i+1} returns with equal probability any one of the remaining $n - i$ available addresses. Nonrepeating uniform hashing is neither practical (try to find such a family of functions!) nor significantly better than practical approximations (such as double hashing, which produces a key-dependent increment to determine the probe sequence of a key), but offers the great advantage of lending itself to analysis and thus providing a tight lower bound on the behavior of actual hashing schemes.

Let α be the loading factor of the table (i.e., the ratio of m, the number of items present within the table, to n, the size of the table) and consider the insertion of another key. Since all hash functions in the family provide perfectly uniform distributions, the probability of a collision at the address returned by f_1 is simply α. If a collision occurs, then we use f_2 to provide an alternate address; among the remaining $n - 1$ locations, $\alpha n - 1$ of which are used, f_2 chooses randomly, so that a second collision occurs with conditional probability $(\alpha n - 1)/(n - 1)$. Continuing in this fashion until an empty location is found, we derive the probability of needing at least i probes. Denote this probability by q_i; we have $q_1 = 1$ (the initial address within the table), $q_2 = \alpha$ (one collision occurred), and in general

$$q_i = \prod_{j=0}^{i-2} \frac{\alpha n - j}{n - j}$$

(where we use the convention that an empty product equals 1).

We want to derive the average length of a probe sequence, which is a sum of the type $\sum_i i \cdot p_i$, where p_i is the probability of needing exactly i probes; unfortunately, p_i is difficult to derive. But we have $q_i = \sum_{j \geq i} p_j$ and thus $\sum q_i = \sum i \cdot p_i$. Hence the average length of a probe sequence is

$$l_{av}(\alpha, n) = 1 + \alpha + \alpha \frac{\alpha n - 1}{n - 1} + \alpha \left(\frac{\alpha n - 1}{n - 1} \right) \left(\frac{\alpha n - 2}{n - 2} \right) + \cdots .$$

Note that the maximum number of probes cannot exceed (one plus) the number of items already in the table, αn, so that we can write the exact sum and simplify it:

$$
\begin{aligned}
l_{av}(\alpha, n) &= \sum_{i=1}^{\alpha n + 1} \prod_{j=0}^{i-2} \frac{\alpha n - j}{n - j} \\
&= \sum_{i=1}^{\alpha n + 1} \frac{(\alpha n)! \, (n - i + 1)!}{n! \, (\alpha n - i + 1)!} = \sum_{i=0}^{\alpha n} \frac{(\alpha n)! \, (n - i)!}{n! \, (\alpha n - i)!} .
\end{aligned}
$$

This avenue of enquiry does not look promising. We shall solve it yet, but consider for the moment the following simple derivation of an upper bound for l_{av}. Most of the problems encountered in the derivation of l_{av} arise as a consequence of the avoidance by function f_{i+1} of all locations so far returned by f_1 through f_i. Suppose, instead, that successive functions just return any location within the table, subject to the single condition that the probability of collision of any two functions of the family on any key is $1/n$; this approach also obeys our requirement for uniform hashing, namely, that all possible table configurations be equally likely. Then we have the much simpler relationship for the average insertion probe length, call it $\hat{l}_{av}$:

$$\hat{l}_{av}(\alpha) = \sum_{i=0}^{\infty} \alpha^i .$$

The sum is now taken to ∞, since we cannot be sure to terminate in finite time, due to the possibility of repetition. Now this is just our most basic sum, so that we get

$$\hat{l}_{av}(\alpha) = \frac{1}{1 - \alpha} . \tag{2.15}$$

That $\hat{l}_{av}$ is an upper bound for the desired l_{av} follows immediately from the fact that the conditional probability of collision in the latter steadily decreases and never exceeds the probability of collision in the former.

Let us now return to our derivation of l_{av}. The product term, which we rewrote as factorials, can be rewritten again so as to isolate the summation variable, i, in one binomial coefficient as follows:

$$\frac{(\alpha n)!\,(n-i)!}{n!\,(\alpha n - i)!} \;=\; \frac{m!\,(n-i)!}{n!\,(m-i)!}$$

$$= \frac{m!\,(n-m)!}{n!}\binom{n-i}{n-m}$$

$$= \binom{n-i}{n-m}\Big/\binom{n}{m}$$

Substituting in the expression for l_{av}, we get (in terms of m and n—we shall restore α later)

$$l_{av}(m/n, n) = \sum_{i=0}^{m}\binom{n-i}{n-m}\Big/\binom{n}{m}.$$

Now we apply a standard formula for manipulating binomial coefficients (which the reader may want to verify quickly by using induction on n),

$$\sum_{i=k}^{n-1}\binom{i}{k} = \binom{n}{k+1},$$

to yield, after some simplification and after reintroducing αn for m,

$$l_{av}(\alpha, n) = \frac{n+1}{(1-\alpha)n + 1}.$$

Note that, interestingly, nonrepeating uniform hashing behaves just as repeating uniform hashing performed on a table larger by one location (in (2.15), replace α with $m/(n+1)$, the loading factor for m keys stored in a table one larger), so that, for all practical purposes, the two behave identically. Since double hashing approximates very closely the behavior of uniform hashing, we conclude that hashing with open addressing is a very efficient data structure as long as the table is not heavily loaded. For instance, a loading factor of $\alpha = 0.5$ results in an average of just two probes for insertion, regardless of the size of the table; by comparison, a binary search tree can handle only a few items with an average of two comparisons and will require on the order of 20 comparisons for a million items. Even at much higher loading factors, the behavior remains excellent; for instance, with $\alpha = 0.8$, the expected number of probes is just five. Best of all, we can afford to aim for truly outstanding performance: at 50% loading, we do not even pay a storage penalty when compared with a binary search tree.

So far, we have analyzed only the behavior of insertion—or unsuccessful search; what about successful search? Note that locating an item in the table requires exactly as many probes as it took to insert it. This observation gives us a simple way to compute the average number of probes needed to locate an item within the table:

$$
\begin{aligned}
f_{av}(m,n) &= \frac{1}{m} \sum_{i=0}^{m-1} l_{av}(i/n, n) \\
&= \frac{1}{m} \sum_{i=0}^{m-1} \frac{n+1}{n-i+1} \\
&= \frac{n+1}{m} \left(\sum_{i=1}^{n+1} \frac{1}{i} - \sum_{i=1}^{n-m+1} \frac{1}{i} \right) \\
&= \frac{n+1}{m} \left(H_{n+1} - H_{n-m+1} \right) \\
&\approx \frac{n+1}{m} \ln\left(\frac{n+1}{n-m+1} \right).
\end{aligned}
$$

The last transformation follows from our earlier work with harmonic numbers. For large values of n and m, the last expression can be rewritten in terms of α only to give

$$
f_{av}(\alpha) \asymp \frac{1}{\alpha} \ln\left(\frac{1}{1-\alpha} \right).
$$

Note that, as expected, the average number of probes needed to locate an item (successful search) is less than the average number of probes needed to insert a new item (unsuccessful search).

2.3.2 Amortized Complexity

The method of analysis employed in Section 2.3.1, when applied to the concrete implementation of an abstract data type, usually amounts to determining the worst-case running time for each of the basic operations viewed in isolation. This type of analysis ignores the fact that algorithms perform sequences of operations; operations in such sequences often exhibit strong correlations so that the running time of the most complex possible sequence of operations, taken as a whole, may still be smaller than the bound computed by summing the bounds for the individual operations in the sequence. *Amortized complexity* is a technique for dealing with the complexity of sequences of operations.

Let us first place the goals of amortized complexity analysis in perspective. When we state that the amortized complexity of a sequence of m operations applied to a data structure of size n is $O(m \log n)$, we imply that, no matter how cleverly the sequence of m operations is designed by an adversary, the running time of the entire sequence is bounded by a constant times $m \log n$. Note that this is a worst-case analysis—the sequence of operations used in deriving the bound is designed by an adversary, who always picks the worst sequence possible. In comparing amortized analysis to traditional worst- and average-case analysis, we must note an essential difference. While both worst- and average-case complexity measures apply to individual operations, amortized complexity applies only to sequences of operations and says nothing about the actual running time of any particular operation. In fact, it is only possible to talk about the "amortized time of a particular (type of) operation" in a purely formal sense.

From the perspective of an algorithm that uses an abstract data type, an implementation that guarantees worst-case time per operation of $O(\log n)$ is no better than one that guarantees an amortized complexity for a sequence of m operations of $O(m \log n)$—unless the algorithm is real-time, in which case the existence of a bound on a per-operation basis is essential. This difference in style is also felt when we compare amortized and average-case analysis. If the average running time of an operation is $O(\log n)$, we expect each operation to take $\log n$ time and expect the entire sequence to take $O(m \log n)$ time. We must be prepared, however, to be disappointed, because the running time of a particular operation can exceed $\log n$ time and, what is worse, a particularly bad sequence of operations can take more than $O(m \log n)$ time. With amortized complexity we have no expectation that all operations in the sequence will take $\log n$ time, but occasional long running operations must be balanced by faster ones, since the overall running time for any sequence of length m is $O(m \log n)$.

One other aspect of amortized analysis is worth stressing: the technique is meant to be applied in environments where there are different types of operations, such as the implementation of an abstract data type. The sequences of operations are therefore heterogeneous and the mix by type arbitrary—even though a particular algorithm using the abstract data type may generate only biased mixes.

To provide a conceptual framework for understanding amortized complexity analysis, we consider an analogy. Imagine a physicist who is observing a system upon which certain forces act from time to time. Each action puts energy into the system but also releases energy to the outside world; the amounts of energy entering and leaving the system can be measured. For illustrative purposes, consider the system depicted in Figure 2.3. Associated with every possible state of the physical system is a potential, Φ. In the physical world this is a very common notion: objects such as the block of Figure 2.3 have potential energy

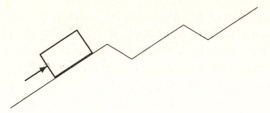

Figure 2.3: A Physical System Demonstrating the Principles of Amortized Complexity Analysis

that is accumulated as the object is raised above the surface of the earth; nuclei of radioactive isotopes have potential energy that is released during fission; and so on. The outside forces that act on the physical system provide energy to the system; some of the energy is absorbed, thereby raising the potential, and the rest is transmitted back to the outside world. Occasionally, after the potential has been raised sufficiently, the next small amount of energy added to the system can cause the release to the outside world of a significantly greater quantity of energy, energy taken from the system. In our concrete example of Figure 2.3, the outside forces might be small shoves in the uphill direction. Most of the energy of each shove is converted into potential energy, but a small amount is dissipated as heat caused by friction. Once in a while, however, a small shove will send the block over an edge, converting a large amount of potential energy into kinetic energy. More formally, our physicist observes that the following equation holds when each action is performed:

$$t_i + f_i = a_i + \Phi_{i-1} - \Phi_i. \tag{2.16}$$

In words, the useful energy transmitted to the environment, t_i, plus the amount of energy dissipated as heat due to friction, f_i, equals the amount of energy input, a_i, plus the amount of potential energy converted to kinetic energy, $\Phi_{i-1} - \Phi_i$. If the potential energy goes up ($\Phi_i > \Phi_{i-1}$), then not all of the available new energy can be released to the environment. Nothing in this equation prevents raising the potential energy of the system by more than a_i through absorption of energy from the environment, i.e., by having a negative t_i or f_i—although, in the physical world, such behavior is forbidden by the laws of thermodynamics.

In our analogy, the physical system represents the data structure that implements the abstract data type, and the outside forces that act on the system stand for the individual operations in the sequence. The quantity t_i is the actual (observed) running time of the ith operation, while a_i is the *amortized time* of the operation. Note that a_i and Φ_i are "artificial" quantities—artificial in the sense that they are human constructs and not "natural," like the potential energy of physical systems. We intend the amortized time of an operation, unlike its actual running time, to be a constant, or at least a "stable" value, just like the amount of energy imparted to the block by each little shove. The f_i term is used to balance the equation; as in the physical world, f_i must be nonnegative. Even though each operation in the sequence may be the same, e.g., a FIND, the t_i may vary widely; in our analogy, some shoves send the object over the edge, whereas most just inch it slightly uphill. The equivalent of the second law of thermodynamics is that all operations take real computing time, i.e., even the simplest operations take a few CPU cycles.

Notice that, if we can establish (2.16) by suitable choices for the amortized time of the basic operations and for the potential function, then we can bound the time of the entire sequence of operations, because we have

$$\sum_{i=1}^{m}(t_i + f_i) = \sum_{i=1}^{m} a_i + \Phi_0 - \Phi_m,$$

where each f_i is nonnegative and the potential function is designed so that $\Phi_0 - \Phi_m$ is nonpositive. The initial potential, Φ_0, is typically zero, corresponding to an empty initial data structure. In this case and if, in fact, a_i is "stable" (i.e., the sum $\sum_{i=1}^{m} a_i$ is easy to compute), we can obtain a bound on $\sum_{i=1}^{m} t_i$. It is important that a_i depend only on the basic operation being performed (such as whether it is a FIND, INSERT, or DELETE) and on the current size of the data structure, but not on the position of the operation in the sequence, i.e., not on i. In this way the bound applies to any sequence of length m. The amortized time of an operation is sometimes referred to as "the average time of an operation in a worst-case sequence," since it is essentially $\sum_{i=1}^{m} t_i / m$, if the losses due to friction and $\Phi_0 - \Phi_m$ are small constants. Lastly, notice that the bound on $\sum t_i$ is not necessarily tight for each sequence of operations. As long as we have $\sum f_i \geq 0$ and $\Phi_0 - \Phi_m \leq 0$, then $\sum a_i$ is a bound for $\sum t_i$, but if we have $\sum f_i \gg 0$ or $\Phi_0 - \Phi_m \ll 0$ for some particular sequence, then the bound is not tight for that sequence.

Amortized complexity is closely associated with *self-adjusting data structures*. A self-adjusting data structure is one that changes its shape as a side effect of the operations performed upon it. Of course, all data structures change shape in response to certain operations—a binary search tree clearly must grow or shrink in response to INSERTs and DELETEs. The data structures we have in mind also change shape when innocuous operations, such as FIND, are performed. To see why self-adjusting data structures and amortized complexity are closely allied, consider binary search trees, both in their simple, unbalanced form (for which we performed an average-case analysis in Section 2.3.1) and in their balanced forms, such as AVL or red-black trees (see Section 3.3), where the height of the tree never exceeds a small constant times the logarithm of the size. Neither of these data structures is self-adjusting. In the unbalanced form, if a sequence of INSERTs produces a leaf at depth n, then this sequence can be extended by an arbitrarily long sequence of FINDs for the key in this leaf and the total running time for the sequence will be $\Theta(mn)$. The inability to readjust the tree during the sequence of FINDs means that the tree cannot react to the particular sequence of operations and the total running time of the sequence cannot be bounded by a constant times $m \log n$. On the other hand, the balanced forms of binary search trees avoid the need for reorganization during FINDs—the rebalancing work done during INSERT and DELETE guarantees that each FIND takes no more than $\log n$ time. Balancing exemplifies the classical approach to ensuring efficient operations: guarantee a strong bound on the running time of each operation by complex reorganization rules that are applied every time the data structure must change shape. There is a middle ground. In the self-adjusting data structure known as a *splay tree*, the details of which we shall present shortly, searching for the element with key x makes subsequent FIND operations less costly. The freedom to reorganize during FINDs has an additional benefit: not only does the running time of the worst sequence of m operations not exceed $m \log n$, but also that of biased sequences of operations, especially where the bias changes over time—a very realistic model of real-world computation—may well be noticeably smaller and thus outperform the more rigid balanced tree structures.

The notion of having a data structure sense the reference pattern and adjust itself accordingly is not new. The effectiveness of the heuristic of path compression in UNION-FIND, the topic of Section 3.2, was known long before a formal analysis was derived. In another context entirely (virtual memory management), the self-adjusting data structure with perhaps the greatest impact on daily computing is the unsorted linear list coupled with a heuristic known as *move-to-front*. At the logical level, we maintain an array of records on which we perform a linear search for each FIND. As part of the internal workings of the FIND operation, when the record with key x is found in position i, it is promoted to position 1, while the records currently in positions 1 through $i-1$ are demoted to positions 2 through i. Of course, a linked list implementation, while not saving any time during the search, allows the move to the front to be accomplished in constant time. This basic strategy, implemented in yet a different manner, is the essence of the page-replacement policy known as *least recently used* (LRU). Here the keys are ranges of addresses, and the records are page table entries. Since the memory management hardware needs to detect rapidly whether a page is currently in memory, the linear search must be avoided and the linear list of page table entries is organized so that direct lookup by key is possible. The linear list is maintained logically by having the hardware place a time stamp in the associated record whenever the page is referenced. The current ordering of the elements of the list can be reconstructed by sorting on the time stamps. This maintenance is done in software whenever a page fault occurs—actually all that needs to be done is to find the page in physical memory with the oldest time stamp, since the logical shift of positions 1 through $i-1$ into positions 2 through i will bump only this one page out of memory. As a consequence of the locality of reference of most programs, use of this self-adjusting structure yields an effective page-replacement algorithm. Despite its good performance in real systems, where the sequences are strongly biased, the worst-case performance of this algorithm is poor because the wrong sequence of FIND operations can cause each operation to take linear time—in the virtual memory environment certain programs exhibit thrashing.

Let us now move from motivation and intuition to a specific example of a self-adjusting data structure and its amortized complexity analysis. Our example, the *splay tree*, looks like an ordinary binary search tree: the binary search tree property always holds at every node, and there are no extra fields for flags, counts, or height information. The only operation that is directly performed upon the tree is *splaying*. The standard operations of FIND, INSERT, and DELETE are all defined in terms of this basic operation. The operation SPLAY(x) is essentially a FIND, but it differs in one major respect: after the record with key x is found, this node is promoted to the root of the tree by a sequence of rotation operations. These rotations, of which there are three basic templates (and their mirror images), are pictured in Figure 2.4. Depending on the relationship between the node with key x, its parent, and its grandparent (if any), the tree is locally reorganized as indicated. This local reorganization is repeated until the node with key x becomes the root of the tree. Figure 2.5 shows the step-by-step reorganization that occurs during a typical SPLAY operation. There is one additional detail: when the search phase is unsuccessful, the last leaf examined before reaching an empty child is promoted to the root. This node is always the inorder successor or inorder predecessor of the key for which we are searching, depending on whether the last downward move was to the left or to the right, respectively.

All three operations, FIND, INSERT, and DELETE, can be implemented in terms of SPLAY. FIND(x) is nothing but SPLAY(x), followed by a constant-time check of the root to see whether or not the desired key was in the tree. INSERT(x) is SPLAY(x), followed by a constant-time correction: assuming that key x was not in the tree, it is added at the root as indicated in Figure 2.6. The figure is drawn under the assumption that the key promoted to the root is the inorder predecessor of x; a similar correction is performed if the key promoted to the

(a) The node being accessed, x, has no grandparent.

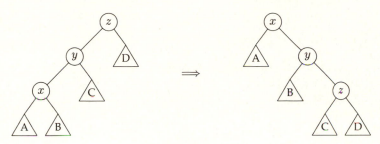

(b) The zig-zig pattern

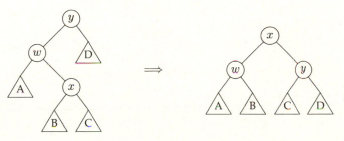

(c) The zig-zag pattern

Figure 2.4: The Three Basic Rotations Used to Implement SPLAY

root is the inorder successor of x. Since a well-balanced tree certainly cannot be harmful, the correction performed as the final step of INSERT is counterintuitive: it pushes down by one level all of the nodes in half the tree. A better practice is to insert key x as a leaf and then promote it to the root as if it were already present—although this approach slightly complicates the analysis (see Exercise 2.37). DELETE is the most complex of the three standard operations, requiring two calls to SPLAY. First we perform SPLAY(x) to bring the required node to the root. If we now remove the root, we are left with two splay trees that we need to join into one. This last task is relatively easy because every key in what was the right subtree of the root is larger than any key in what was the left subtree. To perform the join, we first reorganize one of the subtrees, say the

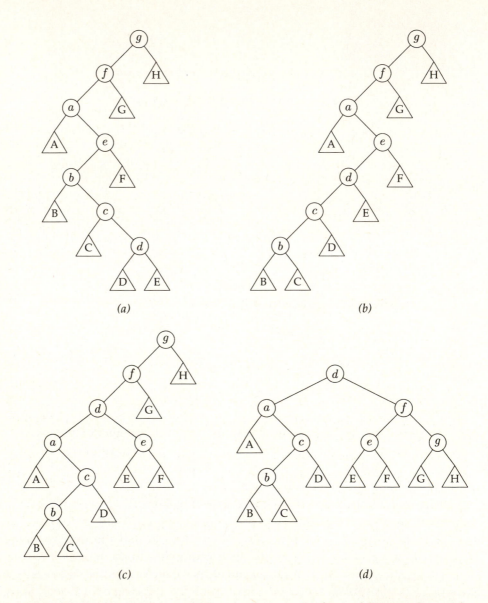

(a)

(b)

(c)

(d)

Figure 2.5: The Sequence of Transformations Performed During SPLAY(d)

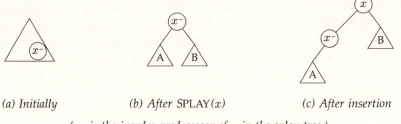

(a) Initially   (b) After SPLAY(x)   (c) After insertion

(x^- is the inorder predecessor of x in the splay tree.)

Figure 2.6: Insertion of Key x into a Splay Tree

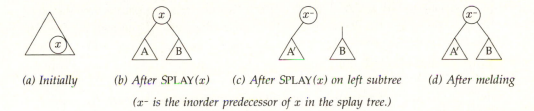

(a) Initially   (b) After SPLAY(x)   (c) After SPLAY(x) on left subtree   (d) After melding

(x^- is the inorder predecessor of x in the splay tree.)

Figure 2.7: Deletion of Key x from a Splay Tree

left one, by again performing SPLAY(x), this time on this subtree. As neither x nor its inorder successor is present within the tree, this splaying must return the inorder predecessor of x, and the root of the reorganized tree has no right child. We then attach the former right subtree as the right child of this new root. Figure 2.7 traces the process pictorially.

Looking at the three basic rotations of Figure 2.4, one may easily doubt that every sequence of m FIND, INSERT, and DELETE operations, starting with an empty tree that grows to a maximum size of n, consumes only $O(m \log n)$ time. Two of the three rotations, the first and second, do not seem to decrease the height of the tree, while the third does raise subtrees B and C, but lowers subtree D. Nonetheless, an amortized analysis verifies that the $O(m \log n)$ bound on total running time is correct. First we need to define the potential, Φ, of a splay tree. Define $w(x)$, the weight of node x, to be the number of nodes in the subtree rooted at x (including node x) and define $r(x)$, the rank of node x, to be $\lg w(x)$. The potential of the splay tree is then defined to be $\Phi = \sum r(x)$, as x varies over all nodes in the tree. Notice that, although the root has the largest rank ($\lg n$) of any node in the tree, leaves contribute more to the potential than the root, since a leaf contributes to the weight of each of its ancestors. Also, leaves at greater depth contribute more than leaves that are relatively nearer the root. In computing the running time of a SPLAY operation, we shall use as the measure of time the distance of the node from the root. This choice is in line with the measure used in the previous subsection and is also equivalent to counting the number of rotations that need to be performed, since the ratio is essentially two-to-one. We are now in a position to prove our crucial result.

Lemma 2.1 The amortized time to splay a tree of n nodes at node x is $O(\log n)$.

$\square$

Proof: In terms of the general presentation given earlier, we prove: if the energy input by the action of splaying at node x is $3(\lg n - r(x)) + 1$, then Equation 2.16 can be satisfied, with t_i equal to the depth of x and with f_i positive. As we have $r(x) \geq 0$, the lemma follows. Note that $\lg n$ is the rank of the root of the tree regardless of the shape of the tree, because the weight of the tree is n.

Our proof proceeds by tallying the effect of each rotation on the terms of (2.16); in particular, we examine the change in potential induced by a single rotation. If node x is already at the root, no rotation is performed, the potential of the splay tree remains unchanged, $r(x)$ equals $\lg n$, and the right-hand side of (2.16) reduces to 1. Since the depth of x is zero, our time measure for the splaying is zero. To satisfy (2.16), we record that one unit of energy is lost to "friction."

In what follows, primes will be used to distinguish ranks and weights after completion of a rotation from ranks and weights before completion of the rotation. We shall show that, when a rotation is applied, $3(r'(x) - r(x))$ (or $3(r'(x) - r(x)) + 1$ in the case of the first rotation) is greater than the change in potential (new minus old) plus the time charged for performing the rotation. It then follows that $3(\lg n - r(x)) + 1$ is the correct amount of input energy to associate with a SPLAY action: the sequence of rotations results in a sequence of ranks for node x, $r(x)$, $r'(x)$, $r''(x)$, ..., $r^{(k)}(x)$, and

$$3(r^{(k)}(x) - r^{(k-1)}(x)) + \cdots + 3(r''(x) - r'(x)) + 3(r'(x) - r(x)) + 1$$
$$= 3(r^{(k)}(x) - r(x)) + 1$$
$$= 3(\lg n - r(x)) + 1$$

bounds the accumulated change in potential, $\Phi_i - \Phi_{i-1}$, plus the total cost of the rotations. The addition of one is only necessary if the first template is applied. Also, as $3(r^{(j)}(x) - r^{(j-1)}(x))$ is strictly greater than the change in potential plus the time charged for performing a basic step, the excess energy is lost to friction.

There are three cases, each corresponding to one rotation template of Figure 2.4:

1. Referring to Figure 2.4(a), we see that only nodes x and y can change rank, so the change in potential (plus one charged to the rotation) is given by

$$1 + r'(x) + r'(y) - r(x) - r(y)$$
$$< 1 + r'(x) - r(x) \qquad \text{since } w(y) > w'(y)$$
$$< 1 + 3\big(r'(x) - r(x)\big) \qquad \text{since } w'(x) > w(x).$$

2. Referring to Figure 2.4(b), we see that the charge for the running time is two and that the change in potential is due entirely to changes in the ranks of nodes x, y, and z; thus we have

$$2 + r'(x) + r'(y) + r'(z) - r(x) - r(y) - r(z)$$
$$= 2 + r'(y) + r'(z) - r(x) - r(y) \quad \text{since } w'(x) = w(z)$$
$$< 2 + r'(x) + r'(z) - 2r(x) \qquad \text{since } w'(x) > w'(y) \text{ and } w(y) > w(x)$$
$$< 3\big(r'(x) - r(x)\big).$$

Proving the correctness of this last inequality requires a number of algebraically straightforward, but obscure, steps. The most important realization is that for s and t in the triangle bounded by $s > 0$, $t > 0$, and $s + t \leq 1$, the sum $\lg s + \lg t$ is maximized for $s = t = \frac{1}{2}$, with $\lg s + \lg t = -2$. (Clearly the maximum occurs along the line $s + t = 1$, and then the application of some simple calculus gives us this result.) After eliminating one multiple of $r'(x) - r(x)$ from both sides of the inequality, we rearrange $2 + r'(z) - r(x) < 2r'(x) - 2r(x)$ into the equivalent inequality, $\big(r(x) - r'(x)\big) + \big(r'(z) - r'(x)\big) < -2$. Now $r(x) - r'(x) = \lg\big(w(x)/w'(x)\big)$ and $r'(z) - r'(x) = \lg\big(w'(z)/w'(x)\big)$ and, considering the situation depicted in Figure 2.4(b), we see that $w(x) + w'(z) < w'(x)$ (in fact, the left-hand side is exactly one less than the right, due to the presence of the node with key y), so that we can conclude that $w(x)/w'(x) + w'(z)/w'(x) < 1$ and thus $\lg\big(w(x)/w'(x)\big) + \lg\big(w'(z)/w'(x)\big) < -2$, so that the inequality is established.

3. Proceeding as in the previous case, we get

$$2 + r'(x) + r'(w) + r'(y) - r(x) - r(w) - r(y)$$
$$< 2 + r'(w) + r'(y) - 2r(x) \quad \text{since } w'(x) = w(y) \text{ and } w(x) < w(w)$$
$$< 2\big(r'(x) - r(x)\big)$$
$$< 3\big(r'(x) - r(x)\big),$$

where the result on the maximum of $\lg s + \lg t$ on the triangle bounded by $s > 0$, $t > 0$, and $s + t \leq 1$ is again used to establish the inequality $2 + r'(w) + r'(y) - 2r(x) < 2\big(r'(x) - r(x)\big)$.

Q.E.D.

Table 2.2: The Effect of Splaying on Rank and Potential

(a) Weights of subtrees A–H used in part (b)

Subtree	A	B	C	D	E	F	G	H
Weight	20	15	12	15	14	8	30	22

(b) Rank and potential changes

Step	$r(d)$	Δr	Contribution of nodes a–g to Φ	$\Delta\Phi$	Frictional loss
Initially	4.524		42.406		
1	5.883	1.359	43.314	1.108	0.969
2	6.476	0.593	41.514	−1.800	1.579
3	7.160	0.684	39.989	−1.525	1.577

This proof does not fully capture the interplay of potential, tree shape, and splaying. In order to illustrate this interplay, consider the splaying operation depicted by Figure 2.5. First let the weights of subtrees A–H be as given in part (a) of Table 2.2. Part (b) shows the resulting values for the three steps of the splaying operation depicted in Figure 2.5. The crucial argument buried in the proof is that $3\bigl(r'(d) - r(d)\bigr)$ must be greater than the change in potential plus two—plus two because all rotations during the splaying of node d involve the grandparent. As the essence of amortized complexity is utilizing potential energy, energy stored in the data structure during previous steps, to pay for occasional operations where the running time exceeds the allocation of the energy associated with the current action, step 2 is very interesting: $3\bigl(r'(d) - r(d)\bigr)$ is not large enough to cover the cost of the rotation, and potential energy must be extracted from the tree. In step 1, $3\bigl(r'(d) - r(d)\bigr)$ is greater than two, and the algorithm stores energy in the tree—energy which can be released later, if necessary. Step 3 offers an example of frictional losses: the change in the rank of node d is large enough to pay for the rotation, but energy is released from the data structure and dissipated. Actually, in every step there is some loss of energy, since the inequality in the proof is strict. One must understand that, were the weights of the subtrees to be different, the values of Table 2.2(b) would change accordingly, even though exactly the same sequence of rotations would be performed. For instance, if the subtrees A–H are all empty, then the change in potential is nonpositive at every step, as the resulting values of Table 2.3 show. In particular, potential energy is now used to pay for step 3. Notice that the minimum potential energy is associated with

Table 2.3: The Effect of Setting the Weights of Subtrees A–H to Zero

Step	$r(d)$	Δr	Contribution of Nodes a–g to Φ	$\Delta\Phi$	Frictional loss
Initially	0		12.300		
1	1.585	1.585	12.300	0.000	2.755
2	2.322	0.737	10.300	−2.000	2.211
3	2.807	0.485	6.977	−3.322	2.777

a well-balanced tree. Since SPLAY will take no more than logarithmic time in a balanced tree, there is no need to store a lot of potential energy in the tree. Only as the tree gets unbalanced does the algorithm need to store potential energy, to guard against a time-consuming SPLAY step where the node is at the end of a linear path. Note that each rotation modifies the balance of the tree; moreover, each rotation within the same sequence of rotations may have a positive or a negative effect on the balance of a tree, depending on the relative sizes of the subtrees moved in the process. This variability is reflected in the values of $\Delta\Phi$ in each of the two tables—where, for example, the first step leaves the balance unchanged in one case, while damaging it in the other.

What does hold for any assignment of weights to the subtrees is that, at each step, the sum of the cost of the rotation and the change in potential is less than $3(r'(x) - r(x))$; by telescoping the individual steps into a single splaying action, it follows that $3\lg n + 1$ units of energy, plus any potential energy extracted from the tree, suffice to cover the cost of the splaying step. This relationship is the essence of the proof of Lemma 2.1

Exercise 2.3 Study the effect of each rotation of Figure 2.4 on the rank of node x and the potential of the tree, under various assumptions about the sizes of the subtrees. In particular, consider the cases of a balanced tree, in which a subtree one level higher in the tree is twice as large, and of an unbalanced tree, such as one in which the unexplored subtrees attached to the search path are all the same, large size.   □

We now need to look at the running times of our standard operations: FIND, INSERT, and DELETE. FIND is no problem, since it is just SPLAY, but the final adjustments made by INSERT and DELETE affect the potential of the tree, and this energy must be accounted for in order to bound the time of a sequence of user-visible operations.

Theorem 2.2 The amortized time complexity of FIND, INSERT, and DELETE operations on a tree of size n is $O(\log n)$.   □

Proof: With each INSERT, we associate $4 \lg n + 2$ units of energy, where n is the size of the tree after insertion. Of this amount, $3 \lg n + 1$ is allocated to the SPLAY step. The additional $\lg n$ is more than enough to cover the change in potential caused by the actual insertion: all nodes maintain their ranks, except the old root, which loses its right subtree; the new root has rank $\lg n$. The additional $+1$ covers the time needed to do the actual insertion. Similarly, for DELETE, an input of $7 \lg n + 3$ units of energy is enough to perform the two SPLAY steps, cover the constant-time overhead of the deletion, and account for the change in potential during the joining of the two subtrees. (In fact, looking at the actual sizes of the trees involved in DELETE, we see that $6 \lg n + 3$ suffices.)

Q.E.D.

As an empty tree has a potential of zero and a nonempty tree has nonnegative potential, this theorem implies that a sequence of m FIND, INSERT, and DELETE operations, performed on an initially empty tree, cannot take more than $O(m \log n)$ real time. The sequence of operations can run faster and, to reiterate an essential feature of amortized complexity, a given step can take more than the average amount of time. A single example serves to show both of these facets of amortized complexity: the sequence of INSERTs with arguments $1, 2, \ldots, n$, followed by FIND(1) takes a total of $2n$ real time, with the FIND accounting for half the total. On the other hand, some sequences of operations must take time proportional to $m \log n$, so that the worst-case running time for a sequence of m operations that results in a tree of n keys is $\Theta(m \log n)$. It is easy for an adversary to design a sequence of FIND operations which take $\log n$ time each, since a tree of n nodes must have at least one node at $\lfloor \lg n \rfloor$ depth.

The linear worst-case performance for a single operation may make splay trees inappropriate for real-time applications. Another problem arises from the need to maintain the path back to the root, a path that might grow on occasion to the size of the tree. Several alternatives exist which eliminate the need for this potentially large amount of additional storage. If one bit per node is available and the programming language permits the necessary manipulations, we can invert links on the way down the tree, recording the path in the tree itself. Another approach, also a standard data structure "trick," is to store the tree in left-child, right-sibling representation, where the right pointer of a right or only child points to the parent. This trick requires no additional storage within the node, but increases the coefficient that governs the real running time and makes the code more complex. Readers not familiar with these techniques are referred to the standard textbooks on data structures listed in the bibliography.

An interesting third alternative, known as *top-down splaying*, is pictured in Figure 2.8. This algorithm, unlike the simple splaying algorithm discussed so far, does its work on the way down the tree, but, like that algorithm, leaves the node being searched for at the root of the tree. On the downward search for key x, the original tree is at all times broken into three binary search trees: a middle tree, M, which contains key x; a left tree, L, in which every node has a key smaller than the smallest key of the middle tree; and a right tree, R, in which every node has a key larger than the largest key in M. Initially, L and R are empty and M is the entire tree. The algorithm is as follows:

- Repeat the following until the root of the tree is the node for which we are searching, at which time perform the final relinking step of Figure 2.8(d) and stop.

  - If the child of the root is the node for which we are searching, perform the single rotation of Figure 2.8(a), or its mirror image, to bring the node to the root.

  - Determine which search pattern from Figure 2.8(b) and (c), and their mirror images, describes the situation and apply the appropriate rotation.

The obvious modifications are needed to deal with keys not present in the tree. Notice that only five pointers need be maintained: pointers to the three subtrees and pointers to the inner corners of the outer subtrees. While the amortized time for a top-down splay is also $O(\log n)$, the algorithm does not reorganize the tree in the same manner as the splaying algorithm described earlier—in consequence of which a different proof must also be developed.

We shall have occasion to use amortized analysis in later chapters. For now, let us point out that, in the analysis of combinatorial algorithms, amortized analysis is often to be preferred to worst- or average-case analysis for the data structures involved. Putting things in proper perspective, we see that there are two underlying reasons for this: first, no algorithm ever uses an operation on a data structure in isolation, but always uses an abstract data type, so that the interaction of the various operations defined in the package must be taken into account; and secondly, each combinatorial algorithm uses a given package in a unique manner, in that only certain request sequences can be produced, so that the overall time spent may differ considerably from the same measure applied to all conceivable sequences. On the other hand, worst- and average-case analyses remain the tools of choice for the analysis of the combinatorial algorithm itself, because it typically pursues a single goal rather than the combination of goals and operations offered by a data structure package.

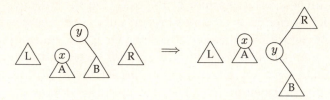

(a) The node being accessed, x, is the child of the root.

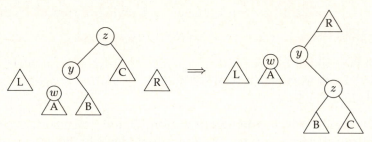

(b) The zig-zig pattern: x is in the subtree rooted at w.

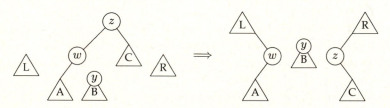

(c) The zig-zag pattern: x is in the subtree rooted at y.

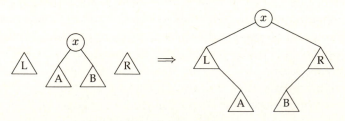

(d) The relinking step

Figure 2.8: Top-Down Splaying

2.4 Analysis as a Design Tool

As we saw at the end of Section 2.1, a problem is defined to be intractable if the performance of the most efficient known algorithm is exponential in the size of the problem for at least some instances. This definition does not, however, make the situation of a programmer faced with an intractable problem totally hopeless. Even if the worst-case performance of an algorithm is bad, it may have better average performance; many backtracking algorithms, for which see Volume II, fall into this category. Furthermore, the instances of theoretically intractable problems generated in the commercial/industrial environment in the normal course of business are often not average, since they do not range uniformly or randomly over the set of possible instances. The presence of additional structure in the instances encountered in practice often biases the distribution of instances toward a subset of easier instances, on which an otherwise exponential algorithm may run to completion within reasonable time. At this point, even small gains in the constant factors describing the behavior of the algorithm may mean all the difference between solving only toy-size instances and solving real ones. The reader may wonder why anybody must be reminded to code as efficiently as possible—who would do otherwise? In the framework of a complete program, however, it is surprisingly hard to produce with any consistency code that is both readable and efficient.

As an example of the required mix of algorithmic design and efficient coding, let us consider a naïve method for solving the n-queens problem of Section 1.5: try all possible placements for the n queens until a solution is found or all placements have been tried. Using a top-down design methodology, we first produce a skeleton of the main program, illustrated in Program 2.3.

The first potential pitfalls are to consider board to be an $n \times n$ array of Boolean values modelling the physical chessboard, and to consider a placement to be any way of positioning the queens, save placing two on the same square. This approach would result in n^2 ways to place the first queen, $n^2 - 1$ ways to place the second queen after the first has been placed, etc., for a total of

$$n^2(n^2 - 1)(n^2 - 2) \cdots (n^2 - n + 1) = \frac{n^2!}{(n^2 - n)!}$$

placements. For $n = 8$, this formula evaluates to 178,462,987,637,760. A moment's reflection shows that there must be exactly one queen per column, so a better approach is to declare

```
type board = array [1..n] of 1..n;
```

where $A[i]=j$ means that the queen in column i is located in row j. The solution to the four-queens problem given in Figure 1.14 would be represented by

```
program NQueens(output);
  label 1;
  const n = ...;
  type board = ...;
  var placement: board;
  function Solution(var (* for speed *) A: board): boolean;
    (* Determine whether placement in A solves the problem. *)
    begin
      ... not shown ...
    end; (* Solution *)
  function Next(var A: board): boolean;
    (* Given a placement of the n queens, return the "next" placement
       in some ordering or an indication that the placement was
       the final one (Next := false).  A is changed as a side effect.
       The calling routine should not change A between calls.
       A must be initialized externally to the first placement. *)
    begin
      ... not shown ...
    end; (* Next *)
  begin
    ...; (* Initialize variable placement to first placement. *)
    while not Solution(placement) do
      if not Next(placement)
        then begin
                writeln('No solutions to ',n:1,'-queens problem');
                goto 1 (* stop *)
              end;
    ...; (* Write out a solution. *)
1:
  end. (* NQueens *)
```

Program 2.3: Skeleton for a Solution to the n-Queens Problem Based on Successively Trying all Possible Placements for the Queens

A=[2,4,1,3]. This representation reduces the number of placements to n^n; for $n = 8$, this formula yields 16,777,216 placements. Though not a particularly difficult transition to make in this problem, this new representation of the board is interesting because it no longer directly models the physical board of the problem statement. This encoding of the board has effectively changed an explicit constraint (no two queens may occupy the same column) into an implicit one. The representation has the additional property that it suggests an ordering of the placements.

Definition 2.5 Let Σ be a finite set ordered by a total ordering relation, $<$. If x and y are strings in Σ^*, with x_i the ith character in the string x, then x is *lexicographically less* than y, written $x \prec y$, if either

1. there exists j such that $x_j < y_j$ and, for all $i < j$, $x_i = y_i$; or

2. length$(x) <$ length(y) and, for all $i \leq$ length(x), $x_i = y_i$.

$\square$

In plain English, the strings are compared until they disagree or until one string runs out of characters. The term *lexicographic* comes from the fact that this is the ordering (more or less) used in the dictionary. In our problem, Σ is the set of integers in the range 1 through n (the integers, not their representations as strings of Arabic numerals) and the strings must all be of length n. For instance, $[2, 5, 4, 7, 1, 8, 3, 8] \prec [2, 5, 4, 7, 3, 6, 2, 7]$, since they first differ in the fifth place and $1 < 3$. That all strings have fixed length, n, means that the concept of "next placement" can be formalized; $y = next(x)$ if $x \prec y$ and $\nexists z$ such that $x \prec z \prec y$. Intuitively, $next(x)$ is formed by advancing the rightmost queen one position, if possible. If not, then the rightmost queen is placed on row 1 and the next rightmost queen is advanced one position, unless it is also on the final row. For instance, we have $next([2, 5, 4, 7, 4, 8, 5, 3]) = [2, 5, 4, 7, 4, 8, 5, 4]$ and $next([5, 4, 7, 6, 2, 8, 8, 8]) = [5, 4, 7, 6, 3, 1, 1, 1]$.

Further analysis suggests another improvement to the general strategy: convert another explicit constraint into an implicit constraint by allowing only one queen per row as well as per column. This conversion reduces the number of placements to $n!$, since there are n placements for the first queen, $n - 1$ placements for the second queen, given that the first has been placed, $n - 2$ placements for the third queen, given that the first two have been placed, etc., and reduces the work that needs to be performed by Solution to checking only for conflicts along diagonals. While a complexity of $n!$ is still considered intractable, 8! is only 40,320 and thus well within our ability to compute. Although the logical functioning of Next has not changed, the strings returned by Next are no longer chosen from all strings of length n, but from the permutations of one through n. That is, we retain the lexicographic ordering, but consider only strings, all elements of which are distinct. For instance, we have $next([2, 5, 3, 1, 4, 8, 7, 6])$ $= [2, 5, 3, 1, 6, 4, 7, 8]$. Note that enforcing the condition A[i] <> A[j] for i <> j appears to take considerable computation time, while enforcing the range of 1 through n on elements of A does not, so that the full savings expected from reducing the number of placements from n^n to $n!$ might not be realized.

Exercise 2.4 Without looking at the programs on the following pages, write (and debug!) the version of the function Next that returns the next permutation of 1 through n.

$\square$

```
const n = ...;
type board = array [1..n] of 1..n;
function Next(var A: board): boolean;
  (* Given a board position A with all queens in distinct rows and
      columns, return the next board position with the same property.
      A should not be changed by the caller between calls and must be
      initialized by the caller to the first such placement, A[i] := i.
      If no further placement exists, then Next returns false. *)
  label 1;
  var inuse: array [1..n] of boolean;
        (* records rows that are currently occupied *)
      i, j, k, m: integer;
  begin
    (* Since there is only one possible place for queen n,
        queen n-1 will need to be repositioned as well. *)
    for i := 1 to n-2 do inuse[A[i]] := true;
    inuse[A[n]] := false;
    i := n - 1; (* Attempt to push queen i forward. *)
    repeat
      inuse[A[i]] := false;
      for j := A[i]+1 to n do
        (* Look for an unoccupied row farther along. *)
        if not inuse[j]
          then begin
                  A[i] := j;
                  inuse[j] := true;
                  for k := i+1 to n do
                    (* Place the next queen on as low a row as possible. *)
                    begin
                      m := 1;
                      while inuse[m] do m := m + 1; (* cannot push m to n+1 *)
                      A[k] := m;
                      inuse[m] := true (* row now in use *)
                    end;
                  Next := true;
                  goto 1 (* return *)
                end;
      (* No way to push queen i onward. *)
      i := i - 1
    until i = 0; (* Last placement was in A. *)
    Next := false;
1:
  end; (* Next *)
```

Program 2.4: An Inefficient Algorithm for Generating the Next Placement

Table 2.4: Running Times for Generating All Permutations of n Elements

n	4	5	6	7	8
Statement count	705	4206	28,681	223,518	1,967,601
$T(n)$	1.00	1.19	1.36	1.51	1.66

Table 2.4 shows the running time for the code of Program 2.4 for small values of n. The cost of running the simple driver that repeatedly calls Next has been removed from the data. The entry in the row labelled $T(n)$ measures the average time spent computing the next placement from the present placement, where the average time to compute the next placement for permutations of length 4 is taken as one time unit. That the values of $T(n)$ increase as n increases indicates that the routine does steadily more work per call, which implies that the overall algorithm is not $O(n!)$. Ideally, $T(n)$ should remain constant, which would indicate that the time to compute the next permutation is independent of n.

This program is a direct encoding of the method which a human would most likely employ to find the next placement on a physical chessboard. It finds the rightmost queen that can be pushed forward without creating a row conflict with any queen to its left and then successively places the queens to its right on the lowest numbered rows possible. The code has the merit of matching our intuitive approach to the problem. Unfortunately it is inefficient.

Two coding, as opposed to algorithmic, changes can improve this program considerably. The more important change is to move the initialization of inuse,

```
for i := 1 to n-2 do inuse[i] := true;
```

outside the procedure. This loop (one line of code!) takes linear time and thus causes the total time spent in Next to be at least $n \cdot n!$, so that $T(n)$ must continue to grow as n grows. By making inuse global and initializing all its elements to true, the repeated initialization can be avoided. As the queens are placed, the innermost loop resets those elements of inuse previously made false, so that, on subsequent entry to Next, all elements of inuse are true. The less important change is to replace the loop

```
for k := i+1 to n do
    (* Place the next queen on as low a row as possible. *)
    begin
      m := 1;
      while inuse[m] do m := m + 1; (* cannot push m to n+1 *)
      A[k] := m;
      inuse[m] := true (* row now in use *)
    end;
```

with the loop

```
m := 1;
for k := i+1 to n do
  (* Place the next queen on as low a row as possible. *)
  begin
    while inuse[m] do m := m + 1; (* cannot push m to n+1 *)
    A[k] := m;
    inuse[m] := true; (* row now in use *)
    m := m + 1
  end;
```

which recognizes that the queens to the right of the one pushed forward will be given successively higher row numbers, so that one pass through inuse is possible. Even with these improvements, however, $T(n)$ continues to grow with n: assigning the positions to the queens to the right of the current queen takes linear time—one pass through inuse that goes more than halfway through on average—so that the running time of the algorithm still grows at least as fast as $n \cdot n!$. A complete analysis of the running time of the code of Program 2.4 with the two modifications is quite complex since the loop that begins

```
for j := A[i]+1 to n do
```

runs a variable number of times during a call, depending on which queen is ultimately pushed forward. The column number of this queen varies nonuniformly from 1 to $n-1$, with the next to last queen being pushed forward half the time and the first queen being pushed forward only n times out of $n!$ calls to Next.

A more efficient, indeed essentially optimal, program generates the $n!$ permutations directly using a recursive strategy. Since recursive procedures cannot be interrupted and restarted, we write the program nonrecursively, with the information describing the state of the recursion kept in a stack (stored in SwapWithWhom in the implementation given below). The recursive version is presented in Program 2.5 and the nonrecursive version in Program 2.6. This algorithm generates permutations by fixing the next element to each available remaining value (which it obtains without searching) and recursively completing the family of permutations between successive assignments. Since we operate on the array directly and since the for loop which chooses available values for the next element assumes that the permuted array remains unchanged from choice to choice, each recursive invocation, upon completion, must restore the permuted array to the value it had when the invocation was made. The properties of lexicographic order allow us to do this with a simple rotation of the affected part of the array.

That $T(n)$ is 1.00 on theoretical grounds (except for a slight perturbation due to initialization) can be seen by analyzing the running time of the recursive

```
const n = ...;
type board = array [1..n] of 1..n;
var A: board;
procedure Permute(i: integer);
  (* Form all permutations of 1 through n, in lexicographic order, that
     have A[1..i-1] fixed, i.e., permute A[i..n] in every possible way.
     It is assumed that A[i..n] holds the lexicographically smallest
     arrangement of A[i..n] to start with.  The ordering in A[ ] is
     restored upon procedure exit, which is required for correct
     functioning.  A[ ] should be initialized to 1,2,...,n before the
     external call to the procedure, which is Permute(1). *)
  var j: integer;
  begin
    if i < n
      then begin
              (* Form all permutations with successively higher values
                 in A[i].  The first value is already in place. *)
              Permute(i+1);
              (* Successively swap in next higher value. *)
              for j := i+1 to n do
                begin
                  SWAP(A[i],A[j]);
                  (* A[i+1..n] is the lexicographically smallest way
                     of arranging the data currently in A[i+1..n]. *)
                  Permute(i+1)
                  (* Invariant: upon return, A is identical to what
                     it was immediately after the SWAP. *)
                end;
              (* Maintain invariant: do a circular shift left one place of
                 A[i..n], which restores A to the way it was when called. *)
              ROTATE(i)
           end
      else EMIT(A) (* Announce new complete permutation. *)
  end; (* Permute *)
```

Program 2.5: An Efficient Algorithm for Generating the Next Placement (Recursive Version)

version when called from the outside with a value of 1. Since each SWAP produces a different permutation, SWAP is executed $n! - 1$ times. ROTATE, which returns the elements of A to their positions at the time of the call, does a nonconstant amount of work, but essentially the same amount of work as all the SWAPs within an invocation of the procedure Permute, for a total of $\Theta(n!)$ additional work. The number of calls to Permute inside the for loop equals the number of SWAPs, for $\Theta(n!)$ work once again, and the number of calls to Permute at the head of the procedure equals the number of ROTATEs executed, which is less than

```
(* Successively generate the permutations of 1 through n using an
   interruptible, nonrecursive version of Program 2.5. *)
var SwapWithWhom: array [1..n] of integer;
      (* Static variable for function Next.  SwapWithWhom[i] is the position
         to the right of i with which A[i] will be swapped to form
         the next subset of permutations.  SwapWithWhom holds the state
         of the process in the nonrecursive version of the function.
         SwapWithWhom[i] = n+1 means that all swaps have been completed.
         Initialize SwapWithWhom (for i := 1 to n do SwapWithWhom[i] := i + 1)
         before the first call to the function Next. *)
function Next(var A: board): boolean;
  (* Given a board position A with all queens in distinct rows and
     columns, return the next board position with the same property.
     A should not be changed by the caller between calls and must
     be initialized by the caller to the first such placement, A[i] := i.
     If no further placement exists, then Next returns false. *)
  label 1;
  var i, t, stacktop: integer;
  begin
    stacktop := n - 1;
    while stacktop > 0 do
      if SwapWithWhom[stacktop] = n + 1
        then begin
               (* Do the circular shift left... *)
               t := A[stacktop];
               for i := stacktop+1 to n do A[i-1] := A[i];
               A[n] := t;
               (* ...and next time start swapping process over. *)
               SwapWithWhom[stacktop] := stacktop + 1;
               stacktop := stacktop - 1
             end
        else begin
               (* Do the SWAP... *)
               t := A[stacktop];
               A[stacktop] := A[SwapWithWhom[stacktop]];
               A[SwapWithWhom[stacktop]] := t;
               (* ...and next time SWAP with the next element. *)
               SwapWithWhom[stacktop] := SwapWithWhom[stacktop] + 1;
               Next := true;
               goto 1 (* return *)
             end;
    Next := false;
1:
  end; (* Next *)
```

Program 2.6: An Efficient Algorithm for Generating the Next Placement (Nonrecursive, Interruptible Version)

Table 2.5: Comparative Running Times for Generating All Permutations of n Elements

n	Program 2.4		Program 2.4 modified		Program 2.6	
	Statement count	$T(n)$	Statement count	$T(n)$	Statement count	$T(n)$
4	705	1.00	597	1.00	382	1.00
5	4,206	1.19	3,198	1.07	1,923	1.01
6	28,681	1.36	20,759	1.16	11,542	1.01
7	223,518	1.51	155,568	1.24	80,785	1.01
8	1,967,601	1.66	1,325,409	1.32	646,254	1.01

the total work done by the ROTATEs. Therefore the entire procedure takes time proportional to $n!$.

Table 2.5 shows the running time for Program 2.4 (in its original form and with the two modifications) and for Program 2.6 for small values of n. The experimental data thus confirm our analysis of the code of Program 2.6: it is essentially optimal and cannot be further improved, except by a constant factor.

2.5 Exercises

2.5.1 Practice with Asymptotic Notation and Recurrences

Exercise 2.5 Order the following functions by their growth rates from smallest to largest:

1. $\log n \log n^{\sqrt{n}}$ 2. $n^2 \log n$

3. $2^{\lg n \lg \lg n}$ 4. $3^{\lg n}$

5. $n 2^{\lg \lg n}$ 6. $n \sqrt{n}$

Solution: 1, 5, 6, 4, 2, 3.   □

Exercise 2.6 Show that:

1. 3^n is not $O(2^n)$, but $\log 3^n$ is $O(\log 2^n)$.

2. n^n is not $O(n!)$, but $\log n^n$ is $O(\log n!)$.

3. For $\alpha > 1$, $n^{\alpha \log n}$ is not $O(n^{\log n})$, but $\log n^{\alpha \log n}$ is $O(\log n^{\log n})$.

     □

Exercise 2.7 Consider the following functions of n:

$$
\begin{aligned}
f_1(n) &= n^2 \\
f_2(n) &= \begin{cases} n, & \text{for } n \text{ odd} \\ n^3, & \text{for } n \text{ even} \end{cases} \\
f_3(n) &= \begin{cases} n, & \text{for } n \le 100 \\ n^3, & \text{for } n > 100 \end{cases} \\
f_4(n) &= n^{2+1/n}.
\end{aligned}
$$

For each distinct pair, i and j, determine whether $f_i(n)$ is $O\big(f_j(n)\big)$ and whether it is $\Omega\big(f_j(n)\big)$.

Solution: The $O(\ )$ relation holds for pairs $(1,3)$, $(1,4)$, $(2,3)$, $(4,1)$, and $(4,3)$; the $\Omega(\ )$ relation holds for pairs $(1,2)$, $(1,4)$, $(2,1)$, $(2,3)$, $(2,4)$, $(3,1)$, $(3,2)$, $(3,4)$, $(4,1)$, and $(4,2)$. $\qquad\square$

Exercise 2.8 Let $f_1(n)$ be $\Omega\big(g_1(n)\big)$ and $f_2(n)$ be $\Omega\big(g_2(n)\big)$. Disprove these claims:

1. $(f_1 + f_2)(n)$ is $\Omega\big(\max(g_1(n),\ g_2(n))\big)$.

2. $(f_1 \cdot f_2)(n)$ is $\Omega\big((g_1 \cdot g_2)(n)\big)$, even if $g_i(n) > 0$.

$\qquad\square$

Exercise 2.9 Prove or disprove: $\Omega(\ )$ is a transitive relation. $\qquad\square$

Exercise 2.10 Find two monotone increasing functions such that neither is $O(\ )$ of the other. $\qquad\square$

Exercise 2.11 Some authors define $\Theta(\ )$ by limits, stating that $f(n)$ is $\Theta(g(n))$ whenever $\lim_{n\to\infty} f(n)/g(n) = c$ holds for some $c > 0$. Is this definition more restrictive than or equivalent to ours? $\qquad\square$

Exercise 2.12 Let us define a new notation, $o(\ )$, as follows: $f(n)$ is $o(g(n))$ whenever $\lim_{n\to\infty} f(n)/g(n) = 0$. This notation is typically used in connection with "breaking barriers" because it denotes that the first function does not grow as fast as the second. Thus, one might ask whether or not it is possible to search an ordered list in $o(\log n)$ average time, i.e., asymptotically faster than binary search. (The answer is yes, for which see Exercise 2.35.) Investigate the connections between this notation and our other notations; in particular, if f is $o(g)$, does it follow that f is $O(g)$? if f is $O(g)$ and g is not $O(f)$, does it follow that f is $o(g)$? $\qquad\square$

Exercise 2.13 Derive the identity

$$
\frac{1}{(1-x)^2} = 1 + 2x + 3x^2 + \cdots
$$

from the identity

$$\frac{1}{1-x} = 1 + x + x^2 + \cdots$$

(i) by differentiation; and (ii) by multiplication.   □

Exercise 2.14 Derive the identity

$$\frac{1}{(1-x)^n} = 1 + \binom{n}{1}x + \binom{n+1}{2}x^2 + \binom{n+2}{3}x^3 + \cdots + \binom{n+m-1}{m}x^m + \cdots.$$

□

Exercise 2.15 Find the closed form formula for the nth term of the sequence given by the following recurrence relation:

$$\begin{cases} a_n = a_{n-1} + a_{n-2} \\ a_1 = 1 \\ a_0 = 0. \end{cases}$$

This is possibly the most famous of all recurrences; it generates the Fibonacci numbers, named after Leonardo of Pisa, also known as Leonardo Fibonacci (*circa* 1175–1250). The arithmetic gets somewhat unpleasant due to the presence of irrational characteristic roots; the answer is:

$$a_n = \frac{1}{\sqrt{5}}\left[\left(\frac{1+\sqrt{5}}{2}\right)^n - \left(\frac{1-\sqrt{5}}{2}\right)^n\right].$$

□

Exercise 2.16 Solve the following recurrences by the method of characteristic roots:

1. $\begin{cases} a_n = 5a_{n-1} - 6a_{n-2} + 4{\cdot}3^n \\ a_1 = 36 \\ a_0 = 0 \end{cases}$

2. $\begin{cases} a_n = 3a_{n-1} - 2a_{n-2} + 2^{n-1} + 2{\cdot}3^n \\ a_1 = 29 \\ a_0 = 9 \end{cases}$

3. $\begin{cases} a_n = a_{n-2} + 4n \\ a_1 = 4 \\ a_0 = 1 \end{cases}$

4. $\begin{cases} a_n = 3a_{n-1} + a_{n-2} - 3a_{n-3} + 16n + 8 \cdot 3^n \\ a_2 = 117 \\ a_1 = 10 \\ a_0 = -1 \end{cases}$

5. $\begin{cases} a_n = 3a_{n-1} - 2a_{n-2} + 3 \cdot 2^{2n-1} \\ a_1 = 12 \\ a_0 = 0. \end{cases}$

Solutions:

1. $a_n = 12n3^n$ 2. $a_n = n2^n + 3^{n+2}$
3. $a_n = (n+1)^2$ 4. $a_n = (9n-2)3^n - 2n^2 - 10n + 1$
5. $a_n = 4(4^n - 1)$.

□

Exercise 2.17 Use the method of characteristic roots to derive the asymptotic solution (in $\Theta(\ )$ terms) of the following recurrences:

1. $a_n = 2a_{n-1} - a_{n-2} + \Theta(n)$

2. $a_n = 3a_{n-1} - 2a_{n-2} + \Theta(n2^n)$

3. $a_n = 4a_{n/2} - 4a_{n/4} + \Theta(n \log n)$

4. $a_n = 5a_{n/2} - 6a_{n/4} + \Theta(n)$.

Solutions:

1. $a_n = \Theta(n^3)$ 2. $a_n = \Theta(n^2 2^n)$
3. $a_n = \Theta(n \log^3 n)$ 4. $a_n = O(n^{\lg 3})$.

□

Exercise 2.18 Use generating functions to derive closed forms for the following sums. Then attempt to derive the closed form solutions more rapidly, using relationships between the various sums (such as summands of one expression being derivatives of summands of another expression).

1. $\displaystyle\sum_{i=0}^{n} a^i$ 2. $\displaystyle\sum_{i=0}^{n} i2^i$

3. $\displaystyle\sum_{i=0}^{n} i^2 3^i$ 4. $\displaystyle\sum_{i=1}^{n} 2^i/i$.

Solutions:

1. $F(z) = \dfrac{1}{(1-z)(1-az)}$ $f(n) = \dfrac{a^{n+1}-1}{a-1}$ (for $a \neq 1$)

2. $F(z) = \dfrac{2z}{(1-z)(1-2z)^2}$ $f(n) = (n-1)2^{n+1} + 2$

3. $F(z) = \dfrac{3z(1+3z)}{(1-z)(1-3z)^3}$ $f(n) = \dfrac{1}{2}(n^2 - n + 1)3^{n+1} - \dfrac{3}{2}$

4. $F(z) = \dfrac{1}{1-z}\ln\dfrac{1}{1-2z}$ no simple closed form.

□

Exercise 2.19 By considering the recurrence relation

$$\begin{cases} a_n = a_{n-1} + n^2 \\ a_0 = 0, \end{cases}$$

derive both

$$\sum_{i=0}^{\infty} \frac{i^2}{2^i} = 6 \quad \text{and} \quad \sum_{i=1}^{n} i^2 = \frac{n(n+1)(2n+1)}{6}.$$

□

Exercise 2.20 Solve the following recurrences using various methods. (*Hints:* The third recurrence needs two successive substitutions—the first obvious, the second involving logarithms; treat the solution to the fourth recurrence as a fraction, replacing a_n with the fraction b_n/c_n, and solve for b_n and c_n separately; to solve the fifth recurrence, generate several terms.)

1. $\begin{cases} a_n = 3a_{n/2} - 2a_{n/4} + \lg n, & \text{for } n \text{ a power of } 2 \\ a_2 = 3 \\ a_1 = 3 \end{cases}$

2. $\begin{cases} a_n = a_{n-1}{\cdot}a_{n-2}{}^2 \\ a_1 = 2 \\ a_0 = 4 \end{cases}$

3. $\begin{cases} a_n = na_{n/2}^2, & \text{for } n \text{ a power of } 2 \\ a_1 = 8 \end{cases}$

4. $\begin{cases} a_n = \dfrac{2}{3 - a_{n-1}} \\ a_0 = 1/2 \end{cases}$

5.
$$\begin{cases} a_n = \dfrac{a_{n-1} + 1}{a_{n-2}} \\ a_1 = 2 \\ a_0 = 1. \end{cases}$$

Solutions:

1. $a_n = 3n - \frac{1}{2} \lg^2 n - \frac{5}{2} \lg n$ 2. $a_n = \begin{cases} 2^{2^n + 1}, & \text{for } n \text{ even} \\ 2^{2^n - 1}, & \text{for } n \text{ odd} \end{cases}$

3. $a_n = \dfrac{32^n}{4n}$ 4. $a_n = 1 - \dfrac{1}{3 \cdot 2^n - 1}$

5. $a_n = a_{n \bmod 5}$

(with the obvious five initial conditions for the fifth solution). $\qquad\square$

Exercise 2.21* Derive a recurrence relation to describe the number of binary trees of height not exceeding h; derive a lower bound for its solution; then attempt to make your bound as tight as possible. (Aho and Sloane show that the exact solution is $\lfloor k^{2^h} \rfloor$ for some suitable constant k.) $\qquad\square$

2.5.2 Regular Exercises

Exercise 2.22 Generalize the Towers of Hanoi problem to arbitrary initial and/or final configurations. $\qquad\square$

Exercise 2.23 [P] Attempt to solve the Towers of Hanoi problem with n pegs. (Note that no optimal strategy is known even for just four pegs!) $\qquad\square$

Exercise 2.24 [P] Attempt to generalize the Towers of Hanoi problem to graphs. Each vertex of the graph corresponds to a peg, and moves from one peg to another can take place only if there is an edge between the two corresponding vertices. In this context, the standard version is played on a triangle. $\qquad\square$

Exercise 2.25 (generalization of Exercise 2.1) Divide-and-conquer algorithms, treated in Chapter 7, have a time complexity described by the recurrence

$$t(n) = g(n) + \sum_{i=1}^{p} t(s_i(n)), \text{ with } t(1) \text{ some constant,}$$

where $p > 1$ is the number of pieces, $s_i(n)$ is the size of the ith piece, and $g(n)$ is the cost of dividing the problem into pieces and of reconstructing a solution to the original problem from the solutions to the pieces. Assume that all pieces have the same size, say n/q for some integer $q \geq 1$, not necessarily equal to p.

1. Solve the recurrence when $g(n)$ is $\Theta(1)$, $\Theta(\log n)$, $\Theta(n)$, $\Theta(n \log n)$, $\Theta(n^k)$, $\Theta(a^n)$, and $\Theta(na^n)$. Be sure to consider the influence of the relative values of p and q. Note that, as the driving function is given only in $\Theta(\ )$ terms, your solution need only be in $\Theta(\ )$ terms as well.

2. (harder) Solve the recurrence when $g(n)$ is $\Theta(\log^i n)$ for any positive integer i.

3. When does $g(n)$ start dominating the overall cost? That is, when does the particular solution start dominating the homogeneous solution?

$\square$

Exercise 2.26* Solve the recurrence

$$\begin{cases} T(n) = T(pn) + T(qn) + \Theta(n) \\ T(1) = \Theta(1), \end{cases}$$

considering separately the cases where $p + q$ is less than, equal to, and greater than one.

$\square$

Exercise 2.27 Consider the recurrence

$$\begin{cases} f(n) = (i+1)f(i) \\ f(1) = 1, \end{cases}$$

where i is a uniformly distributed random integer between 1 and $n-1$, inclusive. What are the possible values of $f(n)$, and what is its average value?

$\square$

Exercise 2.28 The following are fairly complete tables of "magical facts" about generating functions. Once you have proved each relation in it, this table will become a very useful tool both for deriving the generating function of a complex sum or recurrence and also for obtaining the coefficient of the nth term of a known generating function. Prove each relationship listed in the tables that follow.

Common generating functions

$G(z)$	c_n	$G(z)$	c_n
$\dfrac{1}{(1-z)^k}, \ k \in \mathcal{Z}^+$	$\dbinom{n+k-1}{n}$	e^z	$1/n!$
$(1+z)^k, \ k \in \mathcal{Z}^+$	$\begin{cases} \binom{k}{n}, & \text{for } n \le k \\ 0, & \text{for } n > k \end{cases}$	$\ln \dfrac{1}{1-z}$	$\begin{cases} 1/n, & \text{for } n \ge 1 \\ 0, & \text{for } n = 0 \end{cases}$

Useful relationships

Let $G(z) = \sum_{i=0}^{\infty} c_i z^i$ and $H(z) = \sum_{i=0}^{\infty} d_i z^i$; then we have the following:

form of $F(z) = \sum_{i=0}^{\infty} a_i z^i$	form of a_n
$(G + H)(z)$	$c_n + d_n$
$(G \cdot H)(z)$	$\sum_{j=0}^{n} c_j d_{n-j}$
$\dfrac{1}{1-z} G(z)$	$\sum_{j=0}^{n} c_j$
$aG(z)$	ac_n
$G(az)$	$a^n c_n$
$z^k G(z)$	$\begin{cases} c_{n-k}, & \text{for } n \geq k \\ 0, & \text{for } n < k \end{cases}$
$z\, dG(z)/dz$	nc_n
$\displaystyle\int_0^z \dfrac{G(u) - G(0)}{u}\, du$	$\begin{cases} c_n/n, & \text{for } n \geq 1 \\ 0, & \text{for } n = 0 \end{cases}$
$G(z^k), \; k \geq 1$	$\begin{cases} c_{n/k}, & \text{for } n \text{ divisible by } k \\ 0, & \text{otherwise} \end{cases}$
$\dfrac{1}{k} \displaystyle\sum_{j=1}^{k} G(e^{j\frac{2\pi i}{k}} z^{1/k}), \; k \geq 1$	$c_{kn} \qquad (i = \sqrt{-1})$

$\square$

Exercise 2.29 Let the denominator of a generating function, $G(z)$, be of the form

$$\prod_{i=1}^{m} (1 - a_i z)^{k_i}.$$

Prove the following results:

1. If the factor $(1 - a_i z)$ has exponent 1, i.e., if its corresponding term in the partial fraction decomposition is $\alpha_0/(1 - a_i z)$, then α_0 is given by

$$\left[(1 - a_i z) G(z) \right]_{z=1/a_i}.$$

2. If the factor $(1 - a_i z)$ has exponent k_i, i.e., if its corresponding term in the partial fraction decomposition is

$$\frac{\alpha_{k_i - 1} z^{k_i - 1} + \alpha_{k_i - 2} z^{k_i - 2} + \cdots + \alpha_0}{(1 - a_i z)^{k_i}},$$

then α_{k_i-1} is given by

$$\frac{\left[H^{(k_i-1)}(z)\right]_{z=1/a_i}}{(k_i-1)!},$$

with $H(z) = \left((1 - a_i z)^{k_i} G(z)\right)$.

□

Exercise 2.30 The following program finds the maximum element of an array in a clearly inefficient manner. Analyze its running time in $\Theta(\ )$ terms.

```
type list = array [1..Max] of real;

function FindMax(var A: list; first, last: integer): real;
  (* Find the maximum element between positions first and last. *)
  var mid: integer;
      leftmax, rightmax: real;

  function Middle(first, last: integer): integer;
    (* Return the value halfway between first and last. *)
    begin
      while first < last do
        begin
          first := first + 1;
          last := last - 1
        end;
      Middle := last
    end; (* Middle *)

  begin (* FindMax *)
    if first = last
      then FindMax := A[first]
      else begin
              mid := Middle(first,last);
              leftmax := FindMax(A,first,mid);
              rightmax := FindMax(A,mid+1,last);
              if leftmax >= rightmax
                then FindMax := leftmax
                else FindMax := rightmax
           end
  end; (* FindMax *)
```

□

Exercise 2.31 The following program does nothing of much interest other than offering an interesting exercise. Analyze its running time in $\Theta(\ )$ terms, when it is called with parameters 1 and n.

```
type list = array [1..Max] of integer;

procedure Stuff(var A: list; l, n: integer);
  var k: integer;

  procedure Move(l, m: integer);
    var j: integer;
    begin
      for j := l+1 to l+m-1 do A[j-1] := A[j]
    end;

begin
  if n = 1
    then A[l] := 0
    else begin
           Stuff(A, l, n div 2);
           Stuff(A, l + n div 2, n - n div 2);
           k := 1;
           while k * k < n do
             begin
               Move(l,k);
               k := k + 1
             end
         end
end; (* Stuff *)
```

□

Exercise 2.32 Define the complexity, $L(n)$, of the procedure `Trial` to be the number of digits printed when the procedure is called with argument n. Characterize, in $\Theta(\ )$ terms, the asymptotic behavior of $L(n)$.

```
procedure Trial(n: integer);
  var i: integer;
  begin
    if n > 0
      then begin
             for i := 1 to n do writeln(n:1);
             Trial(n-1)
           end
  end; (* Trial *)
```

□

Exercise 2.33 A *lucky number* is any positive integer that passes through the following sieve: begin by removing every second number; then remove every third number from the remaining set; then remove every fourth number from the set left by the first two passes; and so forth. The first few lucky numbers are 1, 3, 7, 13, 19, ...

To find all lucky numbers smaller than n, we can use one of two algorithms. The first algorithm is a direct implementation of the definition: it uses a Boolean array of length n and makes repeated passes over the array, removing numbers, until it completes a pass without removing any number. The second algorithm is more efficient; it maintains a linked list of numbers still thought to be lucky and, at each pass, shrinks the list as needed, terminating when it completes a pass in which no number is removed. Analyze the worst-case behavior of these two algorithms as a function of n. ☐

Exercise 2.34 [Buffon's needle] (requires continuous mathematics) Consider the following algorithm for approximating the value of π in social settings. (You must be in a room with a wood floor, for which you can reasonably assume that the parallel lines determined by the floorboards are equally spaced.) Pick up a swizzle stick and cut it so that its length equals the width of a floorboard. Repeatedly throw the stick in the air, recording how often it lands across two floorboards. The ratio of this number to the total number of throws is an approximation of $2/\pi$, one which is asymptotically exact.

1. What are the possible values after one trial? after two? after three? What can you conclude about the algorithm when it is run a finite number of times?

2. Prove that the approximation is asymptotically exact, i.e., that the ratio approaches $2/\pi$ as the number of trials approaches infinity. (*Hint*: Consider a specific position for one endpoint of the stick. Given this position, the probability that the stick lies across two floorboards is a ratio of angles; integrate this expression over all possible positions for the endpoint. Note that $\int \arccos(x/a)\,dx = x\arccos(x/a) - \sqrt{a^2 - x^2} + C$.)

3. (harder) In view of your answers to (1) and (2) above, do you think that this procedure can indeed be used to determine the value of π to arbitrary precision? If so, in what sense? if not, why?

☐

Exercise 2.35** [Interpolation search] When looking up a word in a dictionary, most of us use a search technique which, while similar to binary search, allows us to locate the entry somewhat faster. We take advantage of additional knowledge in the form of an estimate of the approximate location of the key within the sequence. Thus, when looking for the word *besom*, we do not begin by opening the dictionary in the middle (more or less at the letter m), but rather we begin our search much closer to the beginning of the dictionary; when looking up *nimiety*, on the other hand, we do open the dictionary toward the middle; and when looking up *weald*, we open it toward the end.

Define and analyze such an interpolation search algorithm; note that you must be able to do arithmetic on the keys. Verify that the worst case of this search can, in fact, be linear, but that, with a uniform probability distribution of keys, the average search time is $\Theta(\log \log n)$, which is noticeably faster than simple binary search. $\qquad\square$

Exercise 2.36 Verify that, if the zig-zig pattern for splay trees (Figure 2.4) were to be replaced by a single rotation (which better balances the subtree under examination), the resulting data structure would no longer obey the claimed amortized bound. Do this by producing a repeatable sequence of retrievals such that the amortized time per operation is linear. $\qquad\square$

Exercise 2.37 Show that the amortized complexity of INSERT, implemented by inserting the key as a leaf and promoting to the root as if it were already present, is $O(\log n)$. *Hint*: The inserted node affects the weight of only its predecessors.

$\square$

Exercise 2.38 Perform SPLAY(d), using top-down splaying, on the tree of Figure 2.5(a). $\qquad\square$

Exercise 2.39** Prove that the amortized complexity of a top-down splay (see Figure 2.8) is $O(\log n)$. $\qquad\square$

Exercise 2.40 [P] Compare the performance of unbalanced binary search trees, conventional balanced tree structures (such as AVL trees or red-black trees), and splay trees under random FINDs, INSERTs, and DELETEs and under biased sequences where the bias changes over time. $\qquad\square$

Exercise 2.41 Code the function `Solution` for the n-queens example of Section 2.4. It should run in linear time. $\qquad\square$

Exercise 2.42* Refer again to the n-queens example of Section 2.4. The imposed requirement that `Next` return the next placement in lexicographic order forces the function to do more work than necessary in certain circumstances, since lexicographically adjacent placements can occasionally require significant data motion. While the implementation of `Next` in Program 2.6 takes constant time on average, some calls take considerably longer than others. Observe, however, that `Next` is only required to cycle through all permutations in some order. Implement a version of `Next` which does a fixed amount of work per permutation. $\qquad\square$

2.6 Bibliography

The mathematics used in the analysis of algorithms grew through several centuries; we do not propose to discuss its history here, but we do refer the reader to the texts of Knuth [1968] and Greene and Knuth [1982] for details. Both of these texts provide a much more complete discussion of the mathematical basis of the two methods discussed here and also present more advanced techniques for very complex problems. The surveys of Weide [1977] and Lueker [1980] may be the best starting points for further reading; they provide concise and lucid overviews of both elementary and advanced techniques. Purdom and Brown [1985] offer a comprehensive treatment of advanced analysis techniques, with numerous examples. Finally, Graham *et al.* [1989] have written the definitive textbook on mathematical techniques for the analysis of algorithms, including methods discussed in this chapter as well as others. Asymptotic notation has a confused history, discussed by Knuth [1976] in his partially successful attempt to standardize the notation; we use his definitions for $O(\ )$ and $\Theta(\ )$. The `SillySort` example is taken from the delightful article of Broder and Stolfi [1984]; combining a great sense of humor with an excellent feel for the field of algorithmic analysis, these two authors have written an entertaining and very informative satire. The average-case analysis of algorithms is addressed by, among others, Knuth [1968, 1973] and Graham *et al.* [1989], and discussed in great detail by Hofri [1987]. Balanced trees and hash tables are standard topics for a text on data structures; Reingold and Hansen [1983] and Aho *et al.* [1983] provide very readable classical treatments, while Lewis and Denenberg [1991] offer a more modern view. Knuth [1973] provides an in-depth treatment of hashing. Tarjan has been and remains the prime exponent of amortized analysis; not only did he define the terms, but he also contributed most of the significant amortized data structures to date. His brief survey article (Tarjan [1985]) outlines the entire field and gives the reader an idea of the wide range of applicability of amortized techniques. Splay trees were developed by him and one of his students (Sleator and Tarjan [1983]). Further examples of amortized data structures are presented in the next chapter. Generalizations of the Towers of Hanoi problem are discussed by, among others, Xue-Miao [1986, 1988]. Exercise 2.21 is from Aho and Sloane [1973]; Exercise 2.25 is from Bentley *et al.* [1980].

Finally, the reader could not do better at this point than to read the Turing Award Lectures of Richard Karp [1986] and Robert Tarjan [1987]: these two eminent researchers in algorithms and complexity theory describe their field and the history of their contributions to it in a manner both entertaining and instructive and in the process remind us of how young the field is.

CHAPTER 3

Data Structures for Search Algorithms

Of all operations performed in optimization algorithms, the most common is probably "find the best candidate in a collection"; this operation, together with other useful maintenance operations, characterizes a priority queue. As priority queues come in many guises and as they have undergone much evolution in the last few years, we devote considerable attention to their implementation. In the same spirit, we also discuss at some length the implementation of equivalence relations, another important class of data structures for optimization problems. Finally, we present some extensions of binary search trees, which facilitate operations, such as range searches, needed in geometric algorithms.

3.1 Priority Queues

We shall see in subsequent chapters several algorithms where we need repeatedly to find the "best" choice from a collection of choices. "Best" will usually be defined as "the choice that yields the largest improvement in an objective function." More generally, each member of the collection will have an associated key value taken from a totally ordered set, and we shall repeatedly require the record that has the maximum (or the minimum) key. If all the members of the collection were known in advance and if their key values remained unchanged, the items could be sorted by their key values and retrieved in order. In many of our applications, however, processing the retrieved record creates new members to be inserted into the collection or causes change in the key values of existing members. The abstract data type that formalizes these operations is the priority queue.[1]

Definition 3.1 A *priority queue* is an abstract data type based on atomic entities in which each atom contains a key taken from a totally ordered set, the atom's priority. The data type supports the following operations:

- CREATE: → priority queue
  This operation creates an empty priority queue.

- DELETEMIN: priority queue → atom
  This operation returns the atom, the key of which is the smallest among all atoms in the priority queue, and removes this atom from the priority queue; if the priority queue is empty, an error flag is raised.

- INSERT: priority queue × atom → priority queue
  This operation inserts a new atom into the priority queue.

□

These specifications define a min-priority queue; a max-priority queue is the obvious complement and will not be addressed further. As with any abstract data type, the precise set of operations varies from one application to another. For priority queues, the reader will encounter many variations ranging from the simplest (INSERT and DELETEMIN, as above) to the most elaborate (including, for instance, updating the key value of [DECREASEKEY] or deleting arbitrary elements [DELETE]).

There are several obvious, but inefficient, ways of implementing such an abstract data type. First, one can implement it as a set, i.e., an unordered list of atoms; this implementation will guarantee constant-time insertion, since it matters little where an atom is placed. If the implementation is sequential (i.e., the data are stored in an array), then deletion of the minimum element requires a linear-time sequential search followed by a linear-time compaction pass through the array. If the implementation is linked, we avoid the need for compaction following a deletion, but we still require linear time to locate the atom to delete. Secondly, one can implement a priority queue as an ordered list of atoms. This implementation guarantees constant-time deletion of the minimum element, since the atom to be deleted is always at the head of the list and thus can be located instantly and removed easily. If the implementation is sequential, we can use binary search to identify (in logarithmic time) the slot into which the new atom should be inserted, but we still require a linear-time shift to make space for the atom. If the implementation is linked, locating the slot for insertion requires a

---

[1]The phrase *priority queue* should be viewed as one word, and the concept should not be confused with a *first in, first out queue*.

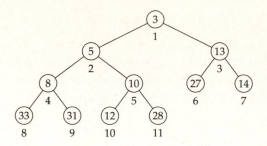

Figure 3.1: An Example of a Heap with the Nodes Labelled in Level Order

linear-time sequential search; the insertion can then be completed in constant time. In summary, all these obvious implementations optimize one operation but lead to linear-time requirements for the other.

3.1.1 Heaps

A simple data structure that allows both operations to be performed in logarithmic time is a *heap*.[2] A heap, or more precisely a 2-heap or binary heap, is a binary tree with two properties:

1. (Heap ordering)   The key associated with every node of the tree is less than or equal to the keys associated with the node's children, if any.

2. The tree is *complete*, that is, as "perfectly balanced" as possible: every level of the tree, except the last, is completely full, and the last level has all its nodes on the left.

Figure 3.1 shows a heap where the nodes have been labelled in level order. The node of the heap with the minimum key is always the root of the tree. Note that there is no relationship between the values of keys on the same level; in fact, a child of the root can have a key value larger than nodes far down in the tree if these nodes occur in the other subtree of the root.

Before showing how heaps can be used to implement priority queues, we address the question of representing heaps themselves. As always, the choice

---

[2]Logarithmic time is much better than linear and only somewhat worse than constant time, at least for reasonable heap sizes, so that we are better off with two logarithmic-time operations than with one constant-time and one linear-time operation. The trade-off is unfavorable only if one of the operations is far more common than the other, an unlikely occurrence for priority queues. An implementation with logarithmic-time operations may easily be devised using some type of balanced tree structure (such as AVL trees), but these trees are really designed for search and are overly complex for the task at hand—although the additional operations which they implement efficiently, such as predecessor and successor, may prove very useful, as we shall see in Section 4.2 (Program 4.11).

is between a sequential representation (using an array and a simple arithmetic computation to determine the index of a node's parent or children given the node's index) and a linked representation (with explicit parent and/or children pointers). The typical representation of trees is linked, despite the fact that any linked representation requires a (rudimentary) memory management package with its accompanying overhead in time and space. This choice of representation is due to the lack of flexibility of sequential representations: if simple index computations are to replace explicit pointers, the various tree nodes must be placed in a fixed pattern in memory, which leads to either an intolerable waste of memory (leaving huge "holes" of unused, yet dedicated, memory) or numerous data moves. However, the perfect balance and utterly predictable structure of heaps makes them ideally suited to sequential representations. If the nodes are labelled in level order, as in Figure 3.1, and placed in that order in the array, no storage whatsoever is wasted since no hole can occur, as ensured by the second property of heaps. Moreover, the level ordering makes for very simple index computations: if a given node's index is i, then the index of its left child (if present) is $2i$, that of its right child is $2i + 1$, and that of its parent is $\lfloor i/2 \rfloor$.[3] The root is always at index 1; the last item in the heap is at index n (the size of the heap). This indexing allows efficient navigation through the tree at no expense in storage: the storage requirements are limited to the atoms themselves, plus a simple integer variable to store the size of the heap. The only drawback of the sequential representation is the need to know the maximum size to which the heap can grow and to preallocate the entire array.

Now we turn to the implementation of priority queues by heaps. The two structural requirements imposed by the heap properties define the INSERT and DELETEMIN processes. Insertion and deletion modify the number of nodes in the heap; by the second heap property, a change in the number of nodes must cause a change in the location of the last element of the heap. In the case of deletion of the minimum element, one fewer element will be present and thus the nth position in the array will become empty; since the element removed from the heap must be taken from position 1 (the root), the nth (last) element can be substituted for the first element. In the case of insertion, one more element will be present and thus the $(n+1)$st position, formerly empty, will contain an element; thus, the newly inserted element should be stored in the $(n+1)$st position. The structure resulting from such changes satisfies the second heap property, but not necessarily the first. At one location in the heap, namely around the new root or newly inserted element, it is possible that the first heap property is not obeyed, either because the key of the changed element is too large (in DELETEMIN) or

---

[3]Multiplications and divisions are generally slower than true pointer references. Analysis of the situation is complicated by the fact that in assembly language (or in the higher-level language C or if the compiler is an optimizing compiler) the multiplications and divisions can be done by shifting.

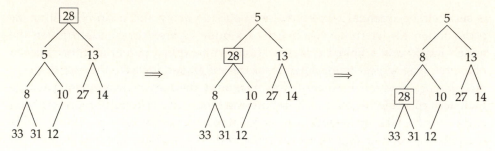

(a) Sift-down operation associated with DELETEMIN

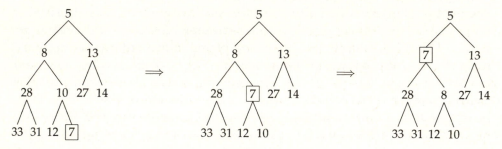

(b) Sift-up operation associated with INSERT

Figure 3.2: Sift-down and Sift-up Operations in a Heap

because it is too small (in INSERT)—see Figure 3.2. If the key is too large, the element needs to "sink" in the heap until it reaches its proper level; if the key is too small, the element needs to "rise." This discussion suggests that a priority queue can be implemented using a heap with the following four fundamental operations:

1. Add a new element at the end of the heap.

2. Replace the root of the heap with its last element and decrement the heap size.

3. "Sift down" an element.

4. "Sift up" an element.

The first two operations are trivial in an array, each requiring only constant time. The last two can be formulated inductively: at any step in the process, either an element has reached its level or it needs to change level. When an element is sifted down, termination occurs when either the element is no larger than its children (or just its child, if it has only one) or has become a leaf in the tree, at which point it cannot sink farther. When an element is sifted up, termination occurs when it is no smaller than its parent or has become the root of the tree, at which point it cannot rise farther. A change of one level is easy to program: as dictated by the first property, we sift down an element by exchanging it with the smaller of its children and sift up an element by exchanging it with its parent. During a sift-down operation, exchanging with the smaller child ensures that the new parent will be no larger than its children. During a sift-up operation, since the parent is already no larger than its other child and the element sifted up is smaller than the parent, the new parent will be smaller than its children. The critical point to notice is that the process propagates along a single path in the heap: when a child and its parent are exchanged, violations of the first property continue to involve only the original element that is being sifted up or down. Thus the number of exchange steps necessary to complete a sifting operation cannot exceed the height of the tree. Since the tree is complete, its height is a logarithmic function of its size; to be precise, the height of a complete binary tree of n nodes is $\lceil \lg(n+1) \rceil$. It follows that the operations run in logarithmic time.

Exercise 3.1 Program the sift-up and sift-down operations without looking at the procedures given in the text. □

The programs for the sift-up and sift-down operations are given in Programs 3.1 and 3.2. Notice that, because the element being sifted is involved in each exchange and does not come to rest until the termination condition is true, unnecessary data movement resulting from the exchange of two items can be avoided by keeping the sifted element in a temporary variable and performing only one half of each exchange. When the last exchange has taken place, the sifted item can be inserted into its final position. In effect, we are treating the location currently containing the sifted element as a "hole." The single assignment statement `elts[i] := elts[j]` moves the data residing in `elts[j]` into `elts[i]` and effectively moves the "hole" from `elts[i]` into `elts[j]`. With this method, no element gets moved more than once.

Also notice that the test for termination involves two separate tests: one for the first heap property and one for a boundary condition (top or bottom of tree). The first condition depends on the data and must be checked at each level, since it could become true at any point in the process. However, the second condition depends only on the size of the heap and holds only at the boundary; hence testing this condition at each iteration should be avoided. In a sift-up operation, the boundary is reached when the sifted element has become the new root; without a boundary check, this element (at location 1) would then be compared with its "parent" at location $\lfloor 1/2 \rfloor = 0$. If we establish a location

```
const HeapSize = ...;
        (* One larger than the true size of the heap,
           for the sentinel on sift-down. *)
      smallestkey = ...;  (* for top sentinel *)
      largestkey = ...;   (* for bottom sentinel *)
type datum = ...; (* any type that can be compared with < *)
     heapelt = record
                  key: datum;
                  rec: ... (* associated data record *)
               end;
     heap = record
                size: integer;
                elts: array [0..HeapSize] of heapelt
                      (* 0 location for sentinel on sift-up *)
            end;

procedure Initialize(var H: heap);
  begin
    with H do
      begin
        size := 0;
        elts[0].key := smallestkey  (* Install sentinel once and for all. *)
      end
  end; (* Initialize *)

procedure SiftUp(var H: heap; i: integer);
  (* i is index in heap of element to be sifted up. *)
  var j: integer;   (* index of parent of i *)
      item: heapelt;  (* stores sifted element until final placement *)
  begin
    with H do
      begin
        item := elts[i];
        j := i div 2;
        (* while parent is larger, exchange and continue *)
        while elts[j].key > item.key do
          begin
            (* Move parent down and go up one level. *)
            elts[i] := elts[j];
            i := j;
            j := i div 2
          end;
        (* Sifted element goes in location i. *)
        elts[i] := item
      end
  end; (* SiftUp *)
```

Program 3.1: The Sift-Up Operation

```
procedure SiftDown(var H: heap; i: integer);
  (* i is index in heap of element to be sifted down. *)
  label 1;
  var j: integer;     (* index of left child/smaller child of i *)
      item: heapelt; (* store sifted element until final placement *)
  begin
    with H do
      begin
        (* Sentinel assumed already placed in elts[size+1]. *)
        item := elts[i];
        j := 2*i;
        (* while i is not a leaf, compare it with its children *)
        while j <= size do
          begin
            (* Find smaller child. *)
            if elts[j].key > elts[j+1].key then j := j + 1;
            (* Do we need to exchange? *)
            if elts[j].key >= item.key
              then goto 1;  (* No: property 1 holds, we are done. *)
            (* Yes, move child up and continue. *)
            elts[i] := elts[j];
            i := j;
            j := 2*i
          end;
    1: (* The element goes in slot i. *)
        elts[i] := item
      end
end; (* SiftDown *)
```

Program 3.2: The Sift-Down Operation

zero and place there, once and for all, a sentinel with the smallest possible key, the sift-up process will always terminate at the root (if it comes up that far) because the first heap property will hold between the root of the heap and its "parent." Hence we can completely dispense with the boundary check at the top of the tree. Unfortunately, the same technique does not work as well when applied to the boundary check at the bottom of the tree. Without a boundary check, the sift-down process would proceed to examine the "children" of a leaf node, thereby requiring one sentinel for each missing child. Since a binary tree of n nodes has $n + 1$ missing children, we would need $n + 1$ sentinels, thereby doubling the size of the array.

Finally (and partly in consequence of our inability to use sentinels at the bottom of the tree) we need to consider, for sift-down operations only, the special case of the one node in the heap that may have only one child. The possible

```
procedure DeleteMin(var H: heap; var smallest: heapelt);
  (* Returns smallest, the min atom in the heap. *)
  begin
    with H do
      begin
        if size = 0
          then error (* Call external procedure not shown. *)
          else begin
                 smallest := elts[1];
                 (* Works correctly on heaps of one element. *)
                 elts[1] := elts[size];   (* replace root *)
                 (* The object already in elts[size] acts as sentinel. *)
                 size := size - 1;
                 SiftDown(H,1)
               end
      end
  end; (* DeleteMin *)

procedure Insert(var H: heap; x: heapelt);
  begin
    with H do
      if size < HeapSize-1
        then begin
               size := size + 1;
               elts[size] := x;   (* append new element *)
               SiftUp(H,size)
             end
        else error (* Call external procedure not shown. *)
  end; (* Insert *)
```

Program 3.3: The Operations DELETEMIN and INSERT in a Priority Queue

existence of such a node would seem to call for one more boundary check, yielding three cases: the element being sifted down is a leaf, an internal node with one child, or an internal node with two children. However, note that, if a missing right child is present, it is at location $n + 1$, directly following the last heap element. Thus we can avoid this boundary case by establishing one sentinel at location $n + 1$ with the largest possible key. Now we need only test whether a given tree node has a left child (a test of the form $2i \leq n$) to handle the bottom of the tree. Once we have procedures for the sift-up and sift-down operations, the code to manage a priority queue is trivial; it is included for completeness in Program 3.3.

In several of the algorithms to be presented in later chapters, we shall need an additional operation:

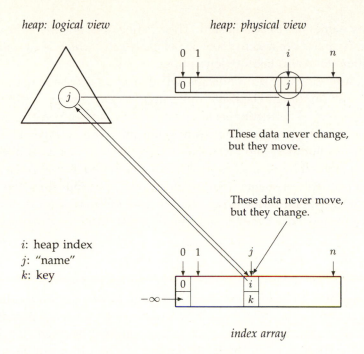

heap: logical view *heap: physical view*

These data never change, but they move.

These data never move, but they change.

i: heap index
j: "name"
k: key

index array

Figure 3.3: A Data Structure for the Efficient Implementation of DECREASEKEY

- DECREASEKEY: priority queue × atom × positive real number → priority queue
  This operation decreases the key of the atom, which is already in the priority queue, by the amount specified by the third argument. If the atom is not present, an error flag is raised.

For this operation to be efficient in any reasonable implementation of priority queues, there must exist an external pointer to the atom. Thus an atom will have two fields: the first is the key that we have already associated with an atom, namely the value that governs its placement in the priority queue; the second is the "name" by which the algorithm that uses the priority queue refers to the atom. When possible, the name space is designed so that an atom can be found in constant time. To consider a concrete example, the atoms may be nodes of a graph, labelled 1 through n so that they can be placed in an array, and the key governing placement in the priority queue might be the degree of the node in the graph. The complete data structure is shown schematically in Figure 3.3. This enhancement adds only a minor complication to the SiftUp and SiftDown procedures of Programs 3.1 and 3.2: keys are referenced indirectly and, when an atom is moved in the heap, the pointer into the heap from the data structure indexed by names has to be adjusted. This change does not affect the asymptotic performance of SiftUp and SiftDown; DecreaseKey, which is essentially a sift-up operation, thus also takes $\Theta(\log n)$ time.

While our primary use of heaps will be as an implementation of priority queues, an important classical application of heaps is the sorting algorithm known as *heapsort*. This sorting technique has a guaranteed performance on a list of n elements of $\Theta(n \log n)$ and uses insignificant extra storage. If it is desired to sort a list of numbers into increasing order, then the elements in the original array are converted into a max-heap. The idea is to find successively the largest, second largest, etc., elements, remove them one at a time from the heap, and place them at the end of the array. Building of the max-heap is done *in place*, i.e., without using extra storage, and can be accomplished by the loop

```
(* At conclusion of each sift-up operation A[1..i] form a heap. *)
for i := 2 to n do SiftUp(A,i)
```

where the data are in array A. (If the sorting routine is part of a library, then the array A presented to heapsort will not normally have a zeroth location to hold the sentinel and the boundary check will have to be added.) A more efficient approach to creating the max-heap exists and will be presented shortly.

Once the heap has been built, the largest element in A can be retrieved by performing a DeleteMax operation. In the process, the size of the heap will decrease by one, i.e., the nth position in the array will be eliminated from the heap. As the largest element must be placed last in array A, and as position n is no longer part of the heap, the retrieved value can safely be assigned to A[n]—this location will never be examined again. The loop

```
for i := n downto 2 do
  begin
    temp := A[1]; A[1] := A[i];
    SiftDown(A,i-1,1); (* i-1 is the size of the heap. *)
    A[i] := temp
  end
```

produces in A the original list sorted into increasing order. Notice that the swapping of A[1] and A[i] is divided into two pieces, with the sift-down operation performed in the middle; as a result, the value in A[i], which equals the value being sifted down, automatically acts as the sentinel during the sift-down operation.

Heapsort is a very peculiar algorithm in that, if the list is already sorted into increasing order on entry to the sorting routine, the algorithm destroys this order during the heap creation phase and then restores the order during the second phase of the algorithm! The worst-case running time for each phase of heapsort, as just described, is $\sum_{i=1}^{n} \lg i$, which is $\Theta(n \log n)$ since the exact sum is easily seen to be between $n/2 \lg(n/2)$ and $n \lg n$.

```
const MaxN = ...;
type data = array [1..MaxN] of datum;

procedure HeapSort(var A: data; n: integer);
  (* Procedure assumes n > 1; it makes no references to A[0] or A[n+1]. *)
  var i: integer;
      temp: datum;
  begin
    (* Build the heap using heapify. *)
    (* Avoid the need for a sentinel in A[0] during the eventual sift-up operation
       by ensuring that the last element is not the largest in the array. *)
    if A[n] > A[1]
      then begin temp := A[1]; A[1] := A[n] end
      else temp := A[n];
    (* Replace the last element with the bottom sentinel:
       treat the array as n-1 long, with sentinel in A[n]. *)
    A[n] := smallestkey;
    for i := (n-1) div 2 downto 1 do
      (* Sift down item i, but do not go past location n-1. *)
      SiftDown(A,n-1,i);
    (* Reinstall the last element and sift it up into the correct place. *)
    A[n] := temp;
    SiftUp(A,n); (* n > 1 is needed here to prevent examining A[0]. *)

    (* Use the heap to sort. *)
    (* Repeatedly remove the largest element and place it in the last slot. *)
    for i := n downto 2 do
      begin
        temp := A[1]; A[1] := A[i];
        SiftDown(A,i-1,1); (* A[i] acts as bottom sentinel. *)
        A[i] := temp (* swap *)
      end
  end; (* HeapSort *)
```

Program 3.4: Heapsort

Although we cannot improve the asymptotic running time of the entire algorithm, it is possible to perform the heap creation phase in linear time by taking an approach first suggested by R. W. Floyd. Instead of successively inserting elements into one continually growing heap that extends from A[1] through A[i], the algorithm starts with a large number of small heaps and repeatedly coalesces two heaps into one larger heap, until only one heap remains. Program 3.4 shows the code for heapsort, and Figure 3.4 shows the contents of A[ ] and the imposed heap structure after each call to SiftDown during the heap creation phase. If we insist that the upper limit on the size of the array be respected—so that we cannot

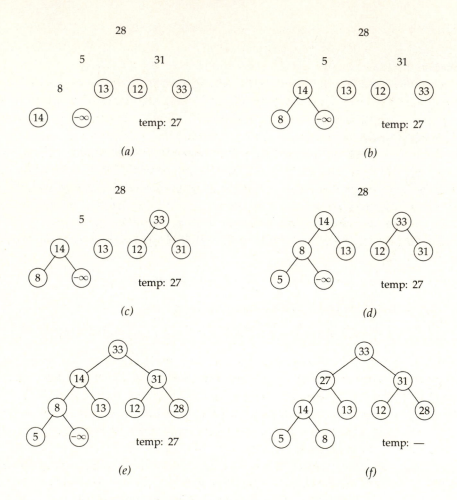

Figure 3.4: The Heap Creation Phase of Heapsort

place a "smallest key" sentinel in position $n + 1$, we have two choices. The first approach modifies our sift-down routine for use in heap creation (no change is required for its use in the sorting phase) by introducing an explicit check for a missing right child. Alternately, we can store the nth element from the array in a temporary variable and process it separately. The code of Program 3.4 takes the latter approach—the only change needed to SiftUp and SiftDown as given in the text is the reversal of the inequalities to account for the use of a max-heap. Which of these two alternatives we select hardly affects the total running time, since, as we shall see in the next paragraph, the heap creation phase of heapsort takes $\Theta(n)$ time. In Figure 3.4, the uncircled numbers at the beginning of the array have not yet been processed and are not part of any heap, while those in circles form a heap of one or more nodes. Notice that, initially, each node between locations $\lfloor n/2 \rfloor + 1$ and n forms a heap of one element.

The following argument shows that the heap creation phase requires linear time. In order to avoid the need for ceiling and floor functions when performing divisions or taking logarithms, we assume, without loss of generality, that there are $2^m - 1$ elements and let $n = 2^m$. Now, $n/2$ elements (those in positions $n/2 + 1$ through n) take no time to insert into their heaps; $n/4$ elements, the parents of the $n/2$ elements that form the initial heaps, have to be sifted down, but can make at most one exchange; $n/8$ elements, the grandparents of the $n/2$ elements that form the initial heaps, can sift down at most two levels. Continuing in this manner, we see that there is only one element, the element initially in location 1, that can sift down at most $\lg n - 1$ levels. The overall worst-case running time is given by

$$(n/2){\cdot}0 + (n/4){\cdot}1 + (n/8){\cdot}2 + \cdots + 2{\cdot}(\lg n - 2) + 1{\cdot}(\lg n - 1) =$$
$$\left(n/4 + n/8 + \cdots + 2 + 1\right) + \left(n/8 + \cdots + 2 + 1\right) + \cdots + 1 =$$
$$(n/2 - 1) + (n/4 - 1) + \cdots + 1 = n - 1 - \lg n.$$

Even if no sifting down were necessary, $n/2$ elements must be examined; thus the heap creation phase takes $\Theta(n)$ time. Heap creation done in this manner is generally referred to as *heapify*. Intuitively, the larger the amount of work that may have to be done on an item, the less numerous such items become: as we move towards the top of the heap, where a sift-down operation may cost the full height of the heap, the number of heap items decreases very fast. Moreover, half the items require no work at all. In contrast, our earlier heap construction through successive insertions saw the number of items grow rapidly as the potential work per item grew, to the point where fully half the items could require $\lg n$ work.

3.1.2 Meldable Heaps

Another useful operation on priority queues is the following:

- MELD: priority queue $\times$ priority queue $\rightarrow$ priority queue
  This operation merges two priority queues into one, destroying the two original queues in the process.

The implementation of priority queues with heaps does not support this operation efficiently. The best that we can do is to copy the second heap immediately behind the first and apply Heapify, a process that requires linear time. However, there are a number of linked implementations of heaps that support this operation efficiently—indeed, where this is the operation through which all others

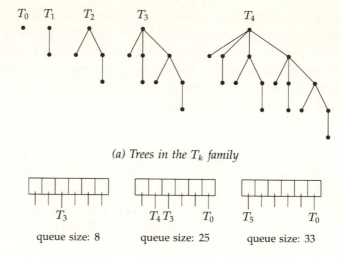

(a) Trees in the T_k family

T_3

queue size: 8

$T_4 T_3$ T_0

queue size: 25

T_5 T_0

queue size: 33

(b) The forests corresponding to various queue sizes

Figure 3.5: The Structure of Binomial Queues

are defined. Exercises 3.13 and 3.15 discuss one such implementation based on swapping children in a binary tree, called a *leftist tree* in its standard version and a *skew heap* in its amortized version. We take up here the standard and amortized versions of a different implementation, this one based on decomposing the queue into a forest of heaps. In their standard version, these heaps are known as *binomial queues* and, in their amortized version, as *Fibonacci heaps*.

A binomial queue implements a priority queue as a forest of trees, where the size of each tree in the forest is a power of 2. Specifically, binomial queues are based on the family of trees, $\{T_k\}$, defined as follows:

- Trees in T_0 are composed of a single node.

- Trees in T_{k+1} are composed of two trees from T_k, where one of the two trees has been attached to the root of the other as its new rightmost child.

This definition immediately implies that a T_k tree has height k, has 2^k nodes, and that its root has exactly k children. The operation which produces a T_{k+1} tree from two T_k trees is called *linking*; it forms the basis of all operations on binomial queues. Let the priority queue have n items and let $b_m b_{m-1} \ldots b_1 b_0$ be the binary representation of n (thus $m = \lceil \lg n \rceil$); then the forest representing the priority queue has a T_i tree whenever b_i equals 1. The structure of binomial queues is illustrated schematically in Figure 3.5. In order to support priority queue operations, each tree in the forest must obey the heap ordering, a requirement which, during linking, forces comparison of the root items of the two trees in order to decide which tree will be attached to the other. Even so, linking takes only constant time.

Since all operations are based on the binary representation of n, a convenient method of access to the forest is through an array of size $\lceil \lg n \rceil$; the ith entry in the array either points to a T_i tree or is nil. The schematic representation of the queue adopted in Figure 3.5(b) reflects this implementation. The various operations on binomial queues are now easily defined: the full-fledged MELD operates exactly like binary addition, starting with the T_0 tree in each forest and moving on up, possibly with a "carry" due to the merging of two T_k trees into a T_{k+1} tree; INSERT simply creates a separate tree of one node containing the new atom and melds this new queue with the existing one; and DELETEMIN locates the smallest element amongst the roots, removes its tree from the forest, breaks it apart by removing its root, and finally melds in turn each child subtree thus produced with the forest. We now describe MELD and DELETEMIN in more detail.

The MELD operation is given by the following algorithm, which the reader will recognize as nothing more than right-to-left addition of binary numbers (just substitute 0 for nil and 1 for a tree):

- Set the carry to nil and set currentbit to 0.

- While there remain trees in either forest, do the following at array position currentbit:

  - There are four cases to consider, depending on the number of trees among the carry and the two array entries.

    (zero trees) The corresponding array entry in the result is set to nil.

    (one tree) The corresponding array entry in the result points to the one tree, and the carry is set to nil.

    (two trees) The corresponding array entry in the result is set to nil, and the carry is assigned the linking of the two trees.

    (three trees) The corresponding array entry in the result points to any one of the three trees, and the carry is assigned the linking of the other two trees.

    Now increment currentbit.

- Let the corresponding array entry in the result be the carry.

Figure 3.6 illustrates the process for binomial queues. Since the body of the loop takes only constant time, the total time spent in a MELD operation is easily seen to be $\Theta(\log s)$, where s is the size of the resulting binomial queue. The reader can verify that the resulting queue has all of the required properties.

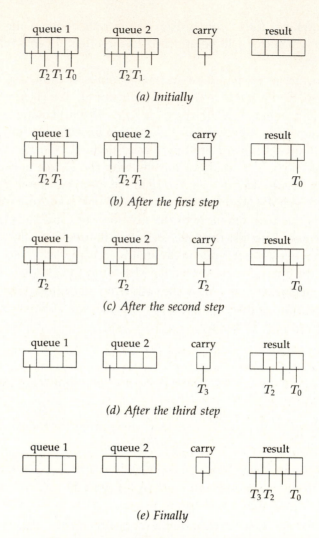

Figure 3.6: MELD in Binomial Queues

A special case of interest is the INSERT operation, because it always merges a binomial queue of size 1 with the existing queue. This operation can easily be implemented as a minor modification of MELD so that it works in place and stops as soon as the carry stops propagating; the resulting procedure, while requiring logarithmic worst-case time (think of adding an item to a queue of size $2^n - 1$ for any value of n), requires only constant time on the average because, assuming that all queue sizes are equally likely, the carry propagates through only $\sum i/2^i$ stages, and $\sum i/2^i$ never exceeds 2. As a reminder of the difference between

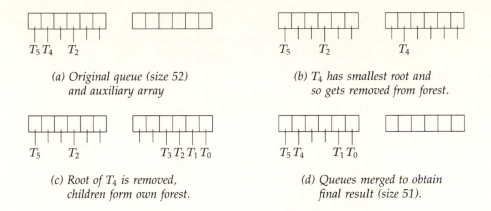

(a) *Original queue (size 52)*
and auxiliary array

(b) *T_4 has smallest root and*
so gets removed from forest.

(c) *Root of T_4 is removed,*
children form own forest.

(d) *Queues merged to obtain*
final result (size 51).

Figure 3.7: DELETEMIN in Binomial Queues

amortized and average analysis, note that the amortized running time of INSERT remains logarithmic: one need only think of a sequence of INSERT and DELETEMIN operations that make the queue size oscillate between sizes $2^n - 1$ and 2^n.

The first step in a DELETEMIN operation is a sweep of the indexing array to carry out a linear search through the roots of the forest for the minimum key. Once this key is found, its corresponding tree, say a T_k tree, is removed from the forest (one pointer change in the array). The third step removes and returns the root of T_k, thereby creating orphan subtrees; note that each of these subtrees is a proper, heap-ordered, T_i subtree itself, for $i = 0, 1, \ldots, k - 1$. Now these trees together form a forest for a priority queue of size $2^k - 1$; thus it is enough to MELD this queue and the existing one to obtain the desired result. The time taken by the whole operation is dominated by the search for the minimum element and is thus logarithmic. Figure 3.7 illustrates the process.

If the application allows amortized, rather than worst-case bounds and makes use of the DECREASEKEY operation, we can improve on binomial queues by using Fibonacci heaps.[4] The amortized time complexity of these heaps is $\Theta(1)$ for INSERT, DECREASEKEY, and MELD and $\Theta(\log n)$ for DELETEMIN, so that their use improves the worst-case performance of a number of classical algorithms that we shall study in Chapter 5 (Prim's algorithm for minimum spanning trees and Dijkstra's algorithm for shortest paths). Note that, in spite of these improved bounds on running time, ordinary heaps may still lead to better performance

---

[4]Note that Fibonacci heaps are not the only way to turn binomial queues into an amortized data structure; Exercise 3.17 discusses a whole family of amortized data structures, called *pairing heaps*, which are also loosely based on binomial queues, and we briefly mention in the bibliography *relaxed heaps*, which achieve bounds similar to those attained by Fibonacci heaps while maintaining the rigid forest structure of binomial queues.

in practice, due first to the hidden costs of Fibonacci heaps (a relatively high space overhead and fairly high coefficients on the time bound) and secondly to the good behavior of ordinary heaps in optimization algorithms (in their use of DECREASEKEY, such algorithms often do not or hardly decrease the key).

Fibonacci heaps are an example of a "lazy" data structure: as little as possible is done during each operation, and time-consuming tasks are delayed as long as possible. As a rule, lazy data structures, as well as data structures on which amortized analysis yields improved bounds, have a less rigid structure than their standard cousins, and Fibonacci heaps are no exception. Like a binomial queue, a Fibonacci heap is a forest of trees, each of which is drawn from a family of similar trees, but we relax two of the constraints placed on binomial queues. First, we no longer require that the forest contain at most one tree of each size. This freedom can lead to very large forests and presents a minor difficulty, as the array of pointers used in binomial queues is no longer applicable. We overcome this difficulty simply by linking all children of a node together in a circular doubly-linked list and by considering the roots of the trees as children of some (nonexistent) supernode (see Figure 3.8). For reasons of convenience, we force the external pointer to point to the root with the minimum key, whereas, for reasons of efficiency in the execution of DECREASEKEY, we allow the child pointer of a node in the forest to point to an arbitrary child. Given this relaxation on the structure of the forest, INSERT and MELD are trivially implemented in constant actual time. MELD, for example, simply joins the two linked lists and adjusts the external pointer. Of course, we shall have to pay for our laziness during DELETEMIN; the new minimum element can be any of the siblings or children of the deleted node.

We also allow a greater variety of tree shapes for use with Fibonacci heaps than we did for use with binomial queues. Recall that, in binomial queues, the number of children of the root of a tree completely characterizes the size and shape of that tree. We again use this measure, which we call the *rank*, to classify trees into families, but we allow a limited amount of pruning to occur at lower levels of the tree. Note that this definition of rank is compatible with that used for splay trees, where the rank of a node was defined to be the base 2 logarithm of its weight; for the trees used in binomial queues, the two definitions are completely equivalent, whereas for the trees used in Fibonacci heaps, a somewhat more complex correspondence exists, which we shall characterize shortly.

The interesting operations are DELETEMIN and DECREASEKEY. We have already noted that deleting the minimum node forces us to examine the siblings and children of the deleted node, an operation that may require linear actual time. Since we may be forced to spend a lot of time searching, we take the opportunity to do additional constant-time work per node in order to reduce the complexity of future operations. Since the complexity is driven by the number of

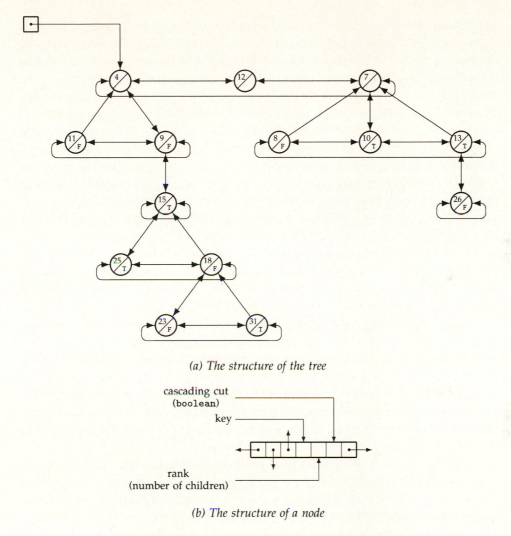

(a) The structure of the tree

cascading cut
(boolean)

key

rank
(number of children)

(b) The structure of a node

Figure 3.8: A Small Fibonacci Heap

nodes at the root level, linking trees to reduce their number should be our goal. The basic step is the same as that used in the maintenance of binomial queues: the linking together of two trees of equal rank. As with binomial queues, the heap ordering determines which root is made the child of the other when linking two trees and linking continues, with possible propagations, until at most one tree of each rank remains. Because we wish to identify candidates for linking in constant time, we use an auxiliary array, indexed by rank, each element of which is a pointer—this is essentially the structure used in binomial queues. This array holds the new forest as we construct it; initially all of its entries are nil. As we remove a subtree from one of the linked lists (either the list of roots or the list of children of the deleted node), we add it to the new forest as follows: if the forest does not contain a tree of the same rank, we place the tree in the forest; otherwise, we link it with the other tree of the same rank and repeat the process. At the end, we use a single pass through the array to reestablish the doubly-linked structure of the forest. We shall eventually prove that the size of this array remains logarithmic in the number of items stored in the priority queue. Each linking step takes constant actual time; we claim that the complete sequence of linking operations takes time proportional to the number of trees to be linked. The only possible objection derives from the cost incurred through the propagations; however, while any particular linking step can propagate through all possible ranks, the total amount of work done during propagation is limited to the total number of nodes examined, since each node can be a "loser" in the linking process at most once. Thus DELETEMIN takes $\Theta\bigl(\max(m,p)\bigr)$ total actual time, where m is the maximum rank of any tree examined and p is the number of trees that are in the forest when the DELETEMIN occurs.

Notice that, using only INSERT, MELD, and DELETEMIN, the only trees that can come into existence remain T_n trees; the difference is in the structure of the forests (for instance, the priority queue formed by a simple sequence of INSERT operations is stored as a forest of trees of one node each). Although we can prove that the amortized complexity of DELETEMIN is logarithmic, the worst-case complexity of this operation remains linear (e.g., in the case of the sequence just mentioned), so that Fibonacci heaps, when compared with binomial queues, have only disadvantages if limited to these three basic operations. Our real interest in the structure lies in its efficient support of the DECREASEKEY operation. Given an external pointer to the item's node in the heap, this operation begins by updating the item's key. If the item sits at the root level, the heap ordering is not affected, so that we need only maintain the external pointer to the node with the minimum key. If, on the other hand, the item has a parent and the parent's key is now larger than the item's own, then the heap order has been damaged; we restore it, in a typically lazy fashion, by cutting off the node from its parent and melding the new subtree into the forest. Cutting off a node involves changes to the node itself, to its immediate siblings, and to its parent; in particular, the parent's child pointer may have to be changed, which can be done in constant time, since the choice of child is arbitrary. This cut, when applied to T_n trees, will not produce other T_n trees, which explains our need for flexibility.

However, unless we restrain the application of cuts, we risk obtaining very lean trees because parents may lose most of their children; yet we cannot avoid cutting off the child, because it is the child-parent ordering which violates the first heap property. What is a properly lazy solution to dealing with the potential for creating lean subtrees? Why, just cut off the parent too! Even though the grandparent thereby loses a child, the effect on the grandparent is less severe, since the child is presumably lean. Of course, such a solution is not applicable at the root level, where we shall have to tolerate trees with roots that have very few children. Such trees look no different from those that were cut off because they were becoming too lean, so we have succeeded in relegating all our problems to the root level. Notice that this solution, like all ideas applying to trees, is recursive: if cutting off the parent results in removing too many children from the grandparent, then the grandparent must also be cut off. The trick is to determine when to cut off the parent and how to maintain the needed information as efficiently as possible. This is the purpose of the Boolean field called "cascading cut" in Figure 3.8. A node, other than a root-level node, is allowed to lose only one child ("suffer one cut"); the next cut must propagate (cascade) to the parent. This propagation is the main reason for the existence of parent pointers in the implementation of Figure 3.8. The actual time of a DECREASEKEY operation can therefore be other than constant. However, there is an important distinction in the behavior of DECREASEKEY between ordinary heaps and Fibonacci heaps: in an ordinary heap the amount of upward propagation depends on the data, whereas in a Fibonacci heap it depends only on the history of operations performed on the heap. It is this data independence which allows the amortized behavior to improve on the actual behavior.

We are now in a position to analyze the properties and behavior of Fibonacci heaps.

Theorem 3.1 Let x be any node in a Fibonacci heap and let the current children of x be ordered from earliest to latest according to the time at which they were linked to x. Then the rank of the ith child is at least $i - 2$. □

Proof: Note that children only come into existence via the linking performed during DELETEMIN operations; although the order in which trees are selected for linking during any such operation is arbitrary, the final result is dictated by the constraint that only trees of equal rank be linked, so that the theorem is well posed. Also note that the ordering is just a convenience for the sake of the proof and has no bearing on the actual implementation, even though the children are easily maintained in this order.

Let y be the current ith child of x. When y was linked to x, x must already have had at least $i - 1$ children, because children could since have disappeared (due to cuts), but any children added subsequently would be farther down in the order. Since x and y were linked, they had the same rank at that time, so that y itself had at least $i - 1$ children. Since y has not been cut, it can have lost at most one child since that time and hence still has at least $i - 2$ children.

Q.E.D.

Note the connection to binomial queues: there the ith child has exactly $i - 1$ children. Yet in both cases the fundamental consequence remains the same: the height of the trees grows only logarithmically with their size, as shown below for Fibonacci heaps.

Corollary 3.1 A node of rank k in a Fibonacci heap has at least F_{k+2} descendants (including itself), where F_k is the kth Fibonacci number. $\square$

Proof: Let S_k be the size of the smallest possible (sub)tree in any Fibonacci heap such that its root has rank k. We claim that we have $S_k = F_{k+2}$. Clearly we have $S_0 = 1$ and $S_1 = 2$. The preceding theorem allows us to derive the recurrence $S_k \geq \sum_{i=2}^{k} S_{i-2} + 2$, since the second through kth children must have ranks at least as large as 0 through $k - 2$ (and thus sizes at least as large as S_0 through S_{k-2}) and since the root itself and its first child each contribute one node (or possibly more in the latter case). A tree with these attributes can indeed be constructed, so that the inequality may in fact be replaced by an equality. By collapsing the full-history recurrence, we obtain $S_k = S_{k-1} + S_{k-2}$, so that the solution is $S_k = F_{k+2}$.

Q.E.D.

At long last we know why Fibonacci heaps are so named! Note that, whereas in a binomial queue of size n the largest tree has rank $\lfloor \lg n \rfloor$, in a Fibonacci heap of equal size the largest tree has rank at most k, with $F_{k+2} \leq n < F_{k+3}$; from Exercise 2.15, we conclude that k does not exceed $\log_\phi n$, where $\phi = (1 + \sqrt{5})/2$ is the golden ratio. This result provides the promised bound on the size of the array needed during DELETEMIN, namely $\lfloor 1.4405 \lg n \rfloor$. This array is the only nontrivial, nondynamic storage used by the data structure; since its size grows only logarithmically with the size of the queue, even moderate sizes (say 100) provide for as large a queue as could ever be handled realistically. We are finally in a position to analyze the amortized time complexity of Fibonacci heaps.

Theorem 3.2 The complexity of Fibonacci heap operations is as follows: MELD, INSERT, and DECREASEKEY run in constant amortized time, and DELETEMIN runs in logarithmic amortized time. $\square$

Proof: The amortized time complexity bounds follow in a straightforward manner once the correct potential function is chosen. We define the potential of a Fibonacci heap to be the number of root nodes plus twice the number of nonroot nodes that have lost one child since last becoming nonroot nodes. We associate an input of two units of energy with INSERT. One of these two units is used to cover the actual constant time of the operation; the other is used to offset the increase in potential, which goes up by one unit. Analysis of MELD is even simpler, because there is no change in total potential and the operation takes constant actual time.

The situation with DECREASEKEY is more complex. Each cut takes constant actual time. If the cut does not cascade, then the maximum increase in the potential is three: promoting a node to the root level raises the potential by one and, if the node's parent is not a root and is losing its first child, the cut causes another increase of two. When the parent is a root, the potential increases by only one. Thus, if there is no cascading of cuts, an associated input energy of four units is sufficient to cover both the actual running time and the changes to the Fibonacci heap. But what of the situation when the parent is not a root and suffers the loss of a second child? In this case the parent is brought to the root level, increasing the potential by one, but a nonroot node that has already suffered a cut is eliminated, decreasing the potential by two, for a net release of one unit of energy. The released unit is used to cover the constant actual time required to move the parent to the root level. As its energy balance is even, this step justifies our mysterious choice of potential function. Eventually we reach either a root or a nonroot node that loses its first child, in the latter case raising the potential by two. Thus an input energy of four, coupled with the use of stored potential energy, covers all situations.

We now turn to the DELETEMIN operation and show that $O(\log n)$ energy suffices to cover its four aspects: initialization of the auxiliary array indexed by rank, time spent in the final scan of this array when the forest is rebuilt, actual time spent processing the children of the deleted node, and assignment of one unit of potential to each root node in the rebuilt forest. Recalling that DELETEMIN takes constant time per node and that the maximum rank of any node in a Fibonacci heap remains logarithmic in the total number of nodes, we see that the cost of each of the four parts is $O(\log n)$. Lastly, the time spent processing the root level nodes in the original Fibonacci heap is exactly compensated by their contribution to the potential of the original heap.

Q.E.D.

Exercise 3.2* Show (by construction) that the height of a tree in a Fibonacci heap can be linear in the number of elements in the heap and that a single DECREASEKEY can take linear actual time. How do you reconcile these facts with Theorem 3.1 and its corollary?   □

Exercise 3.3 Fibonacci heaps also support a DELETE operation. DELETE is normally handled like DECREASEKEY, with one difference: the children of the deleted node are melded in at the root level. Show that the amortized complexity of DELETE is logarithmic.   □

Note that, when DELETEMIN operations follow one upon the other, they are essentially indistinguishable from DELETEMIN operations in a binomial queue: two logarithmic length lists—the remaining nodes from the root level and the children of the node with minimum key—are "added." When a DELETEMIN follows a long sequence of INSERT operations, it acts very much like Heapify in ordinary heaps: it takes all of the little pieces and combines them into successively larger trees, using linear time in the process.

3.2 Equivalence Relations

Another abstract data type that we shall need in the following chapters is the *equivalence relation* (or *partition*). That is, we shall have a set of atoms, S, which is at all times partitioned into a collection of disjoint subsets, the equivalence classes. In most mathematical applications, the equivalence relationship is specified directly, either in English or by some formula or equation, and is used to determine the equivalence classes. Some simple examples are: being congruent modulo N; being in the same connected component of an undirected graph; and occupying the same storage location in computer memory (the effect of the EQUIVALENCE statement of FORTRAN). On a more abstract level, however, any partition of a set into disjoint subsets defines an equivalence relation: two elements are defined to be equivalent if and only if they are in the same subset. Thus the concepts of equivalence relation and of partition into disjoint sets reflect two views of the same underlying mathematical structure.

What kind of operations can one specify on partitions? An obvious choice is a test for equivalence of atoms. In addition, as for all abstract data types, we need an initialization function to provide the first partition and a building function to produce a new partition from an existing one. Since the elements of a partition are just sets, an operation on a partition reduces to some set operation; since the sets in question are disjoint and since the original set of atoms is fixed, most set operations are either trivial (such as intersection, difference, and subset) or irrelevant (such as insertion and deletion). We are left with union and membership. Taking the union of two sets within a partition produces another, "coarser" partition;[5] this is the desired building operation. Membership in the original set of atoms is taken for granted; thus the question of membership becomes "To which equivalence class does the given atom belong?" and the corresponding operation can be used to implement the test for equivalence of atoms. Now we need only provide a label for each equivalence class, as, although the atoms are labelled, the subsets, which vary in number and composition, are not.

---

[5]This suggests another operation, *refinement*, which would produce a "finer" partition. This concept is indeed useful in many areas of mathematics; however, we shall not require it and thus do not consider its implementation.

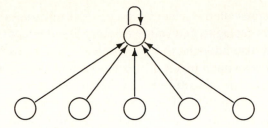

Figure 3.9: An Ideal Structure for FIND Operations

Mathematics suggests an answer to this problem: any element of an equivalence class uniquely characterizes that class. In consequence, an equivalence class can be identified with a chosen representative element—a choice which may even vary, as long as changes do not affect the consistency of the other operations. For instance, the relation "congruent modulo 7" divides the integers into seven equivalence classes; one of these classes contains the integers $\{\ldots, -9, -2, 5, 12, 19, \ldots\}$ and can be characterized by its element 5. To determine that 243 is congruent modulo 7 to 691, one can determine that both integers are congruent to 5 and thus congruent to each other.

In summary, the abstract data type *partition* is described by the following three operations:

- CREATE: set $\rightarrow$ partition
  This operation constructs the trivial partition, in which each atom is the sole element of its equivalence class.

- UNION: partition $\times$ atom $\times$ atom $\rightarrow$ partition
  This operation merges the two equivalence classes given as arguments (as characterized by their representative elements).

- FIND: partition $\times$ atom $\rightarrow$ atom
  This operation returns (the representative element of) the equivalence class to which the given atom belongs.

Now the question "Is x equivalent to y in partition P?" reduces to the question "Is FIND(P, x) equal to FIND(P, y)?"

An effective implementation of this abstract data type must provide easy access to the representative element of an equivalence class from any element of the class. Ideal in this regard would be a collection of nodes, one for each element of the equivalence class, where each node points to the node that contains the representative element. This structure, illustrated in Figure 3.9, would allow constant-time FIND operations, using just one pointer traversal. (Even the node that is the representative element points to itself; this pointer avoids the need for special processing to determine whether the element on which the FIND is being performed also happens to be a representative element.) However, the union of two such structures given by their representative elements is impossible: to provide the proper structure for the result, the pointer of every node in one structure would have to be changed, yet only the representative element is accessible. Suppose that we do start with two sets represented as in Figure 3.9. In accordance with our basic idea of using pointers to the representative element, we can make the representative of one set point to the representative of the other. This change can be accomplished in constant time, but the resulting data structure, a tree in which nodes point to their parents (and the root points to itself), has some elements that are two links away from their representative element. By following a policy of attaching the tree associated with the second argument to the representative element of the tree associated with the first argument, a suitable series of UNIONs can construct a tree that is a linear list—in which a FIND operation requires, on average, $n/2$ pointer traversals.

We can slow down the growth of the longest path by maintaining a balance between the subtrees. This control is exerted by carefully choosing, at each UNION, which subtree to attach to the other.

Theorem 3.3 Let rank(x) be the length of the longest path from a leaf to its representative element, x, and let size(x) be the number of nodes in the equivalence class with representative element x. Either of the following rules for performing UNION(P, x, y), i.e., for merging two trees representing equivalence classes, guarantees that the height of the resulting tree is logarithmic in its size:

- (size rule) If we have size$(x) \leq$ size(y), make the tree rooted at x a subtree of the tree rooted at y; otherwise, make the tree rooted at y a subtree of the tree rooted at x.

- (rank rule) If we have rank$(x) \leq$ rank(y), make the tree rooted at x a subtree of the tree rooted at y; otherwise, make the tree rooted at y a subtree of the tree rooted at x.

$\square$

Proof: More precisely, we show that, for any tree constructed from one-element equivalence classes by repeated UNION operations, we have

$$2^{\text{rank}(x)} \leq \text{size}(x).$$

The conclusion then follows immediately by taking logarithms of both sides. The proof proceeds by induction on the number of UNION operations. Certainly the formula is true initially, since all trees then have one node each, with size of one and rank of zero. We do the induction step for the size rule—the induction step for the rank rule is similar and we leave it to the reader. Without loss of generality, assume that the tree rooted at y has been attached to the tree rooted at x. There are two possible cases: $\text{rank}(x)$ remains unchanged, or $\text{rank}(x)$ becomes $\text{rank}(y)+1$ (the latter because the tree rooted at y has a very long path). In the former case, $2^{\text{rank}(x)}$ remains unchanged, but $\text{size}_{\text{new}}(x)$ increases to $\text{size}_{\text{old}}(x) + \text{size}(y)$, so that the inequality is clearly preserved. In the latter case we have

$$\begin{aligned}
2^{\text{rank}_{\text{new}}(x)} &= 2^{\text{rank}(y)+1} \\
&= 2^{\text{rank}(y)} + 2^{\text{rank}(y)} \leq \text{size}(y) + \text{size}(y) \\
&\leq \text{size}_{\text{old}}(x) + \text{size}(y) = \text{size}_{\text{new}}(x).
\end{aligned}$$

The first inequality comes from the induction hypothesis and the second from the fact that the tree rooted at y has been attached to the tree rooted at x and so is the smaller tree.

Q.E.D.

This approach to merging two equivalence classes was first proposed by Galler and Fischer in 1964.

Exercise 3.4 Show that the analysis presented above cannot be improved upon, i.e., that there are trees formed by repeated UNION operations, the longest path of which is logarithmic in the size of the tree. □

McIlroy and Morris subsequently proposed a heuristic for improving the performance of the algorithm. Since the number of FIND operations generally exceeds the number of UNION operations, which are limited in number to $n-1$, they proposed doing additional work during a FIND operation, with a view to lessening the amount of work done in future FIND operations. As the amount of work done in a FIND is directly proportional to the length of the path from the atom to its representative element, shortening this path through suitable pointer manipulations improves the behavior of future FIND operations along the same path. When a FIND has been completed, we have pointers to both the representative element and the original atom, so that we can retrace the path from the atom to the root of the tree, changing parent pointers as we go to make them point directly to the root of the tree (see Figure 3.10). Not only does this change reduce to one the depth of any node along the path, it also pulls up any nodes hanging down from these nodes. This alteration has become known as *path compression*.

The balancing operation at the time of UNION is easily combined with path compression. Both size and rank criteria require that each root node store the size (respectively, rank) of the tree of which it is the representative element.

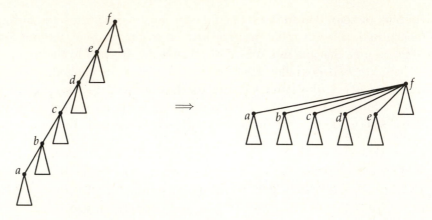

Figure 3.10: The Effect of Path Compression in UNION-FIND

Compression does not alter size, so no updating is necessary. On the other hand, compression does change the rank and, unfortunately, the new rank is difficult to compute. However, the rank cannot increase as a result of compression, so, if we leave it unchanged, the existing value acts as an upper bound on the true rank. This bound is in fact sufficient to guide the merging of two equivalence classes; that is, Theorem 3.3 holds even if "rank" is replaced by "upper bound on rank." Experimental work showed that, if FIND operations were interspersed with UNION operations, the overall work grew more or less linearly with the number of operations. In other words, although a given FIND operation could require logarithmic time, the amortized time complexity of each operation appeared to be constant. (Of course, all of this analysis assumes that we can find in constant time the node that represents an atom, but that task is easily accomplished by using an array to represent the set of atoms, where the ith array element is the node associated with the ith atom and pointers to parents are just array indices.)

In fact, the amortized time complexity of a sequence of the two operations grows imperceptibly faster than linearly. We first need to define a function, $\lg^* n$, read as "log star of n," which grows *very* slowly. This function is defined as the number of times that the lg function must be applied to n in order to reduce the result to a value not exceeding 1. That is, we form the sequence $n = \lg^{(0)} n$, $\lg n = \lg^{(1)} n$, $\lg^{(2)} n$, ..., with $\lg^{(j)} n = \lg(\lg^{(j-1)} n)$, and define $\lg^* n = \min\{ j \mid \lg^{(j)} n \leq 1 \}$. (Note that $\lg^{(j)} n$ is not the logarithm of n raised to the jth power, but the result of repeatedly applying the logarithm function j successive times.) To build intuition as to just how slowly the $\lg^*$ function grows, consider the following values:

$$n: \quad 0 \quad 1 \quad 2 \quad 3\text{--}4 \quad 5\text{--}16 \quad 17\text{--}65{,}536 \quad 65{,}537\text{--}2^{65.536}$$
$$\lg^* n: \quad 0 \quad 0 \quad 1 \quad 2 \quad 3 \quad 4 \quad 5$$

From this table, we see that, for all practical purposes, the $\lg^*$ function never exceeds 5.

Theorem 3.4 If the merge associated with UNION operations uses the heuristic based on rank and the FIND operations use path compression, then, for any sequence of UNION and FIND operations performed on the initially trivial partition of n elements, the total running time is $O(\max(m, n) \lg^* n)$, where m is the number of FIND operations. □

Proof: Much of the proof involves reasoning about the relationship between the rank of a node and the rank of its parent and how path compression affects this relationship over time.

First we extend the notion of rank and size to apply to all nodes in the forest of trees that constitute the partition. The size of a node is always the number of descendants of the node, including the node itself. This number increases monotonically for a time, but, once the node is the "loser" in a UNION operation, its size decreases monotonically, because path compression may only remove descendants. We define the rank of a node at any time to be $\max\{\operatorname{rank}(j) + 1\}$, where j runs over all nodes that are or have been children of the node; the rank of a node which has never had children is zero.

Actually, the rank as just defined is the same as the rank of a node as defined earlier, namely, the length of the longest path from a node to a leaf when path compression is not applied. That the two definitions are equivalent is obscured by the fact that path compression attaches additional children to the roots of trees, additional children that must be taken into account when applying the max function. However, these new children cannot affect the rank of the root of a tree within the forest, because of the following property: starting from any node and proceeding to the root of the tree for this element of the partition, the sequence of ranks is strictly increasing. When viewed from the perspective of a single node, the rank increases monotonically over time until the node is the "loser" in a UNION operation, at which time it never changes again, although the node may lose children over time.

Note that our theorem about the relationship between the rank of a node and its size holds true if we generalize it suitably: if node x has rank r, then at some time the size of the tree rooted at x had size at least 2^r. This assertion always holds, from the time when node x was first assigned rank r until node x either obtains higher rank (which is necessarily $r + 1$) or becomes a child in a UNION operation—and it may hold beyond that time as well.

Finally note that, for a given rank r, a node has, during its entire existence, at most one ancestor of rank r. Our earlier remarks make it clear that, during its entire existence, a node can have at most one parent of rank r; the extension follows from the same remarks, from the monotonicity of the sequence of ranks from a node to a root, and from the rules for performing UNION and FIND. This observation is important because it allows us to prove that at most $\lfloor n/2^r \rfloor$ nodes of rank r exist simultaneously during the execution of the algorithm.[6] First note that any node, when it was assigned a rank of r, had at least 2^r children. Even though these children may no longer be children of the node, they are not now nor have they ever been children of any other node of rank r. Thus the nodes of rank r partition a subset of the n nodes into disjoint sets of at least 2^r elements each.

We are now ready to get to the heart of the proof. Define the jth rank group by

$$S_j = \{\, x \mid \lg^{(j+1)}(n) < \text{rank}(x) \le \lg^{(j)}(n) \,\}.$$

(The lower the rank group, the higher the rank of the node.) The lowest rank group is S_1, which might well be empty. The highest rank group contains exactly those nodes which have remained leaves throughout their entire existence; it is normally $S_{\lg^* n}$, since $\lg^{(\lg^* n)}(n)$ is usually less than one, but it is $S_{\lg^* n+1}$ in the rare case where $\lg^{(\lg^* n)}(n)$ equals 1. We need a precise characterization of the size of a rank group: since there are at most $n/2^r$ vertices of rank r, we have

$$|S_j| \le \sum_i \frac{n}{2^i} < \frac{n}{\lg^{(j)} n}\left(1 + \frac{1}{2} + \frac{1}{4} + \cdots\right) = \frac{2n}{\lg^{(j)} n},$$

where the index of summation runs over the integers in the half-open interval $(\lg^{(j+1)} n, \lg^{(j)} n]$. The second inequality follows because the largest term in the sum is smaller than $n/2^{\lg^{(j+1)} n} = n/2^{\lg(\lg^{(j)} n)} = n/\lg^{(j)} n$ and each successive term is half the previous one.

Now we show how these results may be combined to give the claimed amortized complexity bound. We define the potential of the forest as the sum of the potentials of its trees and the potential of a tree as the sum of the potentials of its nodes. The potential contributed by a node is zero if the node and its parent are in different rank groups (or if the node is a root); otherwise, the contribution to the potential is the distance from the rank of the parent to the "edge" of the rank group, i.e., how much larger the rank of the parent would have to be for the parent to be in a different rank group. (Thus, the larger the difference between

---

[6]In fact, we can strengthen this claim: at most $\lfloor n/2^r \rfloor$ nodes of rank r ever appear during the entire life of the algorithm.

the rank of a node and the rank of its parent, the lower the potential of the node.) Note that the potential contributed by a node decreases with time: if the node gets reattached to a node in a higher rank group, then its contribution drops to zero (permanently); if it is attached to a new node in the same rank group, then the rank of the new parent is higher than the rank of the old parent, and so the potential also drops.

Now let us define our charging policies. Basically, we charge constant time for all the work done during a UNION and for the work done during a FIND on those nodes that keep their parent pointers unchanged (the root and its immediate descendant). We also charge constant time for the work done at each node that has its parent pointer changed during path compression. Since UNION operations add a variable amount of potential to the forest, we do not associate a fixed amount of energy with each UNION, but rather we bound the total amount of potential added to the forest by $O(n \lg^* n)$. The amortized time associated with a FIND, which is $1 + \lg^* n$, accounts for the constant work near the root and for some, but not all, of the pointer manipulations, which can run to $\lg n$ for any FIND. Potential energy stored in the tree is used for any pointer manipulations that cannot be accommodated by the input of $\lg^* n$ units of energy. FIND operations never add potential to the tree. Thus the total running time is bounded by the actual time of the UNION operations (linear); the potential added by the UNION operations, $O(n \lg^* n)$; and the amortized time contributed by the FIND operations, $O(m \lg^* n)$.

Now consider the work done to adjust pointers during a FIND. If a node and its parent are in different rank groups, we use energy associated with the FIND. Since there are at most $\lg^* n$ rank group transitions, the energy associated with the FIND is adequate to cover the cost of the work done at these nodes and the constant time work done at the root. When a node has a parent in the same rank group and is reattached to a new parent in either the same or a lower rank group, there is a decrease in potential of at least one, which can be used to cover the work. Thus, to complete the proof, we must only show that the total amount of potential that must be added during UNION operations can be bounded by $O(n \lg^* n)$. Since the potential of a node is never higher than when it is made a child for the first time and since, when the algorithm terminates, not all nodes of rank r are necessarily children, it follows that the amount of potential added for nodes in rank group j must be less than $(2n / \lg^{(j)} n) \lg^{(j)} n$. The first term of the product is greater than the maximum number of nodes in rank group j, and the second term is an upper bound on the "width" of the rank group, i.e., the maximum potential any node in that rank group can contribute to the potential of the forest. Thus each rank group contributes at most $2n$ to the potential, and there are $1 + \lg^* n$ rank groups, which establishes the result.

Q.E.D.

Exercise 3.5 Show that, if all of the UNION operations occur first in a sequence of UNION and FIND operations, then, provided that path compression is used during the FIND operations, the total running time is linear—regardless of whether or not the rank (or size) heuristic is used during the UNION operations.   □

Tarjan showed that, when path compression is employed and either one of the decision rules on how to perform a UNION is used, the worst-case time required by CREATE and a sequence of m FIND operations interspersed with UNION operations is proportional to $n + m\alpha(m + n, n)$, where $\alpha(m, n)$ is the inverse of Ackermann's function. There is no universally accepted definition of Ackermann's function; that used by Tarjan is:

$$\begin{cases} A(m, n) = A(m - 1, A(m, n - 1)) \\ A(1, n) = 2^n \\ A(m, 1) = A(m - 1, 2) \end{cases}$$

The functional inverse is then defined as

$$\alpha(m, n) = \min\{\, i \geq 1 \mid A(i, \lfloor m/n \rfloor) > \lg n \,\}.$$

Now, Ackermann's function grows extremely fast, even faster than the function given by the recurrence

$$\begin{cases} f(0) = 1 \\ f(i) = 2^{f(i-1)}, \quad i > 0, \end{cases}$$

which forms a sequence of values where the $\lg^*$ function undergoes an increase of one. For instance, with just $m = 2$, $A(m, n)$ equals

$$2^{A(2,n-1)} = 2^{2^{\cdot^{\cdot^{\cdot^2}}}},$$

a tower of $n + 1$ twos, which is exactly $f(n + 1)$. This causes α to grow extremely slowly, even more slowly than $\lg^*$. When m equals n, resulting in a ratio of 1 (the minimum value for the second argument), all values of n less than $2^{A(4,1)}$ result in a value of α of 4 or less; since $A(4, 1) = A(3, 2) = A(2, 16)$ is a tower of 17 twos, all plausible values of n—and a great many more!—are in this range.[7] Moreover, the value of $\alpha(m, n)$ decreases with increasing ratios of m/n; in particular, for

---

[7] One often speaks of "astronomically" large numbers to describe very large numbers; however, the largest numbers arising in the natural sciences are of the order of 10^{90} (which is, within a few powers of 10, the current estimated number of electrons in the known universe). Such numbers are derisively small compared with many numbers arising in mathematics and in algorithmic analysis. In particular, a tower of 5 twos, which is just $A(2, 4)$, is 2^{65536} or about 10^{19728}. Think of what kind of number $A(4, 1)$ is.

```
(* These declarations are common to all three Union-Find routines,
   but not needed elsewhere. *)
const MaxElts = ...;
var sets: array [1..MaxElts] of record
                                    rank, parent: integer
                                end;

procedure CreateUF(N: integer);
  var i: integer;
  begin
    for i := 1 to N do
      begin
        sets[i].rank := 0;
        sets[i].parent := i (* roots point to themselves *)
      end
  end; (* CreateUF *)

procedure Union(i, j: integer);
  (* union by rank;  assumes that i, j are roots *)
  begin
    if sets[i].rank >= sets[j].rank
      then begin
             sets[j].parent := i;
             if sets[i].rank = sets[j].rank
               then sets[i].rank := sets[i].rank + 1
           end
      else (* sets[i].rank < sets[j].rank *)
           sets[i].parent := j
  end; (* Union *)

function Find(i: integer): integer;
  (* uses halving rather than full compression; thus only one pass *)
  var above: integer;
  begin
    above := sets[i].parent;
    while above <> sets[above].parent (* parent is not the root *) do
      begin
        sets[i].parent := sets[above].parent; (* point to my grandparent *)
        i := sets[above].parent; (* move up two levels *)
        above := sets[i].parent
      end;
    Find := above
  end; (* Find *)
```

Program 3.5: UNION-FIND Routines

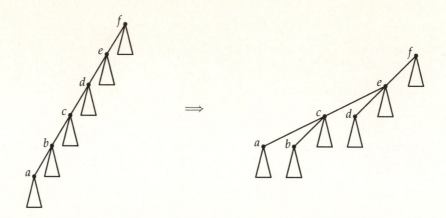

Figure 3.11: The Effect of Path Halving in UNION-FIND

$\lfloor m/n \rfloor \geq 1 + \lg\lg n$, we have $\alpha(m,n) = 1$. Thus $\alpha(m,n)$ is, for all practical purposes, a constant, usually equal to one and never larger than four; hence the implementation of equivalence relations just discussed offers operations that run effectively in constant amortized time.

This bound is tight, so that, in particular, the algorithm is indeed not linear. Several variants have since been proposed and analyzed; these variations only affect the coefficients of the exact running time, not the essential result on the asymptotic performance of the algorithm. The simplest and most efficient version to date does balancing by rank and uses *path halving* rather than full path compression. Path halving only partially compresses the path from an element to the root by making every other node on that path point to what was its grandparent (see Figure 3.11). This heuristic can be implemented in the same pass which performs the FIND, in contrast to path compression, which requires a pass for the FIND and another for the compression. This is the implementation that we present in Program 3.5.

3.3 Search Trees

We have already discussed one species of search tree: the splay tree. Another useful binary search tree based on a totally different approach is the *red-black tree*. Red-black trees offer logarithmic worst-case behavior for standard search tree operations and, as such, are direct competitors of height- and weight-balanced trees; in addition, they support efficiently, in amortized terms, a number of new operations of importance in geometric algorithms. Among existing varieties of red-black trees, we choose one where the items are stored at the leaves; thus the internal tree nodes only store keys. This choice does not affect the behavior of the data structure, but simply proves more convenient in our applications. The keys stored in the internal nodes can duplicate values stored in the leaves or can simply take on any values that are consistent with the binary search tree structure. Once again, this choice can generally be arbitrary, although we shall see one application (intersection of line segments) where it is not; it only affects deletion, and that in a minor way. The tree nodes are partitioned into red nodes and black nodes, where nodes of each color must meet the following conditions:

- (Black rule) All leaves are black, as is the root.

- (Red rule) The parent of a red node is black.

- (Rank rule) The number of black nodes is the same on all paths from the root to a leaf.

It is not strictly necessary for the root to be black. Relaxing the black rule has the advantage that any subtree of a red-black tree is itself a red-black tree; on the other hand, allowing the root to be red increases slightly the complexity of some arguments and has a minor impact on the case-by-case coding for insertion.

These three conditions immediately imply that the length of a longest path from an internal node to a leaf cannot exceed twice that of a shortest path from that node to a leaf: both paths have the same number of black nodes; in the extreme case there are no red nodes at all on a shortest path, while every other node on a longest path is red. Red nodes are best viewed as auxiliary nodes attached to their black parent in order to increase the permissible number of children for a black node. Thus a black node with one red child can be viewed as a node with three (black) children, and one with two red children can be viewed as a node with four (black) children. In this view, the tree is composed entirely of black nodes, each with zero, two, three, or four children. This tree has all of its leaves at the same depth as a consequence of the rank rule. Readers familiar with B-trees may recognize from this description a 2,4-tree; indeed, a very close correspondence between red-black trees and 2,4-trees can be established. These observations lead us to define an additional measure on red-black trees: the *rank* of a node in a red-black tree equals the number of black nodes on a path from the node to a leaf—the rank of a leaf is defined as zero; the rank of a red-black tree is simply the rank of its root. This definition explains the name of the third rule. Red-black trees of minimal size for their rank are composed entirely of black nodes and have exactly 2^r leaves and $2^r - 1$ internal nodes.

Exercise 3.6 Show rigorously that a red-black tree with n internal nodes has height not exceeding $2\lfloor \lg(n+1) \rfloor$.   □

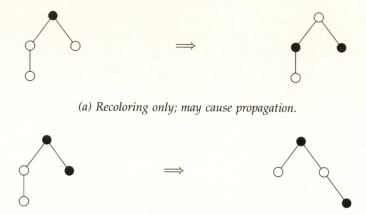

(a) Recoloring only; may cause propagation.

(b) Rotation and recoloring; stops propagation.

Figure 3.12: The Two Patterns for Recoloring After Insertion

In the discussion of insertion and deletion that follows, we shall be concerned primarily with the adjustments required on the red-black tree to ensure that the black, red, and rank rules are obeyed for the resulting tree; we shall take it for granted that all red-black search trees must also obey the binary search tree property, an assumption that implicitly informs much of our discussion on red-black tree maintenance. Insertion takes place at a leaf: the leaf is replaced by a subtree composed of a red root and two (black) leaves, one the old leaf and the other containing the new key; the key assigned to the red root is the lesser of the two keys stored in its children, while these children are ordered accordingly. This strategy ensures that the black rule and the rank rule remain satisfied; however, the new red node thus created could have a red parent, in which case we must do some recoloring. This recoloring proceeds bottom-up from the insertion point until no more recoloring is needed—a process which may move all the way up to the root. The recoloring uses just two patterns (up to symmetry), as illustrated in Figure 3.12. A last recoloring may have to follow applications of the patterns: the root may have to be colored black to satisfy the second clause of the black rule, an adjustment which leads to an increase in the rank of the tree. In the figure, the red node at fault is not given a left *vs.* right orientation, as such is irrelevant to the choice of pattern, although in the second pattern the orientation of the node at fault and the binary search tree property interact to produce two very different rotations. (We do not show the uninvolved children nor the symmetric cases.) Since selection and application of a recoloring step takes constant time, it follows that insertion into a red-black tree is a logarithmic-time operation.

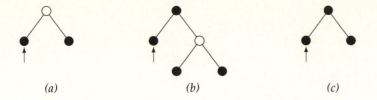

(a)   *(b)*   *(c)*

Figure 3.13: The Situation at a Leaf Before Deletion

Deletion proceeds like insertion. The leaf with the key to be deleted is removed, and then the parent of this leaf is replaced by its other child. Three cases arise, as shown in Figure 3.13. In the first case, a red parent is replaced, so that all three rules remain satisfied after removal and replacement. In the other two cases, a black parent is replaced, so that the remaining leaves end up too close to the root. In the second case, however, it suffices to recolor the red node in black in order to restore the rank rule. There remains only the third case, where recoloring or restructuring of the tree is necessary. Key maintenance can be handled in one of two ways. When the application permits, the simpler solution is to take no special action, with the result that the correspondence between keys stored in leaves and keys stored in internal nodes will be lost, although the binary search tree property still holds. Should one need to retain this correspondence, a small amount of additional work must be done, since the key of one internal node may have to be changed; this node will be on the search path, so that it is easiest to retain a pointer to it and change its key to that of the replaced parent before starting the sequence of recolorings and rotations. The recoloring again proceeds bottom-up, using this time the patterns of Figure 3.14 (where small disks within circles denote nodes of either color); in each pattern, the black node too close to the root is the leftmost node. (Strictly speaking, the "node too close to the root" is actually the root of a subtree in which all leaves violate the rank rule by one.) Pattern (a) is applied as often as necessary; note that, unless the top node of the pattern is itself the root, it will be left too close to the root, so that the need for recoloring propagates. When pattern (a) is no longer applicable and yet recoloring remains necessary, we apply pattern (b) once, if applicable, and then whichever of the other three patterns is applicable. Note that, if the recoloring ends by an application of pattern (a) at the root, the rank of the tree decreases by one. Again, deletion takes logarithmic time overall.

Thus red-black trees join height-balanced and weight-balanced trees, as well as B-trees, in the category of search trees offering logarithmic-time behavior for all three basic operations. Like these other trees, red-black trees also allow logarithmic-time splitting and concatenation, which we shall describe shortly.

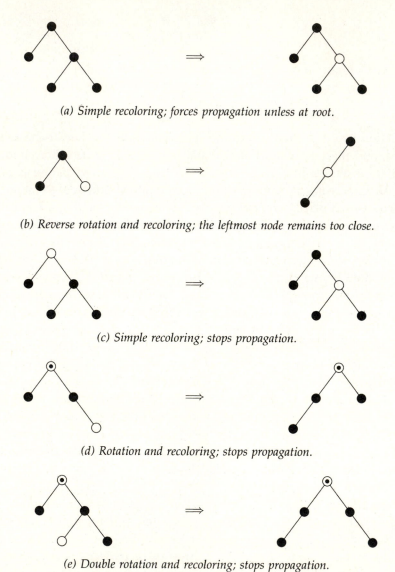

(a) Simple recoloring; forces propagation unless at root.

(b) Reverse rotation and recoloring; the leftmost node remains too close.

(c) Simple recoloring; stops propagation.

(d) Rotation and recoloring; stops propagation.

(e) Double rotation and recoloring; stops propagation.

Figure 3.14: The Five Patterns for Recoloring After Deletion

Table 3.1: The Effect on Potential of an Application of a Recoloring Pattern

Step	Subcase	$\Delta\Phi$	Remarks
Initial insertion	Companion leaf has black parent.	−1 or +2	Depends on color of sibling of leaf.
	Companion leaf has red parent.	0	Recoloring necessary.
	Companion leaf is root.	0	
Insertion pattern (a)	Great-grandparent is black.	+1 or −2	Recoloring propagates.
	Great-grandparent is red.	−1	
	Grandparent is root.	−1	
Insertion pattern (b)		+2	
Root recolored black		+1	
Initial deletion	Red parent	+1 or −2	Depends on color of other child of grandparent.
	Black parent and red sibling	+1	
	Black parent and black sibling	−1	Recoloring necessary.
Deletion pattern (a)		−2	Recoloring propagates.
Deletion pattern (b)		0	One more recoloring needed.
Deletion pattern (c)		0 or −3	Depends on situation at grandparent.
Deletion pattern (d)		−1 or +2	Depends on color of left child of sibling of node too close to root.
Deletion pattern (e)		+2	

Yet red-black trees have something more to offer: a proof that the amortized time of the recoloring phase is constant. Define the potential of a red-black tree as the sum of the number of black nodes with two black children plus twice the number of black nodes with two red children and define the actual cost of the recoloring phase as the number of pattern applications plus one for the initial step of insertion or deletion and the possible recoloring of the root. Intuitively, we ignore the presence of black nodes with three children, since these have slack to grow and shrink, while tallying black nodes in limiting cases, since they store energy which can be used to pay for any manipulations that must be performed on them. Table 3.1 shows the changes in potential that occur during recoloration. Observe that, when propagation occurs, the change in potential is negative, so that the cost of the operation is covered by a release of stored energy, while in situations which can arise only once in any single insertion or deletion, the potential changes by a constant amount. Therefore, the amortized time complexity of the recoloring phase of these two operations is constant, even though the downward search still requires logarithmic time.

In order to take advantage of this recoloring behavior, however, we must use additional storage. Were we to use the space-efficient technique of pointer reversal to move down and up the tree, then we must walk all the way back to the root to reset the pointers, thereby cancelling the benefit of the short propagation of recoloring. If we use an external stack of pointers that records our downward path, then we can terminate the upward walk once the red (for insertion) or rank (for deletion) rule is reestablished, at the expense of logarithmic additional storage. Finally, adding parent pointers throughout the tree simplifies all walks, but requires linear additional storage. However, if the time for comparing two keys is small, we can have our cake and eat it too! During the downward search, we can determine exactly where the upward propagation will stop. For insertion, this point will be the deepest black node along the search path which has either a black parent or black child or, if neither of these occurs, then the root of the entire tree; for deletion, the situation is similar. Thus, if we record the parent of the node where the propagation stops (in case our last recoloring step is a rotation), we can perform all adjustments in a top-down manner on a second downward walk starting from that node.

Level-Linked Trees

In order to support neighborhood searches efficiently, a task of particular importance in geometric applications, we must add pointers to the red-black tree structure, pointers which will allow us to inspect the roots of neighboring subtrees in constant time and also to move easily between levels. Thus we add parent pointers and level links. Level links are pointers between neighboring nodes—for red-black trees, we interpret neighbors to mean black nodes of the same rank. We make these doubly-linked level lists circular by regarding the leftmost and rightmost nodes on a level as neighbors. We also add an additional external pointer to the tree; it points to the leftmost leaf, the item with least value. Figure 3.15 shows an example of a level-linked tree. Such a pointer structure can be imposed on any variety of search tree, but only a few varieties can exploit this additional information efficiently, among which the simplest is the red-black tree.

Level-linked trees, as defined above, behave just like red-black trees under search, insertion, and deletion—the only extra work involves updating the level links, which is easily done in constant time per pattern application. The additional links allow a search for a given item, y, from an arbitrary item, x, in the tree to proceed in time logarithmic in the number of items separating x and y.

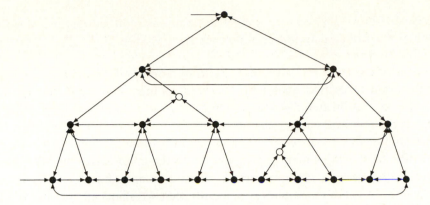

Figure 3.15: An Example of a Level-Linked Tree Based on Red-Black Trees

From item x in the tree, the search for item y proceeds upwards in order to identify a subtree which contains y; once this subtree is found, the search proceeds normally. Without loss of generality, assume that key x is smaller than key y. Starting at the leaf containing x, we follow parent pointers up the tree, considering only black nodes, until we reach some node, u, which meets one of the following three conditions:

1. u lies on the rightmost path of the tree.

2. u lies on the leftmost path of the tree, and its left neighbor (which lies on the rightmost path) contains a key, call it z, no larger than y.

3. u has a right neighbor which contains a key no smaller than y.

In the first case, the subtree rooted at u contains all items with keys larger than x and so must also contain y. In the second case, the subtree rooted at the left neighbor of u contains all items with keys z or larger and thus must contain y. In the third case, we know that y is contained either in the subtree rooted at u or in that rooted at the right neighbor of u. Thus this upward search indeed identifies one or two subtrees in which y must be located; these subtrees are then searched in the conventional manner (without regard to color). The complete process clearly takes time proportional to the height of the subtrees, call it h. Let d be the "distance" between x and y, i.e., the number of items with key values within the interval bounded by x and y, and assume that the level-linked tree contains n items in all. We claim that h is $\Theta(\log \min(d, n-d))$. (The $n-d$ derives from the second stopping condition which, in turn, owes its existence to the circularity of the linked list.)

Exercise 3.7 Prove that our stopping criteria are as tight as possible. Also consider how far from a common root our search may stop.   □

Level-linked trees also support logarithmic-time *concatenation* and *splitting*. Concatenation takes two trees with nonoverlapping key ranges and returns a tree made up of the two trees, destroying both of the original trees. Splitting performs the reverse operation, taking a tree and a key and returning two trees, one containing all keys up to the given key and the other all remaining keys. (The disposition of the single item with key equal to the given key, if such an item in fact exists, depends on our application.) These two operations can be combined to implement a yet more ambitious operation that we shall call *excision*, whereby all items with keys between two values are removed from the tree and made into a tree of their own in time logarithmic in the number of removed items.

Let us first consider concatenation. Let the first tree, with the smaller keys, be T_a and the second be T_b; we simultaneously walk up each tree, along the rightmost path in T_a and along the leftmost path in T_b, ignoring red nodes and keeping at the same distance from the leaves, until we reach the root of one of the trees. During this upward walk, we "zip" the two trees together by updating the level links. Assume that we reach the root of T_a first (the other case is symmetric): we then replace the node reached in T_b, call it x, with a red node, to which we attach T_a as left child and x (with its subtrees) as right child. While this operation satisfies the black rule and rank rule and also ensures the proper ordering of the keys, it may violate the red rule at the new node, in which case we proceed with recoloring in exactly the same manner as described for insertion. The rank of the resulting tree either equals the larger of the ranks of T_a and T_b or is larger by one. The time taken is proportional to the height of the shorter tree, plus a constant, plus the time taken for recoloring (which is constant in amortized terms).

Splitting is more complex; in fact, we shall not solve it directly, but rather reduce it to a series of concatenations. Suppose that we are to split tree T along key x and have located key x (or the largest key not exceeding x) in the tree. From this leaf we proceed upward until we reach the root, deleting every internal node that we encounter, thereby breaking T into two collections of subtrees: those that lie to the left of the path from x to the root (trees in which every key is smaller than x) and those that lie to its right (trees in which every key is larger than x). Each collection can now be separately concatenated into a single tree to yield the desired trees. This process is shown in Figure 3.16, where part (a) of the figure shows a level-linked tree with the path from the splitting key, e, to the root highlighted, part (b) shows the various subtrees which result from the deletion of the internal nodes, and part (c) shows the two trees resulting from the concatenations (parent pointers and level links have been omitted for clarity). The illustrated split arbitrarily places the splitting key in the left tree.

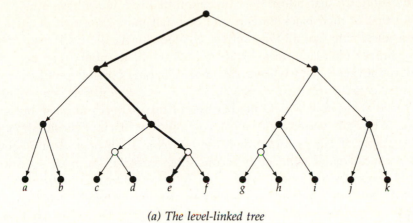

(a) The level-linked tree

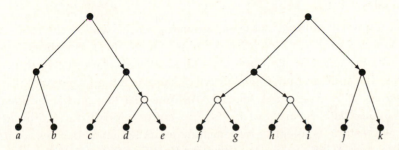

(b) The intermediate subtrees generated by a split along e

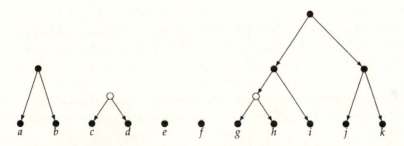

(c) The two trees resulting from the split

Figure 3.16: Splitting a Level-Linked Tree

Although this general schema is clear enough, there are a number of refinements and some critical details that are easily overlooked. In order to simplify our exposition, we shall adopt the convention that red nodes have rank one-half less than that of their black parents and one-half more than that of their black children. First note that all the subtrees created during the walk from x to the root are proper red-black trees, except that some of the roots may be red. Instead of recoloring these, we leave them red. The only possible problem that this choice may cause during the recoloring phase of concatenation is a violation of the red rule at the root, where neither one of our patterns applies; but such a violation is trivially corrected by recoloring the root black. This situation arises in the example of Figure 3.16, when the tree consisting of c, d, and their red parent is concatenated with the tree consisting solely of the node e. Allowing red roots gives rise to some special cases. When two trees of equal rank, both with black roots, are concatenated, we do not recolor the newly created red node that joins the two trees and is the root of the resulting tree. This situation also occurs in Figure 3.16, when the tree containing a and b is concatenated with the newly formed tree containing c, d, and e (this red root is eventually made black because the final trees returned by the splitting operation should be valid red-black trees). When two trees of equal rank, both with red roots, are concatenated, we simply make the newly created root black. Finally, when the tree of smaller rank has a red root, we first make it black, and then proceed normally. All of these rules, and our treating red nodes as having fractional rank, are tied to the following invariant: the rank of the root of the resulting tree exceeds the larger of the ranks of the trees being concatenated by at most one-half. It follows that the root of the resulting tree cannot have rank larger than that of the internal node, the elimination of which spawned one of the two trees involved in the concatenation.

Next note that we need not travel upwards all the way to the root. We can stop as soon as we delete a node, u, on either the leftmost or rightmost path (u can even be the leaf with key x, if x is the smallest or largest key in the tree). What remains of the original tree after we delete u is not a proper red-black tree, but it can be easily repaired as follows. Assume that u is on the leftmost path. The tree rooted at the parent of u loses an entire subtree during the deletion process; we restore its integrity by attaching as its left child the tree, containing keys larger than x, formed by concatenating the trees cast off to the right during the upward walk. At this point, there can be no violation of the binary search tree property or the black rule, but the rank rule can be violated by a large amount, as the rank of the tree that replaces u can be much smaller than the rank of its new parent. We correct this imbalance one step at a time by applying the patterns of Figure 3.14; each such application reduces the rank violation by one, so that the number of these corrective steps equals the difference in the ranks, which is bounded by the rank of u. (The special case of having no right tree to attach can be handled by replacing the parent of u with its right child and taking care of the potential violation of the rank rule by one application of recoloring.) Our previous analysis of the amortized running time of recoloring shows that this is a promising modification of the basic algorithm, because the work done to correct the rank violation cannot exceed that done before reaching u, whereas proceeding onwards to the root of the tree can involve arbitrarily more work.

Exercise 3.8 If the method described in the previous paragraph is applied to the split of Figure 3.16, what two trees are produced?   □

Despite the deceptive simplicity of Figure 3.16, something very important is not happening. When we cast off subtrees, we actually do not cast them off in "pure form": they are not level-linked trees. Each tree produced lacks a pointer to its leftmost leaf; more importantly, the nodes along its leftmost and rightmost paths are not circularly linked—in fact, they are still linked to their original level-linked neighbors. Retaining the original links works to our advantage, since a full concatenation does actual work proportional to the height of the smaller tree while zipping the two trees together, but only constant amortized work while merging in the root of the smaller tree. By not destroying these links, we avoid having to rebuild them later; indeed, we can do the entire splitting operation in a single upward walk using only a constant amount of extra storage. During our walk towards the root, we have three structures to deal with: a single "left tree," a single "right tree," and the remains of the tree being destroyed. The boundaries between these structures are not clearly delineated, since the level links along the leftmost and rightmost paths of the three structures do not point to the correct places. For each of the left and right trees, we maintain two variables: a pointer to the root and a variable that records the rank of the tree. For the remains of the tree being destroyed, we keep a pointer to the internal node about to be eliminated, a variable that holds the rank of this node, and a pointer to the (black) node on the leftmost path of (approximately) equal rank. At all times the level links are fully maintained: for levels below that of the node about to be eliminated, there are two circular level-linked lists, one in what will become the left tree and one in what will become the right tree; for levels at or above the node about to be eliminated, there is only one circular level-linked list. The pointer manipulations that must be performed in eliminating an internal node are complex, involving numerous special cases (coding of this algorithm is not for the faint of heart), but remain manageable due to the invariant discussed earlier, which prevents adjustments from propagating past the node being eliminated. Upon reaching a node on the leftmost or rightmost path, no special action is required to maintain the level links: they have been updated bottom up.

Finally, we note two last details of coding. The key of the node that is created during the concatenation is precisely that stored in the node being eliminated, even though the newly created node may have much lower rank, so that the eliminated node can be reused for this purpose. Secondly, the pointers to the leftmost leaves in the left and right subtrees are easily established once and for all at the start of the algorithm.

We analyze the time complexity of the splitting algorithm in both actual and, more in our favor, amortized terms. If we have direct access to the node with key x, the actual time is proportional to the sum of the length of the path from x to u (the node along the leftmost or rightmost path that allows the algorithm to terminate) and the total number of levels through which recolorings propagate when restoring the rank rule for the tree that loses a child. We only need to verify that the propagation of violations of the red rule during concatenation does not cause each elimination to take more than constant time. While any single concatenation may indeed cause violations of the red rule to propagate, the amount of work for all the concatenations is bounded by h, the length of the path from x to u. This bound is a direct consequence of our earlier invariant (the rank of the root of a concatenation cannot exceed the rank of the node eliminated) and of the fact that the rank of the root of the left (and right) tree increases with each concatenation. The amortized cost has three components: (i) the actual work done while walking from x to u; (ii) the energy added to the trees during the concatenations; and (iii) the energy that must be expended during recolorings, in addition to that withdrawn from the tree. We have seen that the first of these costs is $\Theta(h)$; we also know that there are h concatenations, each requiring input of a constant amount of energy; and, finally, we showed that at most h applications of recoloring are needed, where each application only expends a constant amount of energy. Therefore, the amortized complexity of a splitting operation is $\Theta(h)$.

We are now ready to describe an algorithm for excision. There are a number of versions of this operation, which differ in their assumptions about the exact information available initially. We assume that pointers to both x and y (with x not exceeding y) are given. Were we given only a pointer to x, we could use our fast range search algorithm to find y and proceed as described below (although a more tailored approach could do slightly better). With a small modification of the data maintained in an internal node, we can even efficiently perform an excision of the form "remove x and the next n items." Given just the keys, however, we must search for x, thereby spending time proportional to the height of the entire tree; the search dominates the entire procedure, so we can implement a very simple excision algorithm: split first on x (including x in the right half); then split the tree containing x on y (including y in the left half), yielding one of the two desired trees; and finally concatenate the two trees of elements smaller than x and larger than y.

The difficulty with the simple excision algorithm just described is that each of the splits can propagate all the way to the root even if the distance, d, between x and y is small. We avoid this difficulty by splitting on x and y in parallel, by which we mean that the algorithm proceeds upwards one level at a time, alternating between the ancestors of x and y. This parallel climb up the tree stops when either a common ancestor or two neighboring ancestors (i.e., ancestors u of x and v of y that are neighbors in the level-linking) are found. The excision algorithm thus incorporates aspects of our fast range search. When the parallel search stops, we can simply remove the subtree(s) thus identified, although some repair work on what remains of the original red-black tree, as well as some additional paring on the excised subtree(s), will be necessary.

Before examining the general situation, consider the very simple case—not likely to arise very frequently—where x and y have a common ancestor, w, and where x is the smallest key and y is the largest key in the subtree rooted at w. In this case, the subtree rooted at w is precisely one of the two trees to be returned, and excision is particularly easy. We traverse the leftmost and rightmost paths of the subtree, adjusting the level links; in particular, we stitch together the nodes bordering the portion to be excised. We also detach w and adjust its parent as described for splitting. Overall, the excision in this case requires $\Theta(h)$ real time plus constant amortized time, where h is the height of the subtree rooted at w and is proportional to $\log d$.

In general, when we reach a common ancestor, w, chances are slim that the subtree rooted at w contains exactly the items to be excised; more typically, it will include additional items. Note, however, that the height of that subtree, h, remains proportional to $\log d$; were this not the case, our search would have stopped earlier by reaching neighboring ancestors, as we saw in our discussion of fast range searching. Since the tree rooted at w is thus not too large, we extend the simple approach described earlier by first removing this tree, then splitting it on x and next on y, and finally concatenating the two extreme pieces into a single tree, rooted at w'. Now we replace w with the tree rooted at w', being careful to reestablish the level links from the bottom up. The procedure up to this point takes $\Theta(h)$ actual time and increases the potential by $\Theta(h)$. Finally, correction of the rank violation takes $\Theta(h)$ amortized time, so that the entire procedure runs in $\Theta(\log d)$ amortized time.

We are left with the case where our fast range search reaches two neighboring ancestors, u and v. We can remove both subtrees, split them on x and y, respectively, replace u and v with the extreme pieces from the two splits (one or both may not exist), and process each of them as we processed w' in the previous case. We must also provide the trees that contain x and y with a common root.

This entire procedure can be simplified if the upward search terminates along the leftmost and rightmost paths of the tree: we just apply the simple algorithm for excision described initially. Since the stopping criteria are essentially the same as for fast range searching, the time bound is the same, $\Theta(\log \min(d, n - d))$, but now the bound holds only in the amortized sense because of the propagation of deletions when w, u, or v is replaced by a small subtree.

The excision operation is particularly useful in manipulating lists and collections of intervals. The efficient implementation offered by level-linked trees opens the door to elegant algorithms in computational geometry and other fields; we shall discuss one such application (Jordan sorting) in Section 4.2.3.

3.4 Exercises

Exercise 3.9 Design an algorithm that, given a min-heap and a value, x, determines the relationship between the kth smallest element of the heap and x. Your algorithm should run in $\Theta(k)$ time, regardless of the size of the heap. □

Exercise 3.10* Show that, without affecting the time complexity of sift-up and sift-down, standard heaps can be modified to maintain a stronger version of the first heap property: not only is the key of a parent never larger than the keys of its children, but the key of the left child is never larger than the key of the right child. Can you think of any application for the data structure that supports this stronger invariant? □

Exercise 3.11* Suitably modify standard heaps in order to implement a double-ended priority queue, i.e., a priority queue that includes the operations CREATE, INSERT, DELETEMIN, and DELETEMAX. Verify that all operations run in logarithmic time or better. □

Exercise 3.12 When we can perform arithmetic on key values, i.e., when they are numbers, we can store the key values of a heap implicitly: in each nonroot node we store the difference between the key and the key of its parent. The key field of the root of the heap contains its true value. This representation allows us to perform the operation ADDTOKEYS, which adds a constant value to all keys in the heap, in constant time. For the heap structures presented in Section 3.1, determine how this representation affects the coding and time complexity of the various heap operations. □

Exercise 3.13* [Leftist Trees] In Section 3.1.2 we alluded to *leftist trees*, a tree structure for maintaining priority queues invented in 1971 by C. A. Crane. Leftist trees have the same performance bounds as traditional heaps for INSERT and DELETEMIN, but allow MELD (really the only operation on this data structure) to be performed in logarithmic time. A node of a leftist tree contains a key field, a "depth" field, and two pointer fields. The depth is defined in an unusual way: it is the length of the shortest path from the node to a nil pointer; the depth of a node with a missing child is zero. The two invariants that define a leftist tree are:

1. The first heap property: the key of a node never exceeds the keys of its children.

2. The "leftist" property: at each node, the depth of the right subtree never exceeds that of the left subtree. (This invariant makes the typical leftist tree appear to lean to the left and gives the data structure its name.)

One immediate consequence of the leftist property is that the shortest path to a nil pointer from the root of any subtree repeatedly follows right links; as part of this exercise asks you to prove, the length of this path is always at most logarithmic in the number of nodes of the tree. The MELD operation takes advantage of this consequence to control the amount of work required. We can think of the operation as the merging of two sorted linked lists (the nodes along the rightmost paths) into one, with the left fields (which just happen to be pointers to trees) carried along for the ride. Pictorially, we can think of the trees turned 45° counterclockwise, so that right-child pointers are drawn horizontally and left-child pointers hang downwards—MELD simply merges the two horizontal sorted lists at the tops of their respective figures. This approach clearly preserves the first heap property and takes logarithmic time, but, on righting the tree, we may find that the leftist property is violated for nodes along the rightmost path. These violations can be corrected by walking back up the path, computing the depth as we go and swapping left and right children whenever necessary. Figure 3.17 illustrates leftist trees and the melding process (the depth field of each node is not shown in the figure). This need for a backward walk suggests a recursive implementation—Program 3.6 implements the process. INSERT is simply a MELD of the leftist tree and the one node tree formed by setting `left` and `right` to nil and the `depth` to zero. DELETEMIN is a MELD of `p^.left` and `p^.right` after deletion of the minimum node.

1. Prove that the maximum value of the depth field is $\lfloor \lg n \rfloor$, where n is the number of nodes in the tree.

2. Prove that, if the pattern of INSERT and DELETEMIN operations happens to be last in, first out, then both operations take constant time—an improvement on a traditional heap, where, under these circumstances, both operations take logarithmic time.

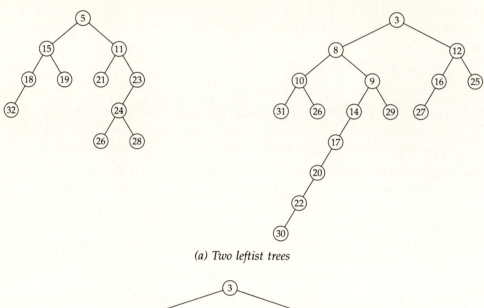

(a) Two leftist trees

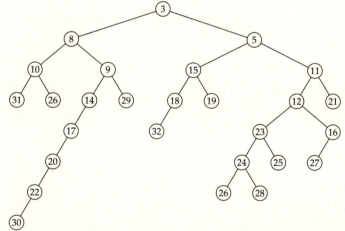

(b) The resulting leftist tree (swaps occurred at nodes with keys 12 and 11)

Figure 3.17: Melding Leftist Trees

```
function Meld(p, q: PtrToNode): PtrToNode;
  (* p and q point to leftist trees. *)
  begin
    (* Call functions key and depth to avoid special cases regarding nil
       (key(nil) = infinity and depth(nil) = -1). *)
    (* Make things uniform--make p point to the node with smallest key. *)
    if key(p) > key(q) then swap(p,q);
    if q <> nil
      then begin
             p^.right := Meld(p^.right,q);
             if depth(p^.left) < depth(p^.right)
               then swap(p^.left, p^.right);
             p^.depth := depth(p^.right) + 1
           end;
    Meld := p
end; (* Meld *)
```

Program 3.6: MELD in Leftist Trees

3. Develop a nonrecursive implementation of MELD that uses link inversion. Note that no bit fields are required to record which pointers are inverted.

4. Using the MELD operation, develop an analogue of Heapify which constructs a leftist tree from a list of items in linear time. The basic idea is the same as in Heapify: start with trivial structures of one element each and repeatedly merge structures two at a time, in a first in, first out manner, until a single leftist tree remains.

5. Consider the two operations of DECREASEKEY and DELETE: can leftist trees support them efficiently?

□

Exercise 3.14[*] [Lazy Leftist Trees] Leftist trees, as developed in the previous exercise, have the advantage of simplicity; however, when compared with Fibonacci heaps, they suffer from two problems: they cannot be melded in constant time and DECREASEKEY takes logarithmic time. Using a lazy approach allows us to reduce the cost of melding to constant time, at the expense of increased time spent during DELETEMIN operations (actually, FINDMIN operations, since a DELETEMIN is implemented as a FINDMIN followed by a DELETE). While the approach does nothing to improve the running time of a DECREASEKEY operation, it automatically provides us with a constant-time DELETE operation. Basically, we allow a leftist tree to accumulate "dummy" nodes through LAZYMELD and DELETE operations and purge some of these nodes at each FINDMIN. When two leftist trees are to be melded, we do it in constant time by introducing a dummy node and attaching to it the two leftist trees. When an element is to be deleted, the deletion is recorded (using an extra bit per node) but not carried out; such "logically deleted" nodes are assimilated to dummy nodes. When carrying out a FINDMIN, we begin by recursively removing dummy and deleted nodes in the vicinity of the root of the tree, terminating the recursion whenever we reach either a nil pointer or a node which is neither a dummy node nor deleted. This recursive procedure creates a collection of disjoint leftist trees, all with roots that represent real objects still present in the heap. We now meld the collection of leftist trees into a single tree using the nonlazy version of MELD and the Heapify strategy of the preceding exercise, but starting now from the existing leftist trees rather than from trivial trees of one node each. Note that nodes that lie along the rightmost path, and happen to be marked as deleted, are carried along during the melding process—they are not physically deleted from the tree at this time; physical removal of a node occurs only during the initial phase of a FINDMIN operation.

Develop the FINDMIN procedure and prove that, when applied to a lazy leftist tree with a total of n nodes, it runs in $O\big(k\log(n/(k+1))\big)$ time, where k is the number of dummy and deleted nodes removed during the FINDMIN operation. (*Hint*: The main problem to solve in the analysis is the time taken by the version of Heapify; if k nodes were removed from the lazy leftist tree, then at most $k+1$ subtrees were created that must be melded into one. Analyze the running time of Heapify in terms of the number of passes through the queue.) □

Exercise 3.15[*] [Skew Heaps] An interesting amortized variation on leftist trees, proposed by Sleator and Tarjan, offers two advantages: there is no need for the depth field, and the MELD operation can be performed as a single top-down walk of the right paths. In leftist trees, after performing p^.right := Meld(p^.right,q), we swap the children of p only when the depth invariant is violated. In skew heaps we always swap the children. For this reason, we need not maintain a depth field and can perform the swap on the way down the right paths, avoiding both recursion and link inversion. Note that, when one of the two right paths becomes nil, the other is simply attached—it is not further explored in order to swap the sibling pairs. Figure 3.18 and Program 3.7 illustrate the melding operation.

The purpose of this exercise is to establish the amortized time bound of $O(\log n)$ for a MELD. As with splay trees, we define the weight of a node, $w(x)$, to be the number of descendants of x (including x). A node is called *heavy* if its weight is greater than half the weight of its parent. The root of the skew heap is, by definition, not heavy. The potential of a skew heap is defined to be the number of heavy nodes that are also right children. The amortized complexity result follows from the following lemmata and observations, which the reader

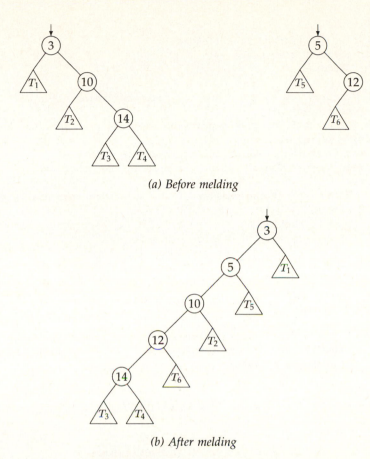

(a) Before melding

(b) After melding

Figure 3.18: Melding Skew Heaps

should prove as part of deriving the amortized complexity bound.

- Only one of a sibling pair of nodes can be heavy.

- On the path from x to a descendant, y, the number of light nodes, counting y, but not x, is at most $\lfloor \lg(w(x)/w(y)) \rfloor$. In particular, any path contains at most $\lfloor \lg n \rfloor$ light nodes.

- During the melding operation, a heavy node can be introduced into a right path, adding to the potential of the skew heap, only if its original sibling was light. Even in this case, creation of a heavy right child is not certain, because the sibling with which it is ultimately swapped during the upward pass is necessarily heavier than the original.

```
function Meld(p, q: PtrToNode): PtrToNode;
  (* p and q point to skew heaps. *)
  var r: PtrToNode;
  begin
    (* Call function key to avoid special cases regarding nil.
        key(nil) = infinity  *)
    (* Make things uniform--make p point to the node with smallest key. *)
    if key(p) > key(q) then swap(p,q);
    if q = nil (* At least one of the two heaps is empty. *)
      then Meld := p (* The result of the Meld is the other. *)
      else begin
              Meld := p; (* the smaller of the two roots--the smallest key *)
              r := p;
              p := p^.right;
              if key(p) > key(q) then swap(p,q);
              while q <> nil do (* p cannot be nil *)
                begin
                  r^.right := r^.left; (* swap siblings on the way down *)
                  r^.left := p;
                  r := p;
                  p := p^.right;
                  if key(p) > key(q) then swap(p,q)
                end;
              r^.right := r^.left;
              r^.left := p
            end
  end; (* Meld *)
```

Program 3.7: MELD in Skew Heaps

- The time spent in processing heavy nodes along the right paths can be covered by a drop in potential.

□

Exercise 3.16* Consider the operations DECREASEKEY and DELETE: can skew heaps support them efficiently? □

Exercise 3.17 [P] [Pairing heaps] Fredman *et al.* have proposed an alternative to Fibonacci heaps, in the form of another amortized version of binomial queues, a version which they call *pairing heaps*. Pairing heaps support all heap operations, including DECREASEKEY and DELETE. They place minimal demands on the structure of the heap: all they insist on is that the heap be stored as a single tree for which the heap property holds. The structure of a node and the structure of the tree are the same as for Fibonacci heaps, except that there is no need for the rank and cascading cut fields; as with Fibonacci heaps, a node can have a variable number of children. In this regard, pairing heaps are more flexible than Fibonacci heaps, since there is no limit on the number of children which a nonroot node can lose. The basic operations remain linking two trees and cutting subtrees out of a tree. Linking immediately give us algorithms for INSERT and MELD. DECREASEKEY operations below the root are accomplished by cutting away the tree rooted at the node of interest and relinking it with the root; there is no cascading. DELETE is similar: if the node being deleted is not the root, the children of the deleted node are joined with the children of the root. The only operation presenting difficulties is DELETEMIN and, indeed, it is the only operation (except for DELETE, which calls upon it if the node being deleted happens to be the root) which takes more than constant actual time. DELETEMIN starts by removing the root, which creates a forest of heap-ordered trees; it then links these together to form a single pairing heap.

The one degree of freedom remaining to us is the order in which we recombine the elements of this forest to form a single tree. The data structure gets its name from the idea of doing the linking by pairs: the simplest approach is to take the first two trees off the front of the list of children of the deleted node, link them together, place the new tree at the end of the list, and repeat this process until only one tree remains. (The equally simple approach of taking the first two trees off the front of the list, linking them together, and placing the new tree at the front of the list is a bad idea, despite the fact that both approaches perform the same number of linking steps. What is the fundamental difference between the two approaches?)

Although experimental results show that pairing heaps are competitive with other heap implementations, all variants appear surprisingly difficult to analyze; Fredman *et al.* have provided approximate analyses of several variants. Design your own heuristics for recombining the elements of the forest into a pairing heap and experiment with them; attempt to establish that the amortized running time of DELETEMIN is logarithmic.   □

Exercise 3.18* Verify that, if we implement UNION-FIND with path compression, but without the merging heuristic, the running time of some sequences of n operations is $\Omega(n \log n)$.   □

Exercise 3.19 An alternative to UNION-FIND as described in Section 3.2 is to use two-way links between the elements of an equivalence class and the canonical element that represents the class. The tree that represents an equivalence class can then easily be maintained so as to have at most two levels. Since the time to perform a UNION operation is linear in the size of the equivalence class that is incorporated into the other, the smaller equivalence class should be incorporated into the larger one.

1. Develop an implementation which: (i) maintains two pointers per node; (ii) carries out FIND in one pointer traversal; and (iii) carries out UNION in time proportional to the smaller of the two equivalence classes involved in the UNION operation.

2. (harder) Determine the worst-case running time of this implementation. Recall that only $n - 1$ UNION operations can be performed before all the elements of S have been merged into one large equivalence class and that only a few of these can involve large, equal-sized sets. Compare this running time with the worst-case running time for the UNION-FIND algorithms (without path compression) given in the text.

□

Exercise 3.20 In our discussion of red-black trees, we noted that such a tree is a binary search tree consisting of interior (key) nodes and exterior (item) nodes in which, from any interior node, the length of a longest path from the node to a leaf cannot exceed twice the length of a shortest path from this same node to a leaf. Prove the converse, i.e., prove that any such tree has a legal red-black coloration.   □

Exercise 3.21 Define the potential of a level-linked red-black tree as the sum of our normal potential plus the rank of its root. Prove that, with this definition of potential, the amortized cost of recoloring remains constant and that the amortized cost of concatenation also becomes constant. Explain this last curious result.   □

3.5 Bibliography

Heaps have a long history, having been introduced as part of heapsort by Williams in 1964; the linear-time algorithm for building heaps is due to Floyd [1964]. Although both authors were concerned with sorting, they pointed out that heaps were particularly well suited to the implementation of priority queues. Modifications of heaps to produce double-ended priority queues are described in Atkinson *et al.* [1986]; Knuth [1973b] attributes the original idea to Williams. Binomial queues were introduced by Vuillemin [1978] and further studied by Brown [1978]. Fibonacci heaps, including their use to improve the worst-case performance of a number of classic algorithms, are due to Fredman and Tarjan [1984]. Crane [1972] invented leftist trees; Knuth [1973b] presents a thorough discussion. Skew heaps, including a variation called *bottom-up skew heaps* that has an amortized time complexity for INSERT and MELD of $O(1)$ and an amortized time complexity for DELETEMIN of $O(\log n)$ (which cannot be performed as a MELD of the two children of the minimum node), were introduced by Sleator and Tarjan [1986]; Jones [1989] points out that they are particularly well suited to parallel implementation. Pairing heaps were first introduced by Fredman *et al.* [1986]; Stasko and Vitter [1987] conducted a thorough experimental investigation which lends support to the conjecture that the amortized running time of DELETEMIN is indeed logarithmic. They also propose numerous variants. Driscoll *et al.* [1988] discuss *relaxed heaps*, yet another variation on heaps, where the first, rather than the second, heap condition is relaxed; these heaps present the same asymptotic behavior as Fibonacci heaps (with one variant strengthening all bounds derived for Fibonacci heaps to worst-case bounds), but appear to suffer from much higher coefficients. Jones [1986] compared heaps, binomial queues, leftist trees, skew heaps, pairing heaps, splay trees, and some other priority queues implementations that we did not present in this chapter (but not Fibonacci heaps and relaxed heaps); he found no significant differences in running time, although splay trees appeared to be fastest. There is no reason to assume that at least one of the three basic operations on priority queues must always require logarithmic time; within the context of certain optimization algorithms, better performance is achievable, as first pointed out by Cheriton and Tarjan [1976] and as discussed at length by Fredman and Spencer [1987].

The UNION-FIND data structure was developed by a number of researchers; its first use is usually credited to McIlroy and Morris. Knuth [1973a] credits path compression to Tritter; the merging heuristic (by size) is due to Galler and Fischer [1964]. The analysis which we present follows Hopcroft and Ullman [1973], while the exact analysis of the algorithm is due to Tarjan [1975]. Merging by rank and size as well as path compression, path halving, and other similar techniques are discussed in detail by Tarjan and van Leeuwen [1984]. Finally, Gabow and Tarjan [1983] discuss a variation of the path compression heuristic which leads to true linear-time behavior for the UNION-FIND data structure under certain patterns of use.

Red-black trees are due to Guibas and Sedgewick [1978] and were further refined by many authors, including Huddleston and Mehlhorn [1982], who showed how to use them to implement level-linked trees (often called *finger trees* in the literature); Tarjan [1983] presents a very thorough discussion of a family of binary search trees which includes red-black trees. Exercise 3.20 is from Olivié [1981]. Level-linked search trees were first proposed by Guibas *et al.* [1977] and can be based on other tree structures besides red-black trees; although they found little use for many years, they have now become an important tool in geometric algorithms. Level linking *per se* has been proposed by many authors, including Brown and Tarjan [1980] (level-linked 2,3-trees) and Hoffman *et al.* [1985] (circular level-linked 2,4-trees).

CHAPTER 4

Fundamental Graph and Geometric Algorithms

Basic graph traversals differ little from basic tree traversals and thus are sure to be known to the reader; however, it is important to realize, first, how closely related all graph traversal methods really are, and, secondly, how powerful even the simplest traversal can be. In particular, graph traversals form the basis of a number of graph decomposition algorithms, such as decomposition into connected components, strongly connected components, and biconnected components. Since these decompositions often save enormous time by allowing one to run an expensive algorithm on small graph pieces rather than on the entire graph, we spend some time discussing them. We then present basic data structures and algorithms for computational geometry; none of the algorithms presented solves any of the geometric problems that we mentioned in the first chapter, but, together with the data structures which they manipulate, they form an indispensable basis for the development of sophisticated geometric algorithms. Also, as geometric applications are getting more pervasive every day, due in large part to the importance of computer graphics in general and of computer-aided design in particular, these basic algorithms can help the reader in solving routine problems in computational geometry. Finally, the field provides a wealth of combinatorial problems, many of which have been solved through particularly beautiful algorithms and data structures.

4.1 Graph Representation and Search

There are many ways to represent graphs, but two representations, based on adjacency relations, tend to dominate algorithmic work: *adjacency matrices* and

```
const MaxVertex = ...;
type vertex = 1 .. MaxVertex;
     PtrToNode = ^node;
     node = record
                  id: vertex;
                  next: PtrToNode
              end;
     graph = record
                  size: integer; (* number of vertices *)
                  AdjLists: array [vertex] of PtrToNode
                    (* array for random access to list heads *)
              end;
```

Program 4.1: Basic Declarations for Graph Search

adjacency lists. If $G = (V, E)$ is a graph, then the adjacency matrix, A, is defined by

$$A_{ij} = \begin{cases} 1, & \text{if } (v_i, v_j) \in E \\ 0, & \text{if } (v_i, v_j) \notin E. \end{cases}$$

If the graph is undirected, then the adjacency matrix is symmetric. We shall consistently distinguish edges from arcs, since the former apply to undirected graphs and the latter to directed graphs; however, we shall also use "edge" in a generic sense. When the edges of a graph have associated costs, it is natural to modify the definition so that A_{ij} is the cost of the edge connecting vertices i and j, if such an edge exists, and a flag if it does not. Figure 4.1(b) shows the adjacency matrix for the graph of Figure 1.3, which is repeated for convenience in part (a) of the figure. The method of adjacency lists associates with each vertex a list of nodes, where each node represents an edge or arc from the vertex associated with the list to that associated with the node. Vertices in each list can, but need not, be sorted according to some useful measure. Figure 4.1(c) shows the same data represented by adjacency lists. Since position in the data structure no longer implicitly defines which two nodes are connected by the edge, we must record both the connection and its cost. Adjacency lists are generally implemented with linked structures, as these are more flexible than sequential implementations; in particular, several links to or from each node can be used to facilitate various updating operations, such as removing a single edge or a vertex and all its associated edges from the graph. Program 4.1 gives our type declarations for adjacency lists.

Which method of representing a graph is preferable depends on the problem, more specifically on the manipulations required and on the storage available. The

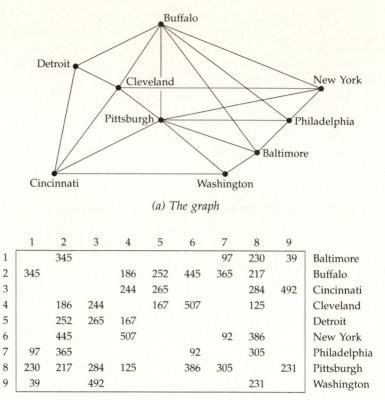

(a) The graph

	1	2	3	4	5	6	7	8	9	
1		345					97	230	39	Baltimore
2	345			186	252	445	365	217		Buffalo
3				244	265			284	492	Cincinnati
4		186	244		167	507		125		Cleveland
5		252	265	167						Detroit
6		445		507			92	386		New York
7	97	365				92		305		Philadelphia
8	230	217	284	125		386	305		231	Pittsburgh
9	39		492					231		Washington

(b) The adjacency matrix representation of the graph

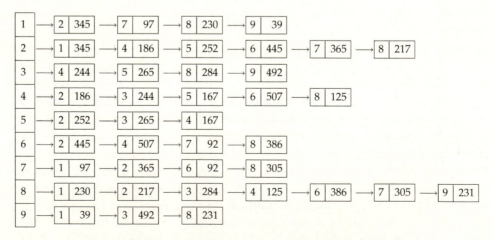

(c) The adjacency list representation of the graph

Figure 4.1: Two Internal Representations of a Graph

adjacency matrix of a directed graph always requires exactly $|V|^2$ locations; thus the storage required is $\Theta(|V|^2 \cdot \log c_{\max})$, where $c_{\max}$ is the largest edge cost. The adjacency lists use only one node per existing edge and thus require exactly $|E|$ nodes, plus an array of $|V|$ positions for the list heads; each node must store the "name" of the associated vertex (which requires $\Theta(\log |V|)$ bits), the cost of the associated edge (which requires $\Theta(\log c_{\max})$ bits), and a pointer to the next node (since there are $|E|$ nodes in all, this requires $\Theta(\log |E|)$ bits), so that the total storage is $\Theta\big(|V|\log |E| + |E|(\log |V| + \log |E| + \log c_{\max})\big)$.[1] In practice, most large graphs, such as transportation and telecommunication networks, are quite sparse ($|E|$ is a small multiple of $|V|$), so that the adjacency list method is clearly preferable to the adjacency matrix method, at least in terms of storage.

In terms of manipulations, the most common operation on graphs is described by the construct "for each vertex adjacent to the current vertex do ..."; if this operation is carried out for each vertex, it takes $\Theta(|V|^2)$ time using an adjacency matrix, but only $\Theta(|V| + |E|)$ time using adjacency lists. The advantage offered by the adjacency matrix representation is its constant-time, random-access capability: if it is necessary to know whether or not there is an edge connecting vertices i and j, only the (i, j)th element of the matrix need be inspected, whereas a traversal of the adjacency list associated with i, looking for j, requires $\Theta(|E|/|V|)$ time on average and $\Theta(|V|)$ time in the worst case. As initializing an adjacency matrix appears to take $|V|^2$ time, the adjacency matrix representation would seem to be inferior, unless used in a $\Omega(|V|^2)$ algorithm that requires random-access capability. In fact, an adjacency matrix can be initialized in $\Theta(|E|)$ time and still support queries regarding edges in constant time, using a data structure known as a *lazy array*. This technique is based on the preposterous notion that we can read from an uninitialized memory cell (which is how we shall represent an edge not present in the graph) and tell, by inspecting the value retrieved, whether the memory cell is, in fact, uninitialized. In order to accomplish this feat, we use extra storage: we associate with each element of the adjacency matrix a "time stamp," which indicates when the element was initialized. Time in this context is not absolute; instead, the time stamp of a newly initialized entry simply indicates how many other entries have already been initialized. The time stamp field of an uninitialized memory cell is whatever random value happens to be stored in it. Consider the querying of a matrix entry: if we discover that the time stamp of the cell is not in the range one through n, where n is the number of memory cells that have been initialized, then we can be sure that

---

[1] These are "theoretical" measures; in practice, all quantities can be stored in one computer word and the log factors are not considered. Thus the adjacency matrix requires $|V|^2$ storage locations and the adjacency lists require $3|E| + |V|$ storage locations. There are only a few applications where the numbers become so large as to require unbounded precision arithmetic and where such theoretical considerations become important; one such application was discussed in Section 1.3: the RSA public-key encryption system.

```
const TotalStorage = ...; (* MaxVertex * MaxVertex *)

var A: array [vertex, vertex] of ...;         (* adjacency matrix *)
    T: array [vertex, vertex] of integer;     (* time stamps *)
    InvT: array [1..TotalStorage] of integer; (* inverted list of time stamps *)
    n: integer;                               (* last time stamp assigned *)

procedure CreateLA;
  (* Initialize lazy array package--user visible. *)
  begin
    n := 0
  end; (* CreateLA *)

function Touched(i, j: vertex): boolean;
  (* Determine if A[i,j] has been initialized--not user visible. *)
  begin
    if (T[i,j] < 1) or (T[i,j] > n)
      then Touched := false (* random value out of range *)
    else if InvT[T[i,j]] <> MaxVertex*i + j
      then Touched := false (* random value within range *)
    else  Touched := true  (* cell initialized in the past *)
  end; (* Touched *)

procedure Touch(i, j: vertex);
  (* Mark A[i,j] initialized, if not already so marked--not user visible. *)
  begin
    if not Touched(i,j) (* If not already initialized... *)
      then begin
             (* ...it is now. *)
             n := n + 1; (* the clock ticks *)
             T[i,j] := n;
             InvT[n] := MaxVertex*i + j
           end
  end; (* Touch *)

function Fetch(i, j: vertex; var defined: boolean): ...;
  (* Return A[i,j] or indication A[i,j] is uninitialized--user visible. *)
  begin
    defined := Touched(i,j);
    Fetch := A[i,j]
  end; (* Fetch *)

procedure Store(x: ...; i, j: vertex);
  (* A[i,j] := x; user visible *)
  begin
    Touch(i,j); (* Harmless if A[i,j] already initialized. *)
    A[i,j] := x
  end; (* Store *)
```

Program 4.2: Lazy Array Implementation of Adjacency Matrices

this entry is uninitialized. To guard against the possibility that the time stamp retrieved from an uninitialized entry just happens to lie within the desired range, we maintain an inverted list, indexed by time, of which entry was initialized at each clock tick. Now, if some matrix entry has a time stamp of i in the required range but the inverted list records that, at time i, a different matrix entry was initialized, we know that the time stamp fell into the allowable range by mere chance. This inverted list is a one-dimensional array of size $|V|^2$, since each of the adjacency matrix elements can be initialized at most once. The code to support adjacency matrices with $\Theta(|E|)$ time for initialization and constant time per query is given in Program 4.2. Although we have tailored the code for adjacency matrices, it is easily generalized to other situations. Since searching down a row of the adjacency matrix still takes $\Theta(|V|)$ time, applications which cycle systematically through all the neighbors of a vertex and require random-access capability can incorporate both data structures, using whichever is better suited to the operation at hand.

4.1.1 Basic Search Methods

As illustrated by the examples in Section 1.2, most graph problems involve some form of graph exploration. Typically, we must search the graph for a vertex or edge with certain properties or examine all vertices or edges in order to verify some property of the graph. Thus we need some basic algorithm for traversing a graph; such an algorithm must visit each node exactly once, presumably examining each edge in the process. In addition, we should like the behavior of the algorithm to reflect the structure of the graph, at least locally; that is, we shall not be content with an algorithm of the type "for each vertex (or edge) of the graph do ...," which processes the elements of the graph in some random order. A family of searches satisfying our needs can be implemented by dividing the vertices of the graph into three disjoint sets: vertices already visited; vertices encountered, but not yet visited; and vertices not yet encountered. The structure of the graph is used to transfer vertices from the "unencountered" to the "encountered" category: when visiting a vertex, all of its unencountered neighbors are placed in the encountered category. The following template describes such a graph traversal:

1. (Initialization) Place all vertices in the unencountered category.

2. (Cycle through graph pieces) While there remain unencountered vertices:

   (a) (Pick a new starting point) Move a vertex from the unencountered to the encountered category.

   (b) (Visit all vertices reachable from the new starting point) While there remain encountered vertices:

   i. Move a vertex from the encountered to the visited category.

   ii. Move all unencountered neighbors of the chosen vertex to the encountered category.

This meta-algorithm produces a proper traversal: each vertex is visited exactly once; each edge is considered exactly once (to be precise, each arc in a directed graph is considered once; each edge in an undirected graph is considered twice, once from each end); and the traversal follows the graph structure. For undirected graphs, step (2b) causes all vertices in a *connected component* to be visited; for directed graphs the same step finds all not yet visited vertices that can be reached from a specified initial vertex. The exact disciplines used for selecting the vertex to move from the unencountered to the encountered category in step (2a) and from the encountered to the visited category were left unspecified. In general, scheduling the next vertex to visit (i.e., selecting the vertex to move from the encountered to the visited category—the more interesting of the two decisions to be made) is done by using a priority queue. The priority itself may be determined through some complex computation, as in the branch-and-bound or game-playing programs presented in Volume II. In two simple special cases, which find a wide range of application in simple graph algorithms, the priority calculation is implicit: (i) the discipline is first in, first out—in which case the category of encountered vertices is implemented with a queue; and (ii) the discipline is last in, first out—in which case this same category is implemented with a stack. The first discipline gives rise to *breadth-first search*, the second to (a variant of) *depth-first search*. In implementing either search mechanism, it is necessary to determine efficiently whether a vertex is still in the unencountered category. The easiest way to record this information is to associate a Boolean flag with each vertex; thus, graph traversals require an extra bit of information per vertex.

   Breadth-first search visits a vertex, then all unvisited neighbors of the vertex, then all unvisited neighbors of these last vertices, and so on. Thus breadth-first search explores the graph on a wide front (hence its name), much like the expanding circular wavelets created by dropping a pebble in a pool. Note that, in an undirected graph, irrespective of the scheduling discipline, the set of edges traversed on the way to unencountered vertices imposes a rooted tree on the connected component: by construction, there is a unique path from the initial vertex to each vertex in the component. Figure 4.2 shows the tree imposed on the graph of Figure 4.1(a) by breadth-first search, starting from Baltimore. Breadth-first search traversal is then recognized as a level order traversal on the imposed tree structure. Program 4.3 implements breadth-first search using adjacency lists. (The comments regarding connectivity apply to undirected graphs.) Because of their simplicity, the queue operations can be placed in-line for added efficiency,

```
procedure BFS(var (* for speed *) G: graph);
  var i, j: vertex;
      p: PtrToNode;
      seen: array [vertex] of boolean;
        (* seen[ ] marks nodes as visited or in queue of nodes to be visited. *)

  (* Program assumes a queue package with operations
        procedure CreateQueue, function IsEmptyQueue: boolean,
        procedure Enqueue(v: vertex), and procedure Dequeue(var v: vertex). *)

begin
  (* Initially, no vertices are visited or in the queue to be visited. *)
  CreateQueue;
  for i := 1 to G.size do seen[i] := false;

  (* The outer loop tries each vertex in turn as the starting point;
     thus all components will be traversed. *)
  for i := 1 to G.size do
    if not seen[i] (* actually "not visited[i]" at this point *)
      then begin (* component traversal *)
              (* Initialize by enqueueing initial vertex. *)
              Enqueue(i);
              seen[i] := true;

              while not IsEmptyQueue do
                begin
                  (* Dequeue the next node seen but not yet visited
                     and visit it... *)
                  Dequeue(j);
                  visit(j);

                  (* ...and now queue all unseen neighbors of j. *)
                  p := G.AdjLists[j];
                  while p <> nil do
                    begin
                      if not seen[p^.id]
                        then begin
                                Enqueue(p^.id);
                                seen[p^.id] := true
                             end;
                      (* else ignore it--either it has been visited
                         or it is in the queue of nodes to be visited *)
                      p := p^.next
                    end
                end
           end
     end
end; (* BFS *)
```

Program 4.3: Breadth-First Search

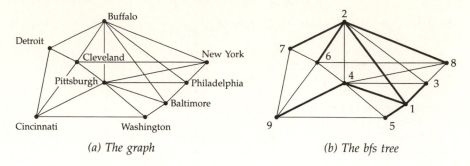

(a) The graph   (b) The bfs tree

Figure 4.2: The Tree Imposed by Breadth-First Search

as can the procedure visit (not shown) since it is frequently short. The outer for loop is needed in order to visit all the components of the graph. Since the queue operations require constant time, the complete algorithm runs in $\Theta(|V| + |E|)$ time. The additional space required is confined to the array of flags and the queue; for some graphs the queue may end up containing all but a few vertices, while on others it will never grow very large. We chose an array implementation for the queue because of its time efficiency; space efficiency concerns would dictate a linked implementation. In any implementation, however, we must conclude that the additional space requirements are $\Theta(|V|)$.

A depth-first search traversal visits a vertex, then immediately traverses an edge to go visit another vertex and continues the search from there. When no further progress is possible (all neighbors, if any, of the last vertex visited have already been visited), the search backs up to the previous vertex and traverses a new edge to an unvisited vertex. When no such new edge exists, the search backs up repeatedly until either it finds a new edge to an unvisited vertex or it attempts to back up from the initial vertex. Depth-first search is the process used to explore a maze: one marks one's path; upon reaching a dead end (either a physical dead end or an intersection that has been encountered before), one backs up to the previous intersection, there to look for an unexplored branch. In the process of traversal, depth-first search maintains one long path from the initial vertex to the vertex currently being explored. As in breadth-first search, the set of edges used to reach unvisited vertices in a given component forms a rooted tree; depth-first search traverses this tree in preorder.

This description suggests a recursive implementation, which we show in Program 4.4. This is the common version of depth-first search. Note that it uses only two categories of vertices, visited and unvisited, in contrast to the brief version that we described earlier, which used a stack to maintain the vertices in the encountered category. The stack-based traversal is identical in every way to the breadth-first search traversal, except that the queue is replaced by a stack;

```
procedure DFS(var (* for speed *) G: graph);
  var i: vertex;
      visited: array [vertex] of boolean;

  (* Auxiliary recursive procedure RecursiveDFS does the work;
     a nonrecursive shell is needed because DFS must initialize visited[ ]
     and scan all the vertices to ensure traversing all the components
     and because visited[ ] must be global to retain values. *)
  procedure RecursiveDFS(i: vertex);
    var p: PtrToNode;
    begin
      (* Visit and mark vertex i... *)
      visit(i);
      visited[i] := true;

      (* ...and proceed recursively on to all unvisited neighbors of i. *)
      p := G.AdjLists[i];
      while p <> nil do
        begin
          if not visited[p^.id]
            then RecursiveDFS(p^.id);
          p := p^.next
        end
    end; (* RecursiveDFS *)

  begin
    (* Initially, no vertex has been visited. *)
    for i := 1 to G.size do visited[i] := false;

    (* Try each vertex in turn as the starting point;
       thus all components will be traversed. *)
    for i := 1 to G.size do
      if not visited[i] then RecursiveDFS(i)
  end; (* DFS *)
```

Program 4.4: Recursive Depth-First Search

since stack operations can also be carried out in constant time, the time and space requirements are the same as for breadth-first search. In fact, the recursive version of depth-first search also uses a stack, albeit implicitly; as a result, the time and space requirements of all three traversals are the same. The ordering imposed upon a graph by depth-first search is called the *dfs numbering*; it is easily computed with a minor modification to Program 4.4, whereby the array visited becomes an array of integers, the elements of which are assigned the dfs number corresponding to the vertex.

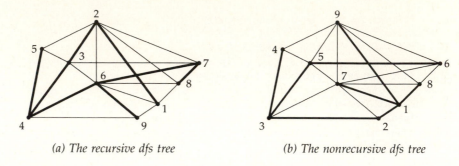

(a) *The recursive dfs tree*   (b) *The nonrecursive dfs tree*

Figure 4.3: The Trees Imposed by the Two Versions of Depth-First Search

Because stacks are intimately tied to recursion, we may be tempted to conclude that the stack version of depth-first search is just the nonrecursive equivalent of Program 4.4. Such is not the case, for two reasons. When the nonrecursive version traverses an adjacency list, it places the unencountered vertices that are near the front of the list deeper into the stack than those that are near the rear of the list; consequently, as the vertices are removed from the stack, the adjacency list is effectively processed in reverse order, in contrast to the recursive version. More importantly, when a vertex is visited in the stack version, all of its neighbors that are unencountered at the time the visit occurs are placed in the stack and their status is switched from unencountered to encountered. In the recursive version of Program 4.4, a vertex adjacent to the vertex being visited may be unencountered when the while loop of RecursiveDFS is entered, but it will have been visited (due to recursive calls and the presence of another path leading to the vertex) by the time p points to it and it is processed by the if statement. Thus, due to the actions during the recursive calls, much time can elapse between entry into the while loop and actual processing of a vertex near the end of the adjacency list, time during which the status of the vertex may change. The trees imposed on the graph of Figure 4.1(a) by the two versions of depth-first search are presented in Figure 4.3.

Topological Sorting

An important application of graph traversal algorithms to directed graphs is *topological sorting*. A *directed acyclic graph*, or *dag* for short, is a directed graph that contains no cycle. Vertices that have no arcs incident upon them are referred to as *sources*, and vertices that have no arcs emanating from them are referred to as *sinks*. A directed acyclic graph must have at least one vertex of each type. To see that it must have a sink, select any vertex of the graph: if it is a sink, we are done; if it is not a sink, then follow any edge to another vertex and repeat this step. This process must terminate since no vertex can be visited twice (or else the graph would have a cycle) and there are only a finite number of vertices. The proof for sources is identical, save that the arcs are followed in the reverse direction. A dag imposes a partial order on the vertices of the graph: the partial order relation is the reflexive transitive closure of the relation described by the set of arcs.

It is always possible to order the vertices of a directed acyclic graph so that, for each vertex, v, all vertices that can be reached in one or more steps from v occur after it in the ordering. In terms of relations, such an ordering, called a *topological ordering*, is a total order on the vertices which satisfies all of the constraints enumerated by the partial order. In general, the topological ordering of a dag is not unique. In view of our discussion of sources and sinks, we can produce a topological ordering in the following manner:

- While $G = (V, A)$ is nonempty:
    - Find any source in G and place it next in the ordering.
    - Remove the source, and all arcs emanating from it, from the graph.

Since removing a vertex and all arcs emanating from it preserves the acyclic property of the graph, each step can be successfully carried out; thus the algorithm terminates. The algorithm can also be used to detect the presence of cycles in a directed graph: if the "find any source ..." step fails while G is nonempty, the graph must contain a cycle.

This meta-algorithm can be implemented in a manner similar to that used to traverse a graph, as shown in Program 4.5. Our implementation uses a stack, but it could equally well use a queue; the abstract data type, known as a *bag*, need only support storage and retrieval of items in constant time, where the item retrieved can be chosen arbitrarily. The vertices are divided into three categories: those already output; those which are sources in the reduced graph; and those that still have arcs incident upon them. When a vertex is transferred from the "sources in the reduced graph" category to the "output" category, it is necessary to remove, at least logically, the vertex from the graph. This removal may cause vertices in the "still have incident arcs" category to become sources in the reduced graph; such vertices must be adjacent to the vertex being visited. The Boolean array seen of Program 4.3 does not retain enough information to determine whether or not a vertex has become a source. Instead we maintain a count of the number of arcs incident upon each vertex (the *in-degree* of the vertex); this information is easily updated when a vertex is removed by decreasing by one the in-degree of each vertex on its adjacency list. If the in-degree of any vertex falls to zero, then this vertex has become a source in the reduced graph and is transferred to the corresponding category. At a practical level, we have

```
type Tsort = array [1..MaxVertex] of vertex;

procedure TopologicalSort(var (* for speed *) G: graph; var T: Tsort);
  (* Assumes that G is a directed acyclic graph. *)
  var i: vertex;
      n: integer; (* number of vertices currently output into T *)
      p: PtrToNode;
      incident: array [vertex] of integer; (* number of incident arcs *)

  (* Program assumes a stack package with operations
        procedure CreateStack, function IsEmptyStack: boolean,
        procedure Push(v: vertex), and procedure Pop(var v: vertex). *)

  begin
    (* Initialize count of number of arcs incident upon each vertex. *)
    for i := 1 to G.size do incident[i] := 0;
    for i := 1 to G.size do
      begin
        p := G.AdjLists[i];
        while p <> nil do
          begin
            incident[p^.id] := incident[p^.id] + 1;
            p := p^.next
          end
      end;

    (* Initialize "sources in reduced graph" to true sources. *)
    CreateStack;
    for i := 1 to G.size do
      if incident[i] = 0 then Push(i);

    n := 0;
    while not IsEmptyStack do
      begin
        (* Retrieve the next "source in reduced graph" and output it. *)
        Pop(i); n := n + 1; T[n] := i;

        (* Effectively remove vertex from graph. *)
        p := G.AdjLists[i];
        while p <> nil do
          begin
            incident[p^.id] := incident[p^.id] - 1;
            (* Is vertex a source in the reduced graph? *)
            if incident[p^.id] = 0 then Push(p^.id);
            p := p^.next
          end
      end
    (* if n <> G.size then graph contains a cycle. *)
  end; (* TopologicalSort *)
```

Program 4.5: Topological Sort

not changed the storage requirements of the algorithm, because we have only replaced an array of Booleans with an array of integers. The upper limit on the size of the stack remains the same. The initialization, which before took $\Theta(|V|)$ time, is now more complex, since it must set up all the in-degree fields; it requires $\Theta(|V| + |E|)$ time, because each field must be initialized to zero, then brought to its proper value by traversing all the adjacency lists. Finally, the stack must be initialized to contain all the sources in the original graph. This is a $\Theta(|V|)$ scan of the in-degree fields looking for zeros. Thus the running time of Program 4.5 is $\Theta(|V| + |E|)$.

4.1.2 Connectivity

Graph traversals, whether by depth-first or breadth-first search, form the basis of a large number of graph algorithms. Several such algorithms will be discussed in the following chapters. In this section, we address some fundamental problems of connectivity in graphs.

Strongly Connected Components

We saw in the preceding section how depth-first search can be used to determine the connected components of an undirected graph. Connectivity is somewhat harder to define in directed graphs. We begin by defining an equivalence relation on the vertices of a directed graph: two vertices, u and v, are related if and only if $u = v$ (the trivial case) or there exists a directed cycle, not necessarily simple, passing through both vertices. (That the directed cycle need not be simple is necessary to establish the transitivity of the relation.) This relation partitions the graph into subgraphs, $G_i = (V_i, A_i)$, $i = 1, 2, \ldots, k$, where the V_i are the equivalence classes determined by the relation and the A_i are those edges of A that have both endpoints in V_i. Each of these subgraphs is called a *strongly connected component* of G; if a graph has only one component, then we say that it is *strongly connected*. Note that, unlike vertices, some of the arcs do not belong to any strongly connected component. We can restate the definition in terms of paths: two vertices are in the same strongly connected component if and only if there exists a directed path from each vertex to the other. In these terms, we can further recast our definition from the perspective of one vertex: the vertices of the strongly connected component characterized by vertex v are simply the elements of the set, $S(v)$, of all vertices for which there exist directed paths to and from v. An immediate consequence of our definitions is that, if each component is collapsed into a single "supervertex," then the resulting graph is acyclic. Figure 4.4 illustrates these definitions and remarks. Partitioning a graph into its strongly connected components before running a complex algorithm (such as a cycle-counting procedure) often results in considerable computational savings.

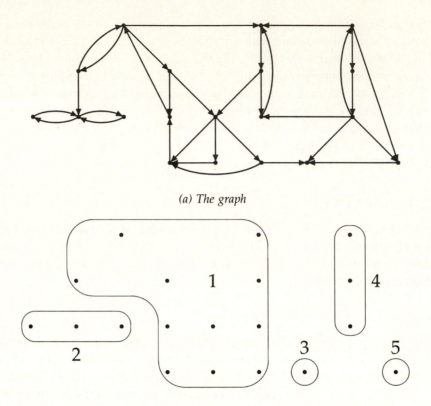

(a) The graph

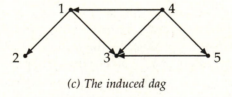

(b) The strongly connected components of the graph (with all arcs removed)

(c) The induced dag

Figure 4.4: Strongly Connected Components

Just as depth-first search can identify connected components in an undirected graph, it can isolate strongly connected components in a directed graph. In view of the definition of strongly connected components, the basic building block is the cycle: a strongly connected component may be viewed as a collection of overlapping simple cycles. Thus we propose to develop an algorithm based on cycles detected through a depth-first search of the graph. However, detecting a cycle in a directed graph is a more complex problem than in an undirected one:

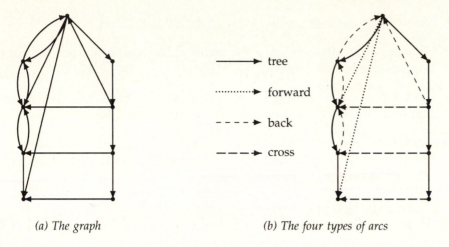

(a) The graph   (b) The four types of arcs

Figure 4.5: The Four Types of Arcs Resulting from a Depth-First Search of a Directed Graph

simply reaching a vertex for the second time, on some alternate path, does not ensure the presence of a cycle passing through that vertex. Therefore, before we proceed with our development of an algorithm for strongly connected components, we examine in detail the process of depth-first search in a directed graph and show how it can be used to detect cycles.

As depth-first search proceeds from a root vertex, v, it develops a tree rooted at v; in the process, it also encounters arcs (other than the tree arcs used for building the tree) connecting nodes in the tree to other, already encountered nodes. Such arcs fall into one of three categories, as illustrated in Figure 4.5 (where we assume that arcs out of a node are explored left to right): (i) forward arcs connect a node to one of its already explored descendants in the tree; (ii) back arcs connect a node to one of its ancestors in the tree; and (iii) cross arcs include all remaining arcs. With a minor modification to our recursive depth-first search routine, we can determine the class into which an arc falls at the time at which it is traversed. In addition to converting the `visited` array into an array of dfs numbers, we need an array of Boolean flags, indexed by vertex number, which indicates which vertices are on the current exploration path. This flag is relevant for only vertices previously encountered, a condition detected by examining the dfs numbers, so it need not be initialized; it is set when we start the exploration of a vertex and reset when we back out of the recursion. (This information is actually redundant, because it is contained in the stack frames of the recursive calls, but we have no programming mechanism for exploring this stack, while the array representation allows constant-time access to the information.)   The four types of arcs are then precisely characterized as follows:

- (Tree arcs) The dfs number of the vertex at the head of the arc has not yet been assigned—it is still zero.

- (Forward arcs) The dfs number of the vertex at the head of the arc is greater than the dfs number of the vertex at the tail.

- (Back arcs) The dfs number of the vertex at the head of the arc is less than the dfs number of the vertex at the tail, and the vertex at the head of the arc is on the current exploration path.

- (Cross arcs) The dfs number of the vertex at the head of the arc is less than the dfs number of the vertex at the tail, but the vertex at the head of the arc is no longer on the current exploration path.

In determining strongly connected components, forward arcs are of no interest to us, since they provide no new information on the connectivity structure of the graph—any forward arc can be replaced by the tree arcs connecting the source node to the destination node. Back arcs, on the other hand, are essential, because each back arc induces a cycle. Cross arcs present a difficulty: they are neither uniformly useful nor uniformly irrelevant. Of the three cross arcs of Figure 4.5(b), the top arc does induce a cycle and is, as such, useful in building the strongly connected component, but it could be dropped from the graph without influencing the result and thus is not essential; the bottom arc is not part of any cycle and is thus irrelevant; and the middle arc is essential because only it allows the incorporation of the vertex from which it emanates into the strongly connected component.

We can now return to the design of an algorithm for the identification of strongly connected components. As we mentioned before, our algorithm will be based on the detection of cycles, which we achieve through depth-first search. Because the difficulties involving cross arcs make it impossible for a simple depth-first search to detect all cycles, we may be unable to find the one cycle which describes all the vertices of a component; instead, we shall record sufficient information about those cycles which our search detects to enable us to identify overlapping cycles and thus place their vertices in the same component. Our task then is threefold: (i) to ascertain that the cycles detected in a depth-first search are sufficient to characterize the strongly connected components; (ii) to store sufficient information about each cycle detected during the search to characterize its extent; and (iii) to identify the vertices of each cycle so as to be able to mark all vertices of each component. We tackle the third task first, because its solution follows immediately from a subtle and elegant relationship between strongly connected components and the forest of dfs trees.

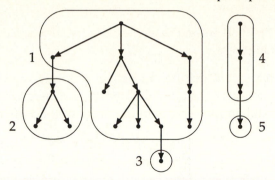

Figure 4.6: The Relationship Between Strongly Connected Components and the dfs Forest

Let the directed graph be $G = (V, A)$. If we form the subgraph, $G' = (V', A')$, by letting V' contain the vertices of a strongly connected component and by restricting A' to exactly those arcs that connect vertices of V' and are also tree arcs of the depth-first search, then G' forms a subtree of the depth-first search forest—not a subtree in the usual sense of a node and all of its descendants, but simply a fragment of the depth-first search forest that itself happens to be a tree. Moreover, the vertex with the lowest dfs number in the strongly connected component is the root of this subtree—for which reason we also call this vertex the root of the strongly connected component. Figure 4.6, based on the graph of Figure 4.4(a), illustrates a dfs forest and the subtrees that correspond to strongly connected components.

Exercise 4.1 Prove these last assertions. *Hint*: let v be the vertex of the strongly connected component with the lowest dfs number. Show that there exists a path, composed exclusively of arcs in A', from v to any other vertex in the component, using the facts that: (i) every vertex on a path between two vertices of a strongly connected component is a member of the component; and (ii) every vertex reachable from v, whether in the strongly connected component or not, will have been assigned a dfs number by the time the recursion backs out of v.

□

We can recast this result in a manner that sheds more light on the situation: let v be the root of its strongly connected component and consider the subtree (in the usual sense), T', rooted at v. Then T' contains A' and A' can be obtained by judiciously pruning away subtrees of T'—subtrees which themselves describe other strongly connected components, although these may also require pruning away of still smaller subtrees. Thus our third task is resolved: in order to keep track of the vertices involved in various cycles and thus in some component, we need only keep track of vertices in the same subtree. Assuming a satisfactory resolution of our first and second tasks, we can use this structural relationship as the basis for an algorithm.

- Walk the depth-first search tree recursively, storing the vertex names in a stack as we encounter them for the first time. (Were we to stop here, the stack would contain the vertices in the order of their dfs numbers.)

- As we back out of the recursion at a given vertex, check whether or not this vertex is the root of its strongly connected component. If so, then the contents of the stack, from the top element to this vertex, describe the vertices of the strongly connected component; pop these elements.

Since we stack the vertices when first encountered, but pop them when last encountered, the entire tree rooted at v is on the stack when the popping takes place, *except for subtrees that have already been removed from the stack*—subtrees which form strongly connected components in their own right. This algorithm effectively uses two stacks: one implicitly to keep track of recursion and the other explicitly to recover the strongly connected components. But, whereas the first stack is popped once for each return from a recursive call, the second remains unchanged in most such occurrences, while "catching up" whenever the root of a strongly connected component is encountered.

We now return to our first two tasks, which, in view of our preceding discussion, we can rephrase simply as: how do we determine, as we back out of a vertex, whether or not that vertex is the root of a strongly connected component? Ideally, we should like to find, for each vertex, v, the vertex with the lowest dfs number that belongs to a cycle passing through v; indeed, this would immediately characterize each strongly connected component. Although we shall eventually extract this information, we cannot expect to find such a vertex and such a cycle directly.

Exercise 4.2 Show, by example, that depth-first search cannot extract enough information to identify, when backing out of some vertex, v, the root of the strongly connected component containing v. (The situation arises in the graph of Figure 4.4(a), although not with the left-to-right ordering used in constructing Figure 4.6.) ☐

Instead, we settle for an approximation: we maintain, for each vertex, v, the dfs number of the lowest-numbered vertex identified by the depth-first search as being part of a cycle passing through v. A vertex will be the root of a strongly connected component if and only if we do not find any cycle passing through it and through a vertex of lower dfs number—if, that is, we can prove that the cycles identified by depth-first search suffice to characterize each component (our first task). Specifically, then, we propose to maintain an array, indexed by vertex name, which stores the dfs number of the lowest-numbered vertex that: (i) is in the same strongly connected component; and (ii) is reachable by traversing zero or more tree arcs followed by at most one cross or back arc. We refer to this value as the *high-water mark*; it provides just the right trade-off between informational content and complexity and solves our second task. On the one hand, it allows us to locate the roots of strongly connected components. On returning from the search of the children of v, we need only compare the dfs number of v with its high-water mark: if they agree, then v, together with any of its children still on the stack, forms a strongly connected component—as we shall shortly prove. On the other hand, maintaining the high-water mark is simple, since it is the minimum of (i) the dfs number of the vertex itself (the initial value, corresponding to a null cycle); (ii) the high-water marks of the children of the vertex in the dfs tree (corresponding to prepending a tree arc to whatever portion of a cycle passes through the descendants); and (iii) the dfs number of any vertex that can be reached directly from the vertex by following a back arc or a relevant cross arc. This last is the one problem we have left: only cross arcs that lead to a vertex within the same component are relevant. Fortunately, we now have the information needed to recognize such arcs. First recall that we can distinguish cross arcs from other types; next consider the cases that might arise: (i) the cross arc is contained within the component; (ii) the cross arc leads to a vertex in another component that has already been popped off the stack; or (iii) the cross arc leads to another, not yet fully explored, component that lies deeper in the stack. The first case is the desired one; the second case is easily recognized through the use of an array of Boolean flags, which indicate whether or not each vertex is on the stack; and the third case cannot arise, because the existence of such a cross arc would form a cycle linking the two components and thus in fact imply that the two components are one.

We now complete our program of three tasks by proving our assertion concerning the root of a strongly connected component; first, however, we prove the basic invariant of our algorithm.

Lemma 4.1 The high-water mark of a vertex v always denotes a vertex included in some common cycle with v (i.e., in the same strongly connected component as v). $\square$

Proof: Our proof proceeds by induction, showing that the invariant holds when the high-water mark is updated. We consider the source of the high-water mark, which is the minimum of the dfs number of the vertex itself and of the values determined by examining the vertices adjacent to v.

- The high-water mark of v is the dfs number of v, i.e., the high-water mark of v denotes itself. In this case, we do not know whether v is part of a substantive cycle or forms a strongly connected component containing only itself (the null cycle), but in either case the lemma is true.

- The high-water mark is determined by the dfs number of a vertex at the head of a back arc emanating from v. The lemma is clearly true.

- The high-water mark is determined by the dfs number of a vertex at the head of a cross arc emanating from v. Our earlier discussion showed that, by use of a Boolean array that records which vertices are on the stack, we can detect when a cross arc leads from v to a vertex within the same component. Since we exclude the cross arc from consideration if it does not remain within the component, the lemma is true in this case.

- The high-water mark is determined by the high-water mark of a vertex at the head of a tree arc. Two cases arise, depending on whether or not the head of the arc is in the same strongly connected component. We could check for this condition explicitly, using our array of Boolean values, but there is no need to do so. If the vertex at the head of the arc is not in the strongly connected component containing v, its high-water mark, which denotes a vertex within its strongly connected component and which has its final value, is greater than the dfs number of v and so cannot be the minimum value. If the head of the tree arc lies in the same connected component, the cycle passing through this vertex and through the vertex denoted by its high-water mark also passes through v.

- The high-water mark is determined by a vertex at the head of a forward arc. This situation cannot arise, as our algorithm ignores forward arcs entirely— any information that could be gleaned from a forward arc will already have been gleaned from a previously encountered tree arc.

All possibilities are thus exhausted and the invariant holds.

Q.E.D.

Theorem 4.1 A vertex is the root of a strongly connected component if and only if its high-water mark equals its dfs number.   □

Proof: The "only if" part follows immediately from the preceding lemma, from the fact that the root of a component has the lowest dfs number of all vertices in the component, and from the fact that the high-water mark of a vertex cannot exceed its dfs number. Assume then that vertex v has a high-water mark equal to its dfs number. The recursive manner in which we compute high-water marks implies that none of the descendants of v (immediate or otherwise) in the dfs tree has a lower high-water mark. It follows that neither v nor any of its descendants in the dfs tree have back or cross arcs (among those that remain within the strongly connected component) leading to a vertex with a dfs number lower than that of v. Therefore, all cycles containing v involve only v and its descendants, so v is the root of a strongly connected component.

Q.E.D.

The last two proofs, based as they are on a recursive definition, have some-what the flavor of existence proofs. The theorem can be proved constructively by considering a cycle including both v and the root of the strongly connected component containing v, which we assume to be other than v. By tracing this cycle, we must eventually come to an arc that leads from a descendant of v to a vertex with dfs number lower than that of v. By replacing, if necessary, the arcs up to this point with tree arcs, which is possible since the tail of the arc is a descendant of v, we see that the high-water mark of a vertex which is not the root of its component must be lower than the dfs number of the vertex.

Although the algorithm is remarkably subtle for what appears to be a simple generalization of connected components from undirected to directed graphs, the code is quite compact, as illustrated in Program 4.6. The reader can easily verify that the procedure runs in time proportional to the number of arcs present in the graph, so that the overall running time of the algorithm on a graph, $G = (V, A)$, is $\Theta(|V| + |A|)$, using $\Theta(|V|)$ extra space.

We conclude this discussion of strongly connected components with two remarks. The reader may still have doubts about this program, due to the fact that the depth-first search traversal of a graph is not unique, whereas the partition of a graph into strongly connected components is unique. Not only does the depth-first search depend on the order in which the starting vertices are chosen (nothing requires that we search for starting points by looping through the vertices in numerical order), it also depends on the order in which vertices are listed in the adjacency lists. Changing the order of visitation may result in shifting arcs among the four categories. This objection is answered simply by noting that the algorithm works in conjunction with the dfs tree which it develops, not with respect to some fixed tree. If a different order of search were chosen, the strongly connected components would still be correctly identified, but the representative element (the root) of each component chosen by the algorithm might vary.

Our second point is that the test to determine, in a general context, whether an arc is a cross arc, and the test to determine, in the context of this problem, whether an arc is a useful cross arc are identical—they both verify that the dfs number of the arc's head is lower than that of its tail and verify that a flag is set. The difference lies in how this flag is maintained. When detecting cross arcs, the flag is reset when we back out of the node—so that an appropriate name for the flag array might be onpath. However, in this algorithm, we delay resetting the

```
type numbering = array [vertex] of vertex;

procedure StrongComponents(var (* for speed *) G: graph;
                              var components: numbering);
  (* The procedure finds all strongly connected components in a directed graph;
     it labels all vertices in a given strongly connected component
     (in components[ ]) by the name of the component's root, which is an
     internally chosen representative for the strongly connected component. *)

  var dfsnumber, highwater: array [vertex] of 0 .. MaxVertex;
      onstack: array [vertex] of boolean;
      lastdfsnumber: 0 .. MaxVertex;
      i: vertex;

  (* Program assumes a stack package with operations
        procedure CreateStack, procedure Push(v: vertex),
        and procedure Pop(var v: vertex). *)

  procedure Strong(v: vertex);
    var p: PtrToNode;
        w: vertex;
    begin
      (* Set up bookkeeping for v. *)
      lastdfsnumber := lastdfsnumber + 1;
      dfsnumber[v] := lastdfsnumber;
      highwater[v] := lastdfsnumber;
      Push(v); onstack[v] := true;

      (* Traverse the adjacency list of v carrying on the depth-first search. *)
      p := G.AdjLists[v];
      while p <> nil do
        begin
          w := p^.id;
          if dfsnumber[w] = 0
            then begin
                   (* (v,w) is a tree arc, continue the depth-first search. *)
                   Strong(w);
                   (* On return, update highwater of parent as needed. *)
                   if highwater[w] < highwater[v]
                     then highwater[v] := highwater[w]
                 end
          else if (* if (v,w) is a back arc or a relevant cross arc and the
                     end vertex improves the highwater mark of the parent... *)
                   (dfsnumber[w] < dfsnumber[v]) and onstack[w] and
                   (dfsnumber[w] < highwater[v])
            then highwater[v] := dfsnumber[w];
          p := p^.next
        end;
```

```
    (* We are ready to leave vertex v, but must first check whether
       or not v is the root of a strongly connected component. *)
    if highwater[v] = dfsnumber[v]
      then repeat (* Pop stack until the root of the component is popped. *)
              Pop(w);
              components[w] := v;
              onstack[w] := false
           until w = v
  end; (* Strong *)

begin
  (* Find all the strongly connected components. *)
  CreateStack;
  lastdfsnumber := 0;
  for i := 1 to G.size do dfsnumber[i] := 0;
  for i := 1 to G.size do
    if dfsnumber[i] = 0 then Strong(i)
end; (* StrongComponents *)
```

Program 4.6: Depth-First Search for Strongly Connected Components

flag until we have backed out of the strongly connected component—hence the name onstack, used for the flag array in Program 4.6.

Biconnected Components

Let us now return to connected undirected graphs. Any pair of points in a strongly connected directed graph is part of a cycle; placing a similar require-ment, phrased in terms of simple cycles, upon undirected graphs leads to bicon-nected graphs. A graph is said to be *biconnected* if and only if any pair of vertices is contained within some simple cycle; equivalently, a graph is biconnected if and only if any pair of vertices is joined by at least two vertex-disjoint paths. The empty graph and the graph consisting of a single vertex are also deemed to be biconnected—we can think of the definition holding vacuously for them; the graph consisting of two vertices joined by a single edge is also deemed to be biconnected, inasmuch as its two vertices are maximally connected. We establish below that the removal of any single vertex from a biconnected graph leaves the graph connected; this result generalizes naturally to k-connected graphs, where the removal of any subset of $k - 1$ vertices leaves the graph connected. Such graphs offer natural models for problems in network reliability: a bicon-nected communications network can still route all packets when one of its nodes has failed—although capacity constraints might then limit the amount of traffic that can be successfully handled. In the same vein, a fault-tolerant computer must have redundant communications paths, while highly parallel computers are most effective when k-connected for some high value of k, because they can then choose minimally loaded routes when transmitting information from one processor to another.

Biconnectivity may also be characterized in terms of vertices and in terms of partitions. A vertex which, when removed from the graph, decomposes the graph into two or more connected components is called an *articulation point*. The presence of an articulation point prevents the existence of more than one vertex-disjoint path between pairs of vertices taken from different connected components, as any path between these pairs must pass through the articulation point. Hence a biconnected graph has no articulation point; in fact, the converse also holds.

Lemma 4.2 A connected graph is biconnected if and only if it has no articulation point.   □

Proof: We have already taken care of the "only if" case. Clearly, the converse holds for the special graphs of one and two vertices. Consider then a graph of three or more vertices without articulation points and consider an arbitrary pair of vertices, say u and v, of the graph. We must show that there exists a simple cycle that includes both u and v; we proceed by induction on the length of the shortest path between these two vertices. The basis corresponds to a path of length one, i.e., a single edge. This case is trivial, since a simple cycle including both u and v then exists if and only if a second path exists between u and v; but this path must exist, lest at least one of u and v be an articulation point. Assume then that our conclusion is true for pairs of vertices up to n edges apart and consider a pair of vertices, u and v, $n + 1$ edges apart. Let the first vertex on a shortest path from u to v be w; now our inductive hypothesis applies to the pair $\{w, v\}$. If the simple cycle that contains w and v also contains u, we are done. Otherwise, note that, as w is not an articulation point, there must exist a path from u to v which does not pass through w. We combine this path with the simple cycle passing through w and v to form a simple cycle passing through u and v, a task easily accomplished through cutting and pasting, as illustrated in Figure 4.7.

Q.E.D.

We can also characterize biconnectivity through an equivalence relation. Recalling our definitions for strongly connected components, we define an equivalence relation on the edges of an undirected graph by deeming two edges, e_1 and e_2, to be related if and only if either $e_1 = e_2$ or there exists a simple cycle containing both e_1 and e_2. The transitivity of this relation is not obvious, but it can be established by using a slight refinement of the cutting and pasting technique illustrated in Figure 4.7(b). The edge partition induced by this equivalence

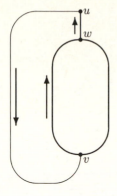
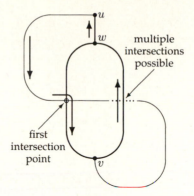

(a) *Path does not intersect cycle.*   (b) *Path intersects cycle.*

Figure 4.7: Merging a Simple Cycle and a Path

relation defines a collection of subgraphs, $G_i = (V_i, E_i)$, $i = 1, 2, \ldots, k$, where the E_i are the equivalence classes and the V_i are the vertices that appear as endpoints of edges in E_i; each G_i is called a *biconnected component* of G. Notice that the relation defining strongly connected components partitions the vertices; in that partition, each edge belongs to at most one subgraph, but may well not belong to any. With biconnected components, we have the dual situation: the relation defines a partition on edges, in which every vertex belongs to at least one subgraph. Those vertices which belong to more than one component, and thus form the boundary of a biconnected component, are precisely the articulation points of the graph. Figure 4.8 illustrates these definitions. We can easily see that a connected graph is biconnected if and only if it contains exactly one biconnected component.

How do we go about identifying the biconnected components of a graph? Once more, we can apply depth-first search. In fact, finding the biconnected components of an undirected graph does not differ significantly from finding the strongly connected components of a directed graph, even though the output previously consisted of collections of equivalent vertices of total size $|V|$ and now consists of collections of equivalent edges of total size $|E|$. Whereas our earlier goal was to find, for each vertex, v, the vertex with the lowest dfs number that was part of any cycle containing v, here we have the same goal, but we restrict our attention to simple cycles. As before, the dfs tree can be partitioned into fragments, each of which is a tree and each of which spans the vertices of, in this case, a biconnected component. Hence, as before, we can stack objects (edges this time) and pop them off all at once when we return to the root of the tree fragment. In contrast to strongly connected components, however, the

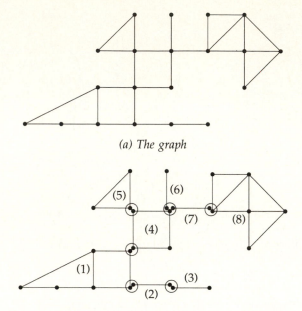

(a) The graph

(b) The biconnected components and articulation points of the graph

Figure 4.8: Biconnected Components

tree fragments overlap at certain nodes of the tree; these points of overlap are precisely the articulation points of the graph. If an articulation point belongs to k biconnected components, the corresponding node in the dfs tree has one parent and at least $k - 1$ children and appears as the root of $k - 1$ of the k overlapping tree fragments. (The root of the entire tree presents a case that differs in details, but not in essence.) Figure 4.9, based on the graph of Figure 4.8, illustrates the subtrees corresponding to the biconnected components, when the depth-first search is started at the uppermost vertex of component (5) and each vertex is searched in counterclockwise order starting at 180°. This overlap appears to produce complications, yet our task is also simplified by the nature of undirected graphs, in which cross arcs do not arise during a depth-first search. By suitably defining the high-water mark of a vertex, Lemma 4.1 (and its proof, which is slightly simpler thanks to the absence of cross arcs) carries over with just one minor change: the vertex v and the vertex denoted by its high-water mark are contained in a common simple cycle. (Here the correct definition of high-water mark is the minimum of the dfs number of the vertex itself and the dfs number of vertices which can be reached by a sequence of tree arcs and a single back arc; we exclude from consideration back arcs that are tree arcs looked at from the opposite endpoint, since these do not contribute to finding simple cycles.) Unfortunately,

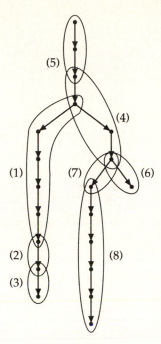

Figure 4.9: The Relationship Between Biconnected Components and the dfs Tree

the overlapping nature of the tree fragments means that Theorem 4.1 does not have an exact parallel: generally, an articulation point will be part of a simple cycle contained in the biconnected component that extends above it in the tree, and its high-water mark will be lower than its dfs number.

Exercise 4.3 Describe exactly under what conditions an articulation point will have its high-water mark equal to its dfs number.   □

Our task, however, is not so much to identify articulation points as to ascertain to which component a given edge belongs; we need to determine when we are backing out of an edge that returns us to an articulation point and thus are most interested in the high-water mark of the child.

Theorem 4.2 A vertex, v, in an undirected graph is an articulation point if and only if there exists a vertex, a, such that: (i) a is a child of v in the depth-first search tree; (ii) the high-water mark of a is at least as large as the dfs number of v; and (iii) there is a vertex, b, other than v, which is not a descendant of a in the depth-first search tree.   □

Proof: Note that the third condition appears in the statement of the theorem only to take care of the root of the tree, since the root must obey the first two conditions whether or not it is an articulation point.

```
procedure Biconnected(var (* for speed *) G: graph;
                      var ... (* output mechanism for components *) );
  (* The procedure finds all biconnected components of a connected
     undirected graph which consist of at least one edge. *)

  type ExtendedVertex = 0 .. MaxVertex; (* 0 is a null parent. *)
  var dfsnumber, highwater: array [vertex] of 0 .. MaxVertex;
      lastdfsnumber: 0 .. MaxVertex;
      i: vertex;

  (* Program assumes a stack package (tailored to edges) with operations
       procedure CreateStack, procedure Push(v, w: vertex),
       and procedure Pop(var v, w: vertex). *)

  procedure BiconnectedComponent(v (* vertex *): vertex;
                                 u (* parent *): ExtendedVertex);
    var p: PtrToNode;
        w, a, b: vertex;
    begin
      (* Set up the bookkeeping for v. *)
      lastdfsnumber := lastdfsnumber + 1;
      dfsnumber[v] := lastdfsnumber;
      highwater[v] := lastdfsnumber;
      (* Traverse the adjacency list of v carrying on the dfs. *)
      p := G.AdjLists[v];
      while p <> nil do
        begin
          w := p^.id;
          if dfsnumber[w] = 0
            then begin
                    (* (v,w) is a tree edge; stack it and continue the dfs. *)
                    Push(v,w);
                    BiconnectedComponent(w,v);
                    (* On return, update highwater of the parent as needed. *)
                    if highwater[w] < highwater[v]
                      then highwater[v] := highwater[w];
                    if dfsnumber[v] <= highwater[w]
                      then (* Either v is the root of the tree or it is an
                              articulation point; all of the edges currently
                              on the stack above (v,w), together with (v,w),
                              form a biconnected component. *)
                        repeat
                          Pop(a,b);
                          ... (* handling of edge (a,b) *)
                        until (a = v) and (b = w)
                 end
```

```
          else if (dfsnumber[w] < dfsnumber[v]) and (w <> u)
              then begin
                      (* (v,w) is a new back edge. *)
                      Push(v,w);
                      if dfsnumber[w] < highwater[v]
                        then highwater[v] := dfsnumber[w]
                    end;
        p := p^.next
      end
  end; (* BiconnectedComponent *)

begin
  CreateStack;
  lastdfsnumber := 0;
  for i := 1 to G.size do dfsnumber[i] := 0;
  (* The graph is connected: one call, with any vertex, is sufficient. *)
  BiconnectedComponent(1,0 (* parent is nonexistent *))
end; (* Biconnected *)
```

Program 4.7: Depth-First Search for Biconnected Components

($\Leftarrow$) We show that every path from a to b must pass through v, which proves our contention. Along any path from a to b, there must be a first arc (directed by the direction of travel) with a tail that is a descendant of a (possibly a itself) and a head that is not a descendant of a. Hence there is a path of tree arcs leading from a to the tail of this arc, and this arc must be a back arc. Condition (ii) implies that the head of this arc must be v, so that the path from a to b goes through v, as claimed.

($\Rightarrow$) First note that an articulation point must have at least degree two. We consider two cases: either v is the root of the depth-first search tree or it is not. If it is, then it must have at least two children in the tree; then any two of these children clearly satisfy the theorem. If it is not, then it has a parent in the tree, call it b. Since v is an articulation point, there is a neighbor of v, call it a', such that b and a' are in different biconnected components. Now the arc from v to a' cannot be a back arc, lest b and a' be part of a simple cycle. Thus this arc is a forward arc or a tree arc; in either case, we may safely choose a to be the first vertex on the path of tree arcs from v to a'. The vertices a and b now meet the conditions of the theorem.

Q.E.D.

This theorem naturally leads to the implementation of Program 4.7, which is easily seen to run in time linear in the number of edges. Two fine details are worth noting: first, we do not test for condition (iii), since we need to output the biconnected component containing the root if it is not an articulation point; secondly, the depth-first search will encounter every edge twice, but our program pushes the edge onto the stack only once (when it encounters it as a tree arc or as nontrivial back arc), so each edge is output only once.

4.2 Geometric Representation and Manipulation

The discipline of computational geometry is quite recent, originating as a unified domain of research with Ian Shamos' dissertation in 1978. Yet the current collection of results, in terms of data structures, algorithms, and insights into both geometry *per se* and other areas of computer science, cannot fail to impress; clearly, this is a rich field of study. In keeping with the computational nature of the area, the main questions addressed by computational geometry to date have been representation, manipulation, and construction, in contrast to classical geometry (i.e., mathematics), which is most concerned with establishing the existence of properties and relations. For instance, typical tasks in computational geometry are deciding whether or not a point is contained within a polygon or constructing the intersection of two polygons, while a typical task in classical geometry is proving the assertion that the bisectors of the angles of a triangle intersect at a single point, which is also the center of the inscribed circle. In this section we present only some very basic ideas about representation and manipulation of two-dimensional geometric objects. We shall return to computational geometry in Chapter 7.

4.2.1 Points, Segments, and Lines

The basic objects of Euclidean geometry are points, lines, and segments. Thus, before anything else, we must address the question of representation of these objects. Let us begin with points. Two different representations immediately suggest themselves: Cartesian and polar coordinates. Both systems are very familiar; both lead to representing points as ordered pairs of numbers. The existence of two coordinate systems does create one difficulty, namely the conversion between the two; while the formulae are well understood, they involve square roots, sines, and cosines, so that the conversion cannot be accomplished without loss of precision. Note, however, that the main purpose of polar representation is to manipulate angles; so the need for conversion really comes down to a question of angle computations. Explicit conversion is unnecessary if the angle computations can be carried out accurately and economically in Cartesian coordinates, in which case polar coordinates can be abandoned altogether. As we shall see, avoiding conversions is indeed possible in most problems.

The problem of representing geometric objects by numbers is actually harder than it appears at first glance: even if we use only Cartesian coordinates and manage to avoid explicit angle and modulus computations, the fact remains that some basic geometric operations will result in loss of precision, unless we use rational arithmetic with variable length representation. Any fixed-length arithmetic—whether derived from the use of variables of type `integer` or of type `real`—induces a finite grid of representable coordinates. An immediate consequence is that even such a simple operation as determining the point of intersection of two lines, which involves only the four basic arithmetic operations, is not closed in computational geometry. Therein lies a major difference between computational geometry, which can only work with representable objects, and classical geometry, which deals with abstract, idealized objects. Yet the boundary is not truly sharp: we can pick two points far apart on the representable grid, declare them to be the endpoints of a segment, and use this segment in many contexts, yet we may be unable to find even one more representable point on the segment itself. Thus the notion of representability of an object depends, appropriately enough, on the use to be made of that object. How much of a concern should this problem of representability be to us? As long as the output devices used in applications of computational geometry remain discrete (as is the case for many graphics devices, robot manipulators, and machine tools), the only problem is one of choosing a suitably precise representation. Moreover, matching the precision available in the input usually suffices, because most tasks involve selecting points and objects from the input data rather than creating new, possibly not representable objects.

In Cartesian coordinates, then, how does one represent a line or a line segment? The segment seems simple enough: we can store both endpoints. The line presents two basic choices: it can be defined either by a subtended segment—and thus represented by a pair of points—or as the solution set of a first-degree equation. The first choice has the advantage of generality and also lets us orient the line, since we can order the pair of points defining it. We can offer an algebraic formulation of this representation: letting the two points be p_1 and p_2, the *parametric representation* of the corresponding line is simply $p_1 + t(p_2 - p_1)$, where operations are carried out independently on each coordinate (and thus are best thought of as vector operations) and where the parameter t varies from $-\infty$ to $+\infty$, describing the segment from p_1 to p_2 as it varies from zero to one. The second choice offers two basic variants, each with some advantages. The familiar *slope-intercept* representation, corresponding to the equation $y = mx + b$, has the advantage of uniqueness; however, it suffers from a very common problem in computational geometry: *degeneracy*—in this case, vertical lines cannot

```
(* Conventions:
     For ordering points--primary key is x, secondary key is y.
       less:      < 0
       equal:     = 0
       greater:   > 0

     For determining on which side of an oriented line a point lies
     or, phrased algebraically, whether a point falls in the positive
     or negative half plane determined by an oriented line.
       left or negative:     < 0
       on line:              = 0
       right or positive:    > 0

     For determining whether two points lie on the same or opposite sides
     of a line.
       same side:                              > 0
       one or both points lie on the line:     = 0
       opposite sides:                         < 0
*)

type point = record
                 x, y: real
              end;
     segment = record
                   e1, e2: point (* endpoints of segment--no order implied *)
                end;

function Compare(p1, p2: point): real;
  (* Sort on x-coordinate, or in the event of a tie, y-coordinate. *)
  var comp: real;
  begin
    comp := p1.x - p2.x;
    if comp = 0
      then (* tie on x-coordinate, so use y-coordinate *)
           comp := p1.y - p2.y;
    Compare := comp
  end; (* Compare *)

function LesserOf(p1, p2: point): point;
  begin
    if Compare(p1,p2) <= 0
      then LesserOf := p1
      else LesserOf := p2
  end; (* LesserOf *)

function GreaterOf(p1, p2: point): point;
  begin
    if Compare(p1,p2) > 0
      then GreaterOf := p1
      else GreaterOf := p2
  end; (* GreaterOf *)
```

```
function WhichSide(p: point; s: segment): real;
  (* Given an oriented line from s.e1 passing through s.e2, determine on
     which side of the line the point p lies.  Alternatively, determine
     in which half plane, positive or negative, the point lies. *)
  (* If the segment degenerates to a point, then the point is always on it. *)
  var a, b: real;
  begin
    a := (p.x - s.e1.x)*(s.e2.y - s.e1.y);
    b := (p.y - s.e1.y)*(s.e2.x - s.e1.x);
    WhichSide := a - b
  end; (* WhichSide *)

function Sides(p1, p2: point; s: segment): real;
  (* Determine whether two points lie on the same side of a line. *)
  begin
    Sides := WhichSide(p1,s) * WhichSide(p2,s)
  end; (* Sides *)
```

Program 4.8: Basic Declarations and Functions for Computational Geometry

be represented. The more general *characteristic equation*, $ax + by + c = 0$, covers all degenerate cases and is easiest to manipulate (in particular, it leads naturally to vector operations), but it is not unique, because multiplying all terms by any nonzero constant does not alter the validity of the equation. Since converting from any of these representations to another entails only rational arithmetic, any form is suitable.

What kind of operations do we need to perform on lines and points? Because a line divides the plane into three regions (two open half planes and the line itself), the most basic question is one of location: given a point and a line, in which of the three regions does the point fall? Analytic geometry provides the answer: the function, $f(x,y) = ax + by + c$, which gives rise to the characteristic equation, $ax + by + c = 0$, and which we shall term the *characteristic function* of the line, equals zero for all points on the line, is positive for all points in one of the half planes, and is negative for all points in the other half plane. A problem of orientation arises, since multiplying the characteristic function by -1 swaps the positive and negative half planes; however, orientation does not affect the answer to such questions as "Do two given points lie on the same side of a given line?" By representing a line as a subtended segment, we can orient it and thus define a notion of "left" and "right." Given the oriented line $\overline{p_1 p_2}$ and given some point p not on the line, we say that p lies to the left of the line if the angle $\angle pp_1p_2$ (measured in the standard counterclockwise direction from $\overline{p_1 p_2}$) measures between zero and π and that it lies to the right otherwise. This

```
function OnSegment(p: point; s: segment): boolean;
  (* Determine whether point p lies on segment s.
     Routine works even if the segment degenerates to a point. *)
  begin
    (* First determine whether p lies on the line passing through s. *)
    if WhichSide(p,s) = 0
      then (* If so, determine whether the point lies within the segment. *)
           OnSegment := (Compare(p,LesserOf(s.e1,s.e2)) >= 0) and
                        (Compare(p,GreaterOf(s.e1,s.e2)) <= 0)
      else OnSegment := false
  end; (* OnSegment *)
```

Program 4.9: A Procedure to Test Whether or Not a Point Lies on a Segment

orientation is easily incorporated into the characteristic function by a suitable choice of coefficients, thereby establishing a polarity for the two half planes: the left half plane then corresponds to negative values and the right half plane to positive ones. Our basic declarations for points, lines, and segments and our implementation of the functions testing the location of one or two points relative to an oriented line are collected in Program 4.8. Testing whether or not a point lies on a given line segment now reduces to testing whether or not the point lies on the subtending line, with an added test to check whether or not the point falls within the segment's range of abscissae and ordinates. Program 4.9 implements a Boolean function which answers this question.

Whether or not a point falls on a line segment can be regarded as an intersection problem. The next task, then, is determining whether or not two segments intersect. This task presents an astounding number of special cases: either segment reduces to a point; both do; the segments are collinear and overlap; they share an endpoint; and so on. Thus we cannot anticipate a short, clean algorithm to test for intersection. Let us first address the general case, where the two segments intersect at a single point that is not either of the segments' endpoints. What do we notice that is characteristic of such an instance? The two segments satisfy a symmetric relationship, in that the endpoints of each lie on opposite sides of the line subtending the other. We know how to test for this situation (Program 4.8); adding various tests to catch all of the special cases, we obtain the Boolean function implemented in Program 4.10. Note that our intersection procedure only decides whether or not two segments intersect and thus can do so even when the intersection point is not representable.

Exercise 4.4 Deciding whether or not two segments intersect can also be done using the parametric representation of a line. If the lines subtending the segments intersect at a unique point, then the segments themselves intersect if the value of t

```
function Intersect(s1, s2: segment): boolean;
   (* Determine whether two line segments, either or both of which can be
      degenerate, intersect. *)
   label 99;
   var sides1, sides2: real;
       max1, min1, max2, min2: point;
   begin
     sides1 := Sides(s2.e1,s2.e2,s1);
     sides2 := Sides(s1.e1,s1.e2,s2);
     (* If both endpoints of segment 2 lie on the same side of line 1
        or vice versa, there is no intersection--even if one segment
        degenerates to a point that does not lie on the line determined
        by the other segment. *)
     if (sides1 > 0) or (sides2 > 0)
       then begin
             Intersect := false;
             goto 99 (* return *)
           end;
     (* If the endpoints of one segment lie on opposite sides of the
        other, there is an intersection: segments form an 'X' or a 'T'. *)
     if sides1 + sides2 < 0
       then begin
             Intersect := true;
             goto 99 (* return *)
           end;
     (* Either the four points are collinear or the two segments form a 'V'.
        Range comparisons handle even the degenerate cases of a point lying
        on a line or of two points. *)
     max1 := GreaterOf(s1.e1,s1.e2); min1 := LesserOf(s1.e1,s1.e2);
     max2 := GreaterOf(s2.e1,s2.e2); min2 := LesserOf(s2.e1,s2.e2);
     Intersect := (Compare(max2,min1) >= 0) and (Compare(max1,min2) >= 0);
99: (* return *)
   end; (* Intersect *)
```

Program 4.10: A Procedure to Decide Whether or Not Two Segments Intersect

corresponding to the intersection point falls within $[0, 1]$ for each line. Whether this condition holds can be determined without finding the point of intersection and without any divisions, which might cause overflow. The special cases are now parallel and coincident lines. Program this version of the algorithm.   □

4.2.2 Simplicity, Convexity, and Intersections

Having thus disposed of points, lines, and segments in isolation, let us move on to more complex geometric objects, namely polygons. A polygon is not entirely characterized by its set of vertices, unless the polygon is known to be convex;

but a polygon is characterized by its perimeter, so that an ordered list of the vertices provides a satisfactory representation. Since the perimeter is a closed curve, a circular list is preferable. Such a representation has the clear advantage of simplicity and economy of storage, but it allows a large number of degenerate cases which do not match our intuitive understanding of polygons. First comes the problem of degenerate line segments, which arises whenever two consecutive points coincide. A generalized version of this problem is collinearity of consecutive segments; this collinearity comprises two varieties: a harmless one, where the consecutive line segments continue in the same direction, sharing only a single common vertex; and a more confusing one, where consecutive segments overlap, with accompanying reversal in the direction of travel along the perimeter. Whereas we may remove the single common vertex present in the first case, thereby merging the two consecutive segments, we may not do the same in the second case, because the removal of a common vertex would eliminate the direction reversals; what is worse still, the entry and exit from the subsequence of collinear segments may be in the middle of the line segment defined by the extreme points, so that a merging of the collinear segments would actually alter the outline of the geometric figure. Fortunately, these difficulties are all of a local nature and thus can be detected in a linear-time preprocessing scan and dealt with before running algorithms that may not be able to deal with them. In consequence, not only shall we make frequent use of the circular linked list of vertices to represent a polygon, but we shall also use this model as our definition of a polygon.

Definition 4.1 A *polygon* is a finite, circular sequence of points. The line segments determined by two consecutive points in the sequence are called the *edges* of the polygon, and the ordered collection of edges is called the *perimeter*.   □

Another reason for not eliminating overlapping consecutive polygon edges from the basic definition is that nonconsecutive edges can intersect and overlap as well; this latter problem, being of a global nature, is much harder to detect. The class of polygons which present none of these problems of overlapping or intersecting edges is of particular importance in computational geometry, because only such polygons possess a well-defined notion of interior.

Definition 4.2 A polygon is called *simple* if and only if no two of its edges intersect, with the exception of consecutive edges that must intersect at one and only one point, their common endpoint.   □

Figure 4.10 shows some nonsimple polygons; we have added indices to the vertices in order to show the order in which the vertices appear along the perimeter.

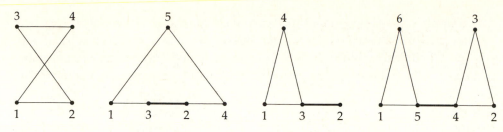

Figure 4.10: Some Nonsimple Polygons

Our definition of polygon implies an orientation to the perimeter, while our visual understanding of a polygon does not; this orientation causes no difficulty and, in fact, is of great help, since now we can define interior and exterior regions algebraically. The existence of an interior also allows us to apply our definition of convexity (Section 1.6) to simple polygons.

Definition 4.3 A polygon is *convex* if and only if it is simple and its interior is a convex region. □

This definition excludes some cases which might otherwise be considered as examples of convex polygons, such as the limiting case of a triangle where the third vertex lies on the opposite segment.

Given a simple polygon, a number of basic decision and construction problems suggest themselves, all based on the existence of a well-defined interior and all revolving around the union or intersection of simple polygons with other geometric objects:

- Decide inclusion of point(s) within a simple polygon.

- Compute the intersection of lines and line segments with simple polygons.

- Compute the union or intersection of simple polygons.

Simplicity Testing

Perhaps the most fundamental task in computational geometry is to determine whether or not a polygon is simple. The very definition of simplicity immediately suggests an algorithm: after scanning the perimeter for overlapping consecutive edges, run Program 4.10 on every pair of nonconsecutive edges; if any pair intersects, the polygon is not simple. Since each test takes constant time, this algorithm requires time quadratic in the number of vertices. Can we do better? And can we derive a lower bound on the complexity of this problem? Observe that simplicity cannot be determined solely on the basis of local tests. No test which is run once at each edge or vertex and involves only a small neighborhood can verify simplicity, since the displacement of a single vertex in a simple polygon can lead to arbitrary edge intersections, in fact, a linear number of them. This observation bodes ill for the development of a linear-time algorithm; indeed, while the best lower bound remains linear, the algorithm described below requires $\Theta(n \log n)$ time, and the current best, a very complex algorithm indeed, runs in $O(n \log \log n)$ time.

The $\Theta(n \log n)$ algorithm for simplicity testing is an application of a more general algorithm which, given n line segments, tests in $\Theta(n \log n)$ time whether or not there exist intersecting pairs. Rather than examine all possible pairs, the algorithm attempts to minimize the number of pairs that must be considered; a rather obvious first step is to consider only segments that share a range of abscissae. We implement this idea by ordering the vertices by their abscissae and traversing the sorted list of vertices, all the while maintaining a list of active segments, i.e., segments for which we have seen the left endpoint, but not yet seen the right endpoint. Viewed abstractly, this process is one of *sweeping* along the x-axis from left to right. When a segment becomes active, we consider potential intersections with the other active segments; when it becomes inactive, we remove it from all further consideration. Unfortunately, if implemented in an obvious manner, this approach does no better than our earlier quadratic-time algorithm (except possibly in terms of average running time), since all segments may very well share a range of abscissae.

In order to limit the number of tests for intersection and, as a consequence, the running time of our algorithm, we need to analyze carefully the spatial relationship between active segments as the sweep line moves to the right. Ignoring vertical segments for the moment, we consider the set of points formed by the intersection of the vertical sweep line with the active segments. The ordering of these points by their ordinates induces an ordering on the active segments and, except at a segment endpoint (which adds or removes an active segment), this ordering does not change as the sweep line moves right, unless an intersection is encountered. It follows that, at any time during the sweep, the only candidates for intersection are adjacent segments in the induced ordering. Hence an algorithm based on such a sweep can proceed inductively, maintaining the invariant that no two adjacent active segments intersect, until either all segments are processed or an intersection is found. While the invariant holds, the only events that can invalidate it are the insertion or deletion of an active segment, since these operations modify the induced ordering. More specifically, we need to check for intersection any two segments newly made adjacent in that ordering. When a segment becomes active, we must test it for intersection with the segments that lie immediately above and below it. When a segment becomes inactive, we must

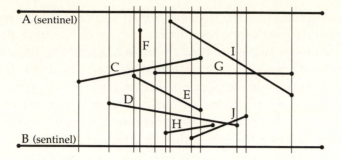

Figure 4.11: A Test Case for Program 4.11

check the segments immediately above and below it, as they now become adjacent and thus candidates for intersection. A maximum of $3n$ tests for segment intersection are thus performed, with $2n$ of these tests occurring at left endpoints and n of these tests occurring at right endpoints.

Note that, if intersections do exist, our algorithm does not necessarily detect the leftmost intersection, nor does it necessarily detect an intersection involving a segment when that segment first becomes active. This somewhat counterintuitive behavior is illustrated in Figure 4.11: our algorithm discovers the intersection of segments G and I when C becomes inactive, rather than when I becomes active— and does not discover the intersection of segments D and J, even though this intersection lies farther to the left.

As our algorithm begins by sorting the vertices by their abscissae, it must run in $\Omega(n \log n)$ time.[2] Although other algorithms might be designed which do not rely on sorting and thus are not subject to this lower bound, it turns out that a lower bound of $\Omega(n \log n)$ can be established for this problem. The proof relies on a known lower bound of $\Omega(n \log n)$ for the problem of *element uniqueness* (given a collection of numbers, are they all distinct?), a result which we discuss in Exercise 8.4 after proving a similar bound for sorting. Given an algorithm for the segment intersection problem, we can easily solve the problem of element uniqueness within the same time bounds by setting up, in linear time, one degenerate segment, with both endpoints at $(x, 0)$, for each element, x: the elements are distinct if and only if their corresponding segments do not intersect. Note that the complexity of the problem does not derive so much from the need to test intersections as from the structure of the problem. Can we run the sweep in $\Theta(n \log n)$ time? In order to do so, we need a data structure for maintaining the induced ordering on the active segments. This data structure must offer efficient support for insertion and deletion of segments and for search

[2]We assume the reader is familiar with this result, which we shall prove in Section 8.1.2.

for inorder predecessor (for the segment below) and inorder successor (for the segment above). As each of the four operations can be executed a linear number of times, none can take more than amortized logarithmic time. A balanced search tree, such as a red-black tree, with all of its leaves held in a doubly-linked list, guarantees logarithmic worst-case behavior for insertion and deletion and constant-time behavior for predecessor and successor operations, thereby meeting our requirements. Note that this structure does not store keys, but segments; the values used to guide the search during insertion and deletion are the ordinates of the segments at the current sweep position. Although these values change as the sweep line moves, we have seen that their relative order does not, so that they can be safely used.

Let us then examine one step of our algorithm in more detail. At a given step, the algorithm processes a new endpoint. If the endpoint is the beginning of a segment, that segment is inserted into the tree and is tested for intersection against its newly acquired inorder predecessor and successor. If the endpoint is the end of a segment, that segment is removed from the tree and its old predecessor and successor are checked for intersection. Vertical segments present a small problem, since both their endpoints appear at once, but are correctly handled if the endpoints are sorted using their ordinates as tiebreakers, as will happen automatically if the function Compare of Program 4.8 is used. Coincident endpoints present another small problem, easily resolved by considering "beginning" points to come before "ending" points in the order, which ensures that a segment is not deleted before its potential intersection with a new segment is detected. The resulting algorithm runs in $\Theta(n \log n)$ time for n segments—which, as we have seen, is optimal. Figure 4.12 illustrates the evolution of the data structure for the instance of Figure 4.11, while Program 4.11 presents an implementation. The introduction of sentinels as shown in the figures and assumed in the program simplifies the handling of boundary cases. A final note concerns the keys (read segments) stored in the internal nodes: they must correspond to segments stored in the leaves, i.e., to active segments. Were an inactive segment to be used to determine the key, that segment would effectively be extended to the right; were this extension to cross an active segment, the induced ordering would be changed and the active segment could no longer be located in the search tree. The situation arises in the last tree of Figure 4.12: the key used in the right child of the root must be the active segment G and not the previously used, and no longer active, segment C.

Now we need only apply this algorithm to our problem of testing for simplicity. The difficulty is that we now expect intersections, since consecutive edges intersect at their common endpoint; the algorithm must judiciously ignore these intersections. Some of the complications are best handled by preprocessing: a simple scan can detect the pathological situation of overlapping consecutive

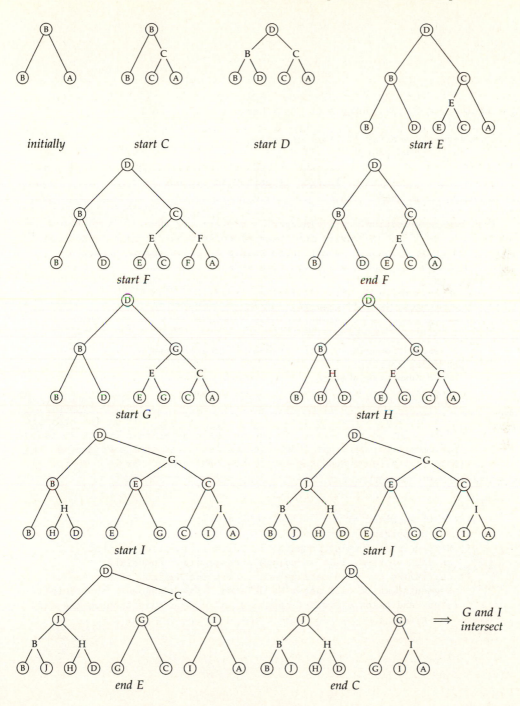

Figure 4.12: The Evolution of the Data Structure for the Instance of Figure 4.11

```
const Max = ...; TwiceMax = ... (* 2*Max *);

type segments = array [1..Max] of segment;
     pointrec = record
                    left: boolean; (* true if left-hand endpoint *)
                    index: integer (* points to segment *)
                end;

function Intersection(    n: integer;
                         var (* for speed *) collection: segments): boolean;
  (* Determines whether or not there exists at least one intersecting
     pair in the input collection of n <= Max segments. *)
  label 99;
  var points: array [1..TwiceMax] of pointrec;
      s, sabove, sbelow: segment;
      i: integer;

  (* We assume the existence of a red-black search tree package
     providing operations
        procedure CreateRBTree,
        procedure Insert(s: segment; var predecessor, successor: segment), and
        procedure Delete(s: segment; var predecessor, successor: segment).
     These operations compute keys on the fly; the key used is the ordinate
     of the point on the segment at the abscissa determined by the left
     (for insertion) or right (for deletion) endpoint of the segment s
     (for vertical segments, the key is the ordinate of the left endpoint).
  *)

  begin
    (* Initialization *)
    (* Set up points[ ] *)
    (* Sort points[ ] using Compare( )--suitably modified so that,
       in case of ties, left endpoints precede right endpoints. *)
    (* Initialize the tree package and insert two horizontal sentinel
       segments, which will never be deleted.  These segments should fall
       above and below all other segments and extend past them on the left
       and right. *)
    ...
```

```
            (* Loop through endpoints until done or until intersection detected. *)
            for i := 1 to 2*n do
              with points[i] do
                begin
                  s := collection[index]; (* get segment in question *)
                  if left
                    then begin
                            Insert(s,sbelow,sabove);
                            if Intersect(s,sbelow) or Intersect(s,sabove)
                              then begin
                                      Intersection := true;
                                      goto 99 (* return *)
                                   end
                         end
                    else begin
                            Delete(s,sbelow,sabove);
                            (* sabove and sbelow are now adjacent in the order;
                               hence we must check them for intersection. *)
                            if Intersect(sbelow,sabove)
                              then begin
                                      Intersection := true;
                                      goto 99 (* return *)
                                   end
                         end
                end;
            Intersection := false;
99:         (* return *)
          end; (* Intersection *)
```

Program 4.11: Deciding Whether or Not an Intersection Exists Among a Collection of Segments

edges and, after sorting the vertices by their abscissae, another scan can be used to check that each vertex occurs as an endpoint exactly twice. The expected intersections are of three types: the point of intersection can be the right endpoint of both segments, or the right endpoint of one and the left endpoint of the other, or the left endpoint of both. While all three situations are easily detected, special attention must be paid to the last case; we must insert the two segments, which are tied in the induced order at the point where they are first encountered, so that they are stored in the search tree in the correct relative order. Despite the excellent performance of this algorithm, it is not asymptotically optimal; the $O(n \log \log n)$ algorithm takes advantage of the additional structure available in a polygon.

We close this discussion by making some remarks about extending this algorithm to one that detects and reports all intersections. We now treat intersections as events in the sweep—events that require two segments to reverse their position in the relative order. By maintaining bidirectional pointers between the leaves and their corresponding internal nodes, the search tree data structure can be updated in constant time to reflect the discovery of an intersection. Unfortunately, as we have pointed out, intersection events are not discovered in the order in which they must be processed. Effectively maintaining these events in sorted order, say by use of a heap, gives us an algorithm running in $\Theta(n \log n + m \log m)$ time overall, where m is the number of intersections; this maintenance strategy allows us to report the intersections in left-to-right order. Unfortunately, when m approaches n^2, our algorithm is outperformed by the obvious $\Theta(n^2)$ algorithm, although this latter does not report the intersections in left-to-right order. The $\Omega(\max(n \log n, m))$ lower bound for this problem is achievable (for which see the bibliography), but the algorithm that attains this bound does not report the intersections in left-to-right order.

Convexity Testing

Let us now address convexity, a problem which we shall solve optimally—which means in linear time, because it is obvious that all vertices must be examined to verify convexity. Recall from elementary geometry that a polygon is convex if and only if, for each edge on a counterclockwise tour of the perimeter, all other vertices of the polygon lie to the left of the line subtending the edge. Unfortunately, this condition is global and verifying it directly requires quadratic time. The standard local definition, that a polygon is convex if and only if none of its interior angles exceeds 180°, does not suffice, since it presupposes that the polygon is simple; Figure 4.13 shows a nonsimple polygon which passes this local test. Nevertheless, we can salvage the idea of an incremental, local test by verifying a slightly more complex invariant: at any time during the exploration of the perimeter, the polygon determined by the vertices visited (i.e., formed by

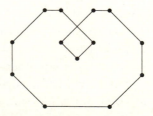

Figure 4.13: A Nonsimple Polygon with All Perimeter Angles Smaller than 180°

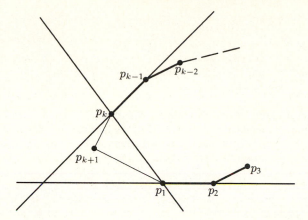

Figure 4.14: Determining the Convexity of a Polygon by Incremental Addition of Points

the explored fraction of the perimeter plus the back edge from the last to the initial vertex) must itself be convex. This new test is one that the polygon of Figure 4.13 does not pass and, in fact, it is a universal test for convexity.

Theorem 4.3 Let the sequence of vertices, $p_1, p_2, \ldots, p_n, p_{n+1} = p_1$, define an arbitrary polygon P and let P_i be the polygon defined by the sequence of vertices $p_1, p_2, \ldots, p_i, p_1$. Then P is convex if and only if, for each i, $i = 3, 4, \ldots, n$, polygon P_i is itself convex. □

Figure 4.14 illustrates how we can turn this lemma into an incremental test: given that P_k is a convex polygon, P_{k+1} is a convex polygon if and only if p_{k+1} lies in the region (a triangle in the figure) formed by the lines $\overline{p_1 p_2}$, $\overline{p_{k-1} p_k}$, and $\overline{p_k p_1}$. This region need not be a triangle, since it can open into an infinite region when $\overline{p_{k-1} p_k}$ and $\overline{p_1 p_2}$ do not intersect or intersect on the other side of $\overline{p_k p_1}$. This test can be implemented in terms of p_{k+1} falling on the proper sides of the lines, preferably without any assumption about the orientation of the polygon. Program 4.12 implements this test in a straightforward way; it is easily seen to run in linear time. Difficulties involving degeneracy can be handled with a linear-time preprocessing step.

Intersection Problems

Now that we know how to test for simplicity and convexity, we can turn our attention to the intersection of points and lines with polygons, problems which presuppose simple polygons. In view of our discussion of convexity testing, there is a simple algorithm for deciding whether or not a point lies inside a convex

```
(* The polygon is represented by a circular linked list. *)
type PtrToElement = ^ListElement;
     ListElement = record
                        vertex: point;
                        next: PtrToElement
                   end;


function Convex(polygon: PtrToElement): boolean;
  (* Assumptions: -- no consecutive collinear points or degenerate segments
                  -- polygon contains at least three vertices.
     NOT assumed: -- orientation, simplicity. *)
  label 99;
  var P1, previous, current, future: PtrToElement;
      (* previous, current, and future stand for P(k-1), P(k), and P(k+1). *)
      s, P1P2: segment;
      a, b, c: real;
  begin
    (* Initialize: set up line from P1 to P2 and the 3 traversal points. *)
    P1 := polygon; P1P2.e1 := P1^.vertex; P1P2.e2 := P1^.next^.vertex;
    previous := P1^.next; current := previous^.next; future := current^.next;

    (* Loop around the perimeter. *)
    while future <> P1 do
      (* Depending on orientation of polygon, future vertex must be either
            to the left of the oriented lines or
            to the right of the oriented lines
        from previous to current, from P1 to current, and from P1 to P2. *)
      begin
        (* Set up oriented line from previous to current and test. *)
        s.e1 := previous^.vertex; s.e2 := current^.vertex;
          a := WhichSide(future^.vertex,s);
        (* Set up oriented line from P1 to current and test. *)
        s.e1 := P1^.vertex;  (* s.e2 := current^.vertex; *)
          b := WhichSide(future^.vertex,s);
        (* Test against oriented line from P1 to P2. *)
          c := WhichSide(future^.vertex,P1P2);
        (* Absence of collinearity implies that a, b, and c are nonzero.
           The requirement on future is that a, b, and c have the same sign. *)
        if abs(a + b + c) <> abs(a) + abs(b) + abs(c)
          then begin
                  Convex := false;
                  goto 99
               end;
        previous := current; current := future; future:= future^.next
      end;
    Convex := true;
99: (* return *)
  end; (* Convex *)
```

Program 4.12: Deciding Whether or Not a Polygon is Convex

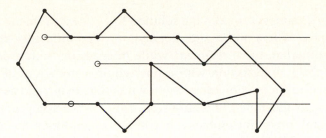

Figure 4.15: Test Cases for Program 4.13

polygon: just verify that the point lies on the same side of all the edges of the polygon. Such a test runs in linear time and leads to a very concise program. However, it fails for simple, but nonconvex polygons, and we want an inclusion test which works for any simple polygon. Suppose that we draw a half line (making it horizontal for simplicity) from the point in question and look at its intersections, if any, with the polygon. If the point lies inside the polygon, then the half line must intersect the polygon at least once, since it must eventually reach a region beyond any of the vertices of the polygon; moreover, the number of intersections must be odd, because the half line alternates between inside and outside. The same reasoning shows that a point lying outside the polygon gives rise to an even number of intersections, because the half line alternates between outside and inside and ends up outside. The only problem with this idea, which is rather simple to implement using our segment intersection procedure, arises whenever the half line actually passes through a vertex of the polygon, since such an occurrence may or may not signal a transition between inside and outside. At each of these vertices, we must find out whether the two segments incident upon the vertex lie on the same side of the half line: a transition between inside and outside occurs when the segments lie on opposite sides. Unfortunately, one more special case must be considered: the half line may cover an edge. Instead of designing some *ad hoc* test for this case, let us instead view the problem from another perspective: our goal is really to determine how many times the perimeter crosses the half line. We can compute this number by travelling around the perimeter, keeping track of the parity of the number of crossings found so far. Program 4.13 implements this test in linear time. Note the manner in which consecutive vertices lying on the half line are handled: their collapse into a single vertex alters the geometry of the polygon (because it creates artificial edges) but does not alter the number of crossings. The reader is urged to trace the execution of the program on the polygon of Figure 4.15 for each of the three points shown.

Program 4.13 almost provides the solution to our next problem: determining the intersection of a line and a simple polygon. The difference resides in the amount of information to be retained: while intersection with a point requires only a parity check, intersection with a line requires storage of all intersection points, because the intersection of an n-gon with a line may yield as many as $n/2$ small segments, as illustrated in Figure 4.16. This intersection problem abstracts aspects of several important problems in computer graphics. One application is known as *polygon filling*: given a simple polygon and a raster device on which it is displayed, fill the interior of the polygon with a given color. This filling may be obtained by computing the horizontal runs of uniform color, i.e., the intersection of the scan lines with the polygon. A closely related application is found in windowing systems, where one window must be *clipped* against another which partially obscures it or one object clipped against the window boundaries. The two-dimensional display of three-dimensional objects entails similar, but much more complex, tasks, usually called the *hidden line* and *hidden surface* problems; the additional complexity arises from the need to resolve the intersections in three dimensions before projecting into two dimensions.

In view of the worst case illustrated in Figure 4.16, the best possible algorithm for computing the intersection of a line and a simple polygon on n vertices requires $\Omega(n)$ time. Using a variant of Program 4.13 which actually computes intersection points, we can easily obtain all intersections of the line with the boundary of the polygon in $\Theta(n)$ time; but we then need to sort all the intersection points in order to obtain the segments themselves, since we must group intersection points two by two into the correct pairs. Using a standard sorting algorithm increases the time requirements to $\Theta(n \log n)$; can this increase be avoided? Since the vertices of a polygon are already ordered, one may be

```
function Interior(p: point; polygon: PtrToElement): integer;
  (* Determines whether p lies inside (+1), on (0), or outside (-1)
     a simple polygon. *)
  (* Assumptions: -- polygon is simple and has at least 3 vertices.
     NOT assumed: -- orientation, absence of consecutive collinear vertices,
                     absence of degenerate segments. *)
  label 1, 99;
  const infinity = ...;   (* beyond any point's abscissa *)
  var previous, current, future: PtrToElement;
      parity: integer;
      edge, halfline: segment;
  begin
    (* Set up horizontal half line with endpoints p and infinity. *)
    halfline.e1 := p; halfline.e2.x := infinity; halfline.e2.y := p.y;
```

```
    (* Invariant: At most one of previous and current can lie on the half
       line.  Establish this condition initially by rotating through the
       polygon until the starting point lies on one or the other side of the
       half line.  Preconditions guarantee that this is always possible. *)
    while WhichSide(polygon^.vertex,halfline) = 0 do polygon := polygon^.next;
    parity := -1;  (* outside by default *)

    (* Prepare to walk around the perimeter--start with the second edge. *)
    previous := polygon; current := previous^.next; future := current^.next;

    (* The main loop walks the perimeter of polygon. *)
    repeat
  1: (* Set up current edge and test. *)
     edge.e1 := current^.vertex; edge.e2 := future^.vertex;
     if Intersect(edge,halfline)
       then if OnSegment(p,edge)
               then begin
                      Interior := 0;
                      goto 99 (* return *)
                    end
        else if OnSegment(edge.e1,halfline) and OnSegment(edge.e2,halfline)
               then (* The half line passes through both endpoints,
                       so shrink the edge to a single vertex. *)
                    begin
                      future := future^.next;
                      goto 1
                    end
        else if OnSegment(edge.e1,halfline)
               then (* The edge intersects the half line at the middle vertex
                       (current) only; determine whether we have a crossing. *)
                    begin
                      if Sides(previous^.vertex,future^.vertex,halfline) < 0
                        then parity := -parity
                    end
        else if not OnSegment(edge.e2,halfline)
               then parity := -parity;  (* clean crossing *)
     (* else the first endpoint is off and the second on the half line,
           so delay the decision until we see further vertices. *)

     (* Move around the perimeter. *)
     previous := current; current := future; future := future^.next
    until previous = polygon;
    Interior := parity;
 99: (* return *)
   end; (* Interior *)
```

Program 4.13: Deciding Whether or Not a Point Lies Inside a Simple Polygon

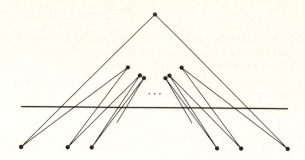

Figure 4.16: A Worst-Case Situation for the Intersection of a Line and a Polygon

tempted to answer yes; however, the order along the perimeter and the order along the line of interest rarely coincide and often diverge to a considerable extent. As a simple example, consider a polygon approximating a thick spiral: the $2k$ intersections with a line bisecting the circular area in which the polygon lies will be found in the order $1, 2k, 3, 2k - 2, \ldots, 2k - 1, 2$. This problem is known as the *Jordan sorting* problem—the name comes from the Jordan curve theorem, because the resulting sorted list automatically establishes which segments lie inside and which lie outside—and has been studied in much detail. In spite of the problem's apparent connection with general sorting, it is possible to solve it in linear time with the help of the proper data structure. Before presenting the solution, we first dispose of a simpler intersection problem that involves only convex polygons.

Computing the intersection of a line or line segment with a convex polygon is easily carried out in linear time, since the result comprises at most one segment. Surprisingly, the intersection of two convex polygons, which can be empty, composed of a single point or segment, or itself a convex polygon, can also be computed in linear time A particularly simple solution uses the line sweep technique introduced earlier. Note that the perimeter of a convex polygon can be divided into two pieces, an upper and a lower boundary, each of which extends from the vertex of minimum abscissa to the vertex of maximum abscissa. The interior of the polygon consists of the points that fall below the upper boundary and above the lower boundary. Whenever there are several vertices with minimum or maximum abscissae, we use the points with largest ordinates for the upper boundary and those with smallest ordinates for the lower boundary; vertical segments determined by such vertices are treated separately. Instead of determining the entire intersection polygon at once, we shall instead use the upper boundaries of the two argument polygons to determine a potential upper boundary for the intersection, do the same for lower boundaries, and

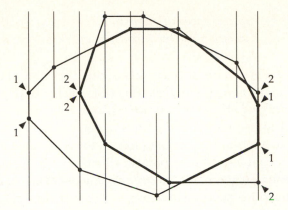

Figure 4.17: Finding the Intersection of Two Convex Polygons Through the Line
Sweep Method

then combine them; to determine each potential boundary, we shall use the line
sweep method.

To determine the potential upper boundary for the intersection, we first restrict our attention to the common range of abscissae. Within this range, we
simply keep whichever of the two upper boundaries is lower; when the two
upper boundaries cross, we add the intersection point to the potential boundary and switch from one polygon to the other. The sweep divides the x-axis
into successive slabs, each delimited by two or more endpoints from the upper boundaries. Within one of these slabs, one of three situations may arise:
(i) one boundary is always lower than the other (although they might intersect
at one endpoint); (ii) the boundaries intersect in the middle; or (iii) they coincide.
Thus each slab contributes one or two segments to the potential upper boundary.
Since, as we traverse the perimeter, the points are already sorted with respect to
their abscissae, no sorting step is required: the operation is essentially a merge.

We have consistently referred to the "potential upper boundary" in order
to stress that the intersection polygon does not simply consist of the upper and
lower boundaries thus obtained. The reason is that, for part or all of its extent,
the potential upper boundary may lie below the potential lower boundary, so
that a final step is needed to combine the two boundaries. This is another merge
operation: we sweep the two potential boundaries from left to right, looking
for the point, if any, where the potential upper boundary equals or exceeds the
potential lower boundary (the leftmost vertex of the intersection polygon) and
ending our scan at the first point where the reverse situation obtains (the rightmost vertex of the intersection). Figure 4.17 illustrates the line sweep method,

including a number of special cases of interest. Note that atypical situations, such as the proper inclusion of one polygon within the other, are handled without any additional code.

Let us comment briefly on three aspects of this algorithm. First, the polygon must be broken into its two boundaries. This task entails finding the points with the smallest and largest abscissae and, due to our representation of a polygon as a circularly linked list, reversing the links of one of the two boundary lists so that all pieces have a left-to-right orientation. Secondly, we must avoid creating output lists which contain collinear points: whenever a long segment from the boundary list of one polygon is chosen over a chain of smaller segments from the boundary list of the other polygon, the long segment crosses several sweep lines, so that a careless design could break this segment into a chain of small collinear segments. Finally, when the two potential boundaries have been processed and the leftmost and rightmost vertices of the intersection polygon determined, we must reverse one of our two boundaries and deal with any vertical edges that may be present. Although these steps lead to additional program lines, the entire algorithm clearly runs in linear time; some efficiency can be gained, at the expense of more complex code, by using a single sweep to form and combine the upper and lower boundaries.

Exercise 4.5 Implement the algorithm that we just discussed, using the following procedure heading.

```
procedure IntersectConvexPolygon(    poly1, poly2: PtrToElement;
                                   var poly: PtrToElement);
   (* Form the intersection of two convex polygons.
      On return poly is one of:
      -- nil, if the intersection is empty;
      -- a circular list of one point, if the intersection is a point;
      -- a circular list of two points, if the intersection is a segment;
      -- a circular list that represents the perimeter of a convex polygon. *)
```

□

Finally, what can be said about the intersection of two simple polygons? In particular, how fast can it be computed? As a quick look back at Figure 4.16 will show, the intersection of two simple polygons of n vertices each may generate up to $n^2/4$ polygons (just picture two polygons such as the one shown in Figure 4.16 intersecting at right angles—two "hands" with interlaced "fingers"), so that any intersection algorithm must sometimes require quadratic time to complete. In general, if the intersection of a polygon of m vertices and one of n vertices produces a number of polygons with a total of k vertices, any intersection algorithm must run in $\Omega(m + n + k)$ time.

4.2.3 Jordan Sorting

We conclude this section on geometric methods by presenting the linear-time algorithm for Jordan sorting to which we alluded earlier. First, let us restate the problem: given an ordered collection of points, a collection which represents the intersection of a simple polygon and a straight line and which is ordered according to a tour of the polygon's perimeter, sort the points according to their abscissae. Note that the polygon itself is not part of the input in this restatement, so that the linear-time requirement on Jordan sorting under these conditions is more demanding than the linear-time requirement for determining the intersection of a line and a polygon. The restatement is natural, however, because it generalizes easily to geometrically more complex, but topologically equivalent, figures: sort the points of intersection of a line with a simple closed curve (known in the mathematical literature as a *Jordan curve* [(Marie Ennemond) Camille Jordan, 1838–1922]).

In spite of the constraints added by our restatement, Jordan sorting is considerably easier than general sorting and the reason can be seen by examining the possible sequences of intersection points. Let us assume, without loss of generality, that the intersecting line is horizontal; furthermore, let us assume that the point of least abscissa occurs first in the ordering—were this not the case, a linear-time search and rotation would make it so. For the sake of simplicity, we deliberately ignore all special cases, such as the Jordan curve touching the line without crossing it. Consequently, every other intersection point is one where the line enters the interior of the curve; this observation allows us to process odd- and even-numbered intersection points separately. Moreover, note that two consecutive points in the input sequence describe an interval within which the Jordan curve lies strictly above or below the line; the first type we call an *upper* interval, the second a *lower* interval. Like intersection points, the intervals must alternate by type. Note that other parts of the curve may well cross the line within an interval, but any such crossings must be paired and properly nested—a study of Figure 4.18 may assist in forming the correct intuition. The intervals thus defined offer a convenient way to express the data.

Specifically, let the input sequence be $p_0, p_1, \ldots, p_{n-1}$ and let $k = n/2$; in addition, let $p_n = p_0$ for convenience of notation. Consider each pair, (p_{i-1}, p_i), as denoting an interval from the abscissa of the leftmost of the two points to the abscissa of the rightmost; there is no presumption that p_{i-1} is to the left of p_i. We say that two intervals *cross* if they overlap without one being wholly enclosed within the other; since the original curve is simple, the intervals (p_{i-1}, p_i) and (p_{j-1}, p_j) cannot cross if they are of the same type (for $i = j \bmod 2$). This property leads us to partition the input sequence into two collections of intervals, $\{ (p_{2i}, p_{2i+1}) \mid 0 \le i < k \}$ and $\{ (p_{2i-1}, p_{2i}) \mid 0 < i \le k \}$. We can always assume

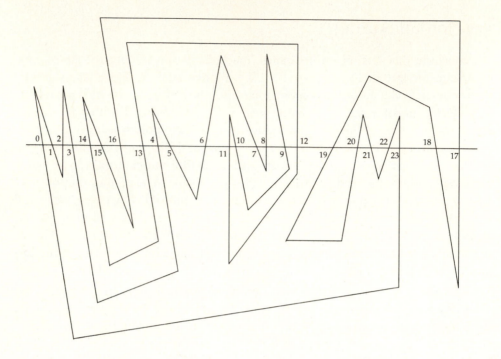

Figure 4.18: A Simple Polygon and Its Intersecting Line

that the upper intervals correspond to the pairs (p_{2i}, p_{2i+1}), since reflecting the Jordan curve around the line of intersection does not change the input. As already noted, intervals must be properly nested within each list. Thus, the relation "is wholly contained in" induces a partial order on each collection of intervals, an order which can be represented by a forest. We make the forests into trees by adding to each collection the interval $(-\infty, \infty)$; we also order the siblings within the tree according to abscissae, a well-defined total order since any two sibling intervals must be disjoint. Thus we can represent the input sequence of intersection points by two trees of intervals, the upper and the lower trees. Figure 4.19 shows the two interval trees corresponding to the simple polygon of Figure 4.18.

The algorithm proceeds by simultaneously building the two trees and the sorted list. Initially, the interval trees each contain only the interval $(-\infty, \infty)$ and the sorted list consists of the three elements $-\infty$, p_0, and ∞. At step i, for $i \geq 1$, the algorithm has built a sorted list of $i + 2$ elements and begins to process point p_i. Without loss of generality, let us consider an odd-numbered step, so that the interval (p_{i-1}, p_i) is to be added to the upper tree, and assume, also

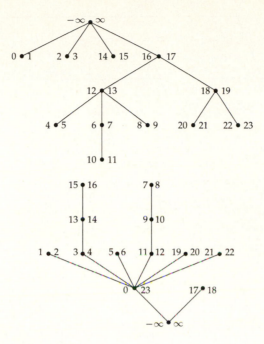

Figure 4.19: The Upper and Lower Interval Trees Corresponding to the Intersection of Figure 4.18

without loss of generality, that p_{i-1} has the smaller abscissa.

- Find the point, call it p, that follows p_{i-1} in the partial sorted list. This point is an endpoint of some interval, (p_{j-1}, p_j), already in the upper tree. (Note that this interval is the smallest interval that contains p.)

- Three cases can arise, depending on the ordering of abscissae of the two intervals; they are shown in schematic form in Figure 4.20.

  (p_{i-1}, p_i) is wholly contained within (p_{j-1}, p_j): Make (p_{i-1}, p_i) the new last child of (p_{j-1}, p_j) and insert p_i after p_{i-1} in the sorted list.

  (p_{i-1}, p_i) is to the left of (p_{j-1}, p_j): Insert (p_{i-1}, p_i) as the immediate left sibling of (p_{j-1}, p_j) and insert p_i after p_{i-1} in the sorted list.

  (p_{j-1}, p_j) is wholly contained within (p_{i-1}, p_i): Find the rightmost sibling of (p_{j-1}, p_j) which is still contained within (p_{i-1}, p_i); call this interval (p_{k-1}, p_k). Now remove from the list of siblings of (p_{j-1}, p_j) the entire sublist from (p_{j-1}, p_j) to (p_{k-1}, p_k) inclusive, replace it with the single node (p_{i-1}, p_i), and attach the sublist just removed as the list of children of (p_{i-1}, p_i). Insert p_i after the larger of p_{k-1} and p_k in the sorted list.

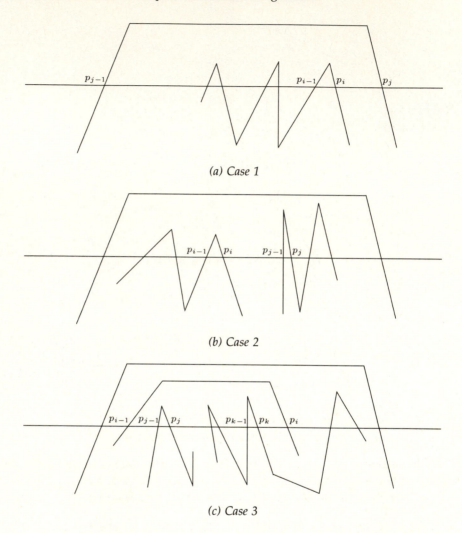

(a) Case 1

(b) Case 2

(c) Case 3

Figure 4.20: The Three Cases for Jordan Sorting

Even-numbered steps are treated similarly, using the lower rather than the upper interval tree; when p_i has the smaller abscissa, the search proceeds to the left, along with the other obvious reversals of handedness.[3]

We need to show that this procedure is correct and to develop some data structure to support its efficient implementation.

---

[3]A slight anomaly arises when (p_{i-1}, p_i) is a lower interval, p_i is to the left of p_{i-1}, and p_0 is the point immediately to the left of p_{i-1}, since p_0 does not appear in the lower interval tree until the very last step. This anomaly is easily dealt with; we leave the details to the reader.

Theorem 4.4 The algorithm described above solves the Jordan sorting problem.

$\square$

Proof: We proceed by induction, showing that the partially sorted list is, in fact, correctly sorted by abscissae. This invariant is trivially true initially, since the initial list consists of only $-\infty$, p_0, and ∞, in that order. The inductive step must then show that the algorithm inserts the ith point in the proper place in the partially sorted list. Since the insertion depends on the interval trees, the step must also prove that the interval is properly placed within the appropriate interval tree.

The purpose of the first step of the algorithm is to provide a reference point for locating the new interval. Because of the two sentinels placed at initialization, we are assured that p_{i-1} is followed by some element. Similarly, the sentinel placed in each tree ensures the existence of at least one interval that meets the requirements. Because p is an endpoint of some interval in the appropriate tree and intervals in the same tree can contain one another, but not cross, this step returns the smallest interval (from among those seen so far) which contains the point immediately to the right of the left endpoint of the new interval. This point can be within the new interval, in which case the interval returned must be wholly contained within the new one (our third case), or the point must lie to the right of the right endpoint of the new interval, in which case the interval returned either contains the new interval or lies entirely to the right of it (our first and second cases). Hence the three cases described in the algorithm cover all possibilities.

We now analyze each case separately; it is critical to keep in mind that every point appears indirectly in both trees, so that we need only look at one tree in order to place the point correctly within the sorted order. In the first two cases, the placement of p_i in the sorted order and the placement of (p_{i-1}, p_i) in the tree are clearly correct. In our third case, the new interval contains at least one previous interval (the returned one), and we must search for the rightmost interval thus contained. This search can be confined to the right siblings of the returned interval. Because intervals in the same tree cannot cross, if a descendant of a right sibling is contained in the new interval, the right sibling must be so contained as well. The parent of the right sibling, on the other hand, must extend farther left than p and so must contain this new interval.

Q.E.D.

We now consider the data structures needed to implement this algorithm efficiently. While Figure 4.19 displays clearly the relationships between intervals, direct conversion to PASCAL does not give a suitable implementation. Some of the required data structures are elementary: we use a record for each point and one for each interval; these records are cross-linked, so we can access the point at the other end of an interval in constant time. In addition, the points are doubly-linked in the order of their abscissae. This structure allows us to locate p, determine which of the three cases applies, and do the insertion of p_i into the sorted list (once the interval tree has been processed) in constant time. Of the operations performed on the interval trees by the algorithm, the only difficult one is that corresponding to the third case: determining the extent of the sublist of consecutive siblings spanned by the new interval, replacing the sublist with a single node, and converting this sublist into a list of children. If we represent the trees of Figure 4.19 using a doubly-linked, left-child, right-sibling representation, we can accomplish this step in time proportional to $\min(d, m-d)$, where m is the number of siblings and d is the size of the sublist to be excised (we can search in parallel in opposite directions for the last interval contained within the new interval). Of the three substeps, only the search takes nonconstant time.

This search cannot proceed linearly, but must return the extent of the sublist in time proportional to $\log \min(d, m-d)$ if we are to achieve linear running time. Thus we must represent the children of a node with a data structure that allows fast range search. We developed, in Section 3.3, a data structure which fits our needs precisely: the level-linked tree. Now each node in an interval tree points to a possibly empty level-linked tree (more precisely, to the root and to the leftmost leaf of such a tree), the leaves of which are in turn nodes of the interval tree—the original node's children in the abstract representation of Figure 4.19. Notice that, no matter which of the three cases of our algorithm applies, we have direct access to the leaf where either an insertion or a search and excision must occur: in the first case, the interval pointed to by p is not the one we desire, but the pointer to the leftmost leaf of the level-linked tree containing its children allows the insertion to be accomplished in constant amortized time; in the second case, the insertion is done, again in constant amortized time, immediately to the left or right of the interval containing p; and, in the third case, we use fast range searching, followed by excision and insertion, to accomplish the operation in $\Theta(\log \min(d, m-d))$ amortized time.

Exercise 4.6 Develop PASCAL declarations for the complete data structure described above. □

Theorem 4.5 With the data structure that we just described, our algorithm for Jordan sorting runs in linear time. □

Proof: As we have already observed, the algorithm does constant-time work per point, except for the work done to maintain the interval trees. We amortize this work over the entire algorithm; depending on which case obtains, the algorithm does $\Theta(1)$ or $\Theta(\log \min(d, m-d))$ amortized work per point. For the sake of analysis, we consider that only one type of operation is ever performed: a combined search, excision, and insertion; while the full-fledged version occurs in only the third case, we can regard the simple insertion taking place in the first two cases as made up of a trivial search, an empty excision, and the insertion itself. With this unified operation, we can amortize the cost over the duration of the algorithm. Let $T(l,m)$ be the worst-case time required to carry out l successive unified operations on a list of initial size m. Note that, as a result of nontrivial excisions, our original list gets broken into separate lists, each represented by a level-linked tree; $T(l,m)$ accounts not only for operations performed on what remains of the original list of length m, but also for operations performed on the sublists created during the sequence of operations. This function obeys the recurrence

$$\begin{cases} T(l,m) = \max_{\substack{0 \le i \le l-1 \\ 0 \le d \le m}} \{T(i,d) + T(l-1-i, m-d+1) + \Theta(\log \min(d, m-d))\} \\ T(0,m) = 0. \end{cases}$$

The second argument of the second call to T on the right-hand side is $m - d + 1$, because the new interval is always inserted among the siblings that are left after the excision. As each interval tree is involved in precisely $n/2$ operations and as the initial list consists of just the interval $(-\infty, \infty)$, the behavior of our sorting algorithm is described by $T(n/2, 1)$.

This recurrence is rather formidable, in part because it involves two variables. We reduce it to a recurrence in one variable by defining the new function of a single argument (with *exactly* the same $\Theta(\ )$ term as in T):

$$\begin{cases} g(n) = \max_{1 \le i \le n-1} \{g(i) + g(n-i) + \Theta(\log \min\{i, n-i\})\} \\ g(1) = \Theta(1). \end{cases}$$

A lengthy induction argument shows that $T(l,m) \le g(4l + m)$, so that we need only show that $g(n)$ grows linearly. Now either $g(n)$ grows no faster than linearly, in which case we are done, or it grows at least as fast as linearly. In the latter case, the maximization can be eliminated by picking $i = n/2$, so that we obtain a simple limiting recurrence of the form $g(n) \approx 2g(n/2) + \Theta(\log n)$, which we can solve with standard methods (see Exercise 2.25) to obtain the desired result. Another way to verify that this result is correct is to consider the difference, $g(n) - g(n-1)$. Let i be the index that maximizes $g(n)$; if we also pick i as index for $g(n-1)$, we can only underestimate $g(n-1)$ and thus overestimate the difference. Let the driving term be the function $f(\ )$; we can write

$$g(n) - g(n-1) \le \big(g(i) + g(n-i) + f(i)\big) - \big(g(i) + g(n-i-1) + f(i)\big)$$
$$= g(n-i) - g(n-i-1).$$

Thus the difference between consecutive values of $g(n)$ never increases, so that $g(n)$ is $\Theta(n)$. (A minor problem arises with $f(\ )$ when $i = n/2$: the term in the expansion of $g(n-1)$ is then $f(i-1)$ rather than $f(i)$. But the difference $f(i) - f(i-1)$ tends to zero as i increases, since $f(i)$ is $\Theta(\log i)$, so that this problem does not affect the answer.)

Q.E.D.

4.3 Exercises

Exercise 4.7 The program for breadth-first search can be modified to save space and reduce overhead by embedding the queue within the array seen, which is no longer a Boolean array: the ith element of seen contains either a flag to mean not yet encountered or the index of the vertex that follows vertex i in the queue. Modify Program 4.3 to implement this suggestion—notice that even a rudimentary memory management package is no longer needed. This suggestion can also be applied to improve the time and space requirements of the program for determining the strongly connected components of a directed graph.   □

Exercise 4.8 Develop a linear-time algorithm to decide whether or not a connected undirected graph is bipartite. (Recall that a graph is bipartite if and only if its vertex set can be partitioned into two subsets such that no edge joins vertices within the same subset.)   □

Exercise 4.9 Devise an efficient algorithm that, given an undirected graph, $G = (V, E)$, and a positive integer, k, finds the largest induced subgraph, $G' = (V', E')$, in which every vertex has degree k or larger, or determines that such a subgraph does not exist.   □

Exercise 4.10 In general, finding the minimum vertex cover (Problem 24) of an undirected graph is $\mathcal{NP}$-hard, but if the graph is a (free) tree, then the problem can be solved in linear time. Devise such an algorithm.   □

Exercise 4.11 Develop a linear-time algorithm on free trees which finds a vertex, the removal of which creates a forest where no single tree includes more than half of the vertices of the original tree.   □

Exercise 4.12 Let T be a binary tree consisting of n nodes and let the nodes be numbered from 1 to n in the order in which they are visited in an inorder traversal. Define the *distance* between two nodes, i and j, to be the length of the path from i to j. Develop an efficient algorithm that takes as input a pointer to a binary tree and returns an upper triangular matrix giving the distances from every node to every other node. How much extra storage is used by your algorithm? Under what circumstances can you reconstruct the binary tree from the distance matrix?   □

Exercise 4.13 Design an efficient algorithm to find the longest path in a directed acyclic graph. Use the same strategy to develop an efficient algorithm to divide the vertices of a directed acyclic graph into the minimum number of groups so that each group forms an *independent set*, i.e., so that no two vertices in the same group are joined by an arc.   □

Exercise 4.14 Consider the variant of topological sorting in which we want to order the vertices of a directed (not necessarily acyclic) graph so that, for every vertex, at least one of its predecessors precedes it in the ordering. Design an efficient algorithm that produces such an ordering or reports that none exists.

□

Exercise 4.15 A subset of the edges of an undirected graph such that every cycle contains at least one edge from the set is called a *feedback-edge set*. Design an efficient algorithm to find the minimum-size feedback-edge set.   □

Exercise 4.16 An *Eulerian circuit* is a path which starts and ends at the same vertex and uses each edge exactly once. A theorem due to Euler states that a connected undirected graph has an Eulerian circuit if and only if every vertex has even degree. (This was the first result in graph theory; it was motivated by the problem of the bridges of Königsberg.) Develop a linear-time algorithm which returns an Eulerian circuit in such a graph.   □

Exercise 4.17 Develop a linear-time algorithm which, given a connected undirected graph, decides whether or not the edges of the graph can be partitioned into a collection of subsets, each of which describes a cycle; your algorithm should construct this partition if it exists. (*Hint*: Refer to the previous exercise.)

□

Exercise 4.18 A *vertex basis* of a directed graph, $G = (V, A)$, is a subset, $B \subseteq V$, of minimum size such that every vertex in V is reachable from a vertex in B. Use a decomposition into strongly connected components to construct a vertex basis in linear time.   □

Exercise 4.19* A *supersource* in a directed graph, $G = (V, A)$, is a vertex of out-degree $|V| - 1$ and in-degree 0. Obviously, at most one such vertex can exist in any given directed graph. Design an algorithm which identifies such a vertex if it exists; your algorithm should run in $\Theta(|V|)$ time when the graph is given by its adjacency matrix.

We can extend this algorithm to graphs given by their adjacency lists by using the lazy array technique of Section 4.1.   □

Exercise 4.20* The notion of strong connectivity in directed graphs is, as its name indicates, more restrictive than that of connectivity in undirected graphs. A possible relaxation of strong connectivity is the following: a directed graph is *unilaterally connected* if and only if, for each pair of vertices, there exists a path from one of the vertices to the other. (In particular, every strongly connected graph is also unilaterally connected.) Design a fast algorithm to decide whether or not a given graph is unilaterally connected.   □

Exercise 4.21* Use depth-first search to determine whether or not the edges of a connected undirected graph can be oriented so that the resulting directed graph is strongly connected.   □

Exercise 4.22 What is the smallest k-connected graph on n vertices?   □

Exercise 4.23** Triconnected and, in general, k-connected components are defined by the obvious generalization of biconnected components: a k-connected component is a maximal k-connected subgraph. We saw how to find 1-connected (connected) and 2-connected (biconnected) components in linear time using graph traversal. Can we detect triconnected or even k-connected components in a similar way and as efficiently? Justify your answer as carefully as possible.   □

Exercise 4.24 An edge in an undirected graph is a *bridge* if its removal leaves the graph with more connected components than it had originally. Design a linear-time algorithm to identify the bridges of a graph, if any.   □

Exercise 4.25* (Refer to the previous exercise.) Let us call an undirected graph *edge-biconnected* if the removal of any single edge does not disconnect it. Define an equivalence relation based on edge-biconnectivity and thus a notion of edge-biconnected components and design an algorithm to decompose a graph into edge-biconnected components.   □

Exercise 4.26 Can you generalize your answer to Exercise 4.25 in a manner similar to the generalization of connected graphs to k-connected ones? What is the smallest edge k-connected graph? In such a graph, how many vertices can always be removed without disconnecting the graph?   □

Exercise 4.27 The *transitive closure* of a graph, $G = (V, E)$, is a graph, $G' = (V, E')$, that includes an edge between vertices v and w whenever one is accessible from the other in G. (The obvious analog can be defined for directed graphs.) Devise an algorithm that computes the transitive closure of an undirected graph in time proportional to the size of the closure. Attempt to generalize your algorithm to directed graphs.   □

Exercise 4.28* A vertex, x, of a rooted direct acyclic graph is called a *dominator* of another vertex, y, if every path from the root to y passes through x. Every vertex is a dominator of itself, and the root is a dominator of every vertex. Like all partial orders, domination can be represented by a dag, the transitive closure of which is the partial order. However, the dominators of a vertex can be linearly ordered by their occurrence on any path from the root to the vertex, so that the partial order can be represented by a tree, the *dominator tree*.

Design a $O(|V| \cdot |E|)$ algorithm for producing the dominator tree of a directed acyclic graph. (Tarjan has given a complex $\Theta(|E| \log |E|)$ algorithm; Lengauer and Tarjan invented a faster, simpler, but more subtle algorithm that runs in $\Theta(|E|\alpha(|E|, |V|))$ time.) □

Exercise 4.29 Devise an efficient algorithm to solve the following problem: given a line and a collection of points, does the line intersect any of the segments determined by two points from the collection? What if the line is just a line segment? □

Exercise 4.30 Devise an efficient algorithm which takes n points in the plane and returns a simple polygon, the vertices of which are the n points. □

Exercise 4.31 Here is a simple problem of geometric nature which can be solved through nongeometric techniques. Assume that all coordinates are positive integers. You are given two positive integers, a and b, which determine a rectangle with vertices $(0,0)$, $(a,0)$, $(0,b)$, and (a,b), as well as a collection of vertices within this rectangle. The problem is to find integers, c and d, such that the rectangle determined by vertices $(0,0)$, $(c,0)$, $(0,d)$, and (c,d) is contained within the given rectangle, has maximum area, and does not properly include any of the given points. □

Exercise 4.32 You are given a convex polygon as an array of n vertices, ordered in a counterclockwise tour of the perimeter (from some arbitrary starting vertex). Design a simple algorithm that, given some new point, P, decides in $\Theta(\log n)$ time whether or not P lies inside the polygon. □

Exercise 4.33* Generalize Exercise 4.32 to suitable families of simple, but not convex polygons. What are sufficient conditions on a simple polygon for your algorithm to work? Can you find necessary conditions as well? □

Exercise 4.34 Prove that, if all vertices of a simple polygon have integer coordinates, the area of the polygon equals $O/2 + I - 1$, where O is the number of points with integer coordinates that lie on the polygon's boundaries (including the polygon's own vertices) and I is the number of points with integer coordinates that lie inside the polygon. □

Exercise 4.35 Devise a linear-time algorithm that, given two intersecting convex polygons, finds their union (a simple polygon). (*Hint*: Use the same sweep method as for the intersection of two convex polygons.)   □

Exercise 4.36** You are given n red points and n blue points in the plane; no two points (of any color) coincide and no four points are collinear. Devise an efficient algorithm (at least in terms of average behavior, but preferably in terms of worst-case behavior) to produce n pairs of red-blue points such that the n segments thus defined do not intersect. (Although it is not obvious, such a matching always exists under the conditions given.)   □

Exercise 4.37** The *stabbing line* problem is posed as follows: given a collection of segments, does there exist a single line which intersects each and every segment? Devise an algorithm that solves this problem in low polynomial time, constructing a stabbing line if one exists. (*Hint*: This exercise is related to the problem of detecting intersecting segments.)   □

Exercise 4.38* Design a $\Theta(n \log n)$ algorithm to decide whether or not any two of n circles in the plane intersect, where each circle is given by its center and its radius.   □

Exercise 4.39* Consider the decision version of polygon intersection: given two simple polygons, do they intersect?

1. Present an informal argument to the effect that the program developed in Exercise 4.5 cannot be improved upon, i.e., that deciding whether or not two convex polygons intersect is as hard as producing the intersection.

2. Design and analyze a fast decision algorithm for the intersection of two simple polygons based upon the segment intersection algorithm of Program 4.11.

                                            □

Exercise 4.40** Design and analyze an efficient algorithm to decide whether or not any two of n simple polygons, each with at most k vertices, intersect.   □

Exercise 4.41* The Jordan sorting algorithm also allows one to test whether or not the input sequence is a proper Jordan sequence (i.e., whether or not it could indeed have been produced by the intersection of a line and a simple closed curve), since an improper sequence will result in crossing intervals within the same tree. Show where to add suitable tests to detect these error conditions.

                                            □

Exercise 4.42 [P] Since there is an intimate connection between Jordan sequences and simplicity, one might suspect that a fast simplicity testing algorithm might be derived from the principles embodied in the Jordan sorting algorithm. Explore this suggestion.   □

4.4 Bibliography

Graph algorithms form a fascinating field of study; two excellent monographs devoted to graph algorithms are those of Christofides [1975] and of Even [1980]. The use of depth-first search in the analysis of connectivity was studied in depth by Tarjan [1972], who invented the algorithms for strongly connected and bi-connected components; Hopcroft and Tarjan [1973] give a linear-time algorithm for triconnected component analysis. Determining arbitrary connectivity can be done through network flow analysis, as we shall see in Section 6.5; for edge-connectivity, the best algorithm to date, due to Matula [1987], runs in $\Theta(|V| \cdot |E|)$ time. The $\Theta(|E| \log |E|)$ algorithm for constructing the dominator tree (Exercise 4.28) is from Tarjan [1973]; Lengauer and Tarjan [1979] give the faster algorithm that runs in $\Theta(|E|\alpha(|E|, |V|))$ time.

Computational geometry can be said to originate with the Ph.D. thesis of Ian Shamos [1978], although many assorted results antedate it; excellent references on the subject include the monograph of Mehlhorn [1984] and the textbooks of Preparata and Shamos [1985] and of Edelsbrunner [1987], as well as the short survey (limited to five fundamental problems) of Dobkin [1987]. Issues of precision in geometric algorithms are just beginning to be studied; Dobkin and Silver [1988] present some preliminary results. The $\Theta(n \log n)$ algorithm for detecting an intersection among n line segments is due to Shamos and Hoey [1976]; the lower bound for element uniqueness was proved by Dobkin and Lipton [1979]. Chazelle and Edelsbrunner [1988] have given an optimal algorithm for reporting all intersections; their algorithm runs in $\Theta(n \log n + k)$ time, where k is the number of intersections. The $O(n \log \log n)$ algorithm for testing simplicity is an application of a more general triangulation algorithm due to Tarjan and van Wyk [1988]. Finding the intersection of two arbitrary simple polygons can be solved in $\Theta(m + n + k)$ time (which is optimal), where m and n are the sizes of the two input polygons and k is the combined size of all output polygons, using techniques invented by Guibas and Seidel [1986]. Hoffman *et al.* [1985] gave the linear-time algorithm for Jordan sorting of Section 4.2.3, a sketch of which appeared earlier in an article by Hoffman and Mehlhorn [1984]. A conjecture of Sleator and Tarjan [1985] implies that Jordan sorting could also be accomplished in linear time by the very simple process, which sorts any list in $\Theta(n \log n)$ time, of inserting the points into a splay tree and then traversing the splay tree; this conjecture has been neither proved nor disproved so far.

CHAPTER 5

Local Search I: The Greedy Method

This and the next chapter discuss optimization methods that run efficiently because they do only local work. By local work we mean that at each step these procedures use only a small fraction of the information available about the problem. *Greedy methods* build solutions piece by piece—for example, by repeatedly adding an object to the knapsack or placing a queen on the $n \times n$ chessboard. Each step increases the size of the partial solution and is based on local optimization: the choice selected is that which produces the largest immediate gain while maintaining feasibility. *Iterative methods* start with any feasible solution and proceed to improve upon the solution by repeated applications of a simple step. The step typically involves a small, localized change which improves the value of the objective function.

Since each application of the elementary step used in local search processes only a small amount of information and examines a small portion of the search space, the resulting algorithms are often very efficient. Unfortunately, local optimization only rarely translates into global optimization, so that local search methods often do not yield optimal solutions. Nevertheless, the inherent efficiency of local search techniques makes them attractive when large instances must be processed and algorithms that guarantee an optimal solution have prohibitive execution times. We shall consider this use of local search in detail in Volume II, but we begin this chapter with two examples (the travelling salesperson and knapsack problems) in order to gain some insight. We continue by discussing some classical problems for which the greedy method yields the global optimum, paying particular attention to issues of implementation. Finally, we develop a mathematical framework through which we characterize the structure of problems for which the greedy method always yields the global optimum.

254

The greedy method builds solutions to optimization problems step by step, according to the following simple precept:

> Whenever faced with a simple decision, make that choice which produces the largest immediate gain.

The wording is intentionally left vague: in general, the same problem may allow several distinct definitions of "choice" and "gain." For this reason the greedy method conceals many subtleties in spite of its apparent simplicity. We begin by presenting the basic paradigm through a simple example.

Recall that an instance of the set cover problem is given by a set and a collection of subsets of the set, the goal being to identify a subcollection of minimum size, the union of which covers the set. In order to apply the greedy method, we must consider the process by which a cover can be formed:

> Start with an empty collection of subsets and successively decide on which subset to incorporate next, until the collection comprises a cover.

The greedy method applied to this sequential decision process would have us select the next subset based on a measure of immediate gain. An obvious choice is "select next that subset which covers the largest number of currently uncovered elements, with ties broken arbitrarily." When this rule is applied to the example from Section 1.1, S_9 is the first subset selected, covering eight of the 16 elements with one subset. Sets S_1, S_2, and S_4 each cover three of the remaining uncovered elements, more than any of the other subsets, each of which now covers only two currently uncovered elements. One of these is selected arbitrarily. Which is selected does not affect the size of the cover produced for this example: although the composition of the cover varies, each consists of five subsets. As the optimal cover contains four subsets, this example points out a fundamental characteristic of the greedy method:

> Even though the greedy method makes each decision optimally from a local perspective, it may fail to achieve the global optimum.

The failure of the greedy method to produce the true optimal solution will be seen repeatedly and raises the following important question:

> How much worse than optimal is the solution produced by the greedy method?

As set covering is apparently intractable (its associated decision problem is $\mathcal{NP}$-complete), a fast heuristic that gets very close to the optimal solution may be the best practical solution. Thus another important issue is raised:

> How efficiently can the greedy heuristic be coded?

5.1 The Travelling Salesperson Problem

If we look at the travelling salesperson problem through the eyes of the salesperson, the simple decision that must be made at each step is "which vertex do we visit next?" Since the travelling salesperson problem is a minimization problem, the "largest gain" translates to the least increase in the objective function and gives rise to the following decision criterion:

> The next vertex to visit should be that unvisited vertex which is closest to the current vertex.

This criterion gives rise to the *nearest neighbor* heuristic. Each decision is made so that the distance travelled so far is increased as little as possible at this step in the process. A single simple path is maintained during the construction; the tour is completed by including the edge that connects the two vertices of degree one at the ends of the simple path.

Let us apply this selection rule to the instance of the symmetric travelling salesperson problem with triangle inequality of Figure 1.3, starting at Washington, D.C. The city closest to Washington is Baltimore, so the salesperson goes there first. From Baltimore the closest city, excluding Washington, is Philadelphia, from which the salesperson proceeds to New York. The greedy solution agrees with the optimal solution so far, but the two diverge at this point. The three cities closest to New York, namely Philadelphia, Baltimore, and Washington, have all been visited; the fourth closest is Pittsburgh, so the selection rule dictates that it be chosen next, whereas the optimal tour proceeds to Buffalo. At

Table 5.1: Comparison of the Tour Dictated by the Nearest Neighbor Heuristic with the Optimal Tour

City	Nearest neighbor heuristic		Optimal tour	
	Next city	Total distance	Next city	Total distance
1	Baltimore	39	Baltimore	39
2	Philadelphia	136	Philadelphia	136
3	New York	228	New York	228
4	Pittsburgh	614	Buffalo	673
5	Cleveland	739	Detroit	925
6	Detroit	906	Cincinnati	1190
7	Buffalo	1158	Cleveland	1434
8	Cincinnati*	1588	Pittsburgh	1559
9	Washington	2080	Washington	1790

*via Cleveland

this point the cycle being built has a path length of 614 miles, while the optimal tour has accumulated a length of 673 miles. Table 5.1 shows how the two tours develop, the optimal tour not having smaller total length until the penultimate city is visited.

An interesting feature of the nearest neighbor heuristic is that the cycle produced, and thus the value of the objective function, depends on the city chosen as the starting point. For this instance of the travelling salesperson problem, each choice of starting city results in a different tour (see Table 5.2). This observation suggests that each possible starting vertex be used in turn and the best resulting tour be chosen.

Unwittingly, by examining this problem from the point of view of the salesperson, we have incorporated hidden, unnecessary structure into the application of the greedy method. Instead of thinking of a tour as a sequence of edges that must be constructed in increasing subscript order (i.e., selecting the first edge of the tour first, the second edge of the tour second, etc.), it is useful to think of the tour as an unordered set of edges, T, which when drawn on a map of the cities to be visited happens to form a simple cycle. Within this framework, a feasible partial solution is any collection of edges which corresponds to a disjoint collection of simple paths (and isolated vertices, which are just degenerate simple paths), since such a collection can always be extended to a tour. The initial collection is empty; the solution is a simple path through all n vertices (which, as with the nearest neighbor heuristic, must be converted into a tour by adding the edge connecting the two vertices of degree one); and at each step, the partial solution grows one larger by inclusion of an edge. Viable candidates for inclusion are those edges which join two simple paths into one: these are precisely the edges that neither raise the degree of a vertex to three nor create a

Table 5.2: Lengths of Tours Produced by the Nearest Neighbor Heuristic Using Different Starting Cities

Starting city	Length of tour
Baltimore	2141
Buffalo	1995
Cincinnati	2297
Cleveland	2086
Detroit	2056
New York	2103
Philadelphia	2114
Pittsburgh	2110
Washington	2080

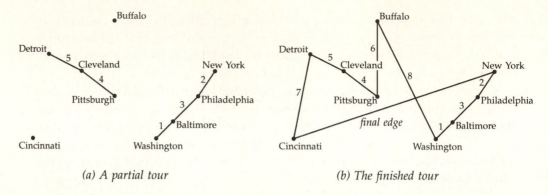

(a) A partial tour   (b) The finished tour

Figure 5.1: Construction of a Tour by the Method of Coalesced Simple Paths

cycle. Notice that, once an edge fails either condition, it can never become viable again. Although the simple paths of a partial solution partition the vertices into equivalence classes, using the UNION-FIND data structure is both inappropriate and unnecessary.

Exercise 5.1 By taking advantage of the bound on the degree of each vertex, develop a data structure which allows a candidate edge to be checked for feasibility in constant time. Updating the data structure to reflect inclusion of a feasible edge should also take constant time, and reconstructing the simple paths should take linear time.   □

The choice of viable edge does not affect the correctness of the algorithm, only the quality of the solution; the greedy method dictates that the chosen edge be the viable edge of least cost. We call the resulting algorithm the method of *coalesced simple paths*. Its execution is illustrated in Figure 5.1; the final tour length is 2056 miles.

We used the same technique for minimizing the objective function in the nearest neighbor heuristic, but we restricted the choices in a different manner. Here the restriction is global, and it allows us to presort the edges and consider them in a fixed order. In contrast, the previous restriction was local, so that the set of candidate edges was altered dynamically, depending on the location of the salesperson. Intuitively, the method of coalesced simple paths is maximally greedy because any edge, the inclusion of which does not lead to an infeasible solution, is a candidate for inclusion at each step. Another aspect of this method is that, if all edge lengths are distinct, the tour produced is unique. Notice that, by specifying the selection of the viable edge of least cost, we have implicitly assumed that the distance measure is symmetric. Indeed, the method of coalesced simple paths as we have outlined it applies only to graphs with a symmetric distance measure—although it can be modified to apply to asymmetric measures as well.

Many other greedy algorithms have been designed for the travelling salesperson problem. Whereas the two methods just discussed build tours edge by edge, a large family of greedy methods, known as *insertion methods*, builds tours vertex by vertex by taking advantage of the triangle inequality. These methods start with a trivial cycle and expand it into a tour by incorporating a new vertex at each step. Call the new vertex x; in order to maintain a cycle, the algorithm replaces a single edge of the cycle, say (u, v), with the two edges (u, x) and (x, v). In order to minimize the increase in the value of the objective function, the edge to be replaced is chosen so as to minimize $d(u, x) + d(x, v) - d(u, v)$, which is nonnegative when the triangle inequality holds. These replacements do not really undo previous work, an important characteristic of greedy methods; they neither remove vertices nor alter their relative order in the cycle. Selection of the next vertex to include can be random or based on additional considerations, in hope of obtaining a better solution. The latter strategies include *nearest insertion*, which chooses the vertex closest to the group of already included vertices; *farthest insertion*, which chooses the vertex farthest from the group of already included vertices (with the goal of obtaining quickly a good "outline" of the solution and refining it in later stages); and *cheapest insertion*, which chooses the vertex that minimizes $d(u, x) + d(x, v) - d(u, v)$ over all choices of edge and vertex.

Exercise 5.2 Devise and analyze an implementation for each insertion method. All should run in quadratic time in the number of vertices, except cheapest insertion, which has an added logarithmic factor. □

All methods in this family require a separate initialization step: selection of the initial cycle. The natural choice is an empty cycle consisting of a single vertex. As with the nearest neighbor heuristic, the resulting tour varies with the choice of vertex. Again we can try every choice and retain the best result, if time permits; otherwise, we can tailor the choice to the specific insertion heuristic. In our experiments, we used a randomly chosen empty cycle as a starting point for random insertion, but we actually started with a two-vertex cycle for the other methods, selecting the shortest such cycle for both nearest insertion and cheapest insertion and the longest such cycle for farthest insertion. Figure 5.2 illustrates the progress of the farthest insertion heuristic in our example.

The results obtained in our small example by all the greedy methods discussed are listed in Table 5.3, which also lists the results obtained with a larger example of 57 cities distributed throughout the United States (this last is a classical example in the literature of the travelling salesperson problem). While the insertion methods generally did better than the simpler greedy methods de-

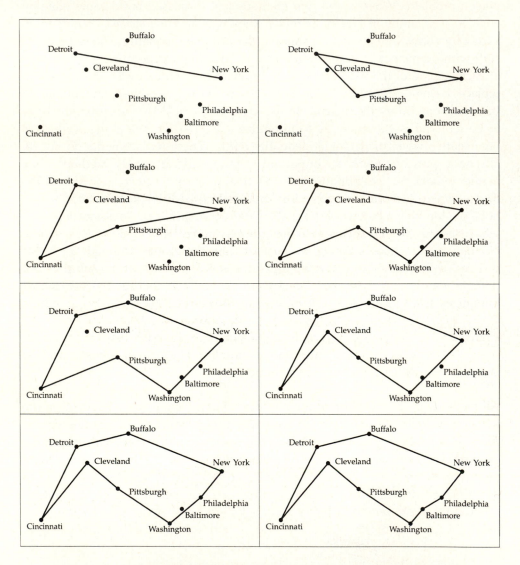

Figure 5.2: Construction of a Tour by the Farthest Insertion Heuristic

Table 5.3: Performance of Greedy Methods on Instances of the Travelling Salesperson Problem

Name of method	Cost of tour		Notes
	9-city map	57-city map	
Optimal	1790	12955	
Nearest neighbor	1995/2109.11/2297	14411/15918.81/18518	Best/Average/Worst
Coalesced simple paths	2056	14583	
Nearest insertion	1790	14667	
Farthest insertion	1790	13352	
Cheapest insertion	1790	14589	
Random insertion	1790/1826.89/1934	13275/14123.35/15018	$|V|$ random orderings

scribed earlier, many graphs can be found for which the simple greedy methods yield better results than the insertion methods.

This discussion should have raised more questions than it answered: how do we evaluate the performance of a given greedy heuristic, both experimentally and analytically? given answers to this first question, how do we choose which heuristics to use? and, more fundamentally, are there problems that can be solved by the greedy method? We give a thorough answer to the third question in the last section of this chapter, but we defer answers to the first two questions to Volume II—although the following section answers these questions for the knapsack problem.

5.2   The Knapsack Problem

We begin by considering briefly two rather naïve applications of the greedy method to the knapsack problem. In the first, we attempt to maximize the value of the knapsack by repeatedly including the most valuable remaining object that fits; in the second, we use an indirect approach: we maximize the number of objects in the knapsack by repeatedly including the smallest remaining object, in hope of obtaining a filling of high value. For the example of Section 1.1, the first approach selects, in order, the food, water purifier, sleeping bag, tent, and mosquito repellent, yielding a filling with a value of 137, while the second approach yields a better filling, with a value of 147, by selecting, in order, the water purifier, mosquito repellent, flashlight, rain gear, novel, dried food, sleeping bag, and first aid kit. The second approach actually does optimize its objective function, as it produces the filling with the most objects (if k objects fit into the

Table 5.4: A Knapsack Where Maximizing the Number of Objects Yields Poor Results

	Objects		
	$1,\dots,N$	$N+1,\dots,2N-1$	$2N$
v_i	1	$N^{1/2}$	$N^{1/2}+\epsilon$
w_i	1	$1+\epsilon$	N

knapsack, then so do the k lightest objects); however, such a filling need not have maximum value.

When the objects are processed in increasing order by weight, the combined weight of the objects included by the algorithm may be less than the weight restriction, because all the light objects may have been included and the next object, of moderate weight, may just barely exceed the remaining capacity. In such a case, many solutions may pack the knapsack with the same number of objects, so that we may be able to exchange the object that failed to fit (or an even heavier object) for a lighter object without violating the weight restriction. This observation suggests an *iterative improvement algorithm* (a member of the class of methods which forms the topic of the next chapter) that can be applied after the initial greedy algorithm is run:

> Repeatedly replace objects of smaller value with objects of larger value as long as the weight restriction is not violated.

In our example, the camp stove, with weight four and value five, can be substituted for the novel, increasing the value of the knapsack to 148.

Both of these naïve approaches are easily misled and neither consistently outperforms the other. The following example shows that maximizing the number of objects carried can produce a solution that is better by an arbitrary factor than the solution produced by processing the objects in decreasing order by value and yet remains an arbitrary factor away from optimal.

Example 5.1 Consider a knapsack of capacity N and $2N$ objects with weights and values given by Table 5.4 (where ϵ is very small). The optimal solution has a value approximately equal to $N^{3/2}$, the solution produced by processing the objects in increasing order by weight has a value of N, and the solution produced by processing the objects in decreasing order by value has a value approximately equal to $N^{1/2}$. Since N is arbitrary, the ratios can be made arbitrarily large.

□

Table 5.5: The Camping Items Arranged in Order of Decreasing Value Density

Object	Value	Weight	Value density
Water purifier	30	1	30.00
Dried food	50	3	16.67
Sleeping bag	25	3	8.33
Mosquito repellent	12	2	6.00
First aid kit	15	3	5.00
Flashlight	6	2	3.00
Rain gear	5	2	2.50
Change of clothes	11	5	2.20
Novel	4	2	2.00
Tent	20	11	1.82
Canteen (filled)	10	7	1.43
Camp stove	5	4	1.25

Exercise 5.3 Give an example in which processing the objects in decreasing order by value outperforms processing the objects in increasing order by weight by an arbitrary factor, yet remains an arbitrary factor below optimal.   □

A more sensible approach is to order the objects according to their value density, where the density of an object is defined as the ratio of its value to its weight. The logic behind this ordering is best seen in an exaggerated example. Consider packing a small crate with valuables; the objects consist of pieces of semiprecious stones (azurite, tiger eye, etc.) and a large block of white marble, which exactly fills the crate. Even though the block of marble is worth more than any of the semiprecious stones, its value density is much lower and we can attain a higher value by packing the crate with as many pieces of the semiprecious stones as will fit, rather than by packing the marble alone. However, if the semiprecious stones are replaced with a large quantity of small glass beads, then the block of marble, despite its large weight, has the higher value density and would be preferable to a crate full of worthless beads. For our example of the hiker, the density ordering is given in Table 5.5. Selecting the next available object that fits, the greedy algorithm yields a filling (the first seven objects plus the novel) with a value of 147.

In fact, applying the greedy method with density ordering to the linear program formed by relaxing the 0-1 integer constraints (allowing the x_i to take on real values between zero and one) produces the optimal solution. With continuous variables, objects are included in the knapsack ($x_i = 1$) until an object, call it k, fails to fit; then that fraction of object k which exactly fills the knapsack is included, i.e., we let $x_k = (M - \sum_{i=1}^{k-1} w_i)/w_k$. To see that this solution is optimal, imagine the objects as being divided into infinitesimally small pieces of equal weight (or just into pieces of unit weight if the weights and knapsack capacity are all integers). Replacing one small piece with another of larger value density improves any solution, so that the optimal packing includes all of the densest objects that fit, plus as much of the next densest object (the first that fails to fit in its entirety) as is necessary to fill the knapsack exactly.

Analysis of the running time of these heuristics is straightforward. All three approaches take $\Theta(n \log n)$ time to sort the objects, then make a single pass (the greedy phase) through the sorted list. Since processing each object to determine the assignment to each x_i and to update the running totals of accumulated value and weight requires constant time, the greedy phase of the algorithm does $\Theta(n)$ work. Thus the preprocessing time dominates the total running time. These results are typical of the greedy method—the order of the entire algorithm usually permits large instances to be run, and often the preprocessing of the data takes longer than making the sequence of decisions.

As another example of the cost of preprocessing, consider the travelling salesperson problem with triangle inequality. If the problem is specified by the distances associated with the direct connections, as in Figure 1.3, then, before we can apply any of our heuristics, we must first solve the all-points shortest-path problem (Problem 5) to produce a matrix of intercity distances. After this preprocessing, all of the greedy algorithms run in either $O(n^2)$ or $O(n^2 \log n)$ time, as seen in Exercise 5.2. We shall return to the all-points shortest-path problem later in this chapter and again in Volume II; for now we only note that its running time must be at least quadratic, since n^2 elements of the matrix of intercity distances must be assigned. Once again the preprocessing is a significant, and possibly dominant, portion of the total computation time.

Our main goal in this section is to answer the question: How badly can the greedy method based on value density perform? Let $G_d(I)$ be the value produced by the greedy method applied to instance I of the knapsack problem (the subscript d is a reminder that objects are sorted by density), and let $OPT(I)$ be the value of the optimal filling; we are interested in the least upper bound for the ratio

$$\frac{OPT(I)}{G_d(I)},$$

as I ranges over all instances. Notice that we are using the ratio of OPT to G_d, as opposed to their difference: the difference can easily be made arbitrarily large by the simple artifice of multiplying the values (but not the weights) by a suitable constant. We use the least upper bound because we want to know the very worst that this ratio can become—though it is possible that the ratio is achieved only as a limit and no instance actually achieves it.

For our heuristic as stated, this ratio is unbounded, i.e.,

$$\text{lub} \left\{ \frac{OPT(I)}{G_d(I)} \right\} = \infty,$$

as demonstrated by the following example.

Example 5.2 Consider a knapsack of capacity N and two objects, the first of weight 2 and value 3, the second of weight and value both equal to $N - 1$. We see that $G_d(I)$ equals 3 since, once the first object is selected, there is not enough room for the second. Thus we have

$$\frac{OPT(I)}{G_d(I)} = \frac{N - 1}{3},$$

a value which grows arbitrarily large as N grows. □

In order to get a better result, we need to modify the method slightly. Consider these two potential fillings: the result of G_d and the filling consisting of the single most valuable object; select whichever of these two has the larger value. We denote the result of the modified heuristic by $G_{md}(I)$. Note that the modification does not affect the overall running time of the algorithm, but does eliminate pathological cases such as that we just examined.

Theorem 5.1 For any instance of the knapsack problem, we have

$$1 \le \frac{OPT(I)}{G_{md}(I)} < 2.$$ □

Before proving the theorem, we note that both bounds are tight. The tightness of the lower bound is obvious. The following construction shows that the value of two cannot be improved upon.

Example 5.3 Consider a knapsack of capacity $2N$ and three objects with weights and values as given in Table 5.6. G_d will select the first object, thereby preventing the inclusion of either remaining object, for a total value of $N+2$. The alternative filling, the single most valuable object, yields the same filling, so G_{md} produces a

Table 5.6: A Knapsack Instance Achieving an Asymptotic Ratio of Two

	Objects	
	1	2 and 3
v_i	$N + 2$	N
w_i	$N + 1$	N
d_i	$1 + 1/(N + 1)$	1

filling of value $N + 2$. The optimal filling consists of the second and third objects and has a value of $2N$. Thus we have

$$\frac{OPT(I)}{G_{md}(I)} = \frac{2N}{N + 2} = 2 - \frac{4}{N + 2},$$

a value which, while always less than two, converges to two as N increases. □

We now prove that $OPT(I)/G_{md}(I) < 2$ holds for any instance I.

Proof: We first modify our heuristic again. Instead of running the first alternative of G_{md} all the way to completion, we terminate it as soon as an object fails to fit. Call this truncated version G_{td} and call the modification of G_{md} which uses G_{td} as its first alternative G_{mtd}. This modification never causes G_{mtd} to perform better than G_{md}, so that it will be sufficient to prove that the ratio of the optimal to G_{mtd} is less than two.

Next we define yet another algorithm, G_l. It is just the greedy algorithm applied to the linear programming problem formed by relaxing the 0-1 constraints. As we have seen, G_l solves this relaxed problem optimally. Note that we have

$$G_l(I) = G_{td}(I) + x_j v_j$$

(where j denotes the first object that fails to fit), because all of our greedy heuristics proceed in the same order and because G_l, when unable to include the next object entirely, includes as much as possible of the next object.

Hence, for any instance I, the following inequalities hold:

$$G_{td}(I) \leq G_{mtd}(I) \leq G_{md}(I) \leq OPT(I) \leq G_l(I).$$

We have two cases, depending on whether or not the value of the first object that failed to fit, v_j, is larger than the value of the truncated greedy filling, $G_{td}(I)$.

Case 1: $v_j \leq G_{td}(I)$. It follows that

$$OPT(I) \leq G_l(I) = G_{td}(I) + x_j v_j < G_{td}(I) + v_j \leq 2G_{td}(I) \leq 2G_{mtd}(I).$$

The strict inequality comes from the fact that x_j is less than 1, since object j did not fit completely into the knapsack.

Case 2: $v_j > G_{td}(I)$. It follows that $G_{mtd}(I) \geq v_j$, as the second alternative of the algorithm will be selected (although the jth object may not be the most valuable, it is more valuable than the filling achieved by the truncated greedy procedure). Hence we have

$$OPT(I) \leq G_l(I) = G_{td}(I) + x_j v_j < G_{td}(I) + v_j < 2v_j \leq 2G_{mtd}(I).$$

Q.E.D.

Although we have seen that the worst-case bound is achievable, at least in the limit, the proof suggests a mechanism for getting a tighter estimate of the error in any particular instance. Since we have

$$G_{md}(I) \leq OPT(I) \leq G_l(I),$$

$G_l(I)/G_{md}(I)$ serves as a conservative estimate for $OPT(I)/G_{md}(I)$. In our running example, we have $G_l(I) = 151.8$ and $G_{md}(I) = 147$, so that the ratio of $OPT(I)$ to $G_{md}(I)$ is guaranteed to be less than 1.04, a much better guarantee than 2. (By noting that all values are integers, we can conclude that $OPT(I) \leq 151$ instead of 151.8.)

5.3 Minimum Spanning Trees

By now the reader may have concluded that the greedy method does not produce the optimal solution to any problem. This conjecture is wrong: minimum spanning trees, shortest paths (both problems from Section 1.2), and optimal encoding are successfully attacked by the greedy approach. We consider these problems in the next three sections, deferring to the last section the more general question of characterizing problems that are solved optimally by the greedy method.

Recall that for a connected, undirected graph, with a positive length associated with each edge, a minimum spanning tree connects all the vertices and minimizes the sum of the lengths of its edges. To apply the greedy method to the construction of the tree, we must, as usual, define a local optimization step. Following the approach taken for the travelling salesperson problem, we consider the family of greedy methods that build a spanning tree by coalescing equivalence classes. Here an equivalence class consists of a set of vertices with an associated set of edges that form a minimum spanning tree for the vertices in the class. Initially, each vertex is the sole element of its equivalence class, and the associated set of edges is empty. When the algorithm terminates, only one equivalence class remains and the associated set of edges is a minimum spanning tree. At each step of the algorithm, we select an edge with an endpoint in each of two equivalence classes and coalesce these classes, thereby combining two trees into one larger tree. Edges, both endpoints of which lie in the same equivalence class, are permanently excluded, since their selection would lead to a cycle. In order to minimize the increase in the value of the objective function, the greedy method dictates that the allowable edge of least cost be chosen next. As in the travelling salesperson problem, this choice can be made with or without additional constraints. At one extreme we can apply no additional constraint and always choose the shortest edge that combines two spanning trees into a larger spanning tree. At the other extreme we can designate a special equivalence class which must be involved in any merge operation. The first approach is again global and can be viewed as selecting edges (producing, at intermediate steps, a forest of spanning trees), while the second is local and, at least for programming purposes, is best viewed as selecting vertices (adding them one by one to a single partial spanning tree).

The first approach is known as Kruskal's algorithm, after J. B. Kruskal, who first presented it in 1956. As discussed in the context of the travelling salesperson problem, the global constraint results in the edges being examined (for inclusion or rejection) in a fixed order. Thus we can presort the edges into nondecreasing order by length, in $\Theta(|E| \log |E|)$ time. The greedy algorithm then examines each edge in turn, including it if and only if its inclusion does not cause a cycle.

The second approach, which restricts the growth to a single partial spanning tree, is known as Prim's algorithm, after R. C. Prim, who presented it in 1957. At all times the vertices of V are partitioned into two classes, V_1 and V_2. The vertices of V_1 (the distinguished equivalence class) are connected by the edges that form a minimum spanning tree for V_1; let E_1 denote this subset of edges. The remaining vertices, those in V_2, are viewed as isolated points since their equivalence classes never grow beyond the initial stage. Initially V_1 consists of an arbitrary vertex. At the end V_1 is V, V_2 is empty, and E_1 is the desired minimum spanning tree. Each simple decision consists of choosing which vertex, v_j, to transfer from V_2 to V_1 and which edge to add to E_1. Using the sum of the lengths of the edges in E_1 as the value to minimize, the locally optimal decision is to select as the vertex to transfer from V_2 to V_1 the one for which $d(v_i, v_j)$ is minimal, with $v_i \in V_1$, $v_j \in V_2$. Stated somewhat less formally, we incorporate the shortest edge, one end of which is in the minimum spanning tree we are building and the other end of which is an isolated vertex. For the graph of Figure 1.3, the eight iterations of Kruskal's and Prim's algorithms are shown in Figure 5.3. (Note that the original graph of Figure 1.3, which contains only the direct connections, is being used rather than the complete graph resulting from the solution of the all-points shortest-path problem.)

We need to prove that both of these algorithms in fact produce a minimum spanning tree for each instance of the problem. We must also devise an efficient implementation for the algorithms. We can prove the correctness of both algorithms at once by proving the correctness of a more general algorithm.

Theorem 5.2 If at each step of the algorithm an arbitrary equivalence class, T, is selected, but the edge selected for inclusion is the smallest that has exactly one endpoint in T, then the final tree that results is a minimum spanning tree.   □

Before giving the proof, we verify that such a proof indeed shows the correctness of both Kruskal's and Prim's algorithms. The correctness of Prim's algorithm follows immediately: we always select as T the equivalence class containing the vertex we have chosen initially to place in V_1. The correctness of Kruskal's algorithm follows as well: the tree chosen in this case can be any that contains an endpoint of a shortest allowable edge.

Proof: As G is connected, there is always at least one allowable edge at each iteration. As each iteration can proceed, irrespective of our choice of T, and as an iteration decreases the number of equivalence classes by one, the algorithm terminates.

The proof is by induction, though we present it somewhat informally. Let T_A be a spanning tree produced by the above algorithm and let T_M be a minimum spanning tree. We give a procedure for transforming T_M into T_A. We will form a sequence of trees, each slightly different from its predecessor, with the property that the sums of the lengths of the edges in successive trees are the same. Since T_A will be at the far end of the sequence of transformations, it must also be a minimum spanning tree. Label the edges of T_A by the iteration on which they entered the tree. Let e_i be the edge of lowest index that is present in T_A but not in T_M. The addition of e_i to T_M forms a cycle (Theorem 1.2). Note that the length of e_i is greater than or equal to that of every other edge in the cycle; otherwise, T_M would not be a minimum spanning tree, because breaking any edge in the cycle would produce a spanning tree and breaking a longer edge, if one such existed, would reduce the total cost. Now, when e_i was added to the forest of trees that eventually became T_A, it connected an arbitrarily chosen tree, T, to some other tree. Traverse the cycle in T_M starting from the endpoint of e_i that was in T and going in the direction that does not lead to an immediate traversal of e_i. At some point in this traversal, we first encounter an edge with exactly one endpoint in T. It might be the first edge we encounter, or it might be many edges into the traversal, but such an edge must exist since the other endpoint of e_i is not in T. Furthermore, this edge, call it $\hat{e}$, cannot be e_i. Now the length of e_i cannot exceed that of $\hat{e}$, because $\hat{e}$ was an allowable edge, but was not selected; thus the two edges have equal length. We replace $\hat{e}$ with e_i in T_M: the resulting tree has the same total length. Note that $\hat{e}$ may or may not be an edge of T_A, but if it is, then its index is greater than i, so that our new tree now first differs from T_A at some index greater than i. Replacing T_M with this new minimum spanning tree, we continue this process until there are no differences, i.e., until T_M has been transformed into T_A.

Q.E.D.

We now turn our attention to the efficient implementation of these algorithms, starting with Kruskal's algorithm. A naïve implementation of the greedy

Kruskal's algorithm   *Prim's algorithm*

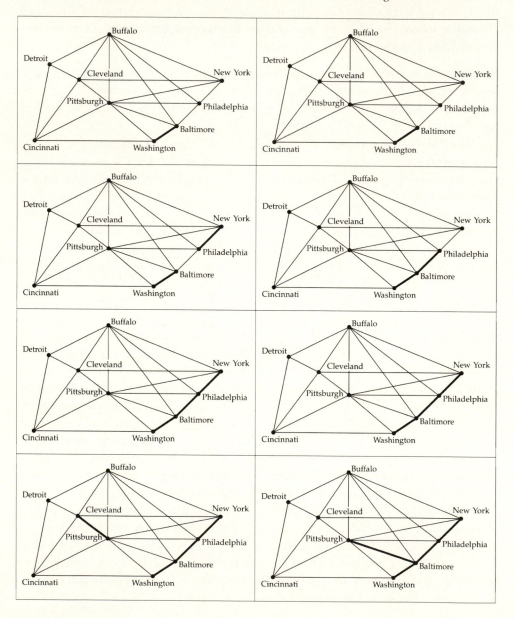

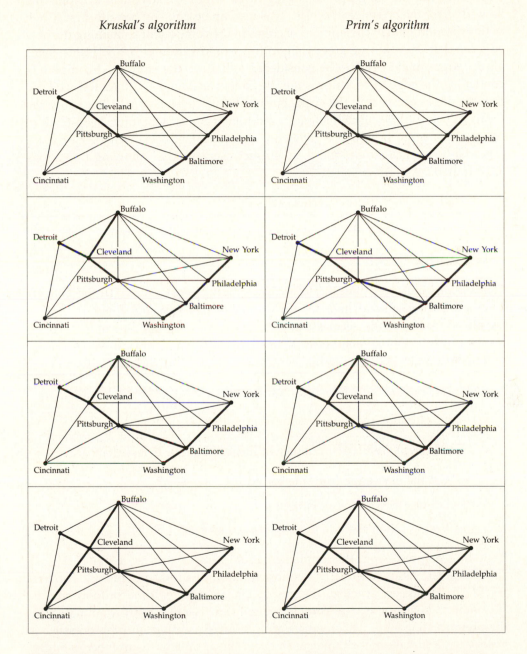

Figure 5.3: The Effect of Successive Iterations of Kruskal's and Prim's Algorithms

step might test the subgraph consisting of all edges already included, plus the new edge, for the presence of cycles. This test can be done by breadth-first search in time proportional to the number of edges in the component containing the new edge, so that the resulting greedy algorithm would run in $\Theta(|E|\cdot|V|)$ time, since all $|E|$ edges might need to be considered and since the connected component containing the edge to be tested might be almost as large as $|V|$. As we need not find the edges composing the cycle, but need only determine that the new edge forms a cycle, our discussion suggests a different implementation: keep track of which vertices are in which equivalence class and just check whether or not a candidate edge has its endpoints in distinct classes. The following operations are required:

- Create classes with one vertex each.

- Detect whether or not two vertices are in the same class.

- Merge two classes.

This abstract data type specification corresponds almost exactly to the UNION-FIND structure discussed in Section 3.2. Indeed, the first and third operations are already present; the second can be implemented simply by comparing the results of FIND run on each vertex. Thus Kruskal's algorithm can be succinctly described as follows:

- (Preprocessing) Sort the edges into nondecreasing order by length.

- (Initialization) Create one set for each vertex.

- (Greedy step) While the number of included edges is less than $|V| - 1$:

    - Get the next edge from the sorted list, say (u, w).

    - Let $x \leftarrow \text{FIND}(u)$, $y \leftarrow \text{FIND}(w)$.

    - If $x \neq y$, then include the edge (u, w) and call $\text{UNION}(x, y)$.

Excluding preprocessing, this implementation of the algorithm requires $|V| - 1$ UNION operations and up to $2|E|$ FIND operations, for a total cost of $\Theta(|E|\cdot\alpha(|E|+|V|, |V|))$. Hence, in practice, the greedy phase requires time proportional to $|E|$ and the behavior of the complete algorithm is once again dominated by the preprocessing step. When edges are presorted (so that no preprocessing is necessary), Kruskal's algorithm runs in quasi-linear time in the number of edges. Program 5.1 presents the implementation discussed.

When the edges are not presorted and the graph is dense, it may be preferable to embed the sorting step within the greedy step rather than to presort the

```
type edge = record
                v1, v2: vertex; (* undirected *)
                length: ... (* integer or real *)
             end;
     tree = array [1..MaxVertexMinus1] of edge;

procedure Kruskal(var G: graph; var mst: tree);
  (* The procedure assumes that the graph is connected. *)

  (* Program assumes a Union-Find package (for holding vertices) with operations
        procedure CreateUF(N: integer), procedure Union(i, j: vertex), and
        function Find(i: vertex): vertex.
     Program assumes a min-heap package (for holding edges) with operations
        procedure DeleteMin(var H: heap) and procedure Heapify(var H: heap).
     For reasons of efficiency, procedure Kruskal has direct access to the heap. *)

  label 99;
  var H: heap;
      s1, s2: vertex;
      count: integer; (* number of edges included in minimum spanning tree *)
  begin
    (* Initially each vertex is its own (degenerate) tree and the heap contains
       all the edges. *)
    CreateUF(G.size);
    ... (* Scan the adjacency lists of G, placing each edge into the heap once. *)
    Heapify(H);

    (* Remove edges from the heap until N-1 are accepted. *)
    count := 0;
    while true do
      begin
        s1 := Find(H.elts[1].v1); s2 := Find(H.elts[1].v2); (* FindMin *)
        if s1 <> s2
          then begin (* This edge does not form a cycle -- include it. *)
                  count := count + 1;
                  mst[count] := H.elts[1];
                  if count = G.size - 1 then goto 99; (* return *)
                  Union(s1,s2) (* Merge the two trees. *)
               end;
        (* Replace the minimum element of the heap with an allowable edge. *)
        while Find(H.elts[H.size].v1) = Find(H.elts[H.size].v2) do
          H.size := H.size - 1;
        DeleteMin(H) (* no need to return minimum element *)
      end;
99:
  end; (* Kruskal *)
```

Program 5.1: An Implementation of Kruskal's Algorithm

edges. As the algorithm rarely examines all the edges, we may save quite a bit of work by just maintaining the edges in a min-heap. We incur a $\Theta(|E|)$ overhead for the initial Heapify operation. Each step involves a DeleteMin operation, which takes $\Theta(\log |E|)$ time. In addition, the last element in the heap can be checked with two Find operations to see whether it remains an allowable edge; if it does not, it can be eliminated and the new last element of the heap can be considered as a candidate to replace the root. In this way we may avoid future DeleteMin operations which retrieve an edge that is no longer allowable, and the additional Find operations, which are very fast already, may cause additional path compression. (On the other hand, a large number of such eliminations can take place, many of elements that would never have risen to the top of the heap anyway, thus wasting time.) Thus we stand to gain on three fronts: (i) the algorithm might not examine all the edges; (ii) some of the edges that are no longer allowable are eliminated before they can rise to the top of the heap and cause an unnecessary DeleteMin; and (iii) any given DeleteMin operation might be completed in less time than the worst case of $\Theta(\log |E|)$, though the value sifted down will generally sink nearly to the bottom, since it came from the bottom in the first place.

Prim's algorithm, as described above, appears to spend most of its time finding the shortest edge that extends E_1 outward. If on each iteration the desired edge is found by simply searching the adjacency lists of the nodes in V_1, then up to $\Theta(|E|)$ time per iteration could be expended, yielding a total work of $\Theta(|V| \cdot |E|)$. It is therefore necessary to maintain additional internal data structures to avoid complete searches through the adjacency lists.

When a vertex, v_i, is added to V_1, the distance from each vertex, v_j, remaining in V_2 to its nearest neighbor in the expanded V_1 cannot increase. Whether or not it decreases depends on whether or not $d(v_i, v_j)$ is less than the distance from v_j to its nearest neighbor in the original V_1. This relationship suggests associating with each vertex in V_2 the following information: the distance to and the identity of its nearest neighbor in V_1. When v_i is incorporated into V_1, this information can be updated by scanning the adjacency list of v_i. The obvious implementation of this approach uses an array, which indicates whether the vertex is in V_1 or in V_2 and (for vertices in V_2) stores the nearest neighbor information. At the time a vertex is transferred from V_2 to V_1, the identity of the nearest neighbor is frozen: the edge from the vertex to its nearest neighbor is an edge of the minimum spanning tree. The resulting implementation runs in $\Theta(|V|^2)$ time. As each vertex gets included in V_1, its adjacency list is scanned; the total accumulated time for this is $\Theta(|E|)$. The step that adversely affects the running time is determining which vertex to add to V_1, a $\Theta(|V|)$ search.

Notice that only two distinct operations are used in our abstract formulation of Prim's algorithm:

- Identify (and remove from further consideration) the closest unincluded vertex.

- Decrease the distance from some unincluded vertices to the set of included vertices.

These are in part the specifications given for a priority queue. We keep the vertices of V_2 in a min-heap with direct access (see Figure 3.3), with the distance of a vertex to its nearest neighbor in V_1 serving as the key. DELETEMIN now returns the vertex that gets transferred from V_2 to V_1. The second operation is just DECREASEKEY. Initialization is most easily accomplished by considering V_1 as initially empty: under this assumption, the values in the array of distances are all infinity, so that any initial ordering results in a valid heap.

The overall running time of Prim's algorithm implemented in this manner is $\Theta(|E| \log |V|)$. The initialization phase takes $\Theta(|V|)$ time; there are $|V|$ DELETEMIN operations, which together contribute $\Theta(|V| \log |V|)$ time; and there are up to $|E|$ DECREASEKEY operations, each of which takes $\Theta(\log |V|)$ time. This is a very pessimistic analysis. Typically, the addition of a vertex to V_1 does not cause the distance fields of all its neighbors to decrease, so there are fewer than $|E|$ DECREASEKEY operations, and even those neighbors which do have to be sifted up may not reach the root. The code for Prim's algorithm is given in Program 5.2. Technically $\Theta(|E| \log |V|)$ cannot be compared with $\Theta(|V|^2)$. On a complete graph we have $|V|^2 < |E| \log |V|$, but typical graphs tend to be sparse, so that we usually have $|V|^2 \gg |E| \log |V|$. Another problem in comparing the running times of the two implementations is that the analysis given accounts for only the worst case. In fact, the $\Theta(|V|^2)$ method requires that much time on any graph—it is essentially unaffected by the data—while the $\Theta(|E| \log |V|)$ algorithm almost never attains its worst-case bound for the reasons previously indicated.

We can modify our implementation of heaps to make Prim's algorithm run in time $\Theta(|E| \log |V|)$ on sparse graphs and in time $\Theta(|V|^2)$ on dense graphs. Observe that the time required for a DECREASEKEY operation depends on the height of the heap; thus the updating of distances can be made more efficient by decreasing the height of the heap, which in turn can be achieved by increasing the branching factor of each heap node. In a binary heap, the height of the heap is proportional to $\lg n$; in a k-heap, the height is proportional to $\log_k n$. While the choice of base makes no difference in asymptotic terms for any fixed value of k, we can adapt k to the situation at hand, increasing it as the number of edges increases. Now, any increase in branching factor adversely affects the behavior of DELETEMIN, which requires time proportional to $k \log_k n$, since all k children must be examined during the sift-down operation. Thus the $|V|$ DELETEMIN operations take $\Theta(|V| k \log_k |V|)$ time. Initialization is still $\Theta(|V|)$, which can be ignored.

```
procedure Prim(var G: graph; var mst: tree);
  (* Program assumes a standard or k-heap package, modified as indicated
     in Figure 3.3, with operations
         procedure DeleteMin(var H: heap; var v: vertex) and
         procedure SiftUp(var H: heap; v: vertex). *)

 var V2: heap;
     (* The information about vertices, indexed by vertex name, is kept
         external to the heap. *)
     d: array [0..MaxVertex] of ...; (* integer or real *)
         (* Distance to nearest vertex in V1:
              positive for vertices in V2, negative for vertices in V1. *)
     who: array [1..MaxVertex] of vertex; (* nearest vertex in V1 *)
     p: PtrToNode;
     vmin: vertex;
     i: integer;
begin
  V2.size := G.size; (* Initially nobody is in V1 and everybody is in V2. *)
  for i := 0 to G.size do
    begin
      V2.elts[i] := i; V2.where[i] := i;
      d[i] := infinity (* maxint or something appropriate *)
    end;
  d[0] := -infinity; (* Install sentinel for SiftUp. *)

  for i := 1 to G.size do
    begin
      (* Find the vertex and edge to incorporate next. *)
      DeleteMin(V2,vmin);
      d[vmin] := -d[vmin]; (* Place chosen vertex in V1. *)
      (* Update distances of vertices in V2 adjacent to vmin. *)
      p := G.AdjLists[vmin];
      while p <> nil do
        begin
          if p^.length < d[p^.id]
              (* The test will fail if p^.id is already included in V1. *)
            then begin
                    d[p^.id] := p^.length;
                    who[p^.id] := vmin;
                    SiftUp(V2,p^.id)
                 end;
          p := p^.next
        end
    end;

  (* Record the answer in standard form. *)
  for i := 2 (* v1 was included without a corresponding edge *) to G.size do
    begin mst[i-1].v1 := i; mst[i-1].v2 := who[i]; mst[i-1].length := -d[i] end
end; (* Prim *)
```

Program 5.2: An Implementation of Prim's Algorithm

Thus the total running time of the algorithm is $\Theta(|V|k\log_k|V| + |E|\log_k|V|)$. Balancing the two terms, so that neither dominates the other, gives

$$k = \max\{2, \lceil|E|/|V|\rceil\}$$

and a running time of $\Theta(|E|\log_k|V|)$. This time varies from $\Theta(|E|\log|V|)$ for very sparse graphs, where the number of edges is a multiple of the number of vertices, to $\Theta(|V|^2)$ for very dense graphs, where the number of edges is a quadratic function of the number of vertices. (The minimum of two on the base of the logarithm is to handle the pathological case of $|E| \leq |V|$.) Calculation of k takes $\Theta(|E|)$ time, the time to count the edges. In theory at least, this implementation is always preferable to either the $\Theta(|V|^2)$ or the $\Theta(|E|\log|V|)$ implementation.

We can further improve the asymptotic behavior, at the cost of using a more complex data structure. The Fibonacci heaps introduced in Section 3.1 have amortized time complexity of $O(\log|V|)$ for each of the $|V|$ DeleteMin operations and an amortized time complexity of $O(1)$ for each of the $|E|$ (or fewer) DecreaseKey operations. With these heaps, therefore, Prim's algorithm runs in $\Theta(|V|\log|V| + |E|)$ time.

Exercise 5.4 Verify that $(|V|\log|V| + |E|)$ is $O(|E|\log_k|V|)$.   □

A $O(|E|\log\log|V|)$ Algorithm

While it can be efficiently implemented, Prim's algorithm suffers from one basic limitation: it never exercises the freedom of choice implied by Theorem 5.2, always choosing the single tree under construction. Kruskal's algorithm does not suffer from this constraint, but operates under the different self-inflicted problem of always using the least costly allowable edge and thus having to choose very carefully, and at significant expense, which pair of subtrees to merge. Yet, the generality of Theorem 5.2 should encourage us to design an algorithm by choosing the tree with a view to efficiency, rather than according to some arbitrary rule. As the cost of handling a tree increases with its size, a reasonable objective is to keep the sizes of the subtrees as equal as possible. This goal can be achieved by a process analogous to that used in Heapify, that is, by scheduling tree merges in a first in, first out manner. (While we did not make it explicit, Heapify in binary heaps can be viewed as merging pairs of heaps of height i, producing heaps of height $i+1$, until no heap of height i remains.) Cheriton and Tarjan developed a $O(E\log\log V)$ algorithm based on this idea; their algorithm is both elegant and subtle, coordinating two distinct data structures discussed in Chapter 3 and requiring careful attention to coding.

Maintaining equal-sized trees is rather difficult, since we only have control over one of the two trees merged—the other must be the tree that is connected to the selected tree by the shortest edge. Moreover, we should be more concerned with the number of edges that extend a tree outward than with the size of the tree itself. For these reasons, the first in, first out merging schedule just proposed only approximates our goal of equal sizes; but it can be implemented efficiently with a queue, so we use it. The high-level algorithm is thus:

- Place the initial trees, each consisting of a single vertex, in the queue.

- Repeat the following steps until only one tree remains:

  - Remove the tree from the front of the queue and find the least-cost edge that has exactly one endpoint in the tree.

  - Remove from the queue the tree which contains the vertex at the other end of the selected edge, merge the two trees by incorporating the selected edge, and place the new tree at the back of the queue.

Figure 5.4 illustrates the construction of the minimum spanning tree using this method.

How closely does this FIFO scheduling approximate that used in `Heapify`, which does a logarithmic number of passes (one for each height) and takes linear time overall? To develop this correspondence, imagine placing at the end of the initial queue (after the vertices of the graph) a special marker; whenever the marker appears at the head of the queue, it is simply removed and placed at the end of the queue again. The time span between two enqueueings of the marker is a pass. As the number of subtrees decreases by a factor of at least two at each pass, we can conclude that at most $\lfloor \lg |V| \rfloor$ passes will be required. This result is encouraging, since it shows that our scheduling strategy makes the same number of passes as `Heapify`, but note that we have to work with trees of different sizes, whereas `Heapify` works with heaps of uniform size within a given pass.

We need to find the least-cost edge extending a tree, and so we need to maintain for each tree a heap similar to that used in Prim's algorithm; since we have a number of trees, we also need a data structure to keep track of equivalence classes, as in Kruskal's algorithm. The equivalence classes are maintained with the familiar UNION-FIND data structure; the representative of each class is what actually gets placed in the queue. The main issue of implementation concerns the heaps: as two subtrees are merged, their heaps must also be merged, so that we must use a meldable heap; moreover, because exactly $|V| - 1$ MELD operations occur (independent of the number of passes through the queue), we cannot afford a logarithmic-time MELD. Fibonacci heaps offer constant-time MELD, but they do not quite fit our needs, because we have one more requirement. The two heaps to be merged store edges that extend out of the trees associated with them: some of these edges connect the two trees and thus must be removed from the merged

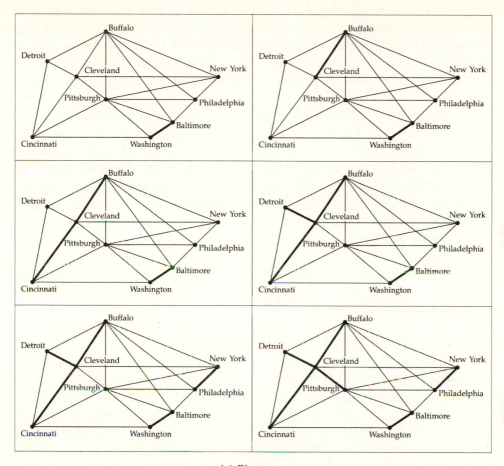

(a) First pass

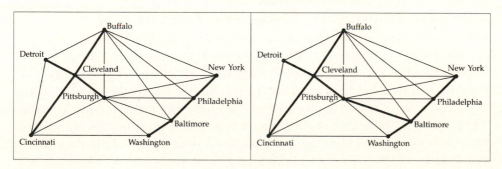

(b) Second pass

Figure 5.4: The Effect of Successive Iterations of Cheriton and Tarjan's Algorithm

heap. We cannot afford to spend logarithmic time on each such deletion. This constraint suggests a lazy data structure: edges which occur in both heaps and which should be deleted will not be physically deleted, but only logically deleted (by marking them, for example). A suitable heap structure is the lazy leftist tree of Exercise 3.14: it achieves constant-time MELD by using dummy nodes as new roots and also uses lazy deletion, paying the price during a FINDMIN, which removes all dummy and logically deleted nodes at the top of a leftist tree prior to searching the resulting subtrees for the minimum element. Observe that unlike the heap used in Prim's algorithm, which stores only one edge per vertex not in the tree, our lazy leftist trees, even immediately after a FINDMIN, may still contain logically deleted edges as well as useless edges, that is, edges that are not the shortest connection from this tree to another tree and will thus never rise to the top of the heap. Figure 5.5 shows the lazy leftist trees for our example at the end of the first pass.

Finding the edges to delete in order to mark them also appears expensive, since we have no way to locate these edges quickly. However, the algorithm only needs to know whether or not an edge is deleted at one step: during a FINDMIN operation. We can use our UNION-FIND data structure to identify deleted edges at that time: with two FIND operations, we can decide whether or not the endpoints of an edge lie in the same tree. The resulting operation does not run in true constant time, but, in amortized terms, the difference is insignificant; and we no longer need to mark the deleted edges.

This overview of the data structures may lead the reader to envision a large collection of nodes allocated dynamically, with the associated overhead of memory management. In fact, we can use a sequential implementation for the data structures and preallocate all of the necessary storage in the form of arrays. The UNION-FIND package of Chapter 3 is already implemented sequentially. We implement the FIFO queue by laying it on top of an array indexed by vertex name, using integer subscripts for the pointers of the doubly-linked list. Random access to the queue (for removing the second tree of the merged pair) is provided by the representative element returned by the FIND operation. The sequential implementation does not cost us any space, since the queue is largest at the start of the algorithm and shrinks at each step. As with the queue, the total size of the lazy leftist trees is largest at the start of the algorithm, when the total number of edges is $2|E|$ (because each appears in two heaps, once from each perspective). The total number of dummy nodes created over the life of the algorithm is $|V|-1$; and all of the dummy nodes can be present along with all of the edges at some stage of the algorithm, at least for some special cases (for instance, when the minimum spanning tree forms a star, i.e., a tree where all but one of the vertices are leaves). Thus we need a minimum of $2|E|$ nodes and may need up to $2|E| + |V| - 1$ nodes for the lazy leftist trees, so that, once again, a sequential

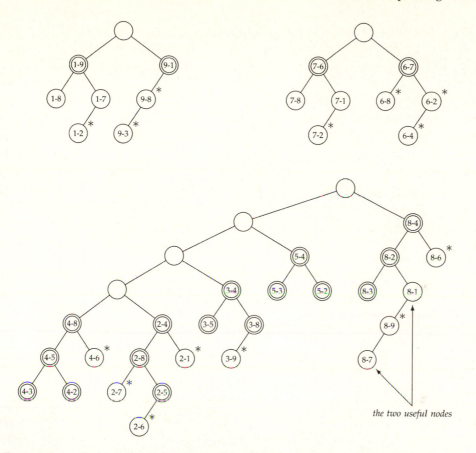

Empty nodes are dummy nodes, circled nodes are logically deleted, and nodes with an asterisk are useless.
Numbers denote the cities in alphabetical order.

Figure 5.5: The Lazy Leftist Trees at the End of the First Pass of Figure 5.4

implementation is natural and increases efficiency. Program 5.3 shows the main body of the code for this implementation. We can implement the FINDMIN operation nonrecursively, using a stack to do the preorder traversal. As the number of unexplored right children plus the number of nodes placed in the queue used by Heapify (a queue which is unrelated to the queue of spanning trees) cannot exceed the number of nodes removed from a lazy leftist tree by more than one, we can store the stack and the queue in the same array in which we keep the leftist trees. Notice also that the implicit check to determine whether or not a node representing an edge has been deleted can be made more efficient: the endpoint H[ ].e.v1 is always in the tree being processed so that, except for dummy

```
const null = 0; (* nil for integers used as pointers *)


(* Declarations used by the queue package laid over an array. *)

type PtrToQNode = integer;
     QueueNode = record
                      prev, next: PtrToQNode
                 end;
     Queue = array [vertex] of QueueNode;
var Q: Queue;
    Qhead, Qtail: PtrToQNode;


(* Declarations shared with the lazy leftist tree package. *)

const MaxNodes = ...;
  (* (V-1) * V {edges} + V-1 {maximum number of dummy nodes} = (V-1)*(V+1),
     or some other a priori limit. *)
type PtrToLeftistNode = integer;
     LeftistNode = record
                       (* public *)
                       e: edge;
                       (* private *)
                       depth: integer;
                       left, right: PtrToLeftistNode
                   end;
     Heap = array [1..MaxNodes] of LeftistNode;
var H: Heap;
    LLtrees: array [vertex] of PtrToLeftistNode;
       (* Pointers to the roots of the lazy leftist trees.  This array is
           indexed by the representative element of an equivalence class/tree. *)


procedure CheritonTarjan(var G: graph;
                             var mst: tree);
  (* Find the minimum spanning tree using Cheriton and Tarjan's
     O(E log log V) algorithm. *)

  (* Program assumes a lazy leftist heap package with operations
         procedure CreateHeap,
         function LazyMeld(u, v: vertex): PtrToLeftistNode, and
         function FindMin(v: vertex): PtrToLeftistNode.
     Program assumes a Union-Find package with operations
         procedure CreateUF(N: integer),
         function Find(v: vertex): vertex, and procedure Union(v, w: vertex).
     Program assumes a queue package (laid over an array) with operations
         procedure CreateQueue(N: integer), procedure Enqueue(v: vertex),
         procedure Dequeue(var v: vertex), and procedure Delete(v: vertex). *)
```

```
    var u, v, w: vertex;
        i: integer;

begin
    CreateUF(G.size);     (* Make each vertex into a tree... *)
    CreateQueue(G.size); (* ...place the initial trees in the queue... *)
    CreateHeap;
    for v := 1 to G.size do LLtrees[v] := ...;
        (* ...and turn each adjacency list into a lazy leftist tree using Heapify. *)

    for i := 1 to G.size - 1 do
        begin
            Dequeue(v); (* v is the representative of its equivalence class/tree. *)

            (* Find the shortest edge that joins this tree with another tree. *)
            LLtrees[v] := FindMin(v);
            mst[i] := H[LLtrees[v]].e;

            (* Find the representative for the other equivalence class/tree. *)
            u := Find(H[LLtrees[v]].e.v2);
            Delete(u);

            (* Merge the two equivalence classes and meld the sets of edges. *)
            Union(u,v);
            w := Find(v); (* constant time as v is a root or a child of a root *)
            LLtrees[w] := LazyMeld(u,v);

            (* Reinstall equivalence class/tree at the end of the queue (under
               its new representative element). *)
            Enqueue(w)
        end
end; (* CheritonTarjan *)
```

Program 5.3: An Implementation of Cheriton and Tarjan's Algorithm

nodes, Find(H[ ].e.v1) will be v, and we need only perform a FIND on the other endpoint.

We analyze the running time of this algorithm one pass at a time, using the invariant that, at the start of a pass, each edge can occur at most twice in the lazy leftist trees associated with entries in the queue.

Lemma 5.1 Let m_i denote the number of nodes (counting edges, logically deleted edges, and dummy nodes) in the ith tree removed from the queue and let k_i denote the number of nodes removed from this tree by the FINDMIN operation. Then we have

$$\sum_{i=1}^{|V|-1} k_i < 2 \cdot |E| + |V| - 1 \text{ and}$$

$$\sum_{i=1}^{|V|-1} m_i < 2 \cdot |E| \cdot \lfloor \lg |V| \rfloor + |V| - 1.$$

$\square$

Proof: Each edge and each dummy node can be deleted only once; thus our first claim follows, since exactly $|V| - 1$ dummy nodes are introduced during the life of the algorithm. To prove our second claim, we begin by partitioning the sum into groups, associating those m_i that are part of the same pass. The number of edges in each group is thus limited to $2|E|$, so that the first term of the bound accounts for the edges (recall that the number of passes is bounded by $\lfloor \lg |V| \rfloor$). The second term simply accounts for the contribution of the dummy nodes.

Q.E.D.

The crucial result for bounding the running time of the algorithm comes from Exercise 3.14, which states that the time taken by Heapify in each application of FINDMIN is bounded by $O\big(r_i \log(m_i - k_i)/r_i\big)$, where r_i is the number of nonempty trees that result from removing dummy and deleted nodes. As the number of trees initially in the queue cannot exceed $k_i + 1$, we can rewrite this bound as $O\big((k_i + 1) \log m_i/(k_i + 1)\big)$. We are now in the position to provide a bound on the running time of the complete algorithm.

Theorem 5.3 Cheriton and Tarjan's algorithm for minimum spanning trees runs in $O(|E| \log \log |V|)$ time. $\square$

Proof: The total amount of time spent manipulating the queue is linear in the number of vertices; the time spent building the initial lazy leftist trees from the adjacency lists is linear in the number of edges; and the time spent in deleting nodes is bounded by $\sum_{i=1}^{|V|-1}(2k_i + 1)$, although each deletion step involves a FIND. There are $|V| - 1$ additional FIND operations, since the algorithm examines one endpoint for the edge that becomes the root after the FINDMIN operation.

The most difficult step is bounding the total time spent in the Heapify operations, using the bound on each such operation that we have just derived. We partition the FINDMIN operations into those for which k_i does not exceed $m_i/(\lg |V|)^2 - 1$ and the others. The work done on the lazy leftist trees that fall into the first category is bounded by some constant times

$$\sum_{i=1}^{|V|-1} \frac{m_i}{(\log |V|)^2} \log m_i < 2 \sum_{i=1}^{|V|-1} \frac{m_i}{\log |V|},$$

which is $O(|E|)$ by our previous lemma, while the work done on those that fall into the second category is bounded by some constant times

$$\sum_{i=1}^{|V|-1} (k_i + 1) \log \frac{m_i}{m_i/(\log |V|)^2} = 2 \sum_{i=1}^{|V|-1} (k_i + 1) \log \log |V|,$$

which is $O(|E| \log \log |V|)$. This last term dominates the running time of the algorithm: we have accounted for everything but the FIND operations and, since there are a linear number of these, their contribution is not significant.

Q.E.D.

The analysis just given may well be overly pessimistic, since it yields only an upper bound; this bound only improves on Prim's algorithm implemented with Fibonacci heaps for sparse graphs.

Even this bound can be improved upon, reaching nearly linear time on both sparse and dense graphs. Consider again Prim's algorithm; much of its cost derives from the need to maintain a heap for the tree under construction, a heap that can grow quite large. When the number of vertices bordering the tree being expanded becomes too large, i.e., when the size of the heap becomes too great, we can simply switch to another tree in order to keep down the costs. In effect, we implement a variation of Cheriton and Tarjan's algorithm by scheduling the selection of trees according to heap sizes. Furthermore, we can use well-chosen graph contractions (which eliminate useless edges and thus shrink the heaps) to reduce the size of the problem. Carefully combining these measures yields an algorithm which, while perhaps not practical (due to its intricacy and overhead), exhibits almost linear asymptotic running time; specifically, it can be shown to run in $O\big(|E|\beta(|E|, |V|)\big)$, where $\beta(m, n) = \min\{ i \mid \log^{(i)} n \leq m/n \}$. Even for the smallest possible value of $|E|$, $\beta(|E|, |V|)$ is five or less for any practical value of $|V|$; on dense graphs, where the ratio is close to $|V|$, $\beta(|E|, |V|)$ is one, irrespective of $|V|$.

Because both Kruskal's and Prim's algorithms rarely attain their worst-case bounds and because their data structures can be maintained with very low overhead, the appropriate algorithm for finding the minimum spanning tree has to be determined by experimentation. Figure 5.6 shows the average running time for the methods presented in this section as applied to three families of graphs. The first two families are random graphs with $|V|^{3/2}$ and $|V| \log |V|$ edges, respectively, and the edge weights were drawn from a uniform distribution. The third family is geometric in nature: $|V|$ points were randomly placed in the unit square, and, for each vertex, arcs were drawn to its five nearest neighbors; finally the graph was made undirected and duplicate edges were removed. We show the ratio of the running times of our algorithms to that of an idealized algorithm,

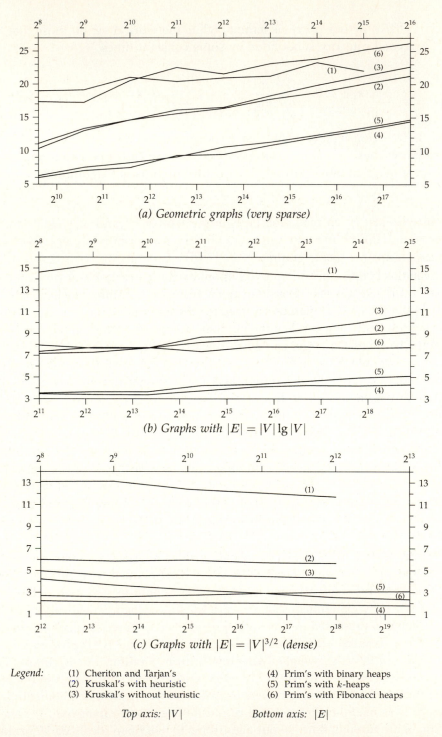

(a) Geometric graphs (very sparse)

(b) Graphs with $|E| = |V| \lg |V|$

(c) Graphs with $|E| = |V|^{3/2}$ (dense)

Legend:
(1) Cheriton and Tarjan's
(2) Kruskal's with heuristic
(3) Kruskal's without heuristic
(4) Prim's with binary heaps
(5) Prim's with k-heaps
(6) Prim's with Fibonacci heaps

Top axis: $|V|$ *Bottom axis:* $|E|$

Figure 5.6: Experimental Results with Algorithms for the Minimum Spanning
Tree Problem

which runs in $\Theta(|E|)$ time with low overhead (our actual benchmark is a program that just counts the number of edges in the graph; it took about 30 seconds to run on a graph of 500,000 edges on a small Vaxstation 2000 computer); therefore our horizontal scale is based on $|E|$ (although we also show $|V|$ for reference). We do not show the data gathered for the quadratic implementation of Prim's algorithm, because these values very quickly become out of range; for Kruskal's and Cheriton and Tarjan's algorithms, which both use $\Theta(|E|)$ additional memory, we were sometimes unable to run the largest size.

From these data we conclude that (unless the graph is presented as a list of edges already sorted by length, in which case Kruskal's algorithm should be used) Prim's algorithm, using binary heaps, is the algorithm of choice. In the very worst case, the running time of the algorithm is only a factor of $\Theta(\log |V|)$ worse than the theoretical limit, but, with the low overhead of the algorithm and a limit on $|E|$ imposed by memory availability, this is not a major concern. Its actual running time is $\Theta(|V| \log |V| + |E| + m \log |V|)$, where the first term corresponds to the $|V|$ DELETEMIN operations, the second term corresponds to the scanning of the adjacency lists (to decide whether or not to apply a DECREASEKEY operation), and the third term corresponds to the time spent in performing the m DECREASEKEY operations which are necessary. The contributions of these three terms are brought to light by the three graphs: note how the contribution of the $\log |V|$ terms dominates the behavior in sparse graphs, but disappears in the dense graphs. The algorithm also uses only $\Theta(|V|)$ additional storage, which means that the limiting factor is the storage used to represent the graph itself.

Whereas, on theoretical grounds, we expect the performance of Prim's algorithm implemented with k-heaps to be better than that of the implementation using binary heaps, it was uniformly worse in practice. The problem is not due to a basic flaw in our reasoning, but to the exact manner in which k was determined. We chose k so as to balance the work of the DELETEMIN operations ($|V| k \log_k |V|$) against the DECREASEKEY operations ($|E| \log_k |E|$). We should, however, balance these two terms based on the actual number of DECREASEKEY operations performed, not on the upper bound of $|E|$. Since m was much less than $|E|$ in our experiments, binary heaps actually balanced these two terms better than k-heaps. (Indeed, notice that the situation is worst on the densest graphs; in particular, for the largest graph k is 91.) The code for binary heaps also has lower overhead.

The running time for Prim's algorithm implemented with Fibonacci heaps fits the theory and practice perfectly. Due to the overhead of using Fibonacci heaps, the code runs comparatively slowly; as $|V|$ increases, its running time slowly approaches that of the traditional implementation of Prim's algorithm, since the $m \log |V|$ term of the latter has greater and greater relative effect. The two curves eventually cross; however, they cross for such large values of $|V|$ that we need not worry about using this implementation in practical applications. The same holds true for Cheriton and Tarjan's algorithm, which has the additional disadvantage of using considerable extra space. The running time tracks $|E|$ almost exactly, since $\log\log|V|$ is essentially constant over the range of sizes used in our experiments, but the overhead makes the algorithm impractical.

A detailed analysis of the running time of Kruskal's algorithm shows that it is made up of three components: the time for Heapify, the cost of the DELETEMIN operations, and the cost associated with the UNION-FIND data structure. The first component takes $\Theta(|E|)$ time; the second, which always dominates the third, takes $\Theta(m\log|E|)$, where m, the number of DELETEMIN operations, varies between $|V|$ and $|E|$. Finally we turn to the heuristic that we proposed for improving Kruskal's algorithm; recall that this heuristic checks (by means of FIND operations) that an edge is still allowable before placing it at the root of the heap and sifting it down. Our experiments do not bring to light any clear pattern: the effectiveness of the heuristic depends heavily on the graphs themselves, having the most impact (whether positive or negative) on the dense graphs. The heuristic only applies when the edges are not presorted—and so may not be that relevant, since Prim's algorithm outperforms Kruskal's in all such cases; yet the heuristic never adds more than $\Theta(|E|)$ overhead and sometimes results in significant savings, so that it is a worthwhile addition. (On a family of random graphs that consisted of two clusters, with the two clusters connected by the longest edge in the entire graph, Kruskal's algorithm ran about three times faster with the heuristic than without.)

5.4   The Shortest-Path Problem

There is a strong connection between Prim's algorithm and the algorithm for solving the shortest-path problem published by E. W. Dijkstra in 1959 and generally known as Dijkstra's algorithm. A few slight changes to procedure Prim are all that will be necessary, in spite of two significant differences between the problems. First, the graph on which the shortest-path problem is defined is directed, whereas the minimal spanning tree problem applies to undirected graphs. Secondly, Prim's algorithm finds a tree connecting all vertices, whereas the problem statement for the shortest-path problem requires finding only a simple directed path between two vertices. This last difference turns out to be moot, as every algorithm known for the shortest-path problem computes a shortest path from one of the vertices (which we shall call the initial vertex and denote by v_I) to each of the other vertices.

In order to develop the similarities between the two problems, we first observe that the arcs composing the collection of shortest paths from v_I to all other

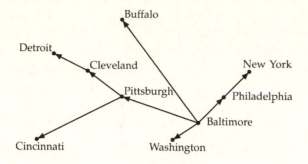

Figure 5.7: The Tree of Shortest Paths from Baltimore

vertices form a directed rooted tree. Figure 5.7 shows the tree that results from solving the shortest-path problem on our graph of the east central United States. Since there are minor complications, we formalize this observation and prove it.

Theorem 5.4 There exists a collection of simple paths from the initial vertex to all other vertices such that: (i) the set of arcs used in these paths forms a directed tree rooted at the initial vertex; and (ii) the path from the initial vertex to any other vertex is a shortest path to that vertex. □

Proof: We are implicitly assuming that there is in fact a path from v_I to every other vertex, an assumption which is just a matter of convenience. We shall prove that, given any collection of shortest paths from v_I to all other vertices, arcs may be deleted until a tree results. Assume that we have a collection of shortest paths from v_I such that the associated set of arcs does not form a tree. Since there exists a path from v_I to every other vertex, the problem must be that there is more than one path to some vertex, say v_T. By tracing the paths from v_T back to v_I, we must find a vertex, v_l, with at least two arcs, a_1 and a_2, incident upon it, as pictured in Figure 5.8. We claim that one of a_1 or a_2 may

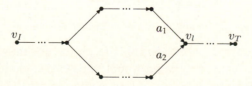

Figure 5.8: A Potential Difficulty in the Construction of Shortest Paths

be deleted from the set of arcs without endangering the construction of shortest paths from v_I to all vertices of V. If the path to v_l via a_1 is longer than that via a_2, then surely no shortest path can use a_1. If the two paths have equal length, then any shortest path that uses a_1 can be rerouted to use a_2. *Mutatis mutandis*, we conclude that one of the two arcs can always be deleted, thereby completing our proof.

Q.E.D.

Therefore, the major difference between the minimum spanning tree and the shortest-paths problems is the choice of objective function: in the former the objective function is the sum of the edge lengths, while in the latter it is the sum of the lengths of the shortest paths. An important aspect of this difference is that each edge of the minimum spanning tree gets counted once, but each arc of the tree of shortest paths gets counted a variable number of times, depending on how many paths use it. This characteristic makes it impossible to account for the contribution of an arc that does not extend the tree rooted at the initial vertex; since the greedy algorithm must be able to evaluate the contribution of each candidate arc, it must at all times maintain a tree of paths rooted at the initial vertex. This is precisely what Prim's algorithm does, except that here the cost of including arc (v_i, v_j) is the sum of $d(v_i, v_j)$ and $D(v_i)$, the length of the unique path from v_I to v_i.

The changes that need to be made to procedure Prim of Program 5.2 to account for the slightly different selection rule are quite minor. We need to replace

```
if p^.length < d[p^.id]   and   d[p^.id] := p^.length
```

with

```
if d[vmin] + p^.length < d[p^.id]   and   d[p^.id] := d[vmin] + p^.length
```

Additionally, as we need the values of d[ ] and need not flag vertices as being in V_1, because the test

```
if d[vmin] + p^.length < d[p^.id]
```

will fail if p^.id is a member of V_1, we remove the line

```
d[vmin] := -d[vmin]; (* Place chosen vertex in V1. *)
```

The input and output parameters to the procedure must also be changed. The input now includes a designated initial vertex; this change causes a minor change in the initialization. A compact representation for the output is the array who (shown for our running example in Table 5.7), from which a shortest path can be reconstructed in time proportional to its number of edges, since the array

Table 5.7: The Array who Corresponding to Figure 5.7

Index	1	2	3	4	5	6	7	8	9
who[i]	–	1	8	8	4	7	1	1	1
d[i]	0	345	514	355	522	189	97	230	39

stores this path in reverse. If the shortest path between two vertices is all that is desired, the algorithm can stop after the destination vertex is transferred to V_1 and the one path can then be reconstructed and returned.

The similarities between Prim's and Dijkstra's algorithms should not cause the reader to assume that a proof of correctness for Dijkstra's algorithm is not needed, because the proof of correctness for Prim's algorithm depended in an essential way on the undirected nature of the graph and the form of the objective function.

Theorem 5.5 Dijkstra's algorithm produces shortest paths from the initial vertex to all other vertices.   □

Proof: We prove, by induction on the size of V_1, that the paths produced by the algorithm are shortest paths in G (not just in the graph induced by V_1) from the initial vertex to the vertices in V_1. The basis is trivial, since no path is needed to go from the initial vertex to itself.

Assume then that our statement is true at some stage characterized by the set V_1 and further assume that Dijkstra's algorithm chooses next to include vertex v_j and arc (v_i, v_j). We need to show that the path, composed of the shortest path from v_I to v_i followed by the added arc, is in fact a shortest path from v_I to v_j; the rest follows since the paths to all other vertices in V_1 are already the shortest paths possible in G and none of these paths is changed by the addition of an arc. *Ad absurdum*, suppose that there is a shorter path from v_I to v_j. Such a path must include at least one vertex from V_2 (even if it is only v_j reached through some other route); denote the first such vertex by v_l and its predecessor on the path by v_m. Let $L(v_I, v)$ be the length of that part of the claimed shorter path which leads from v_I up to v; we have

$$D(v_m) + d(v_m, v_l) \leq L(v_I, v_m) + d(v_m, v_l) = L(v_I, v_l)$$
$$\leq L(v_I, v_j) < D(v_i) + d(v_i, v_j).$$

Because all nodes prior to and including v_m are in V_1, the shortest path to v_m is, by inductive hypothesis, that constructed by the algorithm, so that the first inequality holds. Because all arc lengths are nonnegative and the path to v_l is a part of the complete path to v_j, the second inequality holds. The last inequality is just our assumption *ad absurdum*. The resulting strict inequality between the first and last terms says that the arc (v_m, v_l) should have been selected by Dijkstra's algorithm in preference to the selection actually made, which is the desired contradiction. Thus the inductive step is proved and our proof is complete.

Q.E.D.

As we noted, the difference between Prim's and Dijkstra's algorithms is in the computation of the key, not in the flow of control. Therefore, any priority queue supporting DELETEMIN and DECREASEKEY can be used; in particular using Fibonacci heaps results in a running time of $\Theta(|V| \log |V| + |E|)$. Somewhat unexpectedly in view of our work with minimum spanning trees, this running time is asymptotically optimal. The $|E|$ term is clearly unavoidable; the $|V| \log |V|$ term comes about from a complex reduction to sorting—the difficult part is in ensuring that the reduction runs in $o(|V| \log |V|)$ time.

5.5   Huffman Trees

In this section we consider the problem of compressing a file so as to minimize the number of bits, and thus the time, required to transmit the file. We achieve this minimization at the expense of processing time, because the file must be encoded prior to sending and decoded upon reception. We intend to encode all of the glyphs that compose the alphabet and punctuation symbols of English. Any encoding that uses the same number of bits per glyph, such as the American Standard Code for Information Interchange (ASCII), cannot generally minimize the number of bits transmitted, because it cannot take advantage of the relative frequency of occurrence of the glyphs.[1] For instance, using the same number of bits to represent the lowercase 'e' as the uppercase 'Q' is clearly a very poor decision. Samuel F. B. Morse recognized this inefficiency and attempted to palliate it by introducing, in 1837, what became known as Morse code (formerly used in telegraphy and still used by ham and ship radio operators and for heliography). Morse code is a variable-length code based on dots and dashes, where common characters are assigned short codes; for instance, in international Morse code 'E' is a single dot, whereas 'X' is $- \cdot \cdot -$. Morse code is not strictly binary as, in addition to the dots and dashes, it also makes use of the periods of silence, giving meaning to their various durations. We consider a strictly binary encoding and formalize our problem as follows.

---

[1]A uniform length encoding has many advantages. Among other things, it allows the code to span a range of integers and also allows the assignment of any code word to any glyph: these are crucial properties for indexing arrays and defining an alphabetical collating sequence.

Problem 32 [Optimal Encoding] Devise a binary encoding for messages that minimizes the expected length of the encoded versions.   □

This formulation remains imprecise: we need additional requirements in order to characterize the solution accurately. One important distinction must be made between an encoding tailored to the particular message to be sent and one designed for sending a range of messages: the latter encoding will not accurately reflect the frequencies found in the particular document being compressed, so that the encoding will probably not be optimal for that document. We shall have more to say on this and some related issues after we formalize the problem and present the corresponding algorithm.

We intend to produce a strictly binary code. Therefore, the encoded document will be just one long string of bits; in particular, there will be no indication of where each glyph begins and ends. This is a problem that must be dealt with during decoding. Fixed-length codes avoid this problem by their very nature, but more generally, a simple and elegant solution is obtained by insisting that the code be *prefix-free*, i.e., by requiring that the code for each glyph not be a prefix of the code for any other glyph. Since the code is binary, we can represent all glyph codes in a binary tree, where each edge is labelled with a zero or a one (see Figure 5.9); requiring the code to be prefix-free is then equivalent to requiring that glyph codes correspond only to leaves of the tree and not to internal nodes. To decode a message, we start at the root of the tree and follow the path dictated by the bits of the message until we reach an external node, which is labelled by the glyph. We now return to the root of the tree to decode the next few bits of the message; in this manner, the pattern of the encoded message tells us where the code for a glyph stops. The binary tree representation for the code provides another piece of insight: if the code is to be optimal, then every leaf node must correspond to a glyph and every internal node must have two children. We are now in a position to give a precise statement of the problem.

Problem 33 [Optimal Prefix-Free Encoding] Given an alphabet of N characters, $\Sigma = \{a_1, a_2, \ldots, a_N\}$, with associated frequencies of occurrence, $f_1, f_2, \ldots, f_N$, find the binary tree with N leaves, each labelled with a different character, such that the weighted path length, $\sum_{i=1}^{N} f_i \cdot l_i$, is minimized, where l_i is the length of the path from the root to a_i.   □

The size of the state space at first appears to be the product of $N!$ and the number of binary trees with N leaves (where every internal node has two children):

$$N! \cdot \frac{1}{N} \binom{2N-2}{N-1} = \frac{(2N-2)!}{(N-1)!}.$$

In fact, while very large, it is smaller than this figure, as the total weighted path length of the tree remains invariant under arbitrary swapping of subtrees rooted

Letter	Frequency	Huffman code
A	0.073	1011
B	0.009	000100
C	0.030	01011
D	0.044	0000
E	0.130	100
F	0.028	01010
G	0.016	011110
H	0.035	10100
I	0.074	1100
J	0.002	011100001
K	0.003	01110010
L	0.035	10101
M	0.025	00011

Letter	Frequency	Huffman code
N	0.078	1111
O	0.074	1101
P	0.027	01000
Q	0.003	01110001
R	0.077	1110
S	0.063	0110
T	0.093	001
U	0.027	01001
V	0.013	000101
W	0.016	011101
X	0.005	01110011
Y	0.019	011111
Z	0.001	011100000

The expected code length is 4.189.

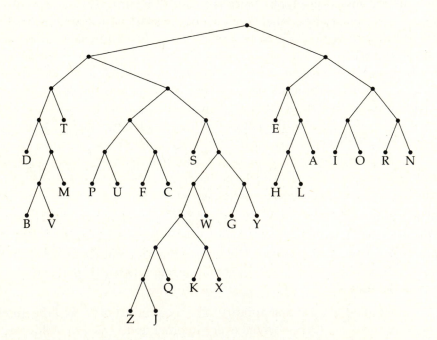

Figure 5.9: A Huffman Code and the Corresponding Huffman Tree

at the same level. While this problem looks similar to the optimal identification tree problem (Problem 12) and even uses the same objective function, there is an essential difference. In the optimal identification tree problem, we begin with a fixed set of tests with known outcomes; when a test is associated with a node, the division of objects into two sets is forced upon us. In our encoding problem, we can effectively construct the tests so that they have the precise outcomes that optimize our objective function; expressed in another way, our encoding problem is just a special case of the optimal identification tree problem, where all possible tests are available. Another very similar problem is the optimal binary search tree problem (Problem 11): consider restricting it by setting the probabilities of successful search to zero and the probabilities of unsuccessful search to the f_i, optimizing the same objective function. The difference now resides in the added flexibility present in our encoding problem: unlike the search tree, the code tree need not return an alphabetized list when traversed in inorder.

The greedy algorithm we present next is due to D. A. Huffman and is known as Huffman's algorithm; by assimilation, the resulting tree and encoding are known as the Huffman tree and the Huffman code. The algorithm is similar to Kruskal's algorithm in that it works bottom up, maintaining a forest of trees that eventually are coalesced into a single tree.

- Initialize by forming N trees of a single node each, with weights f_i, for $i = 1, 2, \ldots, N$.

- Repeat until only one tree remains:

  - Find the two trees of minimum weight. Merge them into one tree by creating a new root and attaching the two trees as its left and right children (in either order); then set the weight of the new tree to the sum of the weights of its two subtrees.

The objective function minimized in this algorithm is the sum, over all trees in the forest, of the weighted path lengths of the trees. Because merging two trees increases the value of the objective function by an amount equal to the sum of their weights, the algorithm is greedy.

Theorem 5.6 Huffman trees have minimum weighted path length.   □

Proof: The algorithm does not produce a unique tree, since it involves many arbitrary decisions. However, these decisions do no affect the total weighted path lengths of the forest at any step. Thus, while the codes produced differ, all possible trees formed by the algorithm have the same value for the objective function. We now show that this value is minimum.

The proof is by induction on N, the number of glyphs. When N equals one or two, there is effectively only one tree. Assume then that the algorithm produces an optimal tree for all instances of the problem with no more than $N-1$ glyphs and consider an instance with N glyphs. *Ad absurdum*, assume that the algorithm produces a nonoptimal tree; denote this tree by T_H and let T_{opt} be some tree with minimum weighted path length. Notice first that the glyph with the least frequency of occurrence must be at the greatest depth in T_{opt}—if such were not the case, we could swap this leaf with a lowest leaf in the tree, for a net reduction in weighted path length, thereby contradicting the assumed optimality of T_{opt}. The optimal tree can be transformed so that the glyph with the second least frequency is made the sibling of the node with the least frequency. Observe that this sibling is also a leaf and at the lowest level in the tree, so that, if the glyph with the second least frequency is elsewhere in the tree, it can be swapped with this sibling without increasing the value of the objective function. These two results allow us to assume, without loss of generality, that both T_{opt} and T_H have the two glyphs of least frequency paired as siblings. Consider then the two trees, T'_{opt} and T'_H, obtained by replacing these two siblings and their parent with a single artificial glyph, with a frequency equal to the sum of the frequencies of the two replaced glyphs. Denote the weighted path length of tree T by $w(T)$. Since the new glyph sits just one level higher than the two replaced glyphs, we have $w(T'_{\text{opt}}) = w(T_{\text{opt}}) - f_{l_1} - f_{l_2}$ and $w(T'_H) = w(T_H) - f_{l_1} - f_{l_2}$, where f_{l_1} and f_{l_2} are the frequencies associated with the two replaced glyphs. Now T'_H is a Huffman tree on the alphabet of $N-1$ glyphs formed by replacing a_{l_1} and a_{l_2} with the new glyph. Because we have $w(T_{\text{opt}}) < w(T_H)$, it follows that $w(T'_{\text{opt}}) < w(T'_H)$; but this latter inequality contradicts the optimality of Huffman's algorithm when applied to alphabets of size not exceeding $N-1$.

Q.E.D.

The proof further illustrates that there are many optimal trees and also shows that some optimal trees cannot be produced by Huffman's algorithm, even when the algorithm never has to break ties. This latter property is rather unusual; such was certainly not the case with the greedy algorithms for the spanning tree and shortest-path problems.

Now, how do we implement Huffman's algorithm? There are really three parts to this problem: the computation of the Huffman code, the encoding of documents, and the decoding of compressed documents. Decoding the file, as we have seen, involves repeatedly traversing a branch of the Huffman tree from its root to a leaf. For encoding the original document, we can build a direct-access table, indexed by the glyphs, where the code for each letter is stored explicitly; this table can be produced in a single inorder traversal of the tree. The choice of mechanism for encoding and decoding affects the implementation of Huffman's algorithm. An efficient implementation that agrees with our prescription is sketched below. We use an array of $2N-1$ entries. The first portion of the

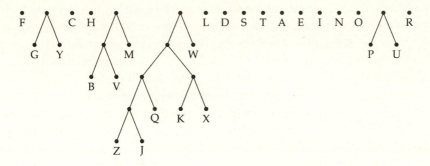

(a) The 17 subtrees after nine steps

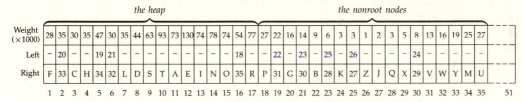

	the heap																the nonroot nodes																				
Weight (×1000)	28	35	30	35	47	30	35	44	63	93	73	130	74	78	74	54	77	27	22	16	14	9	6	3	3	1	2	3	5	8	13	16	19	25	27	
Left	–	20	–	–	19	21	–	–	–	–	–	–	–	–	–	18	–	–	22	–	23	–	25	–	26	–	–	–	–	–	24	–	–	–	–	
Right	F	33	C	H	34	32	L	D	S	T	A	E	I	N	O	35	R	P	31	G	30	B	28	K	27	Z	J	Q	X	29	V	W	Y	M	U	
	1	2	3	4	5	6	7	8	9	10	11	12	13	14	15	16	17	18	19	20	21	22	23	24	25	26	27	28	29	30	31	32	33	34	35	51

(b) The contents of the array after nine steps

Figure 5.10: Storage Allocation in Huffman's Algorithm

array is a heap consisting of the roots of the trees in the forest; initially, this heap includes the first N entries while, at completion, it consists of the single root of the Huffman tree. The middle portion consists of the nonroot nodes; this portion is initially empty and grows to embrace the whole array, with the exception of the first location. The last portion is unused storage into which the middle portion grows. Figure 5.10 illustrates this organization. Once a node is placed in the middle portion, it is never moved nor referred to again during the construction process: it has become part of a tree in the forest, and the trees in the forest are only manipulated through their roots. When the two roots of least weight are merged (they are in the first and second or in the first and third locations of the array), the last element of the heap is placed in the second or third location, as appropriate, and sifted down. One of the nodes being merged (a root no longer) is placed where the last element of the heap used to be; the other is placed at the end of the middle portion; as a result, the first and last portions each shrink by one and the middle portion grows by two. The newly created node, representing the root of the tree obtained by the merge, is then placed in the first location and sifted down. The complete construction takes $\Theta(N \log N)$ time.

Given the large number of distinct optimal Huffman trees, secondary objectives are worth considering. One such objective calls for minimizing the size of the encoding table. If the table is stored as an array of pointers into a pool of variable length codes, then its size is $\sum_{i=1}^{N} l_i$; if it is stored as an array of fixed-length strings (the codes padded with blanks), then its size is $N \cdot \max_i\{l_i\}$. If no tie occurs during the construction of the tree, then there is no freedom of choice: there is only one Huffman tree up to swapping siblings, an operation which does not affect the new objectives. In case of ties, however, processing the nodes in the order of their creation (earliest first) minimizes both $\sum_{i=1}^{N} l_i$ and $\max_i\{l_i\}$.

Although we have solved our formal version of the problem (the optimal prefix-free code for a given set of frequencies), we have not truly solved our informal version (optimal compression). As already noted, the frequency distribution of glyphs differs from document to document, so that the code based on a given set of frequencies will not usually match any given document. Tailoring the Huffman code to each document is of course possible, but then either the code or the set of frequencies must be communicated along with the compressed file. For a very long file, this scheme may make sense, but, for routine transmission of information, the added overhead will probably outweigh the savings due to increased compression. By ignoring this overhead we can obtain a good estimate of the maximum amount of compression that can be expected, since using the data file itself to construct the Huffman code gives the best possible compression for any prefix-free code. As an example, for Ernest Hemingway's short story, *The Snows of Kilimanjaro* (a document of approximately 48,000 characters), the total weighted path length of the Huffman tree is 4.438 and the ratio of the number of bits in the uncompressed version (in 7-bit ASCII) to the compressed version is 1.577.

Huffman codes approximate closely (within the limits imposed by the discrete nature of the transmission media) the theoretical concept known as (communication) *entropy*. C. E. Shannon defined the entropy of a large collection of events in order to capture the informational content of that collection. Consider the following two events: (i) the sun rose this morning; (ii) the sun did not rise this morning. The first conveys almost no information, inasmuch as it is the expected event; on the other hand, the second conveys a lot of information, since no one would have predicted it. More to the point for our discussion, the reception of the character 'e' following the reception of the characters 'T' and 'h' in an English text is the expected event and thus carries little information; an 'r' carries somewhat more; a 'w' carries much more, since almost no English words begin with 'thw'. Thus informational content is directly related to the "surprise" content of the message. High probability events in a collection decrease the entropy of the collection, since they enable one to predict more accurately which event is likely to occur next. The highest informational content, or highest entropy, corresponds to a collection of equally likely events, since we have then no basis for predicting the next event. In particular, the most concise code should be one where the next bit of a message cannot be predicted from the bits already received. Formally, the entropy of a set of events, $\mathcal{E}$, is defined as

$$H(\mathcal{E}) = -\sum_{e \in \mathcal{E}} \big(p(e) \cdot \lg p(e)\big),$$

where $p(e)$ denotes the probability of event e. In particular, the entropy of a set, $\mathcal{E}$, of equally likely events is just $\lg|\mathcal{E}|$, a result which matches our experience that $\lg n$ bits are needed to distinguish n objects.

In terms of our problem, we can use the observed frequency of occurrence in place of the probability of each glyph and define the entropy of the document based on these frequencies. Observe that the formula for the entropy has the same form as our objective function for the prefix-free encoding problem: both are sums of terms, each of which is the product of a weight and another factor. In the encoding problem, the factor is the code length; in the entropy formula it is $-\lg p(e)$, which can be regarded as the ideal code length for event e. Thus the entropy of a set is a lower bound on the total weighted path length of the Huffman tree. The difference between the entropy and the average code length is a measure of the amount of redundancy left in the code—a redundancy, however, that cannot be removed, since an irredundant code would require fractional code lengths. How close the Huffman code gets to these ideal values is illustrated for the letters of the alphabet in Table 5.8; as a further example, the entropy of the set of characters used in Hemingway's short story is approximately 4.278, or only 3.6% smaller than the average code length derived by Huffman's algorithm.

There is also the question of choosing the alphabet—not as obvious a choice as it may seem. For instance, if programs are being compressed, then it makes sense to expand the alphabet to treat reserved words, like begin and procedure, as single letters of the alphabet. More time is spent encoding the text, since a lexical phase is necessary to divide the text file into "characters," but decoding is correspondingly faster, and significantly higher compression ratios may be achieved. This approach applies to English text as well. The 30 most frequently occurring words in ordinary English text account for about one-third of the words (though not one-third of the characters) in a typical document. For example, using such a code for the Hemingway short story yields an average code length of 4.113, for a compression ratio of 1.702, as compared with our previous ratio of 1.577. Prefixes, suffixes, and common letter pairs can also be treated as single letters of the alphabet. Eventually a point of diminishing returns is reached: an accurate frequency determination becomes impossible and the resulting tree might well be worse, rather than better.

Table 5.8: Huffman Code *vs.* Entropy

Letter	$-\lg p$	Code length
A	3.776	4
B	6.796	6
C	5.059	5
D	4.506	4
E	2.943	3
F	5.158	5
G	5.966	6
H	4.836	5
I	3.756	4
J	8.966	9
K	8.381	8
L	4.836	5
M	5.322	5

Letter	$-\lg p$	Code length
N	3.680	4
O	3.756	4
P	5.211	5
Q	8.381	8
R	3.699	4
S	3.988	4
T	3.427	3
U	5.211	5
V	6.265	6
W	5.966	6
X	7.644	8
Y	5.718	6
Z	9.966	9

The entropy is 4.162 and the expected code length is 4.189.

An interesting case of specialized alphabets arises in image processing. Pictures are stored as rows of pixels that record gray levels and typically exhibit high spatial coherence; that is, the value of a pixel only rarely differs from that of its neighbor. In this context, the base alphabet is just the collection of gray levels; however, it makes sense to modify it by adding, for each gray level, a length parameter. The intent is to encode a run of identically valued pixels as a single glyph given by the gray level of the pixels and the length of the run. This new alphabet has many more glyphs, each taking more space, but the spatial coherence ensures that medium to long runs occur with high probability, so that the total number of glyphs needed to describe the image is quite small. This technique is called *run length encoding*.

There are better compression algorithms even for a fixed alphabet. The elaborate Ziv-Lempel algorithm (for which see the references), for example, is an adaptive algorithm that makes no assumptions about the input. The algorithm treats the input as one long string of bits and proceeds to encode it according to observed patterns and frequencies; the compressed document contains within itself the information needed for decoding. Tests have shown that this algorithm slightly outperforms the Huffman code on English text.

The ultimate problem of the most succinct possible encoding of a single text is extremely complex, because the presence of a single sample prevents any probabilistic analysis. However, the problem is a very realistic one; suppose, for instance, that you wanted to archive the text of *War and Peace* or the entire *Oxford English Dictionary*. The code is now a onetime affair, tailored to the text to be encoded and stored along with it. Thus, despite a basic theorem of coding theory which states, in effect, that the entropy decreases monotonically as the size of the alphabet increases, the solution is not to select the largest possible alphabet: the increase in the size of the alphabet might exceed the decrease in the size of the encoding. Furthermore, no simple algorithm exists for determining the optimal trade-off. Dropping the requirement that the code be prefix-free only complicates the problem. The problem now becomes, "Find the smallest program (including data) that, when run, will produce the given text." The size of this smallest program is known as the *Kolmogorov complexity* of the text and will be taken up again briefly in Volume II; suffice it to say for now that this size cannot be computed, but only bounded.

5.6 Epilogue: Matroid Embeddings

Now that we have seen a number of problems which the greedy method can solve optimally, as well as other problems for which the greedy method can only obtain approximate solutions, we characterize the structure of problems that lend themselves to the application of greedy techniques. We do this by abstracting out the essential features of the greedy algorithm. This process leads us to *matroids*, *matroid embeddings*, and other structures which characterize exactly those problems for which the greedy algorithm returns optimal solutions under a variety of objective functions.

Preliminaries

Our first task is to define what is meant by a greedy algorithm. Without loss of generality, we shall restrict our attention to maximization problems. We first note that all of the problems to which we have applied the greedy algorithm share one fundamental property: their feasible solutions can be constructed step by step. Specifically, given any feasible solution to one of these problems, there exists a chain of partial feasible solutions, starting with the empty partial solution, such that two consecutive partial solutions differ by exactly one element (e.g., an edge or a node). In a very strong sense, each partial feasible solution is constructible from the empty partial solution. Phrased differently, the feasibility structure of the problem is independent of the objective function and thus allows the greedy algorithm to build any given feasible set. These observations motivate the following definition.

Definition 5.1 Let S be a finite set and C a nonempty collection of subsets of S; the structure (S, C) is called an *accessible set system* if and only if it obeys the following axiom:

(accessibility axiom) If $X \in C$ and $X \neq \emptyset$, then there exists $x \in X$ such that $X - \{x\} \in C$.

□

The elements of S represent the pieces (such as edges or vertices of a graph) that make up partial feasible solutions and that the greedy algorithm selects one by one. The elements of C represent these partial feasible solutions, for which reason they are called *feasible sets*. The accessibility axiom implies that the empty set always belongs to C; from this starting point, the accessibility axiom asserts that any nonempty feasible set can be constructed element by element through a chain of feasible sets—exactly the fundamental attribute of problems to which the greedy algorithm applies. Note that, since a feasible set is unordered, the manner in which its pieces were put together is immaterial; the accessibility axiom implies that there exists at least one way to construct that feasible set, and there may be others, but which particular way was used to construct it is irrelevant. We have seen this property in the algorithms developed in this chapter: the data structures that they build to represent the partial solutions do not reflect the order in which the elements were added to the partial solution.

A maximal feasible set, i.e., a feasible set which cannot be expanded by the addition of a single element, is called a *basis*. Perhaps unexpectedly, a basis can contain another.

Example 5.4 Let (S, C) be given by $S = \{a, b, c\}$ and $C = \{\emptyset, \{a\}, \{b\}, \{a, c\}, \{a, b, c\}\}$ as follows:

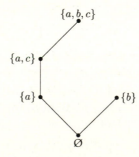

There are two bases, $\{b\}$ and $\{a, b, c\}$, with the first contained in the second.

□

Because such anomalies never arise in practice, we shall assume for the remainder of the section that accessible set systems are free of such problems and so formally redefine them.

Definition 5.2 Let S be a finite set and C a nonempty collection of subsets of S; the structure (S,C) is called an *accessible set system* if and only if it obeys the accessibility axiom and none of its bases is contained in any other. $\qquad\Box$

This change in the definition does not affect any of our results; we use this assumption in only two places, from one of which it can be removed (see Exercise 5.37).

We have already noted that the order in which a feasible set was constructed is not recorded in the structure of an accessible set system. In some problems, any ordering will always result in a chain of feasible sets; we capture this property, a much strengthened version of accessibility, with the following definition.

Definition 5.3 A set system, (S,C), is called a *hereditary set system* if it obeys:

(heredity axiom) If $X \in C$ and $X \neq \varnothing$, then for all $x \in X$ we have $X - \{x\} \in C$.
$\qquad\Box$

Given an arbitrary set system, (S,C), we define its *hereditary closure* as the set system, (S,C^*), where $C^* = \{\, Y \subseteq X \mid X \in C \,\}$. The hereditary closure of any set system is a hereditary set system. Note that a hereditary set system, but not an accessible set system, is completely characterized by its bases.

Many problems can be placed within an accessible or hereditary set system framework, including several for which we know that the greedy algorithm sometimes fails.

- [Uniform set system] For any finite set, S, let C be all subsets of S with k or fewer elements, for some $0 \leq k \leq |S|$. (S,C) is a hereditary set system.

- [Knapsack] Let S be a set of items with associated weights and let C be the collection of all sets of items for which the total weight does not exceed some fixed bound. (S,C) is a hereditary set system.

- [Prim's algorithm] Let S be the set of edges of a graph and let each element of C be a subtree (viewed as a set of edges) of the graph that includes the distinguished vertex v. (S,C) is an accessible set system, but not a hereditary set system, since removing an edge from a tree may disconnect the tree.

- [Kruskal's algorithm] Let S be the set of edges of a graph and let C be the collection of all subforests of the graph. (S,C) is a hereditary set system.

- [Nearest neighbor heuristic for travelling salesperson] Let S be the set of edges of a graph and let each element of C be a simple path. (We are actually modelling a slightly different problem, namely finding the shortest Hamiltonian path, i.e., the shortest path passing through each city.) (S,C)

is an accessible set system, but not a hereditary set system, as removing an edge from a path may split the path.

- [Coalesced simple paths heuristic for travelling salesperson] Let S be the set of edges of a graph and let C be the collection of sets of nonintersecting simple paths of the graph; that is, the elements of C are sets of edges which, when viewed properly, can be decomposed into simple paths, with no two of the simple paths sharing a vertex. (S, C) is a hereditary set system.

- [Matching] Let S be the set of edges of a graph and let C be the collection of matchings on the graph, where a matching (an element of C) is a set of pairwise vertex-disjoint edges. (S, C) is a hereditary set system.

- [Ordered matching] Let $G = (V, E)$ be a bipartite graph, with vertex partition $\{V_l, V_r\}$; recall that, since the graph is bipartite, no edge has both endpoints in the same vertex subset. Let V_l be ordered in some way. We let $S = V_r$ and C be the collection of all ordered matchings, where an ordered matching is a subset, $X \subseteq V_r$, such that the first $|X|$ vertices of V_l and the vertices of X can be paired so as to yield a collection of $|X|$ pairwise vertex-disjoint edges. (Note that, if X and $X \cup \{v\}$ are both feasible, it does not follow that v is matched to the $|X| + 1$st element of V_l; all that matters is that a matching exists, not what its edges are.)[2] (S, C) is an accessible set system, but not a hereditary set system, since removing an arbitrary "suitor" (an element of X) may prevent matching the remaining $|X| - 1$ suitors to the first $|X| - 1$ daughters.

- [Basis of a vector space] Let S be the vectors in some n-dimensional vector space and let C be the collection of all linearly independent subsets of S. (S, C) is a hereditary set system. This example violates our requirement that S be finite; C is not finite either, although all individual members of C have size bounded by n. This slightly weaker condition is sufficient to prove all the following results, provided that the greedy algorithm can make a locally optimal choice in finite time.

- [Gaussian elimination] Recall that a step in the Gaussian elimination process, applied to an $m \times n$ matrix, $\mathbf{A}$, consists of picking a row, k (known as the pivot row), such that $\mathbf{A}_{k1} \neq 0$ and replacing the $m \times n$ matrix, $\mathbf{A}$, with the $(m - 1) \times (n - 1)$ submatrix, $\mathbf{A}'$, obtained by first adding to each row, $j \neq k$, a multiple of its kth row, chosen such that the resulting $\mathbf{A}_{j1}$ becomes zero, and then by dropping the kth row and first column. This step can be

---

[2]This problem is sometimes called the *medieval marriage problem*, because it was the custom in many medieval societies to marry the daughters (the set V_l) of a family in descending order of age, and without much regard for the daughters' individual preferences. Witness Shakespeare's *The Taming of the Shrew*.

repeated on $\mathbf{A}'$, producing a *partial elimination sequence*, $k_1, k_2, \ldots,$ (using the original row indices) of up to m row indices. Let $S = \{1, 2, \ldots, m\}$ and let $\mathcal{C}$ be the set of all partial elimination sequences; note that $\mathcal{C}$ depends on $\mathbf{A}$. This formulation does not fit our definition, since the elements of $\mathcal{C}$ are ordered sets. The need for ordering comes from the fact that pivoting on row i and then on row j does not yield the same matrix as pivoting in the reverse order, possibly making the sets of candidate pivot rows different. Our earlier definitions and subsequent results can be extended to ordered sets; in this expanded framework, Gaussian elimination sequences define structures that lend themselves well to the application of greedy algorithms.

We now have a suitable framework in which to define the greedy algorithm. Let $(S, \mathcal{C})$ be an accessible set system. An *objective function* is an assignment of values to the feasible sets, $f : \mathcal{C} \rightarrow \mathcal{R}$. Given a set system and an objective function, we define the *optimization problem* for f over $(S, \mathcal{C})$ as the problem of finding a basis, $B \in \mathcal{C}$, such that $f(B) = \max\{ f(X) \mid X \text{ is a basis of } (S, \mathcal{C}) \}$. Note that only bases are considered: although all elements of $\mathcal{C}$ are feasible sets, only the bases correspond to feasible solutions for the problem. Given a weight assignment to the elements of S, $w : S \rightarrow \mathcal{R}$, the induced *linear objective function* is defined by $f(X) = \sum_{x \in X} w(x)$ and the induced *bottleneck objective function* is defined by $f(X) = \min_{x \in X} w(x)$. The majority of the objective functions used in this chapter are linear: the length of a tour is the sum of the length of its edges; the value of a knapsack is the sum of the values of the items that it contains; and the cost of a spanning tree is the sum of the lengths of its edges. On the other hand, the cost of a tree of shortest paths is not an induced linear objective function.

Informally, the greedy algorithm, when run on a set system, builds a solution by beginning with the empty set and successively adding the current best element while maintaining feasibility. We formalize this notion as follows.

Definition 5.4 Given an accessible set system, $(S, \mathcal{C})$, and an objective function, $f : \mathcal{C} \rightarrow \mathcal{R}$, the *best-in greedy algorithm* starts with the empty set; at each step, i, it chooses an element $x_i \in S$ such that

1. $\{x_1, x_2, \ldots, x_i\} \in \mathcal{C}$; and

2. $f(\{x_1, \ldots, x_i\}) = \max \{ f(\{x_1, \ldots, x_{i-1}, y\}) \mid \{x_1, \ldots, x_{i-1}, y\} \in \mathcal{C}\};$

the algorithm terminates when it has constructed a basis, i.e., when it can no longer incorporate another element into its partial solution. $\square$

Note that the objective function need not improve at every step: all that the greedy algorithm does is choose the best available extension to the current set.

In order to simplify the exposition throughout, we introduce the following notation and terminology. If (S, C) is an accessible set system and X is some feasible set, we let $ext(X) = \{ x \mid X \cup \{x\} \in C \}$. The termination condition for the best-in greedy algorithm can then be rephrased as: working with the current solution, X, the algorithm terminates when $ext(X) = \emptyset$.

Definition 5.5 A feasible set X is a *greedy set* under f if there exists a sequence, $\emptyset, \{x_1\}, \{x_1, x_2\}, \ldots, \{x_1, \ldots, x_i\}, \ldots, \{x_1, \ldots, x_i, \ldots, x_k\} = X$, of feasible subsets of X such that, for each i, $f(\{x_1, \ldots, x_{i-1}, x_i\}) = \max\{ f(\{x_1, \ldots, x_{i-1}, y\}) \mid \{x_1, \ldots, x_{i-1}, y\}$ is feasible $\}$. A basis with this property is called a *greedy basis*.

□

Observe that the greedy algorithm, for any objective function f, can construct only greedy sets under f and that, breaking ties appropriately, the greedy algorithm can construct any greedy set under f.

Exercise 5.5 Show that, for a particular accessible set system and objective function, not all greedy bases need have the same objective function value, even if all bases have equal cardinality.

□

Towards an Exact Characterization

An accessible set system clearly does not have sufficient structure to ensure the optimality of the greedy algorithm: it ensures only that the greedy algorithm will reach a basis. Indeed, we know that the greedy algorithm does not always return optimal solutions to the knapsack and travelling salesperson problems, although both can be modelled by accessible or even hereditary set systems. In part, this failure derives from the fact that the choices for extending the current set, X, may be overly constrained by the feasibility structure of the set system. In the case of accessible set systems, the greedy set X may be contained in some optimal basis, with $ext(X) \neq \emptyset$, and yet there may be no feasible set, $X \cup \{y\}$, that is also contained in some optimal basis; in such a case the greedy algorithm can build a suboptimal basis.

Example 5.5 Let (S, C) be given by $S = \{a, b, c, d\}$ and $C = \{\emptyset, \{a\}, \{b\}, \{a, c\}, \{b, d\}, \{a, b, c\}, \{a, b, d\}\}$, as follows:

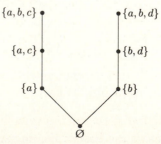

With a weight assignment such that $w(a) > w(b)$, yet with $w(c) < w(d)$, the greedy algorithm constructs a suboptimal basis. □

A traditional remedy for this problem has been to require that the set system also obey the following axiom:

(exchange axiom) If X and Y are members of $\mathcal{C}$ such that $|X| > |Y|$, then there exists $x \in X - Y$ such that $Y \cup \{x\}$ is also in $\mathcal{C}$.

Note that an immediate consequence of this axiom is that all bases must have the same size. A hereditary set system that also obeys the exchange axiom is called a *matroid*. In a matroid, the exchange property allows us to transform one feasible set, X_1, into another feasible set of the same size, X_2, by repeatedly dropping from X_1 an element of $X_1 - X_2$, yielding a feasible set Y, and applying the exchange axiom to X_2 and Y. Of our examples of hereditary set systems, three are matroids—the uniform set system, the system modelling Kruskal's algorithm, and that modelling a vector space—while the other three—knapsack, travelling salesperson, and matching—are not.

Exercise 5.6 Verify this last statement. □

A matroid has an extremely rigid structure, so much so, in fact, that the greedy algorithm, when applied to a matroid, always derives an optimal solution for any linear objective function.

Theorem 5.7 For any linear objective function (even if negative weights are allowed) on any matroid, every greedy basis is an optimal basis. □

Proof: Assume that, for some linear objective function, f, some greedy basis, B_g, is not optimal, and let A be the largest greedy set from which B_g can still be constructed by the greedy algorithm and which is also contained in some optimal basis, call it B. Let x be an element from B_g that the greedy algorithm adds to A when building B_g and let $A' = A \cup \{x\}$; note that $x \notin B$. Now, either A' is B_g, or we can apply the exchange axiom to A' and B and form $A'' = A' \cup \{z\}$, where $z \in B - A'$; repeating this process as often as necessary, we eventually obtain a new basis, call it $\hat{A}$, formed of A, x, and elements of $B - A$. Since all bases have the same size, we have $\hat{A} = B - \{y\} \cup \{x\}$ for some element $y \in B - A$. But x was a choice of the greedy algorithm and, by heredity, y was a potential choice, so that we have $w(x) \geq w(y)$ and thus $f(\hat{A}) \geq f(B)$. Hence $\hat{A}$ is an optimal basis, which contradicts the maximality of A.

Q.E.D.

Matroids thus offer a first characterization of a group of problems for which the greedy algorithm returns optimal solutions. However, we know of problems, such as minimum spanning trees (in Prim's formulation), for which the greedy algorithm returns optimal solutions, but which are not matroids. Hence matroids are too restricted and we need to relax some of the axioms that our set systems must obey.

The exchange axiom was introduced in order to allow an algorithm to extend the current set into a basis which contains it, yet it also allows such extensions between any two sets of unequal sizes. We replace it with a much weaker version, which exactly meets our intent; alternately, we may view this new axiom as a strong version of accessibility. An accessible set system, (S, C), is *extensible* if it obeys the following axiom:

(extensibility axiom) If $X, B \in C$, with B a basis and $X \subset B$, then $\exists y \in B - X$ such that $X \cup \{y\} \in C$.

Any hereditary set system is extensible, but not all accessible and extensible set systems are hereditary. Extensibility eliminates the obstacle illustrated in Example 5.5 (including the special case illustrated in Example 5.4), but it does not suffice to ensure optimality. For instance, as we have observed, the knapsack problem can be modelled by a hereditary, and thus extensible, set system. We introduce a second axiom which enforces a type of congruence on the feasibility structure of an accessible set system. An accessible set system, (S, C), is *closure-congruent* if it obeys the following axiom:

(closure-congruence axiom) If $X \in C$, $x, y \in ext(X)$, and $E \subseteq S - X - ext(X)$, then $X \cup \{x\} \cup E \in C^*$ if and only if $X \cup \{y\} \cup E \in C^*$.

Note that the condition is tested in the hereditary closure, not in the original set system. What this condition has to do with greedy algorithms is not at all obvious. In order to build intuition about closure-congruence, consider an accessible set system that models the minimum spanning tree problem on some connected graph, G. The ground set, S, corresponds to the set of edges of G, and the feasible sets, C, are the subtrees of G. (This is a slight generalization of the structure for Prim's algorithm, since we no longer require the tree to contain a designated vertex; like that structure, this set system is accessible, but not hereditary.) The bases of (S, C) are the spanning trees of G. If T is a feasible set, then $ext(T) = \{e \mid e$ has exactly one endpoint in $T\}$. For this set system, the closure-congruence axiom translates to the assertion:

> Let T be any subtree of G, e and e' be two edges with exactly one endpoint in T, and $E \subseteq S - T - ext(T)$ be any collection of edges; then $T \cup \{e\} \cup E$ is a subforest of G, and hence it is in the hereditary closure of (S, C), whenever $T \cup \{e'\} \cup E$ is one too.

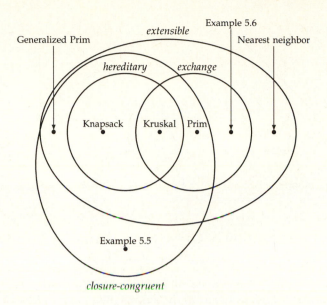

Figure 5.11: The Relationships Among Varieties of Accessible Set Systems

It is readily verified that this condition is obeyed. For any $E \subseteq S - T - ext(T)$, each of $T \cup \{e\} \cup E$ and $T \cup \{e'\} \cup E$ is a subforest if and only if E is an acyclic collection of edges, each member of which is an edge with neither endpoint in T.

The relationships among the four axioms are summarized in the Venn diagram of Figure 5.11. We have already established some of them and presently establish the rest by proving a theorem and presenting an example. First note that, of the real-world problems discussed earlier, all are extensible, but one is not closure-congruent and also fails the exchange axiom: the system for the nearest neighbor heuristic for the travelling salesperson problem.[3]

Theorem 5.8 Every hereditary set system is closure-congruent.   □

Proof: The proof follows immediately from the observation that, in any hereditary set system, for any feasible X, the empty set is the only choice of E that allows $X \cup \{z\} \cup E$ to be in the closure, for any choice of $z \in ext(X)$.

$Q.E.D.$

Example 5.6 Let $(S, \mathcal{C})$ be given by $S = \{a, b, c\}$ and $\mathcal{C} = \{\emptyset, \{a\}, \{b\}, \{a, b\}, \{b, c\}\}$; this set system obeys the exchange axiom, but is not closure-congruent. The hereditary closure of this set system is the matroid given by $\mathcal{C} = \{\emptyset, \{a\}, \{b\}, \{c\}, \{a, b\}, \{b, c\}\}$. The set system and its closure follow:

---

[3]The proofs of extensibility and closure-congruence for the ordered matching problem require a technique discussed in the next chapter.

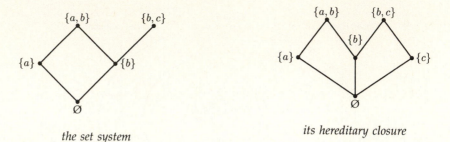

the set system   its hereditary closure

To see that the closure-congruence axiom fails on this set system, take $X = \varnothing$
and $E = \{c\}$.   □

An Exact Characterization of Greedy Structures for Linear Objective Functions

In this section we establish necessary and sufficient conditions for the greedy algorithm to optimize all linear objective functions on an accessible set system. We
begin by establishing necessary conditions on the structure of accessible set systems under which the greedy algorithm optimizes the family of linear objective
functions.

Our first result establishes that, behind every problem structure for which
the greedy algorithm returns optimal solutions, there lurks a matroid.

Theorem 5.9 [Helman]   Let $(S, \mathcal{C})$ be an accessible set system. If, for every
linear objective function, there exists a greedy basis that is also optimal, then the
hereditary closure of $(S, \mathcal{C})$ is a matroid.   □

Proof: The proof proceeds by contradiction. We design a pair of weight assignments such that: (i) the relative ordering of elements by weight is the same under
both weight assignments—so that the same unique greedy basis is constructed
under both weight assignments; and (ii) the two weight assignments share no
optimal basis.

Therefore we assume two sets, X and Y, with $|X| > |Y|$, both feasible in the
closure and between which the exchange axiom does not hold. Because exchange
fails in the closure, no basis that contains all of Y can contain any element of
$X - Y$. Weight assignment w_1 is designed so that no optimal basis can contain
all of Y, while weight assignment w_2 is designed so that any optimal basis must
contain all of Y. The greedy algorithm constructs the same basis under both
w_1 and w_2, and so exhibiting these weight assignments provides the desired
contradiction.

The weight assignments are suggested in Figure 5.12. In w_1, any basis containing all of X has weight greater than that of any basis containing all of Y,

Figure 5.12: The Weight Assignments Used in the Proof of Theorem 5.9

since the additional elements of the latter can only come from $S - X - Y$, all elements of which have small weight. In w_2, any basis containing all of Y has weight at least equal to $|Y|$; as all of the elements of both $S - X - Y$ and X do not have a combined weight of one, no optimal basis can exclude an element of Y.

Q.E.D.

Note the import of this theorem: every accessible set system on which the greedy algorithm returns an optimal basis for every linear objective function has bases which are the bases of a matroid and hence have equal cardinality; thus the greedy algorithm optimizes all linear objective functions only on substructures of matroids.

Our next two theorems expand the collection of necessary conditions for optimality of the greedy algorithm (the set system of Example 5.6 shows that having a matroid as hereditary closure is by no means sufficient). The proofs differ from the proof of Theorem 5.9 in that they make use of the actual mechanism by which the best-in greedy algorithm constructs a basis, setting up a weight assignment under which the greedy solution would not be optimal if the condition were violated.

Theorem 5.10 Let $(S, \mathcal{C})$ be an accessible set system. If, for every linear objective function, there exists a greedy basis that is also optimal, then $(S, \mathcal{C})$ is extensible. $\square$

Proof: Assume that there exist $A, B \in \mathcal{C}$, with $A \subset B$ and B a basis, such that there does not exist $x \in B$ with $x \in ext(A)$. Since $(S, \mathcal{C})$ is accessible, there exists a sequence of feasible sets $\emptyset, \{x_1\}, \{x_1, x_2\}, \ldots, \{x_1, x_2, \ldots, x_k\} = A$; denote the other elements of S by $x_{k+1}, x_{k+2}, \ldots, x_n$. We force the greedy algorithm to construct each set in the sequence leading to A by assigning weights as follows:

$$w(x_i) = \begin{cases} 1 + \epsilon/i & \text{for } 1 \leq i \leq k \\ 1 & \text{for } x_i \in B - A \\ \epsilon & \text{for } x_i \in S - B. \end{cases}$$

Since all bases of (S, C) have equal cardinality, it follows that: (i) B is the unique optimal basis; and (ii) the greedy algorithm cannot construct B, because it must construct A, and B is not accessible from A. This is the desired contradiction.

Q.E.D.

Theorem 5.11 Let (S, C) be an accessible set system. If, for every linear objective function, there exists a greedy basis that is also optimal, then (S, C) is closure-congruent. ◻

Proof: Assume that there exist $A \in C$, $x, y \in ext(A)$, and $E \subseteq S - A - ext(A)$ such that $A \cup \{x\} \cup E$ is in C^*, but $A \cup \{y\} \cup E$ is not. Note that E cannot be the empty set. As in the previous proof, there exists a sequence of feasible sets $\emptyset, \{x_1\}, \{x_1, x_2\}, \ldots, \{x_1, x_2, \ldots, x_k\} = A$; we force the greedy algorithm to construct these sets, followed by the set $A \cup \{y\}$, sending it along a suboptimal course. We accomplish this by giving large weights to elements of A and E, as well as to x and y, and very small weights to all other elements. Denote the elements of E by $x_{k+1}, x_{k+2}, \ldots, x_m$, and let $y = x_{m+1}$ and $x = x_{m+2}$. Our weight assignment is as follows:

$$w(x_i) = \begin{cases} 1 + \epsilon/i & \text{for } 1 \leq i \leq m+2 \\ \epsilon & \text{for } m+3 \leq i \leq n. \end{cases}$$

Since $A \cup \{x\} \cup E$ is in C^*, there is a basis B containing $A \cup \{x\} \cup E$; this basis cannot contain y (or else $A \cup \{y\} \cup E$ would be in C^*) and has objective function value $W - (1 + \epsilon/(m+1)) + r\epsilon$, where W is the sum of the first $m + 2$ weights and r is the number of elements needed to complete the basis. However, the greedy algorithm must begin by constructing $A \cup \{y\}$ and eventually terminates with some basis B'; since $A \cup \{y\} \cup E$ is not in C^*, it follows that E is not a subset of B' and $f(B')$ is not greater than $W - (1 + \epsilon/i) + r\epsilon$ for $i < m + 1$, even if $x \in B'$. Thus we have $f(B') < f(B)$, the desired contradiction.

Q.E.D.

We now have three necessary conditions for the best-in greedy algorithm to be optimal for all linear objective functions on an arbitrary accessible set system. We shall prove shortly that these three conditions are also sufficient. These results justify Definition 5.6.

Definition 5.6 A *matroid embedding* is an accessible set system which is extensible, closure-congruent, and the hereditary closure of which is a matroid. ◻

Our work in the previous section established that every matroid is a matroid embedding; however, the exchange axiom neither implies (Example 5.6) nor is implied by (the generalization of the structure for Prim's algorithm) the matroid embedding structure.

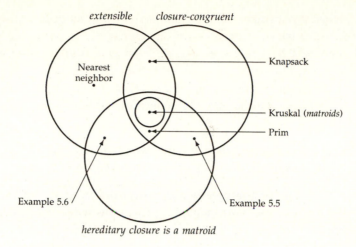

Figure 5.13: Independence of the Three Conditions for Greedy Optimality

The definition of a matroid embedding is well formed, as the three conditions are independent, i.e., no two imply the third; Figure 5.13 shows a Venn diagram with examples for most of the categories.

Exercise 5.7 Provide examples for the two remaining categories.   □

Of our ten earlier examples, five are matroid embeddings: the three matroids (uniform set system, Kruskal's algorithm, and basis for a vector space), plus Prim's algorithm and ordered matching.

We now establish that the structure of a matroid embedding is not only necessary, but also sufficient for the optimality of the greedy algorithm on all linear objective functions.

Theorem 5.12 For any linear objective function (even if negative weights are allowed) on any matroid embedding, every greedy basis is an optimal basis.

□

Observe that this theorem generalizes Theorem 5.7; their statements, as well as their proofs, parallel each other.

Proof: Assume that, for some linear objective function, f, some greedy basis, B_g, is not optimal, and let A be the largest greedy set from which B_g can still be constructed by the greedy algorithm and which is also contained in some optimal basis, call it B. Let x be an element from B_g that the greedy algorithm adds to A when building B_g and let $A' = A \cup \{x\}$; note that $x \notin B$. By extensibility, there exists $y \in B$ such that $y \in ext(A)$; let $E = B - A - ext(A)$. Observe that $A \cup \{y\} \cup E$

is in C^*, since it is a subset of B, so that, by closure-congruence, so is $A \cup \{x\} \cup E$. Because (S, C^*) is a matroid, we can apply the exchange axiom to $A \cup \{x\} \cup E$ with respect to B, yielding some basis B'. Bases B and B' differ by one element: B' contains x at the expense of some other element in $ext(A)$, say z. But x was a choice of the greedy algorithm, so we have $w(x) \geq w(z)$ and thus $f(B') \geq f(B)$. Hence B' is an optimal basis, which contradicts the maximality of A.

Q.E.D.

Combining our previous four theorems, we obtain the following exact characterization of the greedy algorithm run on accessible set systems.

Theorem 5.13 The best-in greedy algorithm run on an accessible set system optimizes all linear objective functions if and only if the set system is a matroid embedding.   □

Bottleneck Objective Functions

Bottleneck functions form an important subclass of functions induced by weight assignments; we have already introduced them, but now we define them formally.

Definition 5.7 A (simple) *bottleneck function* is an objective function of the form $f(A) = \min_{x \in A} w(x)$. By convention, $f(\varnothing) = 1 + \max_{x \in S} w(x)$.   □

Bottleneck functions arise in variations of shortest-path problems, where the question asked is of the form, "What is the widest path from here to there?" They also arise in other graph problems, such as the maximum capacity spanning tree problem, where, given a graph with edge capacities (instead of lengths), we want to find the spanning tree which maximizes the minimum transmission capacity between all pairs of vertices.

It is easily verified that Theorem 5.12 holds for bottleneck functions as well as linear functions, so that we have the following result.

Corollary 5.1 The greedy algorithm is optimal for all bottleneck objective functions when run on an arbitrary matroid embedding.   □

However, the full structure of a matroid embedding is not needed to ensure optimality of the greedy algorithm for accessible set systems with bottleneck objective functions. We need neither closure-congruence nor that the hereditary closure be a matroid.

Example 5.7 The set system given by $S = \{a, b, c, d\}$ with feasible sets $\varnothing$, $\{a\}$, $\{b\}$, $\{a, b\}$, $\{a, c\}$, and $\{b, d\}$, and depicted with its hereditary closure, is such that the greedy algorithm optimizes any bottleneck objective function; yet it is not closure-congruent, and its hereditary closure is not a matroid.

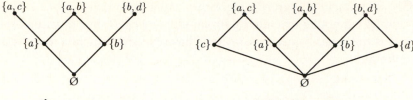

the set system   its hereditary closure

To see that the closure-congruence axiom fails on this set system, take $X = \emptyset$ and $E = \{c\}$; to see that the hereditary closure is not a matroid, consider the sets $\{c\}$ and $\{b, d\}$.   □

The strong extensibility axiom characterizes exactly those accessible set systems on which the greedy algorithm optimizes all bottleneck objective functions. An accessible set system, $(S, \mathcal{C})$, is *strongly extensible* if it obeys the following axiom:

(strong extensibility axiom) If $X, B \in \mathcal{C}$, with B a basis and $|X| < |B|$, then $\exists y \in B - X$ such that $X \cup \{y\} \in \mathcal{C}$.

We observe that the bases of any strongly extensible accessible set system are of the same cardinality, and that a hereditary set system is strongly extensible if and only if it is a matroid.

Exercise 5.8 Prove that a hereditary set system is a matroid if it is strongly extensible. (The other two observations are trivial.)   □

Two lemmata are required before we can establish the exact characterization for bottleneck objective functions. The first lemma establishes (ordinary) extensibility as a necessary condition.

Lemma 5.2 Let $(S, \mathcal{C})$ be an accessible set system. If, for every bottleneck objective function, there exists a greedy basis that is also optimal, then $(S, \mathcal{C})$ is extensible.   □

Proof: Assume that there exists a basis, B, and a feasible set, $A \subset B$, such that, for all $x \in ext(A)$, $x \notin B$. Since $(S, \mathcal{C})$ is accessible, there exists a sequence of feasible sets $\emptyset, \{x_1\}, \{x_1, x_2\}, \ldots, \{x_1, x_2, \ldots, x_k\} = A$; denote the other elements of S by $x_{k+1}, x_{k+2}, \ldots, x_n$. We force the greedy algorithm to construct each set in the sequence leading to A by assigning weights as follows:

$$w(x_i) = \begin{cases} 1 + \epsilon/i & \text{for } 1 \leq i \leq k \\ 1 & \text{for } x_i \in B - A \\ \epsilon & \text{for } x_i \in S - B. \end{cases}$$

With this assignment the greedy algorithm must terminate with a suboptimal basis: since A cannot be extended with an element of B, but must be extended because it is not a basis, any greedy basis has objective function value ϵ, which is not optimal.

Q.E.D.

Lemma 5.3 Let $(S, \mathcal{C})$ be an accessible set system. If, for every bottleneck objective function, there exists a greedy basis that is also optimal, then all bases of $(S, \mathcal{C})$ have equal cardinality.   □

Proof: Assume that at least two sizes of bases exist; let C be an arbitrary non-minimal size basis and let B be a minimal size basis, such that among all minimal size bases, B shares with C a largest size feasible subset, A. Note that A is a proper subset of B and cannot itself be a basis. As before, since the set system is accessible, there exists a sequence of feasible sets $\varnothing$, $\{x_1\}$, $\{x_1, x_2\}$, ..., $\{x_1, x_2, \ldots, x_k\} = A$. Because $(S, \mathcal{C})$ is extensible and because $A \subset C$, there exists some $y \in ext(A)$ such that $y \in C$; note that, by our assumption of the maximality of A, $y \notin B$. Let $y = x_{k+1}$ and denote all other elements of S by x_{k+2}, ..., x_n. We force the greedy algorithm to construct the set $A \cup \{y\}$ and then to complete it in a suboptimal manner by assigning weights as follows:

$$
w(x_i) = \begin{cases} 1 + \epsilon/i & \text{for } 1 \leq i \leq k+1 \\ 1 & \text{for } x_i \in B - A \\ \epsilon & \text{for } x_i \in S - B - \{y\}. \end{cases}
$$

Note that, under this assignment, the basis B has value 1 and is optimal. The greedy bases that can be constructed must all contain $A \cup \{y\}$ and, by our assumption of the minimality of B and the maximality of A, have size greater than $|B|$. Thus at least $|B - A|$ elements must be added to $A \cup \{y\}$; since B is a basis, these elements cannot all come from B. Thus all greedy bases have objective function value ϵ and are suboptimal, the desired contradiction.

Q.E.D.

We are now in a position to prove our main result about bottleneck objective functions.

Theorem 5.14 The best-in greedy algorithm run on an accessible set system optimizes all bottleneck objective functions if and only if the set system is strongly extensible.   □

Proof: We begin with the "only if" part, proceeding, as usual, by contradiction. Assume that there exist a feasible set A and a basis B, with $|A| < |B|$, such that A cannot be extended with respect to B. Note that our previous lemma ensures that A cannot be a basis. As before, we know that there exists a sequence of feasible sets $\emptyset$, $\{x_1\}$, $\{x_1, x_2\}$, $\ldots$, $\{x_1, x_2, \ldots, x_k\} = A$; denote the remaining elements of S by $x_{k+1}, \ldots, x_n$. We force the greedy algorithm to construct the feasible set A and to extend it to a suboptimal basis by assigning weights as follows:

$$w(x_i) = \begin{cases} 1 + \epsilon/i & \text{for } 1 \leq i \leq k \\ 1 & \text{for } x_i \in B - A \\ \epsilon & \text{for } x_i \in S - B - A. \end{cases}$$

Since A is not a basis, it must be extended; but A cannot be extended by an element of B, so that every greedy basis has value ϵ, while B is an optimal basis of value 1, the desired contradiction.

We also use contradiction in proving the "if" part. Assume that, for some bottleneck objective function, f, some greedy basis, B_g, is not optimal, and let A be the largest greedy set from which B_g can be constructed by the greedy algorithm and which is also contained in some optimal basis, call it B. Let x be an element from B_g that the greedy algorithm adds to A when building B_g; note that $x \notin B$. Since the set system is strongly extensible, there also exists $y \in B - A$ such that $A \cup \{y\}$ is feasible; but note that $A \cup \{y\}$ cannot be a greedy set extensible to B_g by the greedy algorithm, since this would contradict the maximality of A. Since $A \cup \{y\}$ is a subset of B, we have $f(A \cup \{y\}) \geq f(B)$. Now, since the set system is strongly extensible (and thus allows $A \cup \{x\}$ to be extended with elements from B), since A is maximal, and since the objective function is determined by the minimum weight of its arguments, we also have $f(B) > f(A \cup \{x\})$. Combining these two inequalities yields $f(A \cup \{y\}) > f(A \cup \{x\})$, which contradicts the fact that the greedy algorithm can choose x.

Q.E.D.

Summary

We have provided exact characterizations of those set systems on which the greedy algorithm always returns an optimal solution, when optimality is measured by a linear or a bottleneck objective function. However, the structure remains dependent on the specific greedy algorithm: for instance, the settings for Prim's and Kruskal's algorithms differ. Given a particular greedy algorithm for a problem, the results of this section may provide an immediate proof of its correctness; on the other hand, given just the problem, they do not enable us to decide whether or not some greedy algorithm can solve it. Finally, matroid embeddings themselves give rise to some difficult problems.

First note that these set systems in general, and matroid embeddings in particular, are normally not given by their feasible sets, nor even by their bases;

rather, they are specified indirectly by a decision procedure which, given any subset of S, decides whether or not this subset is feasible. Such a procedure is usually called a *feasibility oracle*. One obvious question is to decide whether or not a given accessible set system is in fact a matroid or matroid embedding. However, such a question is very difficult to decide; in fact, the following theorem shows that it is an intractable problem.

Theorem 5.15 There is no polynomial-time algorithm to decide whether or not an accessible set system, given by a feasibility oracle, is a matroid.   □

Proof: We give a matroid and a family of accessible set systems such that, for any algorithm that distinguishes the former from all members of the latter, there exist members of the family that cannot be recognized in polynomial time. Let the matroid on S be the uniform matroid of rank $r = \lceil |S|/2 \rceil$; let each member of the family of accessible set systems be given by exactly the same feasible sets, save one: an arbitrary set of size $r - 1$. This missing set becomes the proverbial needle in a haystack: any algorithm to distinguish the matroid from an accessible set system must ask the feasibility oracle about this set. We chose the missing set so that two conditions would be met: (i) its absence causes a violation of the heredity axiom; and (ii) its presence or absence is consistent with any knowledge that the algorithm may have gathered from previous queries to the oracle. Thus any decision algorithm must enumerate, among others, the $\binom{|S|}{r-1}$ subsets of size $r - 1$ in order to determine whether or not one is missing. Therefore, there will be accessible set systems in our family for which the decision algorithm will identify the missing subset only after enumerating an exponential number of these subsets.

Q.E.D.

Finally, we note that the definition of complexity to be used with set systems is quite unclear: since all complexity analyses are done in terms of the size of the input, we must be able to describe the input, yet are clearly unable to do so in the case of a system given by a feasibility oracle. Theorem 5.15 uses the number of calls to the feasibility oracle as its definition of running time, which is clearly unsatisfactory, since this definition ignores the running time of the oracle procedure. Also, there is every reason to think that an examination of the oracle procedure would yield useful information, possibly allowing us to solve our problem more efficiently. Yet avoiding the oracle and presenting the set system through its bases or through its subsets often leads to very large input sizes and thus artificially lowers the complexity estimate. We take up these questions of natural and artificial complexity measures in Volume II.

5.7   Exercises

Exercise 5.9 Devise a linear-time implementation of the greedy method for the set covering problem, assuming that the input is a collection of element lists.

□

Exercise 5.10 You are given a collection of unit-length jobs to be run on a single processor. Each job has an associated deadline and penalty, both positive integers; the penalty is incurred if the job is not completed by the deadline. Devise a greedy algorithm to construct an optimal schedule.

□

Exercise 5.11 This problem addresses optimal file allocation for computer networks. You are given a completely connected network of nodes, a set of files to be allocated among the nodes, and a sequence of retrieval and updating requests (the entire sequence is known in advance). A retrieval or updating request is a triple, consisting of the node initiating the request, the file involved, and the number of bytes to be transferred.

An allocation scheme is an assignment of each file to one or more nodes. Having multiple copies of a file is advantageous in retrieval: the cost of a retrieval is zero when the file is held locally, but equals the number of bytes to be transferred when the file must be accessed remotely. On the other hand, multiple copies of a file increase the cost of an updating operation, because each copy must be updated and thus the number of bytes needed for updating is multiplied by the number of remote copies. Multiple copies are also desirable for reasons of reliability, but only up to a point, since relatively few nodes are expected to fail. The gain in reliability is a function of the number of copies and obeys the law of diminishing returns: each additional copy of a file gives a smaller gain than the previous copy. The cost of an allocation scheme is the cost of the given sequences of retrieval and updating requests minus the gain in reliability.

Develop a greedy algorithm that constructs the optimal allocation scheme and prove its correctness.

□

Exercise 5.12 Show that Kruskal's, Prim's, and Dijkstra's algorithms all still apply when the problem statement requires the inclusion of specific edges (or arcs, in the case of Dijkstra's algorithm).

□

Exercise 5.13 Prove or disprove each of the following statements:

1. If unique, the shortest edge is included in any minimum spanning tree.

2. If unique, the shortest arc is included in any tree of shortest paths.

3. A shortest edge incident upon each vertex is included in any minimum spanning tree.

4. If all edges have different lengths, the minimum spanning tree is unique.

5. If all arcs have different lengths, the tree of shortest paths is unique.

□

Exercise 5.14* *Borůvka's algorithm.* Consider yet another algorithm for constructing minimum spanning trees which lends itself well to parallel implementations. We maintain a forest of partial spanning trees. Initially, the forest is composed of the vertices. At each step we select, for each tree in the forest, the shortest edge incident upon the tree; of course, if the same edge is selected twice, it is added only once.

1. Prove that this algorithm yields a minimal spanning tree if all edge lengths are distinct.

2. Devise an implementation of this algorithm; what is the running time of your implementation?

□

Exercise 5.15* Devise and analyze an algorithm to determine the smallest change in edge cost that causes a change of the minimum spanning tree. Your algorithm need not be efficient. □

Exercise 5.16** You are given a graph and a claimed minimum spanning tree. Devise and analyze a quasi-linear algorithm for verifying the claim of minimality.

□

Exercise 5.17** You are given a graph and its minimum spanning tree, but are later given an additional vertex with its associated edges and edge costs. Devise and analyze an algorithm for rapidly updating the minimum spanning tree. (Linear time is possible.) □

Exercise 5.18* A minimum spanning tree can be obtained by a *worst-out greedy* algorithm; such an algorithm starts with the set of edges and repeatedly removes an edge of greatest cost, while ensuring that the resulting set remains spanning. Devise an implementation of this algorithm; how does your implementation compare with the algorithms discussed in the text? □

Exercise 5.19 An on-line algorithm processes the input as it is read, one item at a time. For the spanning tree problem, such an algorithm processes edges in the order in which they are given, each time deciding how to modify the partial spanning forest. Devise an on-line algorithm for the minimum spanning tree problem. (A running time of $O(|E| \log |V|)$ is possible, but requires a sophisticated representation of trees.) □

Exercise 5.20* Consider *bottleneck* spanning trees; a bottleneck objective function is determined entirely by the cost of one of the edges of the tree. In a minimization problem, the bottleneck cost of a spanning tree is the cost of the costliest edge in the tree; such a formulation models, for instance, a bicyclist who wants to avoid heavily travelled roads. In a maximization problem, the bottleneck cost of a spanning tree is the cost of the least costly edge; such a formulation models, for instance, a network of canals through which one has to move the widest possible barge. The same objective functions can be applied to the shortest-path problem.

Prove or disprove each of the following statements, assuming that the bottleneck function is to be minimized:

1. If unique, the shortest edge is included in any minimum spanning tree.

2. If unique, the shortest edge is included in some minimum spanning tree.

3. If unique, the shortest arc is included in some tree of shortest paths for a fixed initial vertex.

4. If unique and part of some cycle, the longest edge is not included in any minimum spanning tree.

Reprove Theorems 5.2 and 5.5 for bottleneck objective functions.   □

Exercise 5.21 Modify Dijkstra's algorithm so that it returns the number of distinct shortest paths between a pair of vertices.   □

Exercise 5.22 Assume that crossing a vertex also takes work (as it certainly would if each vertex represented a large city); i.e., assign a cost to each vertex as well as to each edge. Show that a simple preprocessing step will allow us to use our standard algorithm to find shortest paths.   □

Exercise 5.23 What is wrong with the following idea for finding the longest path between two points? We let N be a very large integer and let the new length assignment to edges be $d'(u, v) = N - d(u, v)$. We then run Dijkstra's algorithm: the shortest path returned according to the new length assignment is a longest path according to the original length assignment.   □

Exercise 5.24** Modify Dijkstra's algorithm so that it works even when some edges may have a negative length, as long as the graph does not have a cycle of negative total length. (*Hint*: It is enough to add a preprocessing step that changes all edge lengths so that they all become nonnegative; finding the proper scaling values requires an initial breadth-first search of the graph.)   □

Exercise 5.25 There are many cases where finding a shortest path takes second place to finding a feasible path. Referring back to Exercise 5.20, consider finding a feasible or shortest path for a barge. Several versions of the problem arise:

1. Find a feasible path given the width of the barge.

2. Find the maximum possible width for a barge.

3. Find the shortest feasible path given both edge widths and edge lengths.

4. Find the maximum-width path, the length of which does not exceed a given threshold.

The first three variants can be solved efficiently. The fourth cannot—discover why, then do the next exercise.   □

Exercise 5.26* Devise an algorithm for finding the k shortest paths between two specified vertices in an undirected graph. Even with carefully chosen data structures, one cannot expect an efficient algorithm.   □

Exercise 5.27 Let $G = (V, E)$ be an undirected graph, where each node is colored either red or blue, and let s and t be two distinguished vertices of G. Develop a linear-time algorithm to find a path from s to t that passes through the fewest number of blue nodes.   □

Exercise 5.28 The *diameter* of a tree is the length of the longest path between any two vertices. Develop a linear-time algorithm to find the diameter of a tree.

     □

Exercise 5.29 Consider the following greedy algorithm for finding the spanning tree of smallest diameter:

- Let the initial solution be a tree consisting of one arbitrary vertex and no edges.

- While there remain vertices not yet included in the tree, select the edge connecting some vertex in the tree to some unincluded vertex such that the increase in the diameter of the tree is minimized.

Does this algorithm return a spanning tree of minimum diameter?   □

Exercise 5.30 Prove that a necessary condition for the existence of a prefix-free code, where the ith code has length l_i, is $\sum_{i=1}^{n} 2^{-l_i} \leq 1$. (This condition is also sufficient, but sufficiency is harder to show.)   □

Exercise 5.31 Prove the claim made in Section 5.5 that, if nodes of equal weight are sorted on the basis of their creation times, then Huffman's algorithm minimizes both $\sum_{i=1}^{N} l_i$ and $\max_i\{l_i\}$. □

Exercise 5.32 Prove that Huffman codes not only minimize the total weighted path length, but also optimize two natural bottleneck objective functions; namely, Huffman codes minimize $\max_i\{w_i l_i\}$ and maximize $\min_i\{w_i l_i\}$. □

Exercise 5.33 Propose set system frameworks for the optimization problems of Chapter 1. Characterize each set system and objective function and discuss the applicability of the greedy algorithm. □

Exercise 5.34* Although the knapsack problem is in general very difficult to solve and, as we have seen, can only be solved approximately with the greedy method, a special category of knapsack problems can be solved optimally with this approach. This category is that of *change-making* problems in realistic currency systems. When asked to make change for some number of cents with the smallest number of coins, we automatically use as many coins of the largest denomination as possible, continue with the next lower denomination, etc. With real currency systems (e.g., the set $\{1, 5, 10, 25, 50\}$ or the set $\{1, 2, 5, 10, 20, 50\}$), this algorithm is optimal; however, it is easy to devise currencies for which the algorithm fails.

Attempt to place the change-making problem in a matroid embedding framework; can you characterize those currency systems where the greedy algorithm is optimal? □

Exercise 5.35 A ski instructor has available n pairs of skis to be assigned to her n novice pupils; according to the tenets of her ski school, each pupil should receive a pair of skis exactly matching his or her height. The instructor's problem is to assign the n pairs of skis to the n pupils so as to minimize the sum of the absolute values of the differences between the height of a pupil and the length of the assigned pair of skis.

This problem can be solved optimally with the obvious method: assign the shortest pair of skis to the shortest pupil and proceed in increasing order of heights and lengths. Prove this result. (This solution also minimizes the worst-case difference in height.) □

Exercise 5.36** The algorithm described in the previous exercise meets our requirements for a greedy algorithm; however, it is not greedy with respect to the obvious objective function. Attempt to place this algorithm within a matroid embedding framework; also, explain the failure of the greedy algorithm that uses the obvious objective function. □

Exercise 5.37* Prove that Theorem 5.10 holds even in the presence of the anomalies ruled out by the second definition of accessible sets systems. (On the other hand, Example 5.4 shows that Lemmata 5.2 and 5.3 and the "only if" part of Theorem 5.14 do not hold in the presence of such anomalies.)   □

5.8 Bibliography

As we mentioned in Section 1.9, an entire monograph has been devoted to the travelling salesperson problem (Lawler *et al.* [1985]); a very large number of heuristics, including those presented in this chapter, are discussed in that work. A detailed analysis of the nearest neighbor, coalesced-simple-paths, and insertion heuristics is given by Rosenkrantz *et al.* [1977]. The 57-city problem first appeared in Karg and Thompson [1964]. For an overview of experimental studies of heuristics for the travelling salesperson problem, the reader should consult Chapter 7 of the monograph of Lawler *et al.*

Graham and Hell [1985] present a detailed history of the minimum spanning tree problem; rather than repeating here some of their comments, we refer the reader to their excellent article, where further references can also be found. Let us just mention briefly that Prim's algorithm is generally attributed to Prim [1957], although the same algorithm had been published in 1930 in Czech by Jarník; that Kruskal's algorithm is due to Kruskal [1956]; and that the earliest algorithm for the problem is due to Borůvka (see Exercise 5.14) and was published in Czech in 1926. Tarjan [1983] gives a succinct description of various algorithms, including the $O(|E| \log \log |V|)$ algorithm that we presented, which is due to Cheriton and Tarjan [1976]. Some of the fast algorithms for the problem can be found in Cheriton and Tarjan [1976] and Fredman and Tarjan [1984]; the fastest is due to Gabow *et al.* [1984]: it runs in $O(|E| \log \beta(|E|, |V|))$ time; an improved version appears in Gabow *et al.* [1986]. Camerini [1978] has shown that the bottleneck spanning tree problem can be solved in $\Theta(|E|)$ time by taking advantage of the special nature of the objective function. Exercise 5.19 is from Tarjan [1983]; Exercise 5.16 is from Tarjan [1979]; and Exercise 5.17 is from Spira and Pan [1975].

The fastest algorithm for the shortest-path problem is Dijkstra's algorithm, implemented with Fibonacci heaps and thus running in $\Theta(|E| + |V| \log |V|)$ time. Fredman and Tarjan [1987] present this algorithm and mention that it is asymptotically optimal. For graphs where the longest edge has length U, Ahuja *et al.* [1988] present a potentially faster algorithm, running in $O(|E| + |V| \sqrt{\log U})$. Gabow and Tarjan [1988] present an algorithm for bottleneck shortest paths that runs in $O(\min(|V| \log |V| + |E|, |E| \lg^* |V|))$ time.

The text of Abramson [1963] surveys information and coding theory; prefix-free codes are also known as *instantaneous codes*, for obvious reasons, and have long been studied. The concept of entropy was introduced by Shannon [1948], who also proved that the average length of the best possible prefix-free code is bounded below by the entropy of the set and above by the same value plus one (a result generally known as the *noiseless coding theorem*). Huffman [1952] proposed Huffman codes. Improvements using variable-rate coding were proposed by Ziv and Lempel [1978], and a dynamic version of Huffman coding was described by Knuth [1985]. Bentley *et al.* [1986] present an amortized scheme which requires only one pass over the data.

There is a wealth of literature on the subject of matroids, much of it dealing with problems in matroid theory *per se*. For an excellent reference on the latter, consult Welsh [1976]; for a more applied overview of the subject, consult Lawler [1976]. The equivalence between matroids and the optimal behavior of greedy algorithms is due to Edmonds [1971], although Rado [1957] had derived much the same result earlier, and several authors, including Gale [1968], have derived it independently. Recent developments in the characterization of greedy algorithms have been spearheaded by Korte and Lovasz [1981, 1986], who defined greedoids (accessible set systems that obey the exchange axiom) and proved some early results relating greedy algorithms to greedoids. The exact characterization in terms of matroid embeddings is due to Helman and the authors [1989]; Theorem 5.9 is from Helman [1989].

Exercise 5.11 is due to Helman [1987]. Exercise 5.35 is a special case of a class of matching problems studied by Gilmore and Gomory [1964].

CHAPTER 6

Local Search II: Iterative Methods

Unlike greedy methods, which start from an empty structure and build a solution structure step by step, iterative methods start with a solution structure and refine it step by step in an attempt to derive an optimal solution. Iterative methods are also local search methods, since they examine and modify only small parts of the current structure at any step. Like greedy methods, iterative methods may well fail to derive an optimal solution, but typically derive a locally optimal solution quickly and efficiently.

Mathematicians have long used iterative optimization methods known as *gradient methods*. A gradient method optimizes a continuous objective function in multidimensional space by following the gradient vector (the value of the derivative at that point in space), which points in the direction of greatest change for the objective function. The method reaches a solution when the gradient reaches zero, at which point the objective function reaches a local extremum. The size of a step (a move in the direction of the gradient) may be constant or may depend on the value of the gradient and on history. Gradient methods must be used with extreme care: they may not converge (due, for instance, to oscillations around an extremum) or may converge to a local extremum that is not a global extremum. Reconciling them with additional constraints, such as maintaining feasibility, may prove difficult, since it is not clear what step to take when the gradient points out of the feasible region. In all cases the choice of step size is critical. Finally, of course, the objective function must have a computable derivative. Yet gradient methods are close relatives of a family of rather straightforward iterative optimization algorithms for combinatorial problems.

The combinatorial setting simplifies gradient methods considerably: (i) the size of a step is usually not critical, because the discreteness of the problem provides a natural step size; (ii) while the objective function does not have a derivative, one can substitute the change in the objective function corresponding to a move one step away from the current state; and (iii) constraints on the solution region are easily taken into consideration by restricting the choice of possible steps.

Since iterative methods must start with some solution structure, the problem of providing a starting point is very important. While it is true that a trivial solution structure exists for most problems (such as a null flow through a network or an empty knapsack) or can be constructed quickly (such as the travelling salesperson tour which visits all cities in the order in which they are listed), it is generally advantageous to run iterative improvement methods on "good" initial solutions. The goodness of an initial solution should really be gauged by its ability to lead iterative improvement methods quickly to an optimal solution. However, this is not a practical measure, in the sense that no one knows how to compute it in advance; instead, a good initial solution is taken to mean a good approximation to an optimal solution. This interpretation leads naturally to the use of greedy methods for deriving the initial solution. We discussed an example of the use of an iterative algorithm to improve upon a greedy solution when examining the weight-greedy heuristic for the knapsack problem: given a packing, repeatedly replace objects with others of higher value. The examples we are about to discuss will further illustrate this combination of two local search methods.

Perhaps the simplest application of iterative methods is to be found in search problems which ask for the set of objects constructible from an initial set of objects, usually called *generators*, under given rules for construction. In such problems, the following simple algorithm correctly enumerates all constructible objects:

- Initially, the set of constructible objects is set equal to the set of generators.

- All possible rules for generation are used on the current set of constructible objects. If no new object is generated, then the algorithm stops; otherwise, all new objects thus generated are added to the set of constructible objects and the step is repeated.

This approach is clearly iterative, in that it starts with a valid solution—the set of generators is by definition constructible—and proceeds to expand it, maintaining at all times a valid solution. When the process terminates, as it must if the set of constructible objects is finite, the set of constructible objects indeed includes all objects constructible from the generators according to the generation rules. If we look upon the problem as one of maximizing the number of constructible objects enumerated, then we see that each iterative step indeed improves upon the previous solution.

Such problems come from formal languages, where the objects are sentential forms over the alphabet, the generation rules are the productions of the grammar, and the single generator is the sentence symbol of the grammar; from graph theory, where the objects are vertices of the graph and the single rule specifies that a vertex is reachable if and only if it is itself a generator or it is connected by an edge to a reachable vertex; from logic, where the objects can be taken as propositions in a language and the rules are whatever inference rules are allowed (e.g., *modus ponens*); and from many other areas. In its purest form, this type of problem is found in abstract algebra, where we are given a set and an operation on the set and asked which set elements can be generated from a given collection of generators.

These reachability problems serve to underscore the fundamental simplicity of the iterative paradigm; the reader may have noted its close connections with the graph search methods discussed earlier.

6.1 Clustering and Separating

Recall that the clustering problem (Problem 31) asks to find a partition of a set into k clusters, such that the total dissimilitude between members of distinct clusters is maximized (k-max cut) or such that the total dissimilitude between members of the same cluster is minimized (k-min clustering). Once we have obtained a clustering, a natural question is how to determine efficiently to which cluster a new point belongs. Given two clusters in n-dimensional space, the *separating* problem asks that a separating surface, i.e., a surface such that all elements of one cluster lie on one side of the surface, while all elements of the other cluster lie on the other side, be found. For the sake of simplicity, separating surfaces are usually restricted to linear surfaces, known as *hyperplanes*; these surfaces are the natural generalization to higher dimensions of planes in three-dimensional space. With this restriction, however, a solution may not always exist, even with well-defined clusters.

We begin by examining the separating problem, since it offers a range of solutions by gradient methods, solutions which illustrate how these methods naturally lead to other iterative methods. Let us first establish some notation. A point in n-dimensional space will be represented as a column vector,

$$\mathbf{x} = \begin{pmatrix} x_1 \\ \vdots \\ x_n \end{pmatrix}.$$

In vector notation, then, the equation of a hyperplane in n-dimensional space is simply $\mathbf{w}^t \cdot \mathbf{x} = c$, where the superscript t denotes transposition. Hence, given a collection of points in one cluster, $\{\mathbf{x}_1, \ldots, \mathbf{x}_k\}$, and a collection in the other, $\{\mathbf{y}_1, \ldots, \mathbf{y}_l\}$, the separating problem asks to find a *weight* vector $\mathbf{w}$ and a constant c such that the following inequalities hold:

$$\mathbf{w}^t \cdot \mathbf{x}_i > c \qquad \text{for } i = 1, 2, \ldots, k$$
$$\mathbf{w}^t \cdot \mathbf{y}_j < c \qquad \text{for } j = 1, 2, \ldots, l.$$

In order to streamline the notation somewhat further, let us add an extra dimension to all the vectors. The $(n+1)$st coordinate of all points is set to -1, while the unknown c becomes the $(n + 1)$st component of the augmented weight vector. Let us further multiply all vectors from the second cluster by -1 and relabel the resulting patterns according to $\mathbf{x}_{k+j} = -\mathbf{y}_j$. Now the solution to the separating problem is an $(n + 1)$-dimensional weight vector, $\mathbf{w}$, such that

$$\mathbf{w}^t \cdot \mathbf{x}_i > 0, \qquad \text{for } i = 1, 2, \ldots, k + l. \tag{6.1}$$

If a solution exists, then there are an infinity of solutions, since the solution vector can be multiplied by any strictly positive number without affecting its validity; note that they all represent the same hyperplane. The search space for this problem is clearly infinite, yet we shall see that the problem remains combinatorial in nature.

Researchers in artificial intelligence provided the first approach to this problem, designing a so-called *learning* or *training* algorithm. The approach has been characterized as one of "reward and punishment," although we shall recognize it as nothing more than a gradient method. The reward and punishment method attempts to mimic the human approach to learning: from a rough initial concept, such as a guess, the learner reaches a solution through a process of refinement monitored by a teacher, who rewards the learner for taking correct steps and punishes him or her for erroneous ones. In our situation, where the algorithm must "learn" a weight vector, deciding whether to reward or to punish the algorithm means testing its guess against the inequalities of (6.1), "rewarding" it means letting its current guess stand, and "punishing" it means forcing it to change its guess. Testing can be done one inequality at a time (the sequential approach, resulting in small steps) or all at once (the parallel approach, resulting in large, costly steps). It remains only to design a suitable correction to apply whenever punishment is necessary. Punishment must occur whenever the current value of the weight vector fails to satisfy one or another of the inequalities; formally, we have $\mathbf{w}^t(j) \cdot \mathbf{x}_i < 0$, where j indicates the step number and i the failed inequality. (Strictly speaking, we ought to deal with the case where the scalar product equals zero; as this case only rarely arises and introduces complications, we do not address it.) It follows that any correction ought to bring the weight vector closer to satisfying the failed inequality; in other words, we must produce $\mathbf{w}(j+1)$ such that

$$\mathbf{w}^t(j+1) \cdot \mathbf{x}_i > \mathbf{w}^t(j) \cdot \mathbf{x}_i.$$

We could insist that the correction ensure that $\mathbf{w}^t(j+1) \cdot \mathbf{x}_i > 0$, but, as we shall see, this is not necessary: all that is required is a step in the correct direction; we shall also not require that successive weights continue to satisfy previously satisfied inequalities. We can write $\mathbf{w}(j+1) = \mathbf{w}(j) + \mathbf{e}(j)$, where $\mathbf{e}(j)$ is the correction applied at step j; substituting in the previous inequality, we obtain the following simple condition:

$$\mathbf{e}^t(j) \cdot \mathbf{x}_i > 0.$$

We can ensure this outcome by letting $\mathbf{e}(j) = \alpha \mathbf{x}_i$ for $\alpha > 0$. While, at this point, any positive value of α suits our requirements, so that a different α could be used at each correction, we shall see that a fixed positive constant suffices.

The resulting algorithm, known as the *perceptron algorithm*, is based upon the following corrective step:

$$\mathbf{w}(j+1) = \begin{cases} \mathbf{w}(j) & \text{if } \mathbf{w}^t(j) \cdot \mathbf{x}_i > 0 \\ \mathbf{w}(j) + \alpha \mathbf{x}_i & \text{otherwise.} \end{cases}$$

Successive steps cycle through the given points until a complete sweep through the points produces no change at all. Obviously, this process never terminates if the two clusters are not linearly separable, a serious problem which we shall address later; we first need to show that the algorithm converges when the clusters are linearly separable.

Theorem 6.1 The perceptron algorithm terminates when presented with linearly separable clusters. □

Proof: The proof relies upon bounding the norm of the weight vector as a function of the step number and showing that the lower and upper bounds eventually cross, thereby limiting the number of steps.

Since the clusters are linearly separable, there exists some weight vector, $\mathbf{w}^*$, which satisfies all the inequalities. Note that it matters little whether we require a given scalar product to be strictly larger than zero or strictly larger than some small positive constant: as we observed, any solution weight vector can be multiplied by any positive constant to yield another solution vector. Therefore, let us replace the zero on the right-hand side of the inequalities with the positive constant ϵ and assume that our $\mathbf{w}^*$ satisfies the modified inequalities. In discussing the steps taken by the algorithm, we need only consider those in which a correction occurs. Denote by $\mathbf{x}_{i(j)}$ the point which causes the jth correction; then, after j corrections, our weight vector is given by

$$\mathbf{w}(j) = \mathbf{w}(0) + \alpha \sum_{l=1}^{j} \mathbf{x}_{i(l)},$$

and, by assumption, we have $\mathbf{w}^t(j-1) \cdot \mathbf{x}_{i(j)} \leq \epsilon$. (Note that this use of $\mathbf{w}(j)$ differs from our earlier use, which counted all steps.)

We shall derive upper and lower bounds for $\|\mathbf{w}(j)\|^2$ by making judicious use of the existence of $\mathbf{w}^*$. Let us start with the lower bound. We take the scalar product of $\mathbf{w}(j)$ with $\mathbf{w}^*$:

$$\mathbf{w}^t(j) \cdot \mathbf{w}^* = \mathbf{w}^t(0) \cdot \mathbf{w}^* + \alpha \sum_{l=1}^{j} \mathbf{x}_{i(l)}^t \cdot \mathbf{w}^* > \mathbf{w}^t(0) \cdot \mathbf{w}^* + \alpha j \epsilon,$$

where the last step follows from the fact that $\mathbf{w}^*$ satisfies all the inequalities. The left-hand term can be manipulated, using the Cauchy-Schwartz inequality (the norm of the product of two vectors never exceeds the product of the norms of the two vectors):

$$\|\mathbf{w}(j)\|^2 \geq \frac{(\mathbf{w}^t(j) \cdot \mathbf{w}^*)^2}{\|\mathbf{w}^*\|^2}.$$

Combining this inequality with the previous one, for large enough j we obtain

$$\|\mathbf{w}(j)\|^2 > \frac{(\mathbf{w}^t(0) \cdot \mathbf{w}^* + \alpha j \epsilon)^2}{\|\mathbf{w}^*\|^2},$$

which is the desired lower bound.

Now let us derive an upper bound. As we have $\mathbf{w}(l) = \mathbf{w}(l-1) + \alpha \mathbf{x}_{i(l)}$, we can write

$$\|\mathbf{w}(l)\|^2 = \|\mathbf{w}(l-1)\|^2 + 2\alpha \mathbf{w}^t(l-1) \cdot \mathbf{x}_{i(l)} + \alpha^2 \|\mathbf{x}_{i(l)}\|^2.$$

We can bound the last two terms on the right-hand side. The scalar product of the middle term is known to be smaller than ϵ, because each step in our progression involves a correction, and the last term can be bounded in terms of the largest norm, $V = \max_i \|\mathbf{x}_i\|$. Using these two values, we obtain

$$\|\mathbf{w}(l)\|^2 \leq \|\mathbf{w}(l-1)\|^2 + 2\alpha\epsilon + \alpha^2 V^2.$$

Of course, we have one inequality of the type above for each value of l, $1 \le l \le j$. Telescope all the inequalities: all the norms cancel but two, yielding

$$\|\mathbf{w}(j)\|^2 \le \|\mathbf{w}(0)\|^2 + 2\alpha j\epsilon + \alpha^2 j V^2,$$

the desired upper bound.

Now observe that the lower bound is a quadratic function of j, while the upper bound is a linear function of j. Hence there is a value of j at which the two bounds cross: this value is the maximum number of corrective steps that the algorithm may take.

Q.E.D.

Unfortunately, the proof of the theorem is nonconstructive: although it provides us with an equation that determines an upper bound on the number of steps to convergence, one of the terms in the equation is an unknown, the assumed solution weight vector. Thus the perceptron algorithm suffers from a serious drawback: because we cannot set a bound on the time required for convergence, we can only run the algorithm and wait for it to terminate, hardly a tolerable situation from an algorithmic standpoint.

We shall remedy this situation, at least partially, by developing another algorithm, this time purely from the point of view of a gradient method. First, though, let us place the perceptron method within this same context. Since gradient methods attempt to optimize some objective function, we must begin by designing a suitable objective function. This unusual freedom allows us to ensure that the resulting gradient method will indeed produce an optimal solution: it is enough to choose an objective function which has a single extremum. Since gradient methods are based on derivatives, we must also choose a differentiable objective function. Consider then our goal: to satisfy the inequalities of (6.1); and consider our means: to move in the $(n+1)$-dimensional space of the weight vector by following the gradient of the objective function. As any point at which all the inequalities are satisfied is acceptable, we can increase our flexibility by choosing an objective function that has an extremal region instead of a single extremum. The following objective function, to be minimized, satisfies our requirements:

$$J(\mathbf{w}) = - \sum_{\mathbf{w}^t \cdot \mathbf{x}_i < 0} \mathbf{w}^t \cdot \mathbf{x}_i. \tag{6.2}$$

This objective function remains nonnegative for all values of $\mathbf{w}$; it reaches zero only for values of the weight vector which satisfy all of the inequalities of (6.1);

it is differentiable almost everywhere; and, finally, its derivative,[1]

$$\nabla J = \frac{dJ}{d\mathbf{w}} = -\sum_{\mathbf{w}^t \cdot \mathbf{x}_i < 0} \mathbf{x}_i,$$

equals the zero vector when the function itself equals zero (an empty sum) or when the $\mathbf{x}_i$ in the sum happen to cancel each other (a pathological case). Note that the $(n+1)$-dimensional space of the weight vector is composed of regions in which $J(\mathbf{w})$ is differentiable, although the derivative is not defined on the boundaries of these regions, where $\mathbf{w}^t \cdot \mathbf{x}_i$ equals 0 for some $\mathbf{x}_i$. Moving in the direction of the gradient amounts to subtracting (because the function is to be minimized) a positive multiple of the gradient from the current solution vector, so that our iterative scheme becomes:

$$\mathbf{w}(k) = \mathbf{w}(k-1) - \alpha \left. \nabla J \right|_{\mathbf{w} = \mathbf{w}(k-1)} = \mathbf{w}(k-1) + \alpha \sum_{\mathbf{w}^t(k-1) \cdot \mathbf{x}_i < 0} \mathbf{x}_i.$$

This scheme is recognizable as the parallel version of the perceptron algorithm: a step encompasses all given points and the correction consists of adding a positive fraction of all points in error. Hence, the perceptron method is nothing more than the simplest of gradient methods.

How can we then improve upon the perceptron method? Let us recast the problem by replacing our inequalities with equalities; we obtain the set of linear equations:

$$\mathbf{w}^t \cdot \mathbf{x}_i = b_i, \qquad \text{for } b_i > 0.$$

In matrix form, this system of equations can be rewritten as $\mathbf{Xw} = \mathbf{b}$, where the ith row of the matrix $\mathbf{X}$ is the vector $\mathbf{x}_i^t$ and where $\mathbf{b}$ is the N-dimensional vector formed by the b_i. The matrix $\mathbf{X}$ thus has N rows and $n+1$ columns, where N is typically much larger than n; since the resulting linear system is overdetermined, it generally does not admit a solution. But note that the values of $\mathbf{b}$ are arbitrary; we only ask that they remain positive. Thus both $\mathbf{w}$ and $\mathbf{b}$ are variables in this equation and we can derive an iterative scheme that modifies both vectors. Note that, if we had $N = n+1$ and the matrix $\mathbf{X}$ were nonsingular, we could obtain a solution by inverting $\mathbf{X}$ and letting $\mathbf{w} = \mathbf{X}^{-1}\mathbf{b}$. In the general case, $\mathbf{X}$ is rectangular and thus does not have an inverse; yet, like every matrix, it has a *pseudo-inverse* (also known as a *Moore-Penrose inverse*), $\mathbf{X}^{\#}$. Such an inverse always exists and can be computed at no greater expense than the inverse of a

---

[1] The derivative of a scalar function with respect to a vector of n components is a vector of n components, where the ith component is simply the partial derivative of the scalar function with respect to the ith component of the vector variable.

comparably sized nonsingular square matrix, using a similar process of partial diagonalization.[2] When the matrix $\mathbf{X}^t\mathbf{X}$ has an inverse, we define the pseudo-inverse of $\mathbf{X}$ as $\mathbf{X}^{\#} = (\mathbf{X}^t\mathbf{X})^{-1}\mathbf{X}^t$. When that inverse does not exist, one can show that a small perturbation of the matrix $\mathbf{X}^t\mathbf{X}$ to $\mathbf{Y} = \mathbf{X}^t\mathbf{X} + \epsilon\mathbf{I}$ makes the inverse exist and thus allows us to define the pseudo-inverse of $\mathbf{X}$ as the limit of $\mathbf{Y}^{-1}\mathbf{X}^t$ as ϵ goes to zero. Among other things, the pseudo-inverse behaves as closely to an inverse as possible: although $\mathbf{X}\mathbf{X}^{\#}$ is not in general equal to the identity matrix, we do have $\mathbf{X}^{\#}\mathbf{X} = \mathbf{I}$. Most useful to us is the following result, which we quote without proving.

Theorem 6.2 Given an overdetermined linear system, $\mathbf{A}\mathbf{x} = \mathbf{b}$, the vector $\mathbf{x}^{\#} = \mathbf{A}^{\#}\mathbf{b}$ minimizes the squared error, $\|\mathbf{A}\mathbf{x} - \mathbf{b}\|^2$.   □

In other words, although our system normally does not admit a solution, multiplying both sides by the pseudo-inverse will yield the best possible least-square approximation to a solution. And here is the germ of an iterative improvement procedure: let the objective function be the squared error, $J(\mathbf{w}, \mathbf{b}) = \|\mathbf{X}\mathbf{w} - \mathbf{b}\|^2$ and make use of the pseudo-inverse.

While $J(\mathbf{w}, \mathbf{b})$ is a function of two vector variables, it can also be thought of as a function of $N + n + 1$ scalar variables; since the gradient of the latter is zero exactly when the gradients of the former, with respect to each vector variable, are zero, both points of view are equivalent, but it is more convenient to work with the vector variables. We can follow one gradient while keeping the other equal to zero at all times. The two gradients are

$$\frac{\partial J}{\partial \mathbf{w}} = 2\mathbf{X}^t(\mathbf{X}\mathbf{w} - \mathbf{b})$$

and

$$\frac{\partial J}{\partial \mathbf{b}} = -2(\mathbf{X}\mathbf{w} - \mathbf{b}).$$

Since the vector $\mathbf{b}$ is constrained to remain positive at all times, it is simpler to follow its gradient and then to update $\mathbf{w}$, where we have more freedom, to reflect the change in $\mathbf{b}$. Thus we set the gradient with respect to $\mathbf{w}$ to zero:

$$\mathbf{X}^t(\mathbf{X}\mathbf{w} - \mathbf{b}) = 0.$$

If the inverse of $\mathbf{X}^t\mathbf{X}$ exists, we can solve for $\mathbf{w}$:

$$\mathbf{w} = (\mathbf{X}^t\mathbf{X})^{-1}\mathbf{X}^t\mathbf{b} = \mathbf{X}^{\#}\mathbf{b}.$$

---

[2]Most packages for numerical linear algebra include routines for computing the pseudo-inverse.

Moreover, it can be shown that $\mathbf{X}^{\#}\mathbf{b}$ is the correct solution even when $\mathbf{X}^{t}\mathbf{X}$ is singular, an intuitively clear consequence of our definition of the pseudo-inverse. This equation allows us to update $\mathbf{w}$ given a new value of $\mathbf{b}$. As to this latter, updating it is simply a matter of following its gradient subject to keeping all of its components positive. This constraint forces some alteration to the updating scheme. Whereas the simple gradient method suggests

$$\mathbf{b}(k+1) = \mathbf{b}(k) + 2\alpha\big(\mathbf{X}\mathbf{w}(k) - \mathbf{b}(k)\big),$$

which can result in negative values for some components of $\mathbf{b}$, we shall use instead

$$\mathbf{b}(k+1) = \mathbf{b}(k) + \alpha\big(|\mathbf{X}\mathbf{w}(k) - \mathbf{b}(k)| + \mathbf{X}\mathbf{w}(k) - \mathbf{b}(k)\big)$$

(where the absolute value is taken component by component), which limits corrections to nonnegative increments. It remains to define the stopping conditions for this updating scheme. Since we only want to ensure that all points represented by $\mathbf{X}$ fall on the same side of the hyperplane determined by $\mathbf{w}$, we can stop the algorithm as soon as the condition $\mathbf{X}\mathbf{w} > \mathbf{0}$ is fulfilled. What then of nonseparability? Looking at the correction scheme, we note that, whenever $\mathbf{X}\mathbf{w} \leq \mathbf{b}$ (component by component), no correction will be applied, so the scheme would enter an infinite loop: this is our indication of nonseparability.

To summarize, our iterative learning algorithm proceeds as follows:

- Form the matrix $\mathbf{X}$ and compute its pseudo-inverse $\mathbf{X}^{\#}$.

- Pick an arbitrary initial vector $\mathbf{b}(0) > \mathbf{0}$ and arbitrary positive constant α, $0 < \alpha < 1$. (We need $\alpha < 1$ to ensure convergence.)

- At step k, form the weight vector $\mathbf{w}(k) = \mathbf{X}^{\#}\mathbf{b}(k)$, the vector $\mathbf{X}\mathbf{w}(k)$, and the error vector $\mathbf{e}(k) = \mathbf{X}\mathbf{w}(k) - \mathbf{b}(k)$.

- If $\mathbf{X}\mathbf{w}(k) > \mathbf{0}$, then stop: $\mathbf{w}(k)$ is the desired solution. If $\mathbf{e}(k) \leq \mathbf{0}$, then stop: the clusters are not linearly separable. Otherwise, let $\mathbf{b}(k+1) = \mathbf{b}(k) + \alpha\big(|\mathbf{e}(k)| + \mathbf{e}(k)\big)$, and return to the previous step.

The learning scheme thus defined is generally known as the *Ho-Kashyap* or *least-mean-square-error* learning algorithm. Since it is a parallel correction scheme, it may be expected to converge very rapidly, as indeed it does. Since it also terminates whether or not the points are linearly separable, it is clearly preferable to the perceptron method, in spite of the computational expense of determining $\mathbf{X}^{\#}$, a computation which occurs only once and the cost of which depends more on the number of dimensions of the space than on the number of points involved. We still need to prove that our stopping conditions are correct.

Theorem 6.3 The Ho-Kashyap algorithm converges in a finite number of steps to a solution if the clusters are linearly separable and discloses evidence of non-separability otherwise. $\square$

For an outline of the proof, see Exercise 6.5.

The perceptron and the Ho-Kashyap algorithms are two examples of gradient methods applied to a search problem. As is often the case with gradient methods, complexity analysis must be reduced to experimental work, as the speed of convergence cannot be bounded in a meaningful way.

We now turn to the clustering problem and to iterative algorithms that, while clearly inspired by gradient methods, no longer exhibit some of their basic traits. Recall that feasible solutions for k-clustering problems are partitions of the elements into k nonempty subsets. Given any such partition, how can we improve upon it? First we must decide what is an appropriate choice for a step. In the spirit of parallel gradient methods, we can let one step process all the elements and update the composition of all the clusters. Each cluster, $C_i = \{x_{i_1}, x_{i_2}, \dots, x_{i_{k_i}}\}$, contributes the sum of all its pairwise dissimilarities to the total measure. Assume for the moment that the elements are points in n-dimensional space and let the dissimilarity between two such points, $\mathbf{x}$ and $\mathbf{y}$, be defined as the square of the Euclidean distance between them, $\|\mathbf{x} - \mathbf{y}\|^2$. Then the contribution of cluster C_i to the total measure can be written as

$$f(i) = \frac{1}{2} \sum_{j=1}^{k_i} \sum_{l=1}^{k_i} \|\mathbf{x}_{i_j} - \mathbf{x}_{i_l}\|^2.$$

Let $\bar{\mathbf{x}}_i$ stand for the mean of all the points in C_i; we can rewrite $f(i)$ as

$$
\begin{aligned}
f(i) &= \frac{1}{2} \sum_{j=1}^{k_i} \sum_{l=1}^{k_i} \|\mathbf{x}_{i_j} - \mathbf{x}_{i_l}\|^2 \\
&= \frac{1}{2} \sum_{j=1}^{k_i} \sum_{l=1}^{k_i} (\mathbf{x}_{i_j} - \mathbf{x}_{i_l})^t (\mathbf{x}_{i_j} - \mathbf{x}_{i_l}) \\
&= \frac{1}{2} \sum_{j=1}^{k_i} \sum_{l=1}^{k_i} (\|\mathbf{x}_{i_j}\|^2 + \|\mathbf{x}_{i_l}\|^2 - 2\mathbf{x}_{i_j}^t \mathbf{x}_{i_l}) \\
&= \sum_{j=1}^{k_i} \left(k_i \|\mathbf{x}_{i_j}\|^2 - \mathbf{x}_{i_j}^t \sum_{l=1}^{k_i} \mathbf{x}_{i_l} \right) \\
&= \sum_{j=1}^{k_i} (k_i \|\mathbf{x}_{i_j}\|^2 - k_i \mathbf{x}_{i_j}^t \bar{\mathbf{x}}_i)
\end{aligned}
$$

$$= k_i \sum_{j=1}^{k_i} \|\mathbf{x}_{i_j}\|^2 - k_i^2 \|\bar{\mathbf{x}}_i\|^2$$

$$= k_i \sum_{j=1}^{k_i} \|\mathbf{x}_{i_j}\|^2 + k_i^2 \|\bar{\mathbf{x}}_i\|^2 - 2k_i^2 \|\bar{\mathbf{x}}_i\|^2$$

$$= k_i \sum_{j=1}^{k_i} \|\mathbf{x}_{i_j}\|^2 + k_i^2 \|\bar{\mathbf{x}}_i\|^2 - 2k_i \bar{\mathbf{x}}_i^t \sum_{l=1}^{k_i} \mathbf{x}_{i_l}$$

$$= k_i \sum_{j=1}^{k_i} \left(\|\mathbf{x}_{i_j}\|^2 + \|\bar{\mathbf{x}}_i\|^2 - 2\bar{\mathbf{x}}_i^t \mathbf{x}_{i_j} \right)$$

$$= k_i \sum_{j=1}^{k_i} (\mathbf{x}_{i_j} - \bar{\mathbf{x}}_i)^t (\mathbf{x}_{i_j} - \bar{\mathbf{x}}_i)$$

$$= k_i \sum_{j=1}^{k_i} \|\bar{\mathbf{x}}_i - \mathbf{x}_{i_j}\|^2.$$

Thus, with this choice of dissimilarity measure, the total intracluster dissimilarity turns out to be a least-square-error criterion. This last formulation lends itself more easily to iterative improvement than the first: since the criterion depends on the distance of each point to the mean of its cluster, an obvious step is to minimize this distance for each cluster. Because the cluster means will vary as we redistribute points among the clusters, we can let the process take place in two steps: in one step we compute the mean of each existing cluster, and in the other we reassign each point to the closest existing cluster mean. In the process, one or more clusters can conceivably become empty—although such occurrences do not seem to arise in practice; in that case, we can simply decrease the value of k accordingly. These two steps are then repeated until a stable configuration is reached. The resulting algorithm is known as the *k-means* clustering algorithm; its steps are summarized as follows:

- Arbitrarily choose k distinct cluster "means."

- Redistribute the points by associating each point with the closest mean, as computed in the previous step.

- Compute the new mean of each of the k clusters. If the means remain unchanged, then stop; otherwise, return to the previous step.

Since the choice of initial means is arbitrary, one can use a variety of methods (greedy or otherwise) to derive a promising initial clustering. Figure 6.1 illustrates the progress of the algorithm on a population of 205 samples in two

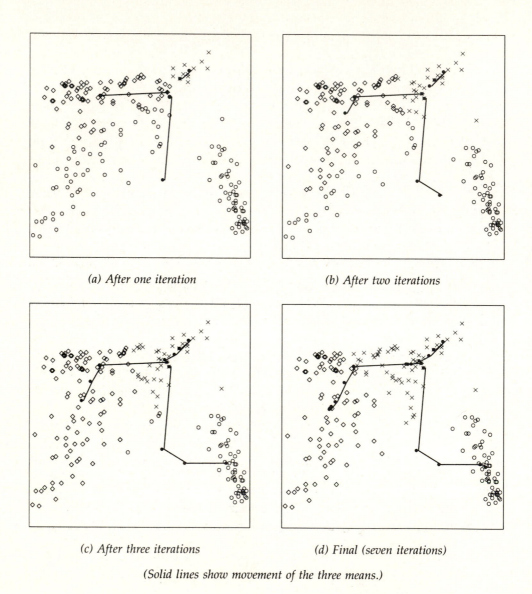

(a) After one iteration   (b) After two iterations

(c) After three iterations   (d) Final (seven iterations)

(Solid lines show movement of the three means.)

Figure 6.1: A Sample Run of the k-Means Procedure

dimensions, with k set to three. Our choice of initial configuration was truly arbitrary: it set the three cluster means to the first three samples in the set. The thin lines show the movement of the cluster means from their initial to their final configuration; the three clusters are shown by using different symbols for their elements.

In practice, the k-means clustering algorithm is widely used (with *ad hoc* modifications), although it suffers from a number of serious drawbacks, namely: (i) no proof of convergence has been found for it, although it appears always to converge in a finite number of steps; (ii) it does not always converge to an optimal solution, and there are no known bounds on the value of the solutions it produces; (iii) the choice of the initial means strongly influences the outcome; and (iv) the least-square-error criterion forces the breakup of large clusters, even very well defined ones. That we appear unable to prove convergence at first seems very surprising in view of the fact that the search space is finite, so that we need only prove that the algorithm does not loop. This proof, in turn, would only require us to show that the objective function decreases at each step—a property that we expect every iterative improvement algorithm to possess, but that we cannot establish for this algorithm. The problem comes from the fact that only a small amount of information, the mean of each cluster, is retained from one step to the next, with the result that successive clusterings can differ considerably.

Now let us address the same clustering problem, with the same objective function, but using iterative approaches that more closely resemble the description given at the beginning of this chapter. In order to keep changes small, we want a sequential rather than a parallel approach. An obvious choice is to choose as the elementary step the transfer of an element from one cluster to another, subject to not leaving any cluster empty; alternate or additional choices are possible, such as exchanges of elements between clusters, but the transfer of a single element has the advantage of being computationally undemanding. At any stage of the algorithm, there are at most n candidates for transfer, each with $k - 1$ new destinations, so that we must choose among $\Theta(kn)$ candidate moves. Moving element x from cluster C_i to cluster C_j induces a change in the total intracluster dissimilitude equal to:

$$\sum_{z \in C_j} d(x, z) - \sum_{y \in C_i} d(x, y).$$

Thus we need not compute the complete measure in order to decide which of the candidate steps will contribute the largest improvement to the objective function; instead we need only look at all elements of the two candidate clusters. This step requires $\Theta(n^2)$ work—a rather expensive step. As any change that improves the current solution is desirable, we need not examine all possible changes, but can accept and execute the first positive change; this modification can considerably shorten the time requirements of an average step. Because each step improves the value of the objective function and because there are only a finite number of feasible solutions, repeated iterations must bring us to a stage where any single transfer is contraindicated, at which time the algorithm has converged. The maximum number of iterations is rather difficult to compute and not likely to be representative of typical applications. Unfortunately, the resulting clustering is not guaranteed to be optimal; in particular, it is easy to devise an example where no single element transfer improves the value of the objective function, but where a multiple element transfer achieves an improvement. In the next section, we encounter another example of this behavior.

6.2 The Travelling Salesperson Problem

Of the problems discussed in the previous chapter, the travelling salesperson problem is the best candidate for application of iterative improvement methods. As we saw in Section 5.1, numerous greedy methods have been developed for this problem, but none leads to an optimal solution. The output of each such greedy method provides an excellent starting point for application of an iterative improvement algorithm.

Given a suboptimal tour, how can we improve it through local changes? We should like to develop a family of increasingly complex steps, each member of the family presumably more computationally demanding, but also more effective. An ideal family is one in which the most complex step is sure to lead to an optimal solution, even though it is also certain to be computationally infeasible. Consider a tour: to modify it with minimal changes, the simplest approach consists of removing some edges, thereby breaking the tour into paths, and then reconnecting the paths in a different manner. Such an approach does yield a family of steps, since its complexity directly depends on the number of paths into which the tour is to be broken, from a minimum of two to a maximum of n, the number of cities.

The simplest member of the family amounts to no more than removing from the tour two nonadjacent edges and reconnecting the two paths thus formed in the only alternate manner possible. Let the two edges be (x, y) and (u, v), where all four vertices are distinct, and let the old tour move from x to y, then along the path from y to u, then from u to v, and finally back to x. Our basic step replaces these two edges with the edges (x, u) and (y, v), and the new tour now moves from x to u, then along the path from u to y (in the opposite direction from the previous tour, which implies that this algorithm makes sense only when applied

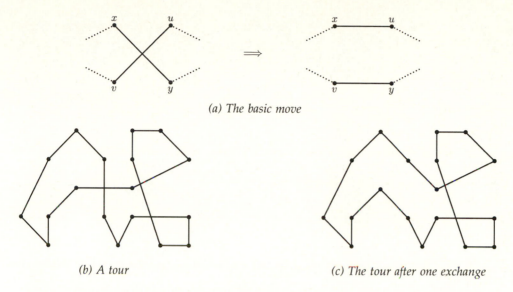

(a) The basic move

(b) A tour

(c) The tour after one exchange

Figure 6.2: Producing a New Tour by Exchanging Pairs of Nonadjacent Edges

to symmetric travelling salesperson problems), then from y to v, and finally back to x (this time in the same direction as before). This process is illustrated in Figure 6.2. Such an exchange induces a change in the length of the tour equal to $d(x, u) + d(y, v) - d(x, y) - d(u, v)$. Our iterative improvement algorithm just scans all eligible edge pairs and, if any such pair can be advantageously replaced, proceeds to replace it. Since the replacement occurs only when the resulting tour is strictly shorter than the existing one, the algorithm must terminate. At termination, the resulting tour is one which cannot be improved upon by any exchange of pairs of edges; such a tour is said to be *2-optimal*.

More complex steps in general remove k edges and reconnect the resulting k paths in a new manner—only now there exist up to $2^{k-1}(k - 1)!$ alternatives; the eight alternatives arising when three nonadjacent edges are broken are shown in Figure 6.3. Again, each such step takes place only if the resulting tour is strictly shorter than the existing one, so that the iterative improvement algorithm must terminate, producing a *k-optimal* tour. The parameter k effectively defines the range of our view in the "landscape" of the state space. A point in the state space may be a local extremum with respect to one member of the family (i.e., k-optimal), but this same point may not be an extremum if we extend the scope of our simple step (e.g., switch to $k+1$ exchanges). In the limit, an n-optimal tour is an optimal tour, although breaking all the edges of a tour and reconnecting the degenerate paths that result is nothing other than solving the original problem.

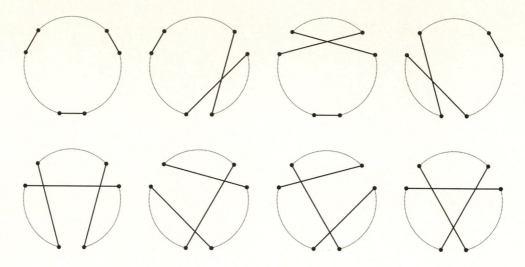

Figure 6.3: The Eight Ways in Which Three Paths Can Be Reconnected

The rapid growth, both in the number of ways to form the k paths and in the number of ways to reconnect them, shows the impossibility of guaranteeing that a tour is k-optimal for even moderate values of k. This limitation raises many questions and opens the door to many heuristics. Notice that, as stated, the method remains rather ambiguous; among all sets of k edges, the replacement of which improves the tour, which are we supposed to choose? Should we simply accept the first improvement found, or should we consider all sets of k edges, searching for the very best improvement possible at each iteration? There is no reason to believe that the sequence of best-possible improvements will converge to a better solution than any other sequence of improvements, but it may converge in fewer steps. The uncertain balance between convergence rate and the cost of a step makes it difficult to say which is the better strategy in general.

Other questions arise, for which there are no firm answers, but only practical advice. What is the initial solution on which an iterative improvement algorithm should be run? Does using a good initial approximation narrow the region of the state space that can be explored to so great an extent that the optimal solution (or better suboptimal solutions) can no longer be found? Can the algorithm be trapped into converging to poor local extrema? If so, should it be run repeatedly, either with different initial solutions or with a random component (especially appropriate if the algorithm accepts the first improvement found)? Because iterative improvement algorithms are typically slow, they are run on good ini-

Table 6.1: The Effect of the k-Optimal Iterative Improvement Algorithm

Algorithm	Tour best/average/worst	Gain in length largest/average/smallest	Iterations fewest/average/most
2-optimal best	13065/13757.7/14742	1643/365.7/0	0/3.7/15
2-optimal first	12985/13752.8/14742	1607/370.6/0	0/4.4/19
3-optimal best	12985/13295.7/13774	1777/827.7/52	1/6.2/14
3-optimal first	12985/13305.6/13886	1804/817.8/52	1/10.9/26

tial solutions, since the number of steps needed to ensure local optimality is then much reduced. While formal analysis of the structure of the state space is usually not possible, experiments indicate that for many problems local extrema abound, many of them not very good. Thus the algorithm must be run several times and the best solution retained. We ran 2- and 3-optimal improvement on the 57-city problem of Section 5.1; the results are given in Table 6.1. Each algorithm was run on each of the tours produced by the random insertion heuristic of Section 5.1. In general, statistical tests can be used to determine when additional trials are not likely to give better results.

Little is known about the rate of convergence of these methods, nor is there much known about the quality of the solutions obtained. For a fixed k, we do not know how fast the method converges from an arbitrary initial tour, nor can we bound the quality of the solution obtained. If we increase the value of k, using as the starting point for the $(k + 1)$-optimal method the tour obtained by the k-optimal method, we know that the new tour can be no worse than the previous and that eventually it converges to the optimum, but we do not know the rate of convergence as a function of k. (One of the few known results is rather discouraging, since it states that, even for values of k as large as $n/4$, the k-optimal solution may be twice as costly as the true optimal solution.)

When the convergence is reasonably fast, we can approximate k-optimality by doing limited searches with larger values of k. Using a method that reconnects k paths in an optimal manner (something that can be achieved, for values of k around 12, with dynamic programming, a technique discussed in Volume II), we can selectively break k edges according to some heuristic criterion. Suitable criteria readily suggest themselves for the travelling salesperson problem in the plane, a special case of particular importance in practice. The algorithm terminates when every set of edges proposed by the heuristic fails to yield an improvement. While not guaranteed to be k-optimal, the tour may be better than k'-optimal tours for $k' < k$. The current best algorithm for solving the travelling salesperson problem, due to Lin and Kernighan, uses a combination of the above ideas (see the bibliography); it routinely finds the optimal solution to problems with 400 cities. Its authors note that the algorithm, when started with many different initial tours, converges to just a few local minima, thus making it likely that the best of these is the true optimum (something that cannot be verified by any known method on large problems).

We mentioned briefly earlier that some controlled random motion may prevent the algorithm from getting trapped at poor local minima. This idea is at the basis of a technique called *simulated annealing*, which allows steps to worsen the current solution with a probability that depends on the amount of disimprovement, the current value of the solution, and the time spent so far in exploring the state space. For certain $\mathcal{NP}$-hard problems, where poor local extrema abound but are not far from good local extrema, this technique outperforms straightforward iterative improvement, at the cost of much longer running times. We consider this and other extensions of iterative improvement in Volume II.

6.3 Marriages and Matchings

In this and the next two sections, we address a family of problems that can be solved with iterative improvement methods. These problems, *matching* and *network flow*, arise often in applications, particularly in the areas of communication, transportation, and scheduling. The algorithms developed for these problems are among the most intriguing polynomial-time algorithms known; while they are based on simple ideas, they have evolved through a large number of refinements, so that the most efficient versions are rather intricate. One author has gone so far as to write that, while network flow algorithms indeed run in polynomial time, they require exponential time for coding by an average programmer. We shall endeavor to show that such is not the case and that, with an understanding of the underlying ideas, one can code any practical matching or network flow algorithm.

Let us begin by introducing some of these problems. We have already seen the bipartite matching, or marriage, problem (Problem 29). Since the condition of heterosexual marriages is purely anthropomorphic, it makes sense to extend the matching problem to general graphs.

Problem 34 [Maximum Cardinality Matching] Given an undirected graph, find the largest subset, M, of edges such that no two edges in M share an endpoint.

□

A variant of this problem is the *perfect matching* problem, where the graph has an even number of vertices and where the question is to determine whether or not there exists a matching that includes all vertices. Matching problems do not appear very serious when phrased in terms of marriages, but they prove very useful as models of various assignment problems, such as allocating tasks among a population of workers, representing constituencies on a committee, preparing interview schedules, and so on.

An important formulation of bipartite matching is the problem known as finding a *set of distinct representatives*. An instance of this problem is given by a set, S, and collection of subsets of that set, $C \subseteq 2^S$; the problem is to find a subset, R, of S, with $|R| = |C|$, such that each subset in the collection C has a distinct representative in R. Note that the representative element of a subset in C may very well belong to other subsets in C. The elements of S can be viewed as people, the elements of C as committees, and the set R as the heads of the committees. Given the committees, the goal is to select committee heads so that no person heads more than one committee. More formally, we seek an injection, $h: C \to S$, such that, for all $C \in C$, $h(C) \in C$; the set R is then $h(C)$. This problem may be rephrased as a bipartite matching problem by setting up one vertex for each subset in C (the left-hand side vertices) and one vertex for each element of S (the right-hand side vertices), with an edge from a subset to each of its elements. An edge of the matching, (C, s), defines s as the head of committee C, so that we can find a set of distinct representatives if and only if the maximum cardinality matching has size $|C|$. Since an arbitrary instance may have no solution, we are interested in conditions which make a solution possible. It turns out that a complete characterization is possible in very simple terms.

Theorem 6.4 [Hall] An instance, (S, C), of the set of distinct representatives problem admits a solution if and only if, for each i, the union of any i subsets in C has at least i elements.

□

This theorem is an alternate formulation of the König-Hall theorem on bipartite matching, which we shall shortly prove.

We can easily devise a greedy approximation algorithm for the general matching problem. As the vertices hardest to match are those with the fewest neighbors, we proceed as follows: begin by assigning to each vertex a priority equal to its degree; then repeatedly pick the remaining vertex of highest priority (i.e., lowest degree), match it with the lowest-degree vertex among its neighbors,

(a) The current matching   (b) The optimal matching

Figure 6.4: A Matching that Cannot be Increased Without Altering Matched Pairs

remove these two vertices from the graph, and update the priority structure to reflect the changed degrees of the other neighbors of these two vertices. A straightforward implementation using Fibonacci heaps runs in $\Theta(|V|\log|V|+|E|)$ time and obtains excellent, if not optimal, results. Even when this greedy approach does not return the optimal solution, it provides a good departure point for an iterative improvement algorithm.

In order to develop a suitable iterative step, let us first consider very small instances of the problem. The smallest matching consists simply of two vertices joined by an edge; the next smallest matching has two pairs of vertices, with each pair joined by an edge; and so on. Thus the iterative step must add two vertices at each step in such a way as to create a matching with one additional edge. In keeping with the idea of iterative methods, each step may well alter the current collection of edges: situations often arise where a matching cannot be increased by simply adding a pair of matched vertices, but only by adding two vertices and reshuffling the matched pairs, as illustrated in Figure 6.4. The change in the set of matched vertices is small (two vertices are added), while the change in the set of matched edges is dramatic (there may be no common edge between the old set and the new set). The path of five edges of Figure 6.4(a) is an example of an augmenting path.

Definition 6.1 Let $G = (V, E)$ be a graph and M be a matching. An *alternating path* with respect to M is a path such that the first and the last edges of the path are not matched and such that every second edge on the path is matched. If the first and last vertices on the path are unmatched, then the alternating path is called an *augmenting path*.   □

An immediate consequence of the definition is that an alternating path has an odd number of edges, with unmatched edges outnumbering matched edges by one. Furthermore, if both the first and last vertices of an alternating path are unmatched, then reversing the status of all edges on the path will produce a larger matching—which explains the name given to such paths. (Note that our greedy algorithm uses augmenting paths, but only trivial ones: each is composed of a single unmatched edge between unmatched vertices.) More significantly, the absence of any augmenting path in a matching guarantees optimality.

Theorem 6.5 [Berge] A matching is of maximum cardinality if and only if the graph has no augmenting path with respect to the matching.   □

Proof: The "only if" part follows immediately from our remarks. Assume then that $G = (V, E)$ has no augmenting path with respect to M. Further assume, *ad absurdum*, that M is not maximum and let M' be a matching of larger cardinality. Let $M \oplus M'$ denote the symmetric difference of M and M', i.e., $M \oplus M' = (M \cup M') - (M \cap M')$, and consider the subgraph $G' = (V, M \oplus M')$. All vertices of G' have degree two or less, because they have at most one incident edge from each of M and M'; moreover, every connected component of G' is one of: (i) a single vertex; (ii) a cycle of even length, with edges drawn alternately from M and M'; or (iii) a path with edges drawn alternately from M and M'. As the cardinality of M' exceeds that of M, there exists at least one path composed of alternating edges from M and M', with more edges from M' than from M. The path must begin and end with edges from M' and the endpoints are unmatched in M, because the path is a connected component of G'. Hence this path is an augmenting path, which yields the desired contradiction.

Q.E.D.

This theorem provides the basis for an iterative algorithm for the maximum matching problem:

- Begin with an arbitrary (possibly empty) matching.

- Repeatedly discover an augmenting path and switch the status of all edges along it, until no augmenting path can be found.

Note that the second step cannot be repeated more than a linear number of times. Hence, maximum matching reduces to the problem of discovering an augmenting path. This turns out to be an easy task in bipartite graphs, but a more complex one in general graphs.

For bipartite graphs, we can produce an exact characterization of maximum matchings and of the conditions under which there exists a *complete* matching, i.e., one in which every vertex from the smaller side of the graph is matched. We begin by restating Hall's theorem in language more appropriate to our setting.

Theorem 6.6 [König-Hall]   A bipartite graph has a complete matching if and only if each subset of vertices on the smaller side is connected to at least as many vertices on the larger side; formally, if we denote the vertex partition by $V = \{V_l, V_r\}$ and choose $|V_l| \le |V_r|$, we require that $|X| \le |R(X)|$ hold for all $X \subseteq V_l$, where $R(X)$ stands for the set of vertices in V_r that are connected by an edge to some vertex in X.   □

Proof: The necessity of the condition is obvious. We prove the sufficiency by induction on the size of V_l. For $|V_l| = 1$, we can choose any edge incident upon the lone vertex of V_l; such an edge must exist, since we have $|V_l| \leq |R(V_l)|$. In the induction step, two cases may arise.

Case 1: $|X| < |R(X)|$ holds for all $\emptyset \subset X \subset V_l$. Pick any element, $v \in V_l$ and use any edge incident upon v to define the matching for this element. Let v' be the corresponding vertex of V_r. Define a new bipartite matching problem with a left side of $V_l - \{v\}$, a right side of $V_r - \{v'\}$, and with those edges of the original problem that had neither v nor v' as an endpoint. This new problem obeys the hypothesis of the theorem, i.e., $|X| \leq |R(X)|$ holds for any subset X, since $|X| < |R(X)|$ holds in the original problem and the new $R(X)$ can be at most one element smaller. Applying the inductive hypothesis now completes the matching.

Case 2: $|X| = |R(X)|$ holds for some X, $\emptyset \subset X \subset V_l$. Since X is a proper subset of V_l, we must have $|X| < |V_l|$, so that the inductive hypothesis applies and we can form a complete matching between X and $R(X)$. Now consider the new problem defined by $V_l - X$ and $V_r - R(X)$. In this problem, any subset, $A \subseteq V_l - X$, obeys $|A| \leq |R(A)|$, since otherwise we would have $|A \cup X| > |R(A \cup X)|$ in the original problem. Thus the inductive hypothesis applies and we can complete the matching.

$$Q.E.D.$$

Recall from Problem 24 that a vertex cover of a graph, $G = (V, E)$, is a subset of the vertices, U, such that every edge in E has at least one endpoint in U. For any graph, one can easily verify that the size of any matching can be no greater than the size of any vertex cover; in particular, the size of the maximum matching can be no greater than the size of the minimum vertex cover. While, in general, the size of the maximum matching can be less than the size of the minimum vertex cover, these two sizes must be equal for bipartite graphs.

Theorem 6.7 [König-Egerváry]   The size of a maximum bipartite matching equals the size of a minimum vertex cover.   □

Proof: We show that a minimum vertex cover, U, can be used to define a matching of equal cardinality. Let S and T be the sets of vertices on the left and right sides. Every edge from S to T falls into one of three classes: (i) both endpoints are in U; (ii) only the left endpoint is in U; and (iii) only the right endpoint is in U. (The fourth potential category, in which neither endpoint is in U, must be empty, as U is a vertex cover.) For each vertex of U, we select an edge from the second or third category so as to form a matching; note that no edge drawn from the second category can share an endpoint with any edge drawn from the third category—a most helpful situation, since we must ensure that no two selected edges share an endpoint. Let $U_S = U \cap S$ and $U_T = U \cap T$; we consider

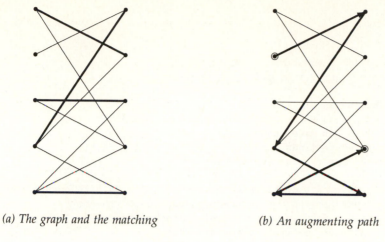

(a) The graph and the matching   *(b) An augmenting path*

Figure 6.5: An Augmenting Path in a Bipartite Graph

only the vertices in U_S, since the situation with respect to U_T is identical. With respect to U_S and the edges in the second category, our problem reduces to finding a complete matching between U_S and $R(U_S)$. There cannot exist $A \subseteq U_S$ with $|A| > |R(A)|$, since replacing A with $R(A)$ in U would yield a vertex cover smaller than U, contradicting our hypothesis. Thus the conditions of Theorem 6.6 are satisfied.

$$Q.E.D.$$

This theorem appears in several formulations and has itself been generalized (see Exercises 6.12 and 6.13). While providing insights into the structure of matchings, these theorems do not lead to a computationally feasible procedure, since the enumeration of all subsets would require exponential time.

We thus return to the construction of augmenting paths. In a bipartite graph, any augmenting path begins on one side of the graph and ends on the other. Thus a search algorithm can simply start at any unmatched vertex on one side of the graph, say the left side, and traverse any edge to the other side. If the endpoint on the right side is also unmatched, then an augmenting path, consisting of a single unmatched edge, has been found. If the other endpoint is matched, then the algorithm traverses that matched edge to the left side and follows any unmatched edge, if one exists, to an unvisited vertex on the right side. The process is repeated until either an augmenting path is found or a dead end on the left side is reached. Unmatched edges are always traversed from the left side to the right side and matched edges in the opposite direction. Figure 6.5 shows a graph with a partial matching and an augmenting path with respect to that matching. If a dead end is reached, we must explore other paths until we find

```
const unmatched = 0;

type PartnerName = unmatched .. MaxVertex;
     partners = array [vertex] of PartnerName;

procedure Match(var G: graph;
                    var error: boolean; (* Set if graph not bipartite. *)
                    var mate: partners);
  (* This procedure finds a maximum matching in a bipartite graph
     in O(V*E) time, recording the answer in mate[ ]. *)

  (* Program assumes the existence of a queue package with operations
         procedure CreateQueue, procedure ResetQueue (to empty),
         function IsEmptyQueue: boolean, procedure Enqueue(v: vertex), and
         procedure Dequeue(var v: vertex). *)

  label 1;
  const null = 0; (* nil *)
  type BackPointers = array [vertex] of integer; (* vertices U {null} *)
       Classification = array [1..MaxVertex] of vertex;
  var NumLefts: integer; (* number of left-side vertices *)
      lefts: Classification; (* the left-side vertices *)
      back: BackPointers; (* backpointers in the breadth-first search *)
      i: integer;
      v, w: vertex;
      p: PtrToNode;

  procedure Augment(l, r: integer);
    (* Augments the matching while traversing the augmenting path in reverse. *)
    var tempR: integer;
    begin
      (* Changing the status of the unmatched edges along the augmenting path
         automatically changes the status of the matched edges as well. *)
      repeat
        tempR := mate[l];
        mate[l] := r; mate[r] := l;
        l := back[l]; r := tempR
      until l = null
    end; (* Augment *)

  begin (* Match *)
    CreateQueue;
    (* Define the bipartite structure of the graph (see Exercise 4.8),
       exiting with an error, if the graph is not bipartite. *)
    ...
    (* Form the empty, or other initial matching. *)
    for v := 1 to G.size do mate[v] := unmatched;
```

```
1: (* Find a shortest augmenting path, if one exists. *)

   (* Reset for the next iteration--keep only previous matching. *)
   ResetQueue;
   for i := 1 to NumLefts do
     begin
       back[lefts[i]] := null; (* set backpointer *)
       if mate[lefts[i]] = unmatched then Enqueue(lefts[i])
     end;

   (* Perform breadth-first search looking for an augmenting path. *)
   while not IsEmptyQueue do (* but leave loop as soon as path found *)
     begin
       Dequeue(v);
       p := G.AdjLists[v];
       while p <> nil do
         begin
           (* If the right-side vertex is unmatched, we have found
              an augmenting path... *)
           if mate[p^.id] = unmatched
             then begin
                    Augment(v,p^.id); (* ...so augment and iterate. *)
                    goto 1
                  end
             else begin
                    (* Continue the search. *)
                    (* As the edge out of a right-side vertex is forced,
                       move directly to the next left-side vertex. *)
                    w := mate[p^.id];
                    if back[w] = null (* as w is matched, it is unseen *)
                      then begin
                             back[w] := v; (* set backpointer *)
                             Enqueue(w)
                           end
                  end;
           p := p^.next
         end
     end
   (* Maximum matching has been found. *)
end; (* Match *)
```

Program 6.1: An Augmenting Path Solution to Bipartite Matching

an augmenting path or run out of possibilities. In developing an augmenting path, choices arise in only two places: in selecting an initial unmatched vertex and in selecting an unmatched edge out of a vertex on the left side. In order to examine all possibilities for augmenting paths, we need to explore these choices in some systematic way; because all augmenting paths make exactly the same contribution of one additional matched edge, we should search for the shortest augmenting paths.

Consider forming an auxiliary directed graph with vertex set $V_l \cup \{s, t\}$ and arc set defined as follows. There is an arc from s to every unmatched vertex in V_l. There is an arc from v_1 to v_2, both in V_l, if there is in G a two-edge path from v_1 to v_2 consisting of an unmatched edge followed by a matched edge. Finally, there is an arc from $v \in V_l$ to t if there is an edge in G from v to an unmatched right-side vertex. Note that, by construction, every augmenting path in G corresponds to a simple path from s to t in the auxiliary graph and vice versa. We can now find the shortest augmenting path, if any, by doing a breadth-first search on the auxiliary directed graph. Note, however, that, while this auxiliary graph shows clearly why a simple breadth-first search on the original graph will uncover a shortest augmenting path, it serves only illustrative purposes and need not be constructed. Program 6.1 implements the complete algorithm—breadth-first search and augmentation; it runs in $\Theta(|V|\cdot|E|)$ time, since it may require $\Theta(|V|)$ iterations and since each iteration requires $O(|E|)$ time, with many taking that much time. On the other hand, Program 6.1 does waste a lot of time. It begins each iteration by setting the back pointers of all the vertices on the left side to nil and enqueueing those that are unmatched, so that it takes $\Omega(|V|)$ time to find any augmenting path—even one of length one, which is just an edge between unmatched vertices. This behavior compares unfavorably with the very simple $\Theta(|E|)$ greedy approximation algorithm that processes the left-side vertices in turn, matching them if possible and discarding them if not. Our algorithm inefficiently mimics this strategy until it needs to search for an augmenting path of length two or more. In general, we can avoid resetting all the back pointers by recording which matched left-side vertices have had their back pointers changed, because these are the only ones that need to be reset to nil. These modifications turn out to be unimportant, however, as we now introduce a major theoretical improvement.

Program 6.1 wastes a lot of potentially useful work at each iteration: while it conducts a breadth-first search from all unmatched vertices on the left side and makes sure to keep all exploration paths disjoint, it discards all but the one augmenting path found and starts anew for the next iteration. It would seem far more profitable to mark the path found and continue the breadth-first search on paths originating from the other unmatched vertices until other augmenting paths are found or the possibilities are exhausted for the current iteration. Multiple iterations would remain necessary, but the worst-case cost per iteration would not change and the number of iterations required might decrease significantly, since it is controlled by the net gain in the size of the matching from one iteration to the next. Before describing an improved algorithm, we establish the gain that we may anticipate through a series of short theorems; although we shall use the results to develop a matching algorithm for bipartite graphs only, the results in fact apply to general graphs as well. We begin by generalizing Berge's theorem (Theorem 6.5).

Theorem 6.8 Let M_1 and M_2 be two matchings in some graph, $G = (V, E)$, with $|M_1| > |M_2|$. Then the subgraph $G' = (V, M_1 \oplus M_2)$ contains at least $|M_1| - |M_2|$ vertex-disjoint augmenting paths with respect to M_2. $\qquad\square$

Proof: The proof is similar to that of Theorem 6.5. Recall that every connected component of G' is one of: (i) a single vertex; (ii) a cycle of even length, with edges alternately drawn from M_1 and M_2; or (iii) a path with edges alternately drawn from M_1 and M_2. Let $C_i = (V_i, E_i)$ be the ith connected component and define $\delta(C_i) = |E_i \cap M_1| - |E_i \cap M_2|$. From our previous observations, we know that $\delta(C_i)$ must be one of -1, 0, or 1 and that it equals 1 exactly when C_i is an augmenting path with respect to M_2. Now we have

$$\sum_i \delta(C_i) = |M_1 - M_2| - |M_2 - M_1| = |M_1| - |M_2|,$$

so that at least $|M_1| - |M_2|$ components C_i are such that $\delta(C_i)$ equals 1, which proves the theorem.

Q.E.D.

Figure 6.6 illustrates the theorem.

Our breadth-first search search process always finds a shortest augmenting path. It turns out that the length of the shortest augmenting path is nondecreasing during the course of successive augmentations.

Theorem 6.9 Let $G = (V, E)$ be a graph, with M a nonmaximal matching, P a shortest augmenting path with respect to M, and P' any augmenting path with respect to the augmented matching $M \oplus P$. Then we have

$$|P'| \geq |P| + |P \cap P'|. \qquad\square$$

Proof: The matching $M \oplus P \oplus P'$ contains two more edges than M, so that, by our previous theorem, $M \oplus (M \oplus P \oplus P') = P \oplus P'$ contains (at least) two vertex-disjoint augmenting paths with respect to M, call them P_1 and P_2. Thus we have $|P \oplus P'| \geq |P_1| + |P_2|$. Since P is a shortest augmenting path with respect to M, we also have $|P| \leq |P_1|$ and $|P| \leq |P_2|$, so that we get $|P \oplus P'| \geq 2|P|$. Since

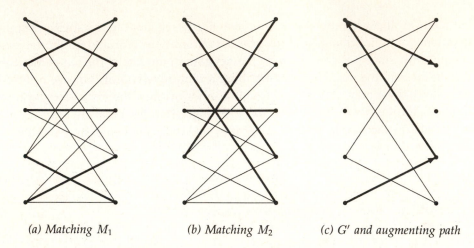

(a) Matching M_1 (b) Matching M_2 (c) G' and augmenting path

Figure 6.6: Multiple Augmenting Paths in the Symmetric Difference of Two
Matchings

$P \oplus P'$ is $(P \cup P') - (P \cap P')$, we can write $|P \oplus P'| = |P| + |P'| - |P \cap P'|$.
Substituting in our preceding inequality yields our conclusion.

Q.E.D.

A consequence is that two augmenting paths in an augmentation sequence have
the same length only if they are vertex-disjoint. Thus all augmenting paths of
the same length can be used at once. This observation provides the desired
foundation for our improved algorithm:

- Begin with an arbitrary (possibly empty) matching.

- Repeatedly find a maximal set of vertex-disjoint augmenting paths, all of
  the same length, and use them all to augment the current matching until
  no augmenting path can be found.

Note that, by a maximal set, we mean one for which we cannot find another
vertex-disjoint augmenting path of the same length, rather than the largest possible set of augmenting paths of this length. This degree of optimization is much
harder to achieve and does not yield any increase in efficiency.

Since all augmenting paths of the same length are used at once, the number
of iterations of this improved algorithm is bounded by the maximum number of
distinct path lengths that may appear in any augmentation sequence.

Theorem 6.10 Let s be the cardinality of a maximum matching and let $P_1, P_2, \ldots ,$
P_s be a sequence of augmenting paths, each as short as possible, that build

on the empty matching. Then the number of distinct integers in the sequence $|P_1|, |P_2|, \ldots, |P_s|$ cannot exceed $2\lfloor \sqrt{s} \rfloor$.   □

Proof: Let $r = \lfloor s - \sqrt{s} \rfloor$ and consider M_r, the rth matching in the augmentation sequence. Since $|M_r| = r$ and since the maximum matching has cardinality $s > r$, Theorem 6.8 states that there exist exactly $s - r$ vertex-disjoint augmenting paths with respect to M_r. (These need not be the remaining augmenting paths in our sequence, $P_{r+1}, P_{r+2}, \ldots, P_s$.) Altogether these paths contain at most all of the edges from M_r, so that the shortest contains at most $\lfloor r/(s - r) \rfloor$ such edges (if the edges of M_r are evenly distributed among the $s - r$ vertex-disjoint paths) and thus at most $2\lfloor r/(s - r) \rfloor + 1$ edges in all. But the shortest augmenting path is precisely the next one picked, so that we get

$$
\begin{aligned}
|P_{r+1}| &\leq 2\lfloor \lfloor s - \sqrt{s} \rfloor / (s - \lfloor s - \sqrt{s} \rfloor) \rfloor + 1 \\
&\leq 2(s - \sqrt{s})/\sqrt{s} + 1 \\
&\leq 2\sqrt{s} - 1 \\
&< 2\lfloor \sqrt{s} \rfloor + 1.
\end{aligned}
$$

Since $|P_{r+1}|$ is an odd integer (all augmenting paths have odd length), we can conclude that $|P_{r+1}| \leq 2\lfloor \sqrt{s} \rfloor - 1$. Hence each of $P_1, P_2, \ldots, P_r$ must have length no greater than $2\lfloor \sqrt{s} \rfloor - 1$. Therefore, these r lengths must be distributed among at most $\lfloor \sqrt{s} \rfloor$ different values and this bound can be reached only if $|P_r| = |P_{r+1}|$. Since $|P_{r+1}|, |P_{r+2}|, \ldots, |P_s|$ cannot contribute more than $s - r = \lceil \sqrt{s} \rceil$ distinct values, the total number of distinct integers in the sequence does not exceed $2\lfloor \sqrt{s} \rfloor$.

Q.E.D.

Careful study of the proof shows that it is not necessary to start with an empty matching: the crucial point is to find the augmenting path where the size of the matching becomes $r = \lfloor s - \sqrt{s} \rfloor$; that there are fewer than r augmenting paths up to this point cannot hurt.

As the cardinality of a maximum matching on an arbitrary graph is $\lfloor |V|/2 \rfloor$, our improved algorithm iterates $\Theta(\sqrt{|V|})$ times, as opposed to $\Theta(|V|)$ times for the original version, a substantial improvement if the worst-case cost of an iteration remains unchanged. Once again, implementing an iteration turns out to be a simple task in bipartite graphs and a difficult one in general graphs.

In bipartite graphs, we need only modify slightly the breadth-first search of Program 6.1. The alterations required arise as a consequence of the multiple augmenting paths sought. Note that when the breadth-first search of Program 6.1 uncovers a coalescing of potential augmenting paths, i.e., when the search uncovers more than one way to reach a vertex in the conceptual auxiliary graph,

```
procedure Match(var G: graph;
                var error: boolean; (* Set if graph not bipartite. *)
                var mate: partners);
  (* This procedure finds a maximum matching in bipartite graphs
     in O(sqrt(V)*E) time, recording the result in mate[ ]. *)

  (* Program assumes the existence of a queue package with operations
        procedure CreateQueue, function IsEmptyQueue: boolean,
        procedure Enqueue(v: vertex), and procedure Dequeue(var v: vertex). *)

  label 1, 99;
  (* The breadth-first search assigns level numbers to left-side vertices;
        unmatched left-side vertices are at level zero.
     Matched right-side vertices are not assigned level numbers,
        because we simply pass through them.
     Unmatched right-side vertices are assigned the level number
        that their mates would be assigned if they were matched. *)
  const Left = -1; (* values that are not valid levels *)
        Right = -2;
  type LevelsAndSides = array [vertex] of integer;
  var level: LevelsAndSides;
      dfs: array [vertex] of PtrToNode;
        (* For right-side vertices, dfs records how far along we are
           in the adjacency list during the depth-first search. *)
      CurrentLevel: integer;
      RightSideEnqueued: boolean;
      v, w: vertex;
      p: PtrToNode;

  procedure DFS(v: vertex; l: integer);
    (* Uses O(E) time and O(V) storage (actually the length of
       the shortest augmenting path) for the implicit stack. *)
    var dummy: boolean;
    procedure RecDFS(v: vertex; l: integer; var success: boolean);
      label 99;
      begin
        (* v is a right-side vertex. *)
        while dfs[v] <> nil do
          begin
            if level[dfs[v]^.id] = l - 1
              then begin
                      if l = 1
                         then success := true
                         else RecDFS(mate[dfs[v]^.id],l-1,success);
                      if success
                         then begin
                                (* Augment.  Switching the status of the
                                   unmatched edges also switches the status
                                   of the matched edges. *)
                                mate[dfs[v]^.id] := v; mate[v] := dfs[v]^.id;
```

```
                          (* Prevent reuse of this left-side vertex. *)
                          level[dfs[v]^.id] := Left;
                          goto 99
                        end
                  end;
            dfs[v] := dfs[v]^.next
          end;
99: end; (* RecDFS *)
  begin (* DFS *)
    dummy := false;
    RecDFS(v,1,dummy);
    level[v] := Right
  end; (* DFS *)

begin (* Match *)
  CreateQueue;
  (* Define the bipartite structure of the graph (see Exercise 4.8),
     exiting with an error if the graph is not bipartite. *)
  ...
  (* Form the empty or other initial matching. *)
  for v := 1 to G.size do mate[v] := unmatched;

  while true do
    begin
      (* Find a maximal set of augmenting paths for the next shortest length.
         Exit loop if no augmenting path exists. *)
      (* O(V) initialization *)
      for v := 1 to G.size do
        case level[v] of
          Left:  if mate[v] = unmatched
                    then begin level[v] := 0; Enqueue(v) end;
          Right: dfs[v] := G.AdjLists[v]
        end;
      CurrentLevel := 1; (* the level about to be enqueued *)
      RightSideEnqueued := false;

      (* Expand the breadth-first search to the next level.  As soon as
         an unmatched right-side vertex has been discovered, we stop
         enqueueing left-side vertices.  We continue the exploration of
         the current level, but only look for additional unmatched right-side
         vertices.  When we advance to the next level, we might have to
         discard some left-side vertices that were enqueued before the first
         unmatched right-side vertex was discovered. *)
      while not IsEmptyQueue do
        begin
          Dequeue(v);
          if level[v] = CurrentLevel
            then if not RightSideEnqueued
                    then CurrentLevel := CurrentLevel + 1
```

```
                             else begin (* Discard useless left-side vertices. *)
                                    while mate[v] <> unmatched do Dequeue(v);
                                    goto 1
                                  end;
                 p := G.AdjLists[v];
                 while p <> nil do
                   begin
                     if mate[p^.id] = unmatched
                       then begin
                              if level[p^.id] = Right (* not already in the queue *)
                                then begin
                                       level[p^.id] := CurrentLevel;
                                       RightSideEnqueued := true;
                                       Enqueue(p^.id)
                                     end
                            end
                       else begin
                              w := mate[p^.id];
                              if (level[w] = Left (* unseen *)) and
                                 not RightSideEnqueued (* and still relevant *)
                                then begin
                                       level[w] := CurrentLevel;
                                       Enqueue(w)
                                     end
                            end;
                     p := p^.next
                   end
              end;
           (* Maximum matching has been found. *)
           goto 99;

       1: (* Start the depth-first search from the right-side vertices,
             searching for a maximal set of shortest augmenting paths. *)
          (* One unmatched right-side vertex has already been dequeued. *)
          DFS(v,CurrentLevel);
          while not IsEmptyQueue do
            begin
              Dequeue(v);
              DFS(v,CurrentLevel)
            end;

          (* Reset level[ ] for the next iteration. *)
          for v := 1 to G.size do
            if level[v] >= 0
              then level[v] := Left
        end;
   99:
     end; (* Match *)
```

Program 6.2: A More Efficient Augmenting Path Solution to Bipartite Matching

it records only a single (shortest) path back to an unmatched left-side vertex. Which path gets recorded depends on the chance ordering of the data. This limited amount of information suffices when only one augmenting path is desired, but fails when a maximal set of shortest vertex-disjoint augmenting paths is sought, since the one recorded path for an unmatched right-side vertex may include a vertex already used in a previously discovered augmenting path. By using $\Theta(|V|)$ additional storage and recording more information about a vertex than simply its membership in the matching, we can find a maximal set of shortest vertex-disjoint augmenting paths in $\Theta(|E|)$ time, after the breadth-first search has revealed all unmatched right-side vertices that are candidate endpoints for shortest augmenting paths. For each left-side vertex encountered during the breadth-first search, we record its distance from the closest unmatched left-side vertex, passing as before through matched right-side vertices. We use this information to run a (backward) depth-first search from each unmatched right-side vertex discovered during the breadth-first search: during these depth-first searches we consider only edges (in the conceptual auxiliary graph) that take us one level closer to unmatched left-side vertices. When we discover an augmenting path, we eliminate the vertices along this path from consideration by any remaining depth-first search, thereby ensuring that our augmenting paths will be vertex-disjoint. The complete program is given in Program 6.2; note that this program is only slightly longer than our simpler, less efficient version. That the program takes only $\Theta(|E|)$ time to perform all the depth-first searches can be seen by studying the behavior of the variable `dfs[ ]`. The pointers in this array, which are defined only for right-side vertices, can only advance down their respective adjacency lists; such a pointer advances past an edge, trivially, when the edge does not lead to a left-side vertex at the next lower level or, more importantly, when there no longer remains any way to follow this edge and still reach an unmatched left-side vertex using vertices not already used in other

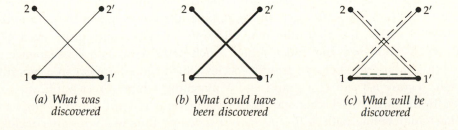

(a) What was   (b) What could have   (c) What will be
discovered   been discovered   discovered

Figure 6.7: The Algorithm Need Not Find the Largest Set of Vertex-Disjoint Augmenting Paths

augmenting paths. (When a right-side vertex lies on an augmenting path, it can never be reached again by any future depth-first search, so there is no need to advance the pointer.) As the breadth-first search and all the depth-first searches take a total of $\Theta(|E|)$ time, each iteration runs in $\Theta(|E|)$ time. Note that not all of the unmatched right-side vertices discovered by the breadth-first search need be part of some augmenting path in the collection constructed during the depth-first searches; thus, while maximal, the set of vertex-disjoint augmenting paths produced by the algorithm need not be the largest possible, as illustrated by the simple example of Figure 6.7, where we augment the empty matching by augmenting paths of length one. Due to the chance ordering of the data, the algorithm finds a maximal set of vertex-disjoint augmenting paths of size one, even though a set of size two exists. Notice that the total number of iterations is nevertheless only two, which is $2\lfloor\sqrt{s}\rfloor$, the bound set by Theorem 6.10.

6.4 Algorithms for General Matching

Now that we have developed an efficient algorithm for maximum cardinality matching in bipartite graphs, let us return to general graphs. As our theorems about augmenting paths hold for general graphs, we explore the possibility of adapting our bipartite matching algorithms to this more general situation. The spirit of the algorithm remains the same. We set up even and odd levels, labelling vertices as we encounter them, in order to preserve a form of alternation—effectively, we attempt to impose a bipartite structure upon the graph. By convention, the starting points of our search, which are the unmatched vertices, are labelled even. The search proceeds from an even vertex along some unmatched edge to an odd vertex and from an odd vertex along a matched edge to an even vertex; the search stops on encountering an unmatched vertex at an odd level.

Unfortunately, this approach may fail to identify augmenting paths in a general graph, because a bipartite structure that is consistent with the current matching does not always exist. In developing alternating paths from an initial unmarked vertex, the algorithm may encounter a vertex both at an even and an odd distance from the initial vertex. Such paths arise as a consequence of the presence of cycles of odd length—cycles which cannot appear in a bipartite graph. Figure 6.8 shows a graph and a matching where direct application of breadth-first search (whether started from A or from K) will fail to identify the unique augmenting path A-B-C-D-E-G-H-J-K and thus will wrongly conclude that the suboptimal matching shown is in fact optimal. The culprits are the odd-length cycles that the search enters at vertices C and J, respectively. Notice that, depending on the direction in which the cycle is traversed, every vertex in the

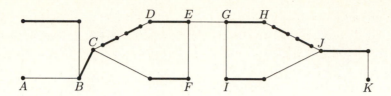

Figure 6.8: The Interaction of Blossoms and Breadth-First Search

cycle (other than the entry point) can be labelled either even or odd. Edmonds, who first studied this problem and offered a solution for it, named these special cycles of odd length *blossoms*. Blossoms only exist with respect to a matching; moreover, only those blossoms that the search encounters present a problem. Every other edge around a blossom is matched, except at the vertex where two unmatched edges meet; this special vertex is called the *base* of the blossom.

Definition 6.2 Let $G = (V, E)$ be a graph, M be a matching, and v_0 be an unmatched vertex. A *blossom* with respect to M and v_0 is a cycle of length $2k + 1$ containing k matched edges and such that there exists an alternating path from v_0 to the base of the blossom (unless v_0 itself is the base) and around the blossom back to its base, a path on which all vertices, with the exception of the blossom's base, are distinct. □

Because the presence of blossoms causes our bipartite matching algorithms to fail on general graphs, we naturally look for a way to eliminate these blossoms while maintaining the basic properties of augmenting paths. We shall eliminate blossoms as we encounter them by shrinking each one into a single supervertex. The edges incident upon this supervertex correspond to those edges in the original graph with one endpoint in the blossom and the other outside the blossom. Notice that at most one edge incident upon the supervertex will be a matched edge, depending on whether or not the base of the blossom is matched. This blossom-shrinking strategy is exactly what we need, because it preserves augmenting paths.

Theorem 6.11 [Edmonds] Let $G = (V, E)$ be a graph, M be a matching, and v_0 be an unmatched vertex. Denote by $G' = (V', E')$ the graph obtained by shrinking a blossom with respect to M and v_0 into a supervertex and let M' be the corresponding matching. Then G has an augmenting path with respect to M beginning at v_0 if and only if G' has an augmenting path with respect to M' beginning at v_0 (or at the supervertex if v_0 is the base of a blossom). □

Proof: We begin with the "if" part. If G' has an augmenting path with respect to M', either this path goes through the supervertex or it does not. If it does not,

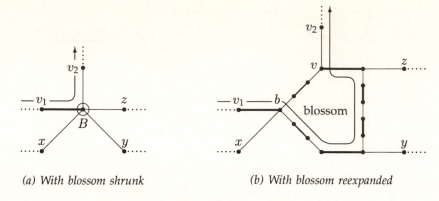

(a) With blossom shrunk   (b) With blossom reexpanded

Figure 6.9: Expanding a Shrunken Blossom

we are done, since the same path exists in G, where it is also an augmenting path with respect to M. If it does, then we expand it into an augmenting path in G by moving around the blossom in the proper direction as follows (refer to Figure 6.9). Let (v_1, B) be the matched edge incident upon B and (v_2, B) be the unmatched edge. The matched edge corresponds to an edge of G connecting to the base, b, of the blossom; we replace it with the edge (v_1, b) of G. Similarly, the unmatched edge is replaced by the (not necessarily unique) edge of G to which it corresponds, (v, v_2). Now we connect b to v by moving around the blossom along the even-length path; as the blossom is a cycle of odd length, such a path always exists. The result is an augmenting path in G with respect to M.

The "only if" part is more complex, because the augmenting path may cross the blossom many times. However, no matter how many times an augmenting path in G, say p, starting from v_0, crosses in and out of the blossom, we can construct an augmenting path in G' that passes through the supervertex at most once. Unfortunately there are numerous cases to consider. If the path, p, does not touch any vertex of the blossom, or if the only vertex of the blossom included in the path is the base, this same path exists in G' and we are done. Let us therefore assume that the augmenting path uses at least one blossom edge. We distinguish two main cases. First, p may enter the blossom for the first time through its base, along the matched edge; it then must leave for the last time through an unmatched edge. The entry and exit points divide p into three sections. Concatenating the first section, which ends at the supervertex, with the last, which starts at the supervertex, yields the desired augmenting path. Notice that the middle section of p, which can be of considerable size (as it may wander in and out of the blossom several times before returning to the blossom for the final time), is eliminated. Secondly, p may enter the blossom for the first time

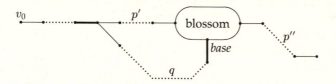

(a) q and p″ do not intersect.

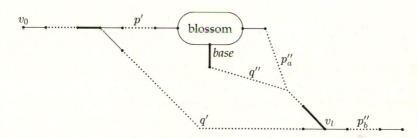

(b) q and p″ intersect, but q″ and p′ do not.

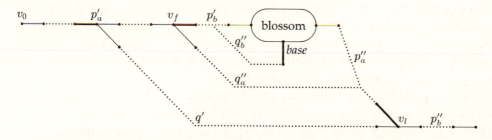

(c) q and p″ intersect, as do q″ and p′—an impossible situation.

Figure 6.10: Constructions Used in the Proof of Theorem 6.11

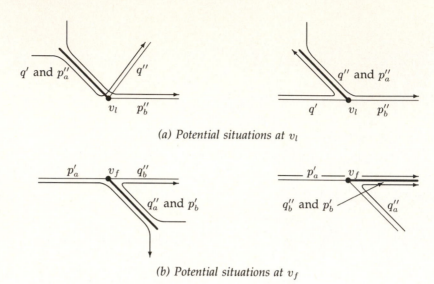

(a) Potential situations at v_l

(b) Potential situations at v_f

Figure 6.11: Details of Cases in the Proof of Theorem 6.11

along an unmatched edge and leave for the last time through an unmatched edge. (If it leaves for the last time through the matched edge touching the base, we return to the previous case.) This case requires closer examination, since the path in G' corresponding to p, after removal of the middle portion of p, has two consecutive unmatched edges and thus is not even an alternating path. We shall construct an augmenting path in G' using pieces of p, the shrunken blossom, and the path, call it q, from v_0 to the base of the blossom (a path which does not intersect the blossom and is an alternating path). Since several such paths may exist, we choose for q that path which has the longest initial segment in common with p. Paths p and q can diverge immediately upon leaving v_0 or they can traverse the same edges for some time, but they must diverge before the blossom is reached. Denote by p' and p'' the sections of path p up to the blossom and beyond the blossom, respectively. If path q and fragment p'' do not intersect or if they share only the base of the blossom (see Figure 6.10(a)), then the path formed by q followed by p'' is an augmenting path in G' with respect to M'.

If q and p'' intersect, let their last common vertex, as defined by a traversal of p'', be denoted by v_l; divide q into segments q' (from v_0 to v_l) and q'' (from v_l to the blossom) and further divide p'' into segments p''_a (from the blossom to v_l) and p''_b (from v_l to the end of p''). Two situations can occur at v_l, as shown in Figure 6.11(a). In the first situation, we follow q up to v_l and then follow p''_b to the unmatched vertex, thereby obtaining an augmenting path in M' which avoids the supervertex. In the second situation, we further subdivide the analysis according

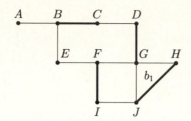

(a) The graph with its current matching

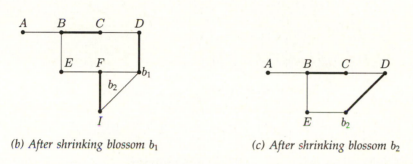

(b) After shrinking blossom b_1 (c) After shrinking blossom b_2

Figure 6.12: Nested Blossoms in a Graph

to whether or not q'' and p' intersect. If they do not, or if they share only the base of the blossom, as depicted in Figure 6.10(b), then the path consisting of p', followed by q'' in reverse, followed by p''_b, is the desired augmenting path. If q'' and p' intersect, let v_f denote the first vertex (as defined by a traversal of p') where they intersect, and divide q'' into segments q''_a and q''_b, as shown (magnified) in Figure 6.11(b). In the first situation, we can simply follow p' up to v_f, switch over to q''_a, traverse it in the reverse direction, and finally switch over to p''_b at v_l, since now we approach it in the correct direction. The second situation would result in the overall diagram shown in Figure 6.10(c). However, this situation cannot arise, due to the properties of q: consider the path starting at v_0, following p' until v_f is reached, and then switching to q''_b. This path starts at v_0 and reaches the base of the blossom; it does not intersect the blossom before reaching the base; and it is an alternating path. Furthermore it coincides with p longer than q coincides with p, which contradicts our hypothesis about q.

$Q.E.D.$

Of course, the new graph G' may itself have blossoms, which will have to be shrunk in turn: blossoms may be nested to any depth. Figure 6.12 shows a graph and a matching with nested blossoms.

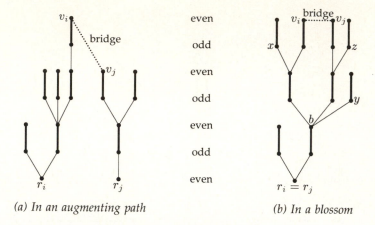

(a) In an augmenting path   (b) In a blossom

Figure 6.13: A Bridge in a Matching

Herein, then, lies the challenge: how to handle blossoms efficiently. First, we must detect their existence; next, we must identify their vertices; and finally, we must be able to shrink and expand them efficiently, allowing for arbitrary nesting. For the sake of convenience, we can regard any single vertex as a degenerate blossom, so that, at any stage, the graph is composed entirely of blossoms.

Whenever the labelling becomes inconsistent, i.e., whenever the search process, working from an even vertex, v_i, finds a neighbor, v_j, that is already labelled even, we have detected either an augmenting path or a blossom. The edge connecting these two vertices is called a *bridge*, since it connects two subtrees;[3] the presence of a bridge thus signals the existence of an augmenting path or a blossom (see Figure 6.13). On encountering a bridge, we backtrack in the forest all the way to the roots, i.e., to the unmatched nodes from which v_i and v_j were reached. Denote these nodes by r_i and r_j, respectively. If they are distinct, then we have found an augmenting path from r_i to r_j. This path goes from r_i to v_i in the tree rooted at r_i, then crosses the bridge to v_j, and finally follows the path in the other tree from v_j to r_j. In general, some of the vertices depicted in Figure 6.13 will be shrunken blossoms, which will have to be expanded (recursively if blossoms are nested) and traversed in the correct direction when constructing the augmenting path in G. As always, once we have augmented the current matching, we move on to the next iteration.

If, however, r_i coincides with r_j, then we have found a blossom. The base of the blossom is the first vertex, b, common to the paths from v_i and v_j to the

---

[3]This choice of language is unfortunate, if descriptive, as the word *bridge* also denotes an edge, the removal of which disconnects a graph—see Exercise 4.24.

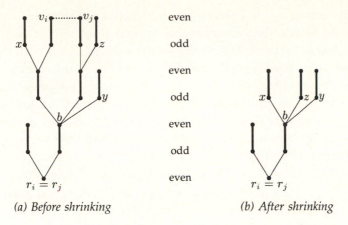

(a) Before shrinking   (b) After shrinking

Figure 6.14: Shrinking a Blossom During the Search

root; the blossom is the odd cycle from b to itself through v_i, the bridge, and v_j. This blossom is duly recorded and shrunk and the search proceeds. That we may continue our search from this point—rather than be forced to start over from scratch in the graph that results from shrinking the blossom—follows from the fact that, after shrinking the blossom (see Figure 6.14), the odd vertices x, y, and z remain at odd levels, even though they are now connected directly to b. Therefore, the search pattern imposed on G' is consistent with respect to the labelling, even though it might differ from that which would result from directly searching G'. As no restriction was placed on the search pattern, we may indeed proceed with our search after shrinking a blossom. (An interesting consequence of this approach is that, at any stage of the search, every odd vertex must be a degenerate blossom.) The search continues until an augmenting path is detected or until all edges have been examined; in the latter case, we have verified that the current matching is optimal.

How efficient is the algorithm sketched in the previous paragraph? Like our first algorithm for bipartite matching, it produces only one augmenting path at each iteration, so that it may iterate $\Theta(|V|)$ times. If implemented by actually shrinking the blossoms, which entails a lot of bookkeeping, each iteration takes $O(|V|\cdot|E|)$ time, for a total running time of $O(|V|^2\cdot|E|)$. However, we can use suitable data structures to search for a single augmenting path in linear time and thus obtain a running time of $\Theta(|V|\cdot|E|)$, the same as for the corresponding bipartite version. In order to attain this running time, we shall make use of two degrees of freedom: (i) we need not merge vertices physically—we can work in the original graph at all times; and (ii) we need not follow a specific traversal order, but can choose any untraversed edge incident upon an even vertex. With respect to data structures, the crucial observation is that, at any time during the search, the vertices of the original graph, G, are partitioned into equivalence classes by their relationship to the vertices of the current graph, G': each blossom in G' is associated with all the vertices in the original graph that the blossom encompasses, directly or through nested blossoms. Thus we can regard the blossoms as equivalence classes of vertices of G: at the beginning of a search all blossoms are degenerate (corresponding to classes of unit size) and, as the search progresses, larger blossoms are found and their vertices joined into larger equivalence classes.

This partitioning of the vertices suggests using the UNION-FIND data structure of Section 3.2. We can explore G' by exploring the original graph G: whenever we encounter an edge, (u, v), in G, we translate the vertices into $\hat{u} = \text{FIND}(u)$ and $\hat{v} = \text{FIND}(v)$ and consider the pair $(\hat{u}, \hat{v})$. If the two elements of the pair are distinct, then $(\hat{u}, \hat{v})$ corresponds to an edge in G'; otherwise, the vertices u and v are part of the same shrunken blossom. However, our translation of u and v is not quite correct. We want to identify a blossom with its base, which simply means that we should like to have the base of the blossom be the representative element for its equivalence class. But, the UNION-FIND routines cannot ensure this identification, since they choose to merge trees according to their rank and not as a function of their root elements. Hence we need to associate the bases of the blossoms with the representative elements of the corresponding equivalence classes; as we sometimes need the true representative element (when merging equivalence classes) and at other times need the base of the blossom (when working in G'), we implement this association externally to the UNION-FIND data structure. All that is required is an array, call it `origin`, the values of which are defined for only the representative elements in the UNION-FIND data structure, and where `origin[v]` is the base of the blossom containing v. Now we can translate edge (u, v) in G into $(\hat{u}, \hat{v}) = (\text{origin}[\text{FIND}(u)], \text{origin}[\text{FIND}(v)])$ in G'. Our algorithm for detecting augmenting paths and blossoms can then be written as follows:

- (Initialize) For every vertex $v \in G$, set `origin[v]` $= v$ and place v in an equivalence class by itself. Label all unmatched vertices even, place the edges incident upon these vertices into a data structure, such as a queue or stack, that supports constant-time insertion and retrieval (this abstract data type is known as a *bag*), and label all other vertices unseen.

- (Process edge) Repeat this step until either the bag is empty, at which point the current matching is optimal, or an augmenting path is found. Remove any edge, (u, v), from the bag and form $(\hat{u}, \hat{v})$. By construction, one endpoint, say $\hat{u}$, is an even vertex in G'; now look at the other endpoint.

($\hat{u} = \hat{v}$) Ignore the edge, since it is degenerate in G'.

($\hat{v}$ is unseen) Make v, which is also $\hat{v}$, an odd vertex. Since v is unseen, it is matched; make its partner, w (also previously unseen), an even vertex, and place the edges incident upon w into the bag.

($\hat{v}$ is odd) Ignore the edge, since it brings no new information.

($\hat{v}$ is even) We have detected either a blossom or an augmenting path. If we have detected a blossom, then do the following:

(Blossom shrinking) Let b be the base of the blossom. For all w in the blossom, do UNION(FIND(b), FIND(w)). If w is labelled odd, place all edges incident upon it into the bag. (These edges were not in the bag, but they now logically emanate from b, which is even.) Finally, set origin[FIND(b)] $= b$.

As just given, the algorithm is incomplete: we must also describe how to trace the paths from v_i and v_j back to r_i and r_j and how to reconstruct an augmenting path when one is found. To make the first task possible, we associate with each odd vertex, v, its predecessor in the search. There are two apparent choices for the predecessor, u and $\hat{u}$. While $\hat{u}$ might seem the more natural, since it appears to avoid an additional reference to the UNION-FIND data structure, it is in fact the wrong choice. First, it actually does not avoid the reference, since $\hat{u}$ may get subsequently collapsed into a blossom not involving v—see x and z of Figure 6.14. Secondly, using u as the predecessor will simplify reconstruction of the augmenting path. Because only odd vertices have predecessors (during reconstruction, even vertices are left through a matched edge), we can coalesce the status and predecessor information into a single array indexed by vertex name, say pred.

When the bridge signals a blossom, it is important, for reasons of efficiency, that we do not retrace our steps all the way to the root vertex, but stop at the base of the blossom. To this end, we search the paths from v_i and v_j to r_i and r_j in parallel, stopping when we reach either two distinct roots or a previously encountered vertex—which is then the base of the blossom. This search strategy detects the base of the blossom in time proportional to the size of the blossom rather than to the size of V. Because only one vertex of the blossom survives and at least two vertices are eliminated from further consideration, the total amount of time spent searching for the bases of blossoms and subsequently shrinking them is $\Theta(|V|)$—not accounting for the $\Theta(|V|)$ FIND operations and for the $\Theta(|E|)$ insertions into the bag. The search for an augmenting path cannot do more than linear work, since each edge is considered at most twice, once from each endpoint. Overall, the algorithm takes $\Theta((|E|+|V|)\alpha(|E|+|V|,|V|))$ time to detect a single augmenting path—where the $\alpha(|E|+|V|,|V|)$ factor accounts for the expense of the FIND operations. The special nature of the problem (the UNION operations always involve the base, and a blossom always eliminates at least two vertices) allows for a specialized version of UNION-FIND that has a true constant-time FIND (see the paper of Gabow and Tarjan mentioned in the bibliography); since the $\alpha(|E|+|V|,|V|)$ factor is irrelevant in practice, this variant remains only of theoretical interest.

Let us now turn to the problem of reconstructing the augmenting path. Unfortunately, our data structures do not record all of the information needed for this task, since, whenever a blossom is shrunk, all knowledge accumulated about that blossom is lost in the internal workings of UNION-FIND. Consider more carefully the conversion of a path from $\hat{v}_i$ to $\hat{r}_i$ in G' into a path from v_i to r_i in G. First note that even vertices present no problem, since the path must follow the matched edge. In contrast, at an odd vertex, the path follows the edge recorded in pred[ ]; following this edge works well in G', where this edge leads to a (possibly degenerate) blossom at an even level, but causes trouble in G, where it may lead into the middle of a blossom or even to a vertex, v, deep within nested blossoms. If v is at an even level in G, no real difficulty arises, since the alternation of levels is preserved and the path can continue from there; we have chanced upon the correct leg of the blossom. If, on the other hand, v is at an odd level, then we have stumbled onto the incorrect leg of the blossom and must walk it in the opposite direction (since every blossom vertex is at both levels, depending on the path direction). Walking in the direction opposite to that in which v was discovered involves marching up to the bridge that signaled this blossom, crossing the bridge, and then, with corrected alternation of levels, returning to the normal walk to the base of the blossom.

It is at this point that the recorded data fail us: information about matched edges and predecessors does not suffice to walk around the blossom in the "wrong" direction. We need one additional datum: the bridge that signaled the blossom; with that information, we can construct the path from the bridge to v by walking along the blossom—thereby obtaining this section of the path in reverse order, a very minor problem. Hence we need an additional array, call it bridge, which records, for each odd vertex that gets collapsed when a blossom is shrunk, the bridge that created that blossom. We record the edge as an arc seen from v, thereby enabling us to distinguish the "near" endpoint from the "far" one. We assign values to the array bridge during the blossom-shrinking step of the algorithm, but use it only during reconstruction of the augmenting path. Let $[v_1, v_2, \ldots, v_n]$ represent a path and denote concatenation of paths by the operator $\|$; if the bridge is (v_i, v_j), with corresponding roots r_i and r_j, then the path we seek is

$$reverse(path(v_i, r_i)) \| path(v_j, r_j),$$

where *path* is defined recursively by

$$
path(u, v) = \begin{cases} [u], \text{ if } u = v; \\[2ex] [u, \texttt{mate}[u]] \parallel path(\texttt{pred}[\texttt{mate}[u]], v), \\ \quad \text{ if } u \neq v \text{ and } u \text{ is even;} \\[2ex] [u] \parallel reverse(path(x, \texttt{mate}[u])) \parallel path(y, v), \\ \quad \text{ if } u \neq v \text{ and } u \text{ is odd, and where } \texttt{bridge}[u] = (x, y). \end{cases}
$$

Notice that the second argument to *path*( ) is always at an even level and that pred[ ] always contains the necessary information. Because each recursive call attempts to build a shorter segment than the caller, the algorithm terminates.

The code for performing a single augmentation is given in Program 6.3. The exact ordering of the many steps ensures that the data remain consistent. Note that the code places vertices into the bag, whereas our high-level description of the algorithm placed edges; also, the program actually explores a vertex thoroughly after removing it from the bag. Neither alteration affects the running time, while together they limit the worst-case size of the bag to $\Theta(|V|)$. More importantly, note that the program does not actually reconstruct the augmenting path. The augmenting path reconstruction takes $\Theta(|V|)$ time and requires $\Theta(|V|)$ additional storage due to the recursion. The overall algorithm thus runs in $\Theta(|V| \cdot |E|)$ time, which matches the bound on our bipartite version; as in the bipartite version, the algorithm can start with any matching, so that greedy heuristics that find a good initial matching make the algorithm much faster in practice.

Since we were able to adapt the simple bipartite matching algorithm to general graphs without loss of performance, we naturally ask next whether or not the same feat is possible with the faster bipartite matching algorithm. The answer is yes: a running time of $\Theta(\sqrt{|V|} \cdot |E|)$ can be attained in the general case as well, but a number of difficult problems arise. Breadth-first search becomes problematic, since, as the graph changes due to the shrinking of blossoms, the distance from a root to a vertex can decrease, even though the parity of the vertex remains unchanged. Our data structures do not allow us to update such information efficiently. More importantly, since the graph is constantly changing, verifying that paths are vertex-disjoint poses quite a challenge, especially in view of the fact that two vertex-disjoint paths can use different parts of the same blossom. These problems necessitate some changes in the strategy used in Program 6.3 and increase considerably the complexity of the resulting algorithm. We do not present the algorithm, but refer the reader to the bibliography at the end of this chapter.

```
(* Assumes type definitions relating to matching used in Section 6.3. *)

procedure AugmentingPath(var G: graph;
                         var mate: partners;
                         var success: boolean);
  (* This procedure finds one augmenting path in a general matching,
     if one exists, in O(|E|) time.

     mate    -- On input, the current matching; on output, the new matching,
                which has one more matched edge, if the input matching was
                not maximum.
     success -- Set true/false depending on whether an augmenting path was
                found. *)

  (* Program assumes a bag package with constant-time operations
        procedure CreateBag, function IsEmptyBag: boolean,
        procedure StoreElement(v: vertex), and procedure GetElement(var v: vertex).
     Program assumes a Union-Find package with operations
        procedure CreateUF(N: integer), procedure Union(u, v: vertex), and
        function Find(v: vertex): vertex
     To achieve the O(|E|) running time, we assume a specialized,
     constant amortized-time version of Find. *)

label 99;

const even = 0; unseen = -1; (* search status flags *)

type VerticesAndFlags = unseen .. MaxVertex; (* vertex name, even or unseen *)
     orientededge = record
                      tail, head: vertex
                    end;

var pred: array [vertex] of VerticesAndFlags;
        (* pred[i] = unseen, even, or (for odd vertices) the other end of the edge
             (in the original graph) that incorporated vertex i into the search.
           Vertices that are both even and odd are part of a blossom.  pred[ ]
           is frozen for vertices in a blossom when the blossom is discovered. *)
    origin: array [vertex] of vertex;
        (* origin[i] identifies the base of the blossom containing vertex i for
           vertices that are roots of trees in the Union-Find data structure. *)
    marked: array [vertex] of boolean;
        (* marked[ ] is used in the parallel search for the base of a newly
           discovered blossom. *)
    bridge: array [vertex] of orientededge;
        (* bridge[ ] records, for odd vertices that become even as the
           result of detecting a blossom, the bridge that made them even. *)
    p: PtrToNode;
    v, (* the vertex being explored *)
    vshrunk, (* the equivalent node in the graph of shrunken blossoms *)
    w, (* the vertex at the other end of an unmatched edge incident upon v *)
    wshrunk, (* the equivalent node in the graph of shrunken blossoms *)
    u: vertex;
```

```
function parent(u: vertex): vertex;
  (* For an odd vertex, u, which must be a degenerate blossom,
     return the predecessor in the current shrunken graph. *)
  begin
    parent := origin[Find(pred[u])]
  end; (* parent *)


procedure Augment(v, root1, w, root2: vertex);
  (* Reconstruct the augmenting path.  Do not actually produce the path in an
     ordered manner; just change the matched/unmatched status of all the edges.
     Note the ordering of operations with respect to recursive calls. *)
  procedure path(v, w: vertex);
    (* Do the actual reconstruction of the path from v to w.  We nominally
       expect v to be even.  If it is odd, then it was also made even by
       shrinking a blossom, so bridge[ ] is defined and we walk around
       the blossom the "long" way. *)
    var t, u: vertex;
    begin
      if v <> w
        then if pred[v] = even
                then begin
                       u := mate[v]; t := pred[u];
                       path(t,w);
                       mate[t] := u; mate[u] := t
                     end
                else begin
                       (* reverse(path(bridge[v].tail,mate[v]));
                          ignore the matched edge *)
                       path(bridge[v].tail,mate[v]);
                       path(bridge[v].head,w);
                       mate[bridge[v].tail] := bridge[v].head;
                       mate[bridge[v].head] := bridge[v].tail
                     end
    end; (* path *)
  begin
    path(v,root1);
    path(w,root2);
    mate[v] := w; mate[w] := v
  end; (* Augment *)


procedure Shrink(base, toofar, b1, b2, bridge1, bridge2: vertex);
  (* Shrink the blossom.  Also clean up the "tail" that came from searching
     too far during the parallel search for the base of the blossom.
     base      -- The base of the blossom in the shrunken graph.
     toofar    -- The furthest vertex, in the shrunken graph, reached
                     by traversing the short side of the blossom.
     b1, b2    -- The vertices in the shrunken graph that form the bridge.
     bridge1,
     bridge2   -- The vertices in the original graph that form the bridge.
  *)
  var t: vertex;
```

```
procedure WalkBack(b, bridge1, bridge2: vertex);
  (* Walk back from one end of the bridge to the base, coalescing all
     nodes into the base of the blossom and placing vertices that were
     newly made even into the bag. *)
  procedure RecWalkBack(t: vertex);
    begin
      if t <> base
        then begin
                marked[t] := false;
                bridge[mate[t]].tail := bridge1;
                bridge[mate[t]].head := bridge2;
                StoreElement(mate[t]);
                RecWalkBack(parent(mate[t]));
                (* It is now safe to change the Union-Find data
                   structure--the recursion is unwinding. *)
                Union(Find(base),Find(t));
                Union(Find(base),Find(mate[t]))
             end
    end; (* RecWalkBack *)
  begin
    RecWalkBack(b);
    origin[Find(base)] := base
  end; (* WalkBack *)
begin
  (* Clean up the tail first. *)
  t := base;
  while t <> toofar do
    begin
      marked[t] := false;
      t := parent(mate[t])
    end;
  marked[t] := false;
  WalkBack(b1,bridge1,bridge2); WalkBack(b2,bridge2,bridge1)
end; (* Shrink *)


procedure HandleBridge(vshrunk, wshrunk, v, w: vertex);
  (* We have detected either a blossom or an augmenting path, determine
     which, and either shrink the blossom or augment the matching. *)
  label 98;
  var xshrunk, yshrunk: vertex;
  procedure StepTowardsBase(var movingvertex: vertex; fixedvertex: vertex);
    (* Take one step back toward the base of the blossom (or root of the tree)
       along one of the legs.  If we detect the base, shrink the blossom. *)
    begin
      movingvertex := parent(mate[movingvertex]);
      if marked[movingvertex]
        then begin (* We have found the base of the blossom. *)
                Shrink(movingvertex,fixedvertex,vshrunk,wshrunk,v,w);
                goto 98
             end
        else marked[movingvertex] := true
    end; (* StepTowardsBase *)
```

```
      begin
        (* Search backwards along both paths in the shrunken graph in parallel. *)
        xshrunk := vshrunk;
        yshrunk := wshrunk;
        marked[xshrunk] := true;
        marked[yshrunk] := true;
        (* while both xshrunk and yshrunk can be moved back one level *)
        while (mate[xshrunk] <> unmatched) and (mate[yshrunk] <> unmatched) do
          begin
            StepTowardsBase(xshrunk,yshrunk);
            StepTowardsBase(yshrunk,xshrunk)
          end;
        (* while one of xshrunk and yshrunk can be moved back one level *)
        while mate[xshrunk] <> unmatched do
          StepTowardsBase(xshrunk,yshrunk);
        while mate[yshrunk] <> unmatched do
          StepTowardsBase(yshrunk,xshrunk);
        (* xshrunk and yshrunk have arrived at distinct roots--an augmenting
           path has been discovered. *)
        Augment(v,xshrunk,w,yshrunk);
        success := true;
        goto 99; (* return from AugmentingPath *)
98: end; (* HandleBridge *)

  begin
    (* Initially, every vertex is a degenerate blossom. *)
    CreateBag; CreateUF(G.size);
    (* Initially, unmatched vertices are at an even level (and unexplored).
       All others are unseen.  No nondegenerate blossom has been found. *)
    for v := 1 to G.size do
      begin
        origin[v] := v;
        if mate[v] = unmatched
          then begin
                  StoreElement(v);
                  pred[v] := even
               end
          else pred[v] := unseen;
        marked[v] := false
      end;

    while not IsEmptyBag do
      begin
        GetElement(v);
        p := G.AdjLists[v];
        (* While we consider the edge in the original graph, we logically
           consider the edge in the graph of shrunken blossoms. *)
        vshrunk := origin[Find(v)];
```

```
            while p <> nil do
              begin
                w := p^.id;
                wshrunk := origin[Find(w)];
                if pred[wshrunk] = unseen
                  then begin
                          (* mate[w] <> unmatched as w is unseen *)
                          u := mate[w]; (* wshrunk = w *)
                          pred[w] := v;
                          pred[u] := even;
                          StoreElement(u)
                       end
                else if (pred[wshrunk] = even)
                          (* If the edge connects an even vertex to an even vertex
                              in the shrunken graph... *) and
                         (vshrunk <> wshrunk) (* ...if they are different... *)
                  then (* ...determine whether they are in the same tree (a blossom)
                            or in different trees (an augmenting path). *)
                       begin
                          HandleBridge(vshrunk,wshrunk,v,w);
                          vshrunk := origin[Find(v)]
                             (* We may not have examined all edges incident upon v;
                                 v is different in the shrunken graph now. *)
                       end;
                (* If pred[wshrunk] indicates that wshrunk is odd,
                    then ignore the edge, since no knowledge is gained. *)
                p := p^.next
              end (* process adjacency list *)
          end; (* not IsEmptyBag *)
        (* We have not found an augmenting path. *)
        success := false;
99:
    end; (* AugmentingPath *)
```

Program 6.3: The Iterative Step for General Matching in $\Theta(|V| \cdot |E|)$ Time

Weighted Matching

As models of real-world optimization problems, the marriage and matching problems leave something to be desired, since they optimize only the number of matches made, not their "quality." We can improve the model by weighting the matches and asking for the matching of maximum total weight.

Problem 35 [Weighted Matching] Given a graph, $G = (V, E)$, and a weight for each edge, $w: E \to \mathcal{R}^+$, find a matching E' of maximum total weight.   □

When the graph is bipartite, the weighted matching problem is usually called the *assignment problem*,[4] because it models the assignment of a crew of workers to a set of tasks. In that setting, the presence of an edge (u_i, v_j) indicates that worker i is capable of carrying out task j, and the weight of that edge represents the profit to be derived from assigning worker i to task j.

The weighted matching problem subsumes the simpler general matching problem: just assign unit weight to all edges. In a weighted matching problem, however, it may well happen that no maximum cardinality matching is optimal, so that any algorithm based on augmentation must include some mechanism to stop the process when an optimal matching is found. In order to use augmenting path methods, we must alter our choice of augmenting paths so as to ensure that the matching obtained does have maximum total weight among all matchings of a given cardinality. When our only goal was to find some larger matching, we had total freedom in choosing the augmenting paths; as our goal now is to maximize the total weight, a sensible choice for an iterative step is to choose an augmenting path which causes the largest weight increase.

Theorem 6.12 Beginning with an empty matching and applying k maximum-weight augmentations yields a matching of maximum total weight among all matchings of size k. $\qquad\qquad\square$

Proof: We proceed by induction on k. The basis is vacuously true. Assume then that we have constructed, by successive maximum-weight augmentations, a maximum-weight matching of size k, call it M_k. Let M_{k+1} denote the matching of size $k+1$ obtained from M_k by one maximum-weight augmentation along path p_{max} and denote by M'_{k+1} some matching of size $k+1$ with maximum total weight. We form $M'_{k+1} \ominus M_k$ and, referring to the proof of Theorem 6.8, we examine the particulars of the three types of connected components. In a cycle of even length, the combined weight of those edges in M'_{k+1} must equal the combined weight of those edges in M_k, for otherwise, reversing the status of these edges will produce either a matching of size k or $k+1$ with total weight greater than that of M_k or M'_{k+1}, respectively. Next we pair off those components with $\delta(C_i) = \pm 1$; there will necessarily be one unaccounted component with $\delta(C_i) = 1$, which is an augmenting path we denote by p. As with even-length cycles, for each such pair, the combined weight of the edges in M'_{k+1} must equal the combined weight of the edges in M_k. Thus the total weight of M'_{k+1} is simply the total weight of M_k plus the weight increase caused by p. Since this increment is, by hypothesis, no larger than the weight increment caused by the maximum-weight augmenting

---

[4]In the literature of operations research, where this problem originally appeared, the underlying bipartite graph is assumed to be complete and to have an equal number of vertices on each side. In such a setting, the optimal solution is a perfect matching.

path, p_{max}, it follows that the total weight of matching M_{k+1} is at least as large as that of matching M'_{k+1}, proving our conclusion.

$$Q.E.D.$$

Exercise 6.1 Demonstrate that the increase due to a maximum-weight augmenting path can in fact be negative, then show that the successive increases form a monotone nonincreasing sequence.   □

An immediate corollary is that a matching has maximum weight exactly when no augmenting path of positive total weight can be found for it. Conceptually, then, our algorithm is:

- Repeat the following iterative step until no augmenting path of positive weight can be found:

  - Find an augmenting path of maximum weight with respect to the current matching.

  - Augment the current matching using this augmenting path.

Implementing this algorithm turns out to be difficult, especially in general graphs. Even in a bipartite graph, finding an augmenting path of maximum weight poses a challenge, since we know of algorithms to find paths of minimum cost, but not of algorithms to find paths of maximum cost; indeed, the latter problem appears to be intractable. Algorithms for weighted matching indeed do reduce the problem of finding augmenting paths of maximum weight to that of finding augmenting paths of minimum cost. An obvious transformation would replace each weight, w, with a cost, $M - w$, for a large value of M, but unfortunately it does not work because augmenting paths differ in length; the correct transformation is subtle. We do not present these algorithms, but refer the reader to the bibliography, noting only that weighted bipartite matching can be solved, using Dijkstra's algorithm with Fibonacci heaps, in $O(|V| \cdot (|E| + |V| \log |V|))$ time and that weighted general matching appears to take somewhat longer, with several algorithms running in $O(|E| \cdot |V| \log |V|)$ time on sparse graphs.

6.5 The Network Flow Problem

The network flow problem (Problem 7) was presented in Section 1.2; we repeat its definition for convenience. A network flow problem is given by an undirected, connected graph, $G = (V, E)$; a capacity function, $c: V \times V \to \mathcal{R}^+$, with $c(v, w) = c(w, v) = 0$ if $\{v, w\}$ is not an edge of G; and two distinguished vertices of V, the source, s, and the sink, t. The objective is to maximize the value of the flow

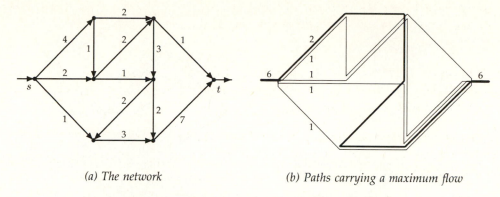

(a) The network　　　　　　(b) Paths carrying a maximum flow

Figure 6.15: Decomposition of Flow into Paths

from the source to the sink, where a flow is a real-valued function on pairs of vertices which obeys five conditions:

1. The flow assigned to an arc does not exceed its capacity: $f(v, w) \leq c(v, w)$.

2. The flow is skew-symmetric: $f(v, w) = -f(w, v)$.

3. There is conservation of flow, i.e., $\sum_w f(v, w) = 0$, at all vertices, v, other than s and t.

4. There is no flow into the source: $f(s, w) \geq 0$.

5. There is no flow out of the sink: $f(w, t) \geq 0$.

The value of a flow from s to t is simply the value of the net flow out of the source, $\sum_w f(s, w)$, which equals the net flow into the sink, $\sum_v f(v, t)$.[5]

6.5.1　Basic Definitions, Results, and Algorithms

A flow from s to t may be viewed as a collection of (possibly overlapping) paths from s to t, each delivering a fraction of the total flow. This view is illustrated in Figure 6.15, where the maximum flow of six is distributed along five paths. (In order to simplify the figure, we have used a directed graph in this example, one which we shall use repeatedly throughout this section.) This viewpoint, together with our experience with augmenting paths in the previous two sections, leads us

---

[5]We could also define the flow problem on a directed graph, $G = (V, A)$, with $c: A \rightarrow \mathcal{R}^+$, but this definition would leave open the possibility of simultaneous positive flow from v to w and from w to v along oppositely directed arcs. Our undirected formulation forces these flows to cancel, leaving at most one of them nonzero. Sometimes one formulation is more natural than the other, and we shall move freely between the two.

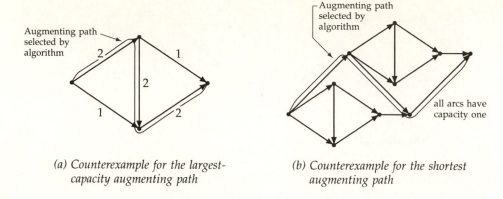

(a) Counterexample for the largest-
capacity augmenting path

(b) Counterexample for the shortest
augmenting path

Figure 6.16: The Naïve Algorithm Fails to Solve the Network Flow Problem

to propose a simple iterative algorithm for deriving a maximum flow: start with
a zero flow and repeatedly find an augmenting path from s to t, using the path
to augment the current flow. In the context of network flow, an augmenting path
is simply one along which no single arc is used to capacity, so that additional
flow may be pushed along the entire path from s to t. Formally, this algorithm
works as follows:

- Initialize the flow to zero: $f(v, w) \leftarrow 0$ for all v and w.

- Repeat these steps until there is no path from s to t:

    - Find any path, P, from s to t in the current graph; let Δ be the capacity
      of the arc of minimum capacity along this path, $\Delta = \min_{(v,w) \in P} c(v, w)$.

    - Record the change to the flow, i.e., let $f(v, w) \leftarrow f(v, w) + \Delta$ for all arcs
      of P and maintain skew-symmetry.

    - Decrease the capacity of all arcs along P by Δ, deleting all arcs for
      which the capacity becomes zero.

Unfortunately, this naïve approach runs into difficulties as soon as some consistent strategy for choosing paths is adopted. Figure 6.16 shows very simple graphs
on which the algorithm, choosing as the next path either that with largest Δ or
that with fewest arcs, fails to derive an optimal solution. In the first example, the
optimal flow has value three, while our naïve algorithm first chooses a path of
capacity two and then can make no further choices. In the second example, the
optimal flow has value two, while our naïve algorithm terminates after producing a flow of value one. (We leave as an open problem—see Exercise 6.29—the
harder question of whether there always exists some sequence of paths which

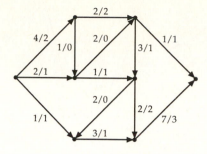
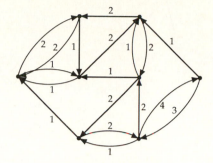

(a) The network, showing capacity/flow　　(b) The residual graph, with residual capacities

Figure 6.17: A Flow in a Network and the Corresponding Residual Network

yields the optimal flow.) The basic difficulty with the naïve approach is not due to an error in our overall design, but to our not having a sufficiently general notion of an augmenting path. Indeed, the naïve approach is essentially greedy, in that it never undoes what it has done in previous stages, whereas we have seen that augmenting path methods must have this capability.

Before proceeding with our discussion, we introduce some terminology. Given a graph, $G = (V, E)$, a capacity function, c, and a flow, f, we define the *residual capacity* of an arc, (v, w), as $r_f(v, w) = c(v, w) - f(v, w)$. The residual capacity of an arc indicates how much more flow can be effectively pushed along this arc: this is obvious if the flow, $f(v, w)$, is positive, while, if $f(v, w)$ is negative, then flow is going from w to v and we can push a total of $c(v, w) + f(w, v)$ (which equals $c(v, w) - f(v, w)$ by skew-symmetry) along the arc, first by pushing enough to cancel the existing flow and then by pushing additional flow equal to the capacity of the arc. Increasing the flow from v to w when there is actual flow from w to v, by "pushing flow against the current," is the fundamental technique used in network flow; viewed in terms of the iterative paradigm, it is what allows us to "correct mistakes" in flow assignments made in past iterations. We say that an arc is *saturated* if its residual capacity is zero. Given a path, P, from s to t, the residual capacity of the path is the minimum of the residual capacities of its arcs, $r_f(P) = \min_{(v,w) \in P} r_f(v, w)$. Finally, we define the *residual graph* of G with respect to f to be the directed graph $G_f = (V, R_f)$, where R_f is the set of unsaturated arcs, each with its residual capacity. Figure 6.17 illustrates this definition for the graph of Figure 6.15(a).

Exercise 6.2 Assume that the original graph of Figure 6.15(a) had been undirected. Draw the residual graph of this undirected graph with respect to the flow of Figure 6.17(a). □

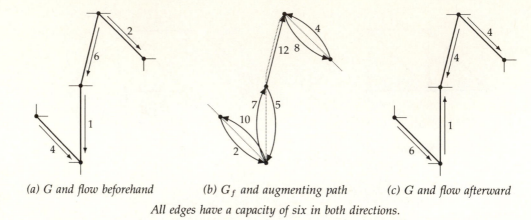

(a) G and flow beforehand   *(b) G_f and augmenting path*   *(c) G and flow afterward*

All edges have a capacity of six in both directions.

Figure 6.18: How Paths in the Residual Graph Reroute Flow in the Original Graph

An augmenting path in the original graph, G, is now defined as a path from the source to the sink in the residual graph, G_f. The move from G to G_f is crucial, because it allows pushing flow against the current. Figure 6.18 shows how an ordinary path in G_f actually reroutes flow in G. Using these terms, we can rephrase our proposed algorithm as follows:

- Initialize the flow to zero: $f(v, w) \leftarrow 0$ for all v and w.

- Repeat the following step until no augmenting path can be found:

  - Find an augmenting path, i.e., a path, P, from s to t in G_f; by construction, $r_f(P) > 0$. If such a path is found, use it to augment the flow: for each arc, $(v, w) \in P$, let $f(v, w) \leftarrow f(v, w) + r_f(P)$ and let $f(w, v) \leftarrow f(w, v) - r_f(P)$. Now rebuild the residual graph.

This is the basic network flow algorithm proposed by Ford and Fulkerson, who proved that it obtains an optimal solution if all capacities are integral but may fail to converge to a solution in a finite number of steps (and may converge in the limit to a local, but not global, optimum) when irrational capacities are allowed. That the algorithm must terminate when all capacities are integral is easily seen, since each augmentation must increase the flow value by a positive integral amount (since $r_f(P)$ is the minimum of a collection of positive integers, the problem remains integral throughout) and since the flow value is bounded by the integer $\sum_w c(s, w)$.

Imagine placing an arbitrary boundary between the source and the sink. Under steady-state conditions, where the flow leaving the source equals the flow

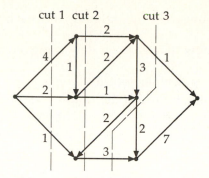

cut 1 cut 2   cut 3

Figure 6.19: Cuts in the Network of Figure 6.15(a)

entering the sink, the net flow crossing the boundary must equal the steady-state flow. The boundary effectively partitions the vertices of the graphs into two subsets, one containing the source, call it X, and the other containing the sink, $\overline{X} = V - X$; more formally, any such partition is called a *cut*, since it cuts all the arcs with an endpoint in each subset. The sum of the capacities of the arcs with tails in X and heads in $\overline{X}$ is known as the capacity of the cut. Figure 6.19 illustrates these concepts: in the figure, the first cut has a capacity of seven, the second has a capacity of eight (note that the arc of capacity two with tail in $\overline{X}$ and head in X is ignored), and the third, which is a minimum cut, has a capacity of six. The reader should not get the impression, which the figure may suggest, that either of X or $\overline{X}$ has to induce connected subgraphs: any partitioning of the vertices into X and $\overline{X}$, with $s \in X$ and $t \in \overline{X}$, is a cut.

From our remark about steady-state conditions, the capacity of any cut acts as an upper bound on the maximum flow. The capacity of the cut can exceed the flow, for two reasons: there may be edges with both endpoints in X (or $\overline{X}$) that restrict how much flow can get to the frontier of X from the source (or can reach the sink from the frontier of $\overline{X}$); and there can be flow crossing the boundary in the wrong direction (from $\overline{X}$ to X), diminishing the net flow from X to $\overline{X}$. Remarkably, the value of the maximum flow actually equals that of the minimum cut.

Theorem 6.13 [Max-flow Min-cut]   Let $G = (V, E)$ be a graph with capacity function c and let f be a flow. Then the following are equivalent:

1. f is a maximum flow.

2. There is no augmenting path in G with respect to f.

3. The value of f equals the capacity of some cut.

□

Proof: We prove the equivalence by setting up a circular chain of implications.

$(1 \Rightarrow 2)$ We have seen how to augment a flow using an augmenting path.

$(2 \Rightarrow 3)$ If there is no augmenting path in G with respect to f, then the set of vertices, X, reachable from s in the residual graph does not contain t, so that the partition, $V = (X, \overline{X})$, is a cut. The capacity of this cut is

$$\sum_{v \in X,\, w \in \overline{X}} c(v, w).$$

We argue that this sum is exactly equal to the value of the flow. Our earlier remarks imply that the value of the flow, the amount of material leaving the source, is equal to the flow across the cut from X to $\overline{X}$, after accounting for any backward flow from $\overline{X}$ to X. Due to the nature of this particular cut, there cannot be any backward flow from a vertex $w \in \overline{X}$ to a vertex $v \in X$; if there were, then the residual graph would have an arc from v to w, w would be reachable from s, and w would be in X rather than in $\overline{X}$. Similarly, every arc from X to $\overline{X}$ is saturated, that is, $f(v, w) = c(v, w)$, and the claim is proved.

$(3 \Rightarrow 1)$ Since the capacity of any cut is an upper bound on the value of any flow, it follows that an equality implies that f is a maximum flow.

Q.E.D.

This theorem embodies a rich mathematical concept known as *duality*, here in the duality between flows and cuts; another example is the König-Egerváry theorem, which establishes the duality between vertex covers and matchings. Together with our remark about termination, the max-flow min-cut theorem proves the correctness of Ford and Fulkerson's algorithm for networks with integral capacities. An immediate corollary is that any network with integral capacities has an integral maximum flow—solving a question which we raised in Exercise 1.10.

We make a few comments about this remarkable theorem. First, note that it places no restrictions on the capacity function; that is, the failure of Ford and Fulkerson's algorithm on some networks with irrational capacities comes from poor convergence properties and is not due to the existence of graphs on which there is a nonmaximum flow, relative to which there is no augmenting path. Secondly, this theorem may be viewed as a generalization of the König-Egerváry theorem. We can rephrase a bipartite matching problem as a network flow problem in the following manner: given the bipartite graph $G = (V, E)$, with $V = V_l \cup V_r$, we set up a network with vertex set $V \cup \{s, t\}$, edge set

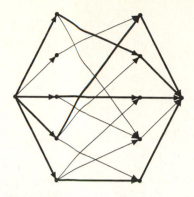

(a) *The graph and a matching*   (b) *The network and a flow*

Figure 6.20: A Bipartite Matching Problem and the Corresponding Network Flow Problem

$E \cup \{ (s,v) \mid v \in V_l \} \cup \{ (w,t) \mid w \in V_r \}$, and capacity function defined by

$$c(v,w) = \begin{cases} 1 & \text{if } v = s \text{ and } w \in V_l \text{ or } v \in V_r \text{ and } w = t; \\ M & \text{if } v \in V_l \text{ and } w \in V_r; \text{ and} \\ 0 & \text{otherwise,} \end{cases}$$

where M is a large number. Figure 6.20 shows a bipartite graph and the resulting network. An integral flow from s to t of value k saturates k arcs from s to vertices in V_l and k arcs from vertices in V_r to t; in between, it just establishes a matching of size k. Hence there exists a one-to-one correspondence between matchings in G and integral flows in the corresponding network; in particular, maximum matchings correspond to maximum flows. Similarly, each vertex cover, V_c, of size k in the bipartite graph gives rise to a cut, $(X, \overline{X})$, of capacity k in the network, where $X = \{s\} \cup (V_l \cap \overline{V_c}) \cup (V_r \cap V_c)$. The partition cuts exactly $|V_l \cap V_c|$ arcs from s to V_l and exactly $|V_r \cap V_c|$ arcs from V_r to t, for a total of $|V_c| = k$ such arcs, so that the capacity of the cut is at least k. Because V_c is a vertex cover, there cannot be an edge connecting $v \in V_l$ and $w \in V_r$ where v and w are both uncovered, that is, where $v \in X$ and $w \in \overline{X}$, so the capacity of the cut is exactly k. Phrased another way, each arc in the network, other than those emanating from the source or terminating at the sink, goes from X to X (uncovered on the left to covered on the right), $\overline{X}$ to $\overline{X}$ (covered on the left to uncovered on the right), or $\overline{X}$ to X (covered on the left to covered on the right). The correspondence is not one-to-one here, since cuts exist where the vertices in $(\overline{X} \cap V_l) \cup (X \cap V_r)$ do not form a cover; in such cases, however, at least one of the cut edges has capacity M, so that the cut is not a cut of minimum capacity. Under this correspondence, the

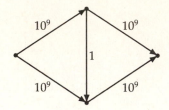

Figure 6.21: A Worst-Case Instance for Ford and Fulkerson's Algorithm

König-Egerváry theorem simply reduces to the max-flow min-cut theorem. As a final remark, note that arcs from V_l to V_r need not be assigned a capacity of M, but can be assigned a capacity of one: the real limiting factor at each node of V_l is that the inflow is limited to one, so that reducing the capacity of arcs from V_l to V_r to one does not diminish any potential flow.

While Ford and Fulkerson's algorithm returns the correct answer in finite time for networks with integral capacities, it suffers from two problems. First, it is inapplicable to networks with irrational capacities—assuming that such networks are of interest. Secondly, it may be very inefficient: Figure 6.21 shows a simple network on which there always exists an augmenting path of unit residual capacity (in the residual graph the middle edge always has unit capacity, but alternates direction) and thus on which the algorithm may take time proportional to the value of the maximum flow. Since this value may be arbitrarily large, Ford and Fulkerson's algorithm might not run in polynomial time. That we might be able to do much better is indicated by the following theorem.

Theorem 6.14 Given an arbitrary network, with underlying graph $G = (V, E)$, a maximum flow can be constructed from the null flow in at most $|E|$ steps, with each step augmenting the flow along a single augmenting path.   □

Proof: Let f^* be a maximum flow and consider the directed graph G^* induced by the set of arcs with positive flow values. Repeat the following steps: find (in G^*) a path, P, from source to sink; augment the current flow in G along the path by $\Delta = \min_{(v,w) \in P} f^*(v, w)$; update the flow values in G^* along the arcs of P (i.e., let $f^*(v, w) \leftarrow f^*(v, w) - \Delta$ for all $(v, w) \in P$); and remove from G^* all arcs with zero resulting flow. The last step always removes at least one arc from G^*; since G^* had at most $|E|$ arcs initially, it follows that at most $|E|$ steps can be taken, at which point the value of the flow in G^* has been reduced to zero and that of the flow in G correspondingly increased to the value of the maximum flow.

Q.E.D.

Note that the augmentation along each augmenting path in G may not use the full residual capacity of the path; on the other hand, it never has to reroute flow. We remarked on this informally when we discussed decomposing a flow into a collection of paths and showed why our naïve algorithm failed. This theorem gives us more information, since it bounds the number of these paths; unfortunately, it only indicates possibilities, but does not provide an algorithm, since the method of construction depends on knowledge of a maximum flow.

A natural suggestion at this point is to augment along augmenting paths of maximum residual capacity; observe, for instance, that such a strategy constructs a maximum flow in just two augmentations on the network of Figure 6.21. Our experience with augmenting path methods in matching, and the close connection between network flow and bipartite matching observed previously, also suggests augmenting along a shortest augmenting path. Maximum-capacity augmentation indeed runs in polynomial time on networks with integral capacities, but it remains dependent on the value of the maximum flow; hence it does not completely fulfill our objectives.

Theorem 6.15 On graphs with integral capacities, the maximum-capacity augmentation algorithm returns a maximum flow in $\Theta(|E| \log c_{\max})$ augmentations, where $c_{\max}$ is the largest capacity. □

Since we want an algorithm that returns a maximum flow for any capacity assignment and the behavior of which depends on only the size of the network, we do not further pursue maximum-capacity augmentation, but turn instead to shortest-path augmentation. We proceed with this idea much as we did with shortest-path augmentation in matching problems, establishing basic results through a series of simple theorems. We begin with a fundamental result, which underlies almost all network flow algorithms; in its basic form, this result can be stated succinctly as "successive shortest augmenting paths have nondecreasing length" or, equivalently, as "when shortest-path augmentation is used, the distance from the source to the sink in successive residual graphs never decreases." A few minutes of thought shows that the behavior of the distance from the source to the sink is in fact tied to the behavior of the distance from the source to any vertex of the residual graph; we now prove this somewhat stronger result.

Lemma 6.1 After a shortest-path augmentation, the distance from the source to any vertex in the new residual graph is no less than it was in the previous residual graph. Moreover, if a shortest augmenting path, P, saturates some edge, e, then the length of the next shortest augmenting path that includes this edge must exceed the length of P by at least two. □

Proof: Let $G = (V, E)$ be the graph, f be the current flow, G_f be the corresponding residual graph, and P be a shortest augmenting path with respect to f. Use breadth-first search to label each vertex of G_f with its distance from the source. A shortest path from the source to any vertex uses only arcs that go from a vertex to another, the label of which is one larger; in particular, this is true of P. Now consider the result of augmenting f using P. This augmentation saturates at least one arc along P, and each such saturated arc gets removed from the residual graph; in addition, backward arcs may be added whenever the augmentation pushes flow through a forward arc that had no flow through it under f. The result of these deletions of forward arcs and additions of backward arcs is the new residual graph. Since shorter paths can only be created by the addition of forward arcs, shortest paths from the source to any vertex cannot have decreased in length.

A similar argument, using distances computed by backward breadth-first search from the sink, shows that successive shortest-path augmentations never decrease the distance from a vertex to the sink. Now consider an edge, $e = \{v, w\}$, saturated by P; assume that P saturates it with a positive flow from v to w. The length of this path is the distance from the source to w plus the distance from v to the sink minus one because the arc (v, w) is counted twice. Because the forward arc, (v, w), is removed from the residual graph after augmentation, and the corresponding backward arc, (w, v), is added if not already present, the next augmenting path to use this edge must use it from w to v. The length of this path is the distance from the source to w plus the distance from v to the sink plus one, since the arc (w, v) must now be counted. As the current distances are no less than the old ones, the result follows.

$$Q.E.D.$$

We can now prove a bound on the total number of augmentations needed to construct a maximum flow.

Theorem 6.16 Starting from the null flow, a series of at most $|E| \cdot |V|/2$ shortest-path augmentations produces a maximum flow. $\square$

Proof: Denote the successive shortest augmenting paths by $P_1, P_2, \ldots, P_n$. We track the history of one edge $\{v, w\}$. Assume that the ith augmentation saturates this edge as arc (v, w); then, when v and w next appear as consecutive vertices in an augmenting path, say in path P_j, it will be as arc (w, v). Our previous lemma shows that P_j is longer than P_i by at least two edges. It follows that the same edge can be saturated (in either direction) at most $|V|/2$ times. Our conclusion follows immediately from applying this result independently to each of the $|E|$

edges and from the knowledge that each augmentation must saturate at least one edge.

Q.E.D.

Since we can find a shortest path in the residual graph in $\Theta(|E|)$ time using breadth-first search and since maintaining the residual graph itself requires only $\Theta(|V|)$ time, it follows that shortest-path augmentation leads to a $\Theta(|V| \cdot |E|^2)$ algorithm—one can devise examples on which the algorithm runs this slowly. As desired, this algorithm runs on all networks and its running time depends only on the size of the networks, not on the capacity values.[6] The bound on the number of required augmentations assumes that no augmenting path saturates more than one edge at a time and that every edge gets saturated $|V|/2$ times; such a conjunction is very unlikely, so that the bound will only rarely be reached.

6.5.2 Blocking Flows and Level Graphs

Since finding one shortest path from the source to the sink involves a breadth-first search exploration of the residual graph, much information is elicited during such a search that our basic algorithm does not put to use. Just as we modified our basic augmentation method for matching so as to use as many paths as possible at once, let us now modify our basic shortest-path augmentation method. Because a shortest augmenting path will, in all likelihood, not saturate all of the arcs it uses, we cannot simply search for a maximal collection of arc-disjoint augmenting paths as we did for the matching problem: in such a collection there may well remain a shortest path of nonzero residual capacity from source to sink, a path that uses nonsaturated arcs from a number of paths in the collection. What we need is a flow that saturates at least one arc on every path from source to sink, a concept known as a *blocking flow*. Note that we made no mention of path length in this definition. We have encountered blocking flows before: our first naïve approach constructed a single blocking flow on G. While a single blocking flow may not yield an optimal solution, we can iterate the process.

- Initialize the flow to zero.

- Repeat until the sink cannot be reached from the source in the residual graph:

    - Find a blocking flow, call it f', on G_f, and increase f by f'.

---

[6]At least, such dependency is not direct, as in Ford and Fulkerson's algorithm; some dependency remains, since all algorithms based on augmentation must compute flow values and such computations take time proportional to $\log F$, where F is the value of the maximum flow. This factor, which we take to be a constant for reasonable capacity assignments, multiplies all running times derived in this section, including those, such as the running time of maximum-capacity augmentation, which already include such a factor.

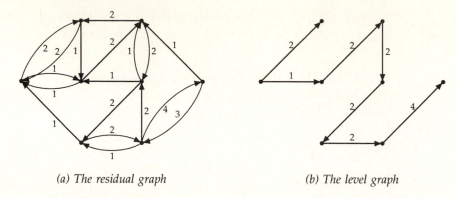

(a) The residual graph   (b) The level graph

Figure 6.22: A Residual Graph and Its Corresponding Level Graph

This is just the Ford and Fulkerson algorithm with a single augmenting path replaced by a blocking flow. As with matching, we hope to gain efficiency by finding a blocking flow without significantly more work than is required to find a single augmenting path. Each iteration of the inner loop, called a *stage*, corresponds to running our naïve algorithm on the residual graph obtained at the end of the previous stage; in view of our previous results, we conclude that the blocking flow algorithm is correct and terminates (at least for integral flows).

While our revision of the basic Ford and Fulkerson algorithm suggests that we find a blocking flow on the residual graph, this is not necessary and not even necessarily a good choice. Instead, we consider a subgraph of the residual graph, the *level graph*, $\hat{G}_f = (V, L_f)$, defined by scanning the residual graph in a breadth-first manner and retaining only the forward arcs, labelled with their capacities. Figure 6.22 illustrates this construction. Level graphs have a very rigid structure: each node is assigned to a single level (given by the length of the shortest path from the source to the vertex), and each arc goes from one level to the next. While level graphs are more rigid than is necessary for the operation of efficient blocking flow algorithms (in particular, a blocking flow on the level graph may not be a blocking flow on the residual graph), they are acyclic, a property that many blocking flow algorithms use to great advantage. Their rigidity also simplifies the task of bounding the number of stages required by blocking flow methods.

Theorem 6.17 From the null flow, a sequence of at most $|V| - 1$ blocking flow augmentations derived from the level graph constructs a maximum flow.

□

Proof: The proof uses the same technique as was used in the proof of Lemma 6.1: in each successive level graph, the sink is farther away from the source.

$$Q.E.D.$$

This theorem further demonstrates the strong similarity between our efficient bipartite matching algorithm and the method of blocking flows: in both algorithms, the length of a shortest augmenting path increases after each stage.

We now turn to developing an efficient algorithm for finding a blocking flow on an acyclic network. We use nonrecursive depth-first search, recording the current search path on the stack, and do additional work when an augmenting path is discovered. Specifically, we find a blocking flow on an acyclic graph, with designated source, s, and sink, t, as follows:

- *Initialize*: Push the source, s, onto the stack; let $v = s$.

- *Advance*: If $v = t$, then go to *Augment*. If $v \neq t$ and there is no arc out of v, then go to *Retreat*. Otherwise, let (v, w) be an arc emanating from v. Push w onto the stack, set v to w, and go to *Advance*.

- *Retreat*: If $v = s$, the algorithm terminates. Otherwise, let (u, v) be the last arc on the path. Delete arc (u, v) from the graph, set v to u, and go to *Advance*.

- *Augment*: Let Δ be the minimum capacity of the arcs along the path recorded on the stack: decrease the capacity of all the arcs along the path by Δ, deleting all arcs of zero remaining capacity. Go to *Initialize*.

The correctness of the algorithm rests on the following invariant: whenever an arc is deleted, there is no path from the source to the sink passing through this arc. The running time of these modifications to depth-first search depends on the cost and number of augmentations. There is one *Advance* step for each *Retreat* step (these are the steps of the depth-first search); in addition there is one *Advance* step for each arc of an augmenting path. Hence the total running time is $\Theta(|A| + \sum_{i=1}^{k} l_i)$, where k is the number of augmenting paths discovered and l_i is the length of the ith augmenting path. While k can be as large as $|A|$, it cannot exceed $|A|$, because each augmenting path deletes at least one edge. Running on the level graph, the resulting flow algorithm, known as Dinic's algorithm, takes $\Theta(|V|^2 \cdot |A|)$ time; once again, the worst case, while realizable, is highly unlikely, and this algorithm runs much faster in practice. Compared with the shortest augmenting path algorithm, Dinic's algorithm gains by replacing a factor of $|A|$ with a factor of $|V|$.

To avoid needless repetition, the declarations that we use for our presentation of graph flow algorithms (a modification of those given in Program 4.1) are

```
const MaxVertex = ...;

type vertex = 1 .. MaxVertex;
     PtrToNode = ^node;
     node = record (* for arc (v,w) *)
               w: vertex;
               c, f: real; (* c(v,w) and f(v,w) *)
               wv, (* pointer to node for arc (w,v) *)
               next: PtrToNode
            end;
     graph = record
                 size: integer; (* number of vertices *)
                 AdjLists: array [vertex] of PtrToNode
                   (* array for random access to list heads *)
             end;
       (* c(v,s) = 0 for all v and c(t,w) = 0 for all w are assumed. *)
```

Program 6.4: Declarations Used in Maximum Flow Algorithms

given in Program 6.4. We assume that, for each edge of G, there are two arcs in the internal representation of the graph, even if the capacity in one direction or the other is zero; we can then avoid explicit construction of the residual graph. Similarly, we avoid explicit construction of the level graphs used by Dinic's algorithm, as shown in Program 6.5. We use the same technique for implicitly deleting edges as we used in Program 6.2. The total amount of additional storage is linear in the number of vertices.

The running time of this algorithm is considerably worse than that of our corresponding bipartite matching algorithm, yet we have argued that finding a maximum bipartite matching is exactly the same problem as that of finding a maximum flow in a special network. As we shall soon see, our improved flow algorithm in fact runs on such networks within the same time bounds as our bipartite matching algorithm. The structure of the network influences both the running time of the blocking flow step and the number of required stages. We look at two specific network structures: those with unit capacities and those with an added structural requirement designed to characterize networks obtained from matching problems.

Lemma 6.2 In a network where all arcs have unit capacity, the length of the shortest path from the source to the sink cannot exceed $(|V|-1)/\sqrt{F^*}$, where F^* is the value of a maximum flow. □

Proof: Let the length of the shortest path from the source to the sink be denoted by L and let the set of vertices of the graph at level i be denoted by $V(i)$. For

```
procedure MaxFlow(var G: graph;
                       s, t: vertex);
  (* Find the maximum flow from s to t for a graph, G=(V,E), with capacity
     function c, using Dinic's algorithm. *)

  (* Program assumes a queue package with the ability to declare queues
     and with operations
         procedure CreateQueue(var Q: queue), ResetQueueEmpty(var Q: queue),
         function IsEmptyQueue(var Q: queue): boolean,
         procedure Enqueue(v: vertex; var Q: queue), and
         procedure Dequeue(var v: vertex; var Q: queue). *)

  label 1, 2, 3, 4, 98, 99;
  var level: array [vertex] of integer;
        (* Depth of vertices in the level graph. *)
      p: array [vertex] of PtrToNode;
        (* For each vertex, a pointer to the next arc to be used in the dfs. *)
      path: array [1..MaxVertex] of vertex;
        (* The current path in the implicit tree of the dfs--a stack. *)
      BFS, (* for performing breadth-first search *)
      InLevelGraph: (* for efficient resetting of level[ ] after a stage *)
        queue;
      q: PtrToNode;
      v: vertex;
      i, j: integer;
      Delta: real;
  begin
    CreateQueue(BFS); CreateQueue(InLevelGraph);
    (* Begin with the null (or arbitrary) flow--O(E). *)
    for v := 1 to G.size do
      begin
        level[v] := G.size + 1; (* infinity *)
        q := G.AdjLists[v];
        while q <> nil do begin q^.f := 0; q := q^.next end
      end;

    while true do (* Escape when no augmenting path is present. *)
      begin
        (* Build the level graph--O(E). *)
        ResetQueueEmpty(BFS);
        Enqueue(s,BFS); Enqueue(s,InLevelGraph);
        level[s] := 0;
        p[s] := G.AdjLists[s];
        while not IsEmptyQueue(BFS) do
          begin
            Dequeue(v,BFS);
            (* Quit building the level graph when the sink is included and a node
               is reached in the bfs that is at the same level as the sink. *)
            if level[v] = level[t] then goto 1;
            q := G.AdjLists[v];
```

```
          while q <> nil do
            begin
              (* if the arc exists in the residual graph and the arc
                 introduces a new vertex into the level graph *)
              if (q^.f < q^.c) and (level[q^.w] = G.size + 1)
                then begin
                        level[q^.w] := level[v] + 1;
                        p[q^.w] := G.AdjLists[q^.w];
                        Enqueue(q^.w,BFS); Enqueue(q^.w,InLevelGraph)
                     end;
              q := q^.next
            end
        end;
    (* We can no longer reach t from s--there are no augmenting paths. *)
    goto 99; (* return *)

    (* Find a blocking flow--O(E + kV). *)
1: (* Initialize *)
   path[1] := s; i := 1; v := s;

2: (* Advance *)
   if v = t then goto 4; (* goto Augment *)
3: while p[v] <> nil do
     begin
       (* if the arc is in the level graph *)
       if (level[p[v]^.w] = level[v] + 1) and (p[v]^.f < p[v]^.c)
         then begin
                 i := i + 1;
                 path[i] := p[v]^.w;
                 v := p[v]^.w;
                 goto 2 (* goto Advance *)
              end;
       p[v] := p[v]^.next
     end;

   (* Retreat *)
   if v = s then goto 98; (* goto Stage_Completed *)
   i := i - 1;
   v := path[i];
   p[v] := p[v]^.next; (* effectively delete edge *)
   goto 3; (* goto Advance, but v cannot equal t *)

4: (* Augment *)
   (* Find the amount of flow we can push along this path. *)
   Delta := p[path[1]]^.c - p[path[1]]^.f;
   for j := 2 to i - 1 do
     if p[path[j]]^.c - p[path[j]]^.f < Delta
       then Delta := p[path[j]]^.c - p[path[j]]^.f;
```

```
              (* Push this much flow. *)
              for j := 1 to i - 1 do
                begin
                  p[path[j]]^.f := p[path[j]]^.f + Delta;
                  p[path[j]]^.wv^.f := -p[path[j]]^.f;
                  if p[path[j]]^.f = 0
                    then p[path[j]] := p[path[j]]^.next (* effectively delete edge *)
                end;
              goto 1; (* Start the search over on what is left of the level graph. *)

        98: (* Stage_Completed *)
            (* Get ready for next iteration. *)
            while not IsEmptyQueue(InLevelGraph) do
              begin
                Dequeue(v,InLevelGraph);
                level[v] := G.size + 1
              end
          end;
  99:
    end; (* MaxFlow *)
```

Program 6.5: Dinic's Algorithm for Finding a Maximum Flow

each $i < L$, the set of vertices $X = \bigcup_{k=0}^{i} V(k)$ defines a cut; the capacity of each such cut is exactly the number of arcs from $V(i)$ to $V(i+1)$, which cannot exceed $|V(i)| \cdot |V(i+1)|$. The max-flow min-cut theorem then implies that this product cannot be less than F^*, which in turn implies that the sum of the sizes of $V(i)$ and $V(i+1)$ is at least $2\sqrt{F^*}$. Hence, by considering levels two at a time, we see that $(2\sqrt{F^*})(L/2) \leq |V| - 1$ holds when L is even (we treat the source separately) and that $(2\sqrt{F^*})((L+1)/2) \leq |V|$ holds when L is odd, which proves our lemma.

$$Q.E.D.$$

We now consider the class of networks in which all arcs have unit capacity and at most one of (v, w) and (w, v) are present. Such networks, called *unit capacity networks*, have the property that, if f is an integral flow on the network, the residual graph with respect to f is also a unit capacity network.

Theorem 6.18 In a unit capacity network, $\Theta(|V|^{2/3})$ stages, using integral blocking flows derived from the level graph, produce a maximum flow from the null flow. □

Proof: Let the value of a maximum flow be F^*. If $F^* \leq |V|^{2/3}$, then we are done, since each blocking flow must increase the flow by at least one unit. Otherwise, consider the step k at which the flow exceeds $F^* - |V|^{2/3}$ for the first time. Let F

be the flow at the start of step k and let F' be the flow at the end of step k; we can write $F \leq F^* - |V|^{2/3} < F'$. After step k, at most $|V|^{2/3}$ stages will be required. As noted above, the residual graph at the start of step k satisfies the conditions of the previous lemma, so that the distance from the source to the sink at the start of step k is less than $|V|/\sqrt{\Delta}$, where Δ is the value of the maximum flow on that residual graph. By construction, we have $\Delta = F^* - F \geq |V|^{2/3}$, so that we can write $|V|/\sqrt{\Delta} \leq |V|/\sqrt{|V|^{2/3}} = |V|^{2/3}$. Since the distance from the source to the sink is the same in the level graph as in the residual graph, and since that distance in the level graph must increase by at least one at each stage, that distance must be at least k at the kth step. We thus obtain $k \leq |V|^{2/3}$, which proves our theorem.

$Q.E.D.$

Now note that, on a unit capacity network, each augmenting path saturates all of its arcs at once; hence the bound on the running time of our depth-first search algorithm for blocking flows becomes simply $\Theta(|A|)$. Putting this new bound together with the theorem above, we conclude that Dinic's algorithm finds a maximum flow on a unit capacity network in $\Theta(|V|^{2/3} \cdot |A|)$ time. It is interesting to note that the algorithm does not change at all (the code of Program 6.5 requires no modifications whatsoever): it is the analysis of the running time of the algorithm that has changed, by making use of the special structure of the network.

The running time of our blocking flow method on unit capacity networks still does not equal the running time of our fast bipartite matching algorithm. The networks corresponding to bipartite matching problems have, in fact, additional structure: each vertex, other than the source and the sink, has associated with it either at most one incoming arc or at most one outgoing arc. A network with this last property is usually termed *simple*; a simple network which is also a unit capacity network is called a *unit network*. Like unit capacity networks, unit networks have the property that, for any integral flow, the corresponding residual graph is also a unit network.

Lemma 6.3 In a unit network, the length of the shortest path from the source to the sink is less than $|V|/F^* + 1$, where F^* is the value of a maximum flow.

□

Proof: The proof is similar to that of Lemma 6.2. Notice that, in a unit network, the maximum amount of flow that can pass through any given vertex (other than the source and sink) is one unit. Hence, since at least F^* units flow from $V(i)$ to $V(i+1)$, it follows that $|V(i)| \geq F^*$ holds for all i in the range from 1 to L. As a result, we can write $F^* \cdot (L-1) \leq |V| - 2$, and our conclusion follows.

$Q.E.D.$

Theorem 6.19 In a unit network, $\Theta(\sqrt{|V|})$ stages, using integral blocking flows derived from the level graph, produce a maximum flow from the null flow.

□

We leave the proof to the reader: it follows along the exact same lines as the proof of Theorem 6.18. The theorem is also a direct analogue of Theorem 6.10, in which we established the number of stages for our fast bipartite matching algorithm. We conclude that the method of blocking flows runs in $\Theta(\sqrt{|V|}\cdot|A|)$ time on unit networks, which is the running time of our fast bipartite matching algorithm.

A particularly interesting application of flow on these special networks is the study of graph connectivity. Given an undirected graph and two distinguished vertices, considered as source and sink, construct a network by replacing each vertex, v, with two vertices, v_{in} and v_{out}, connected by an arc from v_{in} to v_{out} and by replacing each edge, $\{v, w\}$, of the graph with a pair of arcs, (v_{out}, w_{in}) and (w_{out}, v_{in}), assigning unit capacities throughout. (For the source, there is only v_{out} and for the sink there is only v_{in}.) This graph is a unit network, so that we can find the maximum flow from the source to the sink in $\Theta(\sqrt{|V|}\cdot|E|)$ time. The maximum flow in this network is precisely equal to the number of vertex-disjoint paths from the source to the sink, i.e., the degree of connectivity between these two vertices. By letting the choice of source and sink run over all possible vertex pairs, we can determine the connectivity of a graph in $\Theta(|V|^{5/2} \cdot |E|)$ time. This algorithm runs rather slowly when compared with known linear-time algorithms for simple connectivity, biconnectivity, and triconnectivity, but has the significant advantage of complete generality. Exercise 6.26 explores a somewhat faster algorithm based on network flow to determine the edge connectivity of a graph.

6.5.3 The Gravity Flow Method

Is there still room for improvement? Theorem 6.14 states that, using "divine guidance," at most $|E|$ augmentations, each along a single, though possibly non-saturating, augmenting path, suffice to construct a maximum flow. Thus an algorithm running in $O(|V|\cdot|E|)$ time might be possible. While no such algorithm is yet known, a legion of algorithms running in $\Theta(|V|^3)$ time, just as fast as $\Theta(|V|\cdot|E|)$ on dense networks, have been developed. Most use the idea of finding blocking flows on the level graph, but use a method for finding such flows in $\Theta(|V|^2)$ time, whereas Dinic's algorithm finds them in $\Theta(|V|\cdot|E|)$ time. Instead of pursuing this approach, we present a completely different algorithm, not even based on augmentation, which runs in $\Theta(|V|^3)$ time with a simple implementation, in $\Theta(|V|^2\sqrt{|E|})$ time with a dedicated data structure, and in $O(|V|\cdot|E|\log(|V|^2/|E|))$ time with sophisticated data structures. Our new algorithm relies on a basic and very intuitive analogy with gravity: if we hold the source high up and place the sink at ground level, then we should be able just to "pour" flow into the source and have it flow down to the sink and out. In greedy fashion, we pour as much flow into the source as allowed by the total capacity of the arcs leaving it. If excess flow accumulates at a bottleneck (i.e., at a vertex, all downward arcs out of which are saturated), we attempt to reroute it through other vertices by lifting the bottleneck vertex to a higher level in order to allow the excess flow to move downwards. If we cannot reroute some of the excess flow, we eventually send it back into the source, thereby effectively removing it from the network. During execution of this algorithm, we never have a legal flow on the network; it is only when the algorithm terminates that the amounts present in the various arcs define a legal flow—and then it is a maximum flow.

Let us define a *preflow* as an assignment $f: V \times V \to \mathcal{R}$ satisfying all conditions imposed on a flow, except conservation, which is replaced by the weaker condition that the total inflow, $e(v) = \sum_{u \in V} f(u, v)$, be nonnegative at all vertices (except the source). The initial preflow is zero on all arcs except those out of the source, where it equals the capacity of the arc. We can define residual capacities and a residual graph with respect to a preflow in exactly the same way as for a true flow. We shall work on only the residual graph; as the basic operation for altering flow in our algorithm moves it along only one arc, maintenance of the residual graph is trivial.

Essential to our algorithm is a labelling of the vertices, which represents the "height" of the vertices in the current residual graph; the relative height of the two endpoints of an arc determines whether or not gravity can cause flow from the tail to the head of the arc. More importantly for our analysis, we require the labelling to serve as a lower bound on the distance in the residual graph from a vertex to the sink, where we want the excess flow to go; when the sink is no longer reachable from the vertex, we require the labelling to indicate this condition and serve as a lower bound on the distance from the vertex to the source, where we now want the excess flow to go. Since the distance from a vertex to the sink cannot reach $|V|$, we let the labelling indicate unreachability by using values larger than or equal to $|V|$, in which case subtracting $|V|$ from the label must yield the desired lower bound on the distance to the source.

Definition 6.3 Let $G_f = (V, A_f)$ be a residual graph, with source s and sink t. A *valid labelling* on G_f is a function, $d: V \to \{0, 1, \ldots, 2|V| - 1\}$, such that the following hold: $d(s) = |V|$, $d(t) = 0$, and, for each arc $(v, w) \in A_f$, $d(v) \le d(w)+1$.
□

This definition limits the slope of downward arcs, since the tail of such an arc must be exactly one level higher than the head.

Any valid labelling satisfies our requirements as to lower bounds, even if only in trivial and uninteresting ways.

Lemma 6.4 Let $G_f = (V, A_f)$ be a residual graph with a valid labelling. If there exists a path from v to t in G_f, then $d(v)$ is a lower bound on the length of the shortest such path. Similarly, if there exists a path from v to s in G_f, then $d(v) - |V|$ is a lower bound on the length of the shortest such path.   □

Proof: Let $v = v_0, v_1, \ldots, v_l = t$ be the shortest path from v to t. Note that, for all i, $0 \le i < l$, we have $d(v_i) \le d(v_{i+1}) + 1$, which, together with $d(t) = 0$, limits $d(v_0)$ to a maximum value of l, achievable only if equality holds at each step. If paths exist from v to both s and t in G_f, then the preceding remark implies that $d(v) - |V|$ is negative, since the shortest path from v to t has length less than $|V|$; thus $d(v) - |V|$ is surely a (ridiculous) lower bound on the length of the shortest path from v to s. If there is no path from v to t, then an argument similar to our first establishes the claim.

Q.E.D.

The gravity flow algorithm uses two basic operations: one, called PUSH, for moving excess flow, and the other, called RELABEL, for maintaining the labelling. These operations only apply to vertices with excess flow, vertices which we term *active*; the source and the sink are never active. The beauty of the algorithm is that, as we shall see, we can perform these operations in any order and to any vertex to which they apply: the ordering of operations affects efficiency, but it does not affect correctness.

A PUSH operation sends as much excess flow as possible along a downward arc out of an active vertex.

- PUSH: This operation applies to active vertices, v, for which there exists $(v, w) \in A_f$ with $d(v) = d(w) + 1$. It carries out the following four assignments: $e(v) \leftarrow e(v) - \Delta$, $f(v, w) \leftarrow f(v, w) + \Delta$, $f(w, v) \leftarrow f(w, v) - \Delta$, and $e(w) \leftarrow e(w) + \Delta$, where Δ equals $\min\{e(v), r_f(v, w)\}$.

If the residual arc is used to capacity, we call the operation a *saturating push*.

A RELABEL operation applies to a vertex that is no higher than any of the vertices adjacent to it in the residual graph; it lifts that vertex to the highest possible level consistent with a valid labelling, which is also the lowest possible level that allows excess flow to escape.

- RELABEL: This operation applies to active vertices, v, such that $d(v) < d(w) + 1$ holds for all arcs $(v, w) \in A_f$. It carries out the assignment $d(v) \leftarrow \min_{(v,w) \in A_f}\{d(w) + 1\}$.

The two operations are mutually exclusive, but one always applies to an active vertex, since a vertex with excess flow cannot be a sink in the residual graph.

Notice that the label associated with a vertex never decreases, because the only operation affecting labels is RELABEL, which always increases the value of the label. Because both operations depend on a valid labelling, it is crucial that they maintain one.

Lemma 6.5 Any sequence of PUSH and RELABEL operations, starting with an arbitrary preflow and a valid labelling, maintains a preflow and a valid labelling.

$\square$

Proof: We do not show that the label of a vertex cannot exceed $2|V| - 1$, but only that labels must at all times obey the other conditions enumerated in the definition. This omission does not affect the next three results, which we shall use in the proof that the range is also respected.

Flow is affected by only the PUSH operation, which maintains a preflow because it uses the increment $\Delta = \min\{e(v), r_f(v, w)\}$. The initial labelling is valid by hypothesis. Because raising the head of an arc cannot invalidate the labelling for this arc, the RELABEL operation maintains a valid labelling. The PUSH operation, by saturating an arc or pushing some flow through an unused arc, may alter the residual graph: using arc (v, w) may result in its removal from the graph and/or the addition to the graph of arc (w, v). The removal of an arc cannot affect the validity of a labelling (it only removes a constraint); the addition of arc (w, v) does not impair the labelling either, since we must have $d(v) = d(w) + 1$ for the PUSH operation to have applied, so that we can write $d(w) = d(v) - 1 < d(v) + 1$.

Q.E.D.

This lemma allows us to apply any applicable operation at any time while maintaining a valid labelling; and this is indeed the essence of the basic gravity flow algorithm.

- Let the initial preflow saturate all arcs out of the source and be zero everywhere else, and choose any valid labelling.

- While a PUSH or RELABEL operation applies to some vertex, apply it.

Figure 6.23 illustrates the state of our standard example after three relabellings and two pushes (in any of a number of orders), starting from the trivial initial labelling, which assigns $|V|$ to the source and zero to all other vertices. Part (a) shows the network and its current preflow, while part (b) shows the residual graph and its current labelling; note that a PUSH operation is applicable to vertices x and y, while a RELABEL operation is applicable to vertices u and z. In the following, we begin by proving the correctness of this simple algorithm, using a number of lemmata, then discuss its implementation and efficiency.

One striking difference between the gravity flow algorithm and augmentation-based methods is that, with the gravity flow method, the sink is never

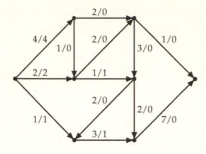
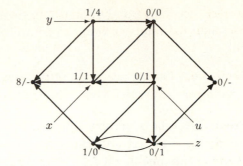

(a) The network, showing capacity/preflow   *(b) The residual graph, showing label/excess flow*

Figure 6.23: A Snapshot During the Execution of the Gravity Flow Algorithm

reachable from the source in the residual graph. This invariant may seem somewhat surprising, but it really only affirms that the algorithm always maintains as much flow out of the source as it possibly can.

Lemma 6.6 If f is a preflow and d a valid labelling, then the sink is not reachable from the source in the residual graph G_f. □

Proof: This result follows immediately from Lemma 6.4. Since $d(s)$ equals $|V|$, if a path from s to t exists in G_f, the path has to have length not less than $|V|$. But a shortest such path can have length at most $|V| - 1$.

Q.E.D.

Now, because of the following theorem, we are done if we can prove termination.

Theorem 6.20 At termination, the gravity flow algorithm has constructed a maximum flow. □

Proof: The algorithm only terminates when neither operation applies at any vertex; since one of the operations is always applicable at any active vertex, it follows that, when the algorithm terminates, no vertex has excess flow. Thus flow must be conserved, so the final preflow is in fact a flow. Since the sink is not reachable from the source in the final residual graph, a residual graph constructed with respect to a true flow, there is no augmenting path in the graph with respect to this final flow. From the max-flow min-cut theorem, we conclude that this final flow is a maximum flow.

Q.E.D.

While the sink is never reachable from the source, the source is always reachable from any vertex with excess flow; this invariant is also required for the

correct functioning of the algorithm, since we may eventually have to push flow
back into the source in order to get rid of excess flow that cannot go anywhere
else.

Lemma 6.7 During execution of the gravity flow algorithm, there always exists
a path from any active vertex to the source.   □

Proof: Let v be a vertex with excess flow and let G_f be the residual graph.
Denote by S the set of vertices reachable from v in G_f and let $\overline{S} = V - S$. *Ad
absurdum*, assume that $s \notin S$. Now we can write

$$\sum_{w \in S} e(w) = \sum_{u \in V, w \in S} f(u, w) = \sum_{u \in \overline{S}, w \in S} f(u, w) + \sum_{u \in S, w \in S} f(u, w) = \sum_{u \in \overline{S}, w \in S} f(u, w).$$

The last of these equalities follows because we have $\sum_{u \in S, w \in S} f(u, w) = 0$ by
skew-symmetry: each arc is included in the sum twice, once from each perspec-
tive. Now, by the definition of S, $f(u, w) \leq 0$ holds for all arcs (u, w) with $u \in \overline{S}$
and $w \in S$; were this not the case, we would have $(w, u) \in G_f$, hence u would
be reachable from v, and so u would belong to S, a contradiction. We conclude
that $\sum_{w \in S} e(w) \leq 0$, which, since $s \notin S$, implies that all the terms in the sum are
zero, and, in particular, $e(v) = 0$, a contradiction.

Q.E.D.

We have already noted that the label of a vertex can only increase. Lemmata 6.4
and 6.7 imply that labels cannot increase without bound.

Lemma 6.8 During execution of the gravity flow algorithm, the label of any
vertex never exceeds $2|V| - 1$.   □

Proof: We proceed by induction. The basis is true, since the initial labelling is
assumed to obey the lemma. Since only active vertices may get new labels, we
need only check that the label of any active vertex is bounded by $2|V| - 1$. By
Lemma 6.7, an active vertex always has a path to the source. Lemma 6.4 implies
that, even after relabelling, which does not affect the residual graph, the label
cannot exceed $2|V| - 1$.

Q.E.D.

We immediately conclude that a RELABEL operation can be applied at most $2|V|-1$
times to any vertex and thus $O(|V|^2)$ times in all. This bound also applies to the
number of saturating PUSH operations that can be applied to an edge.

Lemma 6.9 At most $2|V| - 1$ saturating PUSH operations can be applied to any
given edge.   □

Proof: Consider a saturating PUSH between vertices v and w. After any such operation, the next PUSH along this edge (whether saturating or not) must be in the opposite direction, so that the label of one of v and w must have increased by at least two. It follows that $\max(d(v), d(w))$ must have increased by at least one. Since $\max(d(v), d(w)) \geq 1$ holds initially and since $\max(d(v), d(w)) \leq 2|V| - 1$ holds when the last PUSH occurs, it follows that the maximum number of saturating PUSH operations between v and w is bounded by $2|V| - 1$.

Q.E.D.

There only remains to bound the number of nonsaturating PUSH operations in order to prove that the algorithm terminates and to obtain an upper bound on its running time.

Lemma 6.10 Any implementation of the gravity flow algorithm performs at most $4|V|^2 \cdot |E|$ nonsaturating PUSH operations. $\square$

Proof: We prove this assertion with a simple amortization argument. Let the potential function, Φ, be the sum, over all active vertices, of the vertex labels, and consider the effect on Φ of a nonsaturating PUSH, say from v to w. As the PUSH is nonsaturating, it removes all excess flow from v, so that v is no longer active; consequently, even if w was not active prior to the operation, Φ must decrease, because we had $d(w) < d(v)$. On the other hand, a saturating PUSH can increase Φ (if w was not active before the push), leave Φ unchanged (if the status of both vertices remains active), or decrease Φ (if the saturating PUSH also happened to remove all of the excess flow at v). Therefore, by Lemmata 6.8 and 6.9, the positive contribution to Φ due to saturating pushes is bounded by $(2|V| - 1)^2 \cdot |E|$. A RELABEL operation always increases Φ, but the increase due to all relabellings cannot exceed $(2|V| - 1)(|V| - 2) - \Phi_0$. The sum of these two values is the gross increase in Φ over the running of the algorithm and cannot exceed $4|V|^2 \cdot |E| - \Phi_0$. As the final potential is zero, there are at most $4|V|^2 \cdot |E|$ nonsaturating pushes.

Q.E.D.

Theorem 6.21 The running time of the gravity flow algorithm need not exceed $O(|V|^2 \cdot |E|)$. $\square$

Exercise 6.3 Prove the theorem by developing an implementation of the basic algorithm with the following characteristics: (i) an active vertex can be found in constant time; (ii) a downward arc, if any, out of the selected vertex can be found in constant time; and (iii) relabelling of the selected vertex can be done in time proportional to the number of its neighbors. $\square$

Specific sequencings of the two operations can result in better bounds. We discuss a simple round-robin sequencing that reduces the worst-case running time to $\Theta(|V|^3)$ and mention a different sequencing which achieves a better bound. In order to implement the round-robin, or FIFO, sequencing, we maintain a queue of active vertices. We process the arcs associated with each vertex in some arbitrary, but fixed, order; for this purpose we maintain a pointer to the next arc to be processed, which gets advanced with each saturating push and reset with each relabelling. When a vertex, v, is removed from the queue, it is processed as follows:

- While v is active and there remains some arc, (v, w), to be examined:

  - If flow can be pushed through the arc, then do so and add w to the queue of active vertices if it is not already there; otherwise, or if the arc was saturated as a result of the PUSH, move on to the next arc.

- If v is active, then relabel it and place it at the end of the queue.

This basic step gets repeated until the queue is empty; initially, the queue contains all immediate neighbors of the source. Program 6.6 presents a PASCAL implementation of this algorithm. Since the algorithm does not scan the entire list of arcs before choosing to apply a RELABEL operation, its correctness does not follow immediately from our previous results. We must show that PUSH and RELABEL operations remain mutually exclusive.

Lemma 6.11 When the gravity flow algorithm with FIFO scheduling chooses a RELABEL operation for a vertex, no PUSH operation is applicable to that vertex.

$\square$

Proof: We prove that once we step past an arc, this arc cannot become a candidate for a PUSH operation until the vertex is relabelled. For the pointer into the adjacency list to advance past some arc, (v, w), it must be the case that the arc either is saturated or does not obey the labelling condition, i.e., $d(w) \geq d(v)$. If the latter condition holds, it still holds when the end of the list is reached, since only w can have been relabelled. If the arc is saturated, either it still is when the end of the list is reached, or flow was pushed from w to v, in which case $d(w)$ was raised in the interim and is now greater than $d(v)$. In all cases, the arc (v, w) remains ineligible for a PUSH operation.

Q.E.D.

The running time of this algorithm is determined by the number of passes over the adjacency lists, plus the number of nonsaturating pushes, where we do not advance the pointer into the adjacency list. Since each pass over the list involves a RELABEL, the total amount of work attributable to this source is $\Theta(|V| \cdot |E|)$, which accounts for the work done in skipping over noncandidate arcs, in performing saturating pushes, and in relabelling. We need only bound the number of nonsaturating pushes, which we do indirectly, by bounding the total number of passes over the queue. We define the first pass as the processing of all vertices initially placed in the queue; and we define the $i + 1$st pass as the processing of all vertices added to the queue during the ith pass. (This definition of a pass coincides with that used in our description of Cheriton and Tarjan's algorithm for minimum spanning trees.)

Lemma 6.12 The total number of passes made over the queue by the gravity flow algorithm with FIFO scheduling does not exceed $4|V|^2$.   □

Proof: We prove this assertion by an amortization argument similar to that used in Lemma 6.10. Let the potential function be $\Phi = \max\{d(v) \mid v \text{ is active}\}$ and consider the effect on Φ of one pass over the queue. If no relabelling occurs during the pass, each vertex processed has all of its excess moved to vertices with labels of lower value, so that Φ decreases. Thus, if Φ either increases or remains unchanged during a pass, at least one vertex must get relabelled. We know that the total number of relabellings cannot exceed $2|V|^2$; the same reasoning implies that the gross increase in Φ over the life of the algorithm cannot exceed $2|V|^2 - \Phi_0$. As the final potential equals zero, the number of passes during which no relabelling takes place is also bounded by $2|V|^2$.

Q.E.D.

This lemma provides us with the desired bound on the number of nonsaturating PUSH operations; because at most one such operation can apply to a vertex during each pass and because we now know that there are $\Theta(|V|^2)$ passes, we conclude that Program 6.6 runs in $\Theta(|V|^3)$ time.

As both the choice of initial labelling and the choice of scheduling can affect the running time of the gravity flow algorithm, many variants naturally suggest themselves. Note that the trivial labelling is very crude. A more reasonable choice sets the initial label of a vertex to its distance from the sink; such a labelling is valid and can be computed in $\Theta(|E|)$ time by a backward breadth-first search from the sink. (Vertices not labelled in this process are useless anyway and can be eliminated from the graph.) This labelling gives every vertex the highest initial label consistent with the requirement that the labelling be valid and so saves on needless RELABEL operations and, possibly, on PUSH operations that push flow around aimlessly while the labels start to adjust themselves to something more reasonable. By itself, however, this modification does not improve the worst-case running time of the gravity flow algorithm with FIFO scheduling. A more interesting modification is suggested by this emphasis on maximizing height: select as the next vertex to process the active vertex with the largest label. The excess flow at this vertex will always be discharged, although it might have to undergo a number of relabellings in the process. One can show that the number

```
procedure MaxFlow(var G: graph;
                       s, t: vertex);
  (* Find the maximum flow from s to t for a graph, G=(V,E), with capacity
     function c, using the gravity flow algorithm. *)

  (* Program assumes a queue package with operations
         procedure CreateQueue, function IsEmptyQueue: boolean,
         procedure Enqueue(v: vertex), and procedure Dequeue(var v: vertex). *)

  var d: array [vertex] of integer;
         (* The labelling of the vertices in the gravity flow algorithm. *)
      p: array [vertex] of PtrToNode;
         (* Record of how far along we are in the linked list of arcs
            emanating from each vertex. *)
      e: array [vertex] of real; (* excess flow *)
      q: PtrToNode;
      v: vertex;

  procedure PushRelabel(v: vertex);
     (* Push flow out of v until either we have discharged all excess flow
        or we reach the end of its adjacency list, at which time we relabel
        the vertex and place it again in the queue. *)
     label 99;
     var q: PtrToNode;
         Delta: real;
         h: integer;
     begin
       (* Precondition: e[v] > 0. *)
       q := p[v];
       while q <> nil do
         begin
           if (q^.f < q^.c) (* arc exists in residual graph *) and
              (d[v] > d[q^.w]) (* d[v] = d[w] + 1 *)
              then begin
                      (* Push what can be pushed along this arc. *)
                      Delta := min(e[v],q^.c - q^.f); (* Delta > 0 *)
                      q^.f := q^.f + Delta;
                      e[v] := e[v] - Delta;
                      (* Check to see if w has to be added to the queue of
                         active vertices. *)
                      if e[q^.w] = 0 then Enqueue(q^.w);
                      e[q^.w] := e[q^.w] + Delta;
                      q^.wv^.f := -q^.f;
                      (* Saturating push?  If so, go on to next arc. *)
                      if q^.f = q^.c then q := q^.next;
                      (* If v is no longer active, we are done processing it. *)
                      if e[v] = 0 then goto 99
                   end
           else q := q^.next
         end;
```

```
      (* We have e[v] > 0 and the linked list is exhausted.
         Thus a relabel operation is guaranteed to raise d[v]. *)
      q := G.AdjLists[v];
      h := 2*G.size; (* infinity *)
      while q <> nil do
        begin
          if (q^.f < q^.c) and (h > d[q^.w])
            then h := d[q^.w];
          q := q^.next
        end;
      d[v] := h + 1;
      Enqueue(v);
      q := G.AdjLists[v];

99: p[v] := q
   end; (* PushRelabel *)

begin
  CreateQueue;
  (* Set up the trivial labelling or, better, use backward breadth-first
     search to find the best initial labelling. *)
  for v := 1 to G.size do d[v] := 0; d[s] := G.size;
  (* Begin with the initial preflow. *)
  for v := 1 to G.size do
    begin
      e[v] := 0;
      p[v] := G.AdjLists[v]
    end;
  (* Artificially prevent s and t from ever entering the queue of active
     vertices. *)
  e[s] := 1; e[t] := 1;
  q := G.AdjLists[s];
  while q <> nil do
    begin
      q^.f := q^.c; (* assumed greater than zero *)
      e[q^.w] := q^.c;
      q^.wv^.f := -q^.f;
      if q^.w <> t (* in case there is an arc from s to t *)
        then Enqueue(q^.w);
      q := q^.next
    end;

  while not IsEmptyQueue do
    begin
      Dequeue(v);
      PushRelabel(v)
    end
end; (* MaxFlow *)
```

Program 6.6: The Gravity Flow Algorithm with FIFO Sequencing

of nonsaturating pushes for this scheduling strategy is bounded by $\Theta(|V|^2 \cdot \sqrt{|E|})$ and with suitable, and fairly simple, data structures, the resulting algorithm can be made to run within this time bound. (The necessary data structure, a form of priority queue, is the subject of Exercise 6.30.)

The limiting factor in the running time of Program 6.6 is the time spent on nonsaturating PUSH operations. By maintaining a data structure which keeps track of entire paths to the source and sink, a single step either discharges excess flow from the network or saturates a path. The data structure is quite complex and the analysis considerably more difficult than that of Program 6.6, so that we do not present either here, referring the reader to the bibliography and contenting ourselves with noting that the resulting algorithm runs in $O(|V| \cdot |E| \log(|V|^2/|E|))$ time, which continues to match our goal of $O(|V| \cdot |E|)$ for dense graphs and improves on our two earlier variants for sparse graphs.

As a final question, let us briefly discuss an important variation of network flow. Having seen that the problem of maximum cardinality bipartite matching can be rephrased in terms of network flow and realizing that such was done using only unit capacities, we may well suspect that the weighted version (the assignment problem) can also be rephrased in terms of network flow. Somewhat surprisingly, the answer appears to be no. In fact, to a certain extent, the tables are now turned: the general weighted matching problem can serve as a model for a large variety of network flow problems. The variation of network flow that we need to model the assignment problem is known as the *minimum-cost flow problem*: given a network, with arc costs (given in cost per unit of flow) in addition to arc capacities, find a maximum flow of minimum total cost. The reader may suspect that augmenting along paths of minimum cost will yield an optimal solution; the reader is correct, but the resulting algorithm unfortunately runs in time proportional to, among other things, the value of a maximum flow. In fact, we know of no algorithm for this problem, the running time of which does not depend in some essential fashion on the value of a maximum flow.

6.6 Exercises

Exercise 6.4 Derive other gradient schemes for the linear separation problem by changing the correction step or by using a different criterion function.   □

Exercise 6.5** Prove Theorem 6.3. *Hints*: (i) Start by showing that, if the clusters are linearly separable, then $\|\mathbf{e}(k+1)\| < \|\mathbf{e}(k)\|$; (ii) use this result to show finite convergence in the case of separable clusters; and (iii) show that the other termination condition is reached in the case of nonseparable clusters.   □

Exercise 6.6 Consider both the elementary step of moving an element from one cluster to another and the alternative step of exchanging two elements from different clusters; study their relationship.   □

Exercise 6.7 [P] Consider the following channel layout problem. You are given a complete graph with edge weights—the weights can be thought of as the transmission capacities or the costs per unit length of communication cables. You must place the vertices along a line, spaced at regular intervals, in such a way as to minimize the total cost of the cables.

Design iterative improvement steps for this problem and experiment with them. Note that one obvious step, namely exchanging adjacent vertices, can be implemented so as to take constant time after suitable preprocessing.   □

Exercise 6.8 Design a linear-time algorithm for finding a maximum matching in a free tree.   □

Exercise 6.9 Show how to construct a graph of $2n$ vertices and n^2 edges which has a unique perfect matching.   □

Exercise 6.10 Let f be a function that maps the first n integers into themselves (not necessarily bijectively). Devise an algorithm that finds the largest subset, S, for which $f(S) = S$. Although this problem is similar to a matching problem, it can be solved in linear time by a method that does not involve augmentation.

□

Exercise 6.11[*] [Stable Marriage] The stable marriage problem is a graded version of the perfect marriage problem. Given an equal number of women and men and given, for each person, a ranking of the members of the opposite sex, the problem is to find a *stable* matching, i.e., one that gives no incentive to cheating. Formally, the perfect matching, *wife*: $\{m_1, \ldots, m_n\} \to \{w_1, \ldots, w_n\}$, is stable if there do not exist pairs $(m_i, wife(m_i))$ and $(m_j, wife(m_j))$ such that m_i prefers $wife(m_j)$ to his own wife and $wife(m_j)$ prefers m_i to her own husband.

1. Provide examples to show that there are male- and female-biased stable marriages and that the two can be irreconcilable.

2. Develop an algorithm that finds an optimal male-biased stable marriage, i.e., a stable marriage in which each male fares at least as well as in any other stable marriage. (*Hint*: Marriage customs in Western society have been male-biased and, through long development, have become essentially optimal; thus a strategy for an optimal male-biased stable marriage need only follow traditional marriage customs.) A corollary is that stable marriages always exist.

3. (Harder) Analyze the average-case running time of this algorithm.

4. Prove that an optimal male-biased stable marriage is in fact a pessimal female-biased stable marriage.

5. (Harder) Generalize the algorithm that you developed in part (2) to instances where preference lists are only partial, i.e., where some matches are altogether unacceptable; note that the goal remains a stable perfect marriage. *Hints*: (i) Partial lists can be reduced to full lists by padding them in a suitable manner. (ii) Stable marriage and hashing are very similar problems. In a hashing problem, we must assign each data item to a unique location; each item effectively ranks all locations through its probe sequence; locations do not rank items, but the requirement that each empty location accept the first item to come along gives rise to a condition similar to stability.

6. Investigate the generalization to pairings, where each person has a preference list of other persons. This generalization can model room assignments in college dormitories. Do stable pairings always exist? Is your algorithm for stable marriages usable with pairings?

□

Exercise 6.12 [König-Egerváry] Let the *term rank* of a matrix be the maximum number of entries, no two in the same row or column, all containing nonzero values. Prove this alternate formulation of the König-Egerváry theorem: the term rank of a matrix equals the minimum number of rows and columns that contain all of the nonzero entries of the matrix. *Hint*: Set up a bipartite graph as follows. The vertices of the graph correspond to the rows and columns of the matrix; an edge connects two vertices when the corresponding row and column share a nonzero entry. Then argue in terms of maximum matchings.   □

Exercise 6.13[*] [Birkhoff-von Neumann] A *permutation matrix* is a square matrix where each entry is a zero or a one and where each row and each column has exactly one nonzero entry. (Such matrices derive their name from the fact that, when used to multiply a vector, they simply permute the elements of the vector.) Prove the Birkhoff-von Neumann theorem: if $\mathbf{M}$ is a square matrix with nonnegative entries such that the sum of the elements in each row and column is one (these matrices are termed *doubly stochastic*), then it can be written as a nonnegative linear combination of permutation matrices, $\mathbf{M} = \alpha_1 \mathbf{P}_1 + \alpha_2 \mathbf{P}_2 + \cdots + \alpha_k \mathbf{P}_k$. *Hint*: Use the König-Egerváry theorem as formulated above.   □

Exercise 6.14[*] An *edge cover* for a graph is a subset of the edges such that every vertex of the graph is the endpoint of some edge in the subset (the graph is assumed to be free of isolated points); the edge cover problem asks that an edge cover of minimum size be constructed. Somewhat surprisingly, since the closely related vertex cover problem (Problem 24) is apparently intractable, the edge cover problem can be solved in low polynomial time by reducing it to a matching problem. Show how to use matching techniques to solve the edge cover problem. *Hint*: If M is a matching, then there exists a corresponding edge cover of size $|V| - |M|$. □

Exercise 6.15 Show that the $\Theta(|V| \cdot |E|)$ running time claimed for Program 6.1 is correct by exhibiting a family of graphs on which $\Theta(|V|)$ iterations each take $\Theta(|E|)$ time. □

Exercise 6.16* Construct a family of graphs on which our improved bipartite matching algorithm requires $\Theta(\sqrt{|V|})$ iterations. □

Exercise 6.17 [P] Explore the effectiveness and efficiency of greedy algorithms for the bipartite matching problem. There are many possibilities, ranging from fast, but naïve, to priority-based, as discussed in the text. You may want to extend this experiment to the general matching problem. □

Exercise 6.18 [P] While previous exercises show that both the basic and the improved bipartite matching algorithms can reach their worst-case running times, in practice they are both likely to run considerably faster. Incorporating what you learned in the previous exercise, determine experimentally the ratio of their running times. Do you observe the $\sqrt{|V|}$ ratio that characterizes the worst case? □

Exercise 6.19 Construct an example to show that a blocking flow on the level graph associated with a residual graph need not be a blocking flow on the residual graph. □

Exercise 6.20* This exercise explores a method for finding a blocking flow on the level graph in $\Theta(|V|^2)$ time, which results in a maximum flow algorithm running in $\Theta(|V|^3)$ time, a theoretical improvement over Dinic's algorithm. While Dinic's method builds a blocking flow by saturating paths from the source to the sink one at a time, this method, known as Karzanov's method, builds a blocking flow by saturating vertices one at a time.

For each vertex of the level graph other than the source and sink, we define the *throughput* of a vertex to be the smaller of the potential inflow and the potential outflow. The vertex, v, with minimum throughput, f_v, acts as a bottleneck; in particular, since every vertex has a throughput at least as large as f_v, we know that we can increase the flow from s to t by at least f_v. If we increase the flow by exactly f_v units, all of which pass through the vertex v, then v can be eliminated from the level graph, since either all of its incoming arcs or all of its outgoing arcs become saturated. After adjusting flow values and updating the level graph, we can repeat the step, until the level graph is reduced to two vertices, the source and sink.

Identifying a bottleneck vertex is simple enough; the crux of the method is to send f_v units of flow from s to v and then from v to t as efficiently as possible. We achieve efficiency by pushing the flow from v to t in a breadth-first manner and by pulling flow from s to v, also in a breadth-first manner.

- Find the vertex, v, with minimum throughput, f_v.

- Send f_v units of flow from s to t by pushing flow from v to t and pulling flow from s to v. To push f_v units of flow from v to t (pulling flow from s to v is symmetric), execute these steps:

  - Create a queue and place v in it. This queue will maintain the vertices that have accumulated excess inflow. The queue discipline enforces a breadth-first traversal and thus ensures that all possible inflow into a vertex gets accumulated before any of it is discharged.

  - Dequeue a vertex, call it u, and discharge its inflow in much the same manner as in Dinic's algorithm: moving down the list of arcs emanating from u, saturate one arc at a time in the level graph, until the inflow is discharged. The last arc used may not get saturated. When flow is pushed through an arc: (i) increase the inflow of the vertex at the head of the arc (unless this vertex is the sink) by the amount of the flow and, if the flow into this vertex becomes nonzero, add the vertex to the queue; (ii) if the arc is saturated, remove it from the level graph; and (iii) adjust the throughput of u.

- Remove v from the level graph, adjusting the throughput of adjacent vertices accordingly.

Notice that, as a result of eliminating earlier bottleneck vertices, the vertex of minimum throughput can have a throughput of zero, in which case it is just eliminated. A commonly used heuristic removes from the graph not only the current vertex of minimum throughput, but also (recursively) all vertices with a throughput of zero.

Show that this blocking-flow algorithm can be implemented to run in $\Theta(|V|^2)$ time. *Hints*: (i) Show that the total time spent in finding vertices of minimum throughput is $\Theta(|V|\log|V|)$. (ii) Show that the total number of saturating push and pull operations is $\Theta(|A|)$. (iii) Show that the number of nonsaturating push and pull operations is $\Theta(|V|)$ per saturated vertex.

While the time spent in finding vertices of minimum throughput and in removing saturated edges and useless vertices does not depend on the data, the third component can be less than $|V|^2$, in which case a blocking flow can be found in fewer than $|V|^2$ operations. For unit-capacity and unit networks, the running time of the maximum flow algorithm based on this blocking flow algorithm is, as with Dinic's algorithm, $\Theta(|V|^{2/3}\cdot|A|)$ and $\Theta(|V|^{1/2}\cdot|A|)$.   □

Exercise 6.21 [P] Experiment with Dinic's algorithm, the blocking flow algorithm of Exercise 6.20, and the FIFO and greatest-height versions of the gravity flow method to determine which is best in practice.   □

Exercise 6.22 Assume that the graph underlying a network flow problem forms a tree if the sink is removed. Design a linear-time algorithm to find a maximum flow.   □

Exercise 6.23 Consider the following reduction step on an undirected graph: remove a vertex of degree four or lower, choosing among all candidates, the vertex of lowest degree. Repeat this step until no vertex of degree four or lower remains. Develop an efficient algorithm for this reduction. This reduction is an important preprocessing step in algorithms that color planar graphs with four colors (a special case of Problem 25).   □

Exercise 6.24* Consider the following reduction step on an undirected graph: remove a vertex, v, of degree two and add an edge between its two neighbors, if this edge is not already present. Repeat this step until no vertex of degree two remains. Develop an algorithm for this reduction that runs in $\Theta(|V| + |E|)$ time. This problem is easy if you allow yourself $\Theta(|V|^2)$ extra space. In order to use only $\Theta(|V|)$ extra space, do not attempt to prevent multiple edges and process vertices of degree two in batches; the trick is then to find new vertices of degree two in constant amortized time per vertex.   □

Exercise 6.25* Define a *flow graph* to be a graph such that every edge of the graph is on a simple path from the source to the sink. The simplest flow graph is composed of two vertices connected by an edge. Given two vertex-disjoint flow graphs, $G = (V, E)$ and $G' = (V', E')$, we define two composition operations: (i) the series composition, $G \circ G'$, is obtained by identifying the source of G' with the sink of G; and (ii) the parallel composition, $G \parallel G'$, is obtained by identifying the source of G' with that of G as well as the sink of G' with that of G, eliminating the multiple edge that may arise. Note that both compositions are associative; moreover, parallel composition is also commutative. A flow graph is said to be a *series-parallel graph* if it can be constructed through series and parallel compositions.

We also define a *series-parallel reduction* on a flow graph, G; the step in this reduction is just the step of Exercise 6.24, except that it cannot be applied to the source or the sink.

1. Verify that the smallest flow graph, call it G_O, that is not a series-parallel graph has four vertices, $\{s, t, a, b\}$, and five edges, $\{\{s, a\}, \{s, b\}, \{a, t\}, \{b, t\}, \{a, b\}\}$. Graphs such as G_O are known as *obstructions*.

2. Show that a series-parallel graph has a unique (up to associativity of both operators and commutativity of parallel composition) expression in terms of series and parallel compositions.

3. Show that a flow graph is a series-parallel graph if and only if it can be reduced to a single edge through a series-parallel reduction. (Thus, as a consequence of Exercise 6.24, we can decide in linear time whether or not a graph is a series-parallel graph.)

4. (harder) Show that an arbitrary flow graph is not a series-parallel graph if and only if a series-parallel reduction produces a copy of G_O at some stage. In other words, series-parallel graphs are characterized by a unique obstruction.

5. Design an efficient algorithm to solve the network flow problem on a series-parallel graph.

□

Exercise 6.26* Edge connectivity is defined by analogy with vertex connectivity: a connected undirected graph is edge k-connected if the removal of any $k - 1$ edges does not disconnect the graph. (See also Exercises 4.24 *et seq.*) Show how to use network flow methods to find the edge connectivity of a graph, i.e., the largest value of k for which the graph is edge k-connected, in $O(|V|^{5/3} \cdot |E|)$ time.

□

Exercise 6.27* The *Chinese postman* problem is given by an undirected graph, an assignment of length to the edges, and a distinguished vertex (the post office). The postman must start from the post office and return there, having on his route traversed every edge of the graph at least once (in either direction). The problem is to minimize the length of the postman's route. Show how to use an algorithm for the maximum weighted matching problem to solve the Chinese postman problem in polynomial time. *Hint*: Note that, if every vertex has even degree, then the graph is Eulerian and an Eulerian circuit is an optimal solution. If the graph is not Eulerian, it can be made so by duplicating certain edges, turning the graph into a multigraph. Thus the problem reduces to that of choosing a minimum-cost set of edges to duplicate such that the resulting multigraph has no vertex of odd degree.

□

Exercise 6.28* Consider the following scheduling problem. You are given m identical processors and n jobs; each job has a release time (i.e., a time before which it cannot be started), r_i, a processing time, p_i, and a deadline (i.e., a time by which it must be completed), d_i. (It is assumed that $d_i - r_i \geq p_i$ holds for each job.) Scheduling can be done preemptively, that is, a job can be taken off a processor at any time and that processor given to another job. Show how to reduce this problem to a flow problem in a bipartite network. *Hints*: Let $\{t_1, t_2, \ldots, t_k\}$ be the distinct times (in increasing order) occurring among the release times and deadlines. The problem reduces to determining, for each interval $[t_j, t_{j+1}]$ and for each i, what fraction of the ith job gets completed. Set up a network with nodes corresponding to jobs and nodes corresponding to intervals.   □

Exercise 6.29** Answer the question left open at the beginning of the discussion of the network flow problem: Does there exist an instance of the flow problem for which all sequences of augmenting paths (in the naïve sense) lead to nonoptimal solutions? Either exhibit such an instance or prove that none can exist.   □

Exercise 6.30 Implementing the greatest-height gravity flow algorithm requires a priority queue, since the active vertex with the largest label must be found at each step. As all priority queue implementations discussed in Section 3.1 take logarithmic time for retrieving and removing the largest element, one would expect an additional logarithmic factor in the running time of the algorithm. However, because the keys are integers in the range from 0 to $2|V| - 1$, the priority queue can be implemented so as to allow constant-time retrieval and removal of the largest element, using a technique similar to distribution sort (for which see Section 8.7). Consider the following declarations:

```
const HeapSize = ...; (* 2*|V| - 1 *)
type PtrToHeapNode = ^HeapNode;
     HeapNode = record
                    object: vertex;
                    next: PtrToNode
                end;
     heap = record
                maxbigkey, maxsmallkey: integer;
                H: array [0..HeapSize] of PtrToHeapNode
            end;
```

All vertices with the same label are stored on the appropriate linked list of H[ ]. The fields `maxbigkey` and `maxsmallkey` point to the nonempty lists with the highest key greater than $|V|$ and with the highest key less than $|V|$, respectively. What is the cost of initializing this heap? Show that maintaining this heap in the face of a PUSH or RELABEL takes only constant time. Why is it not necessary to search linearly backwards in H[ ] in order to find a new maximum element once a vertex is fully processed? (This last property follows not from the data structure itself, but from the nature of the gravity flow algorithm.)   □

6.7   Bibliography

Learning algorithms in pattern recognition have a long history, starting with the perceptron algorithm of Rosenblatt [1957]; the Ho-Kashyap algorithm is due to Ho and Kashyap [1966]. For a thorough discussion and an annotated bibliography, see the text of Duda and Hart [1973]. Clustering has an even longer history and finds applications in basically all human pursuits, from sociology to physics; as a result, clustering algorithms used in practice tend to be far more elaborate than the simple methods that we chose to present. For instance, the k-means algorithm forms the basis for more sophisticated methods, such as the *Isodata* algorithm of Ball and Hall [1967]. For a review of clustering algorithms, the reader is referred to the text of Jain and Dubes [1988], where a historical overview and references to applications will also be found.

The k-optimal heuristic is due to Lin [1965]; by refining this heuristic and combining it with lower bounds derived by Held and Karp [1970, 1971], Lin and Kernighan [1973] developed an approximation algorithm that remains the best to date. The example that shows that the k-optimal tour can be twice as long as the optimal even for large values of k can be found in Rosenkrantz *et al.* [1977]. A result due to Papadimitriou and Steiglitz [1977] implies that, for any fixed value of k, the ratio of the length of a k-optimal tour to that of an optimal tour cannot be bounded by any constant, unless $\mathcal{P} = \mathcal{NP}$. While the convergence rate of the k-optimal methods is unknown (the best bound to date, due to Kern [1989], being much larger than the observed behavior), Van Leeuwen and Schoone, as quoted in Lawler *et al.* [1985], show that the heuristic consisting of removing crossings from a Euclidean tour—a weakened form of the 2-optimal heuristic—must terminate after at most n^3 iterations. Limiting the 3-optimal heuristic to the examination of a small subset of triples can still be effective, while greatly improving the running time, as was shown by Or [1976]. Simulated annealing was introduced by Kirkpatrick *et al.* [1983] and has been used by numerous researchers in many fields; Johnson *et al.* [1989] report on the results of extensive experimentation with the method on a variety of problems. Johnson [1990] presents a comprehensive survey of local optimization methods for the travelling salesperson problem, including comparisons of running times.

In our discussion of matching and network flow, we claim a number of $\Theta(\ )$ running times without providing worst-case examples. Indeed, most authors have not provided such examples. We claim a $\Theta(\ )$ running time when the authors gave some indication to that effect; a couple of our exercises address the problem of finding worst-case examples.

Galil [1986] offers a survey of the state of the art in matching algorithms; he covers the material of Sections 6.3 and 6.4, as well as weighted matching problems. Theorem 6.4, often known as the Philip Hall marriage theorem, is due to Hall [1935]; Theorem 6.5, the basic theorem on augmenting paths, is due to Berge [1957], while its extension (Theorem 6.8) and the corollaries and theorems following it were proved by Hopcroft and Karp [1983], who also developed the efficient algorithm for the bipartite case. Blossoms and how to handle them are the work of Edmonds [1963] (whose seminal paper also introduces the idea of a theory of complexity). Edmonds' proposed implementation requires $O(|V|^4)$ time; improvements in the efficiency of blossom-handling are due to Gabow [1976], whose implementation requires $\Theta(|V|^3)$ time. Our $\Theta(|V|\cdot|E|)$ implementation of Gabow's version follows along lines suggested by Tarjan [1983], using the special linear-time equivalence data structure of Gabow and Tarjan [1983]. Even and Kariv [1975] were the first to propose a staged version where each stage constructs a maximal set of disjoint augmenting paths; their complex implementation requires $O(\min\{|V|^{5/2}, |E|\sqrt{|V|}\log|V|\})$ time. The best algorithm to date, which we mentioned in Section 6.4 and which runs in $\Theta(\sqrt{|V|}\cdot|E|)$ time, is due to Micali and Vazirani [1980], who refined the ideas of Even and Kariv; a detailed description of their algorithm was provided by Peterson and Loui [1988]. Stable marriages, the subject of Exercise 6.11, were first discussed by Gale and Shapley [1962]; Knuth [1976] wrote a delightful monograph on the topic. Irving *et al.* [1987] present an algorithm that finds an equitable stable marriage, where neither sex is favored and all spouses fare well; Knuth *et al.* [1990] review known results and present a probabilistic analysis of the problem.

Maximum-weight matchings are most commonly associated with operations research; the main methods for their solution were developed by using linear programming theory. For a very complete introduction to the topic, the reader is referred to the text of Papadimitriou and Steiglitz [1982]; the aforementioned survey of Galil [1986] provides a more in-depth discussion. Methods used in maximum-weight matching are very similar to those used in maximum-cardinality matching, except that one searches for augmenting paths of maximum weight; in the absence of blossoms, this search can be reduced to a search for paths of minimum costs through a linear-time adjustment of parameters. The algorithm then follows closely our first algorithm for bipartite matching, finding one augmenting path at each stage and going through at most $|V|/2$ stages. In consequence, a maximum-weight matching in bipartite graphs (the assignment problem) can be found in $\Theta\big(|V|\cdot(|E| + |V|\log|V|)\big)$ time using Dijkstra's algorithm with Fibonacci heaps. For problems where the largest edge weight is U, the algorithm can use the fast implementation of Dijkstra's algorithm due to Ahuja *et al.* [1988] to run in $O(|V|\cdot|E| + |V|^2\sqrt{\log U})$ time. The fundamental result in general weighted matching, how to handle blossoms, is once again the work of Edmonds [1965a]; his algorithm has remained the basis for most contemporary versions. Galil *et al.* [1986] give a $O(|V|\cdot|E|\log|V|)$ time implementation of Edmonds' algorithm; Gabow *et al.* [1989] present an improved version running in $O(|V|\cdot|E|\lg\lg\log_d|V| + |V|^2\log|V|)$ time, where $d = \max(|E|/|V|, 2)$.

Network flow has a long history, starting with the work of Ford and Fulkerson [1956, 1962], who introduced the notion of an augmenting path and proposed the first algorithm for the problem, proving the max-flow min-cut theorem as part of their work. Our proof of the max-flow min-cut theorem follows closely that of Tarjan [1983]. Edmonds and Karp [1972] proposed and analyzed both augmentation along paths of maximum residual capacity and augmentation along shortest paths and thus derived the first network flow algorithm with a running time dependent on only the size of the network. Augmentation using blocking flows was devised independently by Dinic [1970] and has since been refined by numerous researchers (for a brief overview of these refinements, consult the introduction in the article of Goldberg and Tarjan [1986]); Exercise 6.20 presents one such refinement due to Karzanov [1974], as rephrased by Malhotra *et al.* [1978]. The application of flow augmentation algorithms to graph connectivity problems and their analysis (including Exercise 6.26) is due to Even and Tarjan [1975], who also proved Theorems 6.18 and 6.19; for the specific problem of edge connectivity, Matula [1987] has given an appreciably faster algorithm, also based on network flow, which runs in $O(|E|\cdot|V|)$ time for arbitrary connectivity and in $O(k|V|^2)$ time for k-connectivity. The gravity flow algorithm is due to Goldberg and Tarjan [1986], whose development we follow closely; in the FIFO version that we described, it runs in $\Theta(|V|^3)$ time; its faster version runs in $O(|V|\cdot|E|\log(|V|^2/|E|))$ time, using the dynamic tree structure of Sleator and Tarjan, for which see Tarjan [1983]. Cheriyan and Maheshwari [1989] presented a detailed analysis of the gravity flow algorithm, showing that the time bound for the FIFO version is tight and that the greatest-height scheduling runs in $\Theta(|V|^2\sqrt{|E|})$ time. The scaling algorithm of Gabow [1983] runs in $O(|V|\cdot|E|\log U)$ time on networks where the largest edge capacity is U. Combining scaling techniques with the preflow method and with the dynamic tree structures, Ahuja *et al.* [1989] obtained an algorithm with a running time of $O(|V|\cdot|E|\log(2 + |V|\sqrt{\log U}/|E|))$. Goldberg *et al.* [1989] survey recent results in network flow algorithms, including minimum-cost flow and other variations. Lawler [1976], Tarjan [1983], and Papadimitriou and Steiglitz [1982] all discuss the network flow problem, as well as the minimum-cost flow problem, at some length. The characterization of series-parallel graphs (Exercise 6.25) is due to Valdes *et al.* [1979], as is the algorithm for series-parallel reduction (Exercise 6.24). The Chinese postman problem (Exercise 6.27) was first presented by Edmonds [1965b], who also christened it to acknowledge the nationality of its progenitor, Mei-Ko Kwan; the reduction to matching is due to Edmonds and Johnson [1973]. The scheduling problem of Exercise 6.28 is solved, along with other similar scheduling problems, by Horn [1974].

No structural characterization of problems for which iterative algorithms return optimal solutions has been found so far. Papadimitriou and Steiglitz [1977] and Johnson *et al.* [1985] have explored one avenue: the structure of the neighborhood of a solution within the search space, i.e., the quality and quantity of other solutions reachable from the current one in one step. However, this work remains at a preliminary stage.

CHAPTER 7

Divide-and-Conquer

Divide-and-conquer is a technique where we solve a problem by dividing it into smaller, independent subproblems; solving each subproblem recursively; and finally recombining the solutions into a solution to the original problem. Effective application of this technique depends on the ability to recombine the solutions to the subproblems in an efficient manner. If solving the entire problem by brute force takes more than linear time, then solving a number of independent subproblems will take less time *in toto* and thus lead to a more efficient algorithm, provided that the cost of recombination remains low. A top-down schema for divide-and-conquer is given in Figure 7.1. Viewed in this way, divide-and-conquer appears to be nothing more than recursive problem solving. For many elementary problems where the solution takes on a very simple form, such as counting the number of nodes in a binary tree, translation of the general schema into a PASCAL function is automatic, so much so that it hardly qualifies as an example of the divide-and-conquer technique. More interesting is the application of this approach to problems that have no natural tree structure, such as sorting, finding the convex hull of a set of points, or constructing (nonoptimal) solutions to the travelling salesperson problem. We shall use the recursive formulation inherent in the top-down schema as a design tool and for proving algorithms correct; however, better code often results from viewing the problems in a bottom-up manner.

The divide-and-conquer paradigm highlights the difference between correctness and efficiency. If the correctness of our method for recombining the solutions is unaffected by the manner in which the original problem is divided into subproblems, then any partitioning of the original instance results in a correct algorithm. However, different partitioning methods result in algorithms with different running times. The efficiency of the recombination step is a function of the combined size of the solutions to the subproblems; typically, it takes linear time. When such is the case, the method for partitioning the original problem into

```
procedure Divide_And_Conquer(input P: problem; output S: solution);
  begin
    if small(P)
      then (* If problem P is sufficiently small, solve it directly. *)
            S ← ...
      else begin
              divide P into small problems of type identical to
                the original, P₁, P₂, ..., Pₖ;
              (* k ≥ 2 can be static or a function of P. *)
              Divide_And_Conquer(P₁, S₁);
                    ⋮
              Divide_And_Conquer(Pₖ, Sₖ);
              recombine S₁, S₂, ..., Sₖ into S, a solution to P
            end
  end; (* Divide_And_Conquer *)
```

Figure 7.1: Top-Down Schema for Divide-and-Conquer

subproblems directly affects the efficiency of the algorithm. Consider a scheme that partitions an instance into two independent instances and recombines the two solutions in linear time. The behavior of this scheme is described by the recurrence

$$\begin{cases} T(n) = T(k) + T(n-k) + \Theta(n) \\ T(1) = \Theta(1), \end{cases}$$

the solution of which is minimized when k equals $n/2$ and maximized when k equals 1. Thus the best partitioning cuts an instance into pieces of equal size. Requiring such a partition may add overhead (which may be internal to the algorithm or involve a preprocessing phase) and can affect the precise coefficients; however, if the overhead of partitioning is no larger than the cost of recombination, then the asymptotic running time of the algorithm is not affected.

The independence of the subproblems produced by the partitioning step is also a subtle issue. Independence prevents duplicated effort among the parallel recursive calls; however, independence need not be construed so strictly as to require that the instances produced by the partitioning be completely disjoint. Along with the lack of duplicated effort, a major feature of divide-and-conquer is that the worst-case running time of a recursive call is not affected by the results of earlier calls at the same level. There are problems, such as optimizing the evaluation of a matrix chain product (Problem 10), where the subproblems produced by the partitioning are independent, but the failure to share results between the recursive calls adversely affects the running time. *Dynamic programming*, which can be viewed as a generalization of the divide-and-conquer paradigm, attempts to deal with this difficulty; we take up this topic in Volume II.

There are also problems, such as the travelling salesperson problem, for which recombining the solutions to form an optimal solution to the original instance is not appreciably easier than solving the problem by brute force. In such situations, it is sometimes possible to trade optimality for efficiency and to combine the solutions efficiently into good, but suboptimal, solutions. Hence the divide-and-conquer paradigm can be used to develop efficient approximation algorithms.

Perhaps the simplest and best-known application of divide-and-conquer is searching a sorted array. Although the divide-and-conquer paradigm only appears in a degenerate form, since subsolutions need not be recombined and since only one of the subproblems need be solved recursively, its main attributes are present. The manner in which we partition the problem into subproblems does not affect correctness. We can divide a sorted array of n items into two pieces, one of size one and the other of size $n - 1$ (linear search); into two pieces, one of size $\lfloor n/2 \rfloor$ and the other of size $\lceil n/2 \rceil$ (binary search); or into any k nonoverlapping pieces, each of size smaller than n; in all cases, the correct answer will be returned. However, the partitioning step does affect the running time, which will vary from linear in the first case to logarithmic in the second. This simple problem also demonstrates another attribute of the paradigm: a nonrecursive, bottom-up implementation is preferable to a recursive one, because it avoids the implicit $\Theta(\log n)$ extra storage for the stack and avoids the overhead of procedure invocation.

7.1 Merging and Mergesort

The paradigmatic divide-and-conquer algorithm is *mergesort*, a $\Theta(n \log n)$ sorting algorithm. We develop mergesort by stepwise refinement, using it as a vehicle for explaining the divide-and-conquer technique. The basis of the recursion is simple enough: lists of one element each are trivially sorted. The sorting process thus reduces to two problems: (i) how to break a large problem (a list of more than one element) into nonempty subproblems; and (ii) how to recombine the solutions to the subproblems into a solution to the whole—the more important part. The standard mergesort algorithm breaks the problem into two pieces, although it is easily generalized to any fixed number of pieces. Upon return from the recursive calls, we have two sorted lists, S_1 and S_2, that we must recombine into a single sorted list, S. Here we take advantage of the sorted nature of S_1 and S_2, which

```
procedure mergesort(input P: list (* unsorted *);
                    output S: list (* sorted *));
  var P₁, P₂, S₁, S₂: list;
  begin
    if |P| = 1
      then S ← P
      else begin
             partition P into P₁ and P₂, with P₁ and P₂ both nonempty;
             mergesort(P₁, S₁);
             mergesort(P₂, S₂);
             merge(S₁, S₂, S)
           end
  end; (* mergesort *)
```

Figure 7.2: The Abstract Algorithm for Mergesort

allows us to merge the two lists in $\Theta(|S_1| + |S_2|)$ time. The merging step is quite simple:

- Initialize S, the output list, to empty.

- As long as elements remain in either S_1 or S_2, repeat these steps:

    - Let x_1 be the first, which is also the smallest, element remaining in S_1 (or infinity if S_1 is exhausted); define x_2 similarly.

    - Add the smaller of x_1 and x_2 to the output and eliminate it from S_1 or S_2 as appropriate.

Incorporating this step into the divide-and-conquer schema yields the abstract algorithm of Figure 7.2.

Two natural implementations of the lists suggest themselves: arrays and linked lists. When using the array formulation, the desire for a concise representation of the abstract concept of list suggests that we define a list as a contiguous segment of the original array and represent it by its lower and upper limits, l and r. This choice makes partitioning especially simple, since we need only select an intermediate index, m, with $l \leq m < r$, but makes merging more difficult. The difficulty is that we are faced with a trade-off between time and space: in order to merge the sorted lists A[l..m] and A[m+1..r] efficiently, we need an extra array for temporary storage.[1] In contrast, an implementation using linked lists allows merging without explicit extra storage, but, at least in the top-down

---

[1] The inability of languages like FORTRAN and PASCAL to allocate arrays dynamically makes any use of temporary array storage awkward. The standard solution is to require the user to pass in both the array to be sorted and a "work" array of equal size.

framework that we have established, partitioning is no longer a constant-time operation. Moreover, the linked list itself uses extra storage to hold the pointers. As a result, there is really no gain from using a linked structure when the objects being sorted are of a size comparable to that of the pointer fields.

The algorithm is correct as long as neither P_1 nor P_2 is empty, but it is most efficient if they are of equal length. If P_1 consists of all of P but one datum, the algorithm runs in quadratic time and is essentially *insertion sort*, since the merging operation reduces to the insertion of one element into an already sorted list. Because the algorithm remains correct even when the input list is partitioned into a number of smaller lists, we can, in the extreme, partition P into n pieces, each of size one. The work is now done entirely by the merge operation, and, if it is done by searching through the list for the smallest element, we get the quadratic-time sorting algorithm known as *selection sort*. Only when the input list is partitioned into a constant number of sublists of equal size is the algorithm known as mergesort. Program 7.1 shows a simple, recursive implementation of the basic mergesort algorithm.

The recursion of the top-down schema for divide-and-conquer imposes a tree structure on a problem which may have no natural tree structure of its own. The leaves of the tree correspond to the small instances of the problem, those that we know how to solve directly and often trivially, while the internal nodes of the tree correspond to "merging" or "recombining" operations. From this perspective, we can think of divide-and-conquer as a bottom-up technique: explode the original instance into a myriad of tiny, easily solvable pieces and repeatedly combine solutions to smaller pieces into solutions to larger pieces, stopping when a solution to the original instance has been constructed. For the mergesort algorithm, this view of divide-and-conquer becomes the following:

- Begin with n sorted lists, each of length one.

- Repeat the following step, starting with $i = 1$, until only one list of size n remains:

  - Working on pairs of sorted lists of size i, merge them into sorted lists of size $2i$. Continue merging until no list of size i remains.

If n is not a power of 2, there are slight bookkeeping complications, but no basic changes. This iterative implementation uses neither an implicit nor an explicit stack, although the merge operation still requires an auxiliary work array, which must be of size n to accommodate the final merged list.

Working in this manner actually allows us to use the auxiliary work array more efficiently by avoiding needless copying. Notice that there is enough room in the work array to hold the results of all merge operations performed on pairs of lists at the same level in the tree: if we merge adjacent lists, A[i..j] and

```
procedure MergeSort(var A, work: data; n: integer);
  (* recursive, top-down mergesort algorithm *)

  procedure RecMergeSort(left, right: integer);
    (* Sort A[left..right] using mergesort. *)
    var middle: integer;

    procedure Merge(s, n, m: integer);
      (* Merge A[s..s+n-1] and A[s+n..s+n+m-1], two adjacent sorted sublists,
         of lengths n and m, putting the result in A[s..s+n+m-1]. *)
      var i, (* points to first unprocessed element of sublist 1 *)
          j, (* points to first unprocessed element of sublist 2 *)
          k, (* points to first free space in the output list *)
          t, (* location past first sublist/start of second sublist *)
          u: (* location past second sublist *)
             integer;
      begin
        (* Merge the data into the start of the work array. *)
        k := 1; t := s + n; u := t + m; i := s; j := t;
        while (i < t) and (j < u) do
          if A[i] <= A[j]
            then begin work[k] := A[i]; i := i + 1; k := k + 1 end
            else begin work[k] := A[j]; j := j + 1; k := k + 1 end;
        while i < t do (* Copy any leftover portion of the first segment. *)
          begin work[k] := A[i]; i := i + 1; k := k + 1 end;
        while j < u do (* Copy any left over portion of the second segment. *)
          begin work[k] := A[j]; j := j + 1; k := k + 1 end;
        (* Move merged lists back into A[s..s+n+m]. *)
        i := s;
        for j := 1 to k do begin A[i] := work[j]; i := i + 1 end
      end; (* Merge *)

    begin (* RecMergeSort *)
      if left < right (* Segments of length one are sorted by default. *)
        then begin
                middle := (left + right) div 2;
                RecMergeSort(left,middle);
                RecMergeSort(middle+1,right);
                Merge(left,middle-left+1,right-middle)
             end
    end; (* RecMergeSort *)

  begin
    RecMergeSort(1,n)
  end; (* MergeSort *)
```

Program 7.1: Recursive Mergesort Algorithm Resulting from the Top-Down
Divide-and-Conquer Schema

```
procedure MergeSort(var A, work: data; n: integer);
  (* iterative, bottom-up mergesort algorithm *)
  var inA: boolean; (* where the data currently reside *)
      span, (* current length of sorted lists *)
      i: integer;

    procedure Merge(var inarray, (* lists of length span *)
                        outarray: (* upon return, lists of length 2*span *)
                          data;
                        n, (* total number of elements *)
                        span: integer);
      (* Merge pairs of sorted lists of length span.  The merge operation is
         performed slightly more efficiently than in the previous program. *)
      label 99;
      var i, (* points to first unprocessed element in sublist 1 *)
          j, (* points to first unprocessed element in sublist 2 *)
          k, (* points to first free space in the output list *)
          t, (* location past first sublist/start of second sublist *)
          u: (* location past second sublist *)
            integer;
    begin
      (* There are at least two lists to merge. *)
      i := 1; j := span + 1; k := 1;

        repeat (* until there is at most one list left over *)
          (* Invariant: k = i at the start of the merge operation. *)
          (* Set upper bounds for i and j. *)
          t := j; u := j + span; if u > n then u := n + 1;
      99: if inarray[i] <= inarray[j]
            then begin
                    outarray[k] := inarray[i]; i := i + 1; k := k + 1;
                    if i < t (* only check pointer that changed *)
                      then goto 99
                      else repeat (* copy remainder of sublist 2 *)
                              outarray[k] := inarray[k]; (* k = j at this point *)
                              k := k + 1
                           until k = u
                 end
            else begin
                    outarray[k] := inarray[j]; j := j + 1; k := k + 1;
                    if j < u (* only check pointer that changed *)
                      then goto 99
                      else repeat (* copy remainder of sublist 1 *)
                              outarray[k] := inarray[i]; i := i + 1; k := k + 1
                           until k = u
                 end;
          i := u; j := i + span
        until j > n; (* until sublist 2 is nonexistent *)
        (* Copy over an unmatched list, if one exists. *)
        for j := i to n do outarray[j] := inarray[j]
    end; (* Merge *)
```

```
begin (* MergeSort *)
  inA := true; (* The data are initially in A. *)
  span := 1; (* The array consists of n sublists of length one. *)
  while span < n do (* while we cannot guarantee that the array is sorted *)
    begin
      if inA
        then Merge(A,work,n,span)
        else Merge(work,A,n,span);
      inA := not inA;
      span := 2*span
    end;
  (* If the final result is in the wrong array, then transfer it back. *)
  if not inA then for i := 1 to n do A[i] := work[i]
end; (* MergeSort *)
```

Program 7.2: Nonrecursive Mergesort Algorithm Resulting from the Bottom-Up Divide-and-Conquer Schema

A[j+1..k], the result of the merge operation fits exactly into work[i..k]. If we alternate the roles of the arrays A and work, all copying can be avoided, except for one copying operation if the final result ends up in the work array. The resulting code is given in Program 7.2. (This implementation is only the basic, two-way mergesort algorithm; further improvements are discussed in Section 8.5.) We conclude with two remarks. The top-down schema for divide-and-conquer inherently walks the tree in postorder, while the manner in which the bottom-up schema for divide-and-conquer walks the tree can be tailored to the problem. For mergesort, we chose to walk the tree level by level, since this method avoids use of an auxiliary stack. If n is not a power of 2, the top-down and bottom-up approaches produce slightly different partitions: for instance, if n equals 1000, the final merge operation in the top-down algorithm works with two lists of size 500, whereas in the bottom-up version it works with lists of sizes 512 and 488.

We now turn our attention to the problem of merging: we want to know whether merging can be done in linear time without appreciable extra storage. In order to get a partial answer, we shall proceed in a somewhat roundabout fashion. Consider the question of sorting or merging in a framework in which we are not allowed to maintain any "state information," i.e., local variables dependent on the input data. Phrased more precisely, can we sort or merge using a sequence of comparisons that is fixed in advance and depends only on the number of items to be processed, not on their values? Note that neither heapsort nor mergesort achieves this goal. While the sequence of comparisons performed in a sift-up operation depends only on the index of the object being sifted up (there is no need to stop making comparisons and interchanges before reaching

```
const MaxN = 4;

procedure SortFour(var A: data);
  procedure Comparator(var x,y: datum);
    var temp: datum;
    begin
      if x > y
        then begin
                temp := x;
                x := y;
                y := temp
             end
    end; (* Comparator *)
  begin
    Comparator(A[1],A[2]);
    Comparator(A[3],A[4]);
    Comparator(A[1],A[3]);
    Comparator(A[2],A[4]);
    Comparator(A[2],A[3])
  end; (* SortFour *)
```

(a) Straight-line program   *(b) Equivalent comparator network*

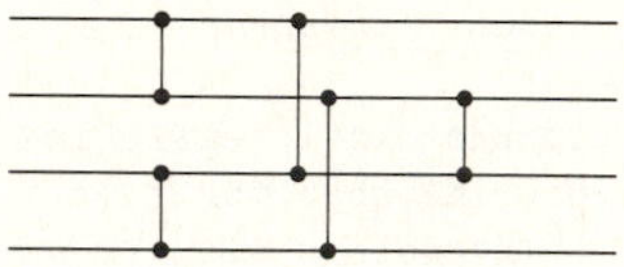

Figure 7.3: Sorting Four Elements with a Comparator Network

the root of the heap—that we normally do so is only for purposes of efficiency), the sequence of comparisons performed during a sift-down operation depends on the values of the two children. In mergesort, the sequence of comparisons performed during the merging depends on the progress through the lists, which, in turn, depends on the actual data.

Let us begin our investigation with a small example. Figure 7.3 shows a straight-line PASCAL program and an equivalent hardware implementation that sorts a four-element array using a simple component called a *comparator*. A comparator either leaves its two inputs unaffected or exchanges them so as to ensure that the value on the upper wire is no larger than the value on the lower wire. The physical appearance of Figure 7.3(b) suggests why we are interested in sorting under the restriction of "no state information": not only are comparators simple enough that they are likely to be fast and inexpensive, but comparator networks exhibit a natural parallelism. For instance, while the sorting network of Figure 7.3(b) uses five comparators, it has a time delay of only three. Thus we can ask the questions, "How many comparators do we need for sorting?" and "What is the minimum delay time for a sorting network?" These questions are similar to the familiar space-time trade-off questions that arise in normal programming tasks.

The divide-and-conquer nature of mergesort makes it an ideal candidate for realization as a comparator network, if we can merge two sorted lists efficiently. The recurrences governing the number of comparators and the time delay for sorting networks based on mergesort are, respectively,

$$\begin{cases} S(n) = S(\lceil n/2 \rceil) + S(\lfloor n/2 \rfloor) + s(\lceil n/2 \rceil, \lfloor n/2 \rfloor) \\ S(1) = 0 \end{cases}$$

and

$$\begin{cases} T(n) = T(\lceil n/2 \rceil) + t(\lceil n/2 \rceil, \lfloor n/2 \rfloor) \\ T(1) = 0, \end{cases}$$

where $s(m, n)$ and $t(m, n)$ are, respectively, the number of comparators and the time delay of optimal networks that merge sorted lists of lengths m and n.

We approach the problem of merging with comparator networks with divide-and-conquer techniques. First, however, we prove two basic theorems that will allow us to restrict our domain of investigation to a standard form of comparator networks. Assume that a technician, while assembling a comparator network, inserts one of them "upside down," i.e., so that the larger output goes onto the upper wire. Does this change add any new capability? What if the technician had crossed two wires? What we are asking here is whether or not the availability of two new components, one a comparator that works upside down and the other a component that always exchanges its inputs, adds anything to the computational power of comparator networks. Comparator networks that make use of these components are called nonstandard, in contrast to the standard comparator networks defined earlier. Clearly, nonstandard networks can perform tasks that standard networks cannot; for example, a standard network cannot sort into decreasing order, while a nonstandard network can. However, this is an artificial difference; indeed all such differences are effectively artificial, as the following theorem shows.

Theorem 7.1 Given a nonstandard comparator network that sorts all permutations of $\{1, 2, \ldots, n\}$, there is an equivalent standard comparator network that uses no more components. □

Proof: Our proof is constructive: we give an algorithm for converting the nonstandard network into a standard one. During this conversion, upside-down comparators will be righted and exchange components will be eliminated. For the purposes of the proof, we break any parallelism in the network. We now proceed from left to right, looking for nonstandard components. Assume that we encounter an upside-down component connecting lines i and j. We replace the component with a standard comparator, followed by an exchange component.

This change clearly has no effect on the performance of the network since no comparator to the right can tell that the change has been made. We eliminate exchange components by uncrossing the wires, which we do by lifting them out of their tracks (with their comparators attached), uncrossing them, and laying them back down. This step has two effects. First, some of the comparators to the right of the replaced exchange component suffer a change in orientation. This is true for precisely those comparators that connect some line k to either of lines i or j, with $i \leq k \leq j$. Secondly, for any input, the output of the network is identical to what it was before, except that the outputs of lines i and j are reversed. We correct this reversal by recrossing lines i and j to the right of all the comparators.

After we have proceeded through the entire network and eliminated nonstandard components, some of which were created during earlier steps, we are left with a standard network followed by a mess of crossed wires at the far right, i.e., a standard network followed by a permutation. This network performs identically to the original, nonstandard network on all inputs. We now use the fact that the original network was a sorting network to show that the permutation is the identity permutation and so can be eliminated. If we pass the permutation $(1, 2, \ldots, n)$ through our equivalent network, the wires at the end of the standard network portion must still carry $(1, 2, \ldots, n)$, since any standard network has no effect on this input; but, at the end of the permutation section, we must also have as output $(1, 2, \ldots, n)$, lest we contradict our hypothesis that the original network was a sorting network. Hence the permutation is the identity.

$Q.E.D.$

Our next theorem, Theorem 7.2, provides us with a mechanism for verifying that a network is in fact a sorting network. The most obvious way to check this property is to pass all $n!$ permutations through the network and verify that they all come out sorted. Theorem 7.2 shows that much less work is required: it suffices to check the 2^n sequences of zeros and ones.

Theorem 7.2 A standard comparator network is a sorting network if and only if it sorts all sequences of zeros and ones. $\qquad\square$

Proof: The "only if" direction is trivial. Suppose then that some network does not sort all permutations of 1 through n. We construct a sequence of zeros and ones that it also cannot sort. Let π be a permutation that is not sorted; then there is a first output wire, k, where the value on wire k is i and the value on wire $k + 1$ is j, with $i > j$. Given the permutation π and the value i, we construct the sequence of zeros and ones as follows: if an input wire carries a value smaller than i, we make the associated input a zero; otherwise, we make it a one. If we sort π on one copy of the network and the sequence of zeros and ones on

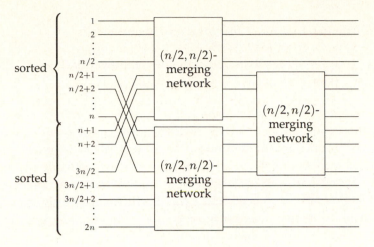

Figure 7.4: A First Attempt at Merging Using a Comparator Network

another, it is easy to see that they stay in strict correspondence: exactly those lines containing a value less than i in one network contain a zero in the other. This is true initially; whenever two values, l and m, go through a comparator in the first network, in the second network we compare either two zeros (if both l and m are less than i), or two ones, or one of each. In this last case, neither or both networks make an exchange. Thus output wire k has a one and output wire $k+1$ has a zero.

Q.E.D.

With these tools, we can approach the question of designing an efficient network for merging two sorted lists of lengths m and n. In order to avoid needless complications, we initially assume that n is a power of 2 and that m equals n. Based on the ideas developed for mergesort, a natural first attempt is suggested by Figure 7.4: we reduce the problem of merging to one of: (i) merging the small elements (upper halves) of the two lists; (ii) merging the large elements (lower halves) of the two lists; and (iii) applying a corrective subnetwork to reposition any misplaced elements. This approach has promise for two reasons. First, the corrective network only need encompass lines $n/2+1$ through $3n/2$, since the smallest and largest $n/2$ elements cannot be out of place. Secondly, the elements on lines $n/2+1$ through n, as well as those on lines $n+1$ through $3n/2$, are already sorted, so that the corrective network need only merge two sorted lists, each of length $n/2$. Unfortunately, the corrective network cannot be further simplified, as we shall see in a moment, so that this approach to merging uses

$n^{\lg 3} \approx n^{1.585}$ comparators, since the governing recurrence is

$$\begin{cases} s(n,n) = 3s(n/2, n/2), & \text{for } n \text{ a power of 2} \\ s(1,1) = 1. \end{cases}$$

Why must the corrective network be a full $n/2$ *vs.* $n/2$ merging network? Consider an input sequence where the first sorted list consists of a sequence of $n/2+r$ zeros followed by ones and the second sorted list consists of a sequence of $n/2-s$ zeros followed by ones. As the wires enter the corrective network, the input consists of two sorted lists, each of length $n/2$, the first having $n/2 - s$ zeros and the second having r zeros. Since r and s can be chosen arbitrarily from 0 to $n/2$, we see that the corrective network must be able to merge any two sorted lists consisting of zeros and ones, each of length $n/2$. The zero-one principle of Theorem 7.2 now implies that the corrective network can merge any two arbitrary sorted lists, each of length $n/2$.

In spite of this pessimistic conclusion, divide-and-conquer does yield an efficient approach to merging—we just did not choose the correct way to divide the problem into subproblems. A better strategy for doing an (m, n)-merge operation, due to K. E. Batcher, proceeds by merging the elements in the odd positions on the two lists while merging in parallel the elements in the even positions, and then applies a corrective subnetwork. The corrective network is, of course, the crux of the problem. This network need not involve the first output line, since the overall smallest element is the first element on one or the other of the two odd sublists. Furthermore, the second and third smallest elements are on output wires two and three, though possibly in reverse order, so that a single comparator connecting these two lines can correct any problem. To verify this assertion, note that two possibilities arise: the three smallest elements come from the same list or two come from one list and one comes from the other. In both cases two of these three smallest elements come from the odd position sublists and one from the even position sublists. The elements from the odd position sublists end up on output wires one and three, and the element from the even position sublist ends up on output wire two.[2] This observation can be extended to the fourth and fifth elements, sixth and seventh elements, etc. The $(4, 7)$- and $(5, 6)$-merging networks are depicted in Figure 7.5.

In order to prove that this corrective network, which uses $\lfloor (m + n - 1)/2 \rfloor$ comparators, actually functions correctly, we use the zero-one principle again. First note that, while we have specified the corrective network mechanistically (place a comparator between output wires $2k$ and $2k + 1$, for all k), we could also have specified it somewhat more abstractly: connect the first output in even

---

[2]The case $m = 1$ is special: the effect is the same, but the two elements in odd positions end up on wires one and two and the element in even position ends up on wire three.

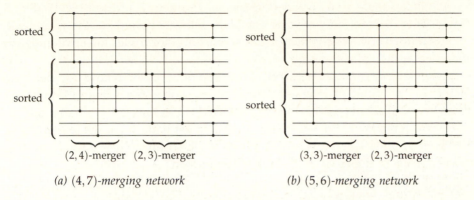

(2,4)-merger   (2,3)-merger   (3,3)-merger   (2,3)-merger

(a) (4,7)-merging network   *(b) (5,6)-merging network*

Figure 7.5: Odd-Even Merging Networks

position to the second output in odd position, connect the second output in even position to the third output in odd position, etc. These two formulations are clearly equivalent. (When m is odd, two elements in odd positions occur on adjacent output wires where the first list stops and the second list starts; this adjacency does not affect the equivalence.) Consider then two sorted lists of lengths m and n, the first having k zeros and the second l zeros. After the independent mergings of elements in odd positions and of elements in even positions, the output wires in odd positions have $\lceil k/2 \rceil + \lceil l/2 \rceil$ zeros and the output wires in even positions have $\lfloor k/2 \rfloor + \lfloor l/2 \rfloor$ zeros. These sums differ by zero, one, or two, depending on whether k and l are odd or even. By examining all four cases, we can verify that at most a single zero and single one can be out of place and thus that one of the comparators of the corrective network can correct the error.

With this construction, we get the following recurrence for $s(m,n)$:

$$\begin{cases} s(m,n) = s(\lceil m/2 \rceil, \lceil n/2 \rceil) + s(\lfloor m/2 \rfloor, \lfloor n/2 \rfloor) + \lfloor (m+n-1)/2 \rfloor \\ s(m,0) = s(0,n) = 0 \\ s(1,1) \; = 1. \end{cases}$$

This recurrence is difficult to solve exactly. For n a power of 2 and $m = n$, we get $s(n,n) = n \lg n + 1$ and $t(n,n) = \lg n + 1$, which yields a sorting network with $S(n) = n(\lg^2 n - \lg n + 4)/4 - 1$ and $T(n) = (\lg^2 n + \lg n)/2$. Therefore, odd-even merging networks improve on our initial design, but still do not perform as well as we might hope; since mergesort runs in $\Theta(n \log n)$ time, we might expect $S(n)$ to be $\Theta(n \log n)$ and $T(n)$ to be $\Theta(\log n)$, because as many as $n/2$ comparisons can be made in parallel.

Achieving these goals is not possible, as Theorem 7.3, due to R. W. Floyd, shows. This theorem allows us to establish a lower bound on the complexity of comparator networks for merging. Establishing nontrivial lower bounds is a fundamental task in the design of algorithms; yet, it is very difficult to derive nontrivial lower bounds. With one exception (the lower bound for detecting whether or not segments intersect, which is based on a lower bound for element uniqueness), all of those that we have seen in previous chapters are derived directly from the lower bound for sorting, the most widely known lower bound. The lower bound of Floyd is independent of the sorting lower bound and thus represents one of the few nontrivial bounds known.

Theorem 7.3 Let $\hat{s}(m, n)$ be the number of comparators in the optimal comparator network for merging sorted lists of lengths m and n. Then we have $\hat{s}(2n, 2n) \geq 2\hat{s}(n, n) + n$.   □

Proof: Using the method developed in the proof of Theorem 7.1, we can assume that the input wires alternate between elements of one list and elements of the other, i.e., the first list is input on wires 1, 3, 5, ..., $4n - 1$ and the second on wires 2, 4, 6, ..., $4n$. We now divide the comparators into three types, based on the indices of the wires, i and j, that they connect: (i) $i < j \leq 2n$; (ii) $2n < i < j$; and (iii) $i \leq 2n < j$. The comparators in the first group must form a (possibly nonoptimal) (n, n)-merging network. In order to verify this assertion, consider merging two lists, each of length $2n$, where the last n elements of each are all equal and all larger than any of the first n elements on either list. The comparators in the second and third groups now make no exchanges, so that all of the work is done by the comparators in the first group. Thus there are at least $\hat{s}(n, n)$ comparators in the first group and, similarly, at least $\hat{s}(n, n)$ comparators in the second group. By considering the input sequence where the first list is all zeros and the second all ones, we see that n elements must be moved from the lower half of the network to the upper half. Only comparators in the third group can move elements between the two halves, so there must be at least n of these.

Q.E.D.

As $\hat{s}(1, 1)$ equals 1, we have $\hat{s}(n, n) \geq \frac{1}{2} n \lg n + n$, for n a power of 2, so that the odd-even merging network is optimal within a factor of two. Thus, merging in the network environment is intrinsically harder than merging in the programming environment, where $2n - 1$ comparisons always suffice. This bound implies that a network sorting algorithm based on mergesort takes $\Theta(n \lg^2 n)$ comparators and $\Theta(\lg^2 n)$ time.

What does this say about our questions, "How many comparators do we need for sorting?" and "What is the minimum delay time for a sorting network?" Actually, the consequences are minimal, as there are other ways to sort besides mergesort. An elegant result, which we do not pursue here, states that finding the median of a list is also intrinsically harder with the network restriction than without, so that a sorting network modelled after quicksort (an algorithm discussed in Section 8.4) will also fail to achieve a $\Theta(n \log n)$ network implementation. However, a complex sorting network that uses $\Theta(n \log n)$ comparators has been devised (for which see the bibliography). On the other hand, by exhaustive examination of cases, one can verify that, for five items, the minimum number of comparisons needed to sort is seven while the optimal sorting network requires nine comparators; hence, sorting by networks requires more work than sorting without the data-independence constraint.

We have also not learned much about merging in place within an array. Floyd's lower bound indicates that this operation cannot be carried out in linear time according to a fixed pattern; yet, merging in place can be accomplished in linear time (for which see the bibliography). Thus, somewhat counterintuitively, a fixed merging pattern is not a condition for a linear-time merging algorithm to use only fixed additional storage.

7.2 Geometric Applications

Divide-and-conquer techniques lead to particularly effective and elegant algorithms for geometric problems. The geometric setting lends itself naturally to partitioning; at the same time, working in two or more dimensions presents new challenges, due to the independence of the coordinates. In this section we consider three simple problems. The first problem centers on the task of merging polygons, a task which illustrates most of the key features of divide-and-conquer techniques in a geometric setting: we discuss the intersection of convex polygons and a special case of the union of convex polygons. The second problem, finding the closest pair in a collection of points, is a special case of more general proximity problems and opens the way to many extensions. Finally, the third problem, finding the convex hull of a set of points (Problem 19), shows how divide-and-conquer techniques can be used to improve the average-case performance of already efficient algorithms. These problems illustrate three principles:

- Devising a solution to a multidimensional problem may be viewed as finding a clever generalization of the often obvious solution in one dimension. Moreover, the two-dimensional problem often can be solved within the same asymptotic bounds as its one-dimensional counterpart, despite a substantial increase in the intricacy of the algorithm.

- Good partitioning often requires a preprocessing step, the running time of which may dominate the running time of the algorithm.

- The size of the solution can be smaller than the sum of the sizes of the sub-solutions. Hence, processing these solutions on return from the recursion may be less costly than the anticipated worst case. Moreover, these savings compound during the execution, so that the running time of the algorithm often improves considerably, at least in the average case.

7.2.1 Merging Polygons

In Section 4.2 we saw how to compute the intersection of two convex polygons in linear time; with the same technique, we can also compute the union of two intersecting convex polygons in linear time. But what of problems that involve a collection of convex polygons? As the intersection of n convex polygons is itself a convex polygon, any algorithm that selects two polygons, computes their intersection, and returns the result to the current set correctly computes the intersection of the collection. As the intersection of a convex polygon of k_1 vertices with one of k_2 vertices is a new convex polygon with at most $k_1 + k_2$ vertices, the intersection of a collection of n convex polygons of k vertices each is a convex polygon with at most kn vertices, so that the result can be described in linear time.

Appealing to our first principle, let us examine the one-dimensional version of this problem: given a collection of line segments, find their intersection. A simple linear-time algorithm for this problem scans each segment in turn: the initial intersection is just the first segment, and updating the intersection (which remains a segment) when scanning a new segment reduces to two constant-time tests. The same algorithm applied to the two-dimensional problem successively intersects the first polygon with the second, the result with the third, etc. While correct, this algorithm takes quadratic time: for example, starting with n polygons of k vertices each, it takes $\Theta(kn^2)$ time.

The problem with the two-dimensional version is that it does not balance the work properly: it spends most of its time working with a potentially large polygon, the intersection of the first i polygons, and, at each step, may make it even larger. The strategy works in one dimension because the intersection is always a single segment and thus cannot grow. This comparison points out the way to a more efficient solution to the two-dimensional problem: we must minimize the number of vertices of the polygons generated during the execution of the algorithm. Because the number of vertices of the polygons generated can grow proportionally to the total number of vertices of the polygons intersected, the obvious solution is a divide-and-conquer approach: partition the collection of polygons into two subcollections of equal size, solve each subproblem recursively, and then compute the intersection of the two resulting polygons. When the collection is composed of n convex k-gons, the running time of this method is described by the standard divide-and-conquer recurrence,

$$\begin{cases} T(n) = 2T(n/2) + \Theta(kn) \\ T(2) = \Theta(k), \end{cases}$$

and thus is $\Theta(kn \log n)$. In particular, given a collection of n half planes (which can be regarded as 1-gons), we can compute their intersection in $\Theta(n \log n)$ time.

Reducing the worst-case running time further is impossible, because we can use an algorithm that computes the intersection of half planes to sort a set of numbers. Given numbers $x_1, x_2, \ldots, x_n$, we form the points (x_i, x_i^2); these points lie on the parabola $y = x^2$. Now let the ith half plane be defined by the tangent to the parabola at the point (x_i, x_i^2), oriented so as to include the positive y-axis. The intersection of these n half planes is an infinite convex region with a boundary defined by $n - 1$ intersection points; these $n - 1$ points can be read sorted by their abscissae in linear time (by following the perimeter of the intersection). Between two consecutive such points lies one of the x_i; hence we can recover the sorted order of the x_i from the list of points by intersecting each successive edge of the polygon with the parabola. Formally, if we denote the ith point on the perimeter by (a_i, b_i), then the $(i + 1)$st number in the desired sorted list is simply $(b_{i+1} - b_i)/2(a_{i+1} - a_i)$; the smallest and largest numbers are found by the obvious linear-time scan of the input. Because the entire construction, with the exception of the procedure for polygon intersection, takes $O(n)$ time and because sorting takes $\Omega(n \log n)$ time, it follows that the intersection of n half planes must also take $\Omega(n \log n)$ time.

In this case, the divide-and-conquer paradigm leads to an efficient scheduling of the intersection operations. Viewed bottom-up, the naïve and the efficient algorithms both start their work with single polygons. Whereas the naïve algorithm schedules intersections by simple iteration (which can also be viewed as a last in, first out policy), the divide-and-conquer algorithm uses a first in, first out policy. This scheduling of operations in a bottom-up algorithm is typical of divide-and-conquer methods. We have already seen several examples of such queue-based scheduling, as well as of the corresponding naïve iterative versions: the Heapify routine builds a heap in linear time in this manner, while building a heap through repeated insertions takes $\Theta(n \log n)$ time; Cheriton and Tarjan's FIFO algorithm for minimum spanning trees improves on Prim's algorithm; and mergesort is the efficient counterpart of insertion sort. Note that, in the case of Cheriton and Tarjan's algorithm, a top-down, recursive divide-and-conquer scheme cannot efficiently determine a valid partition; indeed, while the recursive and the bottom-up approaches generally lead to equally efficient schedules, the bottom-up approach has added flexibility, in that it can choose which objects to merge next on the basis of accumulated knowledge. That such knowledge could be put to use to derive the Cheriton-Tarjan algorithm is tied to the introduction of a second objective: whereas mergesort and `Heapify` need only optimize their running times, an algorithm for the minimum spanning tree problem must also minimize the length of the tree; as we shall see in the last section of this chapter, minimizing running time is not easily reconciled with optimizing some other objective function. Another interesting characteristic of this scheduling mechanism is that it can be varied significantly and yet remain efficient; as we pointed out, the recursive version generally leads to efficient schedules too. We could even use a greedy schedule: select for the next merge operation the two smallest remaining objects. Such a greedy approach works for mergesort and for `Heapify` (but gives the same level-by-level schedule as the simple FIFO schedule), and more interestingly for the intersection of convex polygons and for the other geometric problems discussed in this section. However, since it can work only when the partitioning does not affect the correctness of the algorithm, it cannot be used for the fast Fourier transform problem.

There is more to the divide-and-conquer paradigm than the scheduling of operations, especially within the context of geometric algorithms. In a collection of n polygons, each of the $\lfloor n/2 \rfloor$ intersections computed at the bottom level becomes an operand at the next level. Since the cost of intersecting two polygons is directly proportional to the total number of vertices and since the intersection of two polygons of k_1 and k_2 vertices may have anywhere from zero to $k_1 + k_2$ vertices, the cost of computing the intersections at the next level depends directly on the number of vertices produced at the current level. This dependency, the third major characteristic mentioned earlier, is known as *output-sensitivity* and is common to many geometric applications of the divide-and-conquer technique, as we shall see in our next problems.

Let us now move on to the problem of computing the union of a collection of convex polygons. Unfortunately, the union of an arbitrary collection of convex polygons need not even be a simple polygon and may include up to a quadratic number of simple polygonal pieces, even when the problem is restricted to rectangles in rectilinear geometry; a simple example is illustrated in Figure 7.6. Since the efficiency of algorithms for the general problem is thus limited by the size of the output to be produced, we restrict our attention to a version of the problem, known as the Manhattan skyline problem, in which the output can only grow linearly as a function of the input.

Problem 36 [Manhattan Skyline] Given a set of rectangles (the buildings), all bases of which lie on the x-axis, determine the upper envelope of the collection (the skyline). □

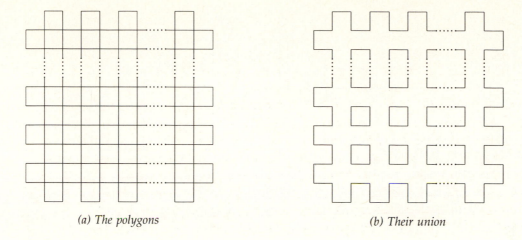

(a) The polygons *(b) Their union*

Figure 7.6: The Union of Convex Polygons May Have a Quadratic Number of Pieces

An instance of this problem is illustrated in Figure 7.7. The skyline can be viewed as an ordered list of horizontal segments, each beginning at the abscissa at which the preceding one ended; this viewpoint leads to a representation as an alternating sequence of abscissae and ordinates, where each ordinate indicates the height of its corresponding segment:

$$(x_1, y_1, x_2, y_2, \ldots, x_{n-1}, y_{n-1}, x_n) \text{ with } x_1 < x_2 < \cdots < x_n.$$

By convention, the skyline is at height zero until x_1 is reached and returns to zero after x_n is passed. We use the same representation for a single rectangle (a building), namely (x_1, y_1, x_2), which specifies the rectangle with vertex coordinates $(x_1, 0)$, (x_1, y_1), (x_2, y_1), and $(x_2, 0)$.

We can begin our design with either the issue of division or the issue of merging. A clever division strategy might result in exceptionally easy merging. On the other hand, a clever merging algorithm might, as with mergesort, make the division trivial. The merging can be made simple by partitioning the x-axis into two disjoint intervals, since merging then reduces to pasting the two partial skylines together. In such a scheme, rectangles on the left are combined into one skyline and the rectangles on the right into another. However, as the data need not be given in sorted order, this strategy requires a sorting step, so that the algorithm must run in $\Omega(n \log n)$ time; moreover, rectangles cannot just be assigned to the left or to the right side, since some rectangles have their left edge clearly in the left half and their right edge clearly in the right half and so must be cut into two rectangles along the partitioning line. (The

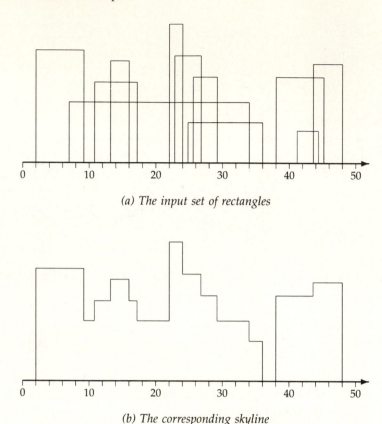

(a) The input set of rectangles

(b) The corresponding skyline

Figure 7.7: An Instance of the Skyline Problem

rectangle $(7, 9, 34)$ of Figure 7.7 is an example.) For these reasons, we take the other approach and consider how to merge two arbitrary skylines. Note that the abscissae of the merged skyline form a subset of the abscissae of the two skylines, since every change in the skyline corresponds to either the left or right edge of a rectangle. Thus merging skylines, like intersecting convex polygons, is output-sensitive; the merging step runs in $\Theta(n_1 + n_2)$ time, where n_1 and n_2 are the sizes of the two skylines and returns a skyline of size varying from 3 to $n_1 + n_2 + 1$. The paradigm for the merging step remains that of mergesort, but it must be modified to accommodate the output-sensitivity (as well as to account for the special cases introduced by the geometric nature of the problem); we present the merging algorithm in detail in Program 7.3. As this implementation is typical of output-sensitive merging steps, we shall not include such code again.

Because of the power of our merging algorithm, the division phase is trivial. We can simply form the skyline for the first $n/2$ rectangles, then form the skyline for the remaining $n/2$ rectangles, and finally merge the two. The worst-case running time of the entire algorithm is given by

$$\begin{cases} T(n) = 2T(n/2) + \Theta(n) \\ T(1) = \Theta(1). \end{cases}$$

Thus the algorithm runs in $\Theta(n \log n)$ time in the worst case. With random or "average" data, the algorithm may run considerably faster because of its output-sensitivity. As mentioned earlier, the exact driving term for the recurrence is really $\Theta(n_1 + n_2)$, and, as we saw in Exercise 2.25, the solution to the divide-and-conquer recurrence is $\Theta(n)$ when $n_1 + n_2$ is $o(n)$.

Can we do better in the worst case? The answer is no, because the skyline problem, like the intersection of convex polygons, is inherently as difficult as sorting. Given n distinct numbers, we can sort them as follows:

- Find two values, one greater than and one less than any value in the list; call these values $\hat{x}$ and $\hat{y}$.

- For each input number, x_i, construct the rectangle $(x_i, x_i - \hat{y}, \hat{x})$. The height of each rectangle basically equals the abscissa of its left edge—the adjustment just avoids negative heights. Thus the skyline of this collection of rectangles defines a step function in which all x values appear.

- Run the skyline algorithm.

- The sorted list of numbers can now be read from the skyline.

As every step, with the possible exception of the skyline algorithm itself, takes $O(n)$ time and as sorting takes $\Omega(n \log n)$ time, it follows that any skyline algorithm based on comparisons must take $\Omega(n \log n)$ time.

Our algorithm for the skyline problem closely resembles mergesort; in particular, the bottom-up coding used in mergesort, which alternates between one array and the next, can be used here as well. We always have sufficient room for this merging strategy for three reasons: (i) the size of a merged list never exceeds the combined size of the two lists by more than one; (ii) we need an array of size $4n - 1$ to hold the largest possible output; and (iii) the input takes only $3n$ storage locations. On the other hand, the size of the merged list may be smaller, so that we must explicitly keep track of the boundaries between the current skylines (with $n + 1$ integer pointers), something that we did not have to do in the mergesort algorithm, where the boundaries are predetermined.

```
const MaxR = ...; (* maximum number of rectangles *)
      MaxSkylineSize = ...; (* 4*MaxR-1 *)
type skyline = array [1..MaxSkylineSize] of real;

procedure Merge(var S1, S2: skyline;
                     n1, n2: integer;
                 var S: skyline;
                 var n: integer);
  (* Merge skylines S1[1..n1] and S2[1..n2] into S[1..n].
     Data are in the form x1, y1, x2, y2, ..., xk,
     so n1 and n2 are necessarily odd and >= 3. *)
  var i, (* points to first unprocessed abscissa of skyline 1 *)
      j, (* points to first unprocessed abscissa of skyline 2 *)
      m: integer;
      k: 1..2; (* Which skyline is currently contributing to the output. *)
      CurHeight1, CurHeight2, CurHeight: real;
  begin
    i := 1; j := 1; n := 0;
    CurHeight1 := 0; CurHeight2 := 0; CurHeight := 0;
    k := 1; (* arbitrarily start with skyline 1 *)
    while (i <= n1) and (j <= n2) do
      (* case S1[i] vs. S2[j] of *)
      if S1[i] < S2[j]
        then begin
                if i < n1 then CurHeight1 := S1[i+1] else CurHeight1 := 0;
                  (* Establish sentinel at end of skyline. *)
                if k = 1
                  (* Skyline can: move up and stay with skyline 1,
                                  move down and stay with skyline 1,
                                  move down and switch to skyline 2, or
                                  stay level and switch to skyline 2. *)
                  then if CurHeight1 >= CurHeight2
                        then begin (* Stay with skyline 1; move up or down. *)
                               S[n+1] := S1[i]; S[n+2] := CurHeight1;
                               CurHeight := CurHeight1;
                               n := n + 2
                             end
                        else begin (* Switch to skyline 2. *)
                               k := 2;
                               if CurHeight2 < CurHeight
                                 then begin (* skyline moves down *)
                                        S[n+1] := S1[i]; S[n+2] := CurHeight2;
                                        CurHeight := CurHeight2;
                                        n := n + 2
                                      end
                                 (* else x value is dropped from the output, because
                                         the skyline accidentally stays level. *)
                             end
```

```
                  else (* k = 2 *)
                       (* Skyline can: move up and switch to skyline 1 or
                                       stay level. *)
                       if CurHeight1 > CurHeight
                         then begin
                                 S[n+1] := S1[i]; S[n+2] := CurHeight1;
                                 CurHeight := CurHeight1;
                                 k := 1;
                                 n := n + 2
                              end;
                       (* else x value is dropped from the output, because
                                 skyline 2 continues to dominate;
                                 this is the source of output-sensitivity. *)
                  i := i + 2
              end
       else if S1[i] > S2[j]
         then ... not shown ... (* symmetric situation *)
       else   begin (* S1[i] = S2[j] *)
                  (* Skyline can: move up,
                                  move down, or
                                  stay level, but switch skylines *)
                  if i < n1 then CurHeight1 := S1[i+1] else CurHeight1 := 0;
                  if j < n2 then CurHeight2 := S2[j+1] else CurHeight2 := 0;
                  if CurHeight1 >= CurHeight2
                    then begin
                            k := 1;
                            if CurHeight1 <> CurHeight (* up or down *)
                              then begin
                                      S[n+1] := S1[i];
                                      if (i<>n1) or (j<>n2) then S[n+2] := CurHeight1;
                                      CurHeight := CurHeight1;
                                      n := n + 2
                                   end
                         end
                    else begin
                            k := 2;
                            if CurHeight2 <> CurHeight (* up or down *)
                              then begin
                                      S[n+1] := S2[j]; S[n+2] := CurHeight2;
                                      CurHeight := CurHeight2;
                                      n := n + 2
                                   end
                         end;
                  i := i + 2; j := j + 2
              end;
       (* Copy remaining portion of either S1 or S2. *)
       for m := i to n1 do begin S[n] := S1[m]; n := n + 1 end;
       for m := j to n2 do begin S[n] := S2[m]; n := n + 1 end
end; (* Merge *)
```

Program 7.3: Merging Algorithm for the Skyline Problem

7.2.2 Finding the Closest Pair

We continue our study of divide-and-conquer techniques in geometric settings by considering the simplest of proximity problems.

Problem 37 [Closest Pair] Given n points in the plane, find the two closest points. If several such pairs exist, find any such pair.   □

An obvious quadratic-time algorithm comes immediately to mind. We appeal to the first of our general principles in order to decide whether additional attention to the problem is warranted: can we solve the one-dimensional version of this problem in better than quadratic time? In the one-dimensional version, we are given a collection of n numbers and must find a pair of numbers with least difference. We can solve this problem in $\Theta(n \log n)$ time by sorting the numbers and scanning the $n-1$ pairs of adjacent elements. However, the one-dimensional and the two-dimensional versions differ in one very important respect: there exists a natural ordering in the former, whereas no such ordering exists in the latter. The natural ordering in the one-dimensional case constrains the choices for closest pairs, because it respects the distance metric: if we have $x < y < z$, then the pair (x, z) cannot be a candidate for the closest pair. The natural ordering of one-dimensional data reduces the number of candidate pairs from a quadratic to a linear function of the number of points, but any artificially imposed ordering on two-dimensional data does very little to save us work.

However, the divide-and-conquer technique allows us to process two-dimensional data so as to reduce the number of candidate pairs from $\Theta(n^2)$ to $\Theta(n \log n)$, a worse bound than in the case of one-dimensional data, but one that will nevertheless enable us to develop a $\Theta(n \log n)$ algorithm. As usual, we start by dividing the input into two pieces of equal size; since proximity is fundamental to the problem, we do not partition the points arbitrarily (and inexpensively) as

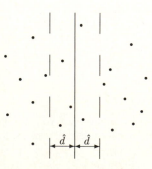

Figure 7.8: Partitioning the Closest Point Problem into Subproblems

we did in our earlier problems, but instead (at some expense) partition the input into two sets by cutting the plane in half. For convenience, we choose a vertical partitioning line. After successive recursions, each subproblem is defined by a thin vertical strip, in which only a few points reside; each such problem can be solved in constant time. A side effect of these successive partitionings is to sort the data into increasing order by their abscissae; thus we may as well begin by sorting the points in this manner, thereby making the partitioning step trivial. Hence the essence of the algorithm is the merging step.

Assume that we have partitioned our n points into two sets of $n/2$ points each and solved each subproblem; that is, for each half of the plane, we have identified the closest pair of points in that half. Comparing the two pairs, we choose the better; denote the distance between its two points by $\hat{d}$. Now, either that pair is the desired solution or there is a better pair. Such a better pair must consist of a point in the left half of the plane and a point in the right half; moreover, no member of the pair can be more than $\hat{d}$ away from the partitioning line, as illustrated in Figure 7.8. Unfortunately, all $n/2$ points from each subcollection can lie within $\hat{d}$ of the vertical line, so it appears that a quadratic number of pairs may still have to be examined. We have not yet made use of all the available information, however. Consider a point, p, lying within $\hat{d}$ of the partitioning line; the only points with which it may be paired must lie within the other strip and within a distance of $\hat{d}$. Thus we can at least restrict our attention to the points that differ from p in ordinate values by at most $\hat{d}$; moreover, as pairing is symmetric, we can further restrict our attention to the points that have ordinate values no smaller than p. These restrictions define a square of side equal to $\hat{d}$, as illustrated in Figure 7.9.

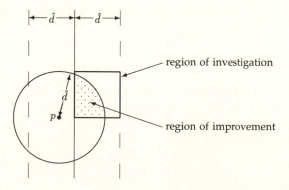

Figure 7.9: Detailed Examination of the Situation at a Point Within $\hat{d}$ of the Partitioning Line

Let us now proceed to an implementation and analysis of our proposed merging step. We begin by temporarily eliminating all points not within $\hat{d}$ of the partitioning line, using a linear-time sweep; let n_1 and n_2 denote the number of points remaining within the left-hand and right-hand strips. We now sort both subcollections by ordinates, an operation which takes $\Theta(\max(n_1 \log n_1, n_2 \log n_2))$ time. Next comes the merging part *per se*: we repeatedly select and delete from the two sorted lists the element with the minimum ordinate and proceed to scan up the other sorted list, computing distances (and updating $\hat{d}$ when appropriate), until a point is reached where the difference between the two ordinates exceeds the current value of $\hat{d}$. This step takes $\Theta(n_1 + n_2)$ time, because at most four points can lie within the region of investigation of Figure 7.9 (since otherwise these points would not be at least $\hat{d}$ apart).

We can summarize our proposed algorithm as follows. The data are stored in an array and a subproblem is defined by two indices; initially the data are sorted by abscissae.

- Divide the current set of points into two subsets of equal size.

- Solve each subproblem recursively.

- Select the better of the two solutions.

- For each subproblem, sort the points within $\hat{d}$ of the partitioning line by their ordinates. Points not included are retained, since they may be needed in a subsequent recombination phase.

- While unprocessed points remain in both sorted lists, run the following steps:

    - Select the unprocessed point with the least ordinate.
    - Scan the other list, computing the distance from each scanned point to the selected point and updating the solution as necessary, until a point is encountered with an ordinate exceeding that of the selected point by at least $\hat{d}$.

In view of our previous discussion, the worst-case running time (not counting the $\Theta(n \log n)$ preprocessing step) occurs when both n_1 and n_2 are $\Theta(n)$ and thus is given by the recurrence

$$\begin{cases} T(n) = 2T(n/2) + \Theta(n \log n) \\ T(1) = \Theta(1). \end{cases}$$

Using the techniques developed in Section 2.2, we obtain that $T(n)$ is $\Theta(n \log^2 n)$. Note that, while it is easy to see that n_1 and n_2 can be $\Theta(n)$ at a particular step, it is much harder to see that this condition can hold at every step. In fact, n_1 and

n_2 can each be $n/2$ at every step: we can construct an example where $\hat{d}$ always exceeds the initial range of abscissae by making the distance between two points depend essentially on their ordinates.

Hence our algorithm improves on the obvious quadratic method; however, it does not yet attain the performance of the one-dimensional version. In fact, we can reduce the running time to $\Theta(n \log n)$ by avoiding the costliest part of the algorithm, namely sorting by ordinates at each stage. All information about the sorted order that the algorithm acquired at such great cost gets discarded when unwinding the recursion; yet, upon return from the recursion, the very same points may again have to be sorted. Had the algorithm somehow retained the sorted subcollections, it could then sort the full collection by a simple merging process in only linear time. We shall thus incorporate mergesort in our current algorithm: our algorithm now returns not only the closest pair, but also the list of points sorted by ordinates. A PASCAL implementation of this algorithm, which incorporates three refinements, is given in Program 7.4. One of the refinements is the use of a global variable to maintain the smallest distance found so far; another is the replacement of the partitioning line with a partitioning "no-man's-land"; the third refinement is the permanent elimination of some points, a refinement that we discuss in the next paragraph. Because the $\Theta(n \log n)$ sorting step has been replaced by a $\Theta(n)$ merging step, the overall running time has been reduced to $\Theta(n \log n)$. What we have done is to balance the various steps: within the recursive body, the main steps each take $\Theta(n)$ time, and, overall, the preprocessing and the recursive body of the algorithm each take $\Theta(n \log n)$ time. Finally, note that, while we chose to do the sorting by abscissae as a preprocessing step, we left the sorting by ordinates embedded within the recursive procedure. The reason for our second choice is basically that we get the sorting for free: we must maintain sets of points that fall within $\hat{d}$ of the partitioning line; these sets depend on both abscissae and ordinates, a dependency that prevents us from using subranges of ordinates (we are already committed to using subranges of abscissae) and thus forces us to merge sets.

We mentioned earlier that points not within $\hat{d}$ of the partitioning line have to be retained for possible use in later recombinations; however, permanent elimination of points can indeed take place. The only points of interest are those that lie within $\hat{d}$ of a boundary; as $\hat{d}$ can only decrease, those points that do not currently lie within $\hat{d}$ of a boundary will never be of interest again and so can be eliminated for all time. This elimination can be done as part of the merging step and may speed up the recursive part of the algorithm considerably, since the running time of the procedure body is $\Theta(n_1 + n_2)$, where n_1 and n_2 are the numbers of points returned by the two recursive calls: if $n_1 + n_2$ is $o(n)$, then the running time of the recursive part of the algorithm is $\Theta(n)$, although the overall running time remains the same in asymptotic terms, since it is now dominated

```
const MaxP = ...;
type SetOfPoints = array [1..MaxP] of point;

procedure ClosestPair(var A, work: SetOfPoints; n: integer;
                        var p1, p2: point; var d: real);
  (* Find the closest pair from among n points in O(n log n) time. *)
  (* p1 and p2 keep track of the closest points and d of their distance. *)
  (* NOTE: the contents of A are destroyed. *)
  var i: integer; MinX, MaxX: real; (* dummy variables *)

  procedure RecClosestPair(    l, r: integer;
                              var newr: integer; var MinX, MaxX: real);
    (* Find the closest pair of points in A[1..r], which is sorted by abscissae.
       On return, A[1..newr] contains the points, sorted by ordinates, which lie
       within d of the boundaries of the vertical strip [MinX,MaxX]. *)
    var m, newml, newmr: integer;
        MaxX1, MinX2: real;

    procedure Merge(l1, r1, l2, r2: integer; var newr: integer;
                    MinX, MaxX1, MinX2, MaxX: real);
      (* Check for closest pairs among A[l1..r1] and A[l2..r2] and merge. *)
      begin
        ... no code shown for this routine ...
        (* The partitioning line is a no-man's-land between MaxX1 and MinX2. *)
        (* Scan both lists and place at the front of the work array, preserving
           the ordering by ordinates, the points of subproblem 1 that lie within d
           of MinX2 and the points of subproblem 2 that lie within d of MaxX1. *)
        (* Scan the work array and update global variables p1, p2, and d. *)
        (* Merge the two sorted lists, retaining only points within d of the
           boundaries of the new vertical strip. *)
      end; (* Merge *)

    begin (* RecClosestPair *)
      if l = r
        then begin newr := r; MinX := A[l].x; MaxX := MinX end
        else begin
               m := (l+r) div 2;
               RecClosestPair(l,m,newml,MinX,MaxX1);
               RecClosestPair(m+1,r,newmr,MinX2,MaxX);
               Merge(l,newml,m+1,newmr,newr,MinX,MaxX1,MinX2,MaxX)
             end
    end; (* RecClosestPair *)

  begin (* ClosestPair *)
    ...; (* Sort the points by their abscissae. *)
    d := infinity; (* suitable constant *)
    RecClosestPair(1,n,i,MinX,MaxX)
  end; (* ClosestPair *)
```

Program 7.4: Algorithm for the Closest Pair Problem

by the $\Theta(n \log n)$ preprocessing step—an illustration of our second principle. In fact, a running time of $\Theta(n \log n)$ is optimal; we can prove this assertion by a simple reduction to the problem of element uniqueness, a problem for which a lower bound of $\Omega(n \log n)$ is known (see Exercise 8.4). Clearly, if two elements are identical, they must form the closest pair; hence we get an immediate answer to the problem of uniqueness (phrased in terms of numbers on the x-axis) by identifying the closest pair.

We can generalize this problem in two natural ways: by moving to higher dimensions or by finding a closest neighbor for each point rather than just one closest pair for the whole collection, a problem called the *all-nearest-neighbors problem*. The same overall approach works well on the k-dimensional version of the closest pair problem, but the recombination phase becomes complex, since we must now consider all points within distance $\hat{d}$ of the $(k-1)$-dimensional hyperplane. Whereas we reduced the two-dimensional recombination to a one-dimensional problem by sorting the points by their ordinates and merging, we now have the problem of sorting points that retain $k-1$ degrees of freedom—the very issue that gave us trouble in the first place. Fortunately, what worked before can be made to work again: by using a similar divide-and-conquer strategy (but with very carefully chosen partitions), we can devise an algorithm that solves the closest-pair problem for n points in k-dimensional space and runs in $\Theta(n \log n)$ time.

The all-nearest-neighbors problem can also be solved in $\Theta(n \log n)$ time, but requires a sophisticated analysis of the geometric properties of neighborhood structures and a divide-and-conquer algorithm with a complex merging step. Although the one-dimensional problem can be solved, like the one-dimensional closest-pair problem, by simply sorting the points, the generalization to two dimensions fails one essential test: a point quite far from the partitioning line can have as its nearest neighbor a point in the other subcollection that also lies quite far from the partitioning line. Fortunately, it can be shown that only a linear number of nearest-neighbor pairs need be rearranged during merging, so that a linear-time merging algorithm remains feasible. We shall not present the $\Theta(n \log n)$ algorithm, but we discuss briefly the two-dimensional neighborhood structure that embodies the solution to the problem and show how to compute it in $\Theta(n^2 \log n)$ time with a less sophisticated divide-and-conquer approach.

Note that the nearest-neighbor relation is not symmetric: if P_1 is the closest neighbor of P_2, it does not follow that P_2 is the closest neighbor of P_1. We can establish a hierarchy of proximity for each point: the one point that is the closest neighbor; then a collection of points that are also immediate neighbors (a single point in one dimension); and finally, all other points. Formally, we capture the notion of immediate neighborhood with the Voronoi polygon, named after G. F. Voronoi (1868–1908).

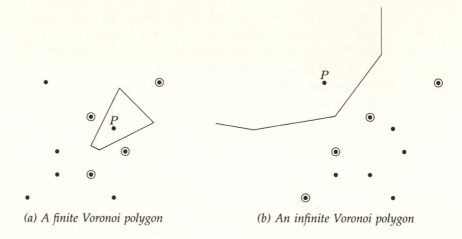

(a) A finite Voronoi polygon   (b) An infinite Voronoi polygon

Figure 7.10: Voronoi Polygons

Definition 7.1 Given a collection of points, $\mathcal{P} = \{P_1, P_2, \ldots, P_n\}$, and a distinguished point, P_i, the *Voronoi polygon* of P_i with respect to $\mathcal{P}$ is the locus of points that are as close to P_i as to any other point in $\mathcal{P}$.   □

We know from elementary geometry that the locus of points as close to P_i as to some other point, P_j, is the half plane that includes P_i and is bounded by the perpendicular bisector of the segment $\overline{P_iP_j}$; the Voronoi polygon is just the intersection of $n-1$ such half planes, one for each point in $\mathcal{P}$. Therefore, Voronoi polygons are convex polygonal regions, which can be finite or infinite, as illustrated in Figure 7.10. Note that some of the half planes may not contribute to the boundary of a Voronoi polygon; in both parts of the figure, the points that contribute part of the polygonal boundary have been highlighted. These points are the immediate neighbors of P_i, in that their Voronoi polygons (their "territory") share an edge with that of P_i. Our algorithm for the intersection of half planes immediately gives us a $\Theta(n \log n)$ algorithm for computing the Voronoi polygon of a point.

Given a collection of points, we want to find the Voronoi polygon of each point in the collection with respect to all other points in the collection. The result is a partition of the plane into n convex regions, each region being a Voronoi polygon.

Definition 7.2 Given a collection of n points, $\mathcal{P}$, the *Voronoi diagram* of $\mathcal{P}$ is the partition of the plane into n convex regions such that each region is the Voronoi polygon of one point of $\mathcal{P}$ with respect to the other points of $\mathcal{P}$.   □

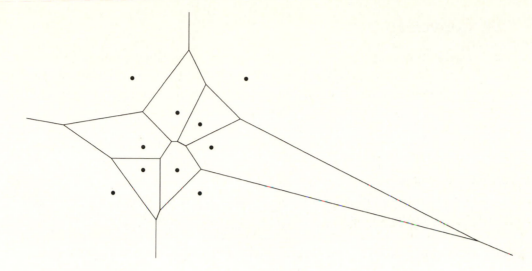

Figure 7.11: The Voronoi Diagram of a Set of Points

Figure 7.11 illustrates the Voronoi diagram of the set of points used in Figure 7.10. From our previous observation, it is clear that we can compute the Voronoi diagram of a set of n points in $\Theta(n^2 \log n)$ time by computing the Voronoi polygon of each point. But this approach does not use the full power of divide-and-conquer; instead, we should sort the points by their abscissae, partition the set of points into two subsets of equal size by cutting the plane with a vertical line, find the Voronoi diagrams of each half recursively, and finally merge the two diagrams. This last step can in fact be done in linear time, so that a $\Theta(n \log n)$ algorithm results; however, the merging step is very complex, so that we do not discuss it, but refer the reader to the bibliography. (Before even starting such a step, one first has to establish that the number of line segments in a Voronoi diagram cannot grow very fast, since otherwise no efficient algorithm could exist; in fact, the size of the Voronoi diagram remains bounded by a linear function of the number of points.)

Note that the Voronoi diagram of a set of points is closely related to the convex hull of that set (recall from Section 1.6 that the convex hull of a set of points in the plane is simply the smallest convex polygon such that all points in the set lie either within or on the polygon). In particular, it can be shown that the Voronoi polygon of a point is infinite if and only if that point is part of the convex hull of the set (see Exercise 7.13). How to compute convex hulls is the topic of our next discussion.

7.2.3 Convex Hulls

We first give an intuitive algorithm, known by the descriptive name of *package wrapping*, which runs in $\Theta(nm)$ time, where n is the number of points in the set and m is the number of points on the convex hull. After identifying the basic weakness of this algorithm, we develop the *Graham scan* algorithm, which constructs the hull in linear time after a $\Theta(n \log n)$ preprocessing step. With a divide-and-conquer algorithm that uses both the idea of the Graham scan and that of mergesort, we can attain linear average-case time for a wide variety of random distributions of points in the plane.

The package-wrapping algorithm is a simple algorithm based on a physical interpretation of the problem. If the points are represented by nails sticking out of a board and if we have a large rubber band, we can stretch the rubber band, place it so that it encloses all the nails, and let it shrink to fit. The nails that it touches are the vertices of the convex hull. In the absence of a suitable rubber band, we can obtain the same result with a long piece of string. We first locate a nail that is certain to lie on the convex hull, such as the point with the smallest ordinate, and tie our string to it. Next, we stretch out the string in a line parallel to the x-axis and begin pivoting the string around our starting nail. The string first touches some nail, then, as we continue our rotation, another and another, until it has completely enclosed all the nails, describing the convex hull. Figure 7.12 illustrates the process.

Package wrapping is very efficient when done by hand using physical materials, but cannot be coded as efficiently. The iterative step in package wrapping simply searches for the point, P, such that the line $\overline{P_1 P}$ forms the minimum angle

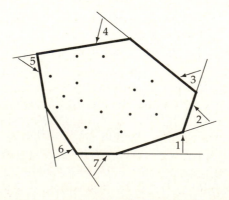

Figure 7.12: An Example of Package Wrapping

```
function Theta(p1, p2: point): real;
  (* Return the pseudoangle between the line from p1 to (infinity,p1.y)
     and the line from p1 to p2.  The pseudoangle has the property that
     the ordering of points by true angle around p1 and the ordering of
     points by pseudoangle are the same. *)
  (* The result is in the range [0,4) (or it is an error indication). *)
  var dx, dy, t: real;
  begin
    dx := p2.x - p1.x;
    dy := p2.y - p1.y;
    if (dx = 0.0) and (dy = 0.0)
      then Theta := -1.0 (* error indication *)
      else begin
              t := dy/(abs(dx) + abs(dy));
              (* Now correct for quadrant--first quadrant: [0,1] *)
              if dx < 0.0 (* inside second or third quadrant: (1,3) *)
                then t := 2.0 - t
              else if dy < 0.0 (* fourth quadrant: [3,4) *)
                then t := 4.0 + t;
              Theta := t
           end
  end; (* Theta *)
```

Program 7.5: Computing the Pseudoangle

with the line $\overline{P_2P_1}$, where P_2 and P_1 are, respectively, the next to last and last points included in the partially formed convex hull. This step requires accurate and efficient determination of angles, an operation that we have avoided up until now. As we need only compare angles, however, we can avoid computing their actual values and thus avoid using transcendental functions; we require only a function, f, such that $f(x) < f(y)$ whenever $x < y$, where x and y represent angles in the range $[0, 2\pi)$. Several trigonometric functions, such as the sine, have the desired property in the first quadrant and can be computed from the Cartesian coordinates without first determining each angle. A better function, because it uses only one division and no multiplication or square root, is given in Program 7.5. We call this function a pseudoangle because it behaves like an angle under comparison and because its range closely approximates that of a real angle: it is $[0, 4)$ instead of $[0, 2\pi)$. This function also behaves much like the sine function in the first quadrant, varying from zero to one as the angle varies from zero to $\pi/2$; but the length of the hypotenuse is computed according to the Manhattan metric rather than the Euclidean metric, with the result that the pseudoangle replaces the unit circle, on which the sine is based, with the triangle formed by the axes and the line connecting $(0, 1)$ to $(1, 0)$.

Although we have coded the pseudoangle function to allow for arbitrary shifts of origin, the reference axis must remain parallel to the x-axis and have the same orientation. This restriction is of no consequence in the context of package wrapping: we simply search for the point of minimal pseudoangle greater than the current pseudoangle (where angles are defined with respect to a horizontal line passing through the current point); in case of ties, we select the point farthest away from our current point, thereby handling collinearity. Because each step changes the perspective from which the vertices are seen, the angles have to be recomputed at each step; therefore, finding the next point on the hull takes time proportional to the number of points, and the resulting algorithm takes time proportional to the product of the total number of points and the number of points on the hull. In the worst case, all the given points lie on the hull and the package-wrapping algorithm takes quadratic time; on the other hand, the convex hull of a set of randomly distributed points includes only a small fraction of the points in the set and the package-wrapping algorithm then runs quickly.

As the change of perspective is the main cause of inefficiency in the package-wrapping algorithm, our next step is to develop an algorithm that follows the same basic idea, but uses a fixed perspective. With respect to a fixed perspective, the points can be ordered in $\Theta(n \log n)$ time by a preprocessing step, after which they can be processed in that fixed order. Let $P_1, P_2, \ldots, P_n$ be the points as they are ordered by the preprocessing phase. The main processing phase then successively finds the convex hull of $H_j = \{P_1, P_2, \ldots, P_j\}$ as j increases. A convenient starting point for this phase is a pair of adjacent points on the hull; thus we pick the point at the bottom of the hull, define it to be the point P_1, and order all other points by their pseudoangles with respect to a horizontal line passing through P_1. An immediate consequence is that the second point, P_2, must also lie on the hull.

The scan through the points uses the following property: if a point is known to lie inside the convex hull of a set of points, then it lies inside the convex hull of any superset. Therefore, once the algorithm determines that P_i is not part of the convex hull of H_j, it need never reconsider P_i. This permanent elimination is the key to the efficiency of the main processing phase. The algorithm, known as the Graham scan, can be summarized as follows:

- (Selection of perspective) Find the point with minimum ordinate and, in the case of equality, with minimum abscissa; this is the "anchor" point, P_1.

- (Static ordering) Using P_1 as the origin, sort the remaining points into ascending order by the pseudoangles formed by a parallel to the x-axis and by the lines from P_1 to the points, breaking ties by using their distances from P_1.

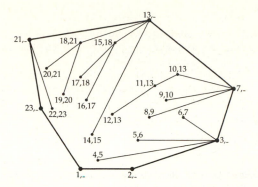

Figure 7.13: An Example of the Graham Scan

- (Graham scan) Create a stack and push onto it P_1 and P_2; generally, denote the points on the stack by $S_1, S_2, \ldots, S_k$, where S_k is on top of the stack. For each value of j, $j = 3, 4, \ldots, n$, execute the following elimination step, then place P_j on the stack:

  - (Elimination) If S_k is on or to the left of the oriented line from S_{k-1} to P_j, then eliminate S_k from the hull and decrease k. Repeat for successively lower values of k until either k equals 1 or no elimination occurs.

- (Closure) Connect S_k to P_1 to complete the convex hull.

Figure 7.13 illustrates the operation of the Graham scan. The thin lines indicate line segments that once connected hull vertices, but were subsequently eliminated. The vertices are labelled with ordered pairs: the first component indicates when the vertex was added to the hull, and the second component indicates which vertex, if any, was the cause of its subsequent elimination.

Each point is pushed onto the stack exactly once and removed from the stack at most once; therefore, although the elimination substep has a variable execution time, the time taken by the scan phase is $\Theta(n)$. A PASCAL implementation of the algorithm is given in Program 7.6. Since the input to a convex hull problem is just a set of points, we present the output polygon not as a circular, singly-linked list of points, as we did in Section 4.2, but as a sequence of points in an array. Our choice does not affect the asymptotic running time of our algorithm, but it makes for clearer and slightly more efficient code. Our algorithm rearranges the data, placing the points that compose the convex hull at the start of the array, in counterclockwise traversal order; the remainder of the array contains the interior points, in no particular order. We use the same conventions for all

```
procedure GrahamScan(    n: integer; (* actual number of points in input *)
                     var m: integer; (* number of points in hull *)
                     var P: SetOfPoints);
(* Points may be collinear and need not even be distinct.  The points of P
   are rearranged so that the m convex hull points come first. *)
label 1;
var i, min: integer;
    q: point;
    l: segment;
begin
  (* Find the minimum point--smallest y and, within equal y values,
     smallest x.  Swap this point with the first point. *)
  min := 1;
  for i := 2 to n do if Compare(P[i],P[min]) < 0 then min := i;
  q := P[1]; P[1] := P[min]; P[min] := q;

  (* Sort the points using polar coordinates, treating the anchor as the
     origin.  The primary key is the pseudoangle of the line from the anchor
     to the point; the secondary key is the distance from the anchor. *)
  ... not shown ...

  (* The stack contains points thought to be on the hull and occupies
     the first m positions of P; initially, it contains P1 and P2. *);
  m := 2; (* Effectively push P[1] and P[2] onto the stack. *)
  for i := 3 to n do
    begin
      (* The new point is always included in the convex hull of the points
         in P[1..i], because it has the largest angle and, in case of a tie,
         is farthest from the anchor. *)
      l.e2 := P[i];
      (* Eliminate points from the hull (stack) due to the inclusion of P[i]. *)
      while m > 1 do
        begin
          l.e1 := P[m-1];
          if WhichSide(P[m],l) <= 0
             (* Points on the left are inside the convex hull.  As we have m > 1,
                there cannot be any subscript problems due to collinearity. *)
             then m := m - 1
             else goto 1
        end;
  1: (* Place P[i] on the stack. *)
     m := m + 1;
     q := P[m]; P[m] := P[i]; P[i] := q
    end
end; (* GrahamScan *)
```

Program 7.6: Graham Scan Algorithm

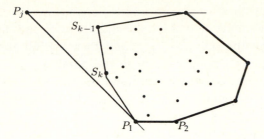

Figure 7.14: The Effect on the Convex Hull of Adding an Exterior Point

our hull-finding programs. Declarations and basic functions are those given in Program 4.8, with one exception: the function Compare must use the ordinate, rather than the abscissa, as the primary key.

We now prove that the Graham scan correctly builds the convex hull. Our proof proceeds by induction, using the following invariant: at the end of the jth step, the stack contains a counterclockwise traversal of the convex hull of the set of points $H_j = \{P_1, P_2, \ldots, P_j\}$. This invariant clearly holds initially, though in a degenerate way: the stack contains only P_1 and P_2, and the convex hull of H_2 is the line segment $\overline{P_1 P_2}$. Now note that P_j always lies on the convex hull of H_j, because the angle formed by the line from the anchor to P_j with the horizontal is the largest of any of the angles determined by the points in H_j; our ordering from nearest to farthest takes care of any ties. We must verify that the elimination step does not eliminate any point that belongs to the hull of H_j and that it does eliminate every point not on the hull. If S_k lies to the left of (or on) the oriented line from S_{k-1} to P_j, then S_k lies inside (or on the perimeter, but is not one of the vertices of) the triangle $\triangle P_1 S_{k-1} P_j$, so that it is not one of the points defining H_j and must be eliminated. Therefore, the scan does not eliminate any point that belongs to the hull. Figure 7.14 shows the effect on the convex hull of incorporating a new point exterior to the present hull. Notice that all of the points that were formerly on the hull and are now interior to it form a single polygonal line; this line is the base of a cone, the apex of which is the new point. Since P_1 is always on the hull, it is one endpoint of the base of the cone. The first point at which the elimination step fails lies to the right of the oriented line from the current S_{k-1} to P_j and thus must be the other endpoint of the base, so that all of the points in between are correctly eliminated.

Can we improve on the worst-case behavior of this algorithm? As with the polygon-merging problems, the answer is no, because we can again reduce sorting to our problem. More precisely, we can use an algorithm that returns the points of the hull in the order in which they appear on the hull to sort a collection of distinct numbers. Let x_i, $i = 1, 2, \ldots, n$ be the numbers; for each number, x_i, we form the point, (x_i, x_i^2), and then ask for the convex hull of the resulting collection of points. Because the parabola, $y = x^2$, is a convex function, all of the points lie on the hull and we can read off the numbers in increasing order by traversing the hull in counterclockwise order from the point of minimum abscissa. The pre- and postprocessing steps both take linear time; as sorting takes $\Omega(n \log n)$ time, so must any comparison-based algorithm for finding convex hulls. Note that this reduction does not rule out the existence of a comparison-based algorithm for convex hulls that would merely return the hull points in any order in $o(n \log n)$ time, although no such algorithm is known.

While we cannot improve the worst-case running time, we can improve the average-case running time by using a divide-and-conquer approach. If we split our collection of points into two subcollections and find the convex hull of each subcollection, the convex hull of the complete collection must be a subset of the points in the convex hulls of the two subcollections; from the opposite viewpoint, any point eliminated by a recursive call need not be considered ever again. Thus, as in our previous examples, we want to take advantage of output-sensitivity. If we can partition the points into subcollections of equal size in constant time, then the running time of the overall algorithm is described by the recurrence,

$$\begin{cases} T(n) = 2T(n/2) + f(n_1, n_2) \\ T(1) = \Theta(1), \end{cases}$$

where n_1 and n_2 are the sizes of the hulls of the two subproblems and f describes the running time of the hull-merging step. Hence we need to devise an efficient algorithm for merging two convex hulls and then to determine the average values of n_1 and n_2. The latter problem is one of stochastic geometry: we shall quote some results without proof and use them in our analysis.

We can merge two convex hulls, viewed as sets of points, by finding the convex hull of their union. A naïve use of the Graham scan leads to a merging step running in $\Theta((n_1 + n_2) \log(n_1 + n_2))$ time. However, such an approach completely ignores the structure present in each hull: the points of the hull are already ordered according to a counterclockwise traversal of their perimeter. As the Graham scan runs in linear time once the points have been sorted, we can hope to derive a linear-time merging step by taking advantage of the ordering of the hull points. In order to use the Graham scan, we need to set up a single ordered list of all the points; unfortunately, we cannot obtain this list by simply merging our two lists, since these are ordered from different perspectives. Hence, our one remaining problem is to reorder a perimeter-ordered list with respect to a different anchor. Figure 7.15 illustrates the basic idea; a high-level description of the algorithm follows:

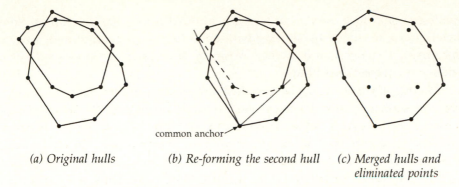

| (a) Original hulls | (b) Re-forming the second hull | (c) Merged hulls and eliminated points |

Figure 7.15: Merging Two Convex Hulls

- (Selection of anchor) Choose as the common anchor, P, that with smaller ordinate, breaking ties by choosing that with smaller abscissa.

- (Re-forming the second hull) Split the hull that does not contain P into an upper and a lower piece as viewed from the perspective of P, as illustrated in Figure 7.15(b). The points along the lower piece are interior points— they are in the interior of the convex polygon consisting of P and the upper piece—and can be discarded; the upper piece is properly ordered with respect to P.

- (Graham scan) Run the Graham scan; points are chosen from one or the other list as dictated by their (pseudo)angle with respect to the horizontal line passing through the common anchor.

The selection of the anchor takes constant time, because the two choices are already the first elements in their respective hulls. Re-forming the second hull takes time proportional to its original size, because we need only identify the vertices with the largest and smallest angles with respect to the horizontal line passing through the common anchor. The Graham scan takes $\Theta(n_1 + n_2)$ time, so that the merging step takes $\Theta(n_1 + n_2)$ time overall. As we always have $n_1 + n_2 \leq n$, the worst-case running time of our divide-and-conquer algorithm is $\Theta(n \log n)$.

As with our previous divide-and-conquer algorithms, this algorithm can be coded nonrecursively, in a bottom-up manner. It must then keep track of where in the array of points the hull of each subproblem begins and ends; this expense is unavoidable in bottom-up divide-and-conquer algorithms that are output-sensitive. Unfortunately, the recursive and nonrecursive versions both suffer from a fairly high overhead; the resulting code is longer and has higher coefficients than either the Graham scan or the package-wrapping algorithm (our complete code, which we do not show, is approximately 400 lines long). Some efficiency can be gained by starting with subcollections of some small size, for which the hull can be found by the Graham scan in much less time than by our divide-and-conquer algorithm.

In terms of worst-case behavior, then, our new algorithm does not improve upon the Graham scan: the two have the same asymptotic behavior and the Graham scan has by far the lower overhead. In terms of average-case behavior, however, we have indeed achieved a significant improvement. Looking back at the recurrence describing the running time of our new algorithm, notice that, if $n_1 + n_2$ is $o(n)$, then the solution to the recurrence is $\Theta(n)$. Thus, if the size of the hull grows more slowly than the number of points, then our divide-and-conquer algorithm runs in linear time. Results from stochastic geometry indicate that the size of the hull grows much more slowly than the number of points.

Theorem 7.4 If n points are chosen uniformly from the unit square or the unit circle, then the expected number of points on the convex hull is $O(\log n)$ or $O(n^{1/3})$.   □

A limitation on the applicability of these results is the hypothesis that the points come from a given distribution; this distribution may well not be preserved by our partitioning. Fortunately, the two distributions mentioned in the theorem are preserved by a random partitioning, which is exactly what our algorithm does. If we suspect that there is an underlying order to the points, we should shuffle them as a preprocessing step; not only will this step place us in a situation that more closely meets the hypothesis of the theorem, it will also tend to make the convex hulls cover more area, so that points are eliminated sooner.

Since the overhead of the divide-and-conquer method may well make it slower than the Graham scan and since the package-wrapping algorithm can run much faster than its worst-case bound indicates, we conducted some experiments to determine the performance of these three algorithms on uniformly distributed data over the unit square. The results are summarized in Table 7.1 (where all running times are given in seconds). The linearity of the divide-and-conquer algorithm is clearly evident, as are the linear and $n \log n$ phases of the Graham scan. The reasonable performance of the $\Theta(nm)$ package-wrapping algorithm is due to the fact that m is $O(\log n)$ for uniformly distributed points over the unit square. The disappointing times turned in by the divide-and-conquer algorithm, in spite of its clearly linear behavior, are due to its higher overhead. Because the running time of the Graham scan is dominated by the sorting phase, special attention must be paid to the coding of that step. We discuss sorting thoroughly in Chapter 8 and so postpone a presentation of the chosen implementation (the quicksort algorithm of Program 8.5), but we comment on one aspect that is peculiar to this application. The quicksort algorithm works through key comparisons

Table 7.1: Performance of Convex Hull Algorithms

(a) Problem characteristics (ten instances)

	Number of points		
	1000	10,000	100,000
Average number of points on hull	19.2	25.8	32.3
Average number of points after running Floyd-Eddy heuristic	517	5274	48,347
Average running time of Floyd-Eddy heuristic	0.48	4.7	49

(b) Running times

		Number of points					
		1000	10,000	100,000	1000	10,000	100,000
Package wrapping		3.9	52.3	655.3	2.4	32.3	366.0
Improved package wrapping		2.6	32.7	415.6	1.9	21.9	258.0
Graham scan	Total	1.2	12.9	142.7	1.1	11.4	116.3
	$\Theta(n \log n)$ sort	0.5	6.0	72.7	0.2	3.0	33.1
	$\Theta(n)$ portion	0.7	6.9	70.0	0.9	8.4	83.2
Divide-and-conquer		1.9	19.1	192.3	1.5	15.5	149.5
Method		without Floyd-Eddy			with Floyd-Eddy (including Floyd-Eddy times)		

and exchanges; as our keys (the pseudoangles) must themselves be computed from the data, we have a choice of computing them as needed or precomputing all of them by taking advantage of the fixed perspective and storing them in a separate array. The former approach results in $\Theta(n \log n)$ rather expensive angle computations, while the latter makes only $\Theta(n)$ angle computations, but uses an additional $\Theta(n)$ storage. Equal angles can be handled in a single linear-time pass after the sort is made: we need not sort each group of points with equal angles, but need only find the point farthest from the anchor, discarding the others. We used this technique in producing the data for Table 7.1. Indeed, computing the pseudoangles as needed slows the code down so much that, in our experiments, the resulting version of the Graham scan is the slowest of the three algorithms, rather than the fastest.

We have also incorporated a general heuristic that improves the performance of all the algorithms and one particular heuristic that improves the performance of package wrapping. The latter heuristic is based on a feature of the Graham scan and allows the package-wrapping algorithm to eliminate efficiently a number of points at each step. When searching for the next hull point, we can permanently eliminate any points that lie inside the convex polygon formed by immediately closing our partial hull. Identifying such points takes only one additional comparison, but this comparison often fails, so that the effectiveness of this heuristic must be balanced against the cost of failed comparisons. We content ourselves with noting that, in our experiments, this heuristic resulted in a 30%–40% gain in running time.

The general heuristic, called the *Floyd-Eddy heuristic* after its independent codiscoverers, is a linear-time preprocessing step that can permanently eliminate a significant fraction of the points. It is based on three trivial results: (i) given any subset of points on the hull, any point that falls within the convex polygon described by this subset must also fall within the convex hull proper; (ii) given any convex k-gon for fixed k, we can determine in constant time whether or not an arbitrary point lies within the polygon; and (iii) given any collection of points, we can find in linear time some constant number of points that must lie on the hull. We can easily get four points on the hull (at least, in general, although we may get as few as two) by selecting the points with minimum and maximum abscissae and ordinates; the expense caused by using additional points is not justified in practice. The number of points eliminated by this heuristic is again a question of stochastic geometry. For a uniform distribution over the unit circle, the result is easy to derive. As n goes to infinity, the four points that delimit the quadrilateral approach the compass points of the circle, so that the ratio of the area of the square that they inscribe to the area of the circle approaches $2/\pi$; therefore, approximately 63.66% of the points

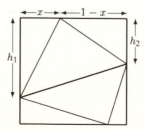

Figure 7.16: Determining the Effectiveness of the Floyd-Eddy Heuristic on the Unit Square

are eliminated. For a uniform distribution over the unit square, the same argument shows that the four points must, in the limit, lie on the four sides of the square, so that the expected percentage of eliminated points is given by the expected area of an inscribed quadrilateral with vertices chosen independently and uniformly along the four sides. A little geometric reasoning (see Figure 7.16) shows that the area of the upper trapezoid outside the inscribed quadrilateral is given by $1/2 x h_1 + 1/2(1-x)h_2$, while the area of the upper trapezoid is $1/2(h_1 + h_2)$. Since x varies uniformly over $[0, 1]$, we conclude that the expected area of the inscribed quadrilateral is $1/2$; the data of Table 7.1(a) clearly demonstrate this behavior.

7.3 The Fast Fourier Transform

The *Fourier transform*, named after Jean-Baptiste Joseph Fourier (1768–1830), is an essential tool of modern applied mathematics, finding application in all areas where information or signals are transmitted or analyzed, from concert hall acoustics, through aerodynamics, broadcasting, and process control, to computer vision. Whereas the Fourier transform can be applied to any periodic continuous function, the *fast Fourier transform* (generally referred to as the FFT) is a divide-and-conquer algorithm for computing discrete Fourier transforms for numerical data; in other words, the first is a tool of mathematics, whereas the second is an algorithm to be used in mathematical applications. We begin with a short description of Fourier's intent and the nature of the Fourier transform, then go on to consider other transforms with which the reader is already familiar, before considering the problem of computing the discrete Fourier transform efficiently.

Fourier developed the transform that bears his name to express *periodic functions* (i.e., functions such that, for some fixed constant, T, known as the *period*, $f(x) = f(x + T)$ holds for all x) as infinite series of sine and cosine functions,

$$f(x) = \sum_{i=0}^{\infty} (a_n \cos nx + b_n \sin nx).$$

Such expressions have the advantage of putting all periodic functions within the same frame of reference: we can think of the sine and cosine functions as the coordinates in which the periodic function is expressed.[3] What has since become known as the Fourier transform is the method for deriving the coefficients of the

---

[3]Notice that the periods of the sine and cosine functions are 2π and the periods of the functions given in the infinite series are $2\pi/n$, whereas the function to be expressed as a sum of sine and cosine functions can have any positive real number for a period. This minor problem is easily remedied by a change of variables: if $f(t)$ has period T, then $f(x)$, where $x = 2\pi t/T$, has period 2π.

sine and cosine functions. We shall not study the general transformation, but look only at its discrete version.

In many applications, a continuous function is sampled at a number of equally spaced points, say $x_1 < x_2 < \cdots < x_n$, and the resulting finite collection of pairs, $(x_1, f(x_1)), (x_2, f(x_2)), \ldots, (x_n, f(x_n))$, defines the function. Under such circumstances, it matters little whether the actual function is periodic or not: we can always assume that the sampled version is periodic, with a period larger than $x_n - x_1$; that is, we can assume that the samples we have taken define the period of the function. As a result, whereas the continuous Fourier transform is limited to periodic functions, its discrete version is universally applicable.

Fourier, who was a physicist, developed a set of mathematical tools for working with these infinite series of functions, enabling him and later scientists to solve important questions in physics. The reader may be familiar with other transform methods; Fourier's compatriot and contemporary, the mathematician Pierre Simon de Laplace (1749–1827), developed the related *Laplace transform* as a tool for solving differential equations; we have seen in Section 2.2 how to transform the problem of solving a recurrence relation into one of deriving the generating function for the recurrence, a method known to engineers as the *z-transform*; finally, all of us (at least, those of us who were not born in the age of hand-held calculators) are familiar with the method of using logarithms in order to transform time-consuming multiplications into additions. Thus transform methods are common in applied mathematics. All of them share one goal: to simplify difficult computations by transforming the problem into a different domain.

An important application of transform methods in modern computing is the computation of the discrete convolution of two sampled functions.

Definition 7.3 The *convolution* of two vectors, $\mathbf{a} = (a_0, a_1, \ldots, a_{n-1})^t$ and $\mathbf{b} = (b_0, b_1, \ldots, b_{n-1})^t$, written $\mathbf{c} = \mathbf{a} \circledast \mathbf{b}$, is the vector, $\mathbf{c} = (c_0, c_1, \ldots, c_{n-1})^t$, given by

$$c_i = \sum_{j=0}^{n-1} a_j b_{i-j},$$

where the subtraction in the subscript is done modulo n.   □

Convolutions are used in signal processing, to filter noise, determine peaks, and other such tasks; they are used in computer vision, for similar purposes, and also to locate a target within a picture; and they are used in many other applications. Locating a target within a picture, which can easily have a million pixels, requires that a very large number of convolutions be computed. The convolution of two vectors can obviously be computed in quadratic time and can be expressed as a matrix product as follows:

$$\mathbf{Ab} = \begin{pmatrix} a_0 & a_{n-1} & a_{n-2} & \cdots & a_1 \\ a_1 & a_0 & a_{n-1} & \cdots & a_2 \\ \vdots & \vdots & \vdots & \ddots & \vdots \\ a_{n-1} & a_{n-2} & a_{n-3} & \cdots & a_0 \end{pmatrix} \begin{pmatrix} b_0 \\ b_1 \\ \vdots \\ b_{n-1} \end{pmatrix}. \tag{7.1}$$

Matrices such as $\mathbf{A}$ are termed *circulant*, for obvious reasons. While multiplying an $n \times n$ matrix by an $n \times 1$ vector generally takes time quadratic in n, the special form of this matrix allows us to compute this product more quickly. In 1965, Cooley and Tukey gave a $\Theta(n \log n)$ algorithm for computing Fourier transforms and, indirectly, convolutions. Their introduction of the fast Fourier transform revolutionized applied mathematics by making it possible to compute Fourier transforms of vectors of several thousand elements very quickly. Furthermore, the FFT algorithm is easily implemented in parallel with a resulting execution time of $\Theta(\log n)$; with the development of special purpose hardware (FFT boards), Fourier transforms and convolutions became computable in real time for very large vectors. As a result, the FFT has become one of the workhorses of engineering and is one of the algorithms used most often in practice, second only to sorting and merging; speech processing, seismic oil exploration, target acquisition and tracking, real-time video enhancement, and many other tasks have been made possible by the FFT.

Rather than start with the Fourier transform itself and its application to the computation of convolutions, let us begin our investigation of transforms with two somewhat simpler transforms, after which we shall investigate convolutions in a slightly different context. One simple example is reducing multiplication to addition by using logarithms. To obtain the product of two numbers, x and y, typically written to about five decimal places, without going through the tedious and error-prone longhand multiplication, we transform the problem into one of longhand addition by using logarithms as follows:

- Take the logarithms of x and y by looking them up in a table.

- Add the logarithms, a much simpler and much faster process than multiplying the original numbers.

- Take the antilogarithm of the result, again by looking it up in a table.

In mathematical notation, we have just taken advantage of the equality $\log xy = \log x + \log y$ to change domains. Because table lookup and addition are both simpler, faster, and more reliable than multiplication, this transformation has been perhaps the most widely used mathematical result for centuries, from its invention by John Napier (1550–1617) to the development of the modern hand-held calculator, which has made it (and the slide rule, which embodied its operation) obsolete as a computational method.

Another simple transformation known to high school students is moving from Cartesian coordinates to polar coordinates to facilitate work with complex numbers. While multiplying complex numbers in Cartesian coordinates is not particularly difficult, it is even easier in polar coordinates: simply multiply the moduli and add the angles. This transformation proves particularly useful when we need to raise some complex number to a power, as we shall shortly need to do. In polar coordinates, the complex number z becomes $z = (r, \theta)$ and its nth power becomes $z^n = (r^n, n\theta)$. From a computational standpoint, unfortunately, this transformation and its inverse use irrational-valued functions: the square root and the sine, cosine, and arctangent.

We mentioned earlier that generating functions, which we discussed in Section 2.2, are another transform method, the z-transform. In solving the recurrence for the Towers of Hanoi problem,

$$\begin{cases} a_n - 2a_{n-1} = 1 \\ a_0 = 1, \end{cases}$$

by generating functions, we moved from the space of coefficients, $g(n) = a_n$, to the space of generating functions, deriving the z-transform of $g(n)$, $G(z) = 1/((1 - z)(1 - 2z))$. We derived $G(z)$ by first using the equality $\sum_{i=0}^{\infty} 1 \cdot z^i = 1/(1-z)$, found in a table (Exercise 2.28), and then manipulating the formal power series, $G(z) = \sum_{i=0}^{\infty} a_i z^i$, as dictated by the recurrence, in order to eliminate all but the a_0 term, for which we had a value. We then operated in the z-domain to decompose $G(z)$ into the two terms $-1/(1 - z)$ and $2/(1 - 2z)$. By using the inverse transform, that is, by using the table in the reverse direction, we moved back into the space of coefficients, obtaining $a_n = 2^{n+1} - 1$.

Closer to our convolution problem, consider the second entry in the second table of Exercise 2.28: it states that, if the z-transform for $g(n) = c_n$ is $G(z)$ and the z-transform for $h(n) = d_n$ is $H(z)$, then the z-transform for the new function $f(n) = a_n$, defined by $a_n = \sum_{j=0}^{n} c_j d_{n-j}$, is the function $F(z) = G(z) \cdot H(z)$. Note that the definition of a_n parallels that of convolution; hence we see that convolution in our original domain is transformed into multiplication of functions in the z-domain. If we could compute efficiently the z-transform of a function and just as efficiently compute the inverse transform, we could then compute convolutions by first transforming our problem into the z-domain, then doing a function multiplication, and then transforming back from the z-domain into our original domain.

As a last example to develop our intuition about Fourier transforms and how to compute them efficiently, consider the problem of multiplying two polynomials. Let the two polynomials be $p(x) = \sum_{i=0}^{n} a_i x^i$ and $q(x) = \sum_{i=0}^{m} b_i x^i$; in the conventional description of this multiplication, we observe that the coefficient of the ith term, $\sum_{j=0}^{i} a_j b_{i-j}$ (where coefficients with subscripts higher than n and m, respectively, are treated as zero), satisfies the same definition as the ith term of a convolution. In fact, polynomial multiplication is precisely convolution when the two vectors of coefficients are padded with zeros to a length of $n + m + 1$. Therefore, a method for computing convolutions in $\Theta(n \log n)$ time also yields a method for multiplying two polynomials that runs faster than the obvious $\Theta(mn)$ method, at least when m and n are approximately equal.

The secret to developing a faster method of multiplication is to transform the problem. Whereas the problem is stated in the domain of coefficients, we can transform it into the domain of sampled values. It is a simple consequence of the Fundamental Theorem of Algebra (which states that a polynomial of degree n has precisely n roots, counting multiplicities) that exactly one polynomial of degree n passes through $n + 1$ distinct points.[4] Thus, as long as the degree of our polynomials does not exceed n, we can represent them as sets of $n + 1$ pairs, $\{(x_0, p(x_0)), (x_1, p(x_1)), \ldots, (x_n, p(x_n))\}$, where we require that all polynomials use the same sampling values, $x_0, x_1, \ldots, x_n$. With this representation, we can add and, more importantly, multiply polynomials on a point-by-point basis; in mathematical notation, the product polynomial $r(x) = p(x) \cdot q(x)$ is represented by the pairs $\{(x_0, p(x_0) \cdot q(x_0)), (x_1, p(x_1) \cdot q(x_1)), \ldots, (x_n, p(x_n) \cdot q(x_n))\}$. In effect, we can either multiply two polynomials in the coefficient domain, and then evaluate their product at the sample points, or evaluate the multiplicands at these points, and then take their product in the "point domain." Multiplying in the point domain is a linear-time operation, in contrast to the quadratic-time multiplication in the coefficient domain. Yet we cannot discard the coefficient domain, since how to perform other operations on polynomials (such as evaluating the polynomial at a new point or differentiating it) in the point domain is unclear; hence we need efficient means of transforming polynomials from one domain to the other. The transformation from the coefficient domain to the point domain could hardly be simpler: it suffices to evaluate the polynomial at a number of points; the inverse transformation is known as polynomial interpolation.

---

[4]While a polynomial of degree n is usually understood to have a nonzero coefficient for its term of degree n and zero coefficients for all terms of higher degree, here we only require that the second condition be met. For example, the unique polynomial of degree two passing through $(-1, 2)$, $(1, 8)$, and $(2, 11)$ is $p(x) = 3x + 5$.

In a matrix formulation, we need to evaluate the product,

$$\mathbf{Va} = \begin{pmatrix} 1 & x_0 & x_0^2 & \cdots & x_0^{m+n} \\ 1 & x_1 & x_1^2 & \cdots & x_1^{m+n} \\ \vdots & \vdots & \vdots & \ddots & \vdots \\ 1 & x_{m+n} & x_{m+n}^2 & \cdots & x_{m+n}^{m+n} \end{pmatrix} \begin{pmatrix} a_0 \\ a_1 \\ \vdots \\ a_n \\ 0 \\ \vdots \\ 0 \end{pmatrix},$$

and the similar product, $\mathbf{Vb}$, then to multiply the two vectors point by point, and finally to take the inverse, yielding

$$\mathbf{V}^{-1}(\mathbf{Va} \cdot \mathbf{Vb}).$$

Matrices such as $\mathbf{V}$, in which successive columns are increasing powers of a vector with distinct elements, are known as *Vandermonde matrices* and always have an inverse. Since the inverse of $\mathbf{V}$ need be computed only once (because the x_i are the same for all polynomials), after which it can be used whenever the inverse transform must be applied, the time expended in computing the inverse is immaterial. Even so, the matrix multiplication appears to require $\Theta((m+n)n)$ time and thus to be at least as time consuming as direct multiplication of the polynomials.

Example 7.1 Consider multiplying the two polynomials, $2x + 1$ and $3x - 2$; in our notation, we have $\mathbf{a} = (1\ 2\ 0)^t$ and $\mathbf{b} = (-2\ 3\ 0)^t$. We can choose any three values for x_0, x_1, and x_2; we choose 0, 1, and -1. The resulting Vandermonde matrix and its inverse are

$$\mathbf{V} = \begin{pmatrix} 1 & 0 & 0 \\ 1 & 1 & 1 \\ 1 & -1 & 1 \end{pmatrix} \quad \text{and} \quad \mathbf{V}^{-1} = \begin{pmatrix} 1 & 0 & 0 \\ 0 & 1/2 & -1/2 \\ -1 & 1/2 & 1/2 \end{pmatrix}.$$

We now compute the products, $\mathbf{Va} = (1\ 3\ -1)^t$ and $\mathbf{Vb} = (-2\ 1\ -5)^t$; their pointwise product is $(-2\ 3\ 5)^t$, and its inverse transform is $(-2\ -1\ 6)^t$, which represents the polynomial $6x^2 - x - 2$.

These same $\mathbf{V}$ and $\mathbf{V}^{-1}$ work for any two first-degree polynomials; that is, we can use them to compute the convolution $\mathbf{a} \circledast \mathbf{b}$ as long as both a_2 and b_2 equal zero. However, if we attempt to use them for general convolutions, things go awry: if we let $\mathbf{a} = (1\ 2\ 3)^t$ and $\mathbf{b} = (2\ 1\ 2)^t$, then the convolution is $(9\ 11\ 10)^t$, but $\mathbf{V}^{-1}(\mathbf{Va} \cdot \mathbf{Vb}) = (2\ 12\ 16)^t$.   □

In our quest for an efficient multiplication algorithm, we still have a major degree of freedom at our disposal: the x_i in the Vandermonde matrix are arbitrary. We must choose them distinct, but otherwise may attempt to choose them so as to minimize the time needed to compute the three products $\mathbf{Va}$, $\mathbf{Vb}$, and $\mathbf{V}^{-1}(\mathbf{Va} \cdot \mathbf{Vb})$. It turns out that the correct choice, which allows us to compute these products in $\Theta(n \log n)$ time, makes $\mathbf{V}$ a Fourier transform matrix—which returns us to our principal objective.

Consider again the formulation of convolution in terms of a circulant matrix, as given in (7.1). If the matrix were diagonal, i.e., if its only nonzero elements were on the diagonal, then the product would become

$$
\begin{pmatrix}
d_{11} & & & \\
& d_{22} & & \textbf{0} \\
& & \ddots & \\
\textbf{0} & & & d_{nn}
\end{pmatrix}
\begin{pmatrix}
u_1 \\
u_2 \\
\vdots \\
u_n
\end{pmatrix}
$$

and would be computable in linear time. In order to obtain this form, we must apply a transformation that will transform the circulant matrix $\mathbf{A}$ into the diagonal matrix $\mathbf{D}_A$ and the vector $\mathbf{b}$ into the new vector $\hat{\mathbf{b}}$; of course, we also need the corresponding inverse transformation in order to recover our answer. Moreover, we want a transformation that is independent of the particular entries in the circulant matrix, so that the same transformation can be applied to all convolutions of n-vectors. Such requirements on a single transformation appear formidable; yet the very special form of circulant matrices makes such a transformation possible.

There exists a single matrix, the Fourier transform matrix, which we shall denote by $\mathbf{F}$, that transforms any circulant matrix into a diagonal matrix by $\mathbf{FAF}^{-1} = \mathbf{D}_A$. The Fourier transform matrix is as follows:

$$
\mathbf{F} =
\begin{pmatrix}
1 & 1 & 1 & \cdots & 1 \\
1 & \omega & \omega^2 & \cdots & \omega^{n-1} \\
1 & \omega^2 & \omega^4 & \cdots & \omega^{n-2} \\
\vdots & \vdots & \vdots & \ddots & \vdots \\
1 & \omega^{n-1} & \omega^{n-2} & \cdots & \omega
\end{pmatrix}.
$$

The symbol ω stands for a *primitive nth root of unity*, $\sqrt[n]{1}$ (a complex number). In polar form, the n roots of unity are the complex numbers $(1, 2\pi k/n)$, $k = 0, 1, \ldots, n-1$; in the complex plane, these numbers are equally spaced around the unit circle. It is easily seen that the sum of the roots of unity equals zero; in terms of the unit circle, their "center of gravity" is the origin. A primitive nth root of unity is a root of unity, ω, such that the sequence $\omega, \omega^2, \ldots, \omega^n$ cycles through all of the roots of unity before arriving at 1. The root $(1, 2\pi/n)$ is a primitive root of unity, as is any root of unity for which k is relatively prime to n.

The (i, j)th element of the Fourier transform matrix is simply ω^{ij}, with the powers computed modulo n, since ω^n equals one. (For instance, the element in row 2 and column $n - 1$ is just $\omega^{2(n-1)} = \omega^{2n-2} = \omega^{n-2}$.) Notice that $\mathbf{F}$ is a Vandermonde matrix. The inverse of $\mathbf{F}$ has an especially simple form as well:

$$
\mathbf{F}^{-1} = \frac{1}{n} \cdot \begin{pmatrix} 1 & 1 & 1 & \cdots & 1 \\ 1 & \omega^{n-1} & \omega^{n-2} & \cdots & \omega \\ 1 & \omega^{n-2} & \omega^{n-4} & \cdots & \omega^2 \\ \vdots & \vdots & \vdots & \ddots & \vdots \\ 1 & \omega & \omega^2 & \cdots & \omega^{n-1} \end{pmatrix}.
$$

Note that $\mathbf{F}^{-1}$ is essentially the same matrix as $\mathbf{F}$: except for the factor of $1/n$, $\mathbf{F}^{-1}$ is just $\mathbf{F}$ with ω replaced by $\omega^{-1} = \omega^{n-1} = 1/\omega$. Thus the inverse Fourier transform differs from the forward Fourier transform only by a scaling factor and by the use of a different primitive root of unity.

By design and construction, $\mathbf{FAF}^{-1}$ is a diagonal matrix, as we now verify. Evaluating the first product yields

$$
\mathbf{FA} = \begin{pmatrix} S & S & S & \cdots & S \\ X & \omega X & \omega^2 X & \cdots & \omega^{n-1} X \\ Y & \omega^2 Y & \omega^4 Y & \cdots & \omega^{n-2} Y \\ \vdots & \vdots & \vdots & \ddots & \vdots \\ Z & \omega^{n-1} Z & \omega^{n-2} Z & \cdots & \omega Z \end{pmatrix},
$$

with $S = \sum_{i=0}^{n-1} a_i$, $X = \sum_{i=0}^{n-1} a_i \omega^i$, $Y = \sum_{i=0}^{n-1} a_i \omega^{2i}$, ..., $Z = \sum_{i=0}^{n-1} a_i \omega^{(n-1)i}$. Now multiplying on the right by $\mathbf{F}^{-1}$ yields, as desired, a diagonal matrix:

$$
\mathbf{FAF}^{-1} = \begin{pmatrix} S & & & & \\ & X & & \mathbf{0} & \\ & & Y & & \\ & & & \ddots & \\ & \mathbf{0} & & & Z \end{pmatrix}.
$$

Since the diagonal of the matrix is exactly the first column of $\mathbf{FA}$, we can compute $\mathbf{FAF}^{-1}$ by computing $\mathbf{Fa}$, the Fourier transform of $\mathbf{a}$. Rather than writing $\mathbf{Fa}$ for the Fourier transform of $\mathbf{a}$, we shall write $\mathcal{F}(\mathbf{a})$ whenever our emphasis is on the use of the transform, rather than on its computation.

Let us now return to our convolution problem. By using the Fourier transform, we obtain

$$\mathbf{Ab} = (\mathbf{F}^{-1}\mathbf{F})\mathbf{A}(\mathbf{F}^{-1}\mathbf{F})\mathbf{b} = \mathbf{F}^{-1}(\mathbf{FAF}^{-1})(\mathbf{Fb}) = \mathbf{F}^{-1}\mathbf{D}_A(\mathbf{Fb}).$$

We have just proved the convolution theorem.

Theorem 7.5 Given two vectors of equal length, **a** and **b**, we have

$$\mathbf{a} \circledast \mathbf{b} = \mathcal{F}^{-1}\big(\mathcal{F}(\mathbf{a}) \cdot \mathcal{F}(\mathbf{b})\big),$$

where the product of vectors is done pointwise. $\square$

The convolution theorem, while elegant and mathematically important, does not directly give rise to a more efficient algorithm for computing convolutions: each Fourier transform appears to take quadratic time, so that computing the convolution takes quadratic time whether computed directly or through Fourier transforms. What the convolution theorem does yield, though, is a method of computing convolutions, the running time of which depends entirely on the time needed to compute Fourier transforms. Thus, when Cooley and Tukey showed how to compute a Fourier transform in $\Theta(n \log n)$ time, they also gave us a $\Theta(n \log n)$ algorithm to compute the convolution of two vectors of length n. As we shall see, the FFT is restricted to values of n that are powers of 2 (a true restriction, unlike our usual assumption made strictly for purposes of analysis); in practice, however, this restriction is of little importance.

Now that we have seen what a discrete Fourier transform is, and before we plunge into the derivation of the FFT algorithm, let us summarize our results and relate them to our original setting. Recall that the Fourier transform is the expression of a function in terms of an infinite sum of sines and cosines; the discrete Fourier transform, because it works with finite samples, is the expression of the sampled function in terms of a finite sum of sines and cosines. Given a sampled function as the vector of function values, $\mathbf{x} = (x_1, x_2, \ldots, x_n)^t$, the discrete Fourier transform of **x** is the vector $\mathbf{y} = \mathcal{F}(\mathbf{x})$, where the kth component of **y** is given by

$$y_k = \sum_{j=0}^{n-1} x_j \omega^{kj},$$

or, equivalently, the kth component of **x** is given (through the inverse Fourier transform) as

$$x_k = \frac{1}{n} \sum_{j=0}^{n-1} \frac{y_j}{\omega^{kj}}.$$

What happened to the sum of sines and cosines? To make the connection, we need to remember that ω is a complex number; given a complex number in polar form, say $z = (r, \theta)$, we can write $z = r(\cos \theta + i \sin \theta)$. Now, we mentioned that ω could be chosen as $(1, 2\pi/n)$ and ω^j as $(1, 2j\pi/n)$; hence the kth component of $\mathbf{x}$ can be rewritten as

$$x_k = \frac{1}{n} \sum_{j=0}^{n-1} y_j (\cos \frac{2kj\pi}{n} - i \sin \frac{2kj\pi}{n}),$$

where we have used the identity $1/\omega = (1, -2\pi/n)$, and the sines and cosines have reappeared. However, there is a major difference between the infinite sum of sines and cosines that we wrote at the beginning of this section and this formula for x_k: while the former uses only real numbers, the latter uses complex numbers. Indeed, in its general form, the Fourier transform of an arbitrary function, f, is a complex function, $\mathcal{F}(f)$; the transform pair is defined in continuous terms by integrals:

$$g(x) = \mathcal{F}(f) = \frac{1}{\sqrt{2\pi}} \int_{-\infty}^{\infty} f(u)(\cos ux + i \sin ux) du$$

and

$$f(x) = \mathcal{F}^{-1}(g) = \frac{1}{\sqrt{2\pi}} \int_{-\infty}^{\infty} g(u)(\cos ux - i \sin ux) du.$$

Now that we have placed the discrete Fourier transform in perspective, we can finally consider the problem of devising an efficient divide-and-conquer algorithm for its computation. The crucial observation for developing such an algorithm is that rows i and $i + n/2$ of $\mathbf{F}$ are intimately related when n is even. Since we then have $\omega^{i+n/2} = -\omega^i$, the even-indexed elements of rows i and $i + n/2$ are equal (because they are, respectively, ω^i and $-\omega^i$ raised to an even power) and the odd-indexed elements of these rows are negatives of each other. Therefore, instead of computing the scalar product of row i of $\mathbf{F}$ with $\mathbf{x}$ and of row $i + n/2$ of $\mathbf{F}$ with $\mathbf{x}$, operations which cost us n multiplications and $n - 1$ additions each, we can proceed as follows. We begin by computing the scalar product of the even-indexed elements of the ith row with the even-indexed elements of $\mathbf{x}$ and do the same with the respective odd-indexed elements; call the first product u and the second v. The two desired scalar products are now just $u + v$, for row i, and $u - v$, for row $(i + n/2)$. As this computation is valid for any i, we can view it in matrix terms. We need to compute

$$\mathbf{u} = \begin{pmatrix} 1 & 1 & 1 & \cdots & 1 \\ 1 & \omega^2 & \omega^4 & \cdots & \omega^{n-2} \\ 1 & \omega^{2\cdot 2} & \omega^{2\cdot 4} & \cdots & \omega^{2\cdot(n-2)} \\ \vdots & \vdots & \vdots & \ddots & \vdots \\ 1 & \omega^{(n/2-1)\cdot 2} & \omega^{(n/2-1)\cdot 4} & \cdots & \omega^{(n/2-1)\cdot(n-2)} \end{pmatrix} \begin{pmatrix} x_0 \\ x_2 \\ x_4 \\ \vdots \\ x_{n-2} \end{pmatrix}$$

and

$$\mathbf{v} = \begin{pmatrix} 1 & 1 & 1 & \cdots & 1 \\ \omega & \omega^3 & \omega^5 & \cdots & \omega^{n-1} \\ \omega^2 & \omega^{2\cdot 3} & \omega^{2\cdot 5} & \cdots & \omega^{2\cdot(n-1)} \\ \vdots & \vdots & \vdots & \ddots & \vdots \\ \omega^{n/2-1} & \omega^{(n/2-1)\cdot 3} & \omega^{(n/2-1)\cdot 5} & \cdots & \omega^{(n/2-1)\cdot(n-1)} \end{pmatrix} \begin{pmatrix} x_1 \\ x_3 \\ x_5 \\ \vdots \\ x_{n-1} \end{pmatrix}.$$

We can then combine these two vectors to obtain $\mathcal{F}(\mathbf{x})$: its first $n/2$ elements are $\mathbf{u} + \mathbf{v}$, and its remaining $n/2$ elements are $\mathbf{u} - \mathbf{v}$. Note that $\mathbf{u}$ is itself a Fourier transform of size $n/2$, since ω^2 is the corresponding primitive root of unity; in fact, so is $\mathbf{v}$, since it is the pointwise product of $(1 \ \omega \ \omega^2 \cdots \omega^{n/2-1})^t$ and

$$\begin{pmatrix} 1 & 1 & 1 & \cdots & 1 \\ 1 & \omega^2 & \omega^4 & \cdots & \omega^{n-2} \\ 1 & \omega^{2\cdot 2} & \omega^{2\cdot 4} & \cdots & \omega^{2\cdot(n-2)} \\ \vdots & \vdots & \vdots & \ddots & \vdots \\ 1 & \omega^{(n/2-1)\cdot 2} & \omega^{(n/2-1)\cdot 4} & \cdots & \omega^{(n/2-1)\cdot(n-2)} \end{pmatrix} \begin{pmatrix} x_1 \\ x_3 \\ x_5 \\ \vdots \\ x_{n-1} \end{pmatrix}.$$

Thus we have the recursive formulation needed for a divide-and-conquer algorithm. The recombination requires $n/2$ multiplications, $n/2$ additions, $n/2$ subtractions, and n assignments. The base case, $n = 1$, reduces to a simple assignment. Hence the running time is governed by the recurrence,

$$\begin{cases} T(n) = 2T(n/2) + \Theta(n) \\ T(1) = \Theta(1), \end{cases}$$

so that we have $T(n) = \Theta(n \log n)$. Notice that n must be a power of 2 for the algorithm to work, since n must be even at each stage. Having n a power of 2 is thus necessary for correctness, not just a convenience for analysis as in our previous work with divide-and-conquer algorithms.

Our analysis does not take into account implementation problems and one such problem looms large: it appears that, in order to pass the proper parameters to the recursive calls, we may have to move large amounts of data to form the

```
const MaxN    = ...;   (* MaxN = 2**p - 1 *)
      MaxNdiv2 = ...;   (* MaxNdiv2 = 2**(p-1) *)

type ComplexArray = array [0..MaxN] of complex;

procedure FFT(var x: ComplexArray; n: integer; PRofU: complex);
  (* Given a vector, x = [x(0) x(1) ...  x(n-1)], return the discrete
     Fourier transform of x, overwriting x.
     The procedure assumes that n is a power of 2.
     PRofU is a primitive nth root of unity. *)
  var RofU: array [0..MaxNdiv2] of complex;
        (* The extra element is to avoid subscript-out-of-range errors. *)
      omega, temp: complex;
       i, j, k, l, m: integer;
  begin
    (* For efficiency reasons, precompute the roots of unity. *)
    RofU[0] := (1.0,0.0);
    RofU[1] := PRofU;
    for i := 2 to n div 2 - 1 do RofU[i] := RofU[i-1]*RofU[1];

    (* Shuffle the data so that the recombination phase is orderly. *)
    (* i and j are the bit reversals of each other to lg n bits. *)
    j := n div 2; (* bit reversal of 1 *)
    for i := 1 to n-2 do
      begin
        (* Swap the pair, but swap them only once. *)
        if i < j then begin temp := x[i]; x[i] := x[j]; x[j] := temp end;
        (* Compute the value of j corresponding to the next i--with a bitwise
           addition of 1 from high bit (left) to low bit (right).
           Normal machine hardware addition is used to do the same
           operation low bit (right) to high bit (left) on i. *)
        k := n div 2;
        while j div k = 1 do
          begin
            j := j - k;
            k := k div 2
          end;
        j := j + k
      end;

    (* Remarks on variables:
         k is the size of the subarrays;
         l is the spacing within the nth roots of unity at which the kth roots
           of unity are found;
         j runs down each position of u, v, and w;
         m runs, in parallel to j, down the kth roots of unity; and
         i allows the computation to be done bottom-up, level by level. *)
```

```
  k := 1; l := n div 2;
  while k < n do
    begin
      m := 0;
      omega := RofU[0];
      for j := 0 to k-1 do (* Combine u(j) and v(j). *)
        begin
          i := j;
          while i < n do
            (* The bottom-up approach allows us to proceed across vectors. *)
            begin
              temp := x[i];
              x[i]   := temp + omega*x[i+k];
              x[i+k] := temp - omega*x[i+k];
              i := i + 2*k
            end;
          m := m + 1;
          omega := RofU[m] (* undefined value on last fetch *)
        end;
      k := 2*k; l := l div 2
    end
end; (* FFT *)
```

Program 7.7: The Fast Fourier Transform

smaller Fourier transform matrices. Fortunately, we need not even store the Fourier transform matrix: from its size and its generator, the primitive root of unity in the second row and column, all of its elements can easily be derived as needed. We still need to rearrange the elements of **x**, in order to pass a subrange of the array to the recursive calls, but this rearrangement takes only linear time.

We can now describe more carefully the recursive procedure at the heart of the FFT. Passed to the routine are: the size of the current problem, n; a subarray of size n of coefficients, **x**; and a primitive nth root of unity, ω. The routine returns $\mathcal{F}(\mathbf{x})$, stored in place of **x**. Assume that n is larger than one, since otherwise the transform reduces to the identity; the algorithm runs through these three steps:

- Rearrange the elements of **x** so that the even-indexed elements occupy the first half of the subarray and the odd-indexed elements occupy the second half.

- Call the FFT routine recursively twice, passing once the first half of the rearranged **x** and the other time its second half; in both cases, the other two parameters are $n/2$ and ω^2. Call the results **u** (in the first half of the subarray) and **v** (in the second half).

- Combine **u** and **v** to form **w** by computing, for $i = 0, 1, \ldots, n/2 - 1$,

$$w_i = u_i + \omega^i v_i \qquad \text{and} \qquad w_{i+n/2} = u_i - \omega^i v_i,$$

and storing w_i in place of u_i and $w_{i+n/2}$ in place of v_i.

We can easily verify that the routine runs in linear time, not counting the time taken by the recursive calls.

As we did with our other divide-and-conquer algorithms, we can eliminate the recursion and program the FFT bottom-up. The procedure of Program 7.7 uses this approach. (The code is in nonstandard PASCAL, because it assumes a type complex, similar to that of FORTRAN, with associated constants and operations and with the natural coercions. Conversion to standard PASCAL is straightforward.) An interesting consequence of the bottom-up approach, evident from the layout of the code, is that the complete rearrangement of the elements of **x** is done first, with the recombination of the elements of **x** done in an orderly way, always using contiguous portions of the array and never moving the data. Moreover, the rearrangement, unlike the recombination, is independent of the data, depending only on the value of n. The data-dependency of the recombination phase prevents us from improving its $\Theta(n \log n)$ running time, but the data-independence of the rearrangement phase gives us an opportunity for significant improvement. If implemented by unwinding the recursion, the rearrangement phase takes $\Theta(n \log n)$ time, since every element is moved $\lg n$ times. When n is fixed, as it often is in image- and signal-processing applications, we can code the permutation directly into the program, reducing the running time of this phase from $\Theta(n \log n)$ to $\Theta(n)$. For this gain, it would seem that we have to pay a price, in the form of $\Theta(n)$ extra storage in which to store the permutation. However, if we study the permutation carefully, we discover an interesting phenomenon: whenever i and j are the reversal of each other as bit patterns of length $\lg n$, the ith and jth elements exchange places. For instance, with $n = 32$, elements 11 and 26 exchange places, since their bit patterns are 01011 and 11010. Such a regular pattern suggests that the extra storage may not be needed; on the other hand, reversing a bit pattern takes $\lg n$ time. Fortunately, we can do the reversal incrementally: if j is the bit reversal of i, then the bit reversal of $i + 1$ can be computed from j by incrementing j, but in the reverse direction: the incrementation is done left to right, and the carry, if any, propagates from high bit to low bit. We cannot rely on the hardware of a general-purpose computer to do this reverse incrementation, but we can do it with additions, subtractions, and integer divisions, as shown in Program 7.7. With this additional improvement, even though any particular reverse incrementation can still take $\lg n$ steps, the total number of operations as i runs from 1 to $n - 2$ is $\Theta(n)$.

7.4 Divide-and-Conquer for Approximation

Like the other algorithmic paradigms that we have discussed, the divide-and-conquer paradigm does not apply equally well to all problems. We have seen a number of problems that it can solve efficiently; we noted that all of these are search problems, not optimization problems. Basically, in all but the FFT problem, we were dealing with problems where the partitioning did not affect the correctness of the algorithm, only its efficiency; it was then just a matter of designing a partitioning that led to an efficient algorithm. In other words, our sole objective was to minimize the running time of the algorithm. When the problem includes an objective function of its own, conflicts often arise: either the algorithm is efficient, but does not return the optimal solution, or it is optimal, but does not run quickly. The first case arises when the partitioning affects the quality of the solution; the second arises when the merging step must do too much work. In both cases, however, we can use the algorithm for purposes of approximation: in the first case, we may be able to find a partition that leads to good, if not optimal, solutions (an approach that has very strong ties to the greedy method), while, in the second case, we may be able to simplify the merging step (at the expense of optimality) so as to obtain reasonable running times. We present one illustration of each case.

Binary Search Trees

The problem of constructing an optimal binary search tree (Problem 11) illustrates the first case. We shall see in Volume II that this problem can be solved in quadratic time by the method of dynamic programming. However, quadratic time can be prohibitive for large input sizes, so that a faster algorithm may prove useful, even if suboptimal. Since insertion in binary search trees takes place at the leaves and since the best binary search trees place high-probability items close to the root and low-probability items far down in the tree, we may be tempted to use a simple greedy approach: sort the items into decreasing order by frequency, then insert them, in that order, into the tree. This approach has two fatal flaws: it ignores the failure probabilities and it can take quadratic time. For the example of the original 13 states given in Section 1.4, this approach builds a tree in which the average search length is 3.82, a value almost 17% worse than the optimal value of 3.27.

Let us instead attempt to apply the divide-and-conquer paradigm to this problem. We are given a list, ordered by keys, of n items and their associated probabilities, together with $n + 1$ failure probabilities. In the spirit of divide-and-conquer, let us partition this list into two sublists by choosing the root of the search tree to be the item that most nearly balances the sum of the probabilities

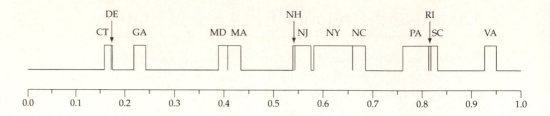

Figure 7.17: Success and Failure Probabilities Viewed as Intervals

on its left- and right-hand sides. Consider our problem in terms of intervals on
the real line: the leftmost and rightmost intervals correspond to failures, and
failures and successes alternate; each interval is given a width proportional to its
probability. This view is illustrated for our example of the 13 original states in
Figure 7.17. In this framework, our divide-and-conquer strategy simply chooses
for the root the item associated with the interval, the center of which is closest
to the 50% mark. In the example of the 13 original states, the 50% mark falls
within the failure interval separating Massachusetts and New Hampshire; applying our algorithm to this example produces the tree illustrated in Figure 7.18,
which has an average path length of 3.36. The algorithm can be implemented
by setting up an array containing the intervals corresponding to the items and
by using binary search on this array. With this implementation, the algorithm
runs in $\Theta(n \log n)$ time; moreover, when the probabilities are fairly uniform,
so that the chosen roots consistently split their trees evenly, the running time
is linear.

Unfortunately, the resulting partition may be very poor, especially in the
presence of items with large probabilities. Consider, for instance, a problem
where the first item has a probability slightly larger than 0.5 and all other probabilities are equal; the optimal search tree places this item at the root, yet our
divide-and-conquer strategy chooses the second item. In general, balancing the
two subtrees as evenly as possible may lead the algorithm to some very poor
choices: when two adjacent items have very different probabilities, with the item
of smaller probability yielding a better split than the item of larger probability,
our algorithm chooses the item of smaller probability. Yet selecting items of
large probability for the roots should also be a priority of the algorithm. This
miscalculation in fact happened in our small example: New Hampshire, the state
with the second smallest probability, was chosen for the root, even though it was
adjacent to both Massachusetts and New Jersey, states with much higher probabilities. In such cases it pays to shift the root slightly to the left or right. Perhaps
the simplest way to choose a root is to choose the item with highest probability

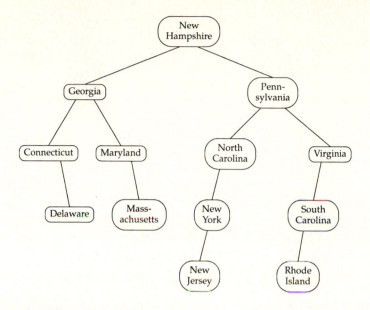

Figure 7.18: The Binary Search Tree Developed by the Divide-and-Conquer Approximation Algorithm

from a fixed number of neighbors, say c on each side—although we may do better by letting c vary with the size of the problem and the probability distribution. Figure 7.19 shows graphically why the divide-and-conquer approach works well for this problem and also why it cannot be optimal. For our example of the 13 states, the graph shows the average path length of the optimal binary search tree for each choice of root; that is, each choice of root is fixed in turn, and the resulting two subproblems are solved optimally. The concave nature of the curve describing the average path length indicates that balancing the probabilities of the subproblems is important; the peaks and troughs correspond to anomalies created by items of very low or very high probability and account for the nonoptimality of the procedure. Had we run the same experiment on data with uniform probabilities, the concave curve would have been smooth and symmetric. Extensive tests on larger problems show that this simple algorithm, improved as discussed, typically returns solutions within a few percent of optimal.

For the more demanding problem of constructing an optimal identification tree (Problem 12), the divide-and-conquer approach has been shown to be asymptotically optimal—even though no polynomial-time algorithm is known that solves the problem.

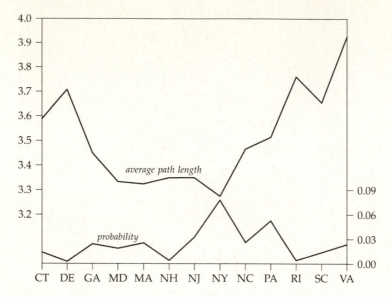

Figure 7.19: Average Path Length of the Binary Search Tree as a Function of the
Choice of Root

The Euclidean Travelling Salesperson

Our second example is the Euclidean travelling salesperson problem in the plane.
In this problem, the merging step is critical; even with excellent partitioning, the
merging step may be unable to take advantage of the solutions to the subproblems to derive an optimal solution. As in the binary search tree problem, we are
interested in a $\Theta(n \log n)$ algorithm, because our greedy heuristics of Section 5.1
may be too slow for large applications. (Large applications, with 10,000 to 100,000
points, do arise in practice, in such fields as VLSI design, channel routing, and
plotting.) The setting of the problem and its dependency on distance lead to
natural partitions: we want to cut the plane so as to define subproblems with
equal numbers of cities and to keep neighboring cities together. We are already
familiar with an efficient method for partitioning the plane to obtain subproblems
of equal size: sort the points by their abscissae and divide the plane into two
half planes based on the abscissa of the median element. However, this method
ignores entirely our second criterion: to keep neighboring points together. As
an inexpensive improvement, we keep each subproblem confined in as square a
box as possible, by partitioning on whichever coordinate has the larger spread.
When only a few points are left within a box, we solve the problem optimally by
some exhaustive search method (as discussed in Volume II); the more points we
include within such boxes, the closer our overall solution will be to the optimal

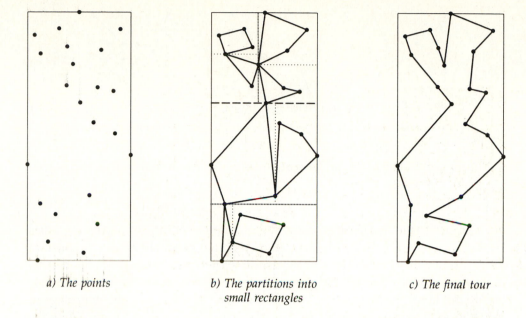

a) The points

b) The partitions into small rectangles

c) The final tour

Figure 7.20: Divide-and-Conquer Applied to the Euclidean Travelling Salesperson Problem

solution, at least on average, but also the longer it will take to run the algorithm. The basic divide-and-conquer step is as follows:

- (Partitioning) Partition the rectangle horizontally or vertically into two rectangles so that: (i) the direction of the dividing line is parallel to the shorter side; and (ii) the dividing line passes through a point, placed in both subproblems, chosen so that the two subproblems contain an equal number of points.

- (Recursion) Solve both halves recursively.

- (Merging) Combine the two subtours, which must meet at exactly one point, into a single tour.

Figure 7.20 illustrates the process; it was constructed with a threshold of four.

In order to implement this algorithm, we need to keep the points of each subproblem sorted by both abscissae and ordinates. The initialization thus requires two sorting passes. Maintaining the sorted lists requires linear time in any implementation, because we must distribute the list sorted on the coordinate not selected. A linked-list implementation is preferable, because an array implementation, while allowing the partitioning line to be found in constant time, does

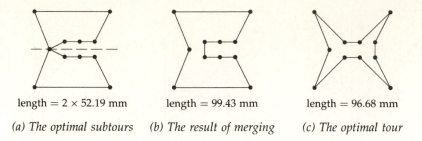

length = 2 × 52.19 mm   length = 99.43 mm   length = 96.68 mm

(a) The optimal subtours   *(b) The result of merging*   *(c) The optimal tour*

Figure 7.21: Failure of Divide-and-Conquer for the Euclidean TSP

not lend itself well to the duplication of the common point. Preprocessing takes $\Theta(n \log n)$ time; each small problem takes constant time, although the constant may be quite large, so the small problems together take linear time; finally, the divide-and-conquer heart of the algorithm, excluding for now the cost of merging two tours, takes $\Theta(n \log n)$ time as usual. Thus, not counting the contribution made by the merge operations, the algorithm runs in $\Theta(n \log n)$ time.

We mentioned that this problem illustrates the second type of failure of the divide-and-conquer paradigm: the merge step cannot be done both efficiently and optimally. As Figure 7.21 shows, the optimal recombination may require breaking a large fraction of the edges of the two subtours and hence may be unable to derive much useful information from the knowledge of the subtours. In order to remain efficient, we resort to a simple heuristic for merging two subtours, as illustrated in Figure 7.22: for each of the four pairs of segments (e_1, e_1'), (e_1, e_2'), (e_2, e_1'), and (e_2, e_2'), consider the effect of replacing the pair with the segment $\overline{P_1 P_1'}$, $\overline{P_1 P_2'}$, $\overline{P_2 P_1'}$, or $\overline{P_2 P_2'}$. Each of these four transformations merges the two subtours into a single tour by bypassing the common vertex; we simply choose the best of the four. This algorithm was used in producing the tours of Figures 7.20(b) and 7.21(b). Using this merging step, our overall approximation algorithm runs in $\Theta(n \log n)$ time, although an imprudent choice of the threshold for solving subproblems exhaustively may result in a linear term with such a large factor that it dominates the running time.

This divide-and-conquer approximation algorithm, while efficient, remains fairly unsophisticated, since it only makes a modest attempt at keeping neighboring points within the same partition. A more ambitious attempt, which remains in the style of divide-and-conquer, but must be implemented bottom-up, is to determine the partition based on a clustering of the points. We discussed the clustering problem in Section 6.1 and noted that it is an intractable problem. Fortunately, the two-dimensional geometry of the Euclidean travelling salesperson problem simplifies the clustering problem somewhat; in particular, we can use

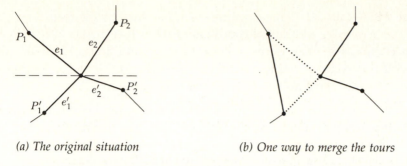

(a) *The original situation*   (b) *One way to merge the tours*

Figure 7.22: Recombining Subsolutions in the Euclidean TSP

the Voronoi diagram or the Euclidean minimum spanning tree, both structures based on proximity and both computable in $\Theta(n \log n)$ time, as the basis for efficient and good, if not optimal, clustering algorithms. Several authors have tried clustering approaches for the Euclidean travelling salesperson problem and report encouraging results.

7.5   Exercises

Exercise 7.1 The obvious algorithm for finding the maximum and minimum elements of an array does $2n$ comparisons. Show how the number of comparisons can be reduced to $3n/2$ by using a divide-and-conquer strategy.   □

Exercise 7.2 Develop an algorithm for finding the kth smallest element when the data are presented as two already sorted arrays; your algorithm should run in $\log \min(k, n - k)$ time.   □

Exercise 7.3 Let $a_1, a_2, \ldots, a_n$ be a sequence of integers stored in an array such that successive elements of the sequence differ by at most one. Devise an efficient algorithm to determine whether a given number appears in the sequence.   □

Exercise 7.4** Consider a new network element, called a *switch*; a switch either passes its two inputs unchanged or exchanges them. Whether a switch passes or exchanges its two inputs does not depend on the data, but on some external control. Show how to construct a network of $\Theta(n \log n)$ switches that, depending on its external control, can implement any of the $n!$ permutations of its inputs.
       □

Exercise 7.5 Recall that Fibonacci numbers are defined by the recurrence $F(n) = F(n-1) + F(n-2)$, with initial conditions $F(0) = 0$ and $F(1) = 1$. Computing the nth Fibonacci number is easily done in $n-1$ additions. However, we can use divide-and-conquer techniques to compute the nth Fibonacci number with $\Theta(\log n)$ arithmetic operations. Derive such an algorithm.   □

Exercise 7.6 Show that two first-degree polynomials can be multiplied with just three multiplications, rather than the obvious four. Use this result as the basis for a divide-and-conquer algorithm that multiplies two polynomials of degree n in $\Theta(n^{\lg 3})$ time. This algorithm is asymptotically slower than the $\Theta(n \log n)$ method that uses the fast Fourier transform, but has lower overhead; moreover, if the coefficients are integers, no roundoff error can occur. Empirically determine the crossover point.   □

Exercise 7.7 Use the result of Exercise 7.6 to show that two n-bit integers can be multiplied in $\Theta(n^{\lg 3})$ time, where each basic operation handles only a constant number of bits.   □

Exercise 7.8* Verify that two 2×2 matrices can be multiplied using only seven scalar multiplications, rather than the obvious eight, at the expense of many additional additive operations (i.e., additions and subtractions); the products of interest are:

$$
\begin{array}{ll}
a_{11}b_{11} & (a_{12} - a_{21} + a_{11} - a_{22})b_{22} \\
a_{12}b_{21} & a_{22}(b_{11} + b_{22} - b_{12} - b_{21}) \\
(a_{11} - a_{21})(b_{22} - b_{12}) & (a_{21} + a_{22} - a_{11})(b_{22} - b_{12} + b_{11}) \\
(a_{21} + a_{22})(b_{12} - b_{11}) &
\end{array}
$$

Note that, by avoiding the recomputation of common subexpressions, these products and the four matrix entries require a total of 15 additive operations.

Now consider replacing the four elements of each matrix with square submatrices: this modification leads to a divide-and-conquer scheme for multiplying two $2^k \times 2^k$ matrices.

1. Formalize this divide-and-conquer algorithm.

2. Generalize it to handle square matrices, the sizes of which are not a power of 2.

3. Analyze the worst-case running time of your algorithm; you should find that it computes the product of 2 $n \times n$ matrices in $\Theta(n^{\lg 7})$ time, faster than the $\Theta(n^3)$ time required by the obvious algorithm. For matrices, the size of which is a power of 2, derive the exact numbers of multiplications and additive operations required by your algorithm and by the obvious algorithm.   □

Exercise 7.9 Suppose that the results of a tournament in which each player played every other are given in a array. While, in general, it is not possible to rank the players (because a player may have defeated another, who defeated a third, who in turn defeated the first), it is always possible to order the players so that each player defeated the next player in the ordering. Develop a $\Theta(n \log n)$ algorithm to produce this ordering; note that the running time of the algorithm is smaller than the time required to read the input.

Use a reduction from sorting to prove that no algorithm for this problem can run in better than $\Omega(n \log n)$ time; this reduction differs from those we have seen in that it must use the array only implicitly.   □

Exercise 7.10* Design an algorithm to produce tournament schedules: every player is to play every other player and the tournament must take the minimum number of rounds to complete. *Hint*: Begin by developing an algorithm for instances where the number of players is a power of 2.   □

Exercise 7.11* The Manhattan skyline problem is a very restricted version of the problem of computing the union of polygons; what constraints can be removed while preserving the $\Theta(n \log n)$ running time of the divide-and-conquer approach?   □

Exercise 7.12 While the construction we suggested on page 447 suffices to show that, at every step, all points can lie within $\hat{d}$ of the partitioning line, it does not suffice to show that the total number of candidate pairs can be $\Omega(n \log n)$. Refine the construction to prove this bound.   □

Exercise 7.13 Show that, given a collection of points, $\mathcal{P}$, the Voronoi polygon of a point in $\mathcal{P}$ is infinite if and only if the point lies on the convex hull of $\mathcal{P}$. (A purely geometric argument suffices.)   □

Exercise 7.14 [P] The Floyd-Eddy heuristic can be tailored to suit the distribution of points. Assume that the points are distributed uniformly in the unit square; the following version can be shown to eliminate all but $O(\sqrt{n})$ points: select one point in each corner of the square by choosing the point closest to the corner under the Manhattan metric. Run experiments to compare this version with the version presented in the text.   □

Exercise 7.15** In k-dimensional space, a point $(x_1, x_2, \ldots, x_k)$ *dominates* another point $(y_1, y_2, \ldots, y_k)$ whenever we have $x_i \geq y_i$, for $i = 1, 2, \ldots, k$, with at least one inequality being strict. Given a collection of points, S, in k-dimensional space, a point P is a *maximum* if it is not dominated by any point in S. Devise an efficient algorithm, based on the divide-and-conquer paradigm, to compute the maxima of a set of points; $O(n(\log n)^{k-2} + n \log n)$ time is possible.   □

Exercise 7.16* A *Toeplitz matrix* is a square matrix such that $a_{ij} = a_{i-1.j-1}$, for $1 < i,j \leq n$. (Thus a Toeplitz matrix is closely related to a circulant matrix.) Devise a $\Theta(n \log n)$ algorithm to multiply two Toeplitz matrices.   □

Exercise 7.17 [P] Compare the divide-and-conquer approach for the Euclidean travelling salesperson problem with the greedy or iterative improvement methods discussed in the previous two chapters.   □

7.6 Bibliography

Mergesort is part of the folklore of computer science. The linear-time merging algorithm that uses only a constant amount of extra storage was given by M. A. Kronrod in 1969, as reported in Knuth [1973] (Exercise 5.2.4.18). Batcher [1968] developed two sorting networks with comparable performance: the odd-even networks that we presented and networks based on bitonic sorting. Knuth [1973] surveys the results known at that time, including lower bounds on selection using networks. The $\Theta(n \log n)$ sorting network was developed by Ajtai *et al.* [1983], but it has a very high coefficient and the networks based on the odd-even merge are better unless n is quite large. One point of interest in hardware implementations of sorting networks is periodicity: a network is periodic if it is composed of a sequence of identical blocks, so that it can be implemented with a single block by recirculating the output of the block to its input in a controlled fashion. Dowd *et al.* [1989] present some improved designs for periodic sorting networks.

Opening any text on computational geometry, such as that of Preparata and Shamos [1985], will convince the reader of the importance of divide-and-conquer techniques in that discipline. Voronoi diagrams, mentioned at the end of our discussion of closest pairs, are due to Voronoi [1908], as well as other authors; the $\Theta(n \log n)$ divide-and-conquer algorithm for constructing the Voronoi diagram of a set of n points in two dimensions is due to Shamos and Hoey [1975], as is the simpler algorithm for finding the closest pair of points that we presented; the extension to k-dimensional space, as well as a detailed treatment of Voronoi diagrams and their applications, can be found in the text of Preparata and Shamos. The divide-and-conquer algorithm for constructing the intersection of a collection of convex polygons is due to Shamos and Hoey [1976]; Manber [1989] proposes and discusses at some length the Manhattan skyline problem. Convex hull algorithms have been proposed in more articles than anyone could track down, mostly because they find applications in areas from social science to biology to engineering. The package-wrapping technique, also known as Jarvis march, is due to Jarvis [1973]; the Graham scan is due to Graham [1972]; and the divide-and-conquer algorithm first appeared in Shamos' Ph.D. thesis [1978]. Exercise 8.12 in the next chapter presents another algorithm, based on quicksort, for computing the convex hull of a set of points.

Fourier transforms have a very large literature of their own; for a complete mathematical treatment, the reader should consult the text of Titchmarsh [1948]. The fast Fourier transform is commonly attributed to Cooley and Tukey [1965], although various authors appear to have developed the basic idea much earlier— claims go back as far as the turn of the century with the work of C. Runge. A comprehensive survey of various formulations of the FFT algorithm is offered by Brigham [1974].

The divide-and-conquer approach to binary search trees was studied by Walker and Gottlieb [1972]. That the divide-and-conquer strategy is asymptotically optimal for identification trees is mentioned in Moret [1982], where other references to similar work can be found. The divide-and-conquer approach to the travelling salesperson problem in the unit square is due to Karp [1977]. His approach is somewhat more elaborate than ours: by fixing some ϵ in advance and adapting the partitioning procedure, his algorithm ensures that the resulting tour cannot exceed the optimal tour by more than $\epsilon\sqrt{n}$ for a uniform distribution of points in the unit square. On the other hand, the expected value of the optimal tour is proportional to $\sqrt{n}$ under these circumstances. Supowit et al. [1983] present an enhanced algorithm that produces a tour, the expected length of which converges to the expected length of the optimal tour as n grows; the algorithm proceeds by solving optimally subproblems of size $\log \log n$ and combines these solutions in a more complex manner than our basic divide-and-conquer algorithm, but it still runs in $\Theta(n \log n)$ time. Using clustering as part of the partitioning step has proved successful, as reported by Litke [1984].

Exercise 7.5 is from Gries and Levin [1980]. Exercise 7.8 develops the algorithm known as Strassen's matrix multiplication, due to Strassen [1969], and as modified by Winograd [1973] to decrease the number of additive operations from 18 to 15. While Strassen's algorithm uses a fast way to multiply two 2×2 matrices as the base case, similar algorithms have since been developed that rest on more complex base cases (for instance, Pan [1978] proposed one based on an efficient scheme for multiplying two 70×70 matrices), and the exponent has been steadily reduced over the years. However, Strassen's algorithm remains the only one of practical interest.

CHAPTER 8

Sorting: A Case Study in Efficient Coding

Without doubt sorting has received more attention in the computer science literature than any other algorithmic task. As a result, one might be tempted to conclude that sorting is a well-solved problem. If "well-solved" is construed to imply the existence of a universally applicable and ultimately efficient sorting algorithm, it is an unachievable goal. On the other hand, several algorithms that use only slightly more comparisons than the provable minimum have been developed for sorting objects held in sequential locations of a random-access memory. In this chapter, we examine in considerable depth five well-known al-

Table 8.1: Characteristics of Sorting Methods

Method	Extra storage	Running time	Stable	Comments
Insertion	None	n^2	$\checkmark$	Very low overhead
Shell's	None	Unknown ($n^{1.2}$ experimental)		
Quicksort	$2 \log n$	$n \log n$ average case n^2 worst case		
Mergesort	n	$n \log n$	$\checkmark$	Generalizes to sorting large files held on disk.
Heapsort	None	$n \log n$		Poor virtual memory performance Efficient for incremental sorting
Radix sort	$n + 2^m$	$\lceil M/m \rceil \cdot n$	$\checkmark$	$M =$ object size, $m =$ subkey size Poor virtual memory performance Machine representation dependent

gorithms for sorting objects on a sequential computer: Shell's method, quicksort, mergesort, heapsort, and radix sort. Throughout the first section, we assume that the reader is already acquainted with these five sorting methods (though not necessarily with all of the fine details), is aware of general issues relating to sorting, and has an elementary understanding of machine architecture. Readers unfamiliar with heapsort or mergesort may want to consult Sections 3.1 and 7.1, respectively; readers unfamiliar with the other methods may want to consult the introductory discussion of and PASCAL code for these algorithms in this chapter before reading the next section. Alternatively, the section on general considerations can be skimmed to get a perspective on the basic issues and then studied in detail at a later time. For convenience, Table 8.1 summarizes the main characteristics of each sorting method. Since we shall be comparing algorithms that all have excellent performance and since sorting routines often receive heavy use, our emphasis will be on fine tuning the algorithms.

We begin with an examination of the desirable attributes of a universal sorting routine, of the performance that can be expected of such a routine, and of the factors that can affect this performance.

8.1   General Considerations

Throughout this chapter we shall assume that the data are stored in sequential locations of a random-access memory and that the computer is a single-instruction, single-data (SISD) machine—a classical CPU that executes one instruction at a time, with each instruction processing a small number of operands. Even within this framework, there remain many issues to consider. What are the attributes of a good sorting routine: how does it interact with its environment, and how does it handle its data? How do we measure the performance of a sorting routine: what are suitable criteria, and what can be expected of the best possible routines? What influence is exerted by the architecture of the machine, in particular, by its instruction set and paging mechanism?

8.1.1 Algorithmic Requirements

We take up four important attributes of sorting routines: universality, use of extra storage, the influence of data distributions, and stability.

Universality

A library utility cannot be limited to sorting just one type of data. For example, the sort utility of the standard C library, qsort, has the following declaration:

```
void qsort(void *base, size_t nmemb, size_t size,
        int (*compar)(const void *, const void *));
/* void *base     starting address of sequential storage containing data */
/* size_t nmemb   number of elements to sort */
/* size_t size    size of an element in bytes */
/* int (*compar)(const void *, const void *))
      A user-supplied function that returns an integer less than, equal to,
      or greater than zero if the first object is, respectively, less than,
      equal to, or greater than the second. */
```

This interface incorporates sufficient information to implement any internal sorting algorithm based on comparisons and data moves. The objects to be sorted may even be records with key fields: the move operations need only know the size of a record and the comparisons rely on the knowledge of the internal structure of the records that is embedded within the comparison function supplied by the user. Note, however, that this interface is not truly universal: its emphasis on comparisons and moves prevents the use of radix sort.

Achieving universality also requires that two related issues be addressed: (i) can an algorithm reference a storage location beyond the stated bounds of the array (such as A[0] or A[NumElements+1]); and (ii) can the algorithm use the smallest or largest possible value associated with the data type of the objects being sorted? These questions are motivated by the desire to use a sentinel in order to guarantee the termination of inner loops, a practice that simplifies the code and avoids explicit boundary checks at every iteration. The guaranteed presence of a sentinel can reduce the size of an inner loop by as much as 40%, with a noticeable, though smaller, effect on the running time. Since there may be valid data or even code bordering the array, storing a sentinel outside the array bounds may have disastrous consequences. While such consequences could be avoided by storing the current content of the sentinel location in a temporary location and restoring it before leaving the sorting routine, there are machines where this measure does not work. For instance, in a segmented memory environment where the hardware forbids addressing violations, reference to the sentinel location can cause a fault if the array occupies a segment of its own. Therefore, to achieve universality, we shall not let any of our routines address memory outside the stated array bounds. On the other hand, we shall make use of the smallest and largest values associated with a data type, although, in the absence of a sentinel location, we shall have only limited need for this capability. Using such values rarely affects universality, since these values are constants for a given data type and machine representation. (Note that for some data types, such as variable length strings over some alphabet, the existence of a largest element is debatable.) In order to accommodate the requirements of a library routine, we can modify the calling sequence to include lower or upper bounds on the values being sorted as additional arguments.

Extra Storage

All sorting algorithms require at least a few bookkeeping variables and one or two temporary variables for the purpose of exchanges or comparisons. A few sorting algorithms, such as heapsort and Shell's method, require only a small fixed quantity of extra storage. However, many sorting algorithms, such as mergesort, quicksort, and radix sort, have storage requirements that grow as the amount of data increases. Mergesort uses a work array as large as the array to be sorted. Quicksort, if carefully implemented, requires $2 \log n$ additional integer storage locations. While this quantity is a function of the amount of data and so theoretically unsatisfactory, it is sufficiently small that the necessary storage can safely be declared inside the sorting routine. An array of length 256—roughly the amount of storage required for the code of the routine—allows at least 2^{128} elements to be sorted; these many data cannot be read or even generated in one lifetime. Radix sort, besides using a work array of size n, uses a nontrivial constant amount of additional storage to hold frequency counts and addresses. The number of passes which radix sort makes over the data is a function of the size of the frequency count array; unless this array is moderately large (larger in practice than the internal array used by quicksort), the algorithm is outperformed by $\Theta(n \log n)$ sorting algorithms for realistic data sizes.

Data Distributions

Most of the algorithms that we consider in this chapter are essentially insensitive to data distributions. The exception is quicksort, which takes $\Theta(n \log n)$ time on average, but takes $\Theta(n^2)$ time on certain initial orderings. Carefully programmed versions of quicksort incorporate code that decreases the likelihood of observing $\Theta(n^2)$ performance, although the possibility cannot be eliminated altogether without adding intolerable overhead.

One important class of biased initial orderings deserves mention: already sorted or nearly sorted data. Nearly sorted input arises frequently in practice for two reasons. First, the gathering and preprocessing of data often results in partial sorting; for instance, rough alphabetization of names is common and two-dimensional data are often clustered. Secondly, the manipulation of sorted data by algorithms often results only in small local perturbations of the ordering, thereby giving rise to nearly sorted data. What is meant by this qualification is necessarily somewhat vague. Indeed, one might expect it to depend on the chosen sorting algorithm, on the principle that what is good for one algorithm is bad for another. However, as all sorting algorithms except radix sort work by exchanging data within the array, some common measure of disorder is possible. Such a measure is the number of *inversions* present in the input, i.e., the number of pairs, x and y, such that x appears before y in the input, and yet y is less than x.

When sorting nearly sorted data, we might expect a significant improvement in running time, as fewer exchanges are required. Unfortunately, none of the common sophisticated sorting algorithms is able to take advantage of this property; indeed, special precautions must be taken to ensure that quicksort does not exhibit quadratic behavior on such data. If the data are guaranteed to be nearly sorted, insertion sort or bubble sort (with repeated alternation of the direction of traversal, sometimes called *shaker sort*) are linear-time algorithms. One must be careful, however, about the meaning of "nearly sorted" in this context, as a small percentage of elements ($\log n$ out of n, that is, 10 out of 1000 or 20 out of 1,000,000) badly out of place is sufficient to cause nonlinear performance.

The presence of ties in the data also offers the potential for faster execution. Quicksort has received the most attention in this regard, and special versions exist that perform exceptionally well in the presence of a significant number of ties. Unfortunately, the overhead of these versions is such that their performance is worse than that of nonspecialized versions on random data.

Stability

A sorting algorithm is said to be *stable* if, whenever s equals t and s precedes t in the original ordering, s also precedes t in the final sorted order. Stability is important when s and t are key fields of a larger record. For instance, consider an array which is to be sorted on a primary key and, in the event of ties, on a secondary key; the telephone book is organized in this manner. The obvious way to sort such an array is to sort it first on the primary key and then to search the array for groups of ties, each of which can then be sorted on the secondary key. Perhaps surprisingly, sorting the entire array first on the secondary key and then on the primary key also works, provided that the sorting algorithm is stable. Figure 8.1 illustrates this method on ordered pairs of integers, where the first component is the primary key and the second component is the secondary key.

$$(5,8) \quad (7,6) \quad (5,4) \quad (4,7) \quad (3,9) \quad (5,2) \quad (4,4) \quad (7,3) \quad (2,6) \quad (4,9)$$
(a) Initial order

$$(5,2) \quad (7,3) \quad (5,4) \quad (4,4) \quad (7,6) \quad (2,6) \quad (4,7) \quad (5,8) \quad (3,9) \quad (4,9)$$
(b) After sorting on the secondary key

$$(2,6) \quad (3,9) \quad (4,4) \quad (4,7) \quad (4,9) \quad (5,2) \quad (5,4) \quad (5,8) \quad (7,3) \quad (7,6)$$
(c) After sorting on the primary key

Figure 8.1: Sorting on the Secondary Key, Then on the Primary Key

If two elements disagree on the primary key, then surely they end up in the correct order, since the last pass sorts all items on the primary key. If two elements agree on the primary key, then the element with the smaller secondary key will precede the element with the larger secondary key after completion of the first pass. The second pass will group these two elements together since they have the same primary key; stability of the sorting algorithm guarantees that this second pass will not alter the order of the two elements. This algorithm is known to old-timers who have had to sort punch cards on a mechanical sorter that could process only one column at a time (each column acts as a key field), and it forms the basis of radix sort.

8.1.2 Timing and Counting Issues

The running time of our sorting algorithms, with the exception of radix sort, is determined by three components: internal bookkeeping, data comparisons, and data moves. Depending on what is being sorted, the relative importance of these three components can vary and thereby affect our perception of the efficiency of an algorithm. An example may shed light on this problem.

Consider the task of sorting strings. Assume that the items to sort are character strings of fixed length. A comparison of two strings, done byte by byte, may require that the entire strings be examined, but more often than not their relationship to one another will be resolved by looking at the first few bytes only. In particular, if the data objects are random strings of letters over an alphabet of size k (an unreasonable assumption in practice), then the expected number of bytes that must be examined is given by

$$\frac{k-1}{k} \cdot 1 + \left(\frac{1}{k}\right)\left(\frac{k-1}{k}\right) \cdot 2 + \cdots + \left(\frac{1}{k}\right)^{i-1}\left(\frac{k-1}{k}\right) \cdot i + \cdots.$$

The ith term of the sum is the probability that the first $i-1$ bytes agree while the ith bytes disagree, multiplied by the number of bytes compared. If the strings have fixed length, m, then this sum is truncated after $m-1$ terms and the mth term is $(1/k)^{m-1}m$. The sum of the infinite series, which is an upper bound on our sum, is $k/(k-1)$, barely larger than one. Therefore, the average time taken by a comparison is much smaller than that taken by a move, so that the number of moves dominates the running time of the computation.

This analysis is too simplistic. While the data objects may be initially in random order, data objects of similar value are brought closer together as the sorting process progresses. Thus we would expect the time to do a comparison to increase as the sorting algorithm nears completion, with varying effect on the running time of different sorting algorithms. The other simplifying assumption, namely, that strings are random concatenations of characters, also

Table 8.2: Average Comparison Length when Sorting Strings

Method	Number of comparisons	Average comparison length	Comments
Shell's	546,111	2.53	$h_{2k+1} = 9 \cdot 4^k - 9 \cdot 2^k + 1$ $h_{2k} = 4^{k+1} - 3 \cdot 2^{k+1} + 1$
Quicksort	400,392	2.63	Insertion sort applied to small segments
Mergesort	372,120	2.47	Three-way merge with insertion sort for constructing initial runs
Heapsort	366,240	2.46	2-heaps with bounce

works towards decreasing the average number of comparisons required; the large number of English words sharing common prefixes would lead us to expect a significantly worse result. Table 8.2 presents experimental results on the average number of bytes examined during comparisons. The data are a random reordering of the 24,474 words, comprising a total of 176,565 characters, found in the local UNIX spelling dictionary. Due to the construction of the initial ordering, this sample acts like a random permutation when considering the number of object comparisons and data moves. We see that, even for data as biased as words of a natural language, the length of a comparison remains small on average.

A very different situation arises when the array to sort contains pointers to the actual records. A move is then just an integer assignment, but a comparison involves at least one level of indirection, so that comparisons become the dominant factor. In general, if large records are to be sorted in main memory, the records should remain stationary and an array of pointers to the records should be maintained and sorted; thus, the time taken by comparisons often dominates the computation. In a related vein, the running time of the utility qsort of the standard C library is heavily influenced by the number of comparisons, since each comparison involves a function call.

Since the time taken by the comparisons can dominate the computation, two questions immediately arise: (i) what is the minimum number of comparisons needed to sort an array of n elements? and (ii) what, if any, sorting algorithms achieve or approach this minimal number of comparisons? Deriving the optimal number of comparisons appears to be a mathematically intractable task, so that we content ourselves with the development of a lower bound on the number of comparisons. Because we are only comparing the data and not considering their internal representation, we may assume without loss of generality that the items to sort are n distinct positive integers, say $a_1, a_2, \ldots, a_n$. Formally then, we are interested in lower bounds on the worst case,

$$\min_{\substack{\text{all sorting}\\\text{algorithms}}} \left\{ \max_{\substack{\text{all permutations}\\\text{of } \{a_1, \ldots, a_n\}}} \{\text{number of comparisons needed to sort permutation}\} \right\},$$

and on the average case,

$$\frac{1}{n!} \min_{\substack{\text{all sorting}\\\text{algorithms}}} \left\{ \sum_{\substack{\text{all permutations}\\\text{of } \{a_1, \ldots, a_n\}}} \text{number of comparisons needed to sort permutation} \right\}.$$

We restrict our attention to the essential aspects of sorting algorithms by requiring that all comparisons, which we regard as enquiries to an oracle, be of the form "what is the relationship between the objects in original locations i and j?" We suffer no loss of generality by insisting on this form of enquiry, since any sorting algorithm can keep track of the original positions of the elements as it moves them around. We can look at the problem of sorting in this context in one of two ways: (i) we are given an input array and must produce the sorted version of this array, i.e., choose which of the $n!$ possible configurations to print; or (ii) we do not know the input and must establish it by questions to the oracle, i.e., must ascertain that the ith smallest element was first, the jth smallest element was second, etc. Both views lead to the same proof: we must reduce our uncertainty from a collection of $n!$ possible choices, all initially compatible with our complete lack of knowledge, down to a single choice. That we must reduce the possibilities down to a single choice is easily seen: in our first interpretation, only one of the $n!$ arrangements of the array is correctly sorted and must be identified; in our second, if the algorithm terminates while there remain several compatible permutations, then it operates identically on these permutations and thus can sort at most one of them correctly. Each enquiry to the oracle may eliminate some choices, because each answer establishes an ordering between two elements, which may be incompatible with some of the remaining choices. Let us represent the state of knowledge at any point during the sequence of enquiries as a tree; an example, as viewed from our first perspective, is shown in Figure 8.2. Each node of the binary tree is labelled with those permutations consistent with the outcomes of the tests along the path from the root to the node; internal nodes of the tree also indicate which comparison to perform next.

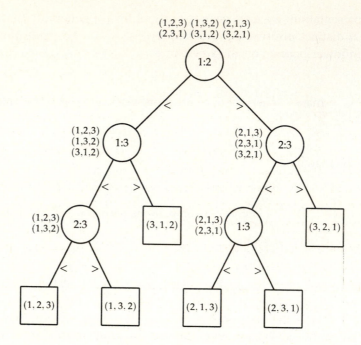

Figure 8.2: The Decision Tree for Sorting (a_1, a_2, a_3)

An enquiry can fail to divide the remaining permutations into two nonempty groups, but it is then redundant, so that the associated algorithm clearly cannot be optimal. Therefore, any algorithm that is a candidate for the optimal algorithm must correspond to a tree with exactly $n!$ external nodes, one for each permutation. A lower bound for the worst-case formulation of our question can be derived by considering the tree of minimum height over all binary trees with $n!$ external nodes, a tree with height $\lceil \lg n! \rceil$. This lower bound is not always achievable, because not every binary tree with $n!$ external nodes corresponds to a decision tree of comparisons. For instance, it has been shown that the optimal decision tree of comparisons for 12 items has a height of 30, while $\lceil \lg 12! \rceil$ is 29. On the other hand, $\lceil \lg n! \rceil$ is only slightly less than $n \lg n$, the ratio of the two expressions approaching one as n approaches infinity. Since two-way mergesort does $n \lg n - n + 1$ comparisons in the worst case (for n a power of 2), we can conclude that the lower bound of $\lceil \lg n! \rceil$ is very close to the actual minimum.

The average number of comparisons for a sorting algorithm is the external path length of the decision tree divided by the number of permutations. For the tree of Figure 8.2, this ratio is $2^2/_3$. In order to derive a lower bound for this value, we first prove a lemma.

Lemma 8.1 Of all trees with a given number of external nodes, the tree which minimizes the external path length has all of its external nodes on two adjacent levels (on a single level when the number of external nodes is a power of 2).

□

Proof: The proof is by induction on the number of external nodes. The lemma is clearly true for trees with one external node. The root of a binary tree with m external nodes divides it into two binary trees with m_1 and m_2 external nodes, with $m_1 + m_2 = m$. Now each of these subtrees must be optimal for m_1 and m_2 external nodes, respectively. Thus the external nodes of the left subtree must be on one level or on two adjacent levels; these external nodes are still at most one level apart when viewed from the root. The same argument can be applied to the right subtree. Hence we have four cases:

1. The nodes of the left subtree are on levels p and $p + 1$, while those of the right subtree are on levels q and $q + 1$.

2. The nodes of the left subtree are on levels p and $p + 1$, while those of the right subtree are all on level q.

3. This is the second case with left and right exchanged.

4. The nodes of the left subtree are all on level p, while those of the right subtree are all on level q.

Let us examine the second case. We need to show that either $q = p$ or $q = p + 1$ holds. *Ad absurdum*, assume $q < p$ and that our tree is nevertheless optimal. Let a be an internal node at level p in the left subtree and let b be an external node at level q in the right subtree. Remove the two children of a and attach them as children of b. The total number of external nodes remains m, and the total external path length decreases by $p - q$, thereby contradicting the optimality of the tree and proving our claim. The subcase of $q > p + 1$ is handled similarly, thereby completing the proof for the second case. The same proof applies directly to the third case; and the other two cases are handled similarly.

Q.E.D.

If we let x be the number of external nodes at level $j - 1$ and y be the number of external nodes at level j, then we obviously have $x + y = m$. Adding two children (external nodes) to each external node at level $j - 1$ yields a tree in which all external nodes are on level j. Such a tree has 2^j external nodes, so that we have the equation $2x + y = 2^j$. Solving for x and y in the previous two equations yields the following expression for the external path length:

$$(j - 1)(2^j - m) + j(2m - 2^j) = m(j + 1) - 2^j.$$

Because we have $j = \lceil \lg m \rceil$ and $m = n!$, our lower bound on the average number of comparisons becomes

$$\frac{(\lceil \lg n! \rceil + 1)n! - 2^{\lceil \lg n! \rceil}}{n!} = \lceil \lg n! \rceil + 1 - \frac{2^{\lceil \lg n! \rceil}}{n!},$$

which is only minutely smaller than $\lceil \lg n! \rceil$. Because the average- and worst-case bounds are so close, an algorithm with excellent worst-case performance must also have excellent average-case performance.

In view of all the comments made so far, it is clear that providing a single measure of the efficiency of a sorting routine is impossible. Yet meaningful statistics can be obtained; our discussion suggests that data should be collected about the number of comparisons, the number of moves, and the running time. In the tables associated with each of the sorting algorithms discussed in the next sections, we shall generally provide this information. In collecting data for the tables, we used randomly generated integers in the range -maxint to maxint; the values reported are averaged over several runs. The number of comparisons and moves are based on the PASCAL versions of the programs given in the text. Timing data for the PASCAL versions of the programs were obtained by running the code produced by the pc compiler (with optimization turned on) on a DEC VAX 11/780 running under UNIX 4.2 BSD in single-user mode.

The overhead associated with the various sorting algorithms becomes most noticeable when basic operations on the types of the objects to be sorted are supported directly in hardware. In order to get a more accurate picture of the true overhead associated with the sorting algorithms and to gauge the effects of instruction set design on the behavior of each algorithm, all our sorting algorithms were hand-coded in assembly language for two machines: the VAX 11/780 and the Ridge. These two machines were chosen because they are roughly comparable in raw computing power and because they offer a striking contrast in design philosophy.

8.1.3 Architectural and Programming Language Considerations

Our sorting algorithms are most sensitive to the relative speeds of different components of the memory hierarchy. If virtual memory is part of the hierarchy, paging performance is most critical, since the time spent processing page faults, in both CPU cycles and in time lost waiting for disk transfers, can easily exceed the total time spent on useful work. Quicksort and mergesort have good locality of reference, whereas heapsort uses the pages that contain the top of the heap heavily, but appears to use the pages that contain the bottom of the heap in a random manner. On the other hand, the use of a work array of length n

means that mergesort uses twice as much virtual memory as heapsort, with a correspondingly lower value of n at which the demand for page frames exceeds the supply. The effect of paging on performance is influenced by both the page allocation and replacement policy (e.g., global *vs.* local) and by the scheduling algorithms and system load (e.g., will jobs with excessive working set requirements be suspended?). At a lower level in the memory hierarchy, cache performance has considerably less influence on the behavior of sorting algorithms than does paging performance, due to the smaller size of cache memory, the considerably smaller penalty for a cache miss, and the simplicity of cache management policies. At the bottom of the memory hierarchy sit registers. The largest factor in the 2.5 speedup ratio observed for the assembly language versions of our code over the PASCAL versions is due to mapping commonly used variables onto registers—assignments that a sophisticated optimizing compiler would make automatically. Use of registers also lessens bus contention, because fewer memory fetches are required; bus contention is important where there is a lot of direct-memory-access activity, since direct-memory-access devices usually have priority when claiming the bus. The visible effect of bus contention is an increase in the effective time to access memory. Experiments run on the VAX indicate that the loss of efficiency for our sorting algorithms due to bus contention can be as high as 40%.

The architecture of the CPU, the instruction set of the computer, and the language used to code the sorting algorithms (and the optimizations employed by the compiler) can also affect the running time. The VAX 11/780 has a rich set of instructions and addressing modes; the Ridge is a RISC (*Reduced Instruction Set* Computer) machine with a very simple instruction set and a fast cycle time. Part of the rationale behind both types of design is to assist compiler writers, in one case by making the target language closer to the high-level language constructs to be compiled and in the other by providing a clean and simple target language which allows effective code optimization.

The VAX supports memory-to-memory operations and indexing, where both the offset and the base address are held in registers. To see the usefulness of this addressing mode, consider the simple assignment statement, `A[i] := A[j]`. If `A` is an array of integers (or other suitably simple objects), this assignment translates into a single instruction on the VAX. The addressing mode, `(Rx)[Ry]`, in which the base address is stored in a register, `Rx`, and the displacement in another, `Ry`, allows us to address an arbitrary item in an array passed to the sorting routine. Furthermore the VAX allows two full addresses in move and comparison instructions, so that it can gain speed by computing both addresses in parallel.

RISC machines are characterized by simple addressing modes. Typically all the operations, except load and store, are register-to-register operations. Even the addressing modes for the load and store operations are simple; on the Ridge, they are essentially of the form offset(Rx), where the offset is a translation-time constant embedded into the instruction. Such a mode is not sufficiently powerful to accommodate the calling sequence of a library routine, because the starting address of the array is a parameter to the sorting routine and thus cannot be at a fixed offset known at translation or linkage time. Therefore, on machines of this type, the addressing calculations have to be made explicit in the code. On the Ridge, fetching A[j], given that j and the starting address of A are in registers, takes four instructions and nine cycles, and another eight cycles are spent storing the result in A[i]. Of course, the addresses of A[i] and A[j] may already have been computed or the value of A[j] already fetched as part of an earlier high-level language instruction.

Yet much of the cost of address calculations can often be saved. If the assignment, A[i] := A[j], is part of an algorithm that sweeps through the array, then using a pointer that advances from array element to array element avoids addressing calculations altogether. Consider an inner loop such as

```
while A[i] > X do
  begin
    A[i+1] := A[i];
    i := i - 1
  end
```

which occurs in insertion sort. (A similar loop, without the assignment statement, appears in quicksort.) By maintaining a pointer to A[i] in a register, this loop can be coded without any index computations, except as needed to initialize the pointer to the correct location within the array A. A sophisticated optimizing compiler will produce such code—the replacement of the local variable i with a pointer that is decremented by the size of the data object is called *elimination of induction variables*. The incrementation of i in A[i+1] can also be removed during compilation—the offset(Rx) addressing mode is powerful enough to handle this situation if the size of the data object is known in advance.

Loops like the one just shown are usually better written as

```
if ⟨boolean condition⟩
  then repeat
          ⟨body of code⟩
       until not ⟨boolean condition⟩
```

with the test occurring at the top, where it guards entry into the loop, and again at the bottom, where it controls the iteration, because the translation into machine code uses only conditional jumps. These considerations are especially important in the innermost loop of an algorithm. By applying the principles just discussed, our earlier while loop can be translated into three assembly language instructions on the VAX,

```
Linner:
        MOVL    (Rx),4(Rx)   ; A[i+1] := A[i]
        CMPL    -(Rx),Ry     ; i := i - 1  and then compare A[i] to X
        JGTR    Linner       ; continue looping, if appropriate
```

where Rx holds the pointer to A[i] and Ry holds the value of X. Notice the use of another of the addressing modes of the VAX, indirect addressing with predecrement, -(Rx).

Using these optimization techniques on machines with simpler architectures is even more important, since the explicit calculations of addresses can take several instructions. Our while loop takes four instructions and ten cycles on the Ridge, only one more than the naïve calculation of the address of A[i] and the fetch of its value—a result which casts some doubt on the value of complex addressing modes. Not all sorting algorithms sweep memory in this manner, however: Shell's method sweeps memory, but with variable increments, while heapsort and radix sort access array elements randomly. The relative performance of these three algorithms suffers correspondingly.

Another feature common to many medium or large CPUs within the SISD family of architectures is pipelining at the instruction level, also known as instruction overlap. Instruction processing is typically divided into four phases: prefetching and decoding of instructions, fetching of operands, execution, and storing of results. In this way a simple instruction like ADD Rx,Ry, which adds the content of Rx to that of Ry and stores the result in Rx, can appear to take just one cycle, the time taken by the addition, because the decoding, fetching of operands, and storing of results are done in parallel with other instructions in different phases of execution. Instructions sets with simple addressing modes simplify the design of pipelined architectures; for instance, the Ridge is a pipelined computer. Pipelining introduces new complications for the compiler writer or assembly language programmer. Because an instruction may produce a result needed by the following instruction, because of the relative speeds of different instructions and of register and memory references, and because of the presence of branch instructions (previously decoded instructions and fetched operands may have to be discarded), pipe bubbles may develop in the pipeline, thus causing idleness. By rearranging logically independent instructions, the number of pipe bubbles can often be reduced, with a consequent reduction in execution time.

Is all this attention to detail worthwhile? As remarked on earlier, the PASCAL versions of the sorting algorithms ran 2.5 times slower than the hand-coded assembly language versions. Better optimizing compilers exist, especially for FORTRAN, where the compilers have had time to mature; with such compilers, the ratio would be less impressive. A language like C gives the programmer tighter control over the generated code: address arithmetic and a rich collection of operators, including incrementation, give the programmer direct access to the addressing modes of the hardware without having to code in assembly language. For example, our earlier `while` loop can be coded as

```
for(...; *p > X; p--)
    *(p+1) = *p;
```

where we declare `register int *p`, i.e., request that the pointer p be kept (if possible) in a register. But even these optimized high-level language versions fall short of the performance that can be obtained with assembly code after a lot of experimentation and fine tuning. For a critical system routine, this amount of effort may be justified. On the other hand, no amount of tuning of the code can overcome fundamental differences in asymptotic behavior, or even in leading coefficients, between algorithms.

8.2   Insertion Sort

We begin our treatment of specific sorting algorithms by looking at the $\Theta(n^2)$ method known as *insertion sort*. Our interest in insertion sort stems from three of its attributes: very low overhead, stability, and linear-time performance on nearly sorted data. The small amount of overhead incurred by insertion sort allows it to outperform more sophisticated $\Theta(n \log n)$ algorithms when n is sufficiently small.

```
procedure InsertionSort(var A: data; n: integer);
   var i, j: integer;
      X: datum;
   begin
     (* Loop invariant: A[1..i-1] are sorted into increasing order. *)
     for i := 2 to n do
       begin
         X := A[i]; (* Move A[i] to a temporary location and create a hole. *)
         (* Shift objects greater than X one position to the right. *)
         for j := i-1 downto 1 do
           if A[j] > X
             then A[j+1] := A[j]
             else goto 1;
         j := 0; (* j undefined on normal loop termination in Pascal. *)
       1: A[j+1] := X (* Fill in the hole. *)
       end
   end; (* InsertionSort *)
```

Program 8.1: Insertion Sort: The Basic Algorithm

As a result, both quicksort and mergesort benefit from using insertion sort as a subprocedure when faced with sorting small pieces of the original array. Finally, insertion sort can be refined and reworked into a fairly efficient sorting method known as Shell's method.

A straightforward coding of insertion sort is given in Program 8.1. On each iteration of the outer loop, the object in location i is inserted into the sorted portion of the array; this is the method used by most people in sorting a bridge hand. This coding of insertion sort is not very good, because each iteration of the inner loop makes an implicit test that only becomes true on normal loop termination. For random data, termination of this loop because of this test occurs rarely: on average, it occurs $H_n - 1$ times, where H_n is the nth harmonic number. If we can guarantee the presence of a sentinel in A[0], then the inner loop of insertion sort can be coded as in Program 8.2.

This modification reduces the size of the inner loops of the assembly language versions from 5 to 4 on the Ridge and from 5 to 3 on the VAX, for a 20% and 40% gain, respectively. The effect on execution time is somewhat more modest, since the number of memory references remains the same. The first set of values in Table 8.3 shows running times in microseconds for sorting integers with both versions of insertion sort.

The $\Theta(n^2)$ behavior of insertion sort does not prevent it from being a very useful sorting method. In the following sections, we shall use insertion sort repeatedly to sort small segments of arrays. The times, in seconds, for sorting all of the small pieces of an array of 100,000 integers are given in parentheses in the table. Notice that the anticipated quadratic growth rate of insertion sort is not supported by the data: neither the first set of values, which should grow quadratically, nor the set of parenthesized values, which should grow lin-

```
(* A sentinel is assumed in A[0]. *)
X := A[i];
j := i - 1;
if A[j] > X
  then begin
          repeat
            A[j+1] := A[j];
             j := j - 1
          until A[j] <= X; (* must become true eventually *)
          A[j+1] := X
        end
```

Program 8.2: The Inner Loop of Insertion Sort with Sentinel

Table 8.3: Running Times for Versions of Insertion Sort With and Without Sentinels

Times are given in microseconds and, in parentheses, seconds.

Size	Without sentinel		With sentinel	
	VAX	Ridge	VAX	Ridge
8	97 (1.21)	42 (0.53)	88 (1.10)	43 (0.54)
12	187 (1.56)	81 (0.67)	161 (1.34)	79 (0.66)
16	306 (1.91)	133 (0.83)	254 (1.59)	126 (0.79)
20	454 (2.27)	197 (0.99)	371 (1.86)	182 (0.91)
24	631 (2.63)	273 (1.14)	503 (2.10)	249 (1.04)

early, grow that fast. In fact, for small n, insertion sort does about the same number of comparisons as $\Theta(n \log n)$ sorting methods. In the sentinel-based version of insertion sort, the worst-case number of comparisons is $(n^2 + n - 2)/2$. The average-case performance can be derived by noting that each element, on average, moves halfway towards the beginning of the array. Accounting for the contribution of the final comparison, we get a mean number of comparisons of $(n^2 + 3n - 4)/4$. The values derived from these formulae justify our contention: for $n = 10$, insertion sort makes 31.5 comparisons on average, whereas our lower bound for the optimal algorithm evaluates to 21.8 and $n \lg n$ to 33.2; even for $n = 16$, insertion sort remains competitive, since it makes 75 comparisons on average, whereas our lower bound evaluates to 44.3 and $n \lg n$ to 64.

The PASCAL code of Program 8.2 assumes that the sentinel is already in place; as discussed in the introductory section, we cannot always ensure the presence of a sentinel by storing one in A[0]. When a sentinel is not already present and when placement of a sentinel is not possible, we can still replace the $\Theta(n^2)$ implicit bounds checks with $\Theta(n)$ element comparisons. Whenever an element is inserted, we use up to one additional comparison by checking the content of A[1]: if our check shows that A[1] can act as a sentinel for the element being inserted, the inner loop proceeds as in Program 8.2; if not, then the element being inserted is the new smallest element and it is placed in the first position by shifting all the preceding elements to the right. At different points in our study of sorting, we shall use all three of these variations on the basic insertion sort algorithm.

8.3 Shell's Method

Shell's method, named after its inventor, D. L. Shell, attempts to improve the worst-case performance of insertion sort by taking advantage of its efficiency on both small arrays and nearly sorted data. Insertion sort moves data inefficiently: to move a single element a given distance takes time proportional to that distance. Thus one may seek to improve upon insertion sort by devising some means by which elements can be moved quickly to the vicinity of their final resting place; the resulting array is nearly sorted and insertion sort can complete the work quickly. Shell proposed a clever way to use insertion sort itself to move elements over large distances. The algorithm makes several passes, each of which considers only subsequences within the array. Within each subsequence there are very few elements, so that insertion sort is efficient; since the array positions considered within a subsequence are far apart, sorting a subsequence results in efficient movement of data over large distances. When the subsequences are all sorted, the resulting array is nearly sorted and can be completely sorted with a final pass of insertion sort.

Consider an array with 200 elements. Let us divide the array into 16 subsequences as follows: treat the elements in positions 1, 17, 33, 49, ... as one subsequence, the elements in positions 2, 18, 34, 50, ... as another, and so forth. Thus each subsequence has 12 or 13 elements each. We can now sort each of the 16 subsequences in place using insertion sort; one move in this phase of Shell's method shifts an array element 16 places, something that would have required 16 moves in insertion sort. When all the subsequences are sorted, the array will, we hope, be nearly sorted, so that insertion sort can be applied to the entire array to complete the sort in an efficient manner. Clearly, we are best off if the smallest element is in the first subsequence, the second smallest is in the second subsequence, and so on, returning to the first subsequence for the 17th smallest, and stepping from subsequence to subsequence; in such a case, the array is completely sorted as soon as the subsequences are sorted and insertion sort takes only linear time. Conversely, we are worst off if the first subsequence contains the 13 largest elements, the second subsequence the next 13 largest, and so on, with the 16th subsequence containing the 12 smallest elements; in such a case, long data moves remain necessary after all subsequences are sorted and insertion sort takes quadratic time.

The problem with the two-phase strategy just proposed is that it appears to break down for large arrays. If we use subsequences 16 elements apart, then these subsequences are of length $n/16$ and the first phase is inefficient. On the other hand, forming many subsequences of small length leads to an inefficient second phase. If the length is m, with the elements n/m locations apart, then the first n/m elements are each the smallest in their respective subsequences,

```
procedure ShellSort(var A: data; n: integer);
  label 1;
  var h, (* increment for current pass *)
      i, (* index of object being inserted *)
      j: (* index of object being compared against X *)
         integer;
      X: datum; (* A[i] at start of insertion operation *)
  begin
    repeat
      ... calculate next value for increment--see text ...
      (* For each element use insertion sort with steps of size h. *)
      for i := h+1 to n do
        begin
          X := A[i];
          j := i - h;
          if A[j] > X
            then begin (* must do some shifting *)
                   repeat
                     A[j+h] := A[j];
                     j := j - h;
                     if j <= 0 then goto 1
                   until A[j] <= X;
                 1: A[j+h] := X
                 end
        end
    until h = 1
end; (* ShellSort *)
```

Program 8.3: Shell's Method

but they are in random order with respect to each other. At best, therefore, the final pass applies insertion sort to m random subintervals of size n/m and takes quadratic time.

The solution is to incorporate more phases. The array is first partitioned into h_k-*chains* of roughly n/h_k elements each, with elements h_k locations apart in each chain, where h_k is chosen so that n/h_k is small. These short chains are sorted by insertion sort. The array is then repartitioned into h_{k-1}-chains, where h_{k-1} is smaller than h_k, and these chains are sorted by insertion sort. Continuing in this manner we form a sequence of diminishing increments, $h_k > h_{k-1} > h_{k-2} > \cdots > h_2 > h_1 = 1$. Thus the algorithm makes k passes over the entire array, with each successive pass sorting fewer, but longer, chains. The final pass, with $h_1 = 1$, is just insertion sort and thus ensures that the entire array is correctly sorted. The PASCAL code for Shell's method and an example of its execution are given in Program 8.3 and Figure 8.3.

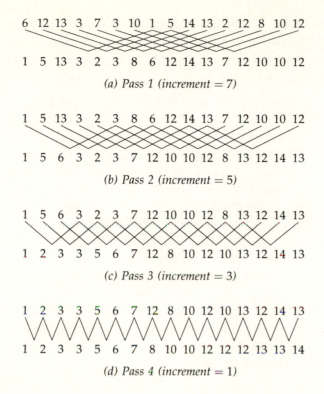

(a) Pass 1 (increment = 7)

(b) Pass 2 (increment = 5)

(c) Pass 3 (increment = 3)

(d) Pass 4 (increment = 1)

Figure 8.3: Shell's Method with Increments 7, 5, 3, and 1

The coding of the algorithm does not parallel the description of Shell's method given in the text, which would yield the following control structure:

```
for h := h_k, h_{k-1}, ..., h_1 do
   for each of the h-chains starting at index 1, 2, ...,h do
      sort the h-chain by insertion sort
```

Instead, the code of Program 8.3 uses the following control structure:

```
for h := h_n, h_{n-1}, ..., h_1 do
   for i := h+1 to n do
      insert A[i], but use backward steps of h instead of 1
```

These two alternatives are logically equivalent: while the first approach works on one chain at a time, the second cycles its attention from one chain to the next. Which approach is taken has a large effect on the appearance of the code, but only a small effect on the number of instructions executed. However, the choice has a significant impact on paging performance. A pass in the first approach makes a scan through the array for each chain, for a total of $\sum_{i=1}^{k} h_i$ scans, whereas a pass in the second approach makes a single scan through the array, for a total of k scans. This analysis ignores the page faults due to the insertions, but we do not expect many such faults, because we do not expect an element to travel more than a few steps to the left.

Outside of paging considerations, efficiency may also depend on the version of insertion sort chosen. Using a sentinel to terminate the innermost loop poses a more subtle problem here than in insertion sort. Due to the use of step sizes larger than one, sentinel locations from A[$-h_k$+1] to A[0] become necessary. Since h_k is of the same order of magnitude as n, quite a large number of sentinel locations would be required. Therefore, we chose the basic insertion sort algorithm of Program 8.1. However, our third version of insertion sort, which manages its own sentinels, can be easily incorporated, so why did we not use it? We observed experimentally that this led to worse performance. The reason lies buried in Table 8.3: as the number of elements decreases, the advantage that accrues to sentinel-based insertion sort declines to the point where, for arrays of fewer than eight elements, simple insertion sort is the faster method. The difference is due to the overhead in getting the sentinel-based methods started if the sentinel must be placed or its presence detected. This overhead is recovered with enough iterations of the inner loop, but the whole point of Shell's method is to avoid more than a few iterations of the inner loop.

In the assembly language versions of Shell's method used to produce the timings given at the end of this section, necessary modifications to the tight inner loop of insertion sort cause about a 33% degradation in performance in this most critical section of the code. The problem is that, instead of A[j+1], we now have A[j+h]; the variable increment prevents us from using the offset(Rx) addressing mode on the Ridge and the -(Rx) addressing mode on the VAX.

While we have discussed the coding of Shell's method in some detail, we have so far ignored the real issue: Does it really work and what sequence of diminishing increments makes it work best? The answer to the first question depends on the answer to the second. If our goal is to develop a $\Theta(n \log n)$ sorting algorithm, then we cannot use more than a logarithmic number of increments, since each pass takes at least linear time. From our previous discussion, we might expect that such a goal is achievable. Determining good sequences is a fascinating and very complex problem involving number theory and combinatorics. While some theory has been developed, there is currently no solution to the problem of selecting an optimal sequence or even to the problem of characterizing the behavior of the algorithm when run with an optimal sequence. The initial tendency is probably to use powers of 2 or some other small integer. Powers of a small number, say k, guarantee a logarithmic number of increments and have intuitive appeal on two counts:

1. They correspond to a recursive application of our initial two-pass idea: the array is divided into k chains, each sorted in the first pass, while the second pass is just insertion sort. The first pass, however, sorts the chains directly only if they are short enough; otherwise, it calls the sorting routine recursively.

2. Sorting an h_i-chain has the effect of merging k independent h_{i+1}-chains. Thus, Shell's method turns into an in-place version of k-way mergesort.

Both points reflect the same basic property: using powers of a number as increments prevents any interaction between chains. As it turns out, however, preventing interaction is a poor idea. As we merge k h_{i+1}-chains into a single h_i-chain, the smaller chains are totally independent, because their elements have never been compared before. A sequence of increments that results in interaction between chains can put us in a position where several elements from each chain have already been compared with several elements from every other chain, so that the relative order of these elements is already correct and the "merging" phase requires less work. Thus it should be better to pick the increments so that there is as much interaction as possible between chains from previous passes. However, a very counterintuitive assumption underlies this assertion, namely, that sorting the h_i-chains does not negate the benefits of sorting the h_{i+1}-chains.

Theorem 8.1 If a k-sorted array is made h-sorted by sorting its h-chains, then it remains k-sorted. $\square$

This statement is clearly true when h divides k, since elements k apart are just some multiple of h apart and, after h-sorting, we have $\texttt{A[j]} \leq \texttt{A[j+h]} \leq \texttt{A[j+2h]} \leq \cdots$. However, the theorem is true for any h and k.

Proof: The proof is by induction on the number of h-inversions in the array, i.e., inversions between elements that are a multiple of h positions apart. We first assign the elements of the k-sorted array to a matrix, A, with k rows and $\lceil n/k \rceil$ columns, proceeding column by column and filling the last column with infinite values if necessary. That the array is k-sorted is equivalent to saying that each of the rows of A is sorted. We shall maintain this latter property as we correct h-inversions. The order in which we correct the inversions does not correspond to the order in which Shell's method corrects them, but the order is clearly immaterial. First note that, if any h-inversions are present, then at least one such involves elements that are exactly h positions apart. We correct the first such h-inversion that we find as we scan the array; since the elements are only h positions apart, correcting this inversion cannot introduce any other. Assume that this inversion involves element $A_{i,j}$; then the other element is $A_{i+h,j}$ or, if we have $i + h > k$, the element $A_{i+h-k, j+1}$. (Throughout the argument that follows, subscripts refer to the original positions of the elements in A.) Consider the former case: we wish to ensure that A remains sorted by rows as we exchange elements in the same column. The following inequalities hold:

$$A_{i, j-1} \leq A_{i, j} \leq A_{i, j+1}$$
$$A_{i+h, j-1} \leq A_{i+h, j} \leq A_{i+h, j+1}$$
$$A_{i, j-1} \leq A_{i+h, j-1}$$
$$A_{i, j} > A_{i+h, j}.$$

The first two inequalities hold because the rows of A are sorted and the last two because of the way in which we selected the inversion to correct. These inequalities imply three more: (i) $A_{i, j-1} \leq A_{i+h, j}$; (ii) $A_{i+h, j-1} < A_{i, j}$; and (iii) $A_{i+h, j} < A_{i, j+1}$. Thus the only possible difficulty in maintaining the rows of A in sorted order arises when $A_{i, j}$ is greater than $A_{i+h, j+1}$. The latter cannot happen when $A_{i, j+1} \leq A_{i+h, j+1}$, but is possible when $A_{i, j+1} > A_{i+h, j+1}$. However, in the latter case, $A_{i, j+1}$ and $A_{i+h, j+1}$ also form an inversion. If we correct this inversion as well, we move our potential difficulty over by one column: only $A_{i, j+1}$ and $A_{i+h, j+2}$ can now be out of order. Continuing in this manner, we

Table 8.4: The Effect of Different Sequences of Diminishing Increments

Sequence	Comparisons	Moves	Comments
256 16 1	36,354	38,901	$h_k = 16^k$
256 64 16 4 1	25,401	28,890	$h_k = 4^k$
128 64 32 16 8 4 2 1	26,045	30,052	$h_k = 2^k$
127 63 31 15 7 3 1	14,600	18,726	$h_k = 2h_{k-1} + 1$
127 31 7 1	16,431	19,596	Every other term of above
129 65 33 17 9 5 3 1	15,169	19,466	$h_k = 2h_{k-1} - 1$
257 65 17 5 1	14,265	17,834	Every other term of above
171 85 43 21 11 5 3 1	15,034	19,312	$h_k = 2h_{k-1} + 1, \quad k$ even $h_k = 2h_{k-1} - 1, \quad k$ odd
85 21 5 1	15,523	18,642	Odd terms of above
122 41 14 5 2 1	14,269	18,005	$h_k = 3h_{k-1} - 1$
121 40 13 4 1	14,377	17,910	$h_k = 3h_{k-1} + 1$
163 79 37 17 7 3 1	13,646	17,631	$h_k = $ next prime $> 2h_{k-1}$
347 113 37 11 3 1	13,518	17,325	$h_k = $ next prime $\geq 3h_{k-1}$
389 97 23 5 1	14,715	18,157	$h_k = $ next prime $> 4h_{k-1}$
209 109 41 19 5 1	13,451	17,217	$h_{2k+1} = 9 \cdot 4^k - 9 \cdot 2^k + 1$ $h_{2k} = 4 \cdot 4^k - 6 \cdot 2^k + 1$

either reach a column, l, with $A_{i,l} \leq A_{i+h,l}$ or run out of columns. In either case, the rows of the matrix remain sorted and the number of h-inversions decreases. The situation for an inversion with $i+h > k$ is basically the same: the number of elements to the right of $A_{i+h-k,j+1}$ is now one less than the number of elements to the right of $A_{i,j}$, but this difference is inconsequential since the row where the potential difficulty arises is the shorter row.

Q.E.D.

This theorem clearly shows the wisdom of choosing the sequence of diminishing increments to be something other than powers of some number. Consider the very last pass, for example. If the diminishing increments are powers of 2, then all we know is that the array is 2-sorted; when we insert an element, we know that it is greater than 50% of the elements to its left, but do not know anything about its relationship to the other 50%. If, on the other hand, the last few increments are 7, 5, 3, and 2, then we know that the element is greater than at least 77% of the elements to its left. Table 8.4 gives experimental results for the number of comparisons and moves performed with various sequences when sorting an array of length 1000. Since each pass requires at least one comparison per element, we can compute a lower bound on the number of comparisons. Comparing this bound with the actual number of comparisons made by Shell's method shows that, on average, just a few comparisons are made per element (for the data shown in the table, between 2.0, for the eighth sequence, and 13.3, for the first sequence); hence, as we claimed earlier, each element moves left only a short distance. Sedgewick argued that a good sequence of increments does not progress strictly geometrically and proposed sequences, such as the last in the table, which include a dominant geometric term as well as some smaller ones. This sequence was used in generating the data for strings given earlier as well as the data for various size arrays of integers given in Table 8.5.

Table 8.5: Sorting Integers with Shell's Method

Size	Comparisons	Moves	Time in seconds		
			PASCAL	VAX	Ridge
500	5,800	7,435	0.12	0.03	0.01
1,000	13,394	17,151	0.27	0.06	0.03
10,000	196,341	249,874	4.07	1.05	0.43
100,000	2,618,997	3,314,356	54.57	14.61	6.16

8.4 Quicksort

Invented in 1962 by C. A. R. Hoare, the divide-and-conquer sorting algorithm known as *quicksort* remains the most popular sorting technique. The algorithm received the nickname "quicksort" because of its low overhead and extremely tight inner loop, which often makes it the fastest sorting algorithm. The main drawback of the method is the possibility of quadratic running time, although such pathological behavior is never observed in practice. As suggested by our study of insertion sort and Shell's method, an in-place sorting algorithm gains speed by moving objects over long distances. Quicksort accomplishes such moves by sacrificing accuracy in the positioning of elements. First it makes a single pass through the array, moving all the "small" elements to the left end of the array and all the "large" elements to the right end of the array; then it sorts the small elements and the large elements separately, which completes the sorting process. In greater detail, the algorithm, applied to a portion of the array, A[l..r], is:

- Select a threshold, T, equal in value to an element of A[l..r].

- Rearrange the elements of A[l..r] into three contiguous pieces, A[l..i], A[i+1..j], and A[j+1..r], such that the elements of A[l..i] are less than T, the elements of A[i+1..j] are equal to T, and the elements of A[j+1..r] are greater than T.

- Recursively sort the first and last segments.

The base cases for the recursive calls are segments of length zero or one, which are trivially sorted. Note that the values of i and j in the second step are implicitly defined by the value of T and by the values of the elements in A[l..r]. Also note that the middle portion, A[i+1..j], is never empty, since T was chosen as an element of A[l..r]; this condition guarantees termination. As a divide-and-conquer algorithm, quicksort has the peculiarity that it does all of its work before the recursive calls and none afterwards. Moreover, unlike the divide-and-conquer algorithms of Chapter 7, the control structure of quicksort is not oblivious, because the manner in which it partitions the problem depends on the actual data; as a result, it cannot be implemented iteratively without an auxiliary data structure.

Our first concern is to develop an efficient algorithm for the second step, which is known as the *partitioning* step. We shall maintain two lists of elements, each starting at one end of the array and growing towards the center, lists which contain, respectively, the elements smaller than T and the elements greater than T; the shrinking region between these two lists contains the unprocessed elements. Where do we keep the elements equal to T and what happens if one of the lists bumps into this middle portion and needs to expand? All elements

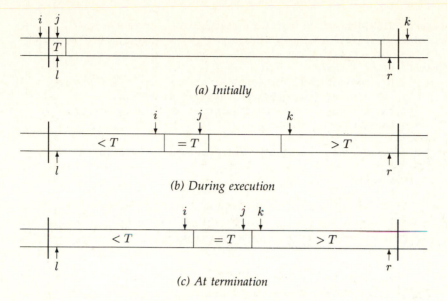

(a) Initially

(b) During execution

(c) At termination

Figure 8.4: Three-Way Partitioning

equal to T can be kept in a third portion of the array, between the first and last portions. Shifting this entire middle portion to the left or right is too inefficient when it is large, but we can take advantage of the fact that all of its elements are equal to accomplish the shift in constant time. To shift the entire middle portion one position left or right, all we need do is pick up the element from one end and place it at the other end. This three-way partitioning algorithm is illustrated in Figure 8.4 and embodied in the code of Program 8.4. Since each iteration of the while loop places one element, the partitioning step takes linear time.

Is the value of A[l] a good choice for the partitioning threshold? To answer this question, we need to analyze the running time of quicksort. We assume no ties in the data: since the middle portion does not require sorting, ties can only serve to decrease the number of elements that remain to be sorted and thus to improve the overall running time. The best case occurs when the two portions to be sorted recursively are of equal length. The governing recurrence is

$$t_{\text{best}}(n) = t_{\text{best}}(\lfloor (n-1)/2 \rfloor) + t_{\text{best}}(\lceil (n-1)/2 \rceil) + \Theta(n),$$

which shows that $t_{\text{best}}(n)$ is $\Theta(n \log n)$. The worst case occurs when one portion has length $n - 1$ and the other has length zero—the middle portion, which is now at one end, consisting of the remaining element. The recurrence is now:

$$t_{\text{worst}}(n) = t_{\text{worst}}(n-1) + t_{\text{worst}}(0) + \Theta(n).$$

```
procedure QuickSort(var A: data; n: integer);
  procedure RecQuickSort(l, r: integer);
    (* Use quicksort to sort A[l..r]. *)
    var T, temp: datum;
        i, (* index of the rightmost value strictly less than T *)
        j, (* index of the rightmost value equal to T *)
        k: (* index of the leftmost value strictly greater than T *)
           integer;
    begin
      (* Zero- or one-element pieces are sorted by default. *)
      if l < r
        then begin
                (* Partition A[l..r] into three pieces.
                   The middle piece cannot be of zero length. *)
                T := A[l];
                i := l - 1; j := l; k := r + 1;

                (* while some elements of A[l..r] are in an unknown state *)
                while j+1 < k do
                  (* case A[j+1] vs. T of *)
                  if A[j+1] < T
                    then (* Logically shift the middle portion one place to the
                            right (to make room for the new element less than T)
                            by moving the leftmost element of the middle portion
                            to the right end of the middle portion.  This works
                            because all elements in the middle portion are equal. *)
                        begin
                          i := i + 1; j := j + 1;
                          A[i] := A[j]; (* effectively swap A[i] and A[j] *)
                          A[j] := T
                        end
                  else if A[j+1] > T
                    then (* Place A[j+1] with the elements greater than T
                            by swapping A[j+1] and A[k-1]. *)
                        begin
                          k := k - 1;
                          temp := A[k]; A[k] := A[j+1]; A[j+1] := temp
                        end
                  else   j := j + 1; (* lengthen the middle portion *)

                RecQuickSort(l,i);
                RecQuickSort(k,r)
             end
    end; (* RecQuickSort *)
  begin
    RecQuickSort(1,n)
  end; (* QuickSort *)
```

Program 8.4: Quicksort—Basic Algorithm

Because the time to detect that the interval has zero length is constant, we have $t_{\text{worst}}(n) = \Theta(n^2)$. If we picture the tree of recursive calls generated by the procedure, we can see that, up to the level of the first leaf, the work done on each level is essentially equivalent to the partitioning of the whole array and so takes linear time. In the best case, all the leaves are on the same or on two adjacent levels at a depth of $\log n$, so that we obtain $\Theta(n \log n)$ behavior; in the worst case, the tree has n levels, there is a leaf at each level, and the other node corresponds to the remaining elements.

Because the running time of quicksort is determined by the number of comparisons, we analyze the average-case behavior of quicksort in terms of the average number of comparisons. Assuming that the partitioning element is selected at random from the array, we get the following recurrence relation:

$$t_{\text{av}}(n) = \frac{1}{n} \cdot \sum_{i=1}^{n} \left(t_{\text{av}}(i-1) + t_{\text{av}}(n-i) \right) + (n-1), \qquad \text{with } t_{\text{av}}(0) = t_{\text{av}}(1) = 0.$$

The terms of the sum correspond to the possible choices of the partitioning element. This is exactly the same recurrence relation as (2.14) of Section 2.3.1; its solution is $t_{\text{av}}(n) = \Theta(n \log n)$.

It only remains to argue that using A[1] as the partitioning element is equivalent to choosing a random element of A[1..r]. We do this loosely because we could just as easily have chosen a random partitioning element and we intend to improve the algorithm anyway. Choosing a random element in a randomly ordered list is no more random than choosing any particular element, but we need to verify that partitioning does not induce any nonrandomness in either of the two remaining unsorted portions. The latter assertion rests on the fact that the partitioning element is excluded from both unsorted portions and thus cannot become the first element of either subinterval or any subsequent subintervals, where it would create a totally imbalanced split.

We make four significant improvements to the basic algorithm. They are directed towards the following:

- Increasing the probability that the two subproblems are roughly equal in size;

- Decreasing the likelihood of observing worst-case behavior;

- Limiting the amount of extra storage even in the worst case; and

- Reducing the overhead.

The first improvement is to choose the partitioning element with more care. As we saw in the best-case analysis, we should prefer the partitioning element to be the median element. We can find the true median in linear time (see Exercise 8.11), but the coefficients are so high as to defeat any gain derived from using the true median. However, we can improve our chances of getting an even split if, instead of picking a random element as the threshold, we choose the median of a small random sample taken from the interval. Whereas choosing one random element results in an expected split of 25–75, choosing the median of three random elements gives an expected split slightly worse than 33–67 and a probability of a 25–75 or worse split of only 31.25%. As with choosing a single element for the threshold, the three random elements do not have to be randomly selected. It is convenient to use the first, middle, and last elements; in this form it is known as "median-of-three partitioning." This choice of sample allows us to find the exact median when the algorithm runs on already sorted data; in contrast, note that already sorted data present a worst-case instance when partitioning with the first element. Our better choice of partitioning threshold both increases the probability of an even split and reduces the likelihood of observing the worst-case behavior.

One way to lessen the overhead of any code is to remove subroutine calls. Because the two recursive calls are independent and not followed by additional code, either call can be considered the final action of the procedure and thus an instance of tail recursion. Hence, we can stack one of the two subproblems for subsequent processing (by storing the bounds of the interval to be sorted) and directly execute the other by setting r to i or l to k and branching to the first line of the procedure. When a return is to be simulated, an unsolved problem is recovered from the stack; if none is left, the procedure terminates. If we systematically stack either the left or right subproblem, the stack can grow to length n. However, by always stacking the larger subproblem and directly solving the smaller, we ensure that the stack does not exceed $\lg n$ records in length. The correctness of this bound can be established using the following invariant: if the stack contains m intervals, then the length of the segment being partitioned does not exceed $n/2^m$. Notice that it is not true that the size of each stacked interval is less than half the size of the interval directly beneath it on the stack. Limiting the size of the stack is possible only in the nonrecursive version: changing the recursive version so that the smaller subproblem is attacked first has no effect on the ultimate growth of the stack, because the stack frame for the parent interval remains on the stack.

We can further lessen overhead by using insertion sort on small intervals. Although the small intervals can be left unsorted as they are created, to be sorted in one long pass at the very end, it is preferable in a paged environment to sort them as they are created. This strategy preserves the excellent locality of quicksort, whereas the final sweep of a single insertion sort pass would trigger another series of page faults. Note that the largest (smallest) element of an interval acts as a sentinel for the interval to its right (left). Since, in our final version of quicksort, we shall know *a priori* if a small interval is a left or right interval, we can use insertion sort with sentinel as presented in Program 8.2 for right intervals and a right-to-left version for left intervals.

We significantly lessen the overhead in one more way, this time by revising our partitioning method. Except in the case of an element equal in value to the partitioning threshold, the three-way partitioning given in Program 8.4 makes more than one assignment to the array in order to decrease the length of the unprocessed portion of the array by one. It is particularly wasteful to exchange A[j+1] and A[k] if A[k] is also larger than T, since a second such exchange follows immediately. This particular inefficiency can be remedied by executing

```
repeat k := k - 1 until A[k] <= T
```

initially and after each such exchange. However, the same technique cannot be applied to elements smaller than T, because the element or elements equal to T always abut the left portion. To avoid this difficulty, we first develop a partitioning scheme that divides A[l..r] into two, instead of three, portions, neither of which is empty. Notice that, after sorting A[l], A[m], and A[r] in place while determining the median of three, we have three landmarks in our array. We shall let the first interval gather elements no larger than the threshold and the second interval gather elements no smaller than the threshold; elements equal to the threshold can end up on either side. Our partitioning algorithm becomes:

```
      i := l;
      j := r;
   1: repeat i := i + 1 until A[i] >= T;
      repeat j := j - 1 until A[j] <= T;
      if i < j
        then begin
               temp := A[i]; A[i] := A[j]; A[j] := temp; (* swap *)
               goto 1
             end
```

In addition to forcing both subintervals to be nonempty, the presence of sentinels in A[l] and A[r] makes explicit checks for subscripts out of range unnecessary. Both assertions about this code fragment remain true even if the left or right element equals the median.

Because an exchange requires three data movements to place two data objects in their correct places, we code this new partitioning method in a somewhat unusual manner which uses only one assignment per element moved. As a secondary benefit we again produce a middle portion, though this time it always has length one, even if there are ties in the data. The idea is to use a hole in much the same way that insertion sort and the sifting operations on heaps use one. The data movement can be viewed as a long rotation rather than a series of exchanges, with only one extra assignment for the entire rotation instead of one extra assignment per exchange. The hole bounces back and forth from the left end of the interval to the right end, converging toward the middle, alternately receiving a value no larger than the threshold and a value no smaller than the threshold. Since moving an object to T creates the hole and since T is the element that gets placed in the hole in the end, the median of the three elements must be placed in A[1] and not in A[m]. The net effect is to use two integer comparisons and two data moves for each two data objects placed instead of one integer comparison and three data moves. The code for the quicksort procedure using this partitioning algorithm and the other improvements we have discussed is given in Program 8.5.

As we noted, partitioning with rotation provides another advantage. By placing T in the hole as the final action of the inner loop, we place T in its final position and so can exclude it from the remainder of the sorting process. The line

```
i := i + 1; (* The element in A[i] is correctly placed. *)
```

and the corresponding line for j accomplish this. Recognizing that one element has been placed correctly may seem like an unimportant nicety, but is in fact useful for two reasons. First, it removes from further consideration a significant fraction of the array elements: assuming no ties and a small interval size of 16, at least $(n - 16)/17$ objects, or approximately 6% of the array, fall into this category. Secondly, these two lines prevent either the rightmost or leftmost element in the new intervals, A[1..j] and A[i..r], from automatically becoming the largest or smallest of the interval. Such an outcome would damage the integrity of our median-of-three partitioning, since one of the three elements considered would be useless. Notice that, on inner loop termination, j = i is possible only if there are ties in the data. When we have j = i, the advantage normally gained by excluding T from both the left and right portions is lost, but the algorithm still works correctly and only slightly more slowly. If many ties are anticipated, a check for j = i can be performed and corrective action taken.

Because of the tightness of the inner loops,

```
repeat i := i + 1 until A[i] >= T
repeat j := j - 1 until A[j] <= T
```

we make a few remarks about the coding of quicksort in assembly language. Computer architectures are not always as cooperative as we should like. On

```
procedure QuickSort(var A: data; n: integer);
   label 1, 2, 3, 4;
   const SmallInterval = 16; SmallIntervalMinus1 = 15;
         (* Sizes between 6 and 25 show less than 10% difference in running times. *)
         StackSize = 100;
   var T, temp: datum;
       i, j, l, r, m: integer;
       stack: array [1..StackSize] of integer;
       (* Sufficient space to sort a list far in excess of the memory
          that can be placed on a computer. *)
       top: integer;
   begin
     if n <= SmallInterval
       then begin
              ...   (* small problem--use insertion sort and return *)
            end;

     (* Use quicksort to sort the array into small pieces that are internally
        jumbled, but with the pieces in correct relative order.
        Use insertion sort to sort these small pieces. *)
     top := 0;
     l := 1;
     r := n;

1:  (* 1, m, and r are all distinct. *)
     (* Put the median element in A[l] so that we can start the hole at the
        left end.  There is an automatic sentinel in both directions of sweep. *)
     m := (l+r) div 2;
     if A[m] > A[l]
       then begin temp := A[l]; A[l] := A[m]; A[m] := temp end;
     if A[l] > A[r]
       then begin
              temp := A[l]; A[l] := A[r]; A[r] := temp;
              (* Only recompare A[m] and A[l] if A[r] was not largest. *)
              if A[m] > A[l]
                 then begin temp := A[l]; A[l] := A[m]; A[m] := temp end
            end;
     T := A[l]; (* Make a hole at A[l] *)

     (* One of i and j points to the hole.  The other points to the last
        element of its portion of A[l..r].  Initially i points to the hole
        and j points to the last element of the portion that contains
        elements >= T. *)
     i := l;
     j := r;
```

```
2: repeat j := j - 1 until A[j] <= T;
   if j <= i
     then begin
                (* j = i-1  or possibly j = i *)
                A[i] := T; (* fill in the hole *)
                i := i + 1; (* The element in A[i] is correctly placed. *)
                goto 3
             end;
   (* Reestablish the invariant by switching the roles of i and j. *)
   A[i] := A[j];
   repeat i := i + 1 until A[i] >= T;
   if j <= i
     then begin
                (* i = j+1  or possibly i = j *)
                A[j] := T; (* fill in the hole *)
                j := j - 1; (* The element in A[j] is correctly placed. *)
                goto 3
             end;
   (* Reestablish the invariant by switching the roles of i and j. *)
   A[j] := A[i];
   goto 2;

3: (* Usually the element T is in neither part, but it is possible in rare
       circumstances that i-j = 1.  In this case no harm is done. *)
   (* Stack the larger and remove tail recursion to solve the smaller. *)
   if r - i > SmallIntervalMinus1
     then if j - l > SmallIntervalMinus1
             then begin
                      (* Both subproblems are large--stack the larger one. *)
                      top := top + 2;
                      if j - l > r - i
                        then begin
                                 stack[top-1] := l;
                                 stack[top] := j;
                                 l := i;
                                 goto 1
                              end
                        else begin
                                 stack[top-1] := i;
                                 stack[top] := r;
                                 r := j;
                                 goto 1
                              end
                   end
             else begin
                      (* The left subproblem is small--work on the right one. *)
                      ... sort left subproblem with right-to-left insertion
                              sort with sentinel ...
                      l := i;
                      goto 1
                   end
```

```
        else begin
                (* The right subproblem is small. *)
                ... same here (left-to-right insertion sort) ...
                if j - 1 > SmallIntervalMinus1
                  then begin (* The left subproblem is large--go work on it. *)
                              r := j;
                              goto 1
                          end
                else begin
                        (* The left subproblem is also small. *)
                        ... same here (right-to-left insertion sort) ...
                        (* Retrieve an unsolved problem from the stack. *)
                        if top > 0
                          then begin
                                  l := stack[top-1];
                                  r := stack[top];
                                  top := top - 2;
                                  goto 1
                              end
                    end
            end
      end;

   (* The entire array is sorted. *)
4: (* exit for arrays sorted entirely by insertion sort *)
  end; (* QuickSort *)
```

Program 8.5: Efficient Implementation of Quicksort

the VAX, for example, the second of these two loops has the following natural
coding:

```
Linner:
        CMPL  -(Rx),Ry       ; Rx points to A[j] and Ry contains T
        JGTR  Linner
```

the predecrement of register Rx corresponding to j := j - 1. But the corresponding increment addressing mode, (Rx)+, is a postincrement. These addressing modes were created for stack manipulations and not for sweeping arrays in
opposite directions. With some care the inner loop on i can also be coded in
two instructions, provided some corrective action is taken both before and after
the loop.

The RISC architecture of the Ridge is even less cooperative. Comparisons
of A[j] and A[i] with T cannot be made without first moving A[j] and A[i]
into registers; for the same reason, a swap takes four instructions. In quicksort,
however, the two elements to swap are already in registers as a result of the
comparisons, so the swap takes only two instructions. Experimental results show

Table 8.6: Sorting Integers with Quicksort

Size	Comparisons	Moves	Time in seconds PASCAL	VAX	Ridge
500	4,845	3,430	0.08	0.01	0.01
1,000	10,881	7,343	0.17	0.03	0.02
10,000	148,152	89,128	2.30	0.48	0.23
100,000	1,898,240	1,048,006	28.65	6.30	2.88

that the "search from both ends and exchange" version of quicksort runs slightly faster on the Ridge than the version based on rotation.

Actually, the tightness of the inner loop is not as relevant as it may seem, because the number of iterations is generally very small. If the median element comes to rest p percent of the way through the interval, then the probability that an element chosen from the future left portion is out of place is $1 - p$ and the expected number of iterations of the inner loop is

$$(1 - p) + 2p(1 - p) + 3p^2(1 - p) + \cdots = 1/(1 - p).$$

For the right subinterval the expected number of iterations is $1/p$. Thus, with perfect partitioning, each loop iterates only twice.

Table 8.6 gives the running times of quicksort, using all of the improvements we have discussed.

8.5   Mergesort

The basic mergesort algorithm was discussed in Section 7.1 as part of our treatment of divide-and-conquer algorithms. In this section, we consider two enhancements that improve its performance.

Each pass of mergesort does approximately the same amount of work: each pass involves exactly n data moves and approximately n comparisons. The latter value varies somewhat, since, whenever one of the two lists being merged is exhausted, the other can simply be copied without further comparisons. As a consequence, mergesort spends a significant percentage of its time just getting started. For instance, building up runs of length 16 accounts for nearly 25% of the time spent in sorting an array of 100,000 elements and 40% of the time spent in sorting an array of 1000 elements. This observation leads to our first

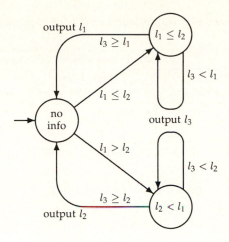

Figure 8.5: Transition Diagram for Three-Way Mergesort

enhancement: as in quicksort, we shall use insertion sort for sorting small arrays; specifically, we replace the first few passes of mergesort with a single insertion sort pass that sorts small contiguous blocks. For all but the initial segment, we can use our most efficient version of insertion sort, since the location for the sentinel falls inside the array. For the initial segment, we can place the sentinel on the right and sort right-to-left.

Our second enhancement is to use multiway merging, i.e., to merge more than two runs into a single long run, in order to reduce the number of passes. The number of passes required for m-way merging is $\lceil \log_m n \rceil$, assuming that we do not use insertion sort to build initial runs; thus m-way merging reduces the number of passes by a factor of $\lg m$ over two-way merging. However, the cost of merging increases with increasing m: the smallest of m objects must be found each time an object is transferred to the output array. Both enhancements have the additional benefit of reducing the amount of paging, because they reduce the number of passes.

We consider three-way merging. If the effect of boundary conditions, such as the exhaustion of one of the runs, is ignored, then the obvious implementation of three-way merging does $2n \log_3 n \approx 1.26n \lg n$ comparisons, or about 25% more than two-way merging, but does only $n \log_3 2 \approx 0.63n$ moves. Moreover, we can "have our cake and eat it too," since we need not always make two comparisons: depending on the outcome of previous comparisons, the ordering of the two list heads not selected for transfer may already be known. The general situation is depicted in Figure 8.5, which shows the transition diagram between the three

Table 8.7: Number of Comparisons and Moves Made by Mergesort

	Number of comparisons and moves					
	Two-way (No insertion sort)		Three-way (No insertion sort)		Three-way (With insertion sort)	
Size	Compares	Moves	Compares	Moves	Compares	Moves
500	3,860	5,000	4,369	3,000	5,169	5,184
1,000	8,719	10,000	9,342	8,000	10,434	8,900
10,000	123,660	140,000	126,322	100,000	140,482	111,572
100,000	1,566,536	1,800,000	1,634,420	1,200,000	1,791,038	1,366,519

possible states of knowledge. Irrespective of the number of comparisons needed on this cycle, one comparison will be needed on the next cycle if the third list head is the smallest element; otherwise two comparisons will be needed. If we ignore boundary conditions, the third list head must be the smallest one-third of the time; therefore, the average number of comparisons per move is $5/3$. We conclude that three-way mergesort makes a total of about $1.05n \lg n$ comparisons—only 5% more than two-way mergesort.

The issue of run length remains: the parenthesized figures of Table 8.3 do not allow us to discriminate between values in the range 8 to 24. Since 8 and 24 are a factor of three apart, we can always save one pass and choose the smallest run length that allows us to do so. A PASCAL implementation of three-way mergesort with all our improvements is given in Program 8.6.

While Table 8.7 shows that Program 8.6 did the most comparisons and more moves than three-way mergesort without insertion sort, it was consistently the fastest; its running times are given in Table 8.8.

Table 8.8: Sorting Integers with Three-Way Mergesort

	Time in seconds		
Size	PASCAL	VAX	Ridge
500	0.11	0.02	0.01
1,000	0.22	0.04	0.02
10,000	2.93	0.51	0.21
100,000	37.29	6.42	2.61

```
procedure MergeSort(var A, work: data; n: integer);
  (* Three-way mergesort with an insertion sort pass. *)
  var inA: boolean; (* where the data currently reside *)
      span, (* current length of runs *)
      runlength, (* length of initial runs *)
      i: integer;

  procedure Merge(var inarray, outarray: data; n: integer; span: integer);
    (* At a minimum, the procedure will do one two-way merge. *)
    label 100, 101, 102, 200, 300, 999;
    var i1, i2, i3, (* iX points to the first unprocessed element in run X. *)
        k, (* points to first free space in receiving array *)
        j1, j2, j3: (* jX points just past the end of run X. *)
            integer;
  begin
    i1 := 1; j1 := i1 + span;
    k := 1;
    repeat  (* until there is no second run *)
        (* The second run starts where the first stops. *)
        i2 := j1; j2 := i2 + span;
        if j2 >= n + 1
            then begin (* There is no third run. *)
                    j2 := n + 1;
                    goto 200 (* goto two-way merge *)
                 end;
        (* The third run starts where the second stops. *)
        i3 := j2; j3 := i3 + span;
        if j3 > n + 1 then j3 := n + 1; (* The third run is incomplete. *)
100: (* general three-way merge *)
        if inarray[i1] <= inarray[i2]
            then begin
                101: (* inarray[i2] is not the smallest *)
                    if inarray[i1] <= inarray[i3]
                        then begin (* order is 1 <= ? <= ? *)
                                outarray[k] := inarray[i1]; i1 := i1 + 1; k := k + 1;
                                if i1 < j1
                                    then goto 100 (* goto general three-way merge *)
                                    else begin (* first run is exhausted *)
                                            (* Maintain stability: do not do
                                                i1 := i3; j1 := j3 *)
                                            i1 := i2; j1 := j2;
                                            i2 := i3; j2 := j3
                                            (* goto two-way merge *)
                                         end
                             end
                        else begin (* order is 3 < 1 <= 2 *)
                                outarray[k] := inarray[i3]; i3 := i3 + 1; k := k + 1;
                                if i3 < j3
                                    then goto 101; (* inarray[i2] is not the smallest *)
                                outarray[k] := inarray[i1]; i1 := i1 + 1; k := k + 1;
```

```
                                 if i1 = j1
                                    then begin
                                            i1 := i2; j1 := j2;
                                            goto 300 (* goto copy remainder *)
                                         end
                                 (* goto two-way merge *)
                               end
                    end
              else begin
                 102: (* inarray[i1] is not the smallest *)
                       if inarray[i2] <= inarray[i3]
                          then begin (* order is 2 <= ? <= ? *)
                                  outarray[k] := inarray[i2]; i2 := i2 + 1; k := k + 1;
                                  if i2 < j2
                                     then goto 100 (* goto general three-way merge *)
                                     else begin (* second run is exhausted *)
                                             i2 := i3; j2 := j3
                                             (* goto two-way merge *)
                                          end
                               end
                          else begin (* order is 3 < 2 < 1 *)
                                  outarray[k] := inarray[i3]; i3 := i3 + 1; k := k + 1;
                                  if i3 < j3
                                     then goto 102; (* inarray[i1] is not the smallest *)
                                  outarray[k] := inarray[i2]; i2 := i2 + 1; k := k + 1;
                                  if i2 = j2
                                     then goto 300 (* goto copy remainder *)
                                  (* goto two-way merge *)
                               end
                    end;

     200: (* two-way merge *)
          if inarray[i1] <= inarray[i2]
             then begin
                     outarray[k] := inarray[i1]; i1 := i1 + 1; k := k + 1;
                     if i1 < j1
                        then goto 200 (* goto two-way merge *)
                        else begin
                                i1 := i2; j1 := j2
                                (* goto copy remainder *)
                             end
                  end
             else begin
                     outarray[k] := inarray[i2]; i2 := i2 + 1; k := k + 1;
                     if i2 < j2
                        then goto 200 (* goto two-way merge *)
                     (* goto copy remainder *)
                  end;
```

```
300: (* copy remainder of remaining run *)
       repeat
         outarray[k] := inarray[i1]; i1 := i1 + 1; k := k + 1
       until i1 = j1;
       i1 := k;
       j1 := i1 + span
     until j1 > n; (* until there is no second run *)

     while i1 <= n do (* Copy over any unmatched first segment. *)
       begin
         outarray[i1] := inarray[i1]; i1 := i1 + 1
       end
   end; (* Merge *)

begin (* MergeSort *)
   (* Insertion sort is used on small pieces to limit the number of passes. *)
   (* Determine the length of the initial runs. *)
   span := 8;
   while span < n do span := 3*span;
   runlength := 8; (* Run lengths of 8 and 24 differ by one pass. *)
   (* Incrementally increase the run length until one pass is saved. *)
   if span > 8
     then begin
             span := span div 3;
             repeat
               span := (span div runlength) * (runlength+1);
               runlength := runlength + 1
             until span >= n
           end;
   if runlength >= n then ... (* just use insertion sort and return *)
   ... (* The first segment must be sorted right-to-left. *)
   ... (* The remaining small pieces can be sorted left-to-right. *)
   inA := true; (* The data are initially in A. *)
   span := runlength;
   repeat (* until we can guarantee that the array is sorted *)
     if inA
       then Merge(A,work,n,span)
       else Merge(work,A,n,span);
     inA := not inA;
     span := 3*span
   until span >= n;
   (* If the final result is in the wrong array, then transfer it back. *)
   if not inA then for i := 1 to n do A[i] := work[i]
999: (* exit for arrays sorted entirely by insertion sort *)
   end; (* MergeSort *)
```

Program 8.6: Three-Way Mergesort

8.6 Heapsort

As was the case for mergesort, we have already discussed the basic algorithm in the text (Section 3.1) and thus only present enhancements in this section. For convenience we repeat the code in Program 8.7, modified slightly to follow the conventions used in this chapter. The basic algorithm makes two data comparisons and one data move with every iteration of the inner loop of the sift-down operation. Since half the elements of the heap are on the bottom level and three-fourths are on the final two levels, a random value will normally filter down to near the bottom. Furthermore, the value being sifted down during heapsort is not random—it comes from a leaf position and so is typically smaller than a randomly selected value. Therefore, by removing the test

```
if X >= A[j] then goto 99
```

from the inner loop, we reduce the number of comparisons by about half; the net result is to create a hole at a leaf position, which is the likely, but not necessarily correct, location for X. The correct location can now be found by sifting X back up into the heap; hence we replace the assignment A[i] := X with the following:

```
(* 1 > 3 at the start of the iteration ensures a sentinel during sift-up. *)
j := i div 2; (* reverse roles of i and j *)
if A[j] < X
  then repeat
          A[i] := A[j];
          i := j;
          j := j div 2
       until A[j] >= X;
A[i] := X
```

Sifting up requires only one comparison per level; moreover, the expectation is that the repeat loop will never execute or will terminate almost immediately. Thus the average number of data object comparisons is cut almost in half, while the number of moves remains about the same. For lack of a better name we call this enhanced program "heapsort with bounce."

Our second enhancement is very similar in nature to the second improvement proposed for mergesort: we can reduce the height of the heap, and thus the average number of moves used in sifting down a value, by using k-heaps, where k, the number of children associated with a node, is larger than two—typically, three or four. We used this approach in Section 5.3 to limit the worst-case behavior of Prim's algorithm on dense graphs. Ignoring the bounce technique for a moment, we note that a single iteration of the inner loop does k comparisons and one move. As k increases, the chances of sifting all the way down to the leaves increases; thus we anticipate $k \log_k n$ comparisons and $\log_k n$ moves. With $k = 3$ we get both fewer comparisons ($1.89 \lg n$ *vs.* $2 \lg n$) and fewer moves ($0.63 \lg n$ vs. $\lg n$); with $k = 4$ we get the same number of comparisons, but half as many moves. Moreover, the number of moves, which equals the number of iterations, also measures the overhead. Thus both 3-heaps and 4-heaps offer an improvement over 2-heaps.

The two enhancements can be combined, as shown in Program 8.8. However, the effectiveness of the bounce technique decreases with increasing k, because it saves only one out of k comparisons per iteration. The analysis of the total number of moves remains the same, although the estimate of $\log_k n$ is too low when the bounce technique is used and too high when it is not. The number of comparisons becomes $(k - 1) \log_k n$; converted to logarithms in base 2, the coefficients are 1, 1.26, and 1.5 for values of k of two, three, and four. Experimental results on an array of 100,000 random integers are reported in Table 8.9. When sorting strings, as in our earlier example, using 2-heaps with bounce is most appropriate since comparisons dominate. (Although heapsort with 2-heaps without bounce compares an average of only 1.86 characters, fewer than the 2.46 reported in Table 8.2 for 2-heaps with bounce, it also makes 1.75 times as many function calls, a losing trade-off.)

```
while l > 3 do (* l is index of end of heap *)
  begin
    X := A[l];
    A[l] := A[l];
    l := l - 1;
    i := 1; (* i is index of parent *)
    j := 2; (* j is index of left/greater child *)
    repeat (* The parent always has two children. *)
      if A[j] < A[j+1] then j := j + 1; (* Find larger child. *)
      if X >= A[j] then goto 99; (* We have found the insertion point. *)
      A[i] := A[j];
      i := j;
      j := 2*j
    until j >= l; (* j points at or past the end of the heap. *)
    if j = l (* i points to a parent with only one child--very rare. *)
      then if X < A[j]
              then begin
                     A[i] := A[j];
                     i := j
                   end;
99: A[i] := X
  end
```

Program 8.7: Inner Loop of Standard Heapsort

```
procedure HeapSort(var A: data; n: integer);
  label 98;
  var i, j, k, l: integer;
      X, temp: datum;
      m, m1, m2: integer;

begin
  (* Heap Creation Phase *)
  (* Avoid the need to check for parents without three children. *)
  m := (n-1) div 3; (* index of last node with three children *)
  m1 := m+m+m+2; (* index of first node not viewed as a child, if any *)
  (* Make sure that any extra nodes have a sentinel for their eventual entry
     into the heap via sift-up operations. *)
  if m1 <= n (* There is at least one extra node. *)
    then begin
            if m1 < n (* There are two extra nodes. *)
              then if A[m1] < A[n]
                      then m2 := n
                      else m2 := m1
              else m2 := m1;
            if A[1] < A[m2]
              then begin
                      temp := A[1]; A[1] := A[m2]; A[m2] := temp
                   end
         end;

  for l := m downto 1 do
    begin (* Sift down element at A[l]. *)
      X := A[l];
      i := l; j := i+i+i;
      repeat (* The parent always has three children. *)
        k := j - 1; (* k points to the largest child *)
        if A[k] < A[j] then k := j;
        if A[k] < A[j+1] then k := j + 1;
        A[i] := A[k];
        i := k; j := i+i+i
      until j > m1; (* j no longer points to a middle child *)
      j := (i+1) div 3; (* reverse roles of i and j *)
      repeat (* no sentinel during heapify *)
        if A[j] >= X then goto 98;
        A[i] := A[j];
        i := j; j := (j+1) div 3
      until j < l;
   98: A[i] := X
    end;
```

```
for l := m1 to n do (* Sift up any extra nodes. *)
   begin
      X := A[l];
      i := l; j := (i+1) div 3;
      if A[j] < X
        then begin
                repeat
                   A[i] := A[j];
                   i := j; j := (j+1) div 3
                until A[j] >= X;
                A[i] := X
             end
   end;

(* Repeatedly remove the maximum element and place it at the end. *)
l := n; (* l marks the end of the heap *)
while l > 4 do
   begin
      X := A[l];
      A[l] := A[1];
      l := l - 1;
      i := 1; j := 3;
      repeat (* The parent always has three children. *)
         k := j - 1;
         if A[k] < A[j] then k := j;
         if A[k] < A[j+1] then k := j + 1;
         A[i] := A[k];
         i := k; j := i+i+i
      until j >= l;
      j := j - 1; (* move to potential leftmost child *)
      if j <= l (* if we are at the very end of the tree--rare *)
        then begin
                if j < l
                  then if A[j] < A[l] then j := l;
                A[i] := A[j];
                i := j
             end;
      (* Sift element up into correct place. *)
      j := (i+1) div 3;
      if A[j] < X (* This is only rarely true. *)
        then repeat
                A[i] := A[j];
                i := j; j := (j+1) div 3
             until A[j] >= X;
      A[i] := X
   end;
   ... special processing for the last four (or fewer) elements ...
end; (* HeapSort *)
```

Program 8.8: Heapsort with 3-Heaps and Bounce

Table 8.9: Number of Comparisons and Moves Made by Heapsort

Variation of heapsort	Comparisons	Moves
2-heap	3,019,742	1,874,981
2-heap with bounce	1,699,595	1,960,276
3-heap	2,897,463	1,312,322
3-heap with bounce	2,084,253	1,356,193
4-heap	3,077,721	1,105,101
4-heap with bounce	2,446,490	1,135,202

By examining the values in Tables 8.2, 8.7, and 8.9 and the running times reported in various tables throughout the chapter, we see that heapsort suffers from higher overhead. The overhead is especially apparent in the assembly language versions, where quicksort and mergesort are roughly twice as fast, despite the fact that the total numbers of comparisons and moves for all three algorithms are roughly the same. In Section 8.1 we gave a brief explanation: the memory reference pattern for heapsort is not sequential and address computations become more complex. To make heapsort competitive at the assembly language level, we had to resort to a number of "dirty tricks." First, there is really no need to maintain the variable i explicitly; it is used only to indicate the location of the hole, which is better maintained as an address kept in a register. The variable j is maintained as the byte offset from the start of the array, rather than in integer format. We cannot, however, just maintain the address of A[j], because the multiplication used in computing the address of the children applies only to the offset. These problems are more serious on the Ridge than on the VAX; the addressing modes of the VAX make a natural translation of the PASCAL implementation of the heapsort algorithm possible, although the offset(Rx)[Ry] addressing mode, which permits direct encoding of memory references like A[j+1], is slower (on the VAX 11/780 implementation of the VAX architecture) than the simpler modes.

A generally useful technique for speeding up inner loops involving successive comparison operations, such as the lines

```
k := j - 1;
if A[k] < A[j] then k := j;
if A[k] < A[j+1] then k := j + 1
```

from Program 8.8, is to use the position in the code to record the state of the computation. Effectively, we replace these three lines with

Table 8.10: Sorting Integers with Heapsort

Size	Time in seconds		
	PASCAL	VAX	Ridge
500	0.13	0.03	0.01
1,000	0.30	0.06	0.03
10,000	3.94	0.91	0.34
100,000	50.60	13.43	4.93

```
if A[j-1] >= A[j]
  then if A[j-1] >= A[j+1]
        then ... (* left child is largest *)
        else ... (* right child is largest *)
  else if A[j] >= A[j+1]
        then ... (* middle child is largest *)
        else ... (* right child is largest *)
```

At each if and at the then and else clauses, we know exactly where the data are located and how to update the address of A[i] for the next iteration. There are no extraneous register-to-register transfers or additions and subtractions.

Lastly we consider the merits of using the bounce technique, which, as we can see from Table 8.9, saves a large number of comparisons for a small increase in the number of moves and loop iterations. Unfortunately, sifting up uses an integer division and divisions are invariably slower than the other operations in the inner loops—so much slower that, on many machines, the time spent on the division exceeds that spent on all the other instructions combined. A similar, but less drastic, situation involves the multiplications during the sift-down phase. In Program 8.8 we have replaced the logical j := 3*i with j := i+i+i, the two additions generally being faster than the multiplication. We have no similar mechanism to reduce the time taken by the integer division by three. For 2-heaps and 4-heaps, however, the multiplications and divisions can be performed by shifting, which is generally a fast operation.

The results of our experiments are presented in Table 8.10. The times given for the PASCAL version are for 3-heaps with bounce, whereas the times for the assembly language versions are for 3-heaps without this addition. Each encoding was the fastest approach for its environment.

Unlike all the other sorting algorithms, heapsort requires that the array be 1-based, i.e., that its first element occupy A[1], because the actual subscripts play a significant role in the algorithm. The C programming language assumes that all arrays are 0-based, while FORTRAN 77, PASCAL, and ADA all allow the user to declare the lower bound of an array. Fortunately, even if the array is not 1-based, most programming languages allow the perspective to be changed across a subroutine boundary: FORTRAN makes this change by declaring the formal parameter to be 1-based; ADA makes it with an explicit type coercion; in C, this change can be made with the code

```
void HeapSort(int *A, unsigned long int n)
{
    const int *B = A-1;
```

and then by referencing the array elements as B[ ]—although this is technically illegal, despite the fact that we never reference B[0] and thus never stray outside the bounds of the array.

Heapsort is the preferred algorithm when incremental sorting is needed, because it finds the m smallest elements in $\Theta(n + m \log n)$ time. Mergesort and Shell's method, on the other hand, must virtually complete the sorting operation before the smallest element is known with certainty. Quicksort can be modified, by always having it sort the left segment before the right segment, to provide the first few elements in order without completing the entire sort; however, this modification, while it runs in linear time with logarithmic extra storage on average, may require quadratic time with linear extra storage in the worst case.

8.7   Distribution and Radix Sort

Radix sort is unique among the sorting algorithms in this chapter in that it deals with the internal representation of the data objects and performs no direct comparisons between items. As a result, the fine details are highly dependent on the design of the CPU. Higher-level language implementations, except for those in C, which has the necessary masking and shifting operators, are inappropriate, and even a C language implementation of the meta-algorithm is dependent on the data type. At the algorithmic level, radix sort is a sophisticated example of *distribution sort*, which we now consider.

Suppose that we wish to sort an array with declarations as follows:

```
type datum = lowvalue..highvalue; (* subrange of ordinal type *)
        (* A ordinal type allows indexing as well as comparison with <. *)
```

If the length of the array exceeds the number of possible keys, M, there will necessarily be ties in the data; the larger the array, the more numerous the ties will be. Distribution sort takes advantage of this situation by basing its work on the range of key values. For each value in the range, it determines the number of items of that value and effectively partitions the array into segments, one for

```
procedure DistributionSort(var A: data; n: integer);
  var count: array [datum] of integer;
      i, j, k: integer;
  begin
    (* M = highvalue - lowvalue + 1 *)
    (* Initialize the distribution counts; this takes M steps. *)
    for i := lowvalue to highvalue do count[i] := 0;

    (* Build the distribution counts; this takes n steps. *)
    for i := 1 to n do count[A[i]] := count[A[i]] + 1;

    (* Refill the array; this takes max(n,M) steps. *)
    k := 0;
    for i := lowvalue to highvalue do
      for j := 1 to count[i] do
        begin
          k := k + 1;
          A[k] := i
        end
  end; (* DistributionSort *)
```

Program 8.9: Sorting by Distribution

each key value. Then the algorithm redistributes the items into the segments. Program 8.9 implements this idea under the assumption that no records are associated with the keys. In this case a final redistribution is unnecessary, since the distribution counts contain all the information present in the original array. When records are associated with keys, the final redistribution can be done in two ways: in place, using "musical chairs" (see Exercise 8.14), or using an extra array of size n, which gives us a stable implementation. Sorting by distribution takes time linear in the size of the array to sort and is linear in space and time in the range of data values. While distribution sort is clearly the best algorithm for sorting values in a narrow range, the importance of the $\Theta(M)$ contribution to the total running time of the algorithm should not be underestimated: as formulated, this algorithm is totally useless for sorting arrays of arbitrary integers.

The basic idea behind radix sort is that of distribution sort, with additional work designed to remedy the fundamental flaw of the latter. The range of values assumed by a key is an exponential function of its length in bits; in order to limit the range, radix sort considers only a small portion of a key at a time, thereby effectively working with subkeys. For expository purposes we initially restrict our attention to unsigned integers.

In our discussion of stability, we proved that a multikey array, when sorted successively from the least significant key to the most significant key by a stable

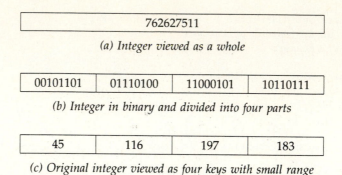

(a) Integer viewed as a whole

(b) Integer in binary and divided into four parts

(c) Original integer viewed as four keys with small range

Figure 8.6: Division of an Integer into a Four-Key Record

sorting algorithm, becomes properly sorted. Radix sort constructs artificial keys
by using the bit patterns within the data and uses distribution sort as a stable
sorting algorithm to sort on each successive key until the entire array is sorted.
The goal is to balance the number of key fields against the range of key values
so that very few passes are made and yet each pass may use distribution sort
and thus take only linear time. Figure 8.6 illustrates the basic concepts involved
in the construction of keys. In the figure, we have assumed a 32-bit word and
a binary representation and have chosen to let each key field correspond to a
byte. This division yields four passes and only moderate overhead (the $\Theta(M)$
portions of the code), since the auxiliary array has size 256. The points of division
are arbitrary—we could have divided the word into one 10-bit and two 11-bit
portions, thereby representing 762,627,511 as (181, 1688, 1463) rather than as
(45, 116, 197, 183) and saving one pass at the cost of increased overhead. It is not
even necessary to restrict ourselves to bit boundaries: nothing prevents us from
expressing the key in a base other than a power of 2. This general approach is at
the origin of the name for this sorting method: the term *radix* is a synonym, now
fallen into disuse, for base. The main advantage of partitioning a word along bit
boundaries is that isolating a key uses only shifting and masking instead of the
more general and considerably slower integer division and remainder required
for general bases.

Thus radix sort orders an array of unsigned integers by successively sorting
the array from the least significant "digit" to the most significant "digit," using a
stable version of distribution sort for each pass. Since the key used by distribution
sort is not the entire integer, the remainder of the integer word effectively forms
a record associated with the key. After the distribution counts are constructed,
it is a simple matter to determine the consecutive range of locations within the
array where the records with any particular key must be placed. If d_j is the

```
type datum = 0..maxint;
procedure RadixPass(var A, work: data; n: integer;
                        lowbit, highbit: integer);
  (* One pass of radix sort.
     Key/digit occupies bit positions lowbit..highbit, inclusive,
     with the least significant bit of the word in position zero. *)
  const UpperBound = ...;
  var count, start: array [0..UpperBound] of integer;
      (* UpperBound must be high enough to accommodate a bit pattern of ones,
          i.e., greater than or equal to 2**(highbit-lowbit+1) - 1. *)
      i, M, d: integer;
  function extract(i: datum; highbit, lowbit: integer): integer;
    (* Extract from i the bits in positions highbit down to lowbit and
       return them as an integer in the range 0 .. 2**(highbit-lowbit+1) - 1.
       This would be done in-line in assembly language with shifting and masking. *)
    ... not shown ...
  function TwoToTheN(n: integer): integer;
    ... not shown ...

begin
  M := TwoToTheN(highbit-lowbit+1) - 1;

  (* Initialize the distribution counts; this takes M steps. *)
  for i := 0 to M do count[i] := 0;

  (* Build the distribution counts; this takes n steps. *)
  for i := 1 to n do
    begin
      d := extract(A[i],highbit,lowbit);
      count[d] := count[d] + 1
    end;

  (* Calculate the starting indices for output; this takes M steps. *)
  start[0] := 1;
  for i := 1 to M do start[i] := start[i-1] + count[i-1];

  (* Move the data to the output array; this takes n steps. *)
  for i := 1 to n do
    begin
      d := extract(A[i],highbit,lowbit);
      work[start[d]] := A[i];
      start[d] := start[d] + 1
    end
end; (* RadixPass *)
```

Program 8.10: One Pass of Radix Sort

number of records that have j as their key value, then the starting index for the records that have key value i is given by $s_i = 1 + \sum_{j=0}^{i-1} d_j$; all of these indices can be computed in a single $\Theta(M)$ pass. During the redistribution phase we rescan the array; using the value of the key field as an index into the array of starting locations, we immediately determine the correct location for each element of A, move it there, and increment the starting location for that key value. To maintain stability, the scan must proceed left to right and so the output must go into a second array. As in mergesort, the algorithm rocks back and forth between the original array and the work array. Program 8.10 implements one pass of radix sort. For the sake of clarity we have restricted the procedure to processing keys delimited by bit boundaries. Since PASCAL is so ill suited to the bit-manipulation operations required for an efficient implementation of radix sort, we did not time the PASCAL code for this algorithm.

Before coding an assembly language version of this algorithm, we must choose the number of pieces into which an integer word is to be divided. For a datum of fixed length, radix sort is linear in the size of the array to sort, since each pass is linear and the number of passes is constant. On the other hand, the inner loop of radix sort is more complex than any that we have seen so far in a sorting algorithm, so that the coefficient of the linear term is relatively high. We need to keep the number of passes small if we are to make radix sort competitive with quicksort, for example. Two passes do not suffice, because a 32-bit integer would yield two keys of 16 bits each and thus require an array of 65,536 words to hold the distribution counts, more storage than used by the array being sorted in all but our largest runs. Splitting the 32-bit word into three pieces of 10 bits, 11 bits, and 11 bits, respectively, requires 2048 words for the distribution counts, not an excessive number; splitting it into four bytes requires only 256 words and has the minor advantage of automatically returning the final sorted output to the original array. When long arrays are sorted, the $\Theta(M)$ time portion of Program 8.10 becomes increasingly unimportant and the three-piece split should take roughly three-fourths of the time taken by the four-piece split.

One improvement that we can make to the code of Program 8.10 saves 50% of the space overhead. Notice that, once the array of starting locations has been constructed, there is no longer any need for the array of distribution counts. Therefore we can overlap their storage. The line start[i] := start[i-1] + count[i-1] becomes start[i] := start[i-1] + start[i], which can be implemented very efficiently in the assembly language of most machines.

We now look at some of the machine-dependent details that are unavoidably part of any implementation of radix sort. Table 8.11 gives the running time of radix sort for our standard test data. These data pose a slight problem: they consist of signed integers. In two's complement representation, the array of starting locations must be initialized on the last pass with

```
start[M div 2 + 1] := 1;
  (* 100... is the first bit pattern to indicate negative values. *)
for i := M div 2 + 2 to M do
  start[i] := start[i-1] + count[i-1];
start[0] := start[M] + count[M]; (* positives start where negatives stop *)
for i := 1 to M div 2 do
  start[i] := start[i-1] + count[i-1];
```

In order to maximize the speed of radix sort, we can replace calls to RadixPass with in-line code; this replacement allows us to take care of special cases directly and, more importantly, allows the use of immediate operands in shift instructions, as is required by many architectures.

As noted earlier, we should expect that division of a key into three subkeys would result in an implementation that runs in three-fourths of the time of an implementation that divides the key into four subkeys, at least if the size of the array to sort dominates the size of the subkey space. Because of specialized byte-oriented instructions, such may not be the case: both the VAX and the Ridge have instructions (MOVZBL and LOADB, respectively) which move a byte from memory to a register and clear the remaining high-order bits of the destination. On the VAX, where the various indexed addressing modes can be used to convert implicitly this 0-based integer index to a byte offset, the shifting and masking operations can be eliminated altogether and the inner loop shortened significantly. Experiments show that the four-pass implementation that divides a word along byte boundaries is faster than the three-pass implementation based on a 10-bit, 11-bit, and 11-bit split. The lack of memory-to-memory data transfer capability and automatic indexing on the Ridge makes it impossible to shorten the length of the inner loop enough to compensate for the extra pass, and the three-way split performs better.

The results reported in Table 8.11 deserve close scrutiny. Since radix sort is a linear-time algorithm, the data in the table are very disconcerting: the ratio

Table 8.11: Sorting Integers with Radix Sort

Size	VAX	Time in seconds Ridge (3 keys)	Ridge (4 keys)
500	0.03	0.02	0.01
1,000	0.06	0.03	0.02
10,000	0.63	0.23	0.26
100,000	7.43	2.85	3.58

of the time taken to sort 100,000 numbers to that taken to sort 10,000 numbers varies from 11.8 to 13.9 instead of being slightly under 10.0. The extra time is due to the architecture of the two computers. The VAX has cache memory, which decreases the effective cycle time of the main memory. Because the redistribution phase of radix sort references the locations of the output array in a random manner, the chance that any given random reference will result in a cache miss increases as the array increases in size. Each instruction not in the constant-time portion of the algorithm executes exactly ten times as often, but the instructions that reference memory appear to execute more slowly. The Ridge computer does not have a cache memory for data, but it does have a page table cache to speed up the translation of virtual addresses. (The VAX also has such a cache.) As the size of the array increases, the page table cache can no longer hold the entire page table and the effective memory cycle time increases as the translation of virtual addresses slows down. The page table cache is large enough to hold the translation information for the input and output arrays as well as for local storage when the arrays do not exceed about 7000 words. Up to this size the running time per element remains virtually constant, with an ever so slight decrease as the array increases in size—just as the theory predicts. Another consequence of the random pattern of reference to the output array is that the working set of the algorithm is very large, so that page faults will overwhelm the computation unless the entire output array can be held in main memory during the redistribution phase.

A significant drawback of radix sort is that it must be recoded for each new data type. With single- or double-precision floating-point numbers, the situation is considerably more complex than with integers. Signed-magnitude representation, with normalized fractional parts and the exponent expressed in excess notation, is widely used. Careful attention must be paid to the representation used on any given machine to make sure that, when the datum is divided into integer key fields and the sort is performed, the net effect is to sort the objects with respect to the original ordering relation. On the other hand, radix sort gains over our other algorithms when sorting floating-point numbers in that it treats the objects as integers and thus takes advantage of the faster integer arithmetic. In particular, on the VAX and the Ridge, radix sort takes the same time to sort an array of single-precision floating-point numbers as it does to sort an array of integers, whereas other sorting algorithms show worse performance when applied to floating-point numbers. On the VAX, where the only change necessary to quicksort is the conversion of CMPL (compare longword) instructions to CMPF (compare floating) instructions wherever data comparisons are performed, quicksort shows a performance degradation from 6.30 seconds to 8.14 seconds on 100,000 numbers. For double-precision numbers, radix sort loses some of this advantage, because it uses twice as many passes. However, if the data are known

Table 8.12: Sorting Double-Precision Numbers

Size	Quicksort VAX	Quicksort Ridge	Radix sort VAX (3 bytes)	Radix sort VAX (4 bytes)	Radix sort Ridge
500	0.03	0.02	0.04	0.04	0.02
1,000	0.08	0.03	0.07	0.09	0.03
10,000	1.11	0.46	0.81	0.99	0.30
100,000	14.42	5.82	8.33	10.14	*

*Excessive page faults with a 2-Mbyte memory

to be widely distributed, then half of these passes can be eliminated. If radix sort is applied to only the significant word, with the extra 32 bits of precision in the lower-order word carried along during the redistribution, then the array will be nearly sorted after completion of radix sort. On both the VAX and the Ridge, two values can be out of order only if they agree on the sign, exponent and 23 or 20 bits of precision, respectively; such should only very rarely be the case. Insertion sort can be used to correct any inversions that are present. Unequal, but very close, data do not normally arise in scientific work, but extreme caution must be exercised to avoid a $\Theta(n^2)$ sorting algorithm. Yet fewer partial keys can be used: on the VAX, for instance, insertion sort continues to have little work to do if only the three most significant bytes of the more significant word are used by radix sort, since 15 bits of precision are still considered during the radix sort phase. Table 8.12 gives running times for quicksort and radix sort on double-precision numbers. Radix sort was applied to only (part of) the most significant word, with a final insertion sort pass to correct any errors. Values ranged from −1.0 to 1.0, thereby forcing the majority of the exponents into a narrow range.

Radix sort can also be run from left to right, i.e., from high-order byte to low-order byte; if nothing else, this order certainly feels more natural. When run in this way, radix sort looks very much like quicksort. After the first pass with a key of m bits, the output array is effectively divided into 2^m segments. If the items are unsigned integers, then the segments are in correct order relative to one another, while the data within each segment are in no particular order; this is exactly the property maintained by the partitioning pass of quicksort. With $m = 1$ the algorithm is known as *radix exchange sort* and behaves exactly like quicksort, except that it blindly chooses as the partitioning threshold the value exactly halfway between the highest and the lowest possible key values. As should be clear, this is not a good choice for the partitioning element.

8.8 Conclusions

We have seen that, in this most common of computing tasks, a large number of issues must be examined and that coding details, which we downplayed in other chapters, have a significant influence on the running time of the various sorting algorithms. Indeed, all of our algorithms benefitted substantially from two types of improvements: improvements in the underlying algorithm and improvements due to coding in assembly language. The two improvements appear to yield about equal benefits, which are evident throughout a wide range of problem sizes.

On the other hand, no amount of fine tuning affected the relative performance of the various algorithms; for instance, even our best PASCAL version of Shell's method does not match the speed of our basic versions of mergesort or quicksort. Hence we can make some general observations about our various sorting methods and their uses:

- In general, use quicksort, since (i) it uses an insignificant amount of extra storage; (ii) high-level language implementations can be mapped naturally by compilers to a wide variety of computer architectures; (iii) it has good virtual memory performance; and (iv) with a careful choice of the partitioning element, it practically never exhibits quadratic-time behavior.

- For applications that require stability, use mergesort; the extra storage requirements are common to all fast and stable sorting algorithms.

- For applications with running times that benefit from incremental sorting, use heapsort, but keep in mind the potential for excessive paging.

- For applications where the data must fall within a small range of values, as in a number of data collection and analysis problems, use distribution sort.

- Do not use radix sort, because it is too specialized and too dependent on the underlying architecture, unless you really need the very fastest sorting method and are willing to spend much time in tuning a program that will not be portable.

- For small problem instances or instances where the data are already nearly sorted, use insertion sort, as it is simple to code and has very low overhead.

8.9 Exercises

Exercise 8.1 Develop an algorithm that, given two lists of numbers, one of length m and the other of length n, determines whether the lists have a number in common. When the two lists have unequal lengths, your algorithm should run faster than the obvious algorithm that sorts both lists and then traverses them.

□

Exercise 8.2 Let $\mathcal{I} = \{I_1, I_2, \ldots, I_n\}$ be a set of intervals on the x-axis. Devise a $\Theta(n \log n)$ algorithm that finds the members of $\mathcal{I}$ that are contained in another member of $\mathcal{I}$. Prove that your algorithm is asymptotically optimal, by reducing the problem of element uniqueness to it.

□

Exercise 8.3 You are given an $n \times n$ matrix of numbers, sorted in increasing order within rows and within columns. Devise a $\Theta(n)$ algorithm that finds the location of an arbitrary value, x, in the matrix or reports that the item is not present. Further show that any algorithm must sometimes examine $\Theta(n)$ matrix entries in order to return the correct answer.

□

Exercise 8.4* Prove, using a decision tree model, a $\Omega(n \log n)$ bound for the problem of *element uniqueness*: given n numbers, decide whether or not two of them are the same. *Hint*: Your decision tree must separate permutations from n-tuples with repeated elements.

□

Exercise 8.5 Prove that, if the last few increments used in Shell's methods are 7, 5, 3, and 2, then each element is known to be greater than 77% of the elements to its left.

□

Exercise 8.6 [P] Study the number of comparisons and moves made during each pass of Shell's method. Use this information to construct better sequences of diminishing increments.

□

Exercise 8.7 Assume that the keys to be sorted have no associated records. Write a code fragment that implements the partitioning phase of quicksort and has the following properties: (i) it partitions the array into three subintervals as described by the invariant of Figure 8.4; and (ii) it moves each array element at most once. This partitioning method improves the performance of quicksort in the presence of many ties.

□

Exercise 8.8 Derive the formula that characterizes the probability of obtaining a split of x vs. $(100 - x)$ with median-of-three partitioning. Extend your formula to median-of-five partitioning; what can you conclude about this possible improvement to quicksort?

□

Exercise 8.9 This and the next two exercises consider the question of selection and median-finding. This exercise addresses the problem of finding the second smallest element; the next exercise generalizes this problem to that of finding the

kth smallest element; and the third leads to a linear-time algorithm for finding the median—a result which allows us to implement quicksort so as to ensure $\Theta(n \log n)$ running time.

The problem of *selection* is: given an array of numbers, find the kth smallest element of the array. This search can easily be done in $\Theta(n \log n)$ time by sorting the array and returning the value in the kth location. That we might do better is indicated by the fact that the smallest or largest element can each be found in exactly $n - 1$ comparisons.

Devise a method that finds the second smallest element in $n + \lg n - 2$ comparisons; this method makes up the first two steps of *tournament sort*. $\square$

Exercise 8.10 The method of the previous exercise generalizes to a selection algorithm that runs in $\Theta(n + \min(k, n-k) \lg n)$ time. A similar algorithm, based on heapsort, has the same running time. For both of these algorithms, the hardest element to find is the median.

The problem of selection can also be approached using ideas taken from quicksort; Program 8.11 implements this approach. What is the worst-case running time of this program? Show that its average-case performance is $\Theta(n)$, irrespective of k. $\square$

Exercise 8.11* [$\Theta(n)$ Median-Finding] In order to ensure that the worst-case running time for selection, as given in the last exercise, be $\Theta(n)$, we must ensure that the partitioning element partition the array into two pieces of roughly equal sizes. The median of a large collection can be closely approximated by first partitioning the large collection into a number of smaller collections, then taking the median of each small collection, and finally taking the median of the medians. This approximation leads to the following algorithm for determining the partitioning element:

- If n is small, find the median of the n elements directly and return the true median as the partitioning element. Since the maximum number of elements is fixed (to what value remains to be determined), this step takes constant time.

- Let m be the largest multiple of 5 not larger than n. Divide m of the n elements into $m/5$ groups of five elements each. Ignore any leftover elements for the present—they are not used in determining the partitioning element, although they are involved in the final partitioning.

- For each group of five elements, find the median; this step takes constant time for each group.

- Find the true median of the $m/5$ medians by recursively calling the procedure of Program 8.11, using the algorithm that we are now describing to find the partitioning element.

```
function Selection(var A: data; n, k: integer): datum;
  (* Return the kth smallest element of A[1..n]. *)
  procedure Partition(l, r: integer; var m: integer);
    (* Partition A[1..r] into A[1..m] and A[m+1..r] so that neither
       portion is empty and A[i] < A[j] if l <= i <= m and m < j <= r. *)
    ... not shown ...

  function Select(l, r, k: integer): datum;
    (* Return the kth smallest element of A[1..r]. *)
    var k1: integer;
    begin
      if l = r
        then Select := A[1] (* k = 1 *)
        else begin
                Partition(l,r,k1);
                (* Determine into which half the kth element falls. *)
                if k <= k1 - l + 1
                  then Select := Select(l,k1,k)
                        (* The kth element of A[1..r] is the kth element
                           of A[1..k1]. *)
                  else Select := Select(k1+1,r,k-(k1-l+1))
                        (* The kth element of A[1..r] is the k-(k1-l+1)st
                           element of A[k1+1..r] as k1 - l + 1 elements are
                           known to be smaller than the kth element. *)
             end
    end; (* Select *)
  begin
    Selection := Select(1,n,k)
  end; (* Selection *)
```

Program 8.11: A Solution to the Selection Problem Based on Quicksort

- Return this median of medians as the partitioning element.

Note that the entire selection algorithm becomes an intertwining of two recursive procedures. Selection calls Select, which calls both Select and Partition, and Partition, after (logically) transferring the medians to a separate array, B, calls Selection, with Selection(B, (r-l+1) div 10, (r-l+1) div 5). The original call to Selection need not have $k = \lfloor n/2 \rfloor$, although the internal calls do.

1. Show that the recurrence

$$\begin{cases} T(n) = T(pn) + T(qn) + \Theta(n) \\ T(1) = \Theta(1), \end{cases}$$

where $p + q < 1$, has solution $T(n) = \Theta(n)$. (See also Exercise 2.26.)

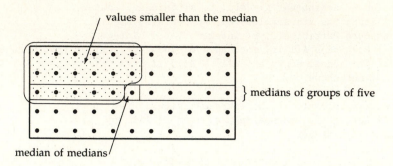

Figure 8.7: Determining the Worst Case for the Median of Medians

2. Show that the worst-case running time of Selection satisfies this recurrence. *Hint*: By considering Figure 8.7, which is drawn as if the data were sorted within groups of five and then sorted by medians, show that the median of medians cannot result in a split worse than 25–75. (The figure seems to imply a 30–70 split, but up to four elements are not included when finding the median of medians, yet are included in the actual partition. This observation can be used to determine the size of a base case.) The expected split is, of course, much better.

3. We need not move the medians of the groups of five elements to a temporary array. Everything can be done without significant extra storage by using the approach taken for doing the insertion sort within Shell's method. Code the $\Theta(n)$ version of Selection just described, as well as a version that uses the median of three as its partitioning element; compare the two versions. While we can now guarantee that quicksort is $\Theta(n \log n)$, does this approach make for a fast sorting algorithm?

□

Exercise 8.12 [P] An algorithm, known as *quickhull*, that finds the convex hull of a set of points closely resembles quicksort. The quickhull algorithm works with two points, P and Q, known to be on the hull and such that all of the other points lie to one side of the line passing through these two points. Selecting two such points initially can be done in linear time, since they are simply adjacent hull points. Thereafter, the algorithm proceeds recursively as follows:

• Find a new point, R, guaranteed to be on the hull. The point furthest from the line passing through P and Q must be on the hull and can be found in linear time.

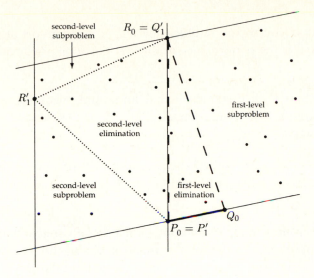

Figure 8.8: The Partition Step of Quickhull

- Use the line segments $\overline{PR}$ and $\overline{QR}$ to partition the set of points into three groups: those to the left of $\overline{PR}$, those to the right of $\overline{QR}$, and those interior to the triangle $\triangle PRQ$.

- Discard permanently any points interior to the triangle and solve each remaining subproblem recursively.

(See Figure 8.8, where the first second-level recursive call is shown in detail.) Program the quickhull algorithm and compare its performance with the algorithms described in Section 7.2. The reason for using the point farthest from the line segment $\overline{PQ}$ is that, from the perspective of the line segment, it appears to be a random choice, so that the partitioning eliminates a good percentage of the points and the two subproblems are of approximately equal size. What is the worst-case running time of quickhull? Its average-case running time? (As in our previous discussion of convex hulls, average-case analysis depends on the distribution of points and requires results from stochastic geometry.)   □

Exercise 8.13* Mergesort can be modified to take advantage of runs in the original data. Instead of merging two or three runs of fixed length, with the length doubling or trebling at each pass, the runs found in the data, whatever their length may be, are merged. The algorithm terminates when only one run remains. This technique is called *natural merging*. Work out the details of the approach. How does it compare in efficiency with the mergesort algorithm given in the text? What is the performance of the algorithm on nearly sorted data?

□

Exercise 8.14 Show that, if stability is not important, records can be sorted in place by distribution sort, using "musical chairs," in $\Theta(\max(M, n))$ time with $\Theta(M)$ extra storage.

□

Exercise 8.15 Show how to sort all the adjacency lists of a graph into increasing order by the degrees of the vertices in $\Theta(|V| + |E|)$ time and with $\Theta(|V| + |E|)$ extra storage.

□

Exercise 8.16 Develop an algorithm that sorts a list of variable-length strings of bits in time proportional to the total number of bits in the list of strings. The input is given as an array of pointers into an array of bits in which the actual strings are located.

□

Exercise 8.17 Assume that you have to sort an array of n items, where $O(\log n)$ distinct keys can occur. Show how to accomplish this task in $\Theta(n \log \log n)$ time. Why were you able to beat the $\Omega(n \log n)$ lower bound? What happens to your solution if the number of distinct keys grows as n^ϵ, for some $0 < \epsilon < 1$?   □

Exercise 8.18* Consider the numbers $x_1 < x_2 < \ldots < x_n$; assume that they are given to you as an unordered collection of ordered pairs, $\{(x_i, x_{i+1}) \mid i = 1, 2, \ldots, n - 1\}$. Show that you can sort these values in linear time.   □

8.10 Bibliography

Sorting is one of the oldest problems in computer science and has been the subject of thousands of publications. The state of the art as of 1973 is comprehensively described by Knuth [1973]; pages 379–388 of his text summarize the various methods and their history. Hence, instead of repeating his comments, we content ourselves with noting that insertion sort, selection sort, bubble sort, tournament sort, and mergesort are all part of the folklore of the discipline (Knuth attributes mergesort to John von Neumann around 1945) and that radix sort is even older, going back to the end of the 19th century and Hollerith's card sorters. On the other hand, several methods have well-defined origins: Shell's method is due to Shell [1959], heapsort to Williams [1964], quicksort to Hoare [1962], and bitonic sort and merge-exchange sort (discussed in Section 7.1) to Batcher [1968]. Knuth [1973] attributes the bounce technique for improving heapsort to R. W.

Floyd. Some of the developments since 1973 include better bounds (Sedgewick [1986]) and better increment sequences (Incerpi and Sedgewick [1986], Weiss and Sedgewick [1990]) for Shell's method; an extremely detailed analysis of the average-case behavior of heapsort (Carlsson [1987]); improved sorting networks, as mentioned in Section 7.1; and a number of results on parallel sorting, both from a worst-case and an average-case perspective (see, for instance, the articles of Shiloach and Vishkin [1981], Alon and Azar [1987], and Rajasekaran and Reif [1989]).

The linear-time algorithm for selection and median-finding is due to Blum *et al.* [1972]. The quickhull algorithm of Exercise 8.12 was first proposed by Eddy [1977]. For detail on natural mergesort, the reader should consult Knuth [1973].

REFERENCES

Aho, A.V., J.E. Hopcroft, and J.D. Ullman [1983]. *Data Structures and Algorithms.* Addison-Wesley, Reading, MA.

Aho, A.V., J.E. Hopcroft, and J.D. Ullman [1974]. *The Design and Analysis of Computer Algorithms.* Addison-Wesley, Reading, MA.

Aho, A.V., and N.A. Sloane [1973], "Some doubly exponential sequences," *Fibonacci Quarterly* **11**, pp. 429–437.

Ahuja, R.K., K. Mehlhorn, J.B. Orlin, and R.E. Tarjan [1988], "Faster algorithms for the shortest path problem," Tech. Rep. CS-TR-154-88, Princeton U., Princeton, NJ; also in final form in *J. ACM* **37** (1990), pp. 213–223.

Ahuja, R.K., J.B. Orlin, and R.E. Tarjan [1989], "Improved time bounds for the maximum flow problem," *SIAM J. Comput.* **18**, pp. 939–954.

Ajtai, M., J. Komlós, and E. Szemerédi [1983], "An $O(n \log n)$ sorting network," Proc. 15th Ann. ACM Symp. Theory Comput. STOC-83, pp. 1–9.

Alon, N., and Y. Azar [1987], "The average complexity of deterministic and randomized parallel comparison sorting algorithms," Proc. 28th Ann. IEEE Symp. Foundations Comput. Sci. FOCS-87, pp. 489–498.

Atkinson, M.D., J.-R. Sack, N. Santoro, and T. Strothotte [1986], "Min-max heaps and generalized priority queues," *Commun. ACM* **29**, pp. 996–1000.

Ball, G.H., and D.J. Hall [1967], "A clustering technique for summarizing multivariate data," *Behav. Sci.* **12**, pp. 153–155.

Batcher, K. [1968], "Sorting networks and their applications," Proc. AFIPS Joint Comput. Conf. **32**, pp. 307–314.

Bentley, J.L., D. Haken, and J. Saxe [1980], "A general method for solving divide-and-conquer recurrences," *SIGACT News* **12**, pp. 36–44.

Bentley, J.L., D.D. Sleator, R.E. Tarjan, and V.K. Wei [1986], "A locally adaptive data compression scheme," *Commun. ACM* **29**, pp. 320–330.

Berge, C. [1957], "Two theorems in graph theory," *Proc. Natl. Acad. Sci.* **43**, pp. 842–844.

Berlekamp, E.R., J.H. Conway, and R.K. Guy [1982]. *Winning Ways for your Mathematical Plays.* Academic Press, New York, NY, in 2 volumes.

Blum, M., R.W. Floyd, V.R. Pratt, R.L. Rivest, and R.E. Tarjan [1972], "Time bounds for selection," *J. Comput. Syst. Sci.* **7**, pp. 448–461.

Brigham, E.O. [1974]. *The Fast Fourier Transform.* Prentice-Hall, Englewood Cliffs, NJ.

Broder, A., and J. Stolfi [1984], "Pessimal algorithms and simplexity analysis," *SIGACT News* **16**, 3, pp. 49–53.

Brown, M.R. [1978], "Implementation and analysis of binomial queue algorithms," *SIAM J. Comput.* **7**, pp. 289–319.

Brown, M.R., and R.E. Tarjan [1980], "Design and analysis of a data structure for representing sorted lists," *SIAM J. Comput.* **9**, pp. 594–614.

Brucker, P. [1981]. *Scheduling.* Akademische Verlaggesellschaft, Wiesbaden (in German).

Camerini, P.M. [1978], "The min-max spanning tree problem and some extensions," *Inf. Process. Lett.* **7**, pp. 10–14.

Carlsson, S. [1987], "Average-case results on heapsort," *BIT* **27**, pp. 2–17.

Chazelle, B., and H. Edelsbrunner [1988], "An optimal algorithm for intersecting line segments in the plane," Proc. 29th Ann. IEEE Symp. Foundations Comput. Sci. FOCS-88, pp. 590–600.

Cheriton, D., and R.E. Tarjan [1976], "Finding minimum spanning trees," *SIAM J. Comput.* **5**, pp. 724–742.

Cheriyan, J., and S.N. Maheswari [1989], "Analysis of preflow push algorithms for maximum network flow," *SIAM J. Comput.* **18**, pp. 1057–1086.

Christofides, N. [1975]. *Graph Theory: An Algorithmic Approach.* Academic Press, New York, NY.

Chvátal, V. [1983]. *Linear Programming.* W.H. Freeman and Company, New York, NY.

Cooley, J.W., and J.W. Tukey [1965], "An algorithm for the machine calculation of complex Fourier series," *Math. Comput.* **19**, pp. 297–301.

Crane, C.A. [1972], "Linear lists and priority queues as balanced binary trees," Tech. Rep. STAN-CS-72-259, Stanford U., Stanford, CA.

Dantzig, G.B. [1965]. *Linear Programming and Extensions.* Princeton U. Press, Princeton, NJ.

Dinic, E.A. [1970], "Algorithm for solution of a problem of maximum flow in networks with power estimation," *Sov. Math. Dokl.* **11**, pp. 1277–1280.

Dobkin, D.P. [1987], "Computational geometry—then and now," Tech. Rep. CS-TR-084-87, Princeton U., Princeton, NJ.

Dobkin, D.P., and R. Lipton [1979], "On the complexity of computations under varying set of primitives," *J. Comput. Syst. Sci.* **18**, pp. 86–91.

Dobkin, D.P., and D. Silver [1988], "Recipes for geometry and numerical analysis; part I: an empirical study," Tech. Rep. CS-TR-144-88, Princeton U., Princeton, NJ.

Dowd, M., Y. Perl, L. Rudolph, and M. Saks [1989], "The periodic balanced sorting network," *J. ACM* **36**, pp. 738–757.

Driscoll, J.R., H.N. Gabow, R. Shrairman, and R.E. Tarjan [1988], "Relaxed heaps: an alternative to Fibonacci heaps with applications to parallel computation," *Commun. ACM* **31**, pp. 1343–1354.

Duda, R.O., and P.E. Hart [1973]. *Pattern Classification and Scene Analysis.* John Wiley, New York, NY (Chapter 5).

Eddy, W. [1977], "A new convex hull algorithm for planar sets," *ACM Trans. Math. Softw.* **3**, pp. 398–403.

Edelsbrunner, H. [1988] *Algorithms in Combinatorial Geometry.* EATCS Monographs in Theor. Comput. Sci. 10, Springer Verlag, New York, NY.

Edmonds, J. [1965a], "Matching and a polyhedron with 0-1 vertices," *J. Res. Natl. Bur. Stand.* **69B**, pp. 125–130.

Edmonds, J. [1965b], "The Chinese postman problem," *Oper. Res.* **13**, p. 373.

Edmonds, J. [1963], "Paths, trees, and flowers," *Can. J. Math.* **17**, pp. 449–467.

Edmonds, J. [1971], "Matroids and the greedy algorithm," *Math. Program.* **1**, pp. 127–136.

Edmonds, J., and E.L. Johnson [1973], "Matching, Euler tours, and the Chinese postman," *Math. Program.* **5**, pp. 88–124.

Edmonds, J., and R.M. Karp [1972], "Theoretical improvements in algorithmic efficiency for network flow problems," *J. ACM* **19**, pp. 248–264.

Even, S., and O. Kariv [1975], "An $n^{2.5}$ algorithm for maximum matching in graphs," Proc. 16th Ann. IEEE Symp. Foundations Comput. Sci. FOCS-75, pp. 100–112.

Even, S., and R.E. Tarjan [1975], "Network flow and testing graph connectivity," *SIAM J. Comput.* **4**, pp. 507–518.

Even, S. [1980]. *Graph Algorithms.* Computer Science Press, Rockville, MD.

Floyd, R.W. [1964], "Algorithm 245: treesort 3," *Commun. ACM* **7**, p. 701.

Gabow, H.N. [1983], "Scaling algorithms for network problems," Proc. 24th Ann. IEEE Symp. Foundations Comput. Sci. FOCS-83, pp. 248–257; also in final form in *J. Comput. Syst. Sci.* **31** (1985), pp. 148–168.

Gabow, H.N. [1976], "An efficient implementation of Edmonds' algorithm for maximum matching on graphs," *J. ACM* **23**, pp. 221–234.

Gabow, H.N., Z. Galil, and T.H. Spencer [1984], "Efficient implementation of graph algorithms using contraction," Proc. 25th Ann. IEEE Symp. Foundations Comput. Sci. FOCS-84, pp. 347–357; also in final form in *J. ACM* **36** (1989), pp. 540–572.

Gabow, H.N., Z. Galil, T.H. Spencer, and R.E. Tarjan [1986], "Efficient algorithms for finding minimum spanning trees in undirected and directed graphs," *Combinatorica* **6**, pp. 109–122.

Gabow, H.N., and R.E. Tarjan [1983], "Algorithms for two bottleneck optimization problems," *J. Algorithms* **9**, pp. 411–417.

Gabow, H.N., and R.E. Tarjan [1983], "A linear time algorithm for a special case of disjoint set union," Proc. 15th Ann. ACM Symp. Theory Comput. STOC-83, pp. 246–251.

Gale, D. [1968], "Optimal assignments in an ordered set: an application of matroid theory," *J. Comb. Theory* **4**, pp. 176–180.

Gale, D., and L.S. Shapley [1962], "College admissions and the stability of marriages," *Am. Math. Monthly* **69**, pp. 9–14.

Galil, Z. [1986], "Efficient algorithms for finding maximum matchings in graphs," *Comput. Surv.* **18**, pp. 23–38.

Galil, Z., S. Micali, and H. Gabow [1986], "Priority queues with variable priority and an $O(EV \log V)$ algorithm for finding a maximal weighted matching in general graphs," *SIAM J. Comput.* **15**, pp. 120–150.

Galler, B.A., and M.J. Fischer [1964], "An improved equivalence algorithm," *Commun. ACM* **7**, pp. 301–303.

Garey, M.R., and D.S. Johnson [1979]. *Computers and Intractability: A Guide to NP-Completeness.* W.H. Freeman, San Francisco, CA.

Giannessi, F., and B. Nicoletti [1979], "The crew scheduling problem: a travelling salesman approach," in *Combinatorial Optimization*, N. Christofides *et al.*, eds., John Wiley, New York, NY, pp. 389–408.

Gilmore, P.C., and R.E. Gomory [1964], "Sequencing a one state-variable machine: a solvable case of the traveling salesman problem," *Oper. Res.* **12**, pp. 655–679.

Goecke, O. [1988], "A greedy algorithm for hereditary set systems and a generalization of the Rado-Edmonds characterization of matroids," *Discrete Appl. Math.* **20**, pp. 39–49.

Goldberg, A.V., and R.E. Tarjan [1986], "A new approach to the maximum-flow problem," Proc. 18th Ann. ACM Symp. Theory Comput. STOC-86, pp. 136–146; also in final form in *J. ACM* **35** (1988), pp. 921–940.

Goldberg, A.V., E. Tardos, and R.E. Tarjan [1989], "Network flow algorithms," Tech. Rep. CS-TR-216-89, Princeton U., Princeton, NJ.

Graham, R.L. [1972], "An efficient algorithm for determining the convex hull of a finite planar set," *Inf. Process. Lett.* **1**, pp. 132–133.

Graham, R.L., and O. Hell [1985], "On the history of the minimum spanning tree problem," *Ann. Hist. Comput.* **7**, pp. 43–57.

Graham, R.L., D.E. Knuth, and O. Patashnik [1989]. *Concrete Mathematics: A Foundation for Computer Science.* Addison-Wesley, Reading, MA.

Greene, D.H., and D.E. Knuth [1982]. *Mathematics for the Analysis of Algorithms.* Birkhauser, Boston, MA.

Gries, D. and G. Levin [1980], "Computing Fibonacci numbers (and similarly defined functions) in log time," *Inf. Process. Lett.* **11**, pp. 68–69.

Guibas, L.J., E.M. McCreight, M.F. Plass, and J.R. Roberts [1977], "A new representation for linear lists," Proc. 9th Ann. ACM Symp. Theory Comput. STOC-77, pp. 49–60.

Guibas, L.J., and R. Sedgewick [1978], "A dichromatic framework for balanced trees," Proc. 19th Ann. IEEE Symp. Foundations Comput. Sci. FOCS-78, pp. 8–21.

Guibas, J.L., and R. Seidel [1986], "Computing convolutions by reciprocal search," Proc. 2nd Ann. ACM Symp. Comput. Geometry, pp. 90–99.

Hales, A.W., and R.I. Jewett [1963], "Regularity and positional games," *Trans. Am. Math. Soc.* **106**, pp. 222–229.

Hall, P. [1935], "On representations of subsets," *J. London Math. Soc.* **10**, pp. 26–30.

Held, M., and R.M. Karp [1970], "The traveling-salesman problem and minimum spanning trees," *Oper. Res.* **18**, pp. 1138–1162.

Held, M., and R.M. Karp [1971], "The traveling-salesman problem and minimum spanning trees: Part II," *Math. Program.* **1**, pp. 6–25.

Helman, P. [1987], "A fast, optimal data allocation algorithm with sensitivity analysis," Tech. Rep. CS87-5, U. of New Mexico, Albuquerque, NM.

Helman, P. [1989], "A theory of greedy structures based on k-ary dominance relations," Tech. Rep. CS89-11, U. of New Mexico, Albuquerque, NM.

Helman, P., B.M.E. Moret, and H.D. Shapiro [1989], "Exact characterizations of greedy structures," Tech. Rep. CS89-13, U. of New Mexico, Albuquerque, NM.

Ho, Y.-C., and R.L. Kashyap [1966], "A class of iterative procedures for linear inequalities," *SIAM J. Control* **4**, pp. 112–115.

Hoare, C.A.R. [1962], "Quicksort," *Comput. J.* **5**, pp. 10–15.

Hoffman, K., and K. Mehlhorn [1984], "Intersecting a line and a simple polygon," *Bull. Eur. Assoc. Theor. Comput. Sci.* **22**, pp. 120–121.

Hoffman, K., K. Mehlhorn, P. Rosenstiehl, and R.E. Tarjan [1985], "Sorting Jordan sequences in linear time using level-linked search trees," Proc. 1st Ann. ACM Symp. Comput. Geometry, pp. 196–203; also in final form in *Inf. & Control* **68** (1986), pp. 170–184.

Hofri, M. [1987]. *Probabilistic Analysis of Algorithms.* Springer Verlag, Berlin.

Hopcroft, J.E., and R.M. Karp [1973], "An $n^{5/2}$ algorithm for maximum matchings in bipartite graphs," *SIAM J. Comput.* **2**, pp. 225–231.

Hopcroft, J.E., and R.E. Tarjan [1973], "Dividing a graph into triconnected components," *SIAM J. Comput.* **2**, pp. 135–158.

Hopcroft, J.E., and J.D. Ullman [1973], "Set merging algorithms," *SIAM J. Comput.* **2**, pp. 294–303.

Horn, W. [1974], "Some simple scheduling algorithms," *Nav. Res. Logist. Q.* **21**, pp. 177–185.

Huddleston, S., and K. Mehlhorn [1982], "A new data structure for representing sorted lists," *Acta Inform.* **17**, pp. 157–184.

Huffman, D.A. [1952], "A method for the construction of minimum redundancy codes," *Proc. IRE* **40**, pp. 1098–1101.

Incerpi, J., and R. Sedgewick [1986], "Practical variations of Shellsort," Tech. Rep. CS-TR-027-86, Princeton U., Princeton, NJ.

Irving, R.W., P. Leather, and D. Gusfield [1987], "An efficient algorithm for the "optimal" stable marriage problem," *J. ACM* **34**, pp. 532–543.

Jain, A.K., and R.C. Dubes [1988]. *Algorithms for Clustering Data.* Prentice-Hall, Englewood Cliffs, NJ.

Jarvis, R.A. [1973], "On the identification of the convex hull of a finite set of points in the plane," *Inf. Process. Lett.* **2**, pp. 18–21.

Johnson, D.S. [1990], "Local optimization and the traveling salesman problem," Proc. 17th Int'l Coll. Automata, Lang. & Progr. ICALP-90, Lecture Notes in Computer Science Vol. 443, Springer Verlag, Berlin, pp. 446–461.

Johnson, D.S., C.R. Aragon, L.A. McGeoch, and C. Schevon [1989], "Optimization by simulated annealing: an experimental evaluation, part I (graph partitioning)," *Oper. Res.* **37**, pp. 865–892. (Parts II and III to appear)

Johnson, D.S., C.H. Papadimitriou, and M. Yannakakis [1985], "How easy is local search?" Proc. 26th Ann. IEEE Symp. Foundations Comput. Sci. FOCS-85, pp. 39–42.

Jones, D.W. [1986], "An empirical comparison of priority-queue and event-set implementations," *Commun. ACM* **29**, pp. 300–311.

Karg, R.L., and G.L. Thompson [1964], "A heuristic approach to solving travelling salesman problems," *Manage. Sci.* **10**, pp. 225–248.

Karp, R.M. [1977], "Probabilistic analysis of partitioning algorithms for the traveling-salesman problem in the plane," *Math. Oper. Res.* **2**, pp. 209–224.

Karp, R.M. [1986], "Combinatorics, complexity, and randomness," *Commun. ACM* **29**, pp. 98–109 (Turing Award Lecture).

Karzanov, A.V. [1974], "Determining the maximal flow in a network by the method of preflows," *Soviet Math. Dokl.* **15**, pp. 434–437.

Kern, W. [1989], "A probabilistic analysis of the switching algorithm for the Euclidean TSP," *Math. Programming* **44**, pp. 213–219.

Kirkpatrick, D., and R. Seidel [1986], "The ultimate planar convex hull algorithm?" *SIAM J. Comput.* **15**, pp. 287–299.

Kirkpatrick, S., C.D. Gelatt, and M.P. Vecchi [1983], "Optimization by simulated annealing," *Science* **220**, pp. 671–680.

Knuth, D.E. [1968]. *The Art of Computer Programming. Vol. 1: Fundamental Algorithms.* Addison-Wesley, Reading, MA.

Knuth, D.E. [1969]. *The Art of Computer Programming. Vol. 2: Semi-Numerical Algorithms.* Addison-Wesley, Reading, MA.

Knuth, D.E. [1973]. *The Art of Computer Programming. Vol. 3: Sorting and Searching.* Addison-Wesley, Reading, MA.

Knuth, D.E. [1976]. *Mariages stables et leur relation avec d'autres problèmes combinatoires.* Les Presses de l'Université de Montréal (in French).

Knuth, D.E. [1976], "Big Omicron and Big Omega and Big Theta," *SIGACT News* **8**, pp. 18–23.

Knuth, D.E. [1985], "Dynamic Huffman coding," *J. Algorithms* **6**, pp. 163–180.

Knuth, D.E., R. Motwani, and B. Pittel [1990], "Stable husbands," *Rand. Struct. & Algorithms* **1**, pp. 1–14.

Korte, B., and L. Lovasz [1981], "Mathematical structures underlying greedy algorithms," Lecture Notes in Computer Science Vol. 177, Springer Verlag, Berlin, pp. 205–209.

Korte, B., and L. Lovasz [1984], "Greedoids and linear objective functions," *SIAM J. Algebr. Discrete Methods* **5**, pp. 229–238.

Korte, B., and L. Lovasz [1986], "Non-interval greedoids and the transposition property," *Discrete Math.* **59**, pp. 297–314.

Kuhn, H.W. [1955], "The Hungarian method for the assignment problem," *Nav. Res. Logist. Q.* **2**, pp. 83–97.

Lawler, E.L. [1976], *Combinatorial Optimization: Networks and Matroids*. Holt, Rinehart, and Winston, New York, NY.

Lawler, E.L., J.K. Lenstra, A.H.G. Rinnooy Kan, and D.B. Shmoys (eds.) [1985]. *The Traveling Salesman Problem: A Guided Tour of Combinatorial Optimization*. John Wiley & Sons, New York, NY.

Lengauer, T., and R.E. Tarjan [1979], "A fast algorithm for finding dominators in a flowgraph," *ACM Trans. Program. Lang. Syst.* **1**, pp. 121–141.

Lewis, H.R., and L. Denenberg [1991], *Algorithms and their Data Structures*. To appear at Harper-Collins, New York, NY.

Lin, S. [1965], "Computer solution of the traveling salesman problem," *Bell Syst. Tech. J.* **44**, pp. 2245–2269.

Lin, S., and B.W. Kernighan [1973], "An effective heuristic algorithm for the traveling-salesman problem," *Oper. Res.* **21**, pp. 498–516.

Lipton, R.J., and R.E. Tarjan [1979], "A separator theorem for planar graphs," *SIAM J. Appl. Math.* **36**, pp. 177–189.

Litke, J.D. [1984], "An improved solution to the traveling salesman problem with thousands of nodes," *Commun. ACM* **27**, pp. 1227–1236.

Luby, M., and P. Ragde [1985], "A bidirectional shortest-path algorithm with good average-case behavior," Proc. 12th Int'l Coll. Automata, Lang. & Progr. ICALP-85, Lecture Notes in Computer Science Vol. 194, Springer Verlag, Berlin, pp. 394–403; also in final form in *Algorithmica* **4** (1989), pp. 551–568.

Lueker, G.S. [1980], "Some techniques for solving recurrences," *Comput. Surv.* **12**, pp. 419–436.

Malhotra, V.M., M.P. Kumar, and S.N. Maheshwari [1978], "An $O(|V|^3)$ algorithm for finding maximum flows in networks," *Inf. Process. Lett.* **7**, pp. 277–278.

Manber, U. [1989], *Introduction of Algorithms: A Creative Approach.* Addison-Wesley, Reading, MA.

Matula, D.W. [1987], "Determining edge connectivity in $O(nm)$," Proc. 28th Ann. IEEE Symp. Foundations Comput. Sci. FOCS-87, pp. 249–251.

Mehlhorn, K. [1984]. *Data Structures and Algorithms.* Springer Verlag, Berlin, in 3 volumes.

Micali, S., and V.V. Vazirani [1980], "An $O(\sqrt{|V|} \cdot |E|)$ algorithm for finding maximal matchings in general graphs," Proc. 21st Ann. IEEE Symp. Foundations Comput. Sci. FOCS-80, pp. 17–27.

Moret, B.M.E. [1982], "Decision trees and diagrams," *Comput. Surv.* **14**, pp. 593–623.

Nemhauser, G.L., and L.A. Wolsey [1988]. *Integer and Combinatorial Optimization.* John Wiley & Sons, New York, NY.

Olivié, H. [1981], "On α-balanced binary search trees," Lecture Notes in Computer Science Vol. 104, Springer Verlag, Berlin, pp. 98–108.

Or, I. [1976], *Traveling Salesman-Type Combinatorial Problems and their Relation to the Logistics of Regional Blood Banking.* Ph.D. thesis, Northwestern U., Evanston, IL.

O'Rourke, J. [1987]. *Art Gallery Theorems and Algorithms.* Oxford U. Press, New York, NY.

Overmars, M.H., and J. van Leeuwen [1981], "Maintenance of configurations in the plane," *J. Comput. Syst. Sci.* **23**, pp. 166–204.

Pan, V. [1978], "Strassen's algorithm is not optimal," Proc. 19th Ann. IEEE Symp. Foundations Comput. Sci. FOCS-78, pp. 166–176.

Papadimitriou, C.H., and K. Steiglitz [1977], "On the complexity of local search for the traveling salesman problem," *SIAM J. Comput.* **6**, pp. 76–83.

Papadimitriou, C.H., and K. Steiglitz [1982]. *Combinatorial Optimization: Algorithms and Complexity.* Prentice Hall, Englewood Cliffs, NJ.

Pearl, Judea [1985]. *Heuristics: Intelligent Search Strategies for Computer Problem Solving.* Addison-Wesley, Reading, MA.

Peterson, P.A., and M.C. Loui [1988], "The general maximum matching algorithm of Micali and Vazirani," *Algorithmica* **3**, pp. 511–534.

Preparata, F., and M.I. Shamos [1985]. *Computational Geometry: an Introduction.* Springer-Verlag, New York, NY.

Purdom, P.W. Jr., and C.A. Brown [1985]. *The Analysis of Algorithms.* Holt, Rinehart, & Winston, New York, NY.

Rado, R. [1957], "A note on independence functions," *Proc. London Math. Soc.* **7**, pp. 300–320.

Rajasekaran, S., and J.H. Reif [1989], "Optimal and sublogarithmic time randomized parallel sorting algorithms," *SIAM J. Comput.* **18**, pp. 594–607.

Reingold, E.M., and W.J. Hansen [1983]. *Data Structures.* Little, Brown and Company, Boston, MA.

Rosenblatt, F. [1957], "The perceptron—a perceiving and recognizing automaton," Tech. Rep. 85-460-1, Cornell Aeronautical Laboratory, Ithaca, NY.

Rosenkrantz, D.J., R.E. Stearns, and P.M. Lewis II [1977], "An analysis of several heuristics for the traveling salesman problem," *SIAM J. Comput.* **6**, pp. 563–581.

Sedgewick, R. [1986], "A new upper bound for Shellsort," *J. Algorithms* **7**, pp. 159–173.

Shamos, M.I., and D. Hoey [1976], "Geometric intersection problems," Proc. 17th Ann. IEEE Symp. Foundations Comput. Sci. FOCS-76, pp. 208–215.

Shamos, M.I., and D. Hoey [1975], "Closest-point problems," Proc. 16th Ann. IEEE Symp. Foundations Comput. Sci. FOCS-75, pp. 151–162.

Shamos, M.I. [1978]. *Computational geometry.* Ph.D. thesis, Yale U., New Haven, CT.

Shannon, C.E. [1948], "A mathematical theory of communication," *Bell Syst. Tech. J.* **27**, pp. 379–423 and 623–656.

Shell, D.L. [1959], "A high-speed sorting procedure," *Commun. ACM* **2**, pp. 30–32.

Shiloach, Y., and U. Vishkin [1981], "Finding the maximum, merging, and sorting in a parallel computation model," *J. Algorithms* **2**, pp. 212–219.

Sleator, D.D., and R.E. Tarjan [1983], "Self-adjusting binary trees," Proc. 15th Ann. ACM Symp. Theory Comput. STOC-83, pp. 235–245; also in final form in *J. ACM* **32** (1985), pp. 652–686.

Sleator, D.D., and R.E. Tarjan [1986], "Self-Adjusting Heaps," *SIAM J. Comput.* **15**, 1, pp. 52–69.

Spira, P.M., and A. Pan [1975], "On finding and updating spanning trees and shortest paths," *SIAM J. Comput.* **4**, pp. 375–380.

Stasko, J.T., and J.S. Vitter [1987], "Pairing heaps: experiments and analysis," *Commun. ACM* **30**, pp. 234–249.

Strassen, V. [1969], "Gaussian elimination is not optimal," *Numer. Math.* **13**, pp. 354–356.

Supowit, K.J., E.M. Reingold, and D.A. Plaisted [1983], "The traveling salesman problem and minimum matching in the unit square," *SIAM J. Comput.* **12**, pp. 144–156.

Tarjan, R.E. [1972], "Depth-first search and linear graph algorithms," *SIAM J. Comput.* **1**, pp. 146–160.

Tarjan, R.E. [1973], " Finding dominators in directed graphs," Proc. 7th Princeton Conf. Inf. Sci. & Sys., pp. 414–418; also in final form in *SIAM J. Comput.* **3** (1974), pp. 62–89.

Tarjan, R.E. [1975], "Efficiency of a good but not linear set union algorithm," *J. ACM* **22**, pp. 215–225.

Tarjan, R.E. [1983]. *Data Structures and Network Algorithms.* SIAM, Philadelphia.

Tarjan, R.E. [1979], "Applications of path compression on balanced trees," *J. ACM* **26**, pp. 690–715.

Tarjan, R.E. [1985], "Amortized computational complexity," *SIAM J. Algebr. Discrete Methods* **6**, 2, pp. 306–318.

Tarjan, R.E. [1987], "Algorithm design," *Commun. ACM* **30**, pp. 204–212 (Turing Award Lecture).

Tarjan, R.E., and J. van Leeuwen [1984], "Worst-case analysis of set union algorithms," *J. ACM* **31**, pp. 245–281.

Tarjan, R.E., and C.J. van Wyk [1988], "An $O(n \log \log n)$-time algorithm for triangulating a simple polygon," *SIAM J. Comput.* **17**, pp. 143–178.

Titchmarsh, E.C. [1948]. *Introduction to the Theory of Fourier Integrals.* Oxford U. Press, New York, NY.

Valdes, J., R.E. Tarjan, and E.L. Lawler [1979], "The recognition of series-parallel digraphs," Proc. 11th Ann. ACM Symp. Theory Comput. STOC-79, pp. 1–12; also in final form in *SIAM J. Comput.* **11** (1982), pp. 298–313.

Voronoi, G. [1908], "Nouvelles applications des paramètres continus à la théorie des formes quadratiques; Deuxième Mémoire: Recherche sur les paralléloèdres primitifs," *J. reine angew. Math.* **134**, pp. 198–287.

Vuillemin, J. [1978], "A data structure for manipulating priority queues," *Commun. ACM* **21**, pp. 309–314.

Walker, W.A., and C.C. Gottlieb [1972], "A top-down algorithm for constructing nearly optimal lexicographic trees," in *Graph Theory and Computing*, R.C. Read, ed., Academic Press, New York, NY, pp. 303–323.

Weide, B. [1977], "A survey of analysis techniques for discrete algorithms," *Comput. Surv.* **9**, pp. 292–313.

Weiss, M.A., and R. Sedgewick [1990], "More on shellsort increment sequences," *Inf. Process. Lett.* **34**, pp. 267–270.

Welsh, D.J.A. [1976], *Matroid Theory*. Academic Press, New York, NY.

Williams, J.W.J. [1964], "Algorithm 232: heapsort," *Commun. ACM* **7**, pp. 347–348.

Winograd, S. [1973], "Some remarks on the fast multiplication of polynomials," in *Complexity of Sequential and Parallel Numerical Algorithms*, J.F. Traub, ed., Academic Press, New York, NY, pp. 181–196.

Xue-Miao, L. [1986], "Towers of Hanoi graphs," *Int. J. Comput. Math.* **19**, pp. 23–38.

Xue-Miao, L. [1988], "Towers of Hanoi problem with arbitrary $k \geq 3$ pegs," *Int. J. Comput. Math.* **24**, pp. 39–54.

Ziv, J. and A. Lempel [1978], "Compression of individual sequences via variable-rate coding," *IEEE Trans. Inf. Theory* **IT-24**, pp. 530–536.

INDEX

ISBN 0-8053-8008-6